INCOME TAX PLANNING

Your unique textbook registration number is below. Please register your new textbook at www.money-education.com for access to our accompanying financial planning software, updated errata, Money Tips™, and other valuable resources.

SPDN142050

INCOME TAX PLANNING

Thomas P. Langdon
E. Vance Grange
Michael A. Dalton

14th Edition

3116 5th Street
Metairie, LA 70002
888-295-6023

Printed in the U.S.A.

ISBN: 978-1-946711-47-2

About the Authors

Thomas P. Langdon, JD, LL.M.

- Professor of Business Law, Gabelli School of Business, Roger Williams University, Bristol, RI
- Principal, Langdon & Langdon Financial Services, LLC (Connecticut-based tax planning & preparation firm)
- Former Professor of Taxation at The American College, Bryn Mawr, PA.
- Former Adjunct Professor of Insurance and Economics at The University of Connecticut Center for Professional Development
- Former Member (and Chair) of the CFP Board's Board of Examiners
- Master of Laws (LL.M.) in Taxation from Villanova University School of Law
- Juris Doctor, from Western New England College School of Law
- Master of Science in Financial Services from The American College
- Master of Business Administration from The University of Connecticut
- Bachelor of Science in Finance from The University of Connecticut, Storrs, CT.
- Chartered Financial Analyst (CFA), Certified Financial Planner (CFP), Chartered Life Underwriter (CLU), Chartered Financial Consultant (ChFC), Accredited Estate Planner (AEP), Chartered Advisor in Philanthropy (CAP), Certified Employee Benefits Specialist (CEBS), Chartered Advisor in Senior Living (CASL), Registered Employee Benefits Consultant (REBC), Registered Health Underwriter (RHU), Associate in Life & Health Claims (ALHC), and Fellow of the Life Management Institute (FLMI)
- Associate Editor of the *Journal of Financial Services Professionals*
- Co-author of *Estate Planning* (1st - 12th editions)
- Co-author of *Income Tax Planning* (1st - 14th editions)
- Contributing author of *Insurance Planning* (1st - 7th editions)
- Faculty member for National Tax Institute

E. Vance Grange, CPA/PFS, PhD, CPA, CFP®

- Director of Tax and Personal Financial Planning Programs in the School of Accountancy at Utah State University
- Teaches courses in income taxation, personal financial planning, retirement planning, and estate planning
- Bachelor's degree in English from Brigham Young University
- Master's of Accountancy degree from Utah State University
- Ph.D. in Accounting (Taxation) from the University of Texas at Austin
- Licensed CPA in the state of Utah
- Investment advisor associate of Beacon Financial Planning, LLC, a registered investment advisory company in Utah
- Former member Board of Examiners of the Certified Financial Planner Board of Standards and a member of the CFP Board of Governors
- Former chair of the Board of Examiners
- Participated in the Model Curriculum project of the Academy of Financial Services and CFP Board
- Has worked with CFP Board staff and other researchers to identify determinants of success on the CFP® Certification Examination since 1999
- Co-author of *Income Tax Planning* (1st - 14th editions)

Michael A. Dalton, Ph.D., JD, CPA, CLU, ChFC, CFP®

- Former Chair of the Board of Dalton Publications, L.L.C.
- Associate professor of Accounting and Taxation at Loyola University in New Orleans, Louisiana (retired)
- Adjunct professor at George Mason University (2014 - 2017)
- Adjunct professor at Georgetown University (2002 - 2014)
- Former Senior Vice President, Education at BISYS Group
- Ph.D. in Accounting from Georgia State University
- J.D. from Louisiana State University in Baton Rouge, Louisiana
- MBA and BBA in Management and Accounting from Georgia State University
- Former board member of the CFP Board's Board of Examiners, Board of Standards, and Board of Governors
- Former member (and chair) of the CFP Board's Board of Examiners
- Member of the Financial Planning Association
- Member of the *Journal of Financial Planning* Editorial Advisory Board
- Member of the *Journal of Financial Planning* Editorial Review Board
- Member of the LSU Law School Board of Trustees (2000 - 2006)
- Author of *Dalton Review for the CFP® Certification Examination: Volume I – Outlines and Study Guides, Volume II – Problems and Solutions, Volume III - Case Exam Book, Mock Exams A-1 and A-2* (1st - 8th Editions)
- Author of *Retirement Planning and Employee Benefits* (1st - 17th Editions)
- Author of *Estate Planning* (1st - 12th Editions)
- Author of *Fundamentals of Financial Planning* (1st - 7th Editions)
- Author of *Insurance Planning* (1st - 7th Editions)
- Co-author of *Income Tax Planning* (1st - 14th Editions)
- Co-author of *Cases in Financial Planning: Analysis and Presentation* (1st - 4th Editions)
- Co-author of *Dalton CFA® Study Notes Volumes I and II* (1st - 2nd Editions)
- Co-author of *Dalton's Personal Financial Planning Series – Personal Financial Planning Theory and Practice* (1st - 3rd Editions)
- Co-author of *Dalton's Personal Financial Planning Series – Personal Financial Planning Cases and Applications* (1st - 4th Editions)
- Co-author of *Cost Accounting: Traditions and Innovations* published by West Publishing Company
- Co-author of the *ABCs of Managing Your Money* published by National Endowment for Financial Education (NEFE)

About the Contributing Authors

James F. Dalton, MBA, MS, CPA/PFS, CFA®, CFP®

- CEO, Money Education
- Adjunct professor at George Mason University (2014 - 2017)
- Adjunct professor at Georgetown University (2002 - 2014)
- Former Executive Vice President, Assessment Technologies Institute LLC
- Former Senior Vice President, Kaplan Professional
- Former President, Dalton Publications LLC
- Former Senior Manager of KPMG, LLP, concentrating in personal financial planning, investment planning, and litigation consulting
- MBA from Loyola University New Orleans
- Master of Accounting in Taxation from the University of New Orleans
- BS in accounting from Florida State University in Tallahassee, Florida
- Member of the CFP Board of Standards July 1996, Comprehensive CFP® Exam Pass Score Committee
- Member of the AICPA and the Louisiana Society of CPAs
- Member of the Financial Planning Association
- Member of the *Journal of Financial Planning* Editorial Review Board
- Author of *Money Education's Quick Sheets*
- Co-author of *Cases in Financial Planning: Analysis and Presentation* (1st - 4th Editions)
- Co-author of *Retirement Planning and Employee Benefits* (1st - 17th Editions)
- Co-Author of *Fundamentals of Financial Planning* (1st - 7th Editions)
- Contributing Author of *Insurance Planning* (1st - 7th Editions)
- Contributing Author of *Estate Planning* (1st - 12th Editions)
- Author of Kaplan Schweser's Personal Financial Planning Understanding Your Financial Calculator
- Author of Kaplan Schweser's Understanding Your Financial Calculator for the CFA® Exam
- Co-author of BISYS CFA® Study Notes Volumes I and II
- Co-author of Kaplan Schweser's Personal Financial Planning Cases and Applications
- Co-author of the Kaplan Schweser Review for the CFP® Certification Examination, Volumes I–VIII and Kaplan Schweser's Financial Planning Flashcards

Sherri Donaldson, CFP®, ChFC®, MSFS, CASL®, CAP®, EA

- Editing Princess for Money Education
- Former Author/Editor/Lead instructor, Keir Educational Resources
- Former Assistant Vice President, Senior Training Specialist, M&T Securities
- Former Associate Financial Consultant, M&T Securities
- Former Financial Sales Specialist, Nationwide Financial
- Former Financial Services Representative, Nationwide Retirement Solutions
- MSFS from The American College Bryn Mawr, PA
- BS in business, concentration in financial services, Pennsylvania State University
- Member of the Financial Planning Association
- Co-Author/Editor of Keir *General Financial Planning Principles* textbook
- Co-Author/Editor of Keir *Risk Management and Insurance Planning* textbook
- Co-Author/Editor of Keir *Introduction to Financial Planning* textbook
- Co-Author/Editor of Keir *Retirement Savings and Income Planning* textbook
- Co-Author/Editor of Keir *Tax Planning* textbook
- Co-Author/Editor of Keir *Estate Planning* textbook
- Co-Author/Editor Keir *Investments Planning* textbook
- Editor Keir *Financial Plan Development* and *Practical Applications for Your Financial Calculator* textbooks
- Co-Author/Editor Keir CFP® exam review books (*Core Knowledge Book 1* and *2*, *Essential Keys* book, *Case Studies* book), practice exams, flashcards, MP3 scripts, Key Concept Infograhics, and Quick Concept videos

About the Reviewers and Contributors

We owe a special thanks to several key professionals for their significant contribution of time and effort with the current and previous editions of this text. These reviewers provided meticulous editing, detailed calculation reviews, helpful suggestions for additional content, and other valuable comments, all of which have improved this edition. To each of these individuals we extend our deepest gratitude and appreciation.

Michelle Bertolini is an assistant professor at Nova Southeastern University, where she teaches Master's level tax and law courses in the Department of Accounting and Taxation. She has a J.D. from Stetson University College of Law in St. Petersburg, Florida and a LL.M. in International Taxation from Thomas Jefferson School of Law in San Diego, CA. Ms. Bertolini is a licensed attorney in the State of Florida and CPA in the State of Georgia and Wisconsin. She is a contributing author for a text book on SEC Audits and has published articles in various tax and accounting journals.

Donna Dalton made a significant contribution to this textbook by her thoughtful and meticulous editing throughout the book. She provided many valuable improvements to both the textbook and instructor materials. This book would not have been possible without her extraordinary dedication, skill, and knowledge.

Harvey Hutchinson is a member of the Money Education team. He is an instructor for Emory University's paralegal program, teaching courses in estate planning, contract law, bankruptcy law, and business organizations; furthermore, he was an instructor for Emory University's CFP® program. He is an adjunct professor with Thomas Jefferson School of Law, teaching courses in wealth management, banking law, tax law, and consumer compliance. Harvey earned three business degrees (B.S.B.A. (Finance), M.B.A., and M.Acc.) and two law degrees (J.D. and LL.M. (Taxation)). He is a licensed attorney holding the following designations: AEP, CTFA, and CFP®.

Randall Martinez is a personal financial planner specializing in personal financial planning, estate, and individual income tax planning. He teaches retirement planning, estate planning, and income tax planning through various CFP Board-Registered Programs as well as comprehensive reviews for the Certified Financial Planner designation. Randy is a contributor to Money Education's *Retirement Planning and Employee Benefits.*

Robin Meyer is a valuable member of our Money Education team. She worked diligently throughout this project by performing numerous reviews and revisions. Robin provided many valuable improvements to both the textbook and instructor materials and this book would not have been possible without her extraordinary dedication, skill, and knowledge. Robin is the joy in our office as she always works tirelessly with a great work ethic and an enormous sense of humor. We are always grateful for her contributions to our products as well as our office happiness.

Kathy Oakley is a CPA and CFP® Certificant. She is a consultant to (and former academic program director of) Rice University's CFP® Certification Education program. She has taught courses in the General Principles of Financial Planning, Income Tax Planning and Case Analysis. She is a co-author of Money Education's *Cases in Financial Planning: Analysis and Presentation*. Mrs. Oakley served on the CFP Board's Council on Education from 2013 - 2017.

Kristi Tafalla is an attorney and personal financial planner specializing in income tax and estate planning. She teaches estate planning, income tax planning and comprehensive case courses through various CFP Board-Registered Programs as well as comprehensive reviews for the Certified Financial Planner designation. She is a contributor to Money Education's *Estate Planning* and *Retirement Planning and Employee Benefits.*

Acknowledgments and Special Thanks

We are most appreciative for the tremendous support and encouragement we have received throughout this project. We are extremely grateful to the instructors and program directors of CFP Board-Registered programs who provided valuable comments during the development stages of this text. We are fortunate to have dedicated, careful readers at several institutions who were willing to share their needs, expectations, and time with us.

We would like to pay special thanks to Donna Dalton and Robin Meyer. It takes more than just the writer to produce a finished book and they are an essential element of our team.

We have received so much help from so many people, it is possible that we have inadvertently overlooked thanking someone. If so, it is our shortcoming, and we apologize in advance. Please let us know if you are that someone, and we will make it right in our next printing.

PREFACE

Income Tax Planning is written for graduate and upperdivision undergraduate level students interested in acquiring an understanding of income tax planning from a professional viewpoint. The text is intended to be used in an Income Tax Planning course as part of an overall curriculum in accounting or financial planning. The text is also intended to serve as an authoritative reference for practicing professionals.

This text was designed to cover many of the tax-related topics required for the Uniform CPA Examination and to meet the educational requirements for an Income Tax Course in a CFP Board-Registered Program. Therefore, one of our goals is to assure CFP Board-Registered Program Directors, instructors, students, and financial planners that we have addressed every relevant topic covered by the CFP Board Exam Topic List and the most recent model curriculum syllabus for this course. The book will be updated, as needed, to keep current with any changes in the law, exam topic list, or model curriculum.

Special Features

A variety of tools and presentation methods are used throughout this text to assist the reader in the learning process. Some of the features in this text that are designed to enhance your understanding and learning process include:

- **Learning Objectives** – At the beginning of each chapter is a list of learning objectives to help you focus your studying of the material. These learning objectives will provide a preview of the important topics covered in the chapter.

- **Key Concepts** – At the beginning of each subsection are key concepts, or study objectives, each stated as a question. To be successful in this course, you should be able to answer these questions. So as you read, guide your learning by looking for the answers. When you find the answers, highlight or underline them. It is important that you actually highlight/underline and not just make a mental note, as the action of stopping and writing reinforces your learning. Watch for this symbol:

Key Concepts

- **Quick Quizzes** – Following each subsection you will find a Quick Quiz, which checks and reinforces what you read. Circle the answer to each question and then check your answers against the correct answers supplied at the bottom of the quiz. If you missed any questions, flip back to the relevant section and review the material. Watch for this symbol:

Quick Quiz 1.1

- **Examples** – Examples are used frequently to illustrate the concepts being discussed and to help the reader understand and apply the concepts presented.

- **Exhibits** – The written text is enhanced and simplified by using exhibits where appropriate to promote learning and application. Exhibits are identified with the following symbol:

- **Cases** – Several chapters contain real world case summaries to help the reader appreciate the application of particular topics being discussed in the chapter.

- **Key Terms** – Key terms appear in **boldfaced type** throughout the text to assist in the identification of important concepts and terminology. A list of key terms with definitions appears at the end of each chapter.

- **End of Chapter Questions** – Each chapter contains a series of discussion questions and a sample of multiple-choice problems that highlight major topics covered in the chapter. The questions test retention and understanding of important chapter material and can be used for review and classroom discussion. Additional problems are available at money-education.com by accessing the Student Practice Portal.

- **Quick Quiz Explanations** – Each chapter concludes with the answers to the Quick Quizzes contained in that chapter, as well as explanation to the "false" statements in each Quick Quiz.

- **Glossary** – A compilation of the key terms identified throughout the text is located at the end of the book.

Student Practice Portal

available by registering your textbook at money-education.com

To my father and tax-practice partner,
Lorenzo W. Langdon,
and my mother,
Patricia E. Langdon,
for their encouragement and support
TPL

To my wife,
Tamara,
for her love and encouragement
in everything I do.
EVG

In loving memory of my father,
James J. Dalton, U.S. Army (1981)
and my mother,
Gertrude Arline Dalton (2010)
MAD

TABLE OF CONTENTS

Chapter 1 | Introduction to Income Tax Planning

Chapter 2 | Working with the Tax Law

Chapter 3 | Fundamentals of Income Taxation

Chapter 4 | Gross Income From Personal and Investment Activities

Chapter 5 | Gross Income from Employment

Chapter 6 | Introduction to Deductions

Chapter 7 | Below-the-Line Deductions

Chapter 8 | Other Deductions, Penalties, and Loss Disallowance

Chapter 9 | Tax Credits

Chapter 10 | Basis Rules, Depreciation, & Asset Categorization

Chapter 11 | The Taxation of Capital Assets

Chapter 12 | Business Assets

Chapter 13 | Nontaxable Exchanges

Chapter 14 | Passive Activity Rules

Chapter 15 | The Alternative Minimum Tax

Chapter 16 | Business Entity Selection and Taxation

Appendices

1

INTRODUCTION TO INCOME TAX PLANNING

LEARNING OBJECTIVES

1. Describe how the system of federal taxation has changed over time.
2. Identify the three separate federal tax systems that impact planning decisions.
3. List and explain the two general rules of income taxation.
4. Describe why categorization of income is important.
5. Define the three key tax principles.

**Ties to CFP Certification Learning Objectives*

INTRODUCTION

Taxes play a significant, although sometimes subtle, role in the daily lives of most Americans. Although some people may only think about the taxes that they file once a year, Americans actually encounter taxes on a daily basis. For example, when someone buys a cup of coffee on his way to work, he generally pays sales tax. When that person fills up his fuel tank on the way home, he pays a federal gasoline excise tax as well as a state tax. And of course, if that person is employed, the wages that he earns during the day are subject to federal income taxes and employment taxes.

Although most people would agree that taxes are pervasive in our country, not everyone would agree on whether that is a good thing. Oliver Wendall Holmes, Jr., a U.S. Supreme Court Justice, believed: "Taxes are what we pay for a civilized society." Winston Churchill, on the other hand, is known for stating: "There is no such thing as a good tax." Regardless of how one feels about taxes, they cannot be avoided. Income taxes have an impact on almost every topical area of financial planning, every type of business entity, every individual who earns income of any kind, and most financial transactions. The federal government imposes income taxes on the taxable income of individual taxpayers at rates up to 37 percent, and most states add additional state income taxes, some at rates up to 11 percent.

HISTORICAL PERSPECTIVE

Over time, the federal, state, and local tax systems in the United States have changed significantly. These changes have occurred as a result of changes in society and in the role of the government. Some changes have been the result of specific events, while others have occurred more gradually. Regardless of how these changes occurred, it is clear that the types and amounts of taxes collected are vastly different than they were even 50 years ago.

Colonial Times

Prior to the Revolutionary War, the most common types of taxes were excise taxes, tariffs, and customs duties. In 1765, England imposed a series of taxes on the American colonies because it needed revenues to pay for its wars against France. Colonists were forced to pay these taxes even though they were not represented in the English Parliament. Consequently, the belief that "taxation without representation is tyranny" became closely associated with the American Revolution and established a persistent wariness regarding taxation as part of the American culture.

The Post Revolutionary Era

Despite their wariness regarding taxation, the writers of the Constitution recognized that the federal government needed a source of revenue, and as a result, the federal government was given the power to raise taxes. However, most of the taxes imposed by Congress were similar to the taxes that existed prior to the Revolutionary War (i.e., excise taxes or tariffs).

In the late 1790s, the federal government imposed the first direct taxes on the owners of houses, land, slaves, and estates. Direct taxes are recurring taxes paid directly by the taxpayer to the government based on the value of certain items. When Thomas Jefferson was elected president in 1802, direct taxes were abolished and for the next 10 years there were no internal revenue taxes other than excise taxes.

To raise money for the War of 1812, Congress imposed additional excise taxes, raised certain customs duties, and raised money by issuing Treasury notes. In 1817, Congress repealed these taxes, and for the next 44 years the federal government collected no internal revenue. Instead, the government received most of its revenue from high customs duties and through the sale of public land.

The Civil War

As a result of the outbreak of the Civil War, Congress passed the Revenue Act of 1861, which restored earlier excise taxes and imposed a tax on personal incomes. The income tax was levied at three percent on all incomes greater than $800 a year (equivalent to $90,582.84 in 2021, assuming a three percent inflation rate). This tax on personal income was a new direction for a federal tax system previously based mainly on excise taxes and customs duties. Certain inadequacies of the income tax were quickly acknowledged by Congress, and thus none was collected until the following year. By the spring of 1862, it was clear that the federal government had significant revenue needs, which resulted in Congress passing many new excise taxes.

After the war ended, the need for federal revenue fell sharply and most taxes were repealed. By 1868, the main source of government revenue was derived from liquor and tobacco taxes. The income tax was abolished in 1872. From 1868 to 1913, almost 90 percent of all revenue was collected from the remaining excise taxes.

The 16th Amendment

Under the Constitution as originally adopted, Congress could impose direct taxes only if they were levied in proportion to each state's population. Thus, when a flat rate federal income tax was enacted in 1894, it was quickly challenged. In *Pollack v. Farmers' Loan and Trust Company* (1895), the U.S. Supreme Court ruled that the federal income tax was unconstitutional because it was a direct tax not apportioned according to the population of each state.

Eventually, a constitutional amendment was proposed that would allow the federal government to impose tax on individuals' incomes without regard to the population of each state. By 1913, 36 states had ratified the 16th Amendment to the Constitution. Congress subsequently passed a new income tax law with rates beginning at one percent and rising to seven percent for taxpayers with income in excess of $500,000 (assuming a three percent inflation rate, that would be the equivalent of an annual income of $12,172,794 in 2021 constant dollars). Less than one percent of the population paid income tax at that time. Form 1040 was introduced as the standard income tax reporting form and, though changed in many ways over the years, remains in use today.

Exhibit 1.1 | Form 1040 for the Year 1913

TO BE FILLED IN BY COLLECTOR.

List. No. ....

.... *District of* ....

Date received ....

Form 1040.

INCOME TAX.

THE PENALTY
FOR FAILURE TO HAVE THIS RETURN IN THE HANDS OF THE COLLECTOR OF INTERNAL REVENUE ON OR BEFORE MARCH 1 IS $20 TO $1,000.
(SEE INSTRUCTIONS ON PAGE 4.)

TO BE FILLED IN BY INTERNAL REVENUE BUREAU.

File No. ....

Assessment List ....

Page .... *Line* ....

UNITED STATES INTERNAL REVENUE.

RETURN OF ANNUAL NET INCOME OF INDIVIDUALS.

(As provided by Act of Congress, approved October 3, 1913.)

RETURN OF NET INCOME RECEIVED OR ACCRUED DURING THE YEAR ENDED DECEMBER 31, 191 ....
(FOR THE YEAR 1913, FROM MARCH 1, TO DECEMBER 31.)

Filed by (or for) .... *of* ....
(Full name of individual.) (Street and No.)

in the City, Town, or Post Office of .... *State of* ....
(Fill in pages 2 and 3 before making entries below.)

1.	Gross Income (see page 2, line 12)	$
2.	General Deductions (see page 3, line 7)	$
3.	Net Income	$

Deductions and exemptions allowed in computing income subject to the normal tax of 1 per cent.

4.	Dividends and net earnings received or accrued, of corporations, etc., subject to like tax. (See page 2, line 11)	$	
5.	Amount of income on which the normal tax has been deducted and withheld at the source. (See page 2, line 9, column A)		
6.	Specific exemption of $3,000 or $4,000, as the case may be. (See Instructions 3 and 19)		
	Total deductions and exemptions. (Items 4, 5, and 6)		$
7.	Taxable Income on which the normal tax of 1 per cent is to be calculated. (See Instruction 3)		$

8. When the net income shown above on line 3 exceeds $20,000, the additional tax thereon must be calculated as per schedule below:

		INCOME.	TAX.
1	per cent on amount over $20,000 and not exceeding $50,000	$	$
2	" " 50,000 " " 75,000		
3	" " 75,000 " " 100,000		
4	" " 100,000 " " 250,000		
5	" " 250,000 " " 500,000		
6	" " 500,000		
	Total additional or super tax		$
	Total normal tax (1 per cent of amount entered on line 7)		$
	Total tax liability		$

The complete Form 1040 for the year 1913 is available in your Money Education Student Study Portal.

World War I and the 1920s

The entry of the United States into World War I greatly increased the need for revenue and Congress responded by passing the 1916 Revenue Act. The 1916 Act raised the lowest income tax rate from one percent to two percent and raised the top rate to 15 percent on taxpayers with income in excess of $1.5 million. The 1916 Act also imposed taxes on estates and excess business profits. However, the federal government's need for revenue was still not met, and as a result, the War Revenue Act of 1917 lowered income tax exemptions and greatly increased income tax rates. In 1916, a taxpayer needed $1.5 million in taxable income to face a 15 percent rate. By 1917, a taxpayer with only $40,000 faced a 16 percent rate and the individual with $1.5 million faced a tax rate of 67 percent.

Another revenue act was passed in 1918, which hiked income tax rates once again, this time raising the bottom rate to six percent and the top rate to 77 percent. These changes increased revenue from $761 million in 1916 to $3.6 billion in 1918, which represented about 25 percent of Gross Domestic Product (GDP). Even in 1918, however, only five percent of the population paid income taxes, and yet the income tax funded one-third of the cost of the war.

The economy boomed during the 1920s and increasing revenues from the income tax followed. These increasing revenues allowed Congress to cut the income tax rates five times, ultimately returning the lowest tax rate to one percent and reducing the top income tax rate to 25 percent. These tax cuts reduced the federal tax burden as a share of GDP to 13 percent. As income tax rates and tax collections declined, the economy was strengthened.

In October of 1929 the stock market crash marked the beginning of the Great Depression. As the economy shrank, government receipts also fell. In the face of rising budget deficits which reached $2.7 billion in 1931, Congress followed the prevailing economic wisdom at the time and increased income tax rates once again. By 1936 the lowest income tax rate had reached four percent and the top rate was 79 percent.

The Social Security Tax

The state of the economy during the Great Depression led to the passage of the Social Security Act in 1935. This law provided payments known as "unemployment compensation" to workers who lost their jobs. Other sections of the Act gave public aid to the aged, the needy, the handicapped, and to certain minors. These programs were financed by a two percent payroll tax, one-half of which was subtracted directly from an employee's paycheck and one-half was collected from employers on the employee's behalf. The tax was levied on the first $3,000 of the employee's salary or wages.

World War II

Even before the United States entered World War II, increased defense spending led to the passage of two income tax laws in 1940 that increased individual and corporate taxes, and they were followed by another income tax hike in 1941. By the end of the war, reductions in exemption levels meant that taxpayers with taxable incomes of only $500 faced a bottom income tax rate of 23 percent, while taxpayers with income over $1 million faced a top income tax rate of 94 percent.

Developments after World War II

Throughout the 1950s, tax policy was increasingly seen as a tool for raising revenue, for changing the incentives in the economy, and also as a tool for stabilizing macroeconomic activity. The economy remained subject to frequent boom and bust cycles and many policymakers readily accepted the new economic policy of raising or lowering income taxes and spending to adjust aggregate demand and thereby smooth the business cycle. Even so, however, the maximum income tax rate in 1954 remained at 87 percent of taxable income. While the income tax underwent some revision or amendment almost every year, certain years marked especially significant changes.

Beginning in the late 1960s and continuing through the 1970s, the United States experienced persistent and rising inflation rates, which ultimately reached 13.3 percent in 1979. Combined with rising inflation and a heavy regulatory burden, the high income tax rates caused the economy to under-perform badly, all of which laid the groundwork for the Reagan tax cut, also known as the Economic Recovery Tax Act of 1981.

The Reagan Tax Cut

The Economic Recovery Tax Act of 1981, which enjoyed strong bipartisan support in Congress, represented a fundamental shift in the course of federal income tax policy. The Act featured a 25 percent reduction in individual income tax rates, phased in over three years, and indexed the rates for inflation thereafter. This brought the top income tax bracket down to 50 percent.

As inflation came down and as more and more of the tax cuts from the 1981 Act went into effect, the economy began a strong and sustained pattern of growth. Though the painful medicine of disinflation slowed and initially hid the process, the beneficial effects of marginal rate cuts and reductions in the disincentives to invest took hold as promised.

Exhibit 1.2 | Highest Marginal Income Tax Rates 1913-2021

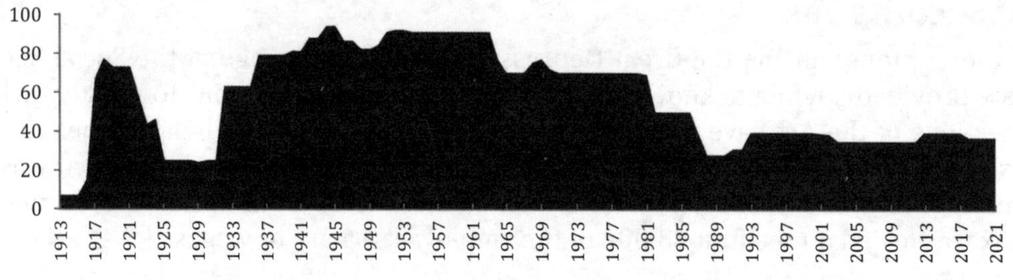

This graph illustrates the highest marginal income tax rate not taking into consideration any surtaxes that may apply to various groups of taxpayers.

The Tax Reform Act of 1986

Following the enactment of the 1981, 1982, and 1984 tax changes, there was a growing sense that the income tax was in need of a more fundamental overhaul. In his 1984 State of the Union speech, President Reagan called for a sweeping reform of the income tax so it would have a broader base and lower rates and would be fairer, simpler, and more consistent with economic efficiency.

The culmination of this effort was the Tax Reform Act of 1986, which brought the top statutory income tax rate down from 50 percent to 28 percent while the top corporate income tax rate was reduced from 50 percent to 35 percent. The number of tax brackets was reduced and the personal exemption and standard deduction amounts were both increased and indexed for inflation, thereby relieving millions of taxpayers of any federal income tax burden. However, the Act also created new personal and corporate alternative minimum taxes.

The 1986 Tax Reform Act was roughly revenue neutral; that is, it was not intended to raise or lower overall tax revenues, but it shifted some of the tax burden from individuals to businesses. Much of the increase in the tax on businesses was the result of an increase in the tax on business capital formation. From a broader perspective, the 1986 Tax Reform Act represented the penultimate installment of an extraordinary process of tax rate reductions. Over the 22-year period from 1964 to 1986 the top individual income tax rate was reduced from 91 to 28 percent. However, because upper-income taxpayers increasingly chose to receive their income in taxable form, and because of the broadening of the tax base, the progressivity of the tax system actually rose during this period.

Between 1986 and 1990 the federal tax burden rose as a share of GDP from 17.5 to 18 percent. Despite this increase in the overall tax burden, persistent budget deficits due to even higher levels of government spending created near constant pressure to increase taxes. Thus, in 1990 Congress enacted a significant tax increase featuring an increase in the top income tax rate to 31 percent. Shortly after his election, President Clinton insisted on, and Congress enacted, a second major tax increase in 1993 in which the top income tax rate was raised to 36 percent and a 10 percent surcharge was added, leaving the effective top income tax rate at 39.6 percent.

The Taxpayer Relief Act of 1997 made additional changes to the income tax code providing a modest tax cut. The centerpiece of the 1997 Act was a significant new tax benefit to certain families with children through the child tax credit. The 1997 Act launched the modern proliferation of individual tax credits and especially refundable credits that are in essence spending programs operating through the tax system.

EGTRRA 2001 (The Bush Tax Cut)

By 2001, the total tax take had produced a projected unified budget surplus of $281 billion, with a cumulative 10-year projected surplus of $5.6 trillion. Much of this surplus reflected a rising tax burden as a share of GDP due to the interaction of rising real incomes and a progressive income tax rate structure. Consequently, Congress halted the projected future increases in the tax burden by passing the Economic Growth and Tax Relief and Reconciliation Act of 2001 (EGTRRA 2001). The centerpiece of the 2001 tax cut was to regain some of the ground lost in the 1990s in terms of lower marginal income tax rates. Though the rate reductions were to be phased in over many years, ultimately the top income tax rate fell from 39.6 percent to 35 percent.

The Patient Protection and Affordable Care Act (PPACA) of 2010

The Patient Protection and Affordable Care Act, or "Affordable Care Act" for short, was signed into law by President Obama on March 23, 2010. Commonly referred to as "Obamacare," the Affordable Care Act required Americans to purchase health insurance coverage by 2014, and imposed income tax penalties on those who do not obtain coverage. The Tax Cuts and Jobs Act (TCJA) of 2017, however, reduced the income tax penalty to zero beginning in 2019. The ACA created tax credits for low income individuals to subsidize the cost of obtaining healthcare coverage. The Act also required business entities employing more than 50 employees to provide health insurance for their employees or pay a tax penalty for failure to provide coverage. Several items affecting individual income taxation were also incorporated into the act to raise revenue to pay for the cost of subsidies, including a 3.8 percent investment income surtax and a 0.9 percent Medicare surtax imposed on high income taxpayers, reductions in pre-tax contribution limits for Medical Flexible Spending Accounts and reductions in the tax deductibility of medical expenses on individual tax returns. A high income taxpayer, as defined in the Affordable Care Act, is an individual with adjusted gross income in excess of $200,000 or a married couple with adjusted gross income in excess of $250,000. The income thresholds for determining whether an individual is a high-income taxpayer are not adjusted for inflation, and have remained the same since the enactment of the Affordable Care Act. If the Affordable Care Act thresholds had been adjusted for inflation (at an assumed 2% rate), the threshold for high income taxpayers in 2021 would be $248,675 for single individuals, and $310,844 for married couples.

TRA 2010

The Tax Relief, Unemployment Insurance Reauthorization, and Job Creation Act of 2010 (herein referred to as TRA 2010), which was signed into law by President Barack Obama on December 17, 2010, extended the majority of the provisions found within EGTRRA 2001 through December 31, 2012.

The American Taxpayer Relief Act of 2012 (ATRA 2012)

In early January, 2013 President Barack Obama signed ATRA 2012 into law. ATRA permanently extended the EGTRRA 2001 tax cuts for most Americans while subjecting "high income taxpayers" to pre-EGTRRA 2001 income tax rates. High income taxpayers are defined by the act as single individuals with adjusted gross income over $400,000 and married couples filing jointly with adjusted gross income in excess of $450,000. The income thresholds for inclusion in the "high income taxpayer" group are not indexed for inflation. ATRA 2012 also increased capital gains and qualified dividend tax rates to 20 percent for high income taxpayers, temporarily extended various tax credits and deductions (including the American Opportunity Tax Credit and the Child Tax Credit), and provided a permanent, though partial, fix for the Alternative Minimum Tax. The provisions included in ATRA 2012 resulted in an increase in federal revenue that was designed to reduce the growth in the federal deficit occasioned by decreasing tax revenues and increasing federal spending during the Great Recession that began in 2008.

Protecting Americans from Tax Hikes Act of 2015

On December 18, 2015, President Obama signed the Protecting Americans from Tax Hikes Act of 2015 (PATH Act) into law. The PATH Act made permanent a number of previously temporary tax breaks for individuals and businesses as well as extending others.

Permanent extensions for individuals include:

- American Opportunity Tax Credit
- Deduction for certain expenses of elementary and secondary school teachers
- Transit benefits parity
- Deduction for state and local sales taxes
- Reduced earnings threshold for additional child tax credit
- Modification of the earned income tax credit
- Tax-free distributions from individual retirement plans for charitable purposes for individuals age 70½ and older

Permanent extensions for businesses include:

- Research tax credit
- Enhanced expensing under IRC Sec. 179
- Charitable deduction for contributions of food inventory
- Basis adjustment to stock of S corporations making charitable contributions of property
- Exclusion of 100 percent of gain on certain small business stock (Section 1202)

The Tax Cuts and Jobs Act of 2017

On December 22, 2017, President Trump signed the Tax Cuts and Jobs Act (TCJA 2017) into law. TCJA 2017 enacted a significant overhaul of the U.S. Income Tax System, and in many ways was akin to the 1986 Tax Changes. Unlike the 1986 Tax Changes, which effectively shifted some of the tax burden away from individuals and towards businesses, TCJA 2017 provided modest individual tax cuts and enacted significant tax cuts for businesses. The policy reasoning behind this shift was to help businesses become more competitive with their international competitors, and to attempt to stop the migration of business activity and business organizations overseas. The act reduced tax rates across the board while removing several deductions and tax preferences. Some of the major highlights of TCJA 2017 include:

- Reduction in the corporate tax rate from 35% to 21%
- Elimination of the Corporate Alternative Minimum Tax
- Creation of a new deduction for pass-through business entities
- Changing tax related inflation adjustments to a chained CPI measure
- Lowering individual tax rates across the board, with the highest rate set at 37% (down from 39.6%)
- Modification of the income ranges for capital gains tax rates (Prior law tied capital gains tax rates to the marginal tax rate of the individual; TCJA changed this methodology to tie capital gains rates to a specified amount of income)
- Suspending several tax benefits until tax years beginning after December 31, 2025, including:
    - Moving expense deductions
    - The personal exemption
    - The overall limitation on itemized deductions
    - Charitable deductions for gifts to educational institutions in return for the right to purchase tickets or seating at an athletic event
    - Casualty and theft losses (unless the loss was attributable to a disaster declared by the President)
    - All miscellaneous itemized deductions subject to the 2% floor
- Increasing the standard deduction for individual taxpayers through December 31, 2025
- Changing the mortgage interest deduction through December 31, 2025
    - Interest on up to $750,000 of acquisition indebtedness may be deducted (down from $1 million)
    - Interest on home equity indebtedness is no longer deductible (unless it qualifies as acquisition indebtedness)
- Limiting the deduction for state and local taxes to $10,000 per year through December 31, 2025
- Expanding the Child Tax Credit (up to $2,000) and increasing the phaseout ranges for qualification
- Increasing the AMT exemption and phaseout amounts
- Expanding the use of Section 529 plans for educational funding
- Eliminating recharacterization of IRA contributions if the recharacterized amount was the result of a conversion to a Roth IRA

- Extending the period for rollover of plan loan offset amounts from a qualified pension plan
- Increasings the Estate, Gift, and Generation skipping transfer tax exemption to $11,700,000 (as indexed in 2021) through December 31, 2025

The Bipartisan Budget Act of 2018

On February 9, 2018, President Trump signed the Bipartisan Budget Act of 2018 (BBA 2018). While most of the provisions of the act dealt with budgetary issues and funding government operations, the act also included several tax related provisions, including extending the credit for residential energy property and the energy credit through 2022.

The Setting Every Community Up for Retirement Enhancement (SECURE) Act of 2019 and The Taxpayer Certainty and Disaster Tax Relief Act of 2019

On December 20, 2019, President Trump signed the Setting Every Community Up for Retirement Enhancement (SECURE) Act of 2019 and the Taxpayer Certainty and Disaster Tax Relief Act of 2019.

The SECURE Act substantially changed several of the rules associated with retirement accounts, including:

- Increasing the age at which an individual must begin to take required minimum distributions from IRAs and retirement accounts from 70½ to 72. This provision is only applicable to taxpayers who were not yet subject to required minimum distributions under the pre-SECURE Act rules as of the end of 2019.
- Requiring IRA and retirement accounts to be paid out to named beneficiaries within 10 years of the death of the plan participant. During this 10 year period, the beneficiary is not required to take required minimum distributions, but the account must have a zero balance at the end of the 10 year period. An exception to the 10 year required payout is available for spousal beneficiaries, disabled and chronically ill beneficiaries, individuals not more than 10 years younger than the original plan participant, and minor children of the original plan participant until they reach the age of majority.
- Eliminating the restriction prohibiting contributions to Individual Retirement Accounts after the age of 70½. Under the SECURE Act, any taxpayer with earned income is permitted to make a contribution to an IRA regardless of their age.
- Creation of a new exception to the 10% early distribution penalty for qualified birth or adoption expenses. The penalty free distribution is limited to $5,000 and must be taken within a year following the birth or adoption event.
- Expansion of eligibility for qualified retirement plan participation, and creation of new incentives for employers to provide qualified retirement plans for their employees.

In addition to the retirement planning changes, the SECURE Act also repealed the changes to the Kiddie Tax imposed by the Tax Cuts and Jobs Act (TCJA) of 2017. TCJA had subjected the net unearned income of a child under the age of 18, or under the age of 24 and a full-time student, to the Trust and Estate tax rates. The SECURE Act repeals this change, and as a consequence the net unearned income of children is again taxed at their parent's marginal tax rate.

Finally, the SECURE Act made some changes to the Section 529 plan rules. Tax-free distributions from 529 plans may now be used to pay for apprenticeship costs, and student loan repayments not exceeding $10,000.

To offset some of the revenue loss created by various provisions of the SECURE ACT, the Act substantially increases the failure to file penalty for individual income tax returns.

The Taxpayer Certainty and Disaster Tax Relief Act of 2019 included the following tax changes:

- Extension, through tax year 2020, of:
  - the exclusion from gross income resulting from the discharge of certain qualified principal residence indebtedness
  - the mortgage insurance premium deduction, which may be claimed by taxpayers itemizing deductions
  - the above-the-line deduction for qualified tuition and related expenses
- Reduced the floor for deductibility of medical expenses from 10% to 7.5% for tax years 2019 and 2020, and applied this threshold to the exception to the 10% penalty for distributions from IRAs and employer-sponsored retirement plans.
- Created a new Qualified Disaster Distribution opportunity from retirement accounts for individuals who have principal residences in Federally declared disaster areas and who suffer an economic loss as result of that disaster, provided the disaster occurred between January 1, 2018 and 60 days after the enactment of the act. Individuals meeting the qualification requirements are:
  - Exempt from the 10% early distribution penalty
  - Exempt from mandatory withholding requirements
  - Eligible to spread the distribution evenly over a 3-year period unless the taxpayer elects to include the full amount in the year of the distribution
  - Eligible to repay the distribution within 3 years of the date of the distribution to avoid tax consequences
- Expanded the availability of retirement plan loans by increasing the maximum permissible loan from $50,000 to $100,000 for qualified disasters. The act also permitted the borrower to delay loan repayments for up to one year.

RECENT TAX LAW CHANGES

The Coronavirus Aid, Relief, and Economic Security (CARES) Act of 2020

On March 27, 2020, President Trump signed the CARES Act; the Federal Government's response to the Coronavirus pandemic. Several temporary tax changes were made to encourage employers to retain employees in light of the economic fallout from the pandemic. Some of the major tax provisions that affect tax planning include:

- Allowing a five-year carry back for net operating losses incurred in 2018, 2019, and 2020 (the carryback provision had been eliminated by TCJA 2017).
- Permitting taxpayers with net operating losses to offset 100% of taxable income with those NOLs (compared with the 80% limitation imposed by TCJA 2017).
- A temporary suspension of the excess business loss limitations imposed by TCJA 2017 (for losses incurred in 2018, 2019, and 2020).
- An increase in the interest expense limitation from 30% to 50% for tax years 2019 and 2020.
- Creation of a charitable deduction that can be taken as an adjustment to income of $300 for 2020.
- Elimination of the adjusted gross income limitations for charitable deductions of cash to a qualified charity for tax year 2020.

- An increase in the charitable deduction limitation for corporations from 10% to 25% of taxable income for tax year 2020.
- A new exclusion from income of student loan payments made by an employer up to $5,250 for tax year 2020.
- Penalty free withdrawals from certain retirement plans for qualified individuals affected by coronavirus or coronavirus-related restrictions. The tax associated with these withdrawals may be paid over a three-year period. To avoid tax on the distribution, amounts distributed can be paid back into the plan within the three-year period.

The Consolidated Appropriations Act of 2020

On December 27, 2020, President Trump signed the Consolidated Appropriations Act into law. This legislation, which included the Taxpayer Certainty and Disaster Tax Relief Act (TCDTRA) of 2020 and the COVID-Related Tax Relief Act (COVIDTRA) OF 2020, provided further coronavirus-related relief, and made some changes to tax rules. The following list summarizes those changes that are most important for income tax planning:

- Increased the allowance for business meals from 50% to 100% for expenses incurred after December 31, 2020 until the end of 2022.
- Increased the above-the-line charitable deduction from $300 to $600 for married couples filing jointly (for tax year 2021). Taxpayers who overstate this deduction, however, are subject to an accuracy related penalty of 50% (up from 20%).
- Repealed the Tuition and Fees deduction for educational expenses for tax years beginning after December 31, 2020.
- Increased the phase-out limits for the Lifetime learning credit. For tax years beginning after December 31, 2020, the phase-out limits match those used for the American Opportunity Credit.
- Increased the corporate charitable contribution deduction, for qualified contributions, to 25% of the corporation's taxable income for tax year 2021.
- Increased the AGI limit on individual charitable contributions of cash to a qualified charity from 60% to 100% through the end of 2021.
- Permanently extended the 7.5% floor for itemizing medical expenses.
- Extended the exclusion from income on discharge of qualified principal residence indebtedness through December 31, 2025. The maximum exclusion is reduced from $2 million to $750,000.
- Created an additional standard deduction for qualified disaster-related personal casualty losses, subject to a $500 per casualty floor.

The American Rescue Plan Act of 2021

On March 11, 2021, President Biden signed the American Rescue Plan Act of 2021 into law. Tax-related provisions include:

- The limit on deductibility of excess business losses for flow-through business entities imposed by TCJA for tax years 2018-2025 is extended for one year, through December 31, 2026.
- For taxpayers with adjusted gross income below $150,000, up to $10,200 of unemployment compensation received during the 2020 tax year is excluded from income.
- For the 2021 tax year only, the child tax credit is increased from $2,000 to $3,000 ($3,600 for children under age 6), with a reduced phaseout on the increased amount. In addition, eligibility is expanded to include 17-year-old children, and the credit is fully refundable.
- For the 2021 tax year only, for a taxpayer with no children the minimum age to qualify for the earned income credit is lowered to age 19 and there is no maximum age (in all other tax years, the taxpayer must be between ages 25 and 64), and the credit percentage and phaseout amount are increased.
- For tax years beginning after December 31, 2020, the earned income tax credit is available for certain married taxpayers who do not file jointly. In addition, the threshold for disqualified investment income is increased to $10,000 for 2021 and will be adjusted for inflation in subsequent years.
- For the 2021 tax year only, the dollar limit and applicable percentage for the dependent care tax credit are increased and the credit is refundable.
- For the 2021 tax year only, the exclusion for employer-provided dependent care assistance is increased from $5,000 to $10,500 ($5,250 for married taxpayers filing separately).
- Certain student loan discharges after December 31, 2020 and before January 1, 2026 are excluded from income.
- For tax years beginning after December 31, 2026, the number of covered employees subject to the $1 million deduction limit on compensation will include the corporation's chief executive officer, chief financial officer, and the five other highest compensated employees (increased from three other highest paid officers); however, the rule stipulating that a covered employee will remain a covered employee in all subsequent years (including after retirement) applies only to the CEO and CFO, and to those who fell into the category of covered employee as one of the three highest paid officers prior to 2027. Those who are covered employees as a result being among the five highest paid employees after 2026 will not remain covered employees indefinitely.

INCOME TAXES AND THE IRS

The Internal Revenue Service, a bureau of the United States Department of the Treasury, is charged with the daunting task of providing America's taxpayers with top quality service by helping them understand and meet their tax responsibilities and by applying the tax law with integrity and fairness to all. The IRS has over 100,000 employees and based on the number of tax returns filed each year, it is easy to see why the IRS requires so many employees.

Exhibit 1.3 | Number of Returns Filed, by Type of Return

Type of Return	*2019*	*2018*	*Percentage Change*
United States, Total	**253,035,393**	**250,321,406**	**1.1%**
Income Tax, Total	191,471,082	190,613,300	0.5%
C or other Corporation	2,146,904	2,127,673	0.9%
S Corporation (Form 1120-S)	5,186,557	5,128,058	1.19%
Partnership (Form 1065)	3,946,342	4,239,198	-6.9%
Individual	154,094,555	152,937,949	0.8%
Forms 1040, 1040A, 1040EZ	153,130,682	151,934,683	0.8%
Forms 1040NR, 1040NR-EZ, 1040-SS, 1040C	963,873	1,003,266	-3.9%
Individual Estimated Tax (Form 1040-ES)	22,225,590	22,387,449	-0.7%
Estate and Trust (Form 1041)	3,116,479	3,096,806	0.6%
Estate and Trust Estimated Tax (Form 1041-ES)	754,655	696,167	8.4%
Employment Taxes	31,566,173	30,942,654	2.0%
Estate Tax	25,742	34,092	-24.5%
Gift Tax	239,618	245,584	-2.4%
Excise Taxes	1,073,183	1,049,493	2.3%
Tax-Exempt Organization	1,590,421	1,603,499	-0.8%
Supplemental Documents	27,069,174	25,832,784	4.8%

Source: Internal Revenue Service Data Book, 2019, Table 2

As shown in **Exhibit 1.3**, the IRS is responsible for processing and reviewing many types of tax returns. In addition to receiving or processing a large number of tax returns (approximately 250 million annually), the IRS also pursues significant collection efforts. As shown in **Exhibit 1.4**, the IRS collected more than $3.5 trillion dollars in 2019. Note that individual income taxes make up both the largest number of returns and the largest amount of net collections. This is consistent with data from the Office of Management and Budget indicating that individual income taxes make up more than 40 percent of the revenues of the federal government.

Exhibit 1.4 | Internal Revenue Collections

Type of Tax	*Gross Collections* for FY 2019*
Total Collections	**$3,564,583,961**
Total Income Taxes	**$2,258,708,451**
Business Income Tax	$277,057,735
Individual Income Tax	$1,942,182,201
Estate & Trust Income Tax	$39,468,515
Employment Taxes	**$1,207,553,842**
Estate Taxes	**$16,001,974**
Gift Taxes	**$1,563,070**
Excise Taxes	**$80,756,624**

**Money amounts are in thousands of dollars.*
Source: Internal Revenue Service Data Book, 2019, Table 6

Overview of Federal Income Taxation

Prior to introducing the technical rules governing income taxation, an overview of the basic themes that will consistently emerge in the text is helpful. Having a broad overview of the income tax system may make some of the specific rules of taxation a bit easier to understand. This section is arranged in three primary parts:

1. the three tax systems
2. basic rules of income taxation
3. the triads of income taxation

Many of the major issues encountered in income taxation will come in sets of three, hence the *triads of taxation*. While we have not included all of the possible triads in this section, the ones included are intended to give a brief introduction and understanding of how the tax system works.

When reviewing these general rules of taxation, keep in mind that there are often exceptions to the rule that may change the tax result. Tax law is often structured so that while a general rule applies, which covers most situations encountered by taxpayers, special circumstances are covered by exceptions to that general rule. To make things even more confusing, there are even some exceptions to the exceptions (which brings you back to the general rule). Some, but not all, of the major exceptions to the general rules covered below are presented here. Remember that the purpose of this section of the text is to give a broad overview of how our tax law is structured; it is not intended to be an exhaustive review of the rules – the rest of the text is designed to achieve that objective.

The Three Tax Systems

In the United States, there are three separate and distinct tax systems that are relevant to tax planning:

1. the income tax system
2. the estate and gift tax system
3. the generation skipping transfer tax system

While many individuals assume that the Internal Revenue Code (IRC) is one set of rules that works together, this is not the case. There are three tax systems, and those systems do not always fit together perfectly. It is important for tax professionals and financial advisors to understand which tax system they are dealing with when contemplating or reviewing a transaction. It is possible, for example, for a single transaction to be treated as a gift for income tax purposes and as a sale for estate and gift tax purposes. Tax consequences under income tax rules may differ from those under the estate and gift tax rules. This text covers income tax rules. The gift and estate tax system, and the generation skipping transfer tax system, are covered in *Estate Planning* by Michael A. Dalton and Thomas P. Langdon.

Basic Rules of Income Taxation

As you study income taxation, you will find that two primary rules apply that can be used to determine the income tax consequences of a transaction. These two rules are:

1. All accretions to wealth, from whatever source derived, constitute income.
2. For every deduction taken for income tax purposes, there must be an inclusion in income. (But keep in mind there are exceptions even to these two rules.)

All Accretions to Wealth Constitute Income

Generally, any accretion (increase) in wealth, from any source and in any form, is subject to income taxation. U.S. citizens are subject to income tax on their worldwide income whether or not that income is reported to the IRS on a tax form (such as a W-2 or Form 1099). Income is not limited to cash compensation – it can be received in many forms, including cash, property, or even as an exchange of services (a bartering transaction) or as forgiveness of a debt that is due. Generally, any time someone's wealth has measurably increased, they will have to pay income tax on that increase in wealth. There are some limitations that apply to this principle. An individual will not have to pay income tax on income that is not yet measurable, or realized. For example, if a taxpayer purchases a stock today, and its value increases by $10 by the end of the year, the taxpayer will not have to pay income tax on the increased value. The value of the stock could increase or decrease by the time the stock is sold, so the taxpayer's actual increase in wealth is not measurable until the stock is sold or transferred. In this case, any gain or loss on the stock will be realized on sale.

The courts, and Congress, have classified certain types of increases in wealth as something other than income, thereby exempting those amounts from income tax. Continuing our example from above, when the taxpayer sells the stock that she purchased, the amount that she paid for the stock, or her taxable basis, will be received income tax free. Basis represents previously taxed income that is invested in an asset, and is exempt from tax to prevent the taxpayer from being subject to a double tax on the same income. In this example, if basis were not received income tax free on the sale of an asset the basis would be taxed twice - once when it was originally earned and then again when the asset it was used to purchase was sold. The tax-free return of basis is sometimes referred to as the capital recovery doctrine.

Another example of an exclusion from income is the receipt of life insurance proceeds upon the death of an insured person. The receipt of the tax-free death benefit is certainly a good thing for the family of the deceased individual, but it is also good for society. By exempting life insurance proceeds from income tax, Congress is encouraging individuals to purchase life insurance to protect their families in the event of their untimely death. To the extent that these risks are privately funded, there is less likelihood that the surviving family members will need to receive government assistance through welfare type payments. Congress is said to pass these types of exclusions for public policy reasons. Keep an eye out for this as you study the income tax rules – many of the exceptions to the general rules (such as the tax-free receipt of death benefits from a life insurance policy) are enacted to serve various public-policy purposes.

For Every Deduction, There Must be an Inclusion

The second basic rule governing our income tax system is that for every deduction taken on an income tax return, there must be an inclusion in income somewhere in the tax system. This principle is important for two reasons:

- to be entitled to deduct something on a tax return, a taxpayer must have included that amount in income, and
- if a taxpayer claims a deduction, that deduction should be income (and therefore subject to income tax) on someone else's return.

A common example of the requirement that taxpayers can only deduct what is already included in their gross income comes into play in charitable giving. Many individuals volunteer time to charitable causes that are important to them, and sometimes they do this in lieu of working for compensation. Since the taxpayer's time is valuable, and represents forgone income, taxpayers often ask if they can deduct the value of their time donated to the charity. The answer, of course, is no. The taxpayer cannot deduct the value of time as a charitable deduction because the value of time was not first included in the taxpayer's taxable income.

When a taxpayer claims a deduction, that deduction usually results in income for someone else. For example, if a taxpayer purchases supplies and equipment, or purchases services in furtherance of some business activity, the taxpayer is entitled to a deduction, but the person from whom the goods or services were purchased now has income. Likewise, when a taxpayer pays mortgage interest to a bank, a mortgage interest deduction is generally available, but the bank has mortgage interest income upon receipt of the interest payment.

The major exceptions to this principle are found in retirement planning and charitable planning.

When a taxpayer makes a gift of cash or property to a charity, a charitable deduction can be claimed on his or her income tax return, but the charity, as a tax-exempt entity, is not required to pay income tax on the amount received. In addition, a special exception applies when a taxpayer makes a gift of appreciated property to a charity, and has met the long-term holding rule requirement with respect to that property. The value of the charitable deduction is the fair market value of the property contributed, even though the taxpayer is not required to recognize the gain on the property and include that gain in income. This is an example of a permanent exemption with the taxpayer getting a deduction but the charity not having any taxable income.

When a business makes a contribution to a qualified retirement plan on behalf of its employees, it is entitled to an income tax deduction for the amount contributed. The employees, however, will not report the income in the current year – they will report and pay tax on the income when they take distributions from the qualified plan many years later. This is an example of a temporary mismatching of the timing of the deduction and the inclusion.

Both of these exceptions to the general rule further public policy objectives of Congress. Private funding of charitable organizations serves the public interest, as does the funding of qualified plans that will provide retirement income benefits for workers. The general rule, in these cases, has thus been modified to achieve the Congressional public policy objectives.

Triads of Income Taxation

As mentioned earlier, income tax rules tend to come in threes. Exposure to these triads of income taxation should help you understand the purpose of the specific income tax rules that are presented in the chapters that follow. In summary, the triads covered here include:

- three types of income
- three types of tax accounting
- three key tax principles
- three components for classifying gains
- three types of assets
- three uses of assets
- three types of rental real estate
- three methods of tax planning
- three anti-abuse provisions
- three types of administrative rulings
- three types of final regulations
- three courts to resolve disputes

Three Types of Income

In the U.S. income tax system, there are three types of income:

1. active (ordinary) income
2. portfolio income
3. passive income

Every bit of income earned by a taxpayer must be classified into one of these three categories.

Active income is income derived from labor, and income connected with the active conduct of a trade or business. Portfolio income is income derived from investments, such as interest, dividends, and capital gains. Passive income is income derived from dealings in real estate and from the conduct of a trade or business in which the taxpayer does not materially participate.

Categorization of income is important for two reasons:

- different tax consequences apply to each type of income
- the "bucket rule" limits a taxpayer's ability to write off losses in one income bucket against the gains in that same bucket

Active income (and loss) is subject to ordinary income tax rates, which are the highest tax rates in our system. Some types of portfolio income are subject to favorable income tax rates, such as the tax rate that applies to long-term capital gains and qualified dividends.[1] Passive income is subject to a host of anti-abuse rules, and therefore constitutes a separate category of income.

1. The three capital gains (and qualified dividend) rates are 0%, 15% and 20%. These rates are much lower than ordinary income tax rates. These rates do not include any surtax imposed by the Affordable Care Act on high income taxpayers.

The "bucket rule" generally limits losses in one bucket to gains in the same bucket. For example, if a taxpayer incurred $5,000 in investment gains and $20,000 in investment losses, $5,000 of the loss could offset the investment gain but could not, under the bucket rule, be used to offset other types of income (such as ordinary or passive income). As in all other areas of tax law, there are exceptions to this rule. In the case of portfolio losses, up to $3,000 of net losses incurred by an individual taxpayer in the portfolio bucket can be used to offset either active or passive income for most taxpayers. These rules will be discussed more fully in the chapters on the taxation of property transactions.

Three Types of Tax Accounting

For income to be reported properly, taxpayers must follow some method to account for income. There are three methods of accounting that are used for federal income tax purposes:

1. the cash method
2. the accrual method
3. the hybrid method

The cash method of accounting is the method used by most individuals and small businesses. Under the cash method, income is taxed when it is received, and allowable deductions are claimed when they are paid. Understanding the cash method is particularly important for advisors, who are typically providing financial advice and planning to individuals and small businesses.

The accrual method of accounting is the method frequently used by larger businesses. Under the accrual method of accounting, income is taxed when it is earned (whether or not it has been received), and deductions are claimed when they are incurred (whether or not they have been paid).

Any method of accounting other than the cash method or accrual method that is approved by the IRS is referred to, collectively, as the hybrid method. The hybrid method is used by some businesses to better reflect their economic income on their income tax returns.

Chapter 3 reviews the methods of tax accounting in more detail, and covers the exceptions to the general rules governing each accounting method listed above.

Three Key Tax Principles

Three key tax principles underlie personal income taxation. They are:

1. the doctrine of constructive receipt
2. the economic benefit doctrine
3. the doctrine of the fruit and the tree

While most individuals account for their income using the cash method, certain circumstances may arise that will subject income that has not yet been received to current taxation. The doctrine of constructive receipt states that if income is permanently set aside in an account for the benefit of a taxpayer, or if a taxpayer is given the choice to receive income now or defer it to the future, that income will be taxed to the taxpayer currently even if he does not receive it until sometime in the future. For example, consider interest that is earned on a three-year certificate of deposit. Even though a taxpayer does not receive the interest until the certificate of deposit matures, he is taxed on the earned interest currently, since the interest earnings are permanently set aside in an account for the taxpayer's benefit.

The doctrine of constructive receipt is a special exception to the cash-basis method of income tax accounting. The doctrine states that even if you have not actually received the income, but have constructively received it, then it is income. For example, if a taxpayer goes to his mailbox on December 31st and sees a check made out to that taxpayer for work he performed, immediately closes the mailbox, and comes back to get the check on January 1st, the income is reported as of December 31st. In fact, the doctrine of constructive receipt is at the cornerstone of retirement planning, and constructive receipt must be avoided if a taxpayer wishes to defer income and taxes into the future to fund his or her retirement.

You may recall from our previous discussion that all income received by a taxpayer, in any form, is subject to income tax. The economic benefit doctrine simply states that if a taxpayer receives an economic benefit as income, the value of that benefit will be subject to tax. For example, if a taxpayer is provided group term life insurance by an employer, the value of that group term insurance is subject to income tax, since it is an economic benefit received in return for labor. Congress has, however, for public policy reasons, exempted part of the value of group term life insurance from income tax, but excess amounts are taxable under the economic benefit doctrine.

The third key principal of income taxation is that income is taxed to either:

- the person who earns it, or
- the person who owns the asset that produced the income.

This principle is referred to as the doctrine of the fruit and the tree or the assignment of income doctrine. He who owns the tree pays income tax on the fruit that the tree produces. This doctrine is really an anti-abuse provision. It is designed to prevent taxpayers from assigning income to a family member in a lower income tax bracket while retaining the asset that produces the income.

Three Components for Classifying Gain

When property is sold, the manner of taxation will depend on:

1. the type of asset that was held
2. the use to which the asset was put
3. the holding period (how long the asset was held)

Two of these criteria are specified in their own sections, below. The holding period requirement is discussed in more detail in Chapter 11 on property transactions.

Three Types of Assets

In the U.S. income tax system, there are only three types of assets:

1. capital assets
2. ordinary income assets
3. IRC Section 1231 assets

To properly determine the tax consequences upon the sale or disposition of property, the taxpayer must first know what type of property was sold. Each type of asset has its own income tax consequences and rules. Depending on the type of asset, different income tax rates may apply, or different loss limitation rules may be imposed. The first step that an advisor should take in determining the tax consequences of a sale of property is to identify the property by its asset type. The rules concerning property transactions are covered in detail in Chapters 11, 12, and 13 of the text.

Three Uses of Assets
Another factor that impacts the tax treatment associated with a sale or disposition of property is how that asset was used by the taxpayer. Individuals can use an asset in one of three ways:

1. they can use it for personal purposes (personal use assets),
2. they can use it in the active conduct of a trade or business (business assets), or
3. they can use it for the production of income (production of income assets).

Personal use assets include such things as personal residences, cars, furniture, and the like. Business assets include any assets used in the active conduct of a trade or business, such as machinery, equipment, and real estate. Production of income assets include stocks and bonds and other assets held for investment.

When attempting to determine the tax consequences resulting from the sale of property, an advisor should:

- determine the type of asset
- determine how that asset was used by the taxpayer

The tax rates and loss limitation rules may differ depending on the use to which a taxpayer puts an asset as well as the type of asset that is sold. The rules concerning property transactions are covered in detail in Chapters 11, 12, and 13 of the text.

Three Types of Rental Real Estate
Real estate has always received special attention in both our legal and our income tax systems. When real estate is held for rental purposes, it is considered trade or business property because of the for-profit purpose. The tax consequences on the sale of rental real estate, however, will depend on how that rental real estate was used. There are three types of rental real estate activities:

1. tax-free rental activities
2. ordinary rental use activities
3. mixed use activities

The income inclusion and deduction rules differ depending on the use to which the rental real estate was put. The tax rules concerning rental real estate activities are covered in detail in Chapter 8.

Three Methods of Tax Planning
Advisors need to know the income tax rules so they can help clients minimize exposure to taxation while achieving their desired financial goals. There are three primary ways to engage in this type of planning.

1. The advisor and client can legally avoid taxation. In addition, the advisor may be able to help clients:
   - shift income to related taxpayers in lower income tax brackets, or
   - realize income in a form that is taxed at lower tax rates (long-term capital gains or qualified dividends).
2. The advisor and client can deduct expenses to reduce taxable income and take tax credits to reduce taxes due.
3. The advisor and client can defer income and thus defer taxation.

Three Anti-Abuse Provisions

While tax planning is useful in assisting taxpayers to minimize their income tax liability, too much tax planning could lead to wealthy individuals paying very little income tax compared to the rest of the population. Congress has imposed three sets of anti-abuse rules that limit the benefits that can be obtained from tax minimization planning. The three sets of anti-abuse income tax rules are:

1. the alternative minimum tax (AMT)
2. the at-risk rule limitations
3. the passive activity rules

The AMT is discussed in Chapter 15, and the at-risk rule limitations and passive activity loss rules are discussed in Chapter 14. These rules are designed to ensure that everybody pays a fair share of income tax on an annual basis.

Three Types of Administrative Rulings

In an attempt to administer the tax system efficiently, and provide taxpayers with information about how to treat various transactions, the Internal Revenue Service issues three types of written rulings:

1. Revenue Rulings
2. Private Letter Rulings
3. Determination Letters

These rulings are important for tax research, and are covered in more depth in Chapter 2.

Three Types of Final Regulations

The Treasury also provides guidance to taxpayers in the form of Treasury Regulations. Once finalized, the Treasury Regulations take one of three forms:

1. Procedural Regulations
2. Interpretative Regulations
3. Legislative Regulations

From a tax-research standpoint, the Treasury Regulations provide a wealth of knowledge about how the statutory law enacted by Congress will be enforced. Some of the regulations constitute law in and of themselves. The types and uses of Treasury Regulations are covered in more depth in Chapter 2.

Three Courts to Resolve Disputes

Sometimes, when the IRS and a taxpayer cannot agree on how to treat a certain transaction for income tax purposes, an independent third party is necessary to resolve the dispute. There are three courts that may resolve income tax matters:

1. the U.S. Tax Court
2. the U.S. District Court
3. the U.S. Court of Federal Claims

The requirements for bringing a case to the various courts will be discussed in detail in Chapter 2.

Summary

While this review is not intended to be a substitute for the detail that follows in the subsequent chapters, it does present a summary of some of the overriding themes that present themselves in a federal income tax course. Understanding these basic principles may assist in developing a deeper understanding of the more complex rules of federal income taxation.

PERSPECTIVE OF THE TEXT

The perspective of this text is that of a professional tax or other financial professional who is providing professional services to clients with a variety of needs, including income tax planning needs. This textbook presents an essential foundation of income tax principles, concepts, and rules and focuses on income tax planning in a manner that will be useful for tax professionals, financial planners, and clients. This focus on the practical application of tax principles and concepts is a distinguishing characteristic of the book.

Although many accountants and other financial professionals are not tax specialists, any competent financial advisor should understand the basic principles of income taxation and be able to recognize tax planning opportunities available to each client. In addition, a competent advisor must know enough about income taxation to avoid giving bad advice because of ignorance of tax laws. Most advisors who are not tax specialists work with Certified Public Accountants (CPAs), tax attorneys and other tax specialists to assure that each client's tax planning needs are adequately considered. Even advisors who are very knowledgeable about taxation frequently work cooperatively with other professionals in tax and other financial fields to best serve the needs of the client.

Income tax planning is a process that matches a client's goals, needs, attitudes, and financial circumstances with available tax planning options. Effective income tax planning requires that the advisor understand:

1. the client's goals and needs (both personal and financial)
2. the client's attitudes (including risk tolerance)
3. the client's financial circumstances
4. the basic principles of income taxation
5. the details of the income tax rules
6. the tax planning opportunities available with respect to the various topical areas

This understanding or knowledge base must then be used by the advisor to identify, recommend, and assist in the implementation of useful tax planning strategies for the client.

Exhibit 1.5 | Overview of Text

- Chapter 2: Working with the Tax Law
- Chapter 3: Fundamentals of Income Taxation
- Chapter 4: Gross Income from Personal and Investment Activities
- Chapter 5: Gross Income from Employment
- Chapter 6: Introduction to Deductions
- Chapter 7: Itemized Deductions
- Chapter 8: Other Deductions, Penalties, and Loss Disallowance
- Chapter 9: Tax Credits
- Chapter 10: Basis Rules, Depreciation, and Asset Categorization
- Chapter 11: The Taxation of Capital Assets
- Chapter 12: Business Assets
- Chapter 13: Nontaxable Exchanges
- Chapter 14: Passive Activity Rules
- Chapter 15: The Alternative Minimum Tax
- Chapter 16: Business Entity Selection and Taxation

Chapter 2 introduces concepts related to working with the tax law. The various sources and types of tax law are described. This chapter also covers the basics of the audit process and the various penalties to which a taxpayer may be subject if he does not follow the tax laws. Finally, the framework within which tax controversies are resolved is described, including taxpayers' options for appealing the decision of a court or administrative body.

Chapters 3 through 9 describe the income tax system and the calculation of gross income and tax liability. Chapter 3 first introduces the basic concepts of income taxation, including how to determine a taxpayer's filing status, how to determine dependency, and how to calculate the tax liability based on a given level of taxable income. Chapter 4 then provides in-depth coverage of various personal and investment activities that generate items that are included and excluded from gross income. Chapter 5 also deals with inclusions and exclusions from gross income, but focuses on items that are related to employment. Chapter 5 includes an extensive discussion of the taxation of fringe benefits. Chapter 6 introduces the concept of a deduction and discusses above-the-line deductions or adjustments to income. Chapter 7 takes this discussion a step further and examines the various itemized deductions to which a taxpayer may be entitled. Chapter 8 considers the limitations on deductions that can be taken against income. Finally, Chapter 9 discusses the tax credits that may be available to help taxpayers reduce their tax liability, or even create an income tax refund.

Chapters 10 through 14 examine the taxation of property transactions including sales and other dispositions. Chapter 10 introduces the concepts of basis, depreciation, and how assets should be categorized for tax purposes. Chapter 11 further examines the tax consequences of transactions involving capital assets. Chapter 12 delves into the tax consequences of transactions involving business assets. Chapter 13 discusses nontaxable exchanges, or transactions that may result in no tax assuming that the specified requirements are met. Chapter 14 contains a discussion of the passive activity rules, which limit a taxpayer's ability to recognize losses associated with the passive activities.

Chapter 15 explores the alternative minimum tax, the stated purpose of which is to prevent taxpayers with high incomes from paying little or no income tax by taking advantage of various preferences in the tax code. However, the number of taxpayers who were affected by the AMT was increasing prior to TCJA 2017. The TCJA attempts to provide much needed relief from AMT.

Finally, Chapter 16 discusses the characteristics and taxation of various legal entities, including C corporations, S corporations, partnerships, and LLCs. This discussion is particularly useful to advisors whose clients may be considering starting a business. Entity selection can affect not only the taxation of the business, but the taxation of the business owner as well.

2

WORKING WITH THE TAX LAW

LEARNING OBJECTIVES

1. Identify the three primary sources of tax law.*
2. Describe the legal basis for the modern income tax system.
3. Explain the process through which statutory law is established.
4. Identify the sources of administrative law.
5. Explain the difference between proposed, temporary, and final regulations.
6. Determine whether a taxpayer engaging in tax planning may rely on proposed, temporary, and final regulations.*
7. Explain the difference between procedural, interpretive, and legislative regulations.
8. Describe the rulings, letters, and procedures that may be issued by the Internal Revenue Service.
9. Determine whether a taxpayer may rely on rulings, letters, and procedures issued by the Internal Revenue Service.*
10. Explain the role of the Internal Revenue Service in the administration of the U.S. Tax System.
11. Describe the statute of limitations applicable to the tax return of a given taxpayer.*
12. Describe penalties imposed for failing to comply with the tax law.*
13. Calculate the failure to file and failure to pay penalties.
14. Describe the penalties that may be imposed on tax preparers.
15. Describe the process through which tax returns are chosen for an audit.
16. Identify the dispute resolution options available to taxpayers.
17. Determine the most appropriate court to hear a taxpayer's case given information about a dispute between taxpayers and the Internal Revenue Service.
18. Identify sources of tax information available to practitioners.

**Ties to CFP Certification Learning Objectives*

INTRODUCTION

To many, the tax law seems to be an endless maze of confusing rules and exceptions. Understanding how these rules and exceptions fit together and how they can be used for planning purposes seems to be a daunting task. Once the structure of the rules is understood, however, the income tax laws are easier to navigate and their significance for planning becomes apparent. The purpose of this chapter is to present the basic structure of our income tax system so that the various components of that system can be used by taxpayers in their planning.

SOURCES OF TAX LAW

There are three primary sources of tax law: statutory, administrative, and judicial. These sources of law reflect the structure of our political system.

Before we elaborate on the direct sources of tax law, however, it is important to understand the origin of our income tax system. As originally adopted, the U.S. Constitution did not give the federal government the ability to collect a tax on income. At the founding of our nation, there was a great deal of suspicion surrounding the new, federal, centralized government, and the states did not want the power of the federal government to get out of control. Consequently, they imposed limitations on the federal government's ability to impose taxes. As time went on, however, and as the federal government began to assume a more active governance role, a source of revenue was needed to fund the cost of these activities. While Congress had enacted an income tax on several previous occasions, these taxes were either temporary, or were declared unconstitutional by the Supreme Court. With the obvious need for revenue, and the Supreme Court's decree that a federal income tax was unconstitutional, it became clear that a constitutional amendment would be needed to grant the Congress the power to lay and collect taxes on income.

On February 25, 1913, the **16th Amendment** to the U.S. Constitution was adopted. This short amendment stated, "The Congress shall have power to lay and collect taxes on income, from whatever source derived, without apportionment among the several States, and without regard to any census or enumeration."

The Constitution, through enactment of the 16th Amendment, became the foundation for income tax law in the United States. Two clauses of the 16th Amendment are particularly important in developing an understanding of our income tax system: (1) the "power to lay and collect taxes on income," and (2) the clause "from whatever source derived."

Key Concepts

1. Identify the three primary sources of tax law.
2. Describe the legal basis for the modern income tax.
3. Explain the process through which statutory tax law is established.
4. Identify the sources of administrative tax law.

As you will see from the in-depth definition of "income" in Chapter 3, the term "income" is not as easily interpreted as it may at first seem. Generally, any accretion to an individual's wealth is income, and is therefore subject to taxation. For reasons of public policy and fairness, however, Congress and the Courts have imposed various limitations on what constitutes income for tax purposes. Exemptions and exclusions also allow some accretions to wealth to avoid income taxes altogether. We will discuss these items more specifically in future chapters.

As the second important clause from the 16th Amendment indicates, a U.S. citizen is subject to income tax on income "from whatever source derived." In other words, the worldwide income of U.S. citizens from any source is subject to taxation by the U.S.

Exhibit 2.1 | Sources of Tax Law

Source	Authority	Law
Statutory (Legislative Branch)	Congressionally enacted law through legislative power provided by the 16th Amendment to the U.S. Constitution.	Internal Revenue Code of 1986, as amended.
Administrative (Executive Branch)	• **Treasury Department:** Executive authority of law enforcement delegated to the Treasury Department. • **Internal Revenue Service:** Tax collection authority delegated by the Treasury Department to the Internal Revenue Service.	• **Treasury Regulations:** a. Proposed Regulations b. Temporary Regulations c. Final Regulations • **IRS Determinations:** a. Revenue Rulings b. Private Letter Rulings c. Determination Letters d. Revenue Procedures
Judicial (Judicial Branch)	Judicial authority to determine if tax laws enacted by Congress and enforced by the President are constitutional. Also, decides whether a regulation or IRS position follows the intent of Congress.	**Case Law:** A case or controversy between a taxpayer and the IRS resulting in case law expressed in the opinion of a court.

Statutory Sources of Tax Law

While the 16th Amendment gave Congress the authority to "lay and collect" an income tax, it did not actually impose an income tax on the citizenry. Shortly after the passage of the 16th Amendment, Congress passed the Revenue Act of 1913 - the first version of the law that would become known as the Internal Revenue Code.

Since 1913, the entire body of statutory law concerning income taxation has been codified three times: 1939, 1954, and 1986. The present Internal Revenue Code is referred to as the "Internal Revenue Code of 1986, as amended."

The Internal Revenue Code (IRC) is the statutory source of law on taxation. Since the 16th Amendment to the Constitution gave Congress the power to collect and levy taxes on income from whatever source derived, taxpayers must adhere to the Code unless the U.S. Supreme Court declares that a provision of the Code is unconstitutional. Given that the 16th Amendment permits Congress to impose a tax on income, but does not impose any restrictions on that power, it is rare to find circumstances where provisions of the income tax code as enacted by Congress will be found unconstitutional by the courts. The relatively few cases that have been heard by the courts on this matter tend to deal with the definition of income. Certainly, if something is not legally classified as income, Congress does not have the power to tax it under the 16th Amendment.

Only Congress can amend the Code, since it is the source of statutory law in the United States. Sometimes, administrative agencies get overzealous in enforcing the Code, and attempt to fix holes left by Congress by enacting regulations that go beyond the language of the statute and the intent of Congress. While the administrative agency's intent may seem proper, its action is not – the administrative branch of government cannot change statutory law without congressional action. When administrative agencies, such as the IRS and the Treasury Department, get overzealous in their interpretation of the tax code, the courts may strike down regulations that are not consistent with the statutory pronouncements of Congress.

A recent example of overreaching by the IRS and Treasury that was struck down by the courts was the IRS' attempt to require all individuals who prepare tax returns for compensation to meet competency requirements. In an attempt to combat erroneous filings and perceived abuses in the preparation of individual income tax returns, The IRS announced that all tax preparers (other than CPAs and Attorneys) would be required to pass a licensing examination and complete 15 hours of continuing education on an annual basis. While this move was supported by many large national tax preparation chains, several individual tax preparers brought suit against the IRS, alleging that Congress had never granted the Treasury or the IRS the authority to impose licensing requirements for tax preparers. In early 2013, the United States District Court agreed, and issued a permanent injunction against Treasury and IRS efforts to require licensing. The court concluded that the Treasury and IRS, as administrative agencies of the government, could not impose requirements that were not specified by statute. The IRS appealed the District Court Decision and the U.S. Circuit Court affirmed the district court ruling. Consequently, the IRS cannot impose those requirements on tax preparers. Of course, should Congress decide that licensing of tax preparers serves the public interest, Congress could overrule the court decision by passing legislation authorizing the IRS to impose licensing and continuing education requirements.

How Tax Laws are Passed

Income tax legislation begins as a revenue bill. All revenue bills must arise in the lower house of Congress, the House of Representatives, and may not be initiated by the executive branch, judicial branch, or Senate. The House Ways and Means Committee has jurisdiction over tax legislation in the House of Representatives. Once tax legislation has passed the House Ways and Means Committee, the entire House of Representatives can consider the tax bill. If the tax bill receives a favorable vote in the House, it is then sent to the Senate for further consideration. The Senate Finance Committee will review the bill, and, if it passes through that Committee, the entire Senate may debate and vote on the proposed legislation.

It is rare to see a proposed income tax bill adopted in exactly the same form in both the Senate and the House. Before the bill can be sent to the White House for the President's action, the bill passed by both houses of Congress must be identical. When the versions of the bill differ, the legislature will form a conference committee consisting of representatives from both the House and the Senate whose purpose is to come to a mutually agreeable version of the legislation. In some cases, the House and Senate cannot agree, and the proposed tax legislation fails. In other cases, a workable compromise is reached, and the revised bill is sent to both houses of Congress for further action. If both houses pass the revised legislation, the bill is then sent to the President of the United States.

When tax legislation arrives at the oval office, the President has three options:

1. sign the bill and enact it into law,
2. veto the legislation, or
3. refuse to sign the bill.

If the President signs the bill, the new legislation is now part of the body of tax law and is incorporated into the Code. If the President vetoes the bill, Congress can override the President's veto by passing the bill with a two-thirds majority vote in both houses. If the override is successful, the legislation becomes part of the Code. Overriding a presidential veto is usually a difficult task for Congress, since it is difficult to solicit enough support to achieve a two-thirds majority vote in both houses of Congress. If the President fails to sign the bill within 10 days, it becomes law without his signature. If Congress is in adjournment and the President fails to sign the bill within the 10 days allowed by the Constitution, however, the bill does not become law. The latter failure to sign and the resulting failure of the bill to become law is called a pocket veto.

The Internal Revenue Code is the only statutory source of federal tax law, and is the starting point for tax determination and research.

Administrative Sources of Tax Law

The President of the United States is the Chief Executive Officer of the U.S. Government. One of the President's primary duties is to enforce the law. As such, the President is responsible for the collection of taxes in the manner set forth in the Internal Revenue Code.

The President has delegated this authority to the Treasury Department, which in turn created, and delegated tax-collection authority to the Internal Revenue Service.

While enforcement of the Internal Revenue Code has been delegated to the Internal Revenue Service (IRS), the Treasury Department remains involved in the interpretation and clarification of tax law from an administrative standpoint by adopting Treasury regulations. The **Treasury regulations** are official interpretations of the Internal Revenue Code (IRC), and give taxpayers insight into how the Code provisions will be enforced by the IRS. Provided that the Treasury regulations are consistent with the literal provisions of the Internal Revenue Code and Congressional intent at the time the law was passed, the regulations are deemed by the courts to have the full force and effect of law.

There are several types of Treasury regulations that are easily classified based upon the stage of adoption and the function of the regulation. Those classified based upon the stage of adoption include proposed regulations, temporary regulations, and final regulations. Procedural regulations, interpretative regulations, and legislative regulations indicate the function served by the regulation.

Stage of Adoption

Proposed regulations have been drafted by the Treasury, but have not yet gone through the process of adoption. To adopt the regulation, the Treasury must comply with the provisions of the Administrative Procedures Act (APA). Under the APA, public comments must be solicited, public hearings must be held, and, after taking into consideration the input from the public, the Treasury will redraft and adopt the regulations. Proposed regulations may be thought of as a first draft of final regulations. They have no legal precedence and are not binding on taxpayers (until the regulations become final).

Temporary regulations are issued when the Treasury feels that guidance must be provided quickly to taxpayers. They are typically issued when the regulations will impact a large number of taxpayers, and the IRS wishes to give taxpayers guidance on how a particular provision of the tax code will be interpreted. Unlike proposed regulations, temporary regulations have the same authority as final regulations and are binding on taxpayers once issued. Issuing temporary regulations does not relieve the Treasury of the obligation to satisfy the requirements of the Administrative Procedures Act – temporary regulations are just that... temporary. Temporary regulations are binding on taxpayers pending the adoption of final regulations in accordance with the Administrative Procedures Act.

Final regulations began as proposed or temporary regulations, but have been formally adopted after compliance with the requirements of the Administrative Procedures Act. Final regulations have the full force and effect of law provided that they are consistent with the Internal Revenue Code provisions they interpret. Final regulations let taxpayers know how the Treasury and IRS will interpret and enforce the tax law. Once issued, they are binding on taxpayers and the Treasury (unless the Treasury takes action to amend the regulations). Courts, however, are not bound by final regulations. To the extent that a court determines that the regulation is not consistent with the Code, that the regulation exceeds the intent of Congress when enacting the Code, or that the regulation is unconstitutional, a court can invalidate a Treasury regulation.

Function of Regulation

Procedural regulations are merely housekeeping instructions indicating how the Treasury and IRS will conduct their affairs. They are useful to a taxpayer, for example, when the taxpayer would like to request a ruling from the IRS and needs to know how to do so. Procedural regulations do not deal with substantive issues of tax law. Instead, they deal with administration of the tax system.

Most Treasury regulations are **interpretative regulations**. That is, they provide an official interpretation of the Internal Revenue Code. Taxpayers may rely on interpretive regulations in tax planning. If, however, the regulations are not consistent with the Code or do not express the intent of Congress, a taxpayer may take a position in opposition to the regulations. Most likely, when this happens the issue will wind up in court, and the court will have to determine whether the regulation appropriately interprets the law. If the court finds that the regulation is not consistent with Congressional intent, it may invalidate the regulation.

The final type of regulation, a **legislative regulation**, permits the Treasury to determine the details of the law. Legislative regulations have the full force and effect of law as if Congress had passed them. Sometimes when Congress enacts tax legislation, Congress has a general idea of what it would like to accomplish, but has not yet worked out all of the details. Instead of waiting until the details are worked out, it passes the legislation, and includes language to the effect that "the Treasury shall promulgate regulations to effectuate the intent of Congress." When Congress does this, it is delegating part of its law-making authority to the Treasury. Provided that the delegation of authority was limited in scope, was definite, and was not overly broad, when the Treasury enacts legislative regulations they are treated as if they were passed by Congress and signed by the President. Unlike interpretative regulations, which can be overturned by the courts if the courts determine that the regulations were inconsistent with the intent of Congress, legislative regulations may only be overturned by the Courts if they are determined to be unconstitutional.

The Internal Revenue Service

Regulations issued by the Treasury are one source of administrative law. Another administrative source of tax law comes from the Internal Revenue Service in the form of:

- revenue rulings
- private letter rulings
- determination letters
- revenue procedures

Revenue rulings are based on a set of facts that are common to many taxpayers, and are issued to the public to give taxpayers insight into how the IRS will treat certain transactions. Once issued, a revenue ruling is binding on the IRS. Therefore, a taxpayer can rely on a revenue ruling when engaging in tax planning. If the taxpayer engages in the same activity covered by the revenue ruling, the IRS must treat the transaction in the manner prescribed in the revenue ruling. Of course, if the taxpayer does not agree with the IRS's position described in the revenue ruling, he or she may take a contrary position. When this happens, the taxpayer and the IRS will likely end up in Court, and the Court will decide whether or not the revenue ruling is consistent with the Code. If the Court finds that the revenue ruling is inconsistent with the Code, or is unconstitutional, it may strike down the revenue ruling. All newly adopted revenue rulings are published weekly in the Internal Revenue Bulletin (which is published by the IRS).

Unlike a revenue ruling, which covers facts applicable to a large number of taxpayers, a **private letter ruling** is issued at the request of an individual taxpayer who would like to know how the IRS would treat an individual transaction that the taxpayer plans to engage in. The advantage of requesting a private letter ruling is that the taxpayer can solicit advice from the IRS on the tax consequences of a proposed transaction before the taxpayer enters into the transaction. Once issued, the private letter ruling binds the IRS with respect to that transaction for that taxpayer. The IRS may, however, change its mind when another taxpayer requests a private letter ruling proposing the same transaction, so it is possible that the tax results for taxpayers entering into the same transaction may differ. Private letter rulings, therefore, cannot be relied on for tax planning purposes, but are helpful in ascertaining IRS thinking on the proposed transaction. If a taxpayer can find a series of private letter rulings covering his or her proposed transaction, and those rulings all come to the same conclusion, there is a substantial likelihood that the IRS will follow its prior rulings, but it is important to remember that the IRS could change its mind. Private letter rulings are only valid for the taxpayer requesting the private letter ruling and only for the facts and law prescribed. If the requesting taxpayer changes the facts or transaction, the private letter ruling is no longer valid. Unlike revenue rulings, private letter rulings are persuasive evidence of how a transaction will be treated for tax purposes, but a taxpayer, who did not request the ruling, may not rely on the result of a private letter ruling as precedent.

Unlike a private letter ruling, which covers a proposed transaction, a **determination letter** may be requested from the district director of the IRS if the taxpayer has already engaged in the transaction. The application must be made to the district director for the district in which the taxpayer's tax return will be filed. The district director will issue a determination letter only if the resolution of the tax issue is clearly covered by statute, Treasury decision or regulation, or a ruling or opinion of a Court decision published in the Internal Revenue Bulletin. If the taxpayer's tax return does not report the transaction in accordance with the advice given in the determination letter, there will likely be an audit of the return. The IRS will look for consistent tax treatment when the tax return is filed, so taxpayers may wish to seek tax determination advice from their tax preparers or financial advisors instead of the district director of the IRS to avoid further IRS scrutiny of their tax returns. Since a determination letter may be issued only if the matter is settled in law, there is no need to rely on determination letters for tax planning purposes.

In addition to issuing rulings and determination letters, the IRS also issues **revenue procedures**, which detail internal practices and procedures within the IRS, and make important announcements to taxpayers. For example, all of the inflation-adjusted thresholds (standard deductions, income tax tables, phaseouts, etc.) for a given tax year are announced in a Revenue Procedure as are the applicable federal rates used for various tax planning techniques. Revenue Procedures are also published in the Internal Revenue Bulletin.

Judicial Sources of Tax Law

If all provisions of the Code were clearly stated so that there was no ambiguity and everyone who read it interpreted it the same way, there would be little need for the courts to review the adequacy of the tax law. In practice, however, there are often disagreements between taxpayers and the IRS concerning the meaning of a Code provision, or how a particular transaction should be reported on a tax return. The role of the courts in our tax system is to interpret ambiguous provisions of the Code, and ensure that the laws enacted by Congress and enforced by the President are constitutional.

The courts are not permitted to review the law on their own initiative and issue advisory opinions. A court can only review tax law when a case or controversy exists between two parties (most likely in this context, between the taxpayer and the IRS). In considering the case or controversy presented, the court can review the law that applies to the facts of the case, and determine whether or not the regulation cited by the IRS is consistent with the intent of Congress, or whether the law itself is constitutional.

When a court issues an opinion on a case or controversy brought before it, that opinion becomes part of the body of the law since the courts have the obligation and duty to state what the law means. Once a court has entered its interpretation on a given case, all lower courts in the same jurisdiction must comply with the opinion of the court. Obviously, once the U.S. Supreme Court has ruled on an issue, all U.S. courts and the administrative branches of government must comply with its decision. Congress must also comply, but can always enact legislation which, if signed by the President, would change how similar transactions are treated in the future.

The body of decisions from U.S. courts is commonly referred to as "case law." Case law is an important resource for tax planning, and reported decisions can be relied on by the taxpayer as law unless the case has been overturned by a higher court or the law relevant to the case has been changed by Congress.

A detailed overview of the courts in the Federal System that rule on tax related matters will be discussed later in this chapter. An overview of the U.S. Court System can be found in **Exhibit 2.10**.

Quick Quiz 2.1

1. The 16th Amendment imposed the income tax on U.S. citizens.
   a. True
   b. False
2. The Internal Revenue Code is one of many sources of statutory tax law.
   a. True
   b. False
3. All Treasury regulations are either proposed, temporary, or final regulations.
   a. True
   b. False
4. Private letter rulings are binding on the IRS with respect to all taxpayers, but revenue rulings are only binding on the IRS with respect to the transaction and taxpayer discussed in the ruling.
   a. True
   b. False

False, False, True, False.

ADMINISTRATION OF THE TAX SYSTEM

Role of the IRS

The IRS was created by the Treasury Department to enforce the Internal Revenue Code and collect the taxes imposed by Congress. In fulfilling its role, the IRS receives and audits tax returns of individual taxpayers, and participates in the administration of the tax system by issuing revenue rulings, private letter rulings, determination letters, and revenue procedures. In addition, the IRS also manages conflict with taxpayers in the early stages of the dispute resolution process.

Statute of Limitations

Key Concepts

1. Explain the IRS' role in the administration of the U.S. tax system.
2. Describe the statute of limitations applicable to the tax returns of a given taxpayer.
3. Describe the penalties imposed for failing to comply with the law.

Under IRC Section 6501, the **statute of limitations** for IRS examination of income tax returns is generally three years from the date a tax return is filed. This means that the IRS must generally review and contest the information submitted in the return within three years of the filing date in order to have a cause of action against a taxpayer. However, there are exceptions to the three-year rule, which are described below.

Remember that tax returns for a given tax year are typically filed in the subsequent year. Cash basis taxpayers (such as individual taxpayers), normally have a calendar-year tax period, and must file their individual income tax returns by the 15th day of the 4th month following the close of the year (April 15, for a calendar year taxpayer. Unless April 15th falls on a national holiday or weekend, or an extension has been granted). When April 15th falls on a national holiday or weekend, individual tax returns are due on the first business day following the holiday or weekend day. Assuming that the taxpayer does not receive an extension to file, the statute of limitations begins to run on April 15. IRC Section 6513 states that returns that are received by the IRS on or before the due date of the return are deemed to be filed on the due date. Therefore, if an individual taxpayer decides to file before the April 15 deadline, the statute of limitations does not begin to run until April 15. Filing early has the effect of giving the IRS a longer period of time to review the tax return.

If a taxpayer does not file by the due date of the income tax return, the statute of limitations does not begin to run until the return is actually filed. This extension of the statute of limitations applies even when the taxpayer has requested an automatic extension of time to file his tax return. If a return is never filed, the statute of limitations never starts and the IRS can review the information at any time.

The statute of limitations is extended to six years if there is a **substantial omission** of gross income on the tax return, defined as an omission of more than 25 percent of the gross income reported on the tax return. For example, the overstatement of asset basis and the resultant understatement of gain may cause an understatement of income sufficient to extend the normal statute of limitations from three years to six years. As with the normal three-year statute of limitations, the statute of limitations starts with the due date of the return, or the actual filing date of the return if the return was filed after the due date (without extensions).

If a taxpayer commits **fraud** when filing his tax return, the statute of limitations never closes.[1] If the IRS ever discovers the fraud, it can open the return for examination, assess additional taxes, and impose interest and penalties without regard to the number of years that have passed since the return was filed. Fraud implies that the taxpayer intentionally disregarded tax rules or misstated information included on the return. Because the legal standard for fraud is actual intent, fraud is difficult to prove, but once proven, can result in significant fines and penalties, and possibly the imposition of criminal sanctions on the taxpayer. Advisors should always encourage clients to truthfully report their income and deductions on their tax returns. The penalty for fraud is 75 percent of any deficiency.

In the event that the IRS assesses a tax deficiency on a taxpayer after auditing a tax return, the statute of limitations for collection of that deficiency is 10 years under Section 6502. Once an assessment is made, the IRS has a relatively long time to collect the tax due. If the IRS had issued an erroneous refund to a taxpayer, however, the statute of limitations for the IRS to file a suit to recover that refund is only two years. Section 6532 extends this time frame to five years if the erroneous refund given to the taxpayer was induced by fraud.

Yet another statute of limitations applies to taxpayers who wish to claim a refund of tax. The statute of limitations for claiming a refund is three years from the date the return was filed, or two years from the date the tax was paid, whichever is later. If no tax return is filed by the taxpayer, the limitation under Section 6511 is two years from the time the tax was paid.

Exhibit 2.2 | Statute of Limitations (In Years)

General Statute of Limitations under Section 6501	3 years
Substantial Understatement of Gross Income >25%	6 years
Fraud	No Limit
Collection of Deficiency by IRS	10 years
Refund Claim by Taxpayer	3 years

1. IRC §6501.

CASE STUDY 2.1

Statute of Limitations

Robert K. and Joan L. Paschall, Petitioners v. Commissioner of Internal Revenue, Respondent. 137 T.C. No. 2 (July 5, 2011).

Robert and Joan liked the prospect of generating tax-free income, and were not happy with the limitations imposed on Roth IRA contributions for each tax year. They opened a self directed Roth IRA in 2000 with a $2,000 contribution. After a series of corporate restructuring transactions, approximately $1.3 million was transferred to their Roth IRA one month later. For all tax years in question, Robert and Joan filed a timely Form 1040, although the filing did not include form 5329 with their tax return. After examination, the IRS assessed a tax deficiency for tax years 2002 through 2006, which included an excess contribution penalty and a failure to file penalty under Section 6651(a)(1) of over $20,000 for each tax year (since Robert and Joan did not file form 5329 with their tax return). The notices of deficiency issued by the IRS were dated February 1 and July 23, 2008. Robert and Joan argued that the IRS assessment for tax years 2002, 2003, and 2004 was barred by the statute of limitations, since Form 5329 is not a separate tax return from Form 1040. The IRS argued that Form 5329 is a separate tax return from Form 1040, and since Robert and Joan never filed the forms, the IRS was permitted to assess the excise tax at any time.

Citing ***Commissioner v. Lane-Wells Co., 321 U.S. 219 (1994) and Springfield v. United States, 88 F.3d 750 (9th Cir. 1996)***, the court stated that the statute of limitations does not start to run by the filing of one return if the return that was filed is insufficient to advise the Commissioner that any liability exists for the tax that should have been disclosed on the return. While Robert and Joan filed Form 1040, the court determined that, upon review of the return, the IRS would not reasonably be able to determine whether they were liable for an excise tax. The court determined that failing to file Form 5329 with the 1040 permitted the IRS to assess the excise tax deficiencies at any time.

Interest and Penalties for Noncompliance

Taxpayers who choose not to comply with the filing requirements are subject to a series of penalties, including the failure to file penalty, the failure to pay penalty, and the accuracy related penalty.

If a taxpayer fails to file his income tax return on time, the **failure to file penalty** under Section 6651 applies. The penalty is five percent of the unpaid tax balance for each month or part thereof that the tax return is late. Since tax returns are typically due in the middle of a month (for example, individual tax returns are due April 15th), when determining the failure to file penalty a month begins on the due date of the return and runs until the corresponding date in the succeeding calendar month (for example, April 15th - May 15th); it is not based on a calendar month.[2] The maximum failure to file penalty is 25 percent of the unpaid tax balance (or, alternatively stated, the failure to file penalty will reach its maximum once five months have passed). If a tax return is filed more than 60 days late, the minimum failure to file penalty is the lower of $435 or the amount of tax due. Since the failure to file penalty applies to the unpaid balance, no penalty is due if the taxpayer who files late is due a refund or owes no income tax. If

2. Treas. Reg. §301.6651-1(b).

the failure to file the tax return is due to fraud, the failure to file penalty is increased to 15 percent per month, up to a maximum penalty of 75 percent of the tax due.

If a taxpayer fails to pay the tax due on the due date, Section 6651 also imposes a **failure to pay penalty**. The failure to pay penalty is 0.5 percent per month or part thereof that the balance due remains unpaid. The maximum failure to pay penalty is 25 percent of the tax liability. Unlike the failure to file penalty, which will stop accruing after five months, the failure to pay penalty will continue to accrue for up to 50 months.

If a taxpayer is subject to both the failure to file penalty and the failure to pay penalty, the failure to file penalty is reduced by the failure to pay penalty for months in which they both apply. Effectively, this creates a maximum potential 25 percent penalty for the initial five months with the 0.5 percent per month failure to pay penalty continuing thereafter for up to 45 additional months.

Exhibit 2.3 | Failure to File and Failure to Pay Penalties

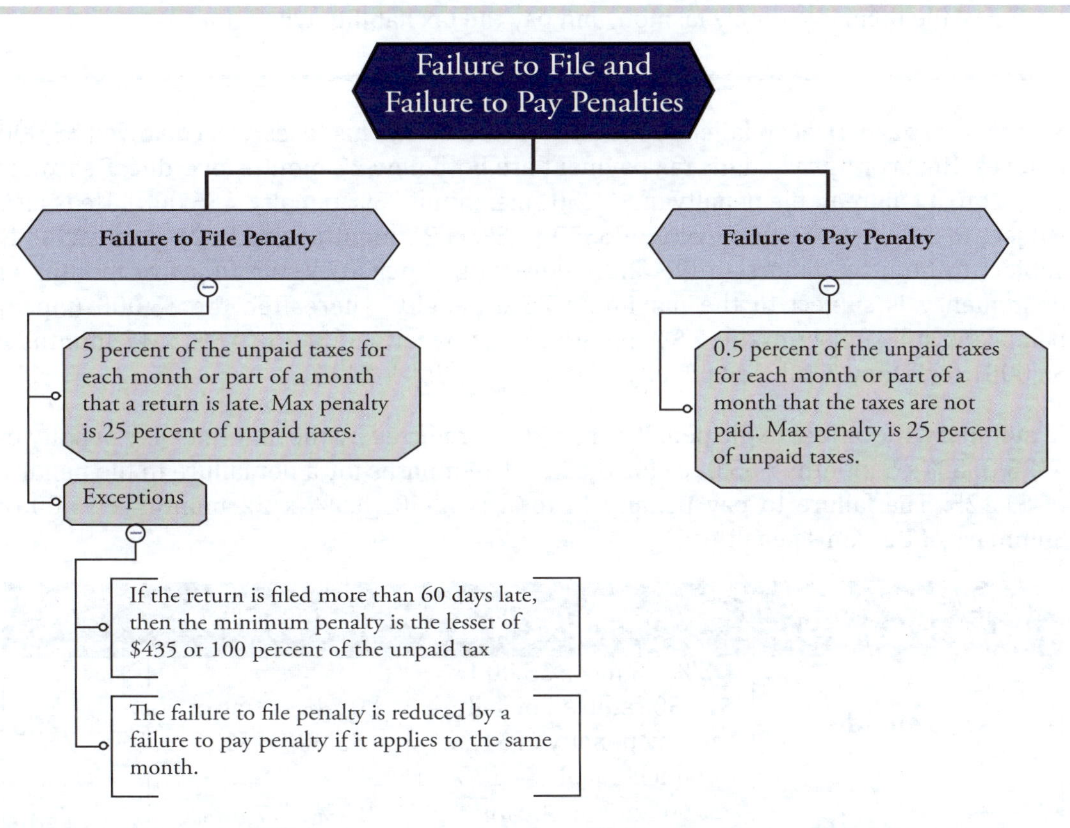

IRC Section 6662 imposes an **accuracy-related penalty** on taxpayers who file incorrect returns as a result of:

1. a failure to make a good faith effort to comply with the tax law,
2. a substantial understatement of tax liability (generally more than 10 percent of the correct tax liability and at least a $5,000 deficiency),
3. a substantial valuation understatement, or
4. a substantial estate or gift tax valuation understatement.

The penalty imposed is generally 20 percent of the underpayment amount, and can be increased to 30 percent for understatement of tax liability due to undisclosed listed transactions (certain transactions listed by the IRS as tax-shelter devices).

The stakes are even higher for those who commit fraud while failing to file or pay, and those who intentionally understate their tax liability. A fraud penalty of 75 percent of the underpayment of tax may be imposed under Section 6663. If a frivolous or incomplete income tax return has been filed, a $5,000 penalty may be imposed under Section 6702 regardless of tax liability. Intentional actions constituting fraud, or a willful failure to file or pay the tax liability that is due can rise to the level of criminal offenses. A willful failure to file an income tax return or pay the tax due is a misdemeanor under Section 7203, carrying penalties of up to $25,000 ($100,000 in the case of a corporation) in fines and up to one year in prison, or both. A willful attempt to evade tax is a felony under Section 7201, with fines up to $100,000 and jail sentences up to five years, or both. If a taxpayer willfully files a false return, he or she can be guilty of a felony under Section 7206, carrying a fine of up to $100,000 and jail sentences up to three years, or both. For obvious reasons, taxpayers should properly report their income and deductions on their tax returns, file them in a timely fashion, and pay the tax liability when due.

Example 2.1

Several years ago, Deacon failed to file a tax return or pay his taxes. Deacon owed $5,000 in taxes. His tax return and his tax payment are both now 22 months overdue. Deacon is subject to a failure to file penalty of $1,250 (maximum 25% penalty x $5,000). He is also subject to a failure to pay penalty of $550 (0.5% x 22 months x $5,000). Because he is subject to both the failure to file and failure to pay penalties, the first five months of delinquency is subject to the maximum 25% penalty. Thereafter, the $5,000 unpaid balance is still subject to the 0.5% failure to pay penalty of $425 (0.5% x 17 months x $5,000), for a total combined penalty of $1,675 ($1,250 + $425).

In summary, the failure to file penalty of $1,250 is reduced by the failure to pay penalty of $125 (0.5% x 5 months x $5,000) for the first five months for a net failure to file penalty of $1,125. The failure to pay penalty in total is $550 (0.5% x 22 months x $5,000). Summary of Deacon's penalties:

$5,000 outstanding for 22 Months	*Failure to File*	*Failure to Pay*	*Total*
1st 5 Months	5% x 5 mo. x $5,000 = $1,250 reduced by failure to pay penalty of $125, which equals $1,125	0.5% x 5 mo. x $5,000 = $125	**$1,250**
Next 17 Months	$0 - not applicable after 1st 5 months	0.5% x 17 mo. x $5,000 = $425	**$425**
Total	**$1,125**	**$550**	**$1,675**

Penalties for Underpayment of Estimated Tax

Taxpayers are required to make payments of tax ratably throughout the year, either through employer withholding or through estimated payments. Self-employed individuals and individuals with large amounts of investment income should determine the amount of tax that needs to be paid annually, and make adjustments to withholding from their employment income, or make quarterly estimated tax payments so that their required payment is made. If a taxpayer underpays estimated taxes, an underpayment of estimated tax penalty applies. When calculating the appropriate amount to pay each year, income, Social Security, and other taxes reported on an individual income tax return must be taken into account.

Estimated tax payments are not required if a taxpayer has no tax liability for the prior year, was a U.S. Citizen or resident alien for the entire year, and the prior tax year covered a 12-month period.

Individuals who will owe $1,000 or more for the current tax year, after subtracting income tax withholding and credits from tax liability, may have to make estimated tax payments. When an individual owes tax liability at the end of the year, the IRS will impose two tests on that income to determine if a penalty is appropriate. First, the IRS will check to see if the total amount of tax withholding and credits was at least 90 percent (66 $^{1}/_{3}$ percent for farmers and fishermen) of the tax due for the year. If the tax payments were less than 90 percent, a penalty will be imposed. Alternatively, the IRS will check to see if the income tax withholding was at least 100 percent of the tax shown on the prior year tax return. If it was, no penalty will be due. For high income taxpayers (those with adjusted gross income over $150,000) to avoid a tax penalty using the second test, the tax payments must have been at least 110 percent of the prior year tax liability.[3] Provided that the taxpayer made payments of an amount necessary to meet one of these tests, no penalty will be applied.

The penalty that applies if the correct amount of tax payment has not been made is really an interest charge on the underpayment. Since the government did not have use of the money on the required quarterly payment dates, it will charge interest for failing to pay the required amount on a quarterly basis even if the tax liability is paid in full by the due date of the return.

Quick Quiz 2.2

1. The statute of limitations for the IRS to examine an income tax return is generally three years.
   a. True
   b. False
2. A substantial understatement of income is an omission of more than 10% of gross income.
   a. True
   b. False
3. If a taxpayer is subject to both the failure to file penalty and the failure to pay penalty, the failure to file penalty will be reduced by the failure to pay penalty.
   a. True
   b. False
4. Willfully filing a false return is a felony.
   a. True
   b. False

True, False, True, True.

For taxpayers who are employees and also have either self-employment or investment income, quarterly tax payments may not be necessary if adjustments to withholding on employment income are made such that the income tax withheld meets the requirements of the tests discussed above. Quarterly payments are due in April, June, September, and January, and if a taxpayer elects to make quarterly estimated payments, interest penalties may be applied if enough estimated tax was not paid in on each quarterly payment due date. Withholding from employment income, however, is deemed to be ratably withheld

3. IRC §6654(d)(1)(C).

from taxpayer income throughout the year regardless of when the withholding is deducted from the taxpayer's paycheck. If a taxpayer will owe an additional tax liability for the current year, instead of making payments in April, June, and September, he or she could wait until near the end of the tax year and then instruct his or her employer (using Form W-4) to withhold additional amounts for federal income tax. This approach allows the taxpayer to have use of the funds until near the end of the year, while still avoiding an IRS penalty for underpayment, since the withheld payments are deemed to have been made ratably throughout the year.

Example 2.2

Last year, Scarlett's federal income tax liability was $28,000, and her adjusted gross income was $130,000. She expects her tax liability this year to be $35,000 due to a particularly profitable year in her consulting practice, which she operates as a sole proprietorship. In addition to being a self-employed consultant, Scarlett is a college professor at Murphy State University. Based on a review of Scarlett's pay stubs, you calculate that Murphy State University will withhold $26,000 from her employment income this year. She will, however, have to make tax payments totaling $28,000 in order to avoid a tax penalty (the lower of 100% of her prior year tax liability, $28,000, or $31,500)(current year tax liability of $35,000 x 90%). Scarlett can make quarterly payments of $500 in April, June, September, and January to cover the shortfall. Alternatively, she could fill out a form W-4 with her employer and request that an additional $2,000 be withheld from her last paycheck of the year. In either case, Scarlett would have paid in enough to avoid an underpayment of estimated tax penalty for the year.

Preparer Penalties

In addition to tax penalties that may be assessed on taxpayers, tax preparers may also be subject to penalties. IRC Section 6694(a) states that if a tax preparer takes an unrealistic position on a tax return and the preparer knew or reasonably should have known of the position, then the penalty is the greater of $1,000 or 50 percent of the income derived by the preparer for preparing the return. If the understatement was due to willful or reckless conduct, the penalty is the greater of $5,000 or 50 percent of income derived by the preparer for the return.

Other penalties may also be assessed, including penalties for failure to sign a return prepared by the tax preparer,[4] failure to provide a copy of the tax return to the taxpayer,[5] failure to keep a copy of the return,[6] and a client list, and failure to comply with due diligence requirements when claiming the earned income credit.[7]

Treasury Department Circular No. 230 (revised 6-2014) establishes standards of conduct for tax preparers; and those who plan to prepare tax returns should become familiar with its content. Practitioners who prepare tax returns should keep abreast of the changes in this area, and make sure that their actions will not subject them to penalties.

4. IRC §6695(b).
5. IRC §6695(a).
6. IRC §6695(d).
7. IRC §6695(g).

Exhibit 2.4 | Summary of Penalties

Failure to File	5% per month or part thereof to 25% maximum
Failure to Pay	0.5% per month or part thereof to 25% maximum
Accuracy Related	20% of underpayment to 30%*
Fraud	75% of underpayment attributable to fraud

**40% if due to substantial valuation misstatement, substantial overstatement of pension liabilities, or substantial estate or gift tax valuation understatement.*

Audits

In the United States, taxpayers self-report their income and deductible expenses, and also calculate the amount of tax due. While the government presumes that most individuals will properly report their taxable transactions and pay the correct amount of tax, an audit system encourages compliance by selecting tax returns for review. The primary purpose of an audit is to test whether or not the tax return filed by the taxpayer truthfully reflects their income and allowable deductions. There are several ways that tax returns are chosen for audit.

Key Concepts

1. Describe the process through which tax returns are chosen for an audit.
2. Identify the dispute resolution options available to taxpayers.
3. Determine the most appropriate court to hear a taxpayer's case given information about the dispute between the taxpayer and the IRS.

The most common type of audit today is a computer generated audit, referred to as the "**Discriminant Inventory Function**" or DIF. Once filed, a tax return is checked against information sources reported to the IRS. These information sources include employer-filed W-2 forms which disclose the amount of money a taxpayer made during the year as well as withholding for income and payroll taxes. Firms that hire independent contractors file Form 1099, disclosing gross payments made to independent contractors. Banks and brokerage firms file Form 1099 forms with the IRS disclosing the amount of interest, dividends, and gross proceeds from the sale of securities. If a tax return filed by a taxpayer does not include at least the amounts reported to the IRS through the above-mentioned information sources, the return is flagged for review. In addition, the DIF assigns scores to each tax return based on the estimated degree of compliance. The formulas used to develop this score are highly confidential, but are known to be based, at least partially, on averages for particular income categories. If a return filed by a taxpayer includes items that are significantly different from the norm, or represents areas of known abuse, the computer will assign a high DIF score to the return. A high DIF score increases the likelihood that the return will be selected for audit.

Exhibit 2.5 | Examination Coverage: Returns Examined Resulting in Refunds, by Type and Size of Return

Type and Size of Return	*Taxable Returns Examined Resulting in Refunds*			*Recommended Refunds (in thousands)*		
	Total	*Field*	*Correspondence*	*Total*	*Field*	*Correspondence*
Individual Income Tax Returns	**22,645**	13,177	9,468	**991,056**	810,856	180,200
Corporation Income Tax Returns (except Form 1120S)	**1,322**	1,303	19	**7,064,808**	7,059,861	4,947
Estate & Trust Income Tax Returns	**199**	135	64	**69,709**	62,862	6,847
Estate Tax Returns	**461**	461	0	**183,708**	183,708	N/A
Gift Tax Returns	**18**	18	0	**3,756**	3,756	N/A
Employment Tax Returns	**389**	389	0	**233,232**	233,232	N/A

Source: Internal Revenue Service Data Book, 2019

Other methods of choosing returns for audit include related party audits, targeted compliance audits, subsequent claims for refund, or financial status audits. A related party audit occurs when the IRS audits a tax return of one individual, and that individual has claimed deductions for payments made to another person. The IRS may audit the return of the recipient to verify that all income was reported. Targeted compliance audits result in checking the tax returns of members of a particular profession (usually professions that have a high potential for engaging in tax evasion, such as cash-basis businesses) to test compliance with the tax laws.

Even when a tax return was not selected for audit under one of the above methods, a subsequent claim for refund may prompt the IRS to take a closer look at the return. The justification for such an audit is that the taxpayer apparently did not carefully file their first return, resulting in the need to file an amended return, or claim for refund. Finally, financial status audits look at the lifestyle of the taxpayer to determine if the income reported on the taxpayer's tax return is sufficient to fund their current lifestyle. Lifestyle audits are used sparingly, and are only permissible under Section 7602 in cases where the IRS has reason to believe that there is a likelihood that the taxpayer has unreported income. Lifestyle audits are typically used with high profile criminal cases when criminals do not report high income, yet live lavishly.

Once selected for audit, an income tax return will be examined by the IRS, and adjustments will be made to correct the tax liability for the taxpayer consistent with the perspective of the IRS. If the taxpayer does not agree with the findings in the audit, the dispute resolution process between the IRS and the taxpayer will begin.

Exhibit 2.6 | Math Errors on Tax Returns

Type of Math Error for 2019 Fiscal Year	*Number*	*%*
Tax Calculation/Other Taxes	1,034,791	44.8%
Exemption Number/Amount	156,497	6.8%
Standard/Itemized Deduction	219,872	9.5%
Earned Income Tax Credit	174,528	7.6%
Child Tax Credit	89,207	3.9%
Adjusted Gross/Taxable Income Amount	157,027	6.8%
Education Credits	48,618	2.1%
First Time Homebuyer Credit Repayment	79,462	3.4%
Refund/Amount Owed	81,677	3.5%
Filing Status	72,794	3.2%
Adjustments to Income	44,653	1.9%
Withholding or Excess Social Security Payments	48,865	2.1%
Other Credits	29,423	1.3%
Other	70,620	3.1%
Total Math Errors	**2,308,034**	***100.0%***

Source: Internal Revenue Service Data Book, 2019

Dispute Resolution

Dispute resolution with the IRS takes two forms. The first is an internal appeals process that permits taxpayers to request a second review of their case from the IRS Independent Office of Appeals, which is separate from the IRS examination division that conducted the initial audit.[8] This appeals process is generally available to individuals and small business taxpayers, with certain limited exceptions. If a taxpayer's request for Independent Appeals is denied, the IRS will provide the taxpayer with procedures to protest the denial. Additionally, a taxpayer may choose the second dispute resolution process, which involves the use of the U.S. court system.

After an audit, if the taxpayer and the IRS do not agree on the amount of tax that should be imposed for a given tax year, the IRS will issue a 30-day letter, and will provide a copy of the examination report that explains the changes proposed by the IRS. Once the 30-day letter is issued, the taxpayer has 30 days to appeal the IRS' decision to the IRS Office of Appeals.

If, during the 30 day period after the issuance of the 30-day letter, the taxpayer decides that the IRS report is correct and pays the tax, the process ends there, and the matter is resolved. When the taxpayer does not agree with the IRS examination report, he or she can take advantage of an internal appeals process within the IRS to resolve the dispute. The appeals office is separate from and independent of the IRS office that examines the taxpayer's return. The internal appeals process is very informal, and conferences with appeals office personnel may be held by correspondence, telephone, or in person. An appeal is requested by filing Form 12203 (**Exhibit 2.8**) within the appropriate time period. In addition to requesting an appeals conference, the taxpayer may have to file either a formal written protest or a

8. The Taxpayer First Act of 2019 renamed the IRS Office of Appeals to the IRS Independent Office of Appeals, the function of which is to resolve federal tax controversies without litigation, on a fair and impartial basis.

small case request. If the taxpayer and the IRS do not agree after the appeals conference, the taxpayer can still take advantage of dispute resolution in the U.S. court system.

If the taxpayer does not respond to the IRS' 30-day letter, and no agreement has been reached with the IRS during this period, the IRS will issue a 90-day letter, also known as a statutory notice of deficiency. Once the 90-day letter is issued, the taxpayer has 90 days to petition the Tax Court for a hearing. If a petition is not made within the 90-day period, the IRS may assess the tax, and begin collection efforts.

Alternatively, taxpayers who receive a 90-day letter may pay the tax due under the notice of deficiency and file an immediate claim for refund. In this case, the IRS generally will not act on the claim for refund. If the IRS fails to respond to the claim for refund within six months, the taxpayer may file a suit for refund against the U.S. in the U.S. District Court, or the U.S. Court of Federal Claims.

For a taxpayer to bring any tax action in the U.S. District Court or the Court of Federal Claims, the tax deficiency asserted by the IRS must be paid in advance. Taxpayers are not required to pay the deficiency in advance of bringing their action in the U.S. Tax Court.

Exhibit 2.7 | Diagram of Dispute Resolution

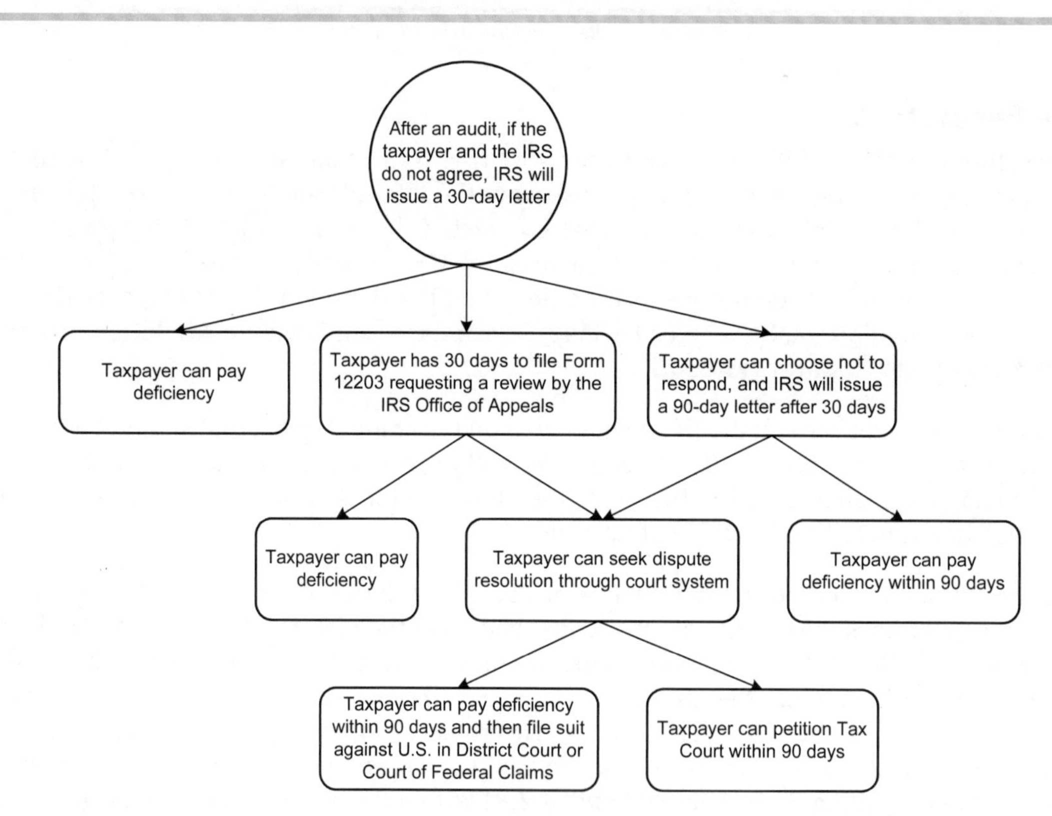

Exhibit 2.8 | Form 12203

Form **12203** (March 2020)	Department of the Treasury - Internal Revenue Service **Request for Appeals Review**

Complete the information in the spaces below, including your signature and the date.

Taxpayer name(s)		Taxpayer Identification Number(s)
Mailing address		Tax form number
City		Tax period(s) ended
State	ZIP Code	
Your telephone number(s)		Best time to call

Identify the item(s) *(for example: filing status, exemptions, interest or dividends)* you disagree with in the proposed change or assessment report you received with the enclosed letter. Tell us why you disagree. You can add more pages if this is not enough space.

Disagreed item	Reason why you disagree
Disagreed item	Reason why you disagree
Disagreed item	Reason why you disagree
Disagreed item	Reason why you disagree

Name of Taxpayer	Signature	Date
Name of Taxpayer	Signature	Date

Name and signature of authorized representative **(If a representative is signing this form, please attach a copy of your completed Form 2848,Power of Attorney and Declaration of Representative.)**

Name	Signature	Date
Your telephone number	Best time to call	

Catalog Number 27136N www.irs.gov Form **12203** (Rev. 3-2020)

Court System

There are three trial courts that may hear tax-related matters: the Tax Court, the U.S. District Court, and the U.S. Court of Federal Claims. In order to bring an action in the U.S. District Court or the U.S. Court of Federal Claims, the taxpayer must pay the tax deficiency alleged by the IRS. If the taxpayer cannot pay the deficiency, or does not want to pay the deficiency before the matter is resolved, the only option available is to bring an action for redetermination of tax liability in the U.S. Tax Court. A cash bond payment may be used in court in lieu of payment of the tax deficiency.

The **Tax Court** is a special purpose court – it only hears tax matters. Any taxpayer who has an ongoing dispute with the IRS after the issuance of a statutory notice of deficiency (a 90-day letter) may bring his or her dispute to the Tax Court. The Tax Court sits in Washington, D.C., but the judges travel (go "on circuit") to hear cases around the country. Typically, a Tax Court case will be held in the state where the taxpayer resides. The special nature of the Tax Court – that it only hears tax cases - may be an advantage or disadvantage to the taxpayer, depending on the issue that is being contested, and the facts of the case. This fact may be a consideration in choosing to bring the case to the U.S. District Court or the U.S. Court of Federal Claims. Decisions of the Tax Court may be appealed if either party – the taxpayer or the IRS – does not like the outcome.

Quick Quiz 2.3

1. The most common type of audit is a lifestyle audit.
   a. True
   b. False
2. Any deficiency must be paid prior to bringing a dispute before the Tax Court.
   a. True
   b. False
3. The U.S. District Court is the only venue for tax controversies that provides jury trials.
   a. True
   b. False

False, False, True.

If the amount in controversy is $50,000 or less, the taxpayer can elect to bring the case to the small claims division of the tax court. The advantage of bringing the case to the small claims division is that the hearing is not as formal as a full tax court proceeding, and does not strictly follow all of the formal rules of legal procedure. Many small claims cases are heard by special trial judges. Since formal rules of procedure are not used, the taxpayer may not need to be represented by a lawyer. Enrolled Agents are members of the tax court bar and can represent clients in tax court, and, in some cases (provided that there is no objection from the opposing party), a CPA may be permitted to describe the positions taken by the taxpayer to the court. Furthermore, small claims cases tend to get resolved faster and easier than full Tax Court proceedings. If a taxpayer chooses to bring a case to the small claims division of the Tax Court, however, there are no appeal rights. The decision of the Tax Court judge is binding on both the taxpayer and the IRS.

If the taxpayer would like to have a jury trial, the dispute must be brought to the **U.S. District Court**. The U.S. District Court is the trial court in the federal system, and there is at least one district per state (some large states, such as Pennsylvania, have Eastern and Western District Courts). Unlike the Tax Court, which specializes in hearing tax-related cases, the U.S. District Court is a court of general jurisdiction. The presiding judge and the members of the jury will not be experts on tax law, which may have a bearing on whether or not the case should be brought to this court. Decisions of the U.S. District Court may be appealed if either party – the taxpayer or the IRS – does not like the outcome.

The final option for trial is to bring the controversy to the **U.S. Court of Federal Claims**. This court sits only in Washington, D.C., and unlike the Tax Court, the judges of the U.S. Court of Federal Claims do not go on circuit. Cases brought in front of this court must be litigated in Washington, D.C. Despite the inconvenience of traveling to Washington to litigate the case, if enough money is at stake, and the prior decisions of the U.S. Court of Federal Claims are more favorable to the taxpayer than the decisions of the U.S. District Court (comparing the decisions of different courts to determine what court to bring the suit to is referred to as 'forum shopping' by lawyers), it may make sense to bring the tax dispute there. The only type of trial available in this court is a bench trial – jury trials on tax matters are reserved for the U.S. District Court. Decisions of the U.S. Court of Federal Claims may be appealed if either party – the taxpayer or the IRS – does not like the outcome.

If a trial court decision is appealed, it goes to the U.S. Court of Appeals for the Circuit that covers the District Court where the trial was brought, or the state where the Tax Court case was heard. Appeals from the U.S. Court of Federal Claims always go to the U.S. Court of Appeals for the Federal Circuit, which sits in Washington, D.C. Either the taxpayer or the IRS can appeal the case to the Circuit Court. Usually, the last step in the dispute resolution process is the decision issued by the Circuit Court. Once a Circuit Court rules on a tax-related issue, all district courts in that Circuit must abide by the decision announced by the Circuit Court. Other Circuit Courts outside the Court of Appeals circuit, other appellate courts, and the Supreme Court, are not bound by the decision.

Exhibit 2.9 | The U.S. Federal Circuit Courts

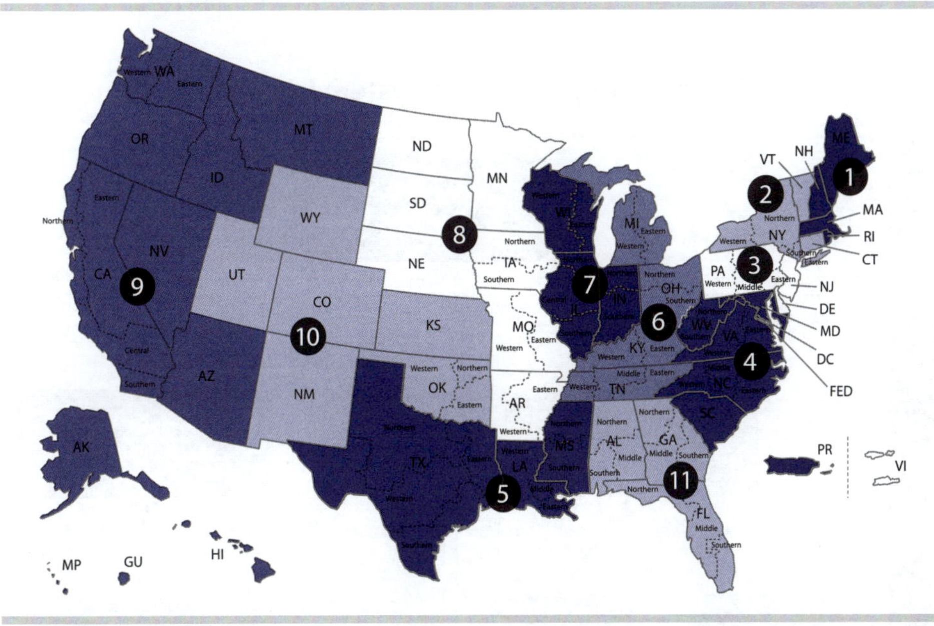

Source: Administrative Office of the U.S. Courts, www.uscourts.gov/uscourts/images/circuitmap.pdf

The U.S. Supreme Court rarely hears cases dealing with tax matters. A party may request the Supreme Court to review a decision of a Circuit Court, a process called petitioning for a *writ of certiorari*, but the Supreme Court will only hear the case if it has the potential to affect a large number of taxpayers, or if it feels that it needs to settle a point of law that is in dispute among the circuits. There is always the possibility, but not the probability of having your case heard in the Supreme Court. If the Supreme Court does decide to hear a tax case, once its decision is announced it is binding on all parties, and all U.S. Courts must follow the ruling in deciding similar cases.

Exhibit 2.10 | U.S. Court System Summary

	Tax Court	*Tax Court - Small Claims*	*U.S. District Court*	*U.S. Court of Federal Claims*
What kinds of cases?	Tax Only	Tax Only	All Types	Claims Against U.S. Government
Is the taxpayer required to pay the tax?	No	No	Yes	Yes
What is the maximum amount of the claim?	N/A	$50,000	N/A	N/A
Is a jury trial available?	No	No	Yes	No
Where is court located?	Around U.S.	Around U.S.	Around U.S.	D.C. Only
To what court are appeals brought?	U.S. Court of Appeals	No Appeals	U.S. Court of Appeals	U.S. Court of Appeals - Federal Circuit

Exhibit 2.11 | U.S. Court System Diagram

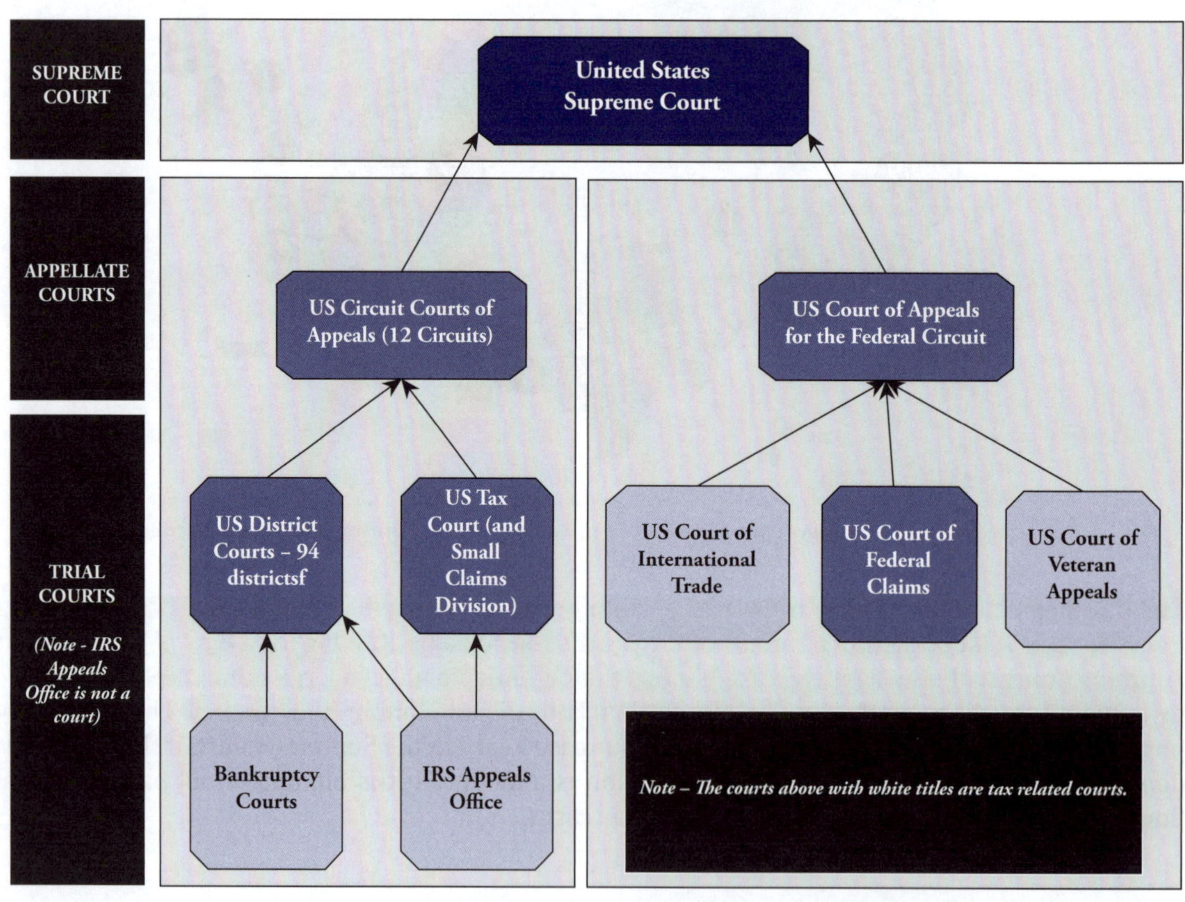

Exhibit 2.12 | Ten Facts from U.S. Courts

1. The Constitution of the United States gives ultimate power to the people, not to the government.
2. The Constitution created a government structure known as federalism, which requires the sharing of power between the federal government and the governments of each of the 50 states. By splitting sovereign power between the state and federal governments, federalism is a form of check and balance on government power.
3. Under federalism, there are two types of court systems—federal and state. Federal courts have jurisdiction over issues mentioned or implied in the Constitution. The state courts have jurisdiction over matters not mentioned in the Constitution and those not specifically denied to the states by the Constitution.
4. The Constitution established three branches of government - the legislative, executive, and judicial. Courts are the judicial branch. As a co-equal branch of government, the judicial Branch is independent of the legislative and executive branches. Courts have the authority to interpret the law based on the Constitution without pressure from the other two branches.
5. Federal courts have the power of judicial review. This means they can review acts of Congress and actions of the President to ensure that they are permitted by the Constitution. If they are not, the Supreme Court of the United States declares such acts or actions unconstitutional, and they do not have the force of law.
6. The federal courts hear both civil and criminal cases. Civil cases involve disputes between private individuals, such as contract disputes. Criminal cases involve offenses against the whole community or society, such as murder. Courts follow different procedures in civil and criminal cases.
7. Within the federal and state court systems, there are two levels—trial courts and appellate courts. Trial courts, called U.S. District Courts, are courts of original jurisdiction.They are the first courts to hear either a civil or criminal case. If parties are not satisfied with the decision of a trial court, they may ask an appellate court, called a U.S. Circuit Court of Appeals, to review the trial court decision.
8. If parties are not satisfied with the decision of the U.S. Circuit Court of Appeals, they may appeal to the Supreme Court of the United States. The Supreme Court selects the cases it will hear. The Supreme Court is the final interpreter of the U.S. Constitution because it is the highest court in the land.
9. In addition to the judges, many other people work together to ensure the success of the judicial system. These include court staff, U.S. attorneys, federal public defenders, lawyers in private practice, and U.S. Marshals.
10. Citizens play a crucial role in the American judicial system. They help to ensure the fair and impartial administration of justice by participating directly in the work of the courts as jurors, witnesses, and court system employees. However, the central role that citizens play in ensuring the rule of law is using courts to settle disputes peacefully and abiding by court orders.

TAX RESEARCH

There are several sources of tax information for practitioners. Primary sources of information include the Internal Revenue Code, Treasury regulations, court opinions, the IRS Manual, and IRS rulings and determination letters. Many of these resources can be obtained from free sources on the internet, such as the IRS website at www.irs.gov. These sources of tax law are used primarily by attorneys and accountants, but may be helpful to other tax professionals as well.

Practice aids index the tax law, making relevant provisions easier to find. The Research Institute of America (RIA), Commerce Clearing House (CCH), and Bureau of National Affairs (BNA) publish internet-based practice aids that can be accessed for a fee.

> ### *Key Concepts*
>
> 1. Identify sources of tax law available to practitioners.
> 2. Identify the sources of secondary tax materials available to practitioners.

Journal articles are perhaps the best source of information for practitioners since they describe the use of the tax law provisions in a planning oriented context, illustrating the direct application of the concepts to client problems. Some journals focus on the legal aspects of tax planning. Journals of this type include *Federal Tax Articles* by CCH, *The Journal of Taxation*, the *Monthly Digest of Tax Articles*, and *Tax Notes*. Other journals focus directly on practical applications that can be useful for practitioners. Some of these journals include: *Estate Planning*, *Trusts & Estates*, *The Journal of Financial Planning*, and *The Journal of the Society of Financial Services Professionals*. Practitioners who are recommending tax-planning strategies to clients should regularly read one or more of these journals to keep up with new developments.

When new tax legislation is adopted by Congress, summaries of that information are often available on accounting firm websites. For those who would like to understand the reasons for the tax law changes, Congressional committee and conference committee reports describing the details of the legislation may be found at the Library of Congress legislative information website at www.congress.gov.[9]

One of the hallmarks of professionalism is to know when to call in an expert. Nobody can be an expert in everything, and if the situation facing your client is complex enough, it may be wise to bring in another advisor that has experience and knowledge in the matter facing the client. A financial advisor typically acts as the captain of the planning team, coordinating the efforts of team members, including accountants, lawyers, trust officers, estate planners, and insurance specialists. For many tax-related problems a client may encounter, either the financial advisor or an existing member of the planning team will be able to resolve the issue. When the issue is beyond the scope of the current team members' research and application skills, however, call in an expert!

CONCLUSION

While at first the tax law in all of its forms (legislative, administrative, and judicial) may seem daunting, repeated exposure to the sources of law and how they apply to client problems will remove the mystique. To successfully navigate through the myriad sources of law, you need to develop a basic understanding of our tax system and how it works. The remaining chapters will walk you through the tax system.

9. Formerly www.thomas.gov.

KEY TERMS

16th Amendment - Amendment to the U.S. Constitution adopted on February 25, 1913 that gave Congress the power to lay and collect taxes on income.

Accuracy-Related Penalty - A penalty of 20 percent of the underpayment amount imposed on taxpayers who file incorrect tax returns in certain situations.

Determination Letter - A letter issued by a district director of the IRS advising a taxpayer on how to report a transaction for tax purposes.

Discriminant Inventory Function System - A computer program used by the IRS to identify tax returns for audit.

Failure to File Penalty - A penalty of 5 percent of the unpaid tax balance for each month or part thereof that a tax return is late; subject to a minimum penalty of $435 or 100% of the tax due if more than 60 days late.

Failure to Pay Penalty - A penalty of 0.5 percent per month or part thereof that a taxpayer fails to pay tax that is owed.

Final Regulations - Regulations issued by the Treasury that have been adopted formally after compliance with the requirements of the Administrative Procedures Act.

Fraud - Implies that the taxpayer intentionally disregarded tax rules or misstated information included on the return.

Interpretive Regulations - Official interpretations of the Internal Revenue Code by the Treasury.

Legislative Regulations - Regulations in which the Treasury determines the details of the law.

Private Letter Ruling - Rulings issued by the IRS that are binding on the IRS only with respect to the transaction and the taxpayer that are the subject of the ruling.

Procedural Regulations - Housekeeping instructions indicating how the Treasury and IRS will conduct their affairs.

Proposed Regulations - Regulations that have been drafted by the Treasury, but have not yet been adopted.

Revenue Procedures - Statements issued by the IRS which detail internal practices and procedures within the IRS and make important announcements to taxpayers.

Revenue Rulings - Rulings issued by the IRS based on a set of facts common to many taxpayers and binding on the IRS.

Statute of Limitations - Specified time within which the IRS may examine an income tax return.

Substantial Omission - An omission from a tax return of more than 25 percent of the gross income reported.

Tax Court - A special purpose court that sits in Washington, D.C. and only hears tax cases. The judges within the court travel throughout the U.S. to hear the cases.

Temporary Regulations - Regulations that have the same authority as final regulations and are issued when guidance must be provided quickly to taxpayers.

Treasury Regulations - Regulations that are official interpretations of the Internal Revenue Code and give taxpayers insight as to how the Code will be enforced by the IRS.

U.S. Court of Federal Claims - Court that may preside over tax controversies and only hears cases in Washington, D.C.

U.S. District Court - Trial court of the federal judicial system which has general jurisdiction and is the only option for tax controversies in which the taxpayer would like a jury trial.

DISCUSSION QUESTIONS

SOLUTIONS to the discussion questions can be found exclusively within the chapter. Once you have completed an initial reading of the chapter, go back and highlight the answers to these questions.

1. What are the three primary sources of tax law?
2. What is the legal basis for today's income tax?
3. What are the statutory sources of tax law?
4. What are the administrative sources of tax law?
5. Compare and contrast proposed regulations, temporary regulations, and final regulations.
6. What is the difference between a procedural regulation and an interpretive regulation?
7. Discuss the two types of rulings issued by the IRS.
8. When can a determination letter be issued?
9. What is the general statute of limitations before which the IRS may examine a tax return?
10. Under what circumstances is the statute of limitations extended?
11. What are the penalties for noncompliance?
12. What are the two forms of dispute resolution with the IRS?
13. What are the three trial courts that may hear tax-related matters and what are the requirements of each?

MULTIPLE CHOICE PROBLEMS

A sample of multiple choice problems is provided below. Additional multiple choice problems are available at money-education.com by accessing the Student Practice Portal.

1. Ashton filed his tax return on April 15. When preparing his return, Ashton accidentally stated that his income was $50,000 when it was really $500,000. What is the statute of limitations prior to which the IRS may examine Ashton's return?
    a. 3 years.
    b. 6 years.
    c. 10 years.
    d. There is no statute of limitations.

2. Mila filed her tax return on April 15. At that time, she owed $800 on a total income tax liability of $10,000 and she submitted a check for $800 with her income tax return. Which of the following penalties will apply to Mila?
    a. Failure to file.
    b. Failure to pay.
    c. Underpayment of estimated tax.
    d. None of the above.

3. Carrie's husband, Drew, died last year. Before his death, Drew exercised a substantial number of incentive stock options (ISOs). Before they could pay the tax, the stock decreased in value, leaving them no cash to pay the alternative minimum tax (AMT) that resulted from the exercise. Carrie would like to challenge the amount due in court, as she has already exhausted the internal IRS review process. Her lawyer believes that the facts of the case may help Carrie if she has a sympathetic audience. However, she is unable to pay the claim currently and her top priority is to choose a court that does not require her to pay up-front. She would like to be able to appeal if the lower court does not render a decision in her favor. Which court is most appropriate for Carrie?
    a. U.S. District Court.
    b. U.S. Court of Federal Claims.
    c. U.S. Tax Court.
    d. U.S. Tax Court: Small Claims Division.

4. Patrick is considering a business transaction. After speaking with his accountant he has determined that the Internal Revenue Code is not clear on the tax treatment of his business transaction. Because the tax dollars at stake are substantial, Patrick is not comfortable completing the transaction without first knowing how the transaction will be treated by the IRS. Which of the following would give Patrick the most peace of mind prior to completing this transaction?
    a. Private Letter Ruling.
    b. Determination Letter.
    c. Revenue Ruling.
    d. Technical Advice Memorandum.

5. Danica failed to file her tax return a few years ago and pay the $5,000 tax liability that was owed at the time. Danica's new tax advisor prepares and files the return in the current year, 21½ months late. How much is her:
   1. Failure to pay penalty.
   2. Failure to file penalty.
   3. Total penalty.
      a. $550; $1,125; $1,675.
      b. $425; $1,250; $1,675.
      c. $550; $700; $1,250.
      d. $1,250; $550; $1,800.

Additional multiple choice problems are available at *money-education.com* by accessing the Student Practice Portal. Access requires registration of the title using the unique code at the front of the book.

QUICK QUIZ EXPLANATIONS

Quick Quiz 2.1

1. False. The 16th Amendment gave Congress the power to impose an income tax, but the amendment itself did not impose an income tax.
2. False. The Internal Revenue Code is the only statutory source of federal tax law.
3. True.
4. False. A private letter ruling binds the IRS with respect to the particular transaction and taxpayer discussed in the letter. A revenue ruling, on the other hand, is binding on the IRS with respect to all taxpayers.

Quick Quiz 2.2

1. True.
2. False. A substantial understatement of income is an omission of more than 25% of gross income.
3. True.
4. True.

Quick Quiz 2.3

1. False. The most common type of audit today is a computer generated audit, referred to as the "Discriminant Inventory Function."
2. False. A taxpayer is not required to pay any tax deficiency prior to bringing a claim before the Tax Court.
3. True.

3
FUNDAMENTALS OF INCOME TAXATION

LEARNING OBJECTIVES

1. Explain the tax formula for individuals.*
2. Define income.*
3. Identify items excluded from gross income.*
4. Identify items included in gross income.*
5. Explain the differences, and the tax consequences, associated with above-the-line (for AGI) deductions, and below-the-line (from AGI or Itemized) deductions.*
6. Define Adjusted Gross Income (AGI).*
7. Explain the difference between the standard deduction and itemized deductions.*
8. List circumstances that will prevent a taxpayer from claiming the standard deduction.*
9. Calculate a taxpayer's standard deduction, based on their filing status and personal characteristics.*
10. Determine a taxpayer's taxable income.*
11. Calculate a taxpayer's federal income tax liability.*
12. Identify common credits that can be used to offset income tax liability.*
13. Describe the three tax accounting methods.*
14. Describe the claim of right doctrine, and identify circumstances where the doctrine may be applied.*
15. Determine a taxpayer's income tax filing status.*
16. List the requirements for an individual to be considered a qualifying child of a taxpayer for purposes of claiming a child credit.*
17. List the requirements for an individual to be considered a qualifying relative of a taxpayer for purposes of claiming a family credit.*
18. Explain how the tie-breaker rules may determine who can claim a qualified child for a given individual.*
19. Calculate the standard deduction for a person who may be claimed by another as a qualifying dependent.*
20. Describe the kiddie-tax rules.*
21. Explain the purpose of the kiddie-tax.
22. Define net unearned income (NUI).*
23. Calculate the net unearned income (NUI) of a child.*
24. Determine how much of a child's income is subject to tax at the parent's tax rate.*
25. Identify the time period for filing a tax return.*
26. Determine when a taxpayer is required to file a tax return.*
27. Calculate FICA and self-employment taxes for a taxpayer.*
28. Identify and give examples of Five Basic Tax Planning Principles.*

**Ties to CFP Certification Learning Objectives*

TAX FORMULA FOR INDIVIDUAL TAXPAYERS

Introduction

Prior to delving into the details of income tax rules, it is helpful to get an overview of how the federal income tax is calculated, and to get an introduction to some of the fundamental income tax concepts that are important in determining tax liability. This chapter begins with an overview of the tax formula for individual taxpayers. The chapter then identifies some of the major categories of income, exclusions, deductions, and credits that are common to income taxation. All of these items will be discussed at length in subsequent chapters of the text. Remember that the important task to accomplish here is to get a general understanding of how the tax formula works.

Key Concepts

1. Explain the basic tax formula.
2. Define income.
3. Identify items excluded from gross income.
4. Identify items included in gross income.

After discussing the individual income tax formula, the chapter turns to fundamental concepts of income taxation that are important for practitioners to know. Topics such as accounting periods and methods, filing status, the calculation of the standard deduction for a dependent, the kiddie-tax rules, and return filing requirements are discussed in detail. The chapter ends with an overview of basic tax-planning strategies that can be used by taxpayers to help manage their tax liability. Many of the techniques used to achieve these planning goals are discussed at length in future chapters.

The Tax Formula

In very general terms, a taxpayer is required to pay a federal income tax on taxable income. **Taxable income** is determined by subtracting allowable deductions from income:

Income – Deductions = Taxable Income

Taxable income is multiplied by the income tax rate to determine the tax liability:

Taxable Income x Tax Rate = Tax Liability

Federal income tax rates are progressive in nature. Higher tiers of income are taxed at higher rates. For example, a single taxpayer with income of $30,000 and deductions of $10,000 has taxable income of $20,000 ($30,000 - $10,000). Using the 2021 tax rate schedule for the single filing status (See Appendix A), the taxpayer's tax is $2,201, calculated as follows: (($9,950 x 10%) + ($10,050 x 12%)) = $2,201.

There is a more extensive tax formula for individual taxpayers than the simple tax calculation presented above. The more complete formula includes exclusions from gross income, different types of deductions, and tax credits. In addition, there are intermediate calculations (such as adjusted gross income) that can be important considerations in tax planning. Each of these items will be discussed in this chapter and throughout the remainder of the textbook.

Income Broadly Defined	**$xx,xxx**
Less: Exclusions	(x,xxx)
Gross Income	**$xx,xxx**
Less: Deductions for Adjusted Gross Income *(above-the-line deductions)*	(x,xxx)
Adjusted Gross Income ("The Line")	**$xx,xxx**
Less: Deductions from Adjusted Gross Income *(below-the-line deductions)* Greater of Standard or Itemized Deductions and the Qualified Business Income Deduction	(xx,xxx)
Taxable Income	**$xx,xxx**
Tax on Taxable Income	**$x,xxx**
Less: Credit for Taxes Withheld	(x,xxx)
Less: Credit for Estimated Tax Payments	(x,xxx)
Less: Other Tax Credits	(x,xxx)
Tax Due or (Refund Due)	**$xxx**

Individuals report their income, deductions, and other information required for the calculation of the federal tax liability on Form 1040.

Subsequent to the enactment of TCJA 2017, the IRS eliminated forms 1040EZ and Form 1040A (which were permitted to be filed by taxpayers with certain levels of income and deductions for tax years 2017 and earlier) and now requires all taxpayers to file Form 1040. Form 1040 has been substantially modified from its prior form, and now consists of a basic, or "Postcard" Form 1040 and three numbered schedules. The information reported on the 1040 and schedules are shown in **Exhibit 3.1**. Beginning with the 2019 tax year, a new version of the Form 1040, the 1040-SR with larger print and a standard deduction chart that includes the additional standard deduction for the aged or blind, is available for taxpayers age 65 or older. Form 1040-SR uses the same Schedules (e.g., Schedules 1-3 and Schedule A) as the Form 1040.

Exhibit 3.1 | Information on Form 1040 and Schedules 1-3

Form 1040	Page 1: Taxpayer and dependent information and a basic tax formula calculation, through the calculation of taxable income. Page 2: A basic tax formula calculation, from taxable income through credits and payments, with refund or payment information and signature lines.
Schedule 1	Additional Income (such as alimony, unemployment compensation, business income, and rental income) and adjustment information (such as student loan interest, self-employment tax, and educator expenses).
Schedule 2	Calculation of tax including Alternative Minimum Tax, Affordable Care Act Advance Premium Tax Credit repayment, self-employment tax, and penalties on early distributions from pension plans and IRAs.
Schedule 3	Non-refundable tax credits other than the child tax credit and the other dependent credit, and other payments and refundable credits other than the earned income credit, American Opportunity credit, or additional child tax credit.

While all taxpayers are required to file the new "Postcard" Form 1040, Schedules 1 through 3 will only be filed if necessary.

Income

Income, broadly defined, means the total amount of money and the fair market value of property, services, or other accretion to wealth received, but it does not include borrowed money or a return of invested dollars (sometimes referred to as return of capital or return of adjusted taxable basis).

Example 3.1

During the year, Seth borrowed $20,000 from a bank and sold an investment for $12,000. He had no other cash inflows. He purchased the investment five years earlier for $5,000. Since the loan and the return of his $5,000 investment are not income, his income for the year is $7,000 ($12,000 sales price - $5,000 investment).

Exclusions

Exclusions are income items that are not subject to income tax. Each exclusion must be specifically authorized by Congress and set forth in the Internal Revenue Code (IRC) or must be determined by the courts to be outside the definition of income as that term is used in the 16th Amendment to the U.S. Constitution. Most exclusions from gross income are allowed by IRC Sections 101 through 150. A more detailed discussion of exclusions is included in Chapters 4 and 5. Some of the more common exclusions permitted by the IRC are listed in **Exhibit 3.2**.

Exhibit 3.2 | Partial List of Exclusions

- Interest income from municipal bonds
- Child support payments received
- Cash or property received by inheritance
- Specified employee fringe benefits
- Qualifying distributions from a Roth IRA during retirement
- Alimony resulting from divorce decrees signed after 2018
- Cash or property received by gift
- Deferral contributions to certain retirement plans
- Gain on the sale of a principal residence (subject to limitations)
- Scholarship or fellowship
- Life insurance proceeds received because of the death of the insured
- Discharge of federal student loan indebtedness in tax years 2021-2025

Exhibit 3.3 | Form 1040 Page 1

Form **1040** Department of the Treasury—Internal Revenue Service (99)
U.S. Individual Income Tax Return **2020** OMB No. 1545-0074 IRS Use Only—Do not write or staple in this space.

Filing Status ☐ Single ☐ Married filing jointly ☐ Married filing separately (MFS) ☐ Head of household (HOH) ☐ Qualifying widow(er) (QW)
Check only one box.
If you checked the MFS box, enter the name of your spouse. If you checked the HOH or QW box, enter the child's name if the qualifying person is a child but not your dependent ▶

Your first name and middle initial	Last name	**Your social security number**
If joint return, spouse's first name and middle initial	Last name	**Spouse's social security number**

Home address (number and street). If you have a P.O. box, see instructions.		Apt. no.	**Presidential Election Campaign** Check here if you, or your spouse if filing jointly, want $3 to go to this fund. Checking a box below will not change your tax or refund. ☐ **You** ☐ **Spouse**
City, town, or post office. If you have a foreign address, also complete spaces below.	State	ZIP code	
Foreign country name	Foreign province/state/county	Foreign postal code	

At any time during 2020, did you receive, sell, send, exchange, or otherwise acquire any financial interest in any virtual currency? ☐ **Yes** ☐ **No**

Standard Deduction **Someone can claim:** ☐ You as a dependent ☐ Your spouse as a dependent
☐ Spouse itemizes on a separate return or you were a dual-status alien

Age/Blindness **You:** ☐ Were born before January 2, 1956 ☐ Are blind **Spouse:** ☐ Was born before January 2, 1956 ☐ Is blind

Dependents (see instructions):
If more than four dependents, see instructions and check here ▶ ☐

(1) First name	Last name	**(2)** Social security number	**(3)** Relationship to you	**(4)** ✔ if qualifies for (see instructions): Child tax credit	Credit for other dependents
				☐	☐
				☐	☐
				☐	☐
				☐	☐

Attach Sch. B if required.

1	Wages, salaries, tips, etc. Attach Form(s) W-2			1	
2a	Tax-exempt interest	2a	b Taxable interest	2b	
3a	Qualified dividends	3a	b Ordinary dividends	3b	
4a	IRA distributions	4a	b Taxable amount	4b	
5a	Pensions and annuities	5a	b Taxable amount	5b	
6a	Social security benefits	6a	b Taxable amount	6b	
7	Capital gain or (loss). Attach Schedule D if required. If not required, check here ▶ ☐			7	
8	Other income from Schedule 1, line 9			8	
9	Add lines 1, 2b, 3b, 4b, 5b, 6b, 7, and 8. This is your **total income** ▶			9	
10	Adjustments to income:				
a	From Schedule 1, line 22	10a			
b	Charitable contributions if you take the standard deduction. See instructions	10b			
c	Add lines 10a and 10b. These are your **total adjustments to income** ▶			10c	
11	Subtract line 10c from line 9. This is your **adjusted gross income** ▶			11	
12	**Standard deduction or itemized deductions** (from Schedule A)			12	
13	Qualified business income deduction. Attach Form 8995 or Form 8995-A			13	
14	Add lines 12 and 13			14	
15	**Taxable income.** Subtract line 14 from line 11. If zero or less, enter -0-			15	

Standard Deduction for—
- Single or Married filing separately, $12,400
- Married filing jointly or Qualifying widow(er), $24,800
- Head of household, $18,650
- If you checked any box under *Standard Deduction*, see instructions.

For Disclosure, Privacy Act, and Paperwork Reduction Act Notice, see separate instructions. Cat. No. 11320B Form **1040** (2020)

Exhibit 3.3 (Continued) | Form 1040 Page 2

Form 1040 (2020) Page **2**

	16	**Tax** (see instructions). Check if any from Form(s): **1** ☐ 8814 **2** ☐ 4972 **3** ☐ ______		16
	17	Amount from Schedule 2, line 3		17
	18	Add lines 16 and 17		18
	19	Child tax credit or credit for other dependents		19
	20	Amount from Schedule 3, line 7		20
	21	Add lines 19 and 20		21
	22	Subtract line 21 from line 18. If zero or less, enter -0-		22
	23	Other taxes, including self-employment tax, from Schedule 2, line 10		23
	24	Add lines 22 and 23. This is your **total tax** ▶		24
	25	Federal income tax withheld from:		
	a	Form(s) W-2	25a	
	b	Form(s) 1099	25b	
	c	Other forms (see instructions)	25c	
	d	Add lines 25a through 25c		25d
• If you have a qualifying child, attach Sch. EIC. • If you have nontaxable combat pay, see instructions.	26	2020 estimated tax payments and amount applied from 2019 return		26
	27	Earned income credit (EIC)	27	
	28	Additional child tax credit. Attach Schedule 8812	28	
	29	American opportunity credit from Form 8863, line 8	29	
	30	Recovery rebate credit. See instructions	30	
	31	Amount from Schedule 3, line 13	31	
	32	Add lines 27 through 31. These are your **total other payments and refundable credits** ▶		32
	33	Add lines 25d, 26, and 32. These are your **total payments** ▶		33
Refund	34	If line 33 is more than line 24, subtract line 24 from line 33. This is the amount you **overpaid**		34
	35a	Amount of line 34 you want **refunded to you.** If Form 8888 is attached, check here ▶ ☐		35a
Direct deposit? See instructions.	▶ b	Routing number ▶ c Type: ☐ Checking ☐ Savings		
	▶ d	Account number		
	36	Amount of line 34 you want **applied to your 2021 estimated tax** ▶	36	
Amount You Owe For details on how to pay, see instructions.	37	Subtract line 33 from line 24. This is the **amount you owe now** ▶		37
		Note: Schedule H and Schedule SE filers, line 37 may not represent all of the taxes you owe for 2020. See Schedule 3, line 12e, and its instructions for details.		
	38	Estimated tax penalty (see instructions) ▶	38	

Third Party Designee

Do you want to allow another person to discuss this return with the IRS? See instructions ▶ ☐ **Yes.** Complete below. ☐ **No**

Designee's name ▶ | Phone no. ▶ | Personal identification number (PIN) ▶

Sign Here

Under penalties of perjury, I declare that I have examined this return and accompanying schedules and statements, and to the best of my knowledge and belief, they are true, correct, and complete. Declaration of preparer (other than taxpayer) is based on all information of which preparer has any knowledge.

Joint return? See instructions. Keep a copy for your records.

Your signature	Date	Your occupation	If the IRS sent you an Identity Protection PIN, enter it here (see inst.) ▶
Spouse's signature. If a joint return, **both** must sign.	Date	Spouse's occupation	If the IRS sent your spouse an Identity Protection PIN, enter it here (see inst.) ▶
Phone no.	Email address		

Paid Preparer Use Only

Preparer's name	Preparer's signature	Date	PTIN	Check if: ☐ Self-employed
Firm's name ▶			Phone no.	
Firm's address ▶			Firm's EIN ▶	

Go to *www.irs.gov/Form1040* for instructions and the latest information. Form **1040** (2020)

Exhibit 3.4 | Form 1040 Schedule 1

SCHEDULE 1 (Form 1040) Department of the Treasury Internal Revenue Service	**Additional Income and Adjustments to Income** ► Attach to Form 1040, 1040-SR, or 1040-NR. ► Go to *www.irs.gov/Form1040* for instructions and the latest information.	OMB No. 1545-0074 2020 Attachment Sequence No. 01

Name(s) shown on Form 1040, 1040-SR, or 1040-NR	**Your social security number**

Part I Additional Income

1	Taxable refunds, credits, or offsets of state and local income taxes	1	
2a	Alimony received	2a	
b	Date of original divorce or separation agreement (see instructions) ►		
3	Business income or (loss). Attach Schedule C	3	
4	Other gains or (losses). Attach Form 4797	4	
5	Rental real estate, royalties, partnerships, S corporations, trusts, etc. Attach Schedule E	5	
6	Farm income or (loss). Attach Schedule F	6	
7	Unemployment compensation	7	
8	Other income. List type and amount ►	8	
9	Combine lines 1 through 8. Enter here and on Form 1040, 1040-SR, or 1040-NR, line 8	9	

Part II Adjustments to Income

10	Educator expenses	10	
11	Certain business expenses of reservists, performing artists, and fee-basis government officials. Attach Form 2106	11	
12	Health savings account deduction. Attach Form 8889	12	
13	Moving expenses for members of the Armed Forces. Attach Form 3903	13	
14	Deductible part of self-employment tax. Attach Schedule SE	14	
15	Self-employed SEP, SIMPLE, and qualified plans	15	
16	Self-employed health insurance deduction	16	
17	Penalty on early withdrawal of savings	17	
18a	Alimony paid	18a	
b	Recipient's SSN ►		
c	Date of original divorce or separation agreement (see instructions) ►		
19	IRA deduction	19	
20	Student loan interest deduction	20	
21	Tuition and fees deduction. Attach Form 8917	21	
22	Add lines 10 through 21. These are your **adjustments to income.** Enter here and on Form 1040, 1040-SR, or 1040-NR, line 10a	22	

For Paperwork Reduction Act Notice, see your tax return instructions. Cat. No. 71479F **Schedule 1 (Form 1040) 2020**

Exhibit 3.5 | Form 1040 Schedule 2

SCHEDULE 2 (Form 1040)
Department of the Treasury
Internal Revenue Service

Additional Taxes

▶ Attach to Form 1040, 1040-SR, or 1040-NR.
▶ Go to *www.irs.gov/Form1040* for instructions and the latest information.

OMB No. 1545-0074
2020
Attachment Sequence No. **02**

Name(s) shown on Form 1040, 1040-SR, or 1040-NR	**Your social security number**

Part I Tax

1	Alternative minimum tax. Attach Form 6251	1	
2	Excess advance premium tax credit repayment. Attach Form 8962	2	
3	Add lines 1 and 2. Enter here and on Form 1040, 1040-SR, or 1040-NR, line 17 . .	3	

Part II Other Taxes

4	Self-employment tax. Attach Schedule SE	4	
5	Unreported social security and Medicare tax from Form: **a** ☐ 4137 **b** ☐ 8919 .	5	
6	Additional tax on IRAs, other qualified retirement plans, and other tax-favored accounts. Attach Form 5329 if required	6	
7a	Household employment taxes. Attach Schedule H	7a	
b	Repayment of first-time homebuyer credit from Form 5405. Attach Form 5405 if required	7b	
8	Taxes from: **a** ☐ Form 8959 **b** ☐ Form 8960 **c** ☐ Instructions; enter code(s)	8	
9	Section 965 net tax liability installment from Form 965-A . . . **9**		
10	Add lines 4 through 8. These are your **total other taxes.** Enter here and on Form 1040 or 1040-SR, line 23, or Form 1040-NR, line 23b	10	

For Paperwork Reduction Act Notice, see your tax return instructions. Cat. No. 71478U **Schedule 2 (Form 1040) 2020**

Exhibit 3.6 | Form 1040 Schedule 3

SCHEDULE 3 (Form 1040) Department of the Treasury Internal Revenue Service	**Additional Credits and Payments** ▶ Attach to Form 1040, 1040-SR, or 1040-NR. ▶ Go to *www.irs.gov/Form1040* for instructions and the latest information.	OMB No. 1545-0074 2020 Attachment Sequence No. 03
Name(s) shown on Form 1040, 1040-SR, or 1040-NR		**Your social security number**

Part I Nonrefundable Credits

1	Foreign tax credit. Attach Form 1116 if required	1	
2	Credit for child and dependent care expenses. Attach Form 2441	2	
3	Education credits from Form 8863, line 19	3	
4	Retirement savings contributions credit. Attach Form 8880	4	
5	Residential energy credits. Attach Form 5695	5	
6	Other credits from Form: a ☐ 3800 b ☐ 8801 c ☐	6	
7	Add lines 1 through 6. Enter here and on Form 1040, 1040-SR, or 1040-NR, line 20	7	

Part II Other Payments and Refundable Credits

8	Net premium tax credit. Attach Form 8962			8	
9	Amount paid with request for extension to file (see instructions)			9	
10	Excess social security and tier 1 RRTA tax withheld			10	
11	Credit for federal tax on fuels. Attach Form 4136			11	
12	Other payments or refundable credits:				
a	Form 2439	12a			
b	Qualified sick and family leave credits from Schedule(s) H and Form(s) 7202	12b			
c	Health coverage tax credit from Form 8885	12c			
d	Other:	12d			
e	Deferral for certain Schedule H or SE filers (see instructions)	12e			
f	Add lines 12a through 12e			12f	
13	Add lines 8 through 12f. Enter here and on Form 1040, 1040-SR, or 1040-NR, line 31			13	

For Paperwork Reduction Act Notice, see your tax return instructions. Cat. No. 71480G **Schedule 3 (Form 1040) 2020**

Gross Income

Gross income includes all income items that must be reported on the federal income tax return and that are subject to the federal income tax. It includes all income as broadly defined, less exclusions. Gross income is discussed in more detail in Chapters 4 and 5. Some of the most common gross income items are listed in **Exhibit 3.7**.

Exhibit 3.7 | Items Included in Gross Income

- Gains from the sale of assets
- Distributions from retirement plans
- Rental income
- Unemployment compensation benefits
- Royalty income
- Compensation (salaries and wages, etc.)
- Interest income
- Dividend income
- Alimony received*
- Gross income from self-employment

** For divorces executed after December 31, 2018, and divorces executed before January 1, 2019 that were subsequently modified with express instructions that the modification incorporates the amendments made by TCJA 2017, alimony received is not included in gross income by the recipient.*

Deductions

Deductions are subtracted from gross income in arriving at taxable income. For individual taxpayers, deductions are divided into two categories: Deductions *for* (before) adjusted gross income and deductions *from* (after) adjusted gross income. Deductions for adjusted gross income are called **above-the-line deductions**, and deductions from adjusted gross income are called **below-the-line deductions**, itemized deductions, or Schedule A deductions. These types of deductions are discussed in more detail in Chapters 6 and 7. A small sample of deductions for adjusted gross income (above-the-line deductions) is listed in **Exhibit 3.8**.

Quick Quiz 3.1

1. Income includes a return of invested capital.
   a. True
   b. False
2. Property obtained by inheritance is not included in gross income.
   a. True
   b. False

False, True.

Exhibit 3.8 | Partial List of Deductions for Adjusted Gross Income

- Alimony paid*
- Contributions to traditional IRAs
- Interest paid on student loans
- Business expenses
- Rental or royalty income expenses
- Losses from the sale of business property
- Moving expenses**

** For divorces executed after December 31, 2018, and divorces executed before January 1, 2019 that were substantially modified with express instructions that the modification incorporates the amendments made by TCJA 2017, alimony paid is not deductible from gross income by the payor.*

*** The moving expense deduction is suspended from 2018 through 2025, except for members of the Armed Forces on active duty that move pursuant to military order or incident to a permanent change of station (TCJA 2017).*

Adjusted Gross Income (AGI)

Adjusted gross income (AGI) is gross income reduced by above-the-line deductions. When determining whether deductions are taken above the line (for AGI) or below the line (from AGI), "the line" is AGI. Adjusted gross income is also used to determine limitations on several below-the-line deductions, on several income tax credits (discussed later in this chapter), and on a few other items on the tax return. Adjusted gross income is a concept that applies to individual tax returns; it does not apply to corporate or other entity tax returns.

Key Concepts

1. Define adjusted gross income.
2. Explain the difference between the standard deduction and itemized deductions.
3. Explain when a taxpayer is not permitted to use the standard deduction.

Deductions from Adjusted Gross Income

Deductions from adjusted gross income (below-the-line deductions, including itemized deductions and the QBI or Section 199A deduction) are those deductions that are subtracted from AGI. They consist of the greater of the standard deduction or certain allowable itemized deductions. Before 2018 and for tax years beginning after December 31, 2025, taxpayers could also claim a personal and dependency exemption as a deduction from adjusted gross income.

Standard Deduction

An individual taxpayer is allowed to deduct the greater of the standard deduction or allowable itemized deductions. Before 2018, approximately 70 percent of individual taxpayers used the standard deduction. In 2018, as a result of TCJA's increase in the standard deduction, 87.3% of taxpayers claimed the standard deduction. The **standard deduction** is a standard amount used to offset AGI that is specified by Congress. The standard deduction is adjusted for inflation on an annual basis. The total standard deduction includes a basic standard deduction plus additional standard deduction amounts for taxpayers age 65 or older and for taxpayers who are blind. The basic standard deduction amounts depend on the taxpayer's filing status (discussed below). The 2020 and 2021 standard deduction amounts for nondependents are listed in **Exhibit 3.9**. The standard deduction for a dependent is different and is discussed later in the chapter.

Exhibit 3.9 | Standard Deduction

Filing Status	*2020*	*2021*
Married Filing Jointly	$24,400	$25,100
Married Filing Separately	$12,200	$12,550
Surviving Spouse	$24,400	$25,100
Head of Household	$18,350	$18,800
Single	$12,200	$12,550

In TCJA 2017, Congress significantly increased the standard deduction for all taxpayer filing categories in an attempt to simplify the tax reporting for the majority of taxpayers in the United States. By increasing the standard deduction and by eliminating personal and dependency exemptions and suspending or modifying several types of itemized deductions, Congress has increased the relative significance of the standard deduction and decreased the relative significance of itemized deductions. As a result, many more Americans will find that they will lower their tax liability by using the standard deduction instead of their itemized deductions, which will save them time and expense when filing their tax return. These changes, while simplifying tax filing for many Americans, do not simplify the Internal

Revenue Code or filing requirements for those taxpayers with more complex financial situations. These taxpayers will continue to need the assistance of financial advisors and CPAs.

Additional Standard Deduction - Aged or Blind

An additional standard deduction is allowed for a taxpayer or spouse (not for a dependent) who is 65 years of age or older or blind. The age of the taxpayer is determined as of the end of the year. It is therefore possible for an unmarried taxpayer to receive one or two additional standard deductions and for a married couple to receive up to four additional standard deductions. The amounts allowed for each additional standard deduction are adjusted for inflation and depend upon the filing status of the taxpayer. The 2020 and 2021 additional standard deduction amounts are listed in **Exhibit 3.10**.

Exhibit 3.10 | Additional Standard Deduction

Filing Status	*2020*	*2021*
Married Filing Jointly	$1,300	$1,350
Married Filing Separately	$1,300	$1,350
Surviving Spouse	$1,300	$1,350
Head of Household	$1,600	$1,700
Single	$1,600	$1,700

Example 3.2

Wyatt (age 66) and Ruth (age 67) file a joint return for 2021. Their standard deduction is $27,800 (basic standard deduction of $25,100 plus two additional standard deductions of $1,350 for age). If Ruth were blind, their standard deduction would be $29,150 (basic standard deduction plus three additional standard deductions).

Example 3.3

Marty (age 65) and Wendy (age 58) are raising their grandson, Jonah, who qualifies as their dependent. Jonah is blind. Their standard deduction on a joint return for 2021 is $26,450 (basic standard deduction of $25,100 plus one additional standard deduction of $1,350 for Marty's age). They do not receive an additional standard deduction for Jonah's blindness because additional standard deductions for age and blindness are allowed only for the taxpayer and spouse, and not for their dependents. It should be noted, however, that a dependent's additional standard deductions can be claimed on the dependent's own tax return.

Example 3.4

Charlotte is 34 years of age, blind, and unmarried as of the end of 2021. She uses the single filing status for her tax return. Her standard deduction is $14,250 (basic standard deduction of $12,550 plus an additional standard deduction of $1,700 for blindness).

Additional Standard Deduction - Qualified Disaster-Related Casualty Losses[1]

The Taxpayer Certainty and Disaster Tax Relief Act of 2020 extended the additional standard deduction for net qualified personal casualty losses related to a presidentially declared disaster, subject to a $500 per disaster floor. Typically, personal casualty losses resulting from a qualified disaster are only deductible as an itemized deduction subject to a $100 per disaster floor, and only the loss in excess of ten percent of AGI is deductible. Additional details regarding the itemized deduction for personal casualty losses are discussed in Chapter 7.

Itemized Deductions

A taxpayer may choose to deduct specific allowable itemized deductions rather than the standard deduction. Itemized deductions, which are below-the-line deductions (also referred to as "from AGI" deductions), are claimed (on Schedule A) when they exceed the total standard deduction and thus reduce taxable income more than the standard deduction. Itemized deductions are explained in more detail in Chapter 7. A partial list of itemized deductions is presented in **Exhibit 3.11**. Prior to 2018, itemized deductions were reduced or phased out for certain high income taxpayers. That reduction/phase-out was eliminated beginning in 2018 by TCJA 2017. In addition, TCJA 2017 modified many itemized deductions, including home mortgage interest, deduction of taxes, casualty losses, and medical expenses. These changes are more thoroughly discussed in later chapters.

Exhibit 3.11 | Partial List of Itemized Deductions

<table>
<tr>
<td>
<ul>
<li>Charitable contributions.</li>
<li>Home mortgage interest.</li>
<li>Investment interest expense.</li>
<li>Up to $10,000 of:
<ul>
<li>State and local income taxes</li>
<li>Real property taxes on home</li>
<li>Property taxes based on the value of a car</li>
</ul></li>
<li>Casualty losses in excess of 10% of AGI due to a Presidentially declared disaster.</li>
<li>Medical and dental expenses in excess of 7.5% of AGI.</li>
</ul>
</td>
<td>
Miscellaneous deductions not subject to the 2% limit:
<ul>
<li>Amortizable premium on taxable bonds.</li>
<li>Casualty and theft losses from income-producing property.</li>
<li>Federal estate tax on income in respect of a decedent.</li>
<li>Gambling losses up to the amount of gambling winnings.</li>
<li>Impairment-related work expenses of persons with disabilities.</li>
<li>Losses from Ponzi-type investment schemes.</li>
<li>Unrecovered investment in an annuity.</li>
</ul>
</td>
</tr>
</table>

Example 3.5

Michael (age 52) and Jordan (age 50) are married and have no qualifying dependents. During 2021, they paid $5,000 in state income taxes, $15,000 in charitable contributions, $4,000 in qualified home mortgage interest, and $1,800 in property taxes on their home. The total of their itemized deductions is $25,800. Their standard deduction is $25,100. Therefore, they should itemize deductions rather than use the standard deduction.

1. A qualified disaster loss is a casualty or theft loss of personal-use property attributable to a major disaster declared by the President by February 26, 2021 under Section 401 of the Stafford Act. The COVID-19 disaster is excluded.

In three situations, a taxpayer is not allowed to use the standard deduction and *must* itemize deductions:

1. A married individual who files a separate return (married filing separately filing status) cannot use a standard deduction if that person's spouse itemizes deductions.
2. A nonresident alien and a dual-status alien is not allowed to use a standard deduction.
3. An individual who files a tax return for less than 12 months because of a change in annual accounting period is not allowed to use a standard deduction (not common for individual taxpayers).

The first special situation that requires use of itemized deductions is particularly important for tax professionals and is often a common area of confusion for clients. This rule applies whether or not the couple is separated, whether or not each spouse has incurred expenses that qualify as itemized deductions, and whether or not the spouses are communicating with each other. Simply stated, if either spouse chooses to itemize deductions, the other spouse must itemize deductions. The purpose of this rule is to deny married individuals the opportunity to claim total deductions in excess of the deductions they actually incur. For example, if this rule did not apply, a married couple could decide to file separately and structure their affairs so that all of the itemized deductions are claimed by one spouse, while the other claims the standard deduction amount. This arrangement would result in an increase in deductions for the couple equal to the standard deduction amount for married individuals filing separately when compared to the deductions permitted on a joint return filed by the couple. In an effort to prevent this type of planning, the special rule forces both spouses to itemize when either spouse itemizes, resulting in total itemized deductions for the couple equal to the deductions that could have been claimed if they had filed jointly.

Key Concepts

1. What is the current status of personal and dependency exemptions?
2. Explain how the tax on taxable income is calculated.
3. Identify various tax credits.

Personal and Dependency Exemptions

Prior to 2018, personal and dependency exemption amounts were also deductions from adjusted gross income. TCJA 2017 suspended the personal and dependency exemptions from 2018 until tax years after December 31, 2025. For tax years after December 31, 2025, taxpayers will be permitted to claim a dependency exemption for each person who qualifies as a dependent. Normally, the child of a taxpayer will qualify as the taxpayer's dependent, but many other people may qualify as well. While a dependent will not generate a dependency exemption for the taxpayer for tax years 2018-2025, dependency status is still important for taxpayers wishing to claim Head of Household filing status, as well as for claiming certain credits, such as the dependent credit.

Qualified Business Income (QBI) Deduction (Section 199A Deduction)

Beginning in 2018, a new below the line deduction is allowed for taxpayers with qualified business income. Subject to certain limitations, the deduction equals 20 percent of qualified business income. This deduction is not an itemized deduction (so taxpayers who qualify for this deduction do not have to be able to itemize deductions in order to receive a tax benefit), and may not be deducted in calculating adjusted gross income (AGI). Consequently, by creating the QBI deduction, TCJA 2017 effectively created a below-the-line deduction that is not impacted by the standard deduction (as is the case with itemized deductions). The QBI deduction will be discussed in more detail later in the text.

Taxable Income

Taxable income is the tax base upon which the income tax is calculated. It is determined by reducing the taxpayer's adjusted gross income (AGI) by (1) the greater of the standard deduction or the taxpayer's itemized deductions and (2) the QBI, or Section 199A deduction.

Tax Rates on Taxable Income

The income tax is determined by applying certain tax rates to taxable income. After 2017, the tax rates range from 10 percent to 37 percent (not including any applicable Affordable Care Act surtaxes). The amount of taxable income subject to tax at each rate (each tax bracket) depends on the filing status of the taxpayer. These tax rates are shown in Appendix A.

Example 3.6

Scott is 32 years of age and unmarried. His taxable income for 2021 is $80,000. Using Tax Rate Schedule X – Single, his tax on taxable income can be computed.

If taxable income is over--	But not over--	The tax is:
$0	$9,950	10% of the amount over $0
$9,950	$40,525	$995.00 plus 12% of the amount over $9,950
$40,525	$86,375	$4,664.00 plus 22% of the amount over $40,525
$86,375	$164,925	$14,751.00 plus 24% of the amount over $86,375
$164,925	$209,425	$33,603.00 plus 32% of the amount over $164,925
$209,425	$523,600	$47,843.00 plus 35% of the amount over $209,425
$523,600	and greater	$157,804.25 plus 37% of the amount over $523,600

For taxable income over $40,525 but not over $86,375, the income tax is $4,664.00 plus 22% of the amount over $40,525. Therefore, Scott's tax is $13,348.50 or ($4,664.00 + $8,684.50); [($80,000 – $40,525) x 22% = $8,684.50].

The total tax consists of:

1. $9,950 taxed at 10%
   $9,950 x 10% = $995.00
2. $30,575 taxed at 12%
   [($40,525 – $9,950) x 12% = $3,669.00]
3. $39,475 taxed at 22%
   [($80,000 – $40,525) x 22% = $8,684.50]

Scott's total tax is $13,348.50.

Scott's marginal income tax rate, the rate assessed on the next dollar of taxable income, is 22%.

Although the tax can be determined by directly applying the tax rates from the tax rate schedules to taxable income (as shown in the example above), taxpayers are required to determine the tax using tax tables provided by the Internal Revenue Service, if possible. These tax tables, published by the Internal Revenue Service in the instructions for individual income tax returns, show small ranges of taxable income and the amount of tax for taxable income within each range.

Exhibit 3.12 | Excerpt From 2020 and 2021 Tax Tables

Excerpt from 2020 Tax Table

If taxable income is -		And you are -			
At least	But less than	Single	Married filing jointly	Married filing separately	Head of a household
		Your tax is -			
80,000					
80,000	80,050	**$13,396**	$9,208	$13,396	$11,954
80,050	80,100	$13,407	$9,214	$13,407	$11,965
80,100	80,150	$13,418	$9,220	$13,418	$11,976
80,150	80,200	$13,429	$9,226	$13,429	$11,987
80,200	80,250	$13,440	$9,232	$13,440	$11,998
80,250	80,300	$13,451	$9,241	$13,451	$12,009
80,300	80,350	$13,462	$9,252	$13,462	$12,020
80,350	80,400	$13,473	$9,263	$13,473	$12,031
80,400	80,450	$13,484	$9,274	$13,484	$12,042
80,450	80,500	$13,495	$9,285	$13,495	$12,053
80,500	80,550	$13,506	$9,296	$13,506	$12,064
80,550	80,600	$13,517	$9,307	$13,517	$12,075
80,600	80,650	$13,528	$9,318	$13,528	$12,086
80,650	80,700	$13,539	$9,329	$13,539	$12,097
80,700	80,750	$13,550	$9,340	$13,550	$12,108
80,750	80,800	$13,561	$9,351	$13,561	$12,119
80,800	80,850	$13,572	$9,362	$13,572	$12,130
80,850	80,900	$13,583	$9,373	$13,583	$12,141
80,900	80,950	$13,594	$9,384	$13,594	$12,152
80,950	81,000	$13,605	$9,395	$13,605	$12,163

Excerpt from 2021 Tax Table

If taxable income is -		And you are -			
At least	But less than	Single	Married filing jointly	Married filing separately	Head of a household
		Your tax is -			
80,000					
80,000	80,050	**$13,354**	$9,205	$13,354	$11,902
80,050	80,100	$13,365	$9,211	$13,365	$11,913
80,100	80,150	$13,376	$9,217	$13,376	$11,924
80,150	80,200	$13,387	$9,223	$13,387	$11,935
80,200	80,250	$13,398	$9,229	$13,398	$11,946
80,250	80,300	$13,409	$9,235	$13,409	$11,957
80,300	80,350	$13,420	$9,241	$13,420	$11,968
80,350	80,400	$13,431	$9,247	$13,431	$11,979
80,400	80,450	$13,442	$9,253	$13,442	$11,990
80,450	80,500	$13,453	$9,259	$13,453	$12,001
80,500	80,550	$13,464	$9,265	$13,464	$12,012
80,550	80,600	$13,475	$9,271	$13,475	$12,023
80,600	80,650	$13,486	$9,277	$13,486	$12,034
80,650	80,700	$13,497	$9,283	$13,497	$12,045
80,700	80,750	$13,508	$9,289	$13,508	$12,056
80,750	80,800	$13,519	$9,295	$13,519	$12,067
80,800	80,850	$13,530	$9,301	$13,530	$12,078
80,850	80,900	$13,541	$9,307	$13,541	$12,089
80,900	80,950	$13,552	$9,313	$13,552	$12,100
80,950	81,000	$13,563	$9,319	$13,563	$12,111

Example 3.7

Using the 2021 tax table above, Scott's federal income tax for 2021 is $13,354. The tax using the tax table is $5.50 more than the $13,348.50 determined from the tax rate schedules. In the tax table, Scott's tax is based on taxable income of $80,025, the mid-point between the $80,000 lower limit and $80,050 upper limit for the bracket he must use from the tax table. Scott is required to use the amount from the tax table. If Scott's taxable income were higher than the amounts listed in the tax tables, he would use the tax rate schedules to determine his tax.

Credit for Estimated Tax Payments

The income earned by a self-employed person, and certain other business and investment income is not subject to tax withholding by an employer. Nevertheless, Congress would like to collect the taxes throughout the year. Therefore, a taxpayer with income not subject to withholding is often required to pay quarterly **estimated tax payments** to the Treasury Department (through the Internal Revenue Service) on:

- April 15,
- June 15,
- September 15, and
- January 15 of the following year.

Estimated payments must also be made (on different dates) by regular C corporations. As with taxes withheld by the employer, the taxpayer can claim a credit against the calculated tax for these quarterly estimated tax payments. Penalties may be imposed if estimated tax payments for the year are insufficient or late. (See Chapter 2 for more specific information on the underpayment penalty.)

Quick Quiz 3.2

1. A nonresident alien taxpayer is allowed to use the standard deduction.
   a. True
   b. False
2. For tax years 2018-2025, personal and dependency exemptions are deducted from AGI.
   a. True
   b. False
3. Tax credits increase the amount that the taxpayer owes.
   a. True
   b. False
4. Tax credits are available for child and dependent care expenses.
   a. True
   b. False

False, False, False, True.

Other Tax Credits

Various other tax credits are allowed to reduce the tax calculated on taxable income. These credits are discussed in more detail in Chapter 9. **Exhibit 3.13** provides a listing of some popular tax credits.

Exhibit 3.13 | Partial List of Tax Credits

Partial List of Tax Credits
Foreign tax credit
Credit for child and dependent care expenses
Credit for the elderly or disabled
Education credits (American Opportunity Tax Credit, Lifetime Learning Credit)
Retirement savings contribution credit
Residential energy credits
Child tax credit
Earned income credit
Other dependent credit
Various business and investment credits

USING THE TAX FORMULA: THE ANDERSON FAMILY

Paul Anderson (age 35) is a school teacher. He participates in two retirement plans and receives medical insurance and other fringe benefits from his employer. His wife, Stacey (age 33), works part-time as an office manager for a small business. Her company provides no retirement plan or other fringe benefits. They are the parents of one child, Amanda, who is almost three years old. Stacey's mother cares for Amanda at no cost while Stacey works. They live in Smithfield, Utah. During 2021, they had the following income and expenses that may be relevant in filing their joint tax return:

		Item
Paul's gross salary	$36,400	1
Paul's payment to his 401(k) retirement plan (withheld from his pay by his employer)	$2,400	2, 5
Stacey's gross salary	$22,000	1
Stacey's cash gift from her mother	$5,000	1, 2
Interest income from a joint savings account	$100	1
Federal income taxes withheld from their paychecks	$2,500	4
State income taxes withheld from their paychecks	$1,680	
Charitable contributions (cash) paid to several charities	$6,000	
Rent paid for apartment	$10,000	
Contribution to a traditional IRA by Stacey	$2,000	3, 5

Their federal income tax for 2021 is calculated as follows:

Item		*2021*
1	**Income Broadly Defined**	**$63,500**
2	Less: Exclusions	($7,400)
	Gross Income	**$56,100**
3	Less: Deductions for Adjusted Gross Income (IRA)	($2,000)
	Adjusted Gross Income	**$54,100**
	Less: Deductions from Adjusted Gross Income: Greater of Standard or Itemized Deductions (Standard Deduction)	($25,100)
	Less: Personal and Dependency Exemptions (Repealed TCJA)	($0)
	Taxable Income	**$29,000**
	Tax on Taxable Income (from tax rate schedule - Appendix A)	$3,082
4	Less: Credit for Taxes Withheld	($2,500)
5	Less: Credit for Qualified Retirement Savings	($400)
	Less: Credit for Other Dependents	$0
	Less: Other Tax Credits (Child Credit)	($2,000)
	Tax Due or (Refund Due)	**($1,818)**

1. *Income broadly defined* includes Paul's gross salary ($36,400), Stacey's gross salary ($22,000), Stacey's gift from her mother ($5,000) and the interest income ($100).
2. *Exclusions* include Paul's deferral of salary (contribution) into his 401(k) retirement plan ($2,400) and Stacey's gift from her mother ($5,000).

Gross income includes the taxable portion of Paul's salary ($36,400 – $2,400 = $34,000), Stacey's gross salary ($22,000), and the interest income ($100). These amounts are reported on the tax return.

3. *Deductions for adjusted gross income* include only Stacey's deductible contribution to a traditional IRA ($2,000). (Note: For the 2021 tax year, the Taxpayer Certainty and Disaster Tax Relief Act (TCDTRA) of 2020 allows married taxpayers who do not itemize deductions to deduct up to $600 of charitable contributions as a deduction for AGI. Because this deduction is limited to one year only (the 2021 tax year), we did not include it in this basic calculation example).

The Andersons' *standard deduction* for 2021 is $25,100, the basic standard deduction on a joint return. This amount is greater than the total of their itemized deductions, $7,680 (state income taxes of $1,680 plus charitable contributions of $6,000). The apartment rent is a personal expense that is not allowed as an itemized deduction.

The *tax on taxable income* can also be determined from tax tables provided in the instructions for Form 1040.

4. A credit of $2,500 is allowed for the amount of federal income taxes withheld from the salaries of Paul and Stacey.
5. The retirement savings contribution credit is a nonrefundable credit with a limit of $1,000 that is based on savings up to $2,000 per taxpayer. The applicable percentage for the credit is based on the taxpayer's AGI. The rate for the Andersons, based on their AGI, is 10%. A credit of $400 (10% of the $2,000 IRA and 10% of $2,000 of the 401(k) contribution (based on AGI) is allowed - see Chapter 9).

The child tax credit of $2,000 is available since Amanda is under the age of 17 and a dependent. This credit was increased by TCJA 2017 from $1,000 to $2,000 for years after 2017 and is now partially refundable up to $1,400 per qualifying child. (Note: For the 2021 tax year, the American Rescue Plan Act (ARPA) of 2021 temporarily increased the child tax credit to $3,600 for children under the age of 6 if the parent's adjusted gross income is no more than $150,000 (for married filing jointly). Based on their AGI and Amanda's age, the Andersons will qualify for the increased child tax credit during 2021; however, due to the limited time of applicability (only for tax year 2021), we did not include the increase in this basic calculation example.)

INTRODUCTION TO INDIVIDUAL INCOME TAXATION

The tax formula for individual taxpayers provides a roadmap for the remainder of this book. Each item in the tax formula will be examined in much more detail, but for now, several fundamental topics will be addressed in this chapter.

Tax Accounting Periods

A tax year, for tax reporting purposes, may be the calendar year, a fiscal year that ends on the last day of a month other than December, or a 52-53 week year that ends on a specified day of the week (such as Friday) that occurs in the last week of the last month of the tax year. The 52-53 week **tax year** may also end on the specified day of the week that falls closest to the last day of the last month of the tax year. A taxpayer normally chooses a tax year by simply filing his first tax return using the desired tax year for reporting purposes.

If a taxpayer wishes to have a tax year other than the calendar year, books and records must be maintained on the basis of the taxpayer's tax year. Since most individual taxpayers do not maintain books and records, their default tax year is the calendar year. Even individuals who do keep accounting records commonly use a calendar year because most tax reporting documents, such as Forms W-2 and 1099, report income on a calendar year basis.

A tax year must be used consistently unless a formal change in accounting period is approved by the Internal Revenue Service. When this happens, special rules apply to the short tax year that results from the change.

Tax Accounting Methods

An overall accounting method must be selected by each taxpayer for tax reporting purposes. This method must be used consistently from year to year unless a formal change in accounting method is made. Such changes normally require:

- the approval of the IRS
- income adjustments in the year of the change

A taxpayer who owns more than one business is allowed to select a different overall accounting method for each business, but taxable income must be computed using the methods normally used in keeping accounting records for each business. Additionally, a taxpayer may use different methods to account for business income and for nonbusiness income and deductions.

Key Concepts

1. Identify the tax accounting periods that can be used by individual taxpayers.
2. Compare and contrast the various accounting methods.
3. Identify the different filing statuses.
4. Describe the requirements for each filing status.

There are three accounting methods that are available for reporting income and deductions:

1. the cash receipts and disbursements method (cash method)
2. the accrual method
3. the hybrid method

Cash Receipts and Disbursements Method

Most individual taxpayers use the **cash receipts and disbursement method** (cash method) of accounting when filing their income tax returns. Under this method of accounting, income items (or revenues) are reported on a tax return for the year in which they are **received** in cash, and expenses are deducted in the year in which they are **paid** with cash. When using the cash method, "cash" includes currency, checks, and similar payments. Payments with credit cards issued by financial institutions are treated the same as paying with cash at the time of purchase, but paying with a credit card issued by a store (such as Sears, Wal-Mart, Home Depot, and the like) is not treated as a cash disbursement until the credit card bill is paid.

While cash method taxpayers normally recognize income when it is received in cash or a cash equivalent, exceptions do apply. Among the more common exceptions that apply to the cash method of accounting are:

1. the doctrine of constructive receipt
2. original issue discount bonds
3. cash received with an obligation to repay

The **doctrine of constructive receipt**, one of the three key tax principles, states that a cash method taxpayer must report income when it is constructively received. Constructive receipt occurs when income is credited to a taxpayer's account or when it is made available to the taxpayer without restriction. A taxpayer need not take possession of income for it to be constructively received. For example, interest income may be credited to the taxpayer's account after the bank closes on the last day of the tax year, or a client may offer to give the taxpayer a check for services already provided while attending a New Year's Eve party. In either case, constructive receipt has occurred and the taxpayer's gross income must include these amounts. The doctrine of constructive receipt underlies most of the retirement planning rules, and must be avoided to allow deferral of income.

A special application of constructive receipt is an **original issue discount (OID) bond**, more commonly known as a **zero coupon bond**. The interest that accrues on the bond each year (determined by a financial calculation that takes into consideration the difference between the maturity value of the bond and its purchase price), is deemed to be constructively received by the taxpayer, and is included in the taxpayer's income. Since the bond does not actually make the interest payment that year, but the taxpayer must include the imputed interest in income, zero coupon bonds generate **phantom income**. As interest is reported in income, the taxpayer's basis in the bond increases by a like amount. The tax treatment of OID bonds will be more fully discussed in Chapter 4.

Finally, if a taxpayer receives cash, but has an obligation to repay the payor, the cash is not included in gross income. This may occur when a landlord receives a deposit for an apartment. If the landlord has an obligation to return the deposit when the renter moves out (provided, of course, that the apartment is left in good condition), the cash received is not included in gross income, since it does not represent an accretion to wealth. If the deposit is really a form of prepaid rent, however, it must be recognized as gross income.

A taxpayer who uses the cash receipts and disbursements method for reporting most items on a tax return may use an accrual or hybrid method for reporting self-employment income or other business income from a proprietorship (on Schedule C), farm (Schedule F), or partnership (Schedule E).

Accrual Method of Accounting

Many businesses use the **accrual method** of accounting, since it provides a better match between income and the expenses associated with producing that income than the cash receipts and disbursements method of accounting. Under the accrual method, income (revenue) is normally reported when it is earned, and expenses are normally deducted when they are incurred.

The "all events" test is commonly used to determine income inclusion under the accrual method of accounting for income tax purposes. Income is includible when all events have occurred that:

- fix the taxpayer's right to receive the income
- allow the amount of income to be determined with reasonable accuracy

There are several exceptions to the accrual method of accounting. Some of the more common exceptions that apply are:

- prepaid income
- advance payment for goods
- advance payment for services
- the claim of right doctrine

For financial accounting purposes, prepaid income is not reported under the accrual method until goods or services are provided to the customer. For income tax purposes, the federal government wants to collect taxes due, even from an accrual basis taxpayer, when the taxpayer has the cash (the wherewithal to pay). Therefore, prepaid income, such as prepaid interest and prepaid rent, must be included in income when the payment is received.

When a business owner receives advance payment for goods to be delivered in the future, financial accounting rules normally require an accrual basis seller to report the revenues only when delivery of the goods is made and the revenues are earned. For tax purposes, the seller is generally allowed similar treatment if the seller elects such treatment and if the same method is used for both tax and financial reporting purposes.

An unusual rule applies when advance payments are received for services to be performed in the future. According to Revenue Procedure 2004-34, an accrual method taxpayer is allowed to use the regular accrual method for the year in which the prepayment is received, but the remainder of the prepayment must be included in gross income for the following year.

Example 3.8

Alma is the owner of a cleaning and custodial business. On November 1 of Year 1, Alma receives $2,400 ($100 per month) for custodial services to be provided from November 1 of Year 1 through October 31 of Year 3. She uses the normal accrual method for Year 1 and therefore reports $200 of the revenues in Year 1. The remaining $2,200 must all be recognized in Year 2. She is not permitted to defer recognition of the $1,000 (for January through October of year 3) until Year 3.

The Claim of Right Doctrine

When an accrual method taxpayer earns income, that income is normally included in gross income. There are circumstances, however, where the amount of income is difficult to ascertain. For example, consider an accrual method taxpayer who sells tires. What happens if the customer is not satisfied? If the customer refuses to pay, the taxpayer is not required to report the contested portion of the bill because the taxpayer's income is in question. The disputed portion of the bill will be reported only when the dispute is settled.

For situations in which the customer pays and then requests or sues for a full or partial refund, courts have established the claim of right doctrine. Under this doctrine, the taxpayer must report the entire payment in gross income in the year of the payment even though part or all of the payment may have to be repaid to the customer. If the customer is repaid in a later year, the taxpayer is allowed a tax deduction in the year of the repayment.

The Hybrid Method

The **hybrid method** of accounting includes any other method of reporting that is permitted by the IRC and regulations as long as it is deemed to clearly reflect income. A common hybrid method of accounting involves use of the accrual method for inventories and property, plant, and equipment and the cash method for everything else. A taxpayer who owns more than one trade or business is allowed to use a different overall accounting method for each business.

Hybrid methods are commonly used in conjunction with special types of transactions or arrangements, such as with long-term contracts. Long-term contracts are contracts that are entered into during the year, but will not be completed within that year. Building, construction, installation, and certain manufacturing contracts are often long-term contracts. The costs associated with a long-term contract are deducted from the revenues generated by that contract under one of two hybrid methods: the completed contract method or the percentage of completion method.

The completed contract method states that no revenue from a contract is included in the taxpayer's income until the contract is completed. The percentage of completion method, on the other hand, requires that a portion of the expected revenues of the contract must be included in the taxpayer's income at regular intervals based upon the percentage of completion of the work. Because revenues from the contract are included in the taxpayer's income, the taxpayer is also allowed to deduct a pro rata share of the expenses during the same period based on the percentage completion method.

Filing Status

The filing status of a taxpayer is used to determine the amount of the taxpayer's standard deduction, the tax rate schedule (or tax table) to be used, and the eligibility of the taxpayer to use various tax benefits. A list of filing statuses is presented in **Exhibit 3.14**.

Exhibit 3.14 | Filing Status for Individuals

Filing Status
Married Filing Jointly
Married Filing Separately
Surviving Spouse/Qualifying Widow(er)
Head of Household / Abandoned Spouse
Single

Marital Status

The determination of whether a taxpayer is married is normally made as of the close (the last day) of the tax year. However, if a taxpayer's spouse dies during the year, the marital status of the taxpayer is determined on the date of the spouse's death. A married person normally has two filing status options: married filing jointly or married filing separately.

Example 3.9

Javi married Darlene on December 31st of this year. They will have to file as married filing jointly or married filing separately for the year.

If a person is not married, then he or she may qualify for the surviving spouse, head of household, or single filing status. A very rare situation is discussed below which may allow a married person to file as a single taxpayer. A taxpayer who is legally separated from his spouse under a decree of divorce or of separate maintenance is not considered to be married for federal income tax purposes.

Married Filing Jointly

Married taxpayers are allowed to choose either married filing jointly or **married filing separately status**. Most married taxpayers use the **married filing jointly filing status**. This filing status allows a married couple to combine their gross income and deductions. If they do not itemize deductions, the basic standard deduction when filing jointly is double the size of the basic standard deduction for a married taxpayer filing separately. Each tax bracket (the 12 percent tax bracket, for example) for joint filers is twice as broad as for a married taxpayer filing separately, subjecting twice as much income to the lower rates. In addition, a married couple is required to file jointly in order to be eligible for certain benefits such as the American Opportunity Tax Credit (discussed in Chapter 9).

Quick Quiz 3.3

1. Only businesses may choose a tax year other then the calendar year.
   a. True
   b. False
2. Two commonly used tax accounting methods are the cash method and the accrual method.
   a. True
   b. False

False, True.

For a taxpayer whose spouse dies during the year, a joint return can be filed. The joint return will include the income and deductions of the taxpayer for the full year and the income and deductions of the spouse for the part of the year that the spouse lived. If the surviving taxpayer remarries before the end of the year, she will be able to file a joint return with the new spouse but not with the deceased spouse. In this situation, the final income tax return for the deceased spouse must use the married filing separately filing status.

Example 3.10

Daniel died in April. His surviving spouse, Ali, married Johnny in November of the same year. Ali will be able to file as married filing jointly with Johnny. A tax return for Daniel for the part of the year he lived will have to use the married filing separately filing status.

Same-Sex Married Couples

A legally married, same-sex couple is required to file as a married person for federal income tax purposes, just as any other married couple. This treatment of same-sex couples is a result of the 2013 landmark case, United States v. Windsor, in which the Supreme Court ruled that Section 3 of the Defense of Marriage Act (DOMA) is unconstitutional under the Due Process Clause of the Fifth Amendment. After the Windsor decision, if a same-sex couple was married in a state that recognized same-sex marriages, they were married for federal income tax purposes, even if they resided in a state that did not recognize same-sex marriages.

The Supreme Court Ruling in Obergefell v Hodges on June 26, 2015 mandated that all states must recognize and license same-sex marriages, extending the ability to file joint returns at the state level to same-sex married couples. Same-sex married couples can file as married filing jointly and receive unlimited spousal deductions related to gifts and estate tax issues. However, if a couple is not in a formal marriage (i.e. registered domestic partnership, civil union or other similar relationships), they will not be treated as being married for federal tax purposes.

Married Filing Separately

A married taxpayer can elect to file separately for any reason. This may be necessary if the husband and wife are separated at the end of the year, or if the taxpayer is not sure that his spouse is accurately reporting income. It may also be used for tax minimization purposes, by permitting one spouse to deduct more of his unusually large medical expenses for the tax year.

Abandoned Spouse

There is one situation in which a legally married taxpayer will be allowed to use a filing status (head of household) generally reserved for unmarried taxpayers. As discussed below, the head of household status is more favorable than filing as married filing separately and when an individual cannot locate his spouse, and does not want to file a tax return with him, it may be available. To be eligible to file as an abandoned spouse (and therefore use the head of household filing status), the taxpayer must meet *all* of the following requirements:

- The taxpayer must be married;
- Must file a separate tax return from the spouse;
- Must maintain as his/her home a household which for more than one-half of the taxable year is the principal place of abode of a child who can be claimed as a dependent;
- Must furnish over one-half of the cost of maintaining the household; *and*
- The spouse must not be a member of the household during the last six months of the tax year.

Example 3.11

Bonnie is married to Clyde, but Clyde moved to another state during March of the current year. Bonnie hasn't talked to Clyde since he moved out. She works as a school teacher and has paid all of the costs of providing for herself and her two minor children who live with her. She will file her own tax return for the year. Although she is legally married at the end of the year, she will be allowed to file using the head of household filing status, a filing status normally used by unmarried taxpayers.

Unmarried Taxpayers

A taxpayer who is not married on the final day of the tax year may be able to file as surviving spouse, head of household, or single. The tax benefits for the surviving spouse filing status are the most favorable, those for head of household are next, and those for the single filing status are the least favorable.

Surviving Spouse/Qualifying Widow(er)

The **surviving spouse filing status** affords the same basic standard deduction and tax rates as the married filing jointly filing status. However, eligibility for this filing status is not something that most people desire. To be eligible, the spouse of the taxpayer must have died within the two preceding tax years of the taxpayer. Specifically, a taxpayer must meet *all* of the following requirements to qualify:

- The taxpayer's spouse must have died during either of the two preceding tax years;
- The taxpayer must maintain (pay more than half the cost of) a household as his home which is also the principal place of residence of a dependent child (son, stepson, daughter, or stepdaughter);
- The taxpayer has not remarried; *and*
- The taxpayer and spouse were eligible to file a joint return for the spouse's year of death.

Quick Quiz 3.4

1. The determination of whether a taxpayer is married is made as of the beginning of the year.
   a. True
   b. False
2. A surviving spouse must not have remarried in order to use the surviving spouse filing status.
   a. True
   b. False

False, True.

Example 3.12

Sam died in 2020. His wife, Diane, filed a joint return with Sam for 2020. Diane did not remarry in 2021, 2022, or 2023, but she maintained a home for herself and her two minor children during those years. During 2021 and 2022, Diane is eligible to use the surviving spouse filing status. In 2023, she will probably be eligible to use the head of household filing status (see below).

The filing status called surviving spouse in the Internal Revenue Code and Treasury Regulations is referred to as the qualifying widow(er) filing status in IRS publications. Surviving spouse and qualifying widow(er) are alternate names for the same filing status.

Head of Household

The **head of household filing status** provides a basic standard deduction and tax bracket sizes that are less favorable to the taxpayer than those for the surviving spouse, but more favorable than those for the single filing status. Head of household filing status can be used by an unmarried taxpayer who is not a surviving spouse and who meets the following requirements:

- The taxpayer must maintain (pay more than half the cost of) a household as his or her home, which is also the principal place of residence for more than half the year for:
  - a qualifying child of the taxpayer who may be claimed as a qualifying dependent (discussed later in this chapter) of the taxpayer,
  - an unmarried qualifying child who lives with the taxpayer but is not a dependent of the taxpayer (for example, a taxpayer's child or grandchild who lives in the taxpayer's household but may be claimed as the qualifying dependent of another person), or
  - a qualifying relative (discussed later in this chapter) who: (1) is claimed as a qualifying dependent of the taxpayer, and (2) is actually related to the taxpayer.

For tax years 2018-2025, TCJA 2017 suspended the deduction available for personal exemptions of the taxpayer and his/her dependents. While taxpayers will not be able to claim a personal exemption for each dependent during this period, the ability to claim a qualifying dependent is important for taxpayers wishing to claim head of household status as well as for certain credits.

If a married child of the taxpayer lives with the taxpayer but cannot be claimed as a dependent of the taxpayer either because the child: (1) files a joint return (married filing jointly) with her spouse or (2) fails to meet a citizenship or residency test, the taxpayer is not allowed to use the head of household filing status.

Example 3.13

Omar, who is not married, rents a home for himself and his two young children. He qualifies to use the head of household filing status.

Example 3.14

Moira is not married. She maintains a household for herself and her dependent son. During the year, Moira's son lived with her during the summer (three months) and lived in an apartment at a distant university during the rest of the year. Even though Moira's son did not live with her for more than half the year, Moira will be allowed to use head of household filing status because her son's absence is considered to be temporary. The taxpayer and the dependent are considered to occupy the household even during temporary absences due to special circumstances such as illness, education, business, vacation, military service, or a custody agreement under which the dependent is absent for less than six months during the tax year.

Example 3.15

June, who is divorced, rents an apartment for herself and for her 14-year-old daughter who lives with her. Under the terms of June's divorce decree, her daughter is claimed as a dependent by her father. June is allowed to use head of household filing status even though she doesn't claim her daughter as a dependent, because she maintains the home for her daughter.

Example 3.16

Luke, who is unmarried, maintains a home in which he and his uncle live. He properly claims his uncle as a dependent. Luke is allowed to use the head of household filing status because he claims his uncle as a dependent and because his uncle is actually related to him.

Example 3.17

Janine is unmarried. She maintains a household in which she and her best friend's daughter live. Her friend's daughter, Hannah, is 8 years old. Hannah's parents, who died in an automobile accident two years earlier, had requested that Janine raise Hannah if they were to die prematurely. Since Hannah meets the definition of a qualifying relative (explained below), Janine is allowed to claim Hannah as a dependent, but she will not be able to use the head of household filing status because Hannah is not actually related to Janine. If Janine were to adopt Hannah, she would be allowed to use the head of household filing status.

Example 3.18

Fred, who is unmarried, owns a large house. He allows his 18-year-old son, Nick, to live in the basement of the home with his wife, Serena. Fred will not be allowed to claim Nick as a dependent because Nick files a joint income tax return with his wife. Fred must use the single filing status rather than head of household.

Special Rule for the Father or Mother of the Taxpayer

In order to use the head of household filing status, a qualifying child or a qualifying relative must normally live with the taxpayer. However, a taxpayer may also qualify for the head of household status by maintaining a separate household for the father or mother of the taxpayer who qualifies as the taxpayer's dependent.

Example 3.19

Lydia provides more than half of the cost of maintaining an apartment (or house or accommodations in a retirement home, etc.) for her mother this year. Lydia properly claims her mother as a dependent. Lydia is eligible to use the head of household filing status.

Single

The **single filing status** must be used by an unmarried taxpayer who is not eligible to use the surviving spouse nor head of household filing status. It provides the least desirable basic standard deduction and tax brackets for an unmarried taxpayer.

Personal and Dependency Exemptions

TCJA 2017 suspended the deduction of personal and dependency exemptions for tax years 2018-2025. While no deduction exists for personal and dependency exemptions during this period, the classification of individuals as dependents is still necessary to take advantage of other tax benefits.

Personal Exemptions

For tax years before 2018 and after 2025, each taxpayer was permitted to take one **personal exemption**. A married couple filing jointly, therefore, was allowed two personal exemptions. During the period from 2018 - 2025, when a deduction for personal exemptions is suspended, personal exemptions may not be claimed and will not generate a tax benefit for the taxpayer.

Dependency Exemptions

The rules for **dependency exemptions** were significantly changed beginning in 2005. Before 2005, a taxpayer was allowed to claim as a dependent each and every person who is considered to be a qualifying child or qualifying relative of the taxpayer. These terms can be confusing, however, because a qualifying child might not be the taxpayer's child at all and a qualifying relative in some cases is not a relative of the taxpayer. Beginning in 2005, in addition to being a qualifying child or a qualifying relative, a dependent must also meet a joint return test and a citizenship or residency test. These two tests are discussed later. A taxpayer who is eligible to be claimed as a dependent of another taxpayer is not allowed to claim any dependents.

Key Concepts

1. Define personal exemption.
2. Define dependency exemption.
3. Describe the requirements for claiming a qualifying child as a qualifying dependent.
4. Describe the requirements for claiming a qualifying relative as a qualifying dependent.

Qualifying Child

A **qualifying child** must meet *all* the requirements of four tests:

1. a relationship test
2. an abode test
3. an age test
4. a support test

These rules for a qualifying child relate not only to dependency status, but also to the definition of a child for purposes of head of household filing status, the earned income tax credit, the child tax credit, and the credit for child and dependent care expenses.

Relationship Test

In order to satisfy the relationship test, a qualifying child of a taxpayer must be:

- the taxpayer's child,
- a descendant of the taxpayer's child,
- the taxpayer's brother, sister, stepbrother, stepsister, half brother, half sister, or
- a descendant of the taxpayer's brother, sister, stepbrother, stepsister, half brother, or half sister.

Stated differently, a qualifying child is the taxpayer's sibling, a descendant of the taxpayer, or the descendant's sibling. Note that a cousin is not a qualifying child.

A taxpayer's child may be a natural child, a stepchild, an adopted child, or an eligible foster child.

Example 3.20

Mike and Carol have a remarkably diverse family. In addition to Mike and Carol, the family includes:

1. Greg, Carol's 10-year-old son from a prior marriage
2. Marcia, Carol's 15-year-old sister
3. Andrei, their 6-year-old son adopted from Russia
4. Cindy, their 4-year old daughter
5. Brady, a 2-year-old foster child placed with them by a state agency

Each of the five children meets the relationship test as a qualifying child of Carol.

Abode Test

To meet the abode test, a qualifying child must live with the taxpayer for more than half the year. The taxpayer and the dependent are considered to occupy the household even during temporary absences due to special circumstances such as illness, education, business, vacation, or military service.

Example 3.21

Lionel and Nicole have an 18-year-old son, Richie. Richie lived at home during the first five months of the year and then entered military service. Since military service is considered to be a temporary absence due to special circumstances, Richie meets the abode test for the year.

Age Test

A qualifying child must either be under the age of 19 and younger than the taxpayer as of the end of the calendar year or, a student under the age of 24 and younger than the taxpayer as of the end of the calendar year in order to satisfy the age test. To be considered a student, the child must be a full-time student at an educational institution during at least five months of the calendar year. Most primary and secondary schools, colleges, universities and similar educational institutions are acceptable for this purpose.

Example 3.22

Samira's 21-year-old son finished his third year of college in May of this year. He spent the remainder of the year serving as a volunteer in a program to assist the victims of a flood. If the son was a full-time student during part or all of the first five months of the year, he meets the age test.

A child who is permanently and totally disabled meets the age test regardless of his or her age.

CASE STUDY 3.1

Dependency Exemption and Head of Household Filing Status

Gabriel M. Daya, ET AL. Petitioners v. Commissioner of Internal Revenue, Respondent. T.C. Memo 2000-360 (November 22, 2000).

At the time petitions were filed for his 1995 and 1996 taxable years, Gabriel resided in Fremont, California. Morhaf resided in Foster City, California. Petitioners are brothers who in August of 1983 emigrated from Syria. Members of the Mahmoud Daya Family include petitioners' father, Mahmoud Gabriel Daya (Mahmoud), petitioners' mother, Laila C. Daya (Laila), and petitioners' younger brother, Mayar Daya (Mayar). Before moving to the United States, Mahmoud, together with his identical twin brother, Fuad Daya (Fuad), purchased a single family residence located at 913 Laguna Circle, Foster City, California. Petitioners did not hold legal title to the Foster City residence at anytime during 1995.

On or about March 20, 1996, a "gift deed" was executed evidencing the transfer of legal title to an undivided one-fifth interest in Mahmoud's undivided one-half interest in the Foster City residence from Mahmoud to Gabriel and Morhaf. California real property tax statements for the Foster City residence were in the names of Mahmoud and Fuad in both 1995 and 1996.

On his 1995 and 1996 federal income tax returns, Gabriel claimed his father as a dependent and head of household filing status. Gabriel also claimed deductions of $9,303 and $9,189 for home mortgage interest and deductions of $1,532 and $1,543 for property taxes in 1995 and 1996. On his 1995 federal income tax return, Morhaf claimed his mother as a dependent and head of household filing status. He also claimed a mortgage interest deduction of $9,303 and a property tax deduction of $1,532.

Gabriel failed to establish the total amount expended on Mahmoud's support from all sources in 1995 and 1996. He likewise failed to establish his own contributions toward his father's support. The record does not provide any evidence from which we could conclude that Gabriel had equitable or beneficial ownership of the residence in 1995.

The court concluded Gabriel is not entitled to the dependency exemptions for his father under Section 151 in 1995 or 1996 and Gabriel is not entitled to head of household filing status in either year. With respect to Morhaf, respondent concedes that he provided more than one-half of the support in 1995 for his mother within the meaning of Section 1.152-1(a)(2)(i), Income Tax Regs., and as such is entitled to a dependency exemption deduction for her.

The IRS, however, maintains that Morhaf is not entitled to head of household filing status in 1995 because he has not established that he paid more than half of the expenses of maintaining a household for his mother. Morhaf has not shown that he paid any of these expenses or any other expenses for the maintenance of the household beyond the $668.74. Morhaf has not established that he provided more than half the cost of maintaining a household for Laila in 1995. Accordingly, the court held the IRS' determination that Gabriel is not entitled to head of household filing status in 1995 and 1996, and Morhaf is not entitled to head of household filing status in 1995.

Support Test

The support test is satisfied if a qualifying child does not provide more than one-half of his or her own support during the year. If a child is the taxpayer's child and is a full-time student, amounts received as scholarships are not considered to be support.

Example 3.23

Alice and Cooper provide $10,000 toward the support of their son, Damon. Damon provides $2,000 toward his own support and receives a scholarship worth $12,000 from the university he attends. Damon is not considered to provide more than one-half of his own support because the scholarship is not considered to be support provided by Damon.

If more than one person is eligible to claim another person as a dependent under the qualifying child rules, the tie-breaker rules shown in **Exhibit 3.15** apply:

Exhibit 3.15 | Tie-Breaker Rules

Eligible Taxpayers	*Taxpayer Allowed to Claim the Dependency Exemption*
Both parents	The parent with whom the child lived longer
Both parents and the child lives with each for the same amount of time	The parent with the higher adjusted gross income
Only one is a parent	The parent
Neither is a parent	The taxpayer with the higher adjusted gross income

Tie-Breaker Rules

Under the tie-breaker rules, when a child lives with each parent for the same amount of time, or if the taxpayers eligible to claim the person as a qualifying dependent are not the parents, the taxpayer with the higher adjusted gross income claims the child as a qualifying dependent. This rule is only important to determine which taxpayer claims the child for filing status and applicable tax credits.

Children of Divorced or Separated Parents

Because of the abode test, a child of divorced or separated parents is normally the qualifying child of the custodial parent. If all four of the following requirements are met, however, the child will be treated as the qualifying child of the noncustodial parent:

1. the parents are divorced or legally separated under a decree of divorce or separate maintenance, are separated under a written separation agreement, or they live apart at all times during the last six months of the year;
2. the child receives over one-half of his support for the year from his parents;
3. the child is in the custody of the parents for more than half the year; and
4. the custodial parent signs a statement that he will not claim the child as a dependent for the year, and the noncustodial parent attaches the statement to his return (may use Form 8332).

For the signed statement or written declaration in requirement four above, the custodial parent may use Form 8332 or a similar statement that contains the same information. The statement may apply to the current year, several years, or to all future years. For divorce or separation agreements after 1984 and before 2009, the requirement for a signed statement can be met by attaching certain pages from the decree or agreement to the tax return of the noncustodial parent. If pages from the decree or agreement are used, they must specify that the noncustodial parent can claim the child as a dependent, that the custodial parent will not claim the child as a qualifying dependent, and the years for which the noncustodial parent is allowed to claim the child. Different rules apply to divorce decrees and separation agreements before 1985. At this point in time (2021), the only children of divorced parents with a separation agreement predating 1985 that would meet the age test are children who are disabled. For post-2008 divorce decrees or separate maintenance agreements, Form 8332 or a similar statement must be provided with the noncustodial parent's tax return.

Example 3.24

Fred and Daphne were divorced in 2007. Daphne was given custody of their daughter, Velma, and Fred was given visitation rights on alternate weekends and other specified times. The divorce decree states that Fred will be allowed to claim Velma as a dependent each year. Fred will be able to claim Velma as a dependent, but he will be required to attach pages from the divorce decree to his income tax return each year. If the right to claim Velma as a dependent had not been given to Fred in the divorce decree, Daphne could allow him to claim Velma by giving him a signed Form 8332 to attach to his tax return.

Qualifying Relative

In addition to the joint return test and the citizenship or residency test (discussed later), **a qualifying relative** must meet the following four tests to qualify as a dependent of a taxpayer:

- relationship test
- gross income test
- support test
- not a qualifying child test

Relationship Test

To satisfy the relationship test for a qualifying relative, the potential dependent of the taxpayer must be:

- the taxpayer's child or a descendant of a child (grandchildren, etc.),
- the taxpayer's brother, sister, stepbrother, or stepsister,
- the taxpayer's father, or mother, or an ancestor (grandparent, etc.),
- the taxpayer's stepfather or stepmother,
- a son (nephew) or daughter (niece) of a brother or sister of the taxpayer,
- a brother (uncle) or sister (aunt) of the father or mother of the taxpayer,
- a son-in-law, daughter-in-law, father-in-law, mother-in-law, brother-in-law or sister-in-law of the taxpayer, or
- any other individual (may be a totally unrelated person) who, for the taxable year of the taxpayer, has the same principal place of abode as the taxpayer and is a member of the taxpayer's household. A person who was married to the taxpayer during part of the year does not qualify.

A child of the taxpayer who does not meet the requirements to be a qualifying child may still meet the requirements to be a qualifying relative of the taxpayer. Note that not all relatives of a taxpayer (a cousin, for example) meet this relationship test. Significantly, individuals who are not actually related to the taxpayer may meet the relationship test if they live with the taxpayer as a member of the taxpayer's household. An unrelated person claimed as a dependent, however, will not qualify a taxpayer for head of household filing status even though the taxpayer filing as a single individual can claim the person as a dependent for purposes of obtaining the dependent tax credit.

Quick Quiz 3.5

1. A taxpayer is entitled to claim as a dependent anyone who lives in his house.
   a. True
   b. False
2. A qualifying child must live with the taxpayer for more than half of the year.
   a. True
   b. False
3. A qualifying relative, unlike a qualifying child, is subject to a gross income test.
   a. True
   b. False

False, True, True.

Gross Income Test

To meet the gross income test, a dependent's gross income must be less than the exemption amount referenced in Section 152(d)(1)(B), which is indexed for inflation annually. The gross income limitation for a qualifying relative was $4,300 in 2020 and is $4,300 in 2021. When applying the gross income test, Social Security income is not counted if it is not included in gross income (taxation of Social Security benefits is covered in Chapter 5). Even though TCJA 2017 suspended the deduction for personal exemptions during the period 2018-2025, the gross income test continues to be a relevant test for the determination of head of household status and the other dependent tax credit (Chapter 9).

Example 3.25

During 2020 and 2021, Sylvester and Adrian provide more than half the support of Adrian's mother, who lives with them. Adrian's mother receives $5,000 (included in gross income) per year from a retirement plan and a small monthly Social Security benefit check. The Social Security is not included in gross income because her other income is so low. Adrian's mother fails the gross income test because her gross income for 2020 and 2021 exceeds $4,300 and $4,300 respectively.

Example 3.26

Paulie provides more than half the support of his son, Apollo. Apollo is a 25-year-old doctoral student at a university. Apollo's only income is a $12,000 fellowship to pay tuition. Even though Apollo is not under 24 years of age and is therefore not a qualifying child, he may be claimed as a qualifying relative if he meets the gross income test. Since a fellowship or scholarship is normally excluded from gross income, and Apollo has no other income, Paulie is allowed to claim Apollo as a dependent.

Support Test

To satisfy the support test, the taxpayer must provide more than one-half of the support of a dependent. Support normally includes providing housing, food, clothing, education, and medical treatment, among other things. Income received by a dependent does not count as support provided by the dependent unless it is actually expended for that purpose. For example, if income earned by an elderly parent is deposited in a savings account rather than expended for his own support, it does not count as support provided by the parent.

Not a Qualifying Child Test
In order to be claimed as a qualifying relative, a dependent cannot be a qualifying child of any taxpayer for the tax year.

Special rules apply to a person who may be claimed as a qualifying dependent by another taxpayer. A person who is a dependent of another taxpayer:

1. may not claim themselves as a dependent
2. may have a reduced basic standard deduction
3. is required to file a tax return based on different rules from the gross income test used by taxpayers who cannot be claimed as a dependent
4. is not allowed to claim any dependents

An overview of issues 1 and 2 is presented in the section on calculating the standard deduction of a dependent, which follows.

Prior to 2018, only one exemption amount was allowed for each taxpayer. Therefore, a taxpayer who would be claimed as a dependent by another taxpayer was not allowed a personal exemption. Due to the enactment of TCJA 2017, for the period 2018-2025, no one may claim a personal exemption in calculating taxable income.

In addition to the four tests for a qualifying child or the four tests for a qualifying relative, anyone who may be claimed as a dependent under the qualifying child or qualifying relative classifications must meet the following two tests:

1. a joint return test
2. a citizenship or residency test

Joint Return Test
To satisfy the joint return test, a married dependent must not file a joint return with a spouse unless a tax return is filed only to claim a refund for tax withheld, if neither spouse is otherwise required to file a tax return, and if no tax liability would exist for either taxpayer on separate returns.

Example 3.27

Fitch and Olivia wish to claim their married daughter, Mellie, as a dependent. They meet all of the tests to claim her except the joint return test. Mellie and her husband file a joint tax return for the year to reduce their income tax liability. They owe money on their joint return and each would have owed money on a separate return. Fitch and Olivia are not eligible to claim Mellie as a dependent.

Citizenship or Residency Test
A dependent must be a citizen or national of the United States or a resident of the United States, Canada, or Mexico during some part of the year. This test does not apply for certain adopted children.

Multiple Support Agreements

Sometimes, no individual taxpayer provides more than one-half the support of a potential dependent. Under these circumstances, over one-half of the support is deemed to be paid by one taxpayer if:

1. the taxpayer provides more than 10 percent of the potential dependent's support;
2. two or more persons who individually provide more than 10 percent of the potential dependent's support also provide more than 50 percent of the individual's total support and meet all other requirements to claim the individual as a dependent;
3. the qualifying persons in item 2 above (other than the taxpayer) sign a statement (Form 2120 can be used) agreeing not to claim an exemption for the potential dependent for the year; and
4. the taxpayer attaches the signed Form 2120 to her tax return.

Example 3.28

No one provides more than half the support of Maya for the year. She is currently unmarried and lives alone in a small apartment, but she only provides 25% of her own support. The remainder of her support is provided by her son, Huck (10%), her daughter, Quinn (22%), her son, Cyrus (30%), and a friend and neighbor, Darby (13%). The qualifying persons are Quinn (22%) and Cyrus (30%) if they meet all other requirements to claim Maya as a dependent. Each of them provides more than 10% of Maya's support and together they provide more than 50% of her support. Either one of them can claim Maya as a dependent for the year if the other person signs an appropriate statement. Huck is not a qualifying person because he does not provide more than 10% of Maya's support. Darby is not a qualifying person because she doesn't meet the relationship test as a qualifying relative.

Personal and Dependency Exemption Phaseouts

TCJA 2017 eliminated the deduction for personal and dependency exemptions, and the phase-out of itemized deductions and personal and dependency exemptions. For tax years 2018 through 2025, therefore, no personal or dependency deductions may be claimed and the phaseout rules do not apply.

Calculation of the Standard Deduction for a Dependent

An individual who can be claimed as a dependent by someone else cannot use the regular basic standard deduction, as discussed above. The basic standard deduction for someone who can be claimed as a dependent by another taxpayer is determined using the following three-step process:

- The minimum basic standard deduction is $1,100 (2021).
- If larger, the basic standard deduction is equal to the earned income (wages, salary, self-employment income, or taxable scholarships or fellowships) of the taxpayer plus $350 (2021); and limited to the normal basic standard deduction for the taxpayer's filing status.
- Any additional standard deductions for age or blindness are added to the basic standard deduction.

Example 3.29

Portia is 17 years old and can be claimed as a dependent by her parents. She earned $500 in wages during 2021. Her basic standard deduction is $1,100. She has no taxable income for 2021 ($500 Gross Income - $1,100 Standard Deduction).

Example 3.30

Rowan is 17 years old and can be claimed as a dependent by his parents.

- He earned $3,000 in wages and $400 in interest income during 2021.
- His basic standard deduction is $3,350 ($3,000 of earned income + $350).
- His taxable income for 2021 is $50.

	2021
Wages	$3,000
Interest Income	$400
Less Personal Exemption (Repealed TCJA)	(0)
Less Standard Deduction	($3,350)
Taxable Income	**$50**

Example 3.31

Khandi is 17 years old and can be claimed as a dependent by her parents.

- She earned $13,000 in wages during 2021.
- Her basic standard deduction for 2021 is $12,550 (the regular basic standard deduction for the single filing status).
- Her taxable income for 2021 is $450.

	2021
Wages	$13,000
Less Personal Exemption (Repealed TCJA)	(0)
Less Standard Deduction	($12,550)
Taxable Income	**$450**

Example 3.32

Naomi is 72 years old, single, and may be claimed as a dependent by her daughter.

- She had $3,000 of interest income during 2021.
- Her basic standard deduction for 2021 is $1,100.
- Her total standard deduction is $2,800 ($1,100 basic standard deduction + $1,700 additional standard deduction for age for 2021).
- Her taxable income is $200 for 2021.

	2021
Interest Income	$3,000
Less Basic Standard Deduction	($1,100)
Less Additional Standard Deduction	($1,700)
Taxable Income	**$200**

Naomi would receive another additional standard deduction if she were blind.

Kiddie Tax

Unearned income of a child under the age of 19, or a child under the age of 24 who is a full time student and qualifies as a dependent by his parents, may be subject to income tax at the highest marginal tax rate of the child's parents. While TCJA 2017 had subjected net unearned income of a child to the trust and estate tax rates, the SECURE Act of 2019 replaced the trust and estate tax rates with the highest marginal tax rate of the child's parent for tax years beginning after December 31, 2019. Taxpayers may also elect to apply the parent's rate to tax years beginning in 2018 and/or 2019.

Key Concepts

1. Explain the purpose of the kiddie tax.
2. Define net unearned income (NUI).
3. Identify the time period for filing a tax return.
4. Identify the taxpayers required to file a tax return.

Unearned income includes interest, dividends, royalties, pension distributions, capital gains distributions, and gains from dealings in property. Unearned Income essentially includes all income that is not generated from work-related activities.

The portion of unearned income taxed at the parents' marginal tax rate is referred to as the **net unearned income (NUI)** of the child. NUI is determined by subtracting the greater of:

- two times the minimum basic standard deduction for a dependent from the child's unearned income; or
- an amount equal to the minimum basic standard deduction for a dependent plus deductible expenses incurred in producing the income from the child's unearned income.

To calculate the amount of income that will be subject to income tax at the child's rate, three steps are required. The first step is to calculate the child's taxable income. When making this calculation, remember the rules for determining the standard deduction of someone who is claimed as a dependent of another. Second, calculate the child's NUI, as described above. Finally, subtract the NUI (which will be taxed at the parent's tax rate) from the child's taxable income to arrive at the amount of income that will be subject to taxation at the child's tax rate.

Example 3.33

Tate is 17 years old, and can be claimed as a dependent by his parents. He earned wages of $4,000 and had interest income of $3,000 during 2021. Tate had no expenses related to producing the income. How much of Tate's income will be subject to tax at his marginal rate, and how much will be subject to tax at the highest marginal tax rate of his parents?

Step 1: Calculate Tate's taxable income. Tate has gross income of $7,000 ($4,000 in wages plus $3,000 in interest income). His standard deduction is the greater of: (1) the minimum basic standard deduction for a dependent of $1,100 (in 2021), or (2) earned income plus $350, limited to the normal standard deduction amount for the year. Since Tate has $4,000 of earned income, his standard deduction will be $4,350. Consequently, his taxable income is $2,650 ($7,000 - $4,350).

	2021
Wages	$4,000
Interest Income	$3,000
Less Personal Exemption	(0)
Less Standard Deduction	($4,350)
Taxable Income	**$2,650**

Step 2: Calculate Tate's net unearned income (NUI). Since Tate does not have deductible investment expenses for the year, his NUI equals his gross unearned income reduced by $2,200 (in 2021), which is two times the minimum basic standard deduction amount. In this example, Tate's NUI is $800 ($3,000 - $2,200). Tate's NUI of $800 is subject to income tax at the highest marginal tax rate of Tate's parents.

Step 3: Calculate the portion of Tate's taxable income that is subject to tax at his marginal tax rate. Since Tate's taxable income is $2,650, and $800 is subject to tax at his parents' tax rates, the difference of $1,850 is subject to tax at Tate's tax rate.

A child's investment income subject to tax at the highest marginal tax rate of the child's parents may be subject to the 3.8 percent surtax on investment income imposed by the Affordable Care Act.

Although the Internal Revenue Code does not refer to it by that name, this tax on NUI is popularly called the **kiddie tax**. The tax was enacted to discourage the shifting of investment income from parents to their minor children (in lower tax brackets) through the gifting of investments to the children.

The first $2,200 for 2021 of the unearned income of a child is not taxed at the highest marginal tax rate of the child's parents. Modest gifting of investment assets to a child can therefore effectively shift a limited amount of income to the child. Some of that income may not be subject to income tax at all and some may be taxed at the lower rates of the child.

Some investment assets do not produce current income. These assets include stocks that do not pay dividends or raw land. These types of deferred income assets could be given to a child and sold after the child reaches the age of 19 (or 24, if a full-time student) to avoid application of the kiddie tax.

Quick Quiz 3.6

1. For the purposes of calculating NUI, unearned income does not include the wages received by the child as a result of his or her own personal efforts.
   a. True
   b. False
2. The kiddie tax only affects children with unearned income greater than $2,200 (2021).
   a. True
   b. False
3. An automatic one-year extension to file a return may be obtained by an individual taxpayer.
   a. True
   b. False

True, True, False.

Filing the Tax Return

If an individual taxpayer is required to file a federal income tax return, the return must normally be submitted and any tax due must be paid by April 15 (within 3½ months after the end of the tax year or, alternatively stated, by the 15th day of the 4th month following the close of the tax year) to avoid any penalties. Taxes can be paid by check, money order, or credit card. A taxpayer who files electronically before the due date of the return is allowed to schedule an automatic withdrawal by the IRS from the taxpayer's checking or savings account at a future date. If the due date of the return falls on a weekend or holiday, the tax return is generally due the following business day. If any tax is due, failing to file on time may result in the imposition of both a failure to file penalty and a failure to pay penalty.

An automatic six-month extension of time to file is normally available to a taxpayer who files a Form 4868 (Application for Automatic Extension of Time to File U.S. Individual Income Tax Return) by the due date of the return. However, an extension of time to file does not grant an extension of time to pay. A taxpayer is expected to estimate the amount of tax due and submit payment with the extension form. A taxpayer who files for an extension without paying the tax due is not normally subject to a failure to file penalty but is subject to a failure to pay penalty until any tax due is paid. Special rules apply to a taxpayer who is out of the country on the due date of the return. Basically, two additional months are allowed to file and pay any taxes due, but interest may be charged on any taxes due from the normal due date of the return until the taxes are paid.

The Internal Revenue Service encourages taxpayers to file tax returns electronically. However, many tax returns are still filed by regular mail. A tax return is considered to be filed in a timely manner if it is postmarked by the due date of the return. The return must be mailed to the Regional Service Center specified in instructions provided by the Internal Revenue Service. Forms, instructions, publications and other information can be obtained from the website of the Internal Revenue Service at www.irs.gov.

All taxpayers required to file a tax return must file Form 1040 or Form 1040-SR (available for taxpayers age 65 or older).

Taxpayers Required to File a Return

The requirement to file is normally based on the gross income of the taxpayer. If the gross income of a taxpayer is equal to or greater than the deductions allowed for personal (not dependency) exemptions, the basic standard deduction, and any additional standard deduction(s) for age (not blindness), then the taxpayer must file a tax return. Self-employed taxpayers must file a return if net self-employment earnings are $400 or greater, even if they would otherwise not be required to file.

Example 3.34

Miguel and Tory are married and normally file a joint return. Miguel is 66 years old and Tory is 64. They must file a return if their gross income is $26,450 or more in 2021.

	2021
Personal exemptions (Repealed TCJA)	$0
Basic standard deduction	$25,100
Miguel's additional standard deduction for his age	$1,350
	$26,450

Example 3.35

Eli is unmarried, age 68, and blind. He must file a return if his adjusted gross income is $14,250 or more for 2021.

	2021
Personal exemption (Repealed TCJA)	$0
Basic standard deduction	$12,550
Eli's additional standard deduction for his age only (note blindness does not count in this calculation)	$1,700
	$14,250

A taxpayer who may be claimed as a dependent of another must follow different rules from those above to determine if a tax return must be filed.

Credit for Taxes Withheld

Although income taxes could (in theory) all be paid at the time the tax return is filed, Congress has decided that federal income taxes should be withheld by an employer from the employee's wages or salary and sent to the government during the year. This not only provides the government with revenues throughout the year, but it also taxes the employee when the employee has the wherewithal (the cash) to pay. This withholding is merely a prepayment of income tax. Therefore, the employee is allowed to subtract any federal income taxes withheld during the year from the tax on taxable income when a tax return is filed. When an amount is subtracted from a tax, it is called a credit or a **tax credit**.

As discussed in Chapter 2, Congress is so intent on receiving tax revenue throughout the year that taxpayers may be subject to an underpayment penalty for not having sufficient federal income tax withheld from their earnings.

FICA

The Federal Insurance Contributions Act (FICA) provides for old-age, survivors, disability, and hospital insurance. This coverage is financed by Social Security and Medicare taxes. Employers are required to withhold Social Security and Medicare tax from an employee's wages with the employer paying a matching amount of tax. The Social Security tax has a wage base limit of $142,800 for 2021. The Medicare tax is not subject to a wage base limit.

Employers who are required to withhold income tax and FICA tax must file a federal return each quarter on Form 941 (see **Exhibit 3.16**). This form must be filed by the last day of the month that follows the end of the previous quarter. Small employers who meet specified requirements may only have to file Form 944 on an annual basis.

Additional Medicare Taxes

Since 2013, high income taxpayers are required to pay a higher Medicare tax. A high income taxpayer includes married individuals (filing jointly) with modified adjusted gross income of more than $250,000, married individuals (filing separately) with modified adjusted gross income of more than $125,000, and all other individuals with modified adjusted gross income of more than $200,000. Modified adjusted gross income, for purposes of classifying individuals as "high income" when imposing the additional Medicare tax, includes adjusted gross income plus excluded foreign source income. The Medicare surtax that applies is an additional 0.9 percent (for a total of 2.35 percent on earned income over the threshold) beginning in 2013.

Self-employed individuals must pay the additional 0.9 percent surtax on the employee portion of the Medicare tax as well, raising the Medicare tax rate for the self-employed to a total of 3.8 percent (up from 2.9 percent rate that was applied through the end of 2012) on income over the threshold. The Medicare surtax will not apply to the employer portion of Medicare for individuals who are not self-employed. The total Medicare tax for self-employed individuals beginning in 2013, therefore, is 3.8 percent on income over the threshold amounts.

Traditionally, the payroll tax only applied to earned income, hence the term "payroll tax." In addition, an investment surtax under the Affordable Care Act may also be applied. The 2010 legislation also imposed an investment surtax of 3.8 percent on investment income beginning in 2013 for high income taxpayers (as defined above). Since the definition of high income taxpayer is not adjusted for inflation, as incomes rise from year to year, more and more taxpayers will be subject to the investment surtax. Furthermore, the government has imposed a significant marriage penalty by failing to double the single "high income" threshold for married taxpayers. Two single individuals, living together, could generate income of $200,000 each (for a total of $400,000) and not be subject to the investment surtax, but if they get married, the investment surtax will apply. The investment surtax is not limited to individuals, as the 2010 legislation imposed the surtax on trusts and estates as well.

For Trusts and estates, the investment surtax applies to the lesser of:

1. the undistributed net investment income of the trust, or
2. net investment income in excess of AGI for which the trust would pay the highest marginal tax rate.

When a person is classified as a "high income" taxpayer, the investment surtax applies to the lesser of:

1. the taxpayer's net investment income, or
2. the amount of modified adjusted gross income over the threshold amount.

Investment income includes dividends, interest, capital gains, rents, royalties, passive activity income, income from a trade or business of trading in financial instruments or commodities, and taxable distributions from annuity contracts.

Some types of investment income are not subject to the surtax, including:

1. distributions from qualified retirement plans;
2. distributions from traditional and Roth IRAs;
3. capital gains from the sale of a principal residence; and
4. business income from an entity (S corporation or partnership) that the taxpayer manages (materially participates in).

FUTA

The Federal Unemployment Tax Act (FUTA) exists in concert with state unemployment systems to pay unemployment compensation to employees who have become unemployed. This tax is paid by the employer only and is taxed at a rate of 6.0 percent (2021) on the first $7,000 that an employer pays in each employee's wages (note: the state wage base may be different). FUTA tax is reported annually on federal Form 940 (See **Exhibit 3.17**). A credit is allowed for unemployment taxes paid to states.

Self-Employment Tax

A self-employed individual pays income tax, as well as self-employment FICA taxes (also called SECA (Self-Employment Contributions Act) taxes) of 15.3 percent (12.4% for Social Security and 2.9% for Medicare) in 2021 on earnings up to the wage base ($142,800 for 2021) and 2.9 percent beyond the wage base for Medicare. However, the self-employed worker is not required to pay FUTA tax on himself. In addition, a self-employed person can take a FICA deduction for adjusted gross income on his own tax return in the amount of one-half of his total FICA taxes paid.

Example 3.36

Laverne is self-employed and has one employee, Lenny. Laverne personally earned $180,000 of self-employment income and paid Lenny $28,000 in salary. The FICA tax and FUTA tax calculations are below:

Laverne's FICA Calculation	
	2021
Net self-employment income	$180,000
Reduction of 7.65% self-employment tax	92.35%
Net earnings subject to FICA tax	**$166,230**
Social Security wage base	$142,800
Self-employment Social Security & Medicare (combined) rate	15.30%
	$21,848.40
Excess earnings over wage base	$23,430
x Medicare rate	2.90%
	$679.47
Total Social Security & Medicare tax for Laverne	**$22,527.87**

An alternative method of calculating the self-employment tax is to calculate separately the Social Security and Medicare portions of the tax. The Social Security portion of the tax is 12.4% (6.2% for the employee portion of the tax plus 6.2% for the employer portion of the tax) of the taxpayer's net self-employment income subject to FICA taxes up to the Social Security wage base. The Medicare portion of the tax is 2.9% (1.45% for the employee portion of the tax plus 1.45% for the employer portion of the tax) on all of the taxpayer's net self-employment income subject to FICA taxes. Note that the total amount of self-employment tax for Laverne is the same if either approach to calculating self-employment tax is used.

Laverne's FICA Calculation (Alternative Approach)	
	2021
Net self-employment income	$180,000
Reduction of 7.65% self-employment tax	92.35%
Net earnings subject to FICA tax	**$166,230**
Social Security wage base	$142,800
OASDI tax rate	12.40%
OASDI tax	**$17,707.20**
Earnings subject to Medicare	$166,230.00
x Medicare rate	2.90%
Medicare tax	**$4,820.67**
OASDI tax	**$17,707.20**
Medicare tax	**$4,820.67**
Total Social Security tax for Laverne	**$22,527.87**

Lenny's FICA Calculation	
	2021
Salary	$28,000
FICA rate (7.65% employer and 7.65% employee)	15.30%
Total FICA tax for Lenny	**$4,284**

Lenny's FUTA Calculation	
Wages subject to FUTA	$7,000
FUTA rate	6.0%
Total FUTA* tax for Lenny	**$420**

**$7,000 is the limit on FUTA. No FUTA on self-employed.*

For more information on payroll and withholding taxes, see Circular E (Publication 15), Employer's Tax Guide, published by the Internal Revenue Service.

BASIC TAX PLANNING PRINCIPLES

A tax professional must have a basic understanding of both income tax rules and the related tax planning strategies that can be beneficial to clients. In doing so, it is important to remember that legal tax avoidance is perfectly acceptable and often desired, but tax evasion is illegal and must be completely avoided.

Income tax planning is emphasized throughout this book. The following tax planning principles provide the foundation for many tax planning strategies:

1. Receive income in a tax-exempt (excludable) form.
   Examples: Income from a Roth IRA, gain on the sale of a personal residence, tax-exempt interest, or employer-provided fringe benefits.

2. Shift income to a related taxpayer with a lower marginal tax rate (tax bracket).
   Example: Gift assets to a family member so that future income generated by the assets can be taxed at the lower tax rates, but beware of the kiddie tax rules.

3. Generate income that is taxed at favorable capital gains rates.
   Example: Sell investment assets held for more than one year or buy investments that pay qualified dividends.

4. Defer income taxes until later.
   Example: Invest in a Traditional IRA or participate in an employer-sponsored retirement plan.

5. Use tax credits to reduce tax liability.
   Example: Qualify for education tax credits or energy tax credits.

Exhibit 3.16 | Form 941

Form **941 for 2020: Employer's QUARTERLY Federal Tax Return** 950120
(Rev. July 2020) Department of the Treasury — Internal Revenue Service OMB No. 1545-0029

Employer identification number (EIN) [ ][ ] – [ ][ ][ ][ ][ ][ ][ ]

Name *(not your trade name)*

Trade name *(if any)*

Address
Number Street Suite or room number
City State ZIP code
Foreign country name Foreign province/county Foreign postal code

Report for this Quarter of 2020
(Check one.)
- ☐ **1:** January, February, March
- ☐ **2:** April, May, June
- ☐ **3:** July, August, September
- ☐ **4:** October, November, December

Go to *www.irs.gov/Form941* for instructions and the latest information.

Read the separate instructions before you complete Form 941. Type or print within the boxes.

Part 1: Answer these questions for this quarter.

1	**Number of employees who received wages, tips, or other compensation for the pay period including:** ***Sept. 12*** **(Quarter 3) or** ***Dec. 12*** **(Quarter 4)**	1	
2	**Wages, tips, and other compensation**	2	.
3	**Federal income tax withheld from wages, tips, and other compensation**	3	.
4	**If no wages, tips, and other compensation are subject to social security or Medicare tax**	☐	**Check and go to line 6.**

		Column 1		Column 2
5a	**Taxable social security wages**	.	× 0.124 =	.
5a	**(i) Qualified sick leave wages**	.	× 0.062 =	.
5a	**(ii) Qualified family leave wages**	.	× 0.062 =	.
5b	**Taxable social security tips**	.	× 0.124 =	.
5c	**Taxable Medicare wages & tips**	.	× 0.029 =	.
5d	**Taxable wages & tips subject to Additional Medicare Tax withholding**	.	× 0.009 =	.

5e	**Total social security and Medicare taxes.** Add Column 2 from lines 5a, 5a(i), 5a(ii), 5b, 5c, and 5d	5e	.
5f	**Section 3121(q) Notice and Demand—Tax due on unreported tips** (see instructions)	5f	.
6	**Total taxes before adjustments.** Add lines 3, 5e, and 5f	6	.
7	**Current quarter's adjustment for fractions of cents**	7	.
8	**Current quarter's adjustment for sick pay**	8	.
9	**Current quarter's adjustments for tips and group-term life insurance**	9	.
10	**Total taxes after adjustments.** Combine lines 6 through 9	10	.
11a	**Qualified small business payroll tax credit for increasing research activities.** Attach Form 8974	11a	.
11b	**Nonrefundable portion of credit for qualified sick and family leave wages from Worksheet 1**	11b	.
11c	**Nonrefundable portion of employee retention credit from Worksheet 1**	11c	.

▶ **You MUST complete all three pages of Form 941 and SIGN it.** Next ▶

For Privacy Act and Paperwork Reduction Act Notice, see the back of the Payment Voucher. Cat. No. 17001Z Form **941** (Rev. 7-2020)

Exhibit 3.17 | Form 940

Form **940 for 2020: Employer's Annual Federal Unemployment (FUTA) Tax Return** 850113
Department of the Treasury — Internal Revenue Service OMB No. 1545-0028

Employer identification number (EIN) ☐☐ – ☐☐☐☐☐☐☐

Name *(not your trade name)* ____

Trade name *(if any)* ____

Address ____
Number Street Suite or room number

____ ____ ____
City State ZIP code

____ ____ ____
Foreign country name Foreign province/county Foreign postal code

Type of Return
(Check all that apply.)

☐ **a.** Amended

☐ **b.** Successor employer

☐ **c.** No payments to employees in 2020

☐ **d.** Final: Business closed or stopped paying wages

Go to *www.irs.gov/Form940* for instructions and the latest information.

Read the separate instructions before you complete this form. Please type or print within the boxes.

Part 1: Tell us about your return. If any line does NOT apply, leave it blank. See instructions before completing Part 1.

1a **If you had to pay state unemployment tax in one state only, enter the state abbreviation** . **1a** ☐☐

1b **If you had to pay state unemployment tax in more than one state, you are a multi-state employer** . . . . **1b** ☐ Check here. Complete Schedule A (Form 940).

2 **If you paid wages in a state that is subject to CREDIT REDUCTION** . . . . **2** ☐ Check here. Complete Schedule A (Form 940).

Part 2: Determine your FUTA tax before adjustments. If any line does NOT apply, leave it blank.

3 **Total payments to all employees** . . . . **3** ____ .

4 **Payments exempt from FUTA tax** . . . . **4** ____ .

Check all that apply: **4a** ☐ Fringe benefits **4c** ☐ Retirement/Pension **4e** ☐ Other
4b ☐ Group-term life insurance **4d** ☐ Dependent care

5 **Total of payments made to each employee in excess of $7,000** . . . . **5** ____ .

6 **Subtotal** (line 4 + line 5 = line 6) . . . . **6** ____ .

7 **Total taxable FUTA wages** (line 3 – line 6 = line 7). See instructions . . . . **7** ____ .

8 **FUTA tax before adjustments** (line 7 x 0.006 = line 8) . . . . **8** ____ .

Part 3: Determine your adjustments. If any line does NOT apply, leave it blank.

9 **If ALL of the taxable FUTA wages you paid were excluded from state unemployment tax, multiply line 7 by 0.054** (line 7 × 0.054 = line 9). Go to line 12 . . . . **9** ____ .

10 **If SOME of the taxable FUTA wages you paid were excluded from state unemployment tax, OR you paid ANY state unemployment tax late** (after the due date for filing Form 940), complete the worksheet in the instructions. Enter the amount from line 7 of the worksheet . . **10** ____ .

11 **If credit reduction applies,** enter the total from Schedule A (Form 940) . . . . **11** ____ .

Part 4: Determine your FUTA tax and balance due or overpayment. If any line does NOT apply, leave it blank.

12 **Total FUTA tax after adjustments** (lines 8 + 9 + 10 + 11 = line 12) . . . . **12** ____ .

13 **FUTA tax deposited for the year, including any overpayment applied from a prior year** . **13** ____ .

14 **Balance due.** If line 12 is more than line 13, enter the excess on line 14.
- If line 14 is more than $500, you must deposit your tax.
- If line 14 is $500 or less, you may pay with this return. See instructions . . . . **14** ____ .

15 **Overpayment.** If line 13 is more than line 12, enter the excess on line 15 and check a box below **15** ____ .

► You **MUST** complete both pages of this form and **SIGN** it. Check one: ☐ Apply to next return. ☐ Send a refund.

Next ►

For Privacy Act and Paperwork Reduction Act Notice, see the back of the Payment Voucher. Cat. No. 11234O Form **940** (2020)

KEY TERMS

Above-the-Line Deductions - Deductions for adjusted gross income, also known as adjustments to income.

Accrual Method - An accounting method under which income is reported when it is earned rather than when it is received in cash, and expenses are reported when they are incurred rather than when they are paid.

Adjusted Gross Income - Gross income less above-the-line deductions.

Below-the-Line Deductions - Deductions from adjusted gross income. Also known as itemized deductions. Personal and dependency exemption amounts are also deducted below-the-line. However, they have been suspended by the TCJA 2017 until 2026. In addition, the new 20% deduction for flow-through entities introduced in the TCJA 2017 is also a deduction that is below-the-line but is taken regardless of whether the taxpayer itemizes deductions.

Cash Receipts and Disbursements Method - An accounting method under which income items are reported for the tax year in which they are received in cash and expenses are deducted in the year in which they are paid with cash.

Deductions - Items that are subtracted from gross income, either below- or above- the-line, in order to arrive at taxable income.

Dependency Exemption - A deduction from adjusted gross income allowed for each person who is a qualifying child or relative of the taxpayer for tax years before 2018 and after 2025. While the dependency exemption cannot be used in calculating taxable income for tax years 2018-2025, it is still used when determining dependency status to qualify for Head of Household filing status.

Doctrine of Constructive Receipt - A cash method taxpayer must report income when it is credited to the taxpayer's account or when it is made available without restriction.

Estimated Tax Payments - Quarterly payments that are paid to the IRS and may be claimed as a credit against tax.

Exclusions - Income items that are specifically exempted from income tax.

Gross Income - All income from whatever source derived unless it is specifically excluded by some provision of the Internal Revenue Code.

Head of Household Filing Status - A filing status that provides a basic standard deduction and tax bracket sizes that are less favorable to the taxpayer than those for the surviving spouse status, but more favorable than those for the single filing status.

Hybrid Method - An accounting method, other than the accrual or cash receipts and disbursements methods, that is permitted by the IRC and regulations as long as it is deemed to clearly reflect income.

Income - Broadly defined as the total amount of money, property, services, or other accretion to wealth received, but it does not include borrowed money or a return of invested dollars.

Kiddie Tax - A tax on the net unearned income of a child at the parent's highest marginal income tax rate.

Married Filing Jointly Filing Status - A filing status that allows married couples to combine their gross incomes and deductions.

Married Filing Separately Filing Status - A filing status used when married couples do not choose to file a joint return.

Net Unearned Income (NUI) - The amount of unearned income of a child that is subject to tax at the parent's marginal tax rate. NUI is equal to the unearned income of the child, less $1,100 (the basic standard deduction of a dependent) and the greater of $1,100 or the amount of the deductions allowed in producing the unearned income (2021 threshold).

Original Issue Discount (OID) Bond - A bond that is issued for a price that is less than its face amount or principal amount on which interest is usually paid only at maturity.

Personal Exemption - A deduction from adjusted gross income for the taxpayer and the taxpayers spouse for tax years before 2018 and after 2025. During the 2018-2025 period, however, the amount of the personal exemption may be relevant in determining whether a taxpayer qualifies for Head of Household filing status.

Phantom Income - Income imputed to taxpayers without a corresponding receipt of cash.

Qualifying Child - A person who meets the relationship test, abode test, age test, support test, joint return test, and citizenship test, and may be claimed as a dependent of the taxpayer.

Qualifying Relative - A person who meets the relationship test, gross income test, support test, joint return test, and citizenship test; is not a qualifying child of any other taxpayer; and may be claimed as a dependent by the taxpayer.

Single Filing Status - A filing status used by an unmarried taxpayer who does not qualify as a surviving spouse or head of household.

Standard Deduction - A standard amount that is specified by Congress and includes inflation adjustments. Taxpayers may deduct the greater of the standard deduction or allowable itemized deductions.

Surviving Spouse Filing Status - A filing status for a surviving spouse with a qualifying child that affords the same basic standard deduction and tax rates as the married filing jointly status.

Tax Credit - An amount that reduces the calculated tax liability of the taxpayer.

Tax Year - Normally a period of 12 months.

Taxable Income - Determined by subtracting allowable deductions from gross income.

Zero Coupon Bond - A bond that is sold at a deep discount, pays no coupons (or periodic interest payments), and matures at its face value.

DISCUSSION QUESTIONS

SOLUTIONS to the discussion questions can be found exclusively within the chapter. Once you have completed an initial reading of the chapter, go back and highlight the answers to these questions.

1. How is income defined?
2. What are exclusions and where do they come from?
3. Define gross income.
4. List some examples of items that would be included in gross income.
5. What are the two types of deductions?
6. What is adjusted gross income and what is its significance?
7. How much can an individual deduct from his AGI?
8. Under what circumstances may a taxpayer be entitled to an additional standard deduction?
9. Under what circumstances will a taxpayer be required to itemize deductions?
10. What types of accounting periods are available to taxpayers?
11. What is the cash receipts and disbursements method of accounting?
12. What is the accrual method of accounting?
13. What is the all events test?
14. What are the different filing statuses available to taxpayers?
15. How is marital status determined for the purpose of selecting a filing status?
16. When is a married taxpayer allowed to file using the head of household filing status?
17. What are the requirements to file as a surviving spouse?
18. For whom is a dependency exemption allowed?
19. What tests must a qualifying child meet?
20. What tests must a qualifying relative meet?
21. How is the standard deduction calculated for someone who can be claimed as a dependent by another taxpayer?
22. What is the kiddie tax?
23. Who must file a tax return?

MULTIPLE CHOICE PROBLEMS

A sample of multiple choice problems is provided below. Additional multiple choice problems are available at money-education.com by accessing the Student Practice Portal.

1. Franklin, a consultant, uses the cash method of accounting for his business. Franklin recently provided consulting services to his best customer, Aretha. When should Franklin recognize income from this service?
    a. When Aretha writes a check, made out to Franklin.
    b. When Franklin deposits Aretha's check.
    c. When Aretha gives the check to Franklin.
    d. When Aretha receives an invoice from Franklin for the service.

2. Which of the following is not an available filing status?
    a. Qualified dependent child.
    b. Married filing jointly.
    c. Head of household.
    d. Surviving spouse.

3. Tina (age 70) and Ike (age 74) are married to each other and file a joint return in 2022 for tax year 2021. Tina is blind. Ike and Tina do not have any dependents. What is their standard deduction for 2021?
    a. $25,100.
    b. $26,450.
    c. $27,800.
    d. $29,150.

4. Luther has been working part-time through college and earned $20,000 last year with a total federal income tax liability of $1,200. This year he will earn $100,000 with an expected income tax liability of $15,000. What is the lowest amount of tax withholding Luther should have to meet the safe harbor rules?
    a. $1,200.
    b. $12,000.
    c. $13,500.
    d. $15,000.

5. Diana is 16 years old. She earned $3,000 during 2021 working at an ice cream store. She earned $4,000 in interest income this year. Diana is claimed as a qualifying dependent by her parents. How much of Diana's income will be taxed at her parents highest marginal tax rate?
   a. $1,100.
   b. $1,800.
   c. $2,900.
   d. $4,000.

Additional multiple choice problems are available at *money-education.com* by accessing the Student Practice Portal. Access requires registration of the title using the unique code at the front of the book.

QUICK QUIZ EXPLANATIONS

Quick Quiz 3.1

1. False. Income, broadly defined, means the total amount received, but it does not include borrowed money or a return of invested dollars.
2. True.

Quick Quiz 3.2

1. False. A nonresident alien is not allowed to use a standard deduction and must itemize his deductions.
2. False. Prior to 2018, personal and dependency exemption amounts were allowed as deductions from adjusted gross income, not for adjusted gross income, but have been repealed by TCJA 2017 for years after 2017.
3. False. Credits reduce the amount of tax that the taxpayer owes.
4. True.

Quick Quiz 3.3

1. False. Although most individual taxpayers report their income and expenses on a calendar year basis, individuals are permitted to choose another tax year under certain circumstances.
2. True.

Quick Quiz 3.4

1. False. The determination of whether a taxpayer is married is normally made as of the close (the last day) of the tax year. However, if a taxpayer's spouse dies during the year, the marital status of the taxpayer is determined on the date of the spouse's death.
2. True.

Quick Quiz 3.5

1. False. Multiple requirements must be met in order to claim a dependency exemption for someone living in the taxpayer's house (dependency exemption repealed TCJA 2017).
2. True.
3. True.

Quick Quiz 3.6

1. True.
2. True.
3. False. An automatic six-month extension of time to file is normally available to a taxpayer who files a Form 4868 (Application for Automatic Extension of Time to File U.S. Individual Income Tax Return) by the due date of the return.

4 GROSS INCOME FROM PERSONAL AND INVESTMENT ACTIVITIES

LEARNING OBJECTIVES

1. Identify permissible accounting methods.
2. Describe when gains on the sale of property are subject to tax.*
3. Explain the taxation of barter transactions.*
4. Identify the three primary sources of taxable income.*
5. Describe the effect of community property laws on the taxation of income.
6. Identify the types of relief available for spouses under Section 66 of the IRC.
7. Identify the various types of investment income.*
8. Describe the taxation of the various types of investment income.*
9. Describe the taxation of annuity payments.*
10. Identify the types of investment income that are excluded from gross income.*
11. Calculate income inclusions resulting from OID (original issue discount) bonds.*
12. Describe the income tax issues associated with a gift of debt securities.*
13. Describe the tax treatment of distributions from mutual funds.*
14. Describe the tax treatment of dividend distributions.*
15. Describe how dividends from corporations are different from dividends declared on a life insurance policy.*
16. Calculate the taxable portion of annuity payments.*
17. Describe the tax treatment of payments and distributions from life insurance and endowment contracts.*
18. Describe the taxation of distributions from pass-through entities.*
19. Describe the taxation of distributions from trusts and estates.*
20. Calculate the equivalent taxable rate for a municipal bond.*
21. List the requirements that must be met for a tax-free distribution from a Roth IRA.*
22. Calculate the taxable portion of Roth IRA distributions for a given taxpayer.*
23. Calculate the amount of savings bond interest that can be excluded from income when part or all of the proceeds from the bond are used to pay qualified education expenses.*
24. Identify the limits imposed on funding 529 plans.*
25. Describe the use of, and funding limitations for Coverdell Education Savings Accounts.*
26. Identify the types of income from personal activities that are included in gross income.*
27. Describe the imputed interest rules for below market loans.*
28. Explain how the imputed interest rules can be used, with particular emphasis on the exceptions to these rules.*
29. Identify personal activity income that is excluded from gross income.*
30. Describe the taxation of prizes and awards received by a taxpayer.*
31. List the requirements for a payment to be considered alimony.*
32. Describe the purpose of the alimony recapture rules, and calculate the amount of alimony recapture given an alimony payment stream for a given taxpayer.*

**Ties to CFP Certification Learning Objectives*

LEARNING OBJECTIVES

33. Describe the tax benefit rule.*
34. Describe the income taxation of gifts and inheritances.*
35. Identify circumstances where scholarship awards must be included in income.*
36. Describe the tax treatment of compensation received for injuries and sickness.*

**Ties to CFP Certification Learning Objectives*

INTRODUCTION

Now that some of the general rules of income taxation and the tax formula have been covered in the text, a review of the specific planning issues that impact the calculation of an individual's tax liability is required. This chapter covers three areas:

1. Determination of when income is taxed
2. Income and exclusions from investment activities
3. Income and exclusions from personal activities

The question of when income is taxed begins with a review of the tax year and the accounting rules covered in Chapter 3. Next, the concepts of realization and recognition of income are covered, followed by an overview of the types of gross income and exclusions, as well as potential sources of income.

Finally, income and exclusions from investment related activities are covered, followed by income and exclusions associated with personal activities. Income and exclusion items associated with employment will be the subject of Chapter 5.

Gross income is defined in the Internal Revenue Code as all income from whatever source derived unless it is specifically excluded by some provision of the Internal Revenue Code.[1] In other words, all income is subject to income tax unless Congress states that it is not. Further, the federal income tax is a global income tax since it is imposed on income earned anywhere unless Congress states otherwise.

Although income is not specifically defined in the Internal Revenue Code, a reading of the IRC and related court decisions makes it clear that income as broadly defined includes the value of benefits received in the form of cash, property, services or any other form. Not all cash inflows are considered income, however. Courts have held that borrowed money and the return of invested dollars to the taxpayer are not forms of income. Borrowed money is not income because it must be repaid, and as such, does not increase the taxpayer's wealth (although the use to which those funds is put may create income and therefore income tax). The return of invested dollars (cost or tax basis) is simply the return to the taxpayer of dollars that have already been subject to income taxation, and the U.S. income tax system only subjects income to tax once during the taxpayer's life.

1. IRC §61.

SUBJECTING GROSS INCOME TO TAXATION

Tax Year and Accounting Method

Gross income must be reported according to the tax year and the tax accounting method of the taxpayer. Most individual taxpayers use the calendar year as their tax year and the **cash receipts and disbursements method** (the cash method) as their accounting method. Basically, gross income of a cash method taxpayer is reported in the tax year in which cash is received or a benefit is conferred in the form of a cash equivalent. Cash includes currency, coin, or a check. Cash equivalents include non-cash property, services, other benefits, electronic credits (such as Bitcoin), or even the value of a promissory note. However, in some circumstances a cash method taxpayer may have to report income when it is constructively, as opposed to actually, received.

> ### *Key Concepts*
>
> 1. Identify the permissible accounting methods.
> 2. Describe when gains are normally taxed.
> 3. Explain the taxation of barter transactions.

While some taxpayers are allowed to use a fiscal, rather than a calendar tax year, it is rare for individuals to do so. Individual taxpayers can use a fiscal year only if they keep a detailed set of accounting books and records. Since most individual taxpayers do not do this, they defer to a calendar year tax period.

A taxpayer may choose to use one of several methods of accounting for reporting gross income and deductions. As discussed in Chapter 3, permissible methods include the cash receipts and disbursements method, the accrual method, or a hybrid method. Under the cash receipts and disbursements method (the cash method), gross income is normally reported as indicated above. Businesses with average gross receipts for the prior three years in excess of $26 million (2021) are not eligible to use the cash method of accounting.[2] Under the **accrual method**, gross income is normally reported when earned rather than when received. An acceptable hybrid method is simply a method other than the cash method or the accrual method unless the IRS decides that it does not "clearly reflect income." For example, under a hybrid method, a taxpayer might report the sale of goods using the accrual method and other types of income using the cash method. Under certain circumstances, the accrual method is required. For example, if inventories are an income-producing factor for a business activity, the accrual method must be used to account for inventory items unless the taxpayer is a qualifying small business taxpayer with average annual gross receipts of $26 million or less for the three prior tax years.[3]

Gains Normally Taxed When Realized

Gains from property transactions are normally taxed when they can be objectively determined through a sale or exchange. A gain that is objectively determined is said to be realized. Unrealized gains are those that cannot yet be objectively determined and therefore, are not subject to tax until they are objectively determined.

2. IRC §448(b)(3). TCJA 2017 expanded the gross receipts limit to determine which taxpayers can use the cash method of accounting from $5 million to $25 million, to be indexed for inflation in subsequent years.
3. Increased from $1 million by TCJA; Rev. Proc. 2018-40.

Example 4.1

Jovi bought stock at the beginning of the current year for $1,000 (which represents his cost basis). At the end of the year, the stock had a value of $1,300. Jovi is not required to report the $300 unrealized gain on his tax return for the current year. However, if he sells the stock next year for $1,450, he will report the $450 realized gain on his tax return for next year.

Barter Transactions

Bartering is an exchange of property and/or services for other property and/or services as opposed to an exchange for cash. The value of goods or services received in a barter transaction must be included in gross income. The value received can be offset by the cost or other tax basis of goods given up in the transaction. When goods or services are received by a taxpayer in exchange for services, the services provided by the taxpayer normally have a tax basis of zero. When barter transactions are made through a barter club or exchange (an organization established to facilitate the trading of goods and services), the transaction must be reported to the taxpayer and the Internal Revenue Service by the barter club or exchange on Form 1099-B (Proceeds from Broker and Barter Exchange Transactions). If a business makes payments of bartered services to another business (except a corporation) of $600 or more in the course of the year, these payments must be reported on Form 1099-MISC.

Exhibit 4.1 | Form 1099-B

7979 ☐ VOID ☐ CORRECTED

PAYER'S name, street address, city or town, state or province, country, ZIP or foreign postal code, and telephone no.

Applicable checkbox on Form 8949

OMB No. 1545-0715

2020

Form 1099-B

Proceeds From Broker and Barter Exchange Transactions

1a Description of property (Example: 100 sh. XYZ Co.)

1b Date acquired | 1c Date sold or disposed

PAYER'S TIN | RECIPIENT'S TIN

1d Proceeds $ | 1e Cost or other basis $

Copy A

1f Accrued market discount $ | 1g Wash sale loss disallowed $

For Internal Revenue Service Center

File with Form 1096.

RECIPIENT'S name

2 Short-term gain or loss ☐ Long-term gain or loss ☐ Ordinary ☐

3 Check if proceeds from: Collectibles ☐ QOF ☐

Street address (including apt. no.)

4 Federal income tax withheld $

5 Check if noncovered security ☐

6 Reported to IRS: Gross proceeds ☐ Net proceeds ☐

7 Check if loss is not allowed based on amount in 1d ☐

City or town, state or province, country, and ZIP or foreign postal code

8 Profit or (loss) realized in 2020 on closed contracts $

9 Unrealized profit or (loss) on open contracts—12/31/2019 $

For Privacy Act and Paperwork Reduction Act Notice, see the **2020 General Instructions for Certain Information Returns.**

Account number (see instructions) | 2nd TIN not. ☐

CUSIP number | FATCA filing requirement ☐

10 Unrealized profit or (loss) on open contracts—12/31/2020 $

11 Aggregate profit or (loss) on contracts $

14 State name | 15 State identification no. | 16 State tax withheld $ $

12 Check if basis reported to IRS ☐

13 Bartering $

Form 1099-B Cat. No. 14411V www.irs.gov/Form1099B Department of the Treasury - Internal Revenue Service

Do Not Cut or Separate Forms on This Page — Do Not Cut or Separate Forms on This Page

Example 4.2

Tommy is a plumber and Gina is a dentist. Tommy has agreed to repair Gina's kitchen plumbing problems in exchange for a crown that Tommy desperately needs. Both Tommy and Gina must include in gross income in the year of receipt the fair market value of goods and services received in exchange for goods or services they provided under the bartering arrangement. In this example, the barter arrangement is informal and not through a barter exchange and, therefore, does not trigger the 1099-B reporting requirement, but there should be reciprocal Form 1099-MISC filed.

TYPES OF GROSS INCOME AND EXCLUSIONS

Types of gross income that are specifically identified in the Internal Revenue Code are presented in **Exhibit 4.2**. The exhibit also lists the various inclusion items, as well as the form upon which each item of income should be reported and the IRS publication in which the item of income is discussed. Some specific exclusions from gross income are presented in **Exhibit 4.3**. This list, however, is not all-inclusive, since Congress taxes income from whatever source derived unless that income is excluded from tax in the Internal Revenue Code.

Exhibit 4.2 | Gross Income - Inclusions

Item	*IRC Section*	*Reported On*	*IRS Publication*
Capital Gains	61(a)(3) & 1001	Schedule D, Form 4797 Form 8949	550/544
Interest Income	61(a)(4)	Schedule B	550
Interest from Original Issue Discount Obligations	1271-1275	Schedule B	550
Dividend Income	61(a)(7)	Schedule B	550
Mutual Fund Distributions	61	Schedules B & D	564
Rental Income	61(a)(5)	Schedule E (pg. 1)	527
Royalty Income	61(a)(6)	Schedule E (pg. 1)	17
Income from Annuities	72	Form 1040	939
Income from Life Insurance & Endowment Contracts	72	Form 1040	525
IRAs (Traditional IRAs)	408(d)	Form 1040	590
Income from Partnerships	61(a)(13)	Schedule E (pg. 2)	525
Income from S Corporations	1366(a)	Schedule E (pg. 2)	525
Income from Trusts and Estates	61(a)(15)	Schedule E (pg. 2)	559
Prizes and Awards	74	Form 1040	17
Alimony and Separate Maintenance Payments[1]	71	Form 1040	504
Imputed Interest on Below-Market Loans	7872	Schedule B	550
Income from Discharge of Indebtedness	61(a)(12)	Form 1040	17
Other Income	61	Form 1040	17

1. For divorce decrees entered on or before December 31, 2018.

Exhibit 4.3 | Gross Income - Exclusions

Item	IRC Section	IRS Publication
Interest Income from Certain State and Local Government Obligations	103	550
Life Insurance Proceeds	101	525
Accelerated Death Benefits	101(g)	525
Income from Roth IRAs (Qualified Distributions)	408A	590
Educational Savings Bonds	135	550
Qualified Tuition Program/Educational Savings Plan	529	970
Coverdell Savings Account	530	970
Improvements by Tenant to Landlord's Property	109	--
Exclusion (50%) of Gain from Sale of Certain Small Business Stock	1202	550
Gifts	102	559
Inheritances	102	559
Scholarships (Tuition and Fees)	117	970
Compensation for Injuries and Sickness	104	17
Alimony and Separate Maintenance Payments[1]	71	504
Child Support	71(c)	504
Property Settlements from Divorce	1041	504
Income from Discharge of Indebtedness (Under Bankruptcy)[2]	108	908/17
Gain on the Sale of Residence (Up to $250,000 or $500,000)	121	523
Amounts Received Under Insurance Contracts for Certain Living Expenses	123	547
Qualified Foster Care Payments	131	17
Disaster Relief Payments	139	547
Tax Benefit Rule	111	17

1. TCJA 2017 repealed the inclusion in income by the payee for alimony decrees entered after December 31, 2018.
2. The American Rescue Plan Act (ARPA) of 2021 added an exclusion for certain federal, state, and private student loans discharged after December 31, 2020 and before January 1, 2026 (IRC Section 108(f)).

Since this chapter focuses on gross income and exclusions related to investments and personal activities, only those items are listed in **Exhibit 4.2** and **Exhibit 4.3**. Chapter 5 focuses on gross income and exclusions related to employment and self-employment. Exclusions from income tend to center around gifts (inheritances, proceeds of life insurance), making one whole (compensatory bodily damage), property transactions where basis is transferred (property transferred in divorce), and statutory exclusions established for public policy reasons (tax free interest income from municipal bonds).

Quick Quiz 4.1

1. Gains on property are normally taxed upon sale or exchange.
   a. True
   b. False

2. Barter transactions are not reportable for income tax purposes.
   a. True
   b. False

True, False.

SOURCES OF INCOME

Individual taxpayers receive income from:

1. investments
2. personal activities
3. employment and self-employment

Key Concepts

1. Identify the various sources of income.
2. Describe the effect of community property laws on the taxation of income.
3. Identify the types of relief available under Section 66.

Investments typically generate dividend income, interest income, and gains from the sale of the investment. The taxation of investment income generally follows the Doctrine of the Fruit and the Tree (introduced in Chapter 1).

Income from personal activities might include items such as the receipt of alimony from a former spouse or receipt of prizes and awards. While the inclusion of alimony in income is repealed under TCJA 2017, it is only applicable to divorce decrees entered into after December 31, 2018 or divorce decrees entered into before that date which were modified and expressly stated that the rules set forth in TCJA 2017 will apply.

Wages, salaries, commissions, fringe benefits, and other types of income can be earned by providing services to an employer. Engaging in the conduct of a trade or business generates self-employment income. These items of earned income will be covered in detail in Chapter 5.

Investment Income

Income from investments is normally taxable to the owner of the investment. A taxpayer cannot attribute investment income to another person who does not own the investment simply by having the income paid to that other person. This is a practical application of one of the three basic principles of Income Taxation: the Doctrine of the Fruit and the Tree. Stated differently, the owner of the tree gets taxed on the fruit that the tree produces.

Income from Personal Activities

Gross income generated from personal activities is normally taxable to the recipient. For example, prizes and awards are taxable to the person who receives them. This flow-through concept is imposed for administrative convenience - it is easier to collect an income tax from the taxpayer who has the cash rather than from the taxpayer who paid the cash.

Employment Income

Gross income from services provided to an employer or from self-employment is normally taxable to the person who performs the services and receives the payment. For example, income earned by a child actor is taxable to the child rather than to the parent of the child. Gross income cannot normally be assigned to another person by the person who earns it since this would violate the Doctrine of the Fruit and the Tree. Employment income is discussed in Chapter 5. The taxation of business income is discussed in detail in several chapters at the end of this text.

Special Issues for Persons Living in Community Property States

Most of the states in the United States follow the common law system for property ownership. However, nine states in the United States use some form of community property regime. These states include Arizona, California, Idaho, Louisiana, Nevada, New Mexico, Texas, Washington, and Wisconsin. Spouses in Alaska can choose to follow community property rules. In **community property** states, one half of the income earned (wages, salaries, etc.) by a spouse is deemed to be earned by each spouse and one half of the income earned from community property is deemed to be the income of each spouse. If a married couple's filing status is married filing jointly, this division of income makes no difference since income is added together. It may make a significant difference, however, if the couple's filing status is married filing separately or if they divorce during the year. If they file as married filing separately, the community property income (earned from employment and community property assets) is divided equally, but any separate property income may be reported by the spouse owning the separate property. After the divorce is final, the community property regime ceases to exist and the income of each of the former spouses is considered to be separate income.

For tax years after June 1, 2010, the IRS has determined that state-level community property laws apply to registered domestic partners and persons in a civil union. Married same-sex couples are allowed to file joint federal returns following the striking down of Section 3 of the Defense of Marriage Act (DOMA). Unless local (state) law states otherwise, registered domestic partners and couples in civil unions are not married and will likely file as unmarried for federal income tax purposes, but community property laws regarding income apply just as they apply to married couples. After the Supreme Court struck down DOMA, some states that had previously permitted civil union status terminated that status under state law, and specified that unless the civil union was terminated by a specified date, those previously in a civil union were deemed to be married under state law.

Exhibit 4.4 | Community Property States

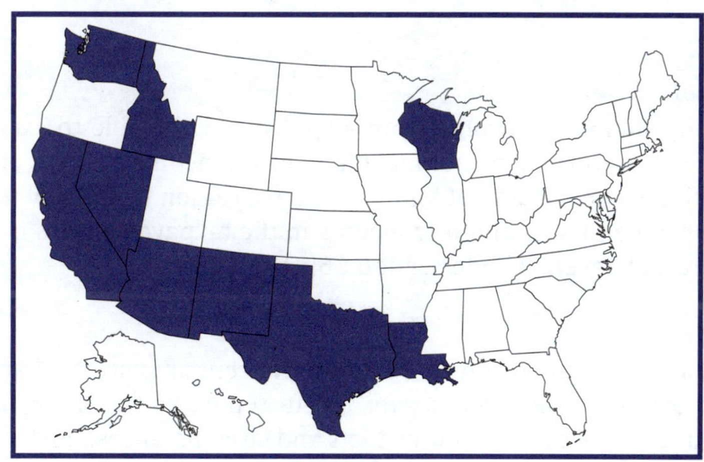

Community property includes property acquired by a married couple during their marriage. Property acquired before the marriage or acquired by gift or inheritance before or after the marriage is generally considered to be the separate property of the spouse. In four states, Idaho, Louisiana, Texas, and Wisconsin, income from separate property is deemed to be community income; in the other community property states, income from separate property is deemed to be the separate income of the spouse who owns the separate property. When allocating income from separate property, gains, losses, and nontaxable returns of capital from separate property may or may not be considered to be community income depending on the community property state (California - no, Louisiana and Texas - yes).

Example 4.3

Skyler and Walter are married and live in Texas (a community property state). During the year, Skyler sold stock that she had inherited from her father five years earlier. The sale of the stock resulted in a long-term capital gain of $12,000. The stock had paid a cash dividend of $500 shortly before the sale. The stock is Skyler's separate property because it was inherited. In Texas, the dividend income is treated as community income, but the gain on the sale is allocated to Skyler because it is considered to be a gain from her separate property rather than income from community property.

The reporting of community income earned through the personal services of either spouse can be complicated or even impossible if the spouses do not live together or if one spouse refuses to completely disclose his earnings. Section 66 of the Internal Revenue Code provides the following solutions for these circumstances.

Separated Spouse Relief

For income earned through personal services, community property laws are ignored and each spouse reports his or her own earned income for federal income tax purposes if the married couple lives apart at all times during the year, they do not file a joint return with each other, and none of the earned community income is transferred between them during the year.

Quick Quiz 4.2

1. In community property states, half of the income earned from community property is deemed to be the income of each spouse.
   a. True
   b. False
2. The only relief available under Section 66 is innocent spouse relief.
   a. True
   b. False

True, False.

Innocent Spouse Relief

A married taxpayer with community income from a spouse may be able to exclude that income if the taxpayer does not file a joint return, does not include in gross income an item of community income of the spouse, establishes that he or she did not know of or have reason to know of that community income, and it is inequitable to include that community income in the taxpayer's gross income. Innocent spouse rules are provided in Internal Revenue Code Section 66(a).

Equitable Relief

Even if the requirements for separated spouse relief or innocent spouse relief are not met, the Internal Revenue Service is authorized to allow a taxpayer not to report half of the community income of the taxpayer's spouse if, taking into account all of the facts and circumstances, the failure to grant such relief would be "inequitable."

Disallowance of Community Property Treatment

The Secretary of the Treasury is given authority in Internal Revenue Code Section 66(d) to disallow the benefits of any community property law (i.e., the splitting of income) to any taxpayer who acts as if he is solely entitled to the community income and who fails to notify his spouse about the income before the due date (including extensions) for filing a tax return for the year.

INCOME FROM INVESTMENT ACTIVITIES

Many different types of investments are available to investors, but the most common investments involve the ownership of assets or the lending of money. Each type of investment has the potential to generate income and/or gain that must be included in gross income for tax purposes. Typically, owning assets carries greater risk of financial loss than loaning money, but the potential rewards are also greater with asset ownership. Some of the more common types of gross income from investment activities are discussed in this section.

Congress has chosen to tax some types of investment income or gains more favorably than other types. Capital gains are normally taxed at lower rates than ordinary income. Advisors need to be aware of how each type of investment income is taxed so that an appropriate after-tax rate of return can be calculated.

Key Concepts

1. Identify the various types of investment income.
2. Describe the taxation of income from investment activities.
3. Describe the taxation of annuities.
4. Identify the types of investment income that are excluded from gross income.

Investment Items Included in Gross Income

Capital Gains

Most investments, including stocks, bonds, and mutual funds fit into the capital asset category. Gains from the sale or exchange of capital assets must be included in gross income and they may be taxed at favorable capital gains rates. The taxation of capital gains is discussed in detail in Chapter 10.

Interest Income

Interest income is generated by a variety of debt instruments, including bank accounts, money market instruments, corporate bonds, government agency securities, Treasury securities, and municipal bonds. Interest income must normally be included in gross income when it is actually or constructively received by a cash basis taxpayer or when it is earned by an accrual basis taxpayer. A cash basis taxpayer is deemed to have constructively received interest income from a savings account or certificate of deposit when it is credited to his account, even if it is not readily available for withdrawal until the next year. This is an application of the doctrine of constructive receipt. Interest income of $10 or more per year is normally reported to a taxpayer on Form 1099-INT by the payor of the interest, but the interest must be recognized by the taxpayer even when this form is not received or when the interest income is less than $10.

Interest income from most municipal bonds can be excluded from federal gross income. It may also be excludable for state income tax purposes. This topic is covered in detail later in this chapter as part of the discussion of exclusions from gross income.

Interest income from U.S. savings bonds and Treasury obligations (bills, notes, and bonds) must normally be included in federal gross income, but is potentially excluded from gross income for state and local income tax purposes.

Exhibit 4.5 | Form 1099-INT

9292 ☐ VOID ☐ CORRECTED

PAYER'S name, street address, city or town, state or province, country, ZIP or foreign postal code, and telephone no.	Payer's RTN (optional)	OMB No. 1545-0112 2020 Form 1099-INT		Interest Income
	1 Interest income $			
	2 Early withdrawal penalty $			Copy A
PAYER'S TIN | RECIPIENT'S TIN	3 Interest on U.S. Savings Bonds and Treas. obligations $			For Internal Revenue Service Center
RECIPIENT'S name	4 Federal income tax withheld $	5 Investment expenses $		File with Form 1096.
Street address (including apt. no.)	6 Foreign tax paid $	7 Foreign country or U.S. possession		For Privacy Act and Paperwork Reduction Act Notice, see the **2020 General Instructions for Certain Information Returns.**
City or town, state or province, country, and ZIP or foreign postal code	8 Tax-exempt interest $	9 Specified private activity bond interest $		
FATCA filing requirement ☐	10 Market discount $	11 Bond premium $		
	12 Bond premium on Treasury obligations $	13 Bond premium on tax-exempt bond $		
Account number (see instructions) | 2nd TIN not. ☐	14 Tax-exempt and tax credit bond CUSIP no.	15 State	16 State identification no.	17 State tax withheld $ $

Form **1099-INT** Cat. No. 14410K www.irs.gov/Form1099INT Department of the Treasury - Internal Revenue Service

Do Not Cut or Separate Forms on This Page — Do Not Cut or Separate Forms on This Page

Original Issue Discount (OID) Bonds

Some debt instruments are issued at a discount from the stated redemption price at maturity. The difference between the redemption price at maturity and the purchase price is called **original issue discount**. The original issue discount really represents interest that will be received by the taxpayer at the time when the bond matures. An accrual basis taxpayer reports this interest as it is earned. Barring the application of the doctrine of constructive receipt, a cash basis taxpayer would report all of the original issue discount as interest income when cash is received at maturity. When a taxpayer purchases debt instruments with maturities of more than one year, the IRC requires cash basis taxpayers to report the interest on the accrual basis, calculated using a constant yield (or effective interest rate) method. For debt instruments issued before July 2, 1982, a straight-line method was used. A cash basis taxpayer must therefore report a portion of the interest each year even though no cash is received during the year, which creates phantom income for the taxpayer and an increase in basis equal to the income recognized. This approach is consistent with the doctrine of constructive receipt, which requires cash basis taxpayers to recognize income when it is permanently set aside in an account for their benefit. The amount of the interest to be included in gross income is calculated by the issuer of the debt instrument and is reported to the taxpayer on Form 1099-OID. Treasury Regulation 1.1272-1(j) provides examples of the calculation of the interest income that must be reported each year.

Example 4.4

zero coupon $1,000 Treasury bond yielding 8% annually. She ury bond on January 1, 2021. (N=30, i=8, PMT=0, FV=$1,000, s bond has an original issue discount, Goldilocks must impute on an annual basis. For 2021, Goldilocks will report $7.95 of x 0.08). In addition, her tax basis in the bond at the beginning of 99.38 + $7.95) since a portion of the OID was recognized nd she paid income tax on that amount).

E U.S. government savings bonds are original issue discount debt ct to recognize all of the interest income when the bonds mature. A cognize the interest each year as with other original issue discount must be used for future purchases of savings bonds as well.

erred by gift, the donor and the donee must report the related interest days that each owned the instrument during the year. This is a direct Fruit and the Tree, which requires income (fruit) to be included in the estment (the tree).

Example 4.5

paid interest of $600 on the first day of January each year. the current year, Hank gave the bond to his daughter, Marie. When Marie receives the $600 of interest next year, Hank will be required to include $300 of interest in his gross income and Marie will be required to include the remaining $300. If Hank is an accrual basis taxpayer (unlikely), he will report his $300 for the current year. If he is a cash basis taxpayer, he will report his $300 of interest income on his tax return for next year, the year in which he would have received the interest if he had retained the bond.

Dividend Income

A C corporation is taxed on its own taxable income. A portion of the corporation's after-tax income is often paid to shareholders in the form of cash dividends. **Dividend income** in the form of cash received by shareholders of a C corporation must be included in the shareholder's gross income to the extent that the issuing corporation has earnings and profits (a concept very similar to retained earnings). If a C corporation makes distributions to shareholders in excess of earnings and profits, the excess is treated as a nontaxable return of invested dollars until the shareholder's entire tax basis in the stock has been recovered. Any distribution in excess of the shareholder's basis is treated as a capital gain to the shareholder. A dividend distribution to a shareholder in the form of property other than

Quick Quiz 4.3

1. Interest income of less than $10 per year does not have to be included in gross income.
   a. True
   b. False
2. Dividend income is reported to a taxpayer on Form 1099-DIV.
   a. True
   b. False

False, True.

cash is treated the same as a cash distribution. Dividend income of $10 or more per year is normally reported to a taxpayer on Form 1099-DIV by the corporation or the pass-through entity (such as a mutual fund) that pays the dividend.

Exhibit 4.6 | Form 1099-DIV

9191 ☐ VOID ☐ CORRECTED

PAYER'S name, street address, city or town, state or province, country, ZIP or foreign postal code, and telephone no.		1a Total ordinary dividends $	OMB No. 1545-0110 2020	Dividends and Distributions
		1b Qualified dividends $	Form 1099-DIV	
		2a Total capital gain distr. $	2b Unrecap. Sec. 1250 gain $	Copy A For Internal Revenue Service Center
PAYER'S TIN	RECIPIENT'S TIN	2c Section 1202 gain $	2d Collectibles (28%) gain $	File with Form 1096.
RECIPIENT'S name		3 Nondividend distributions $	4 Federal income tax withheld $	For Privacy Act and Paperwork Reduction Act Notice, see the 2020 General Instructions for Certain Information Returns.
Street address (including apt. no.)		5 Section 199A dividends $	6 Investment expenses $	
City or town, state or province, country, and ZIP or foreign postal code		7 Foreign tax paid $	8 Foreign country or U.S. possession	
		9 Cash liquidation distributions $	10 Noncash liquidation distributions $	
	FATCA filing requirement ☐	11 Exempt-interest dividends $	12 Specified private activity bond interest dividends $	
Account number (see instructions)	2nd TIN not. ☐	13 State / 14 State identification no.	15 State tax withheld $ $	

Form 1099-DIV Cat. No. 14415N www.irs.gov/Form1099DIV Department of the Treasury - Internal Revenue Service

Do Not Cut or Separate Forms on This Page — Do Not Cut or Separate Forms on This Page

Historically, dividends from C corporations were taxed in the same manner as interest income or other ordinary income. Since 2003, **qualified dividends** are taxed at long-term capital gain tax rates, which range from zero percent to 20 percent, depending on the taxpayer's taxable income. Qualified dividends are not added to long-term capital gains nor do they offset capital losses; they simply generate a tax of:

- **Zero percent:** For single taxpayers and married taxpayers filing separately with taxable income up to $40,400; for married taxpayers filing jointly with taxable income up to $80,800; and for taxpayers claiming head of household status with taxable income up to $54,100,
- **15 percent:** For single taxpayers with taxable income less than $445,850; married taxpayers filing jointly with taxable income under $501,600; married taxpayers filing separately with taxable income less than $250,800; and taxpayers claiming head of household status with taxable income under $473,750, or
- **20 percent:** For single individuals with taxable income over $445,850; married individuals filing jointly with taxable income over $501,600; married individuals filing separately with taxable income over $250,800; and for taxpayers claiming head of household states with taxable income over $473,750.

To achieve favorable tax status, qualified dividends must meet all three of the following requirements:

1. they must be paid by a U.S. corporation or a qualified foreign corporation;
2. the dividend must not be a type of dividend excluded by law from the definition of a qualified dividend such as capital gain distribution, dividends on bank deposits, ESOP dividends, etc.; and
3. the shareholder must meet a holding period requirement of 60 days during the 121 day period beginning 60 days before the ex-dividend date.[4]

Qualified dividends are identified by and reported to the shareholder by the payor of the dividends. Dividends that are not qualified dividends are treated as ordinary income and are subject to tax at the taxpayer's marginal income tax rates. The tax rates for qualified dividends are shown in **Exhibit 4.7**.

Exhibit 4.7 | Qualified Dividend Tax Rates*

Long-Term Capital Gains Rates	*Single Taxpayers*	*Married Filing Jointly*	*Head of Household*	*Married Filing Separately*
0%	Up to $40,400	Up to $80,800	Up to $54,100	Up to $40,400
15%	$40,401 - $445,850	$80,801 - $501,600	$54,101 - $473,750	$40,401 - $250,800
20%	Over $445,850	Over $501,600	Over $473,750	Over $250,800

** Income Thresholds in this Table are Based on Taxable Income*

The most common types of distributions from mutual funds are qualified dividends, ordinary dividends (taxed at ordinary income rates) and capital gain distributions. Qualified dividends and ordinary dividends are included in gross income and are taxed as explained in the preceding paragraphs. Capital gain distributions are treated as long-term capital gains. If these mutual fund distributions are reinvested in more shares of the same fund, the income tax basis in the mutual fund investment is increased by the amount of the distribution that is recognized (included in taxable gross income).

Unlike interest income, dividends do not accrue ratably over time. When stock is sold, the dividend is normally included in the gross income of the person who is listed as the owner of the stock on the record date. Court decisions are inconsistent about whether the donor or donee is to be taxed when the donor gifts stock after the declaration date but before the record date. When stock is gifted before the declaration date, the donee must normally include the dividends in gross income under the Doctrine of the Fruit and the Tree.

Dividends paid on life insurance policies are treated much differently than dividends paid to owners of corporations. Unlike corporate dividends, which are paid from the earnings and profits of the company, a life insurance dividend represents a return of the policy owner's premium payment, and is therefore not subject to income tax. Keep in mind that premiums paid on life insurance policies are paid with after-tax dollars, so a rebate of part of the premium (a life insurance dividend) is a return of capital, not a distribution of income.

Rental and Royalty Income

Rents received from rental real estate and royalties from oil, gas, mineral properties, copyrights, and patents must be included in gross income as ordinary income. Related expenses are subtracted on Schedule E (**Exhibit 4.8**) and the net amount is reported on Form 1040. As discussed later in this chapter, prepaid rent must be included in the gross income of both cash and accrual method taxpayers in the year the rent is received.

4. IRC §1(h)(11)(B).

Income from Annuities

Many individuals purchase commercial annuity contracts from insurance companies with after-tax dollars to generate retirement income on a tax-deferred basis. This type of annuity contract is often referred to as a nonqualified annuity. While money invested in an annuity contract has already been subjected to income tax, income or gains generated inside the contract are taxable when the distributions are received, which will presumably occur during retirement. An annuity is an ordinary income asset, and income generated from an annuity must be reported as ordinary income regardless of how the income was generated (whether the income was earned as interest, dividend, or capital gain) inside the annuity. The timing of the recognition of gross income depends on whether the taxpayer annuitizes the contract, surrenders the contract, or simply takes distributions as needed from the contract.

Annuitization

An annuity contract is **annuitized** when regular periodic (such as monthly or annual) payments begin for life or for a specified period of time in excess of one year. When a contract is annuitized, each payment includes both a portion of nontaxable return of invested capital and a portion of gross income. The amount of each payment that is a nontaxable return of invested capital is determined using the exclusion ratio in the following formula:

$$\text{Excluded Amount} = \frac{\$\ \text{Investment in the Contract}}{\$\ \text{Expected Total Return}} \text{ x Distributions (Payments) Received}$$

The investment in the contract is the total amount of after-tax dollars invested in the contract. The expected return is the total amount of dollar distributions expected under the contract.

Example 4.6

Jessie invested $100,000 in an annuity contract. Many years later, she annuitized the contract. The insurance company agreed to pay her $1,388.89 per month for 15 years. Her expected return is $250,000.20 (15 years x 12 months x $1,388.89 per month). Using the formula above, the exclusion ratio is 0.40 ($100,000/$250,000.20) and the amount of each payment excluded from income tax is $555.56 until Jessie recovers her entire investment in the contract.

$$\text{Excluded Amount} = \frac{\$100{,}000}{\$250{,}000.20} \times \$1{,}388.89 = \$555.56$$

$$\text{Exclusion Ratio} = \frac{\$100{,}000}{\$250{,}000} = 40\%$$

Therefore, the Inclusion Ratio is 60% (1 - 0.40).

The amount excluded from gross income in a twelve month period would be $6,666.67 (12 x $1,388.89 x 0.40) and the amount excluded over the entire 15 years would be $100,000 (15 x 12 x $1,388.89 x 0.40). Note that the total amount excluded from income tax in this example equals Jessie's taxable basis in the contract. The amount included in gross income is the inclusion ratio (60% times each payment received).

Example 4.7

Finn invested $100,000 in an annuity contract. Many years later, he annuitized the contract. The insurance company agreed to pay him $1,388.89 per month for the rest of his life. Using mortality tables provided by the Internal Revenue Service, Finn's life expectancy was determined to be 15 years. As in the preceding example, the expected return is $250,000.20 (15 x 12 x $1,388.89) and the amounts excluded from and included in gross income are the same.

Annuity Payments Received Beyond the Expected Period

In **Example 4.7**, if Finn receives annuity payments for 15 years, he will have recovered his entire investment in the contract (the entire $100,000 basis) free of income taxes. Therefore 100 percent of any payment he receives after 15 years will be included in his gross income.

If an Annuitant Dies Before Recovering His Investment

In **Example 4.7**, if Finn dies after receiving payments for only 10 years, he will have recovered only $66,666.72 (10 x 12 x $1,388.89 x 0.40) of his investment in the contract. A miscellaneous itemized deduction, not subject to a two percent of AGI limitation, of $33,333.28 (representing the unrecovered investment in the annuity contract) can be deducted on Finn's final federal income tax return.

Joint Life Expectancies

In Publication 939, the Internal Revenue Service provides actuarial tables to determine life expectancies used in calculating the expected return from an annuity when payments are to be made for life or for the joint lives of two annuitants. Publication 939 also provides other tables and information to determine the expected return when a refund feature or other features are attached to the annuity.

Taking Distributions as Needed

When distributions (withdrawals) are taken from an annuity before annuitizing, the entire distribution must be included in the taxpayer's gross income until all of the gain in the contract has been distributed. Once all of the gain in the tax contract is distributed, further distributions are treated as a tax-free return of invested dollars. Annuity contracts follow a LIFO (last-in, first-out) approach to income reporting in which the gain in the contract (generated from the investment made in the contract) must be fully distributed before a tax-free return of basis may be received. However, annuities issued prior to August 14, 1982 receive FIFO (first-in, first-out) treatment.

Quick Quiz 4.4

1. All dividends paid by U.S. corporations are qualified dividends subject to favorable tax treatment.
   a. True
   b. False
2. Nonqualified annuity payments include both a nontaxable return of invested money and gross income.
   a. True
   b. False
3. Surrendering an annuity may result in gross income.
   a. True
   b. False

False, True, True.

Surrender of an Annuity

If an annuity is surrendered to an insurance company for its cash surrender value, the difference between the total amount received and the total amount invested in the contract is included in gross income as ordinary income. If the annuity contract has not been owned for the required number of years specified in the annuity contract, the insurance company may impose a surrender charge. Surrender charges are usually specified as a percentage of the contract value and they decrease over time until they are eliminated entirely. The surrender charge usually applies for a period of five to seven years.

Early Distribution Penalty

When gross income is received from an annuity before the recipient (annuitant) reaches the age of 59½, a 10 percent penalty tax (10 percent of the gross income) is imposed unless certain exceptions apply, such as substantially equal periodic payments made to the owner under the provisions of IRC Sections 72(t) or 72(q). This penalty is also waived if the distribution is made due to the disability or death of the annuitant. Prior to annuitization, the last in-first out (LIFO) method is used to determine the character of the distribution. This means all of the income of the contract is distributed prior to any distribution of principal. If an annuity owner takes a distribution before reaching age 59½, and the distribution is greater than the income on the contract, the distribution in excess of income is treated as a return of capital, and is not subject to tax or to the ten percent penalty.

Other Annuity Issues

When distributions are made from a variable annuity, the payments may vary while the expected number of payments remains the same. In this situation, the amount excluded from gross income from each payment is determined by dividing the investment in the contract by the number of periodic payments expected under the contract.

Example 4.8

Jane purchased a variable annuity at a total cost of $120,000. She starts receiving variable annuity payments for life at the age of 65. According to the appropriate actuarial table, her life expectancy at age 65 is 20 years. Jane's annual exclusion amount from the annuity contract is $6,000 ($120,000/20). If she receives $9,000 in the current year, she will be allowed to exclude $6,000 and will include the remaining $3,000 in her gross income. If her payments from the contract are less than $6,000 for a given year (due to investment return fluctuations), she will be able to exclude all of the payments for the year and may choose to allocate her unused exclusion for that year to the remaining years of her life expectancy.

Gross income from an annuity is reported to the taxpayer on Form 1099-R (**Exhibit 4.9**).

Gross income from private and commercial annuities is determined in the same manner as above. Private annuities are non-commercial annuities between two private parties, and are often used to achieve estate planning benefits.

Exhibit 4.8 | Form 1040 Schedule E

SCHEDULE E
(Form 1040)
Department of the Treasury
Internal Revenue Service (99)

Supplemental Income and Loss

(From rental real estate, royalties, partnerships, S corporations, estates, trusts, REMICs, etc.)
▶ Attach to Form 1040, 1040-SR, 1040-NR, or 1041.
▶ Go to *www.irs.gov/ScheduleE* for instructions and the latest information.

OMB No. 1545-0074
2020
Attachment Sequence No. **13**

Name(s) shown on return | **Your social security number**

Part I **Income or Loss From Rental Real Estate and Royalties** **Note:** If you are in the business of renting personal property, use **Schedule C.** See instructions. If you are an individual, report farm rental income or loss from **Form 4835** on page 2, line 40.

A Did you make any payments in 2020 that would require you to file Form(s) 1099? See instructions . . . . . . ☐ **Yes** ☐ **No**
B If "Yes," did you or will you file required Form(s) 1099? . . . . ☐ **Yes** ☐ **No**

1a	Physical address of each property (street, city, state, ZIP code)
A	
B	
C	

1b	Type of Property (from list below)	**2** For each rental real estate property listed above, report the number of fair rental and personal use days. Check the **QJV** box only if you meet the requirements to file as a qualified joint venture. See instructions.		**Fair Rental Days**	**Personal Use Days**	**QJV**
A			**A**			☐
B			**B**			☐
C			**C**			☐

Type of Property:
1 Single Family Residence 3 Vacation/Short-Term Rental 5 Land 7 Self-Rental
2 Multi-Family Residence 4 Commercial 6 Royalties 8 Other (describe)

Income:	**Properties:**		**A**	**B**	**C**
3	Rents received	**3**			
4	Royalties received	**4**			
Expenses:					
5	Advertising	**5**			
6	Auto and travel (see instructions)	**6**			
7	Cleaning and maintenance	**7**			
8	Commissions.	**8**			
9	Insurance	**9**			
10	Legal and other professional fees	**10**			
11	Management fees	**11**			
12	Mortgage interest paid to banks, etc. (see instructions)	**12**			
13	Other interest.	**13**			
14	Repairs.	**14**			
15	Supplies	**15**			
16	Taxes	**16**			
17	Utilities	**17**			
18	Depreciation expense or depletion	**18**			
19	Other (list) ▶	**19**			
20	Total expenses. Add lines 5 through 19	**20**			
21	Subtract line 20 from line 3 (rents) and/or 4 (royalties). If result is a (loss), see instructions to find out if you must file **Form 6198**	**21**			
22	Deductible rental real estate loss after limitation, if any, on **Form 8582** (see instructions)	**22**	( )	( )	( )

23a	Total of all amounts reported on line 3 for all rental properties	**23a**	
b	Total of all amounts reported on line 4 for all royalty properties	**23b**	
c	Total of all amounts reported on line 12 for all properties	**23c**	
d	Total of all amounts reported on line 18 for all properties	**23d**	
e	Total of all amounts reported on line 20 for all properties	**23e**	
24	**Income.** Add positive amounts shown on line 21. **Do not** include any losses	**24**	
25	**Losses.** Add royalty losses from line 21 and rental real estate losses from line 22. Enter total losses here .	**25**	( )
26	**Total rental real estate and royalty income or (loss).** Combine lines 24 and 25. Enter the result here. If Parts II, III, IV, and line 40 on page 2 do not apply to you, also enter this amount on Schedule 1 (Form 1040), line 5. Otherwise, include this amount in the total on line 41 on page 2 .	**26**	

For Paperwork Reduction Act Notice, see the separate instructions. Cat. No. 11344L **Schedule E (Form 1040) 2020**

Exhibit 4.9 | Form 1099-R

9898 ☐ VOID ☐ CORRECTED

PAYER'S name, street address, city or town, state or province, country, ZIP or foreign postal code, and telephone no.			1 Gross distribution $	OMB No. 1545-0119	Distributions From Pensions, Annuities, Retirement or Profit-Sharing Plans, IRAs, Insurance Contracts, etc.
			2a Taxable amount $	2021 Form 1099-R	
			2b Taxable amount not determined ☐	Total distribution ☐	Copy A For Internal Revenue Service Center
PAYER'S TIN	RECIPIENT'S TIN		3 Capital gain (included in box 2a) $	4 Federal income tax withheld $	File with Form 1096.
RECIPIENT'S name			5 Employee contributions/ Designated Roth contributions or insurance premiums $	6 Net unrealized appreciation in employer's securities $	For Privacy Act and Paperwork Reduction Act Notice, see the **2021 General Instructions for Certain Information Returns.**
Street address (including apt. no.)			7 Distribution code(s) IRA/ SEP/ SIMPLE ☐	8 Other $ %	
City or town, state or province, country, and ZIP or foreign postal code			9a Your percentage of total distribution %	9b Total employee contributions $	
10 Amount allocable to IRR within 5 years $	11 1st year of desig. Roth contrib.	12 FATCA filing requirement ☐	14 State tax withheld $ $	15 State/Payer's state no.	16 State distribution $ $
Account number (see instructions)		13 Date of payment	17 Local tax withheld $ $	18 Name of locality	19 Local distribution $ $

Form **1099-R** Cat. No. 14436Q www.irs.gov/Form1099R Department of the Treasury - Internal Revenue Service

Do Not Cut or Separate Forms on This Page — Do Not Cut or Separate Forms on This Page

Income from Life Insurance and Endowment Contracts

When the owner of a life insurance policy surrenders a life insurance policy to the issuing insurance company in exchange for the cash surrender value of the policy, the owner of the policy must recognize gross income equal to the amount of total money received minus the owner's adjusted basis (cost) for the policy. The gain is recognized as ordinary income. The owner's adjusted basis in the policy is equal to the total premiums paid on the policy less any refunded premiums, rebates, dividends, or existing loans against the policy.

An **endowment contract** is a type of insurance contract that pays a specified death benefit to a beneficiary upon the death of the insured owner, but has the added feature of paying the specified benefit (in lieu of the death benefit) to the owner of the policy if the insured person lives to a specified age or date. If the policy matures and the endowment proceeds paid to the owner of the policy exceed the owner's adjusted basis in the policy, the excess must be recognized as ordinary income. When the owner chooses to receive endowment proceeds in installments, the payments are taxed as an annuity with the proceeds of the life insurance contract constituting the initial basis, since the difference between the endowment's proceeds and the owner's cost basis in the policy has already been included in the owner's income.

Other gross income issues related to life insurance and endowment contracts are discussed later in this chapter.

Traditional IRAs

Generally, a contribution to a traditional IRA is deductible in determining adjusted gross income (AGI), the income earned inside the IRA is tax deferred (taxed later), and distributions are taxed at ordinary income tax rates (regardless of the type of investments purchased inside of the IRA). Early distributions (before age 59½) may also be subject to a 10 percent penalty tax unless the distributions are made upon the death or disability of the owner or for certain other specified reasons.

Under certain circumstances, contributions to traditional IRAs may be only partially deductible or not deductible at all. When this occurs, each IRA distribution will consist of both a tax-free return of investment and taxable gross income.

Income from Partnerships

A partnership is not subject to Federal income tax on its income.[5] Instead, the income of the partnership is passed through to the partners and is subject to income tax on the partners' individual income tax returns. Each partner's distributive share of partnership income is determined based upon the profit and loss sharing percentages of the partner. Distributions of cash or other property from the partnership to the partner during the year have no effect on the partner's income from the partnership unless cash distributions to the partner exceed the partner's basis in her partnership interest.

Example 4.9

ABC Partnership has $100,000 of ordinary income for the year. Rosita has a 40% interest in the profits of ABC partnership. She received $30,000 of cash distributions during the year. Rosita must report $40,000 of ordinary income from the partnership for the year. The cash distributions do not affect her current income recognition because they represent either income on which she has already been taxed or money that she invested in the partnership.

Some states do impose a state income tax on partnership income, which is typically referred to as a Pass-Through Business Entity Tax (PTBET). If the state imposes a state income tax at the entity level, that tax is deductible as an ordinary, necessary, and reasonable business expense when calculating federal taxable income for the entity. Some states will give each partner a credit on their state income tax return for some or all of the PTBET paid by the partnership when calculating state taxes due.

Quick Quiz 4.5

1. Distributions from traditional IRAs are generally taxable as ordinary gross income.
   a. True
   b. False
2. An LLC is normally taxed as a partnership.
   a. True
   b. False

True, True.

Income from S Corporations

The tax treatment of the income from an S corporation is similar, but not identical, to that of a partnership. Each stockholder pays income tax on his pro-rata share of the S corporation's income. If the stockholder owns 10 percent of the stock of the corporation, he must report 10 percent of the corporation's income on his individual income tax return. Cash distributions from the corporation to the shareholder are not normally taxable because they represent income that has already been taxed.

Income from Limited Liability Companies

A limited liability company (LLC) is normally taxed as a partnership. Therefore, the income of the LLC is usually passed through the LLC to the members and is subject to income taxation on their individual income tax returns. Under check-the-box regulations discussed in Chapter 16, an LLC may elect to be

5. IRC §701.

taxed as a corporation if certain requirements are met, including being treated as an S corporation if the S election is filed. An LLC can also be treated as a disregarded entity under certain circumstances.

Income from Trusts and Estates

Individuals and C corporations (corporations that have not made an election under subchapter S) pay tax on their own income. Partnerships and S corporations are tax reporting entities that pass their income through to their owners. For income tax purposes, the term partnership includes LLCs, LLPs, and all other unincorporated entities with more than one owner. Trusts and estates may pay tax on their own income, pass through their income to their beneficiaries, or a combination of both. If a trust or estate retains all of its income for the year, it must pay income taxes on its income. If it pays out all of its income to beneficiaries during the year, it simply reports the income and passes it through to the beneficiaries. In this case, each beneficiary must report her share of the income. In some cases, some of the income for the year is retained by the trust or estate and some is paid to beneficiaries. When this happens, the trust or estate must pay income taxes on the income retained and the beneficiaries must pay income taxes on the income paid to them.

Exhibit 4.10 | Income Tax Rate Schedule for Estates and Trusts (for 2021)

If taxable income is:	*The tax is:*
Not over $2,650	**10%** of taxable income
Over $2,650 but not over $9,550	$265 plus **24%** of the excess of such amount over $2,650
Over $9,550 but not over $13,050	$1,921 plus **35%** of the excess of such amount over $9,550
Over $13,050	$3,146 plus **37%** of the excess of such amount over $13,050

Example 4.10

The Simpson Irrevocable Trust earned $25,000 of income during the year and paid $10,000 in cash to one beneficiary of the trust during the year. The trust must report and pay tax on $15,000 of the income and the beneficiary must report and pay tax on the remaining $10,000.

Income from a grantor trust is taxable to the trust's grantor (the person who established and funded the trust) rather than to the trust itself or to the trust beneficiaries. A revocable living trust is one type of grantor trust that is often used to avoid probate. If a Crummey provision is used to qualify a transfer to an irrevocable trust for the gift tax annual exclusion, the trust may be partially or wholly beneficiary defective, causing some or all of the income to be reported on the beneficiary's income tax return.

Investment Items Excluded from Gross Income

Relatively few types of investment income can be excluded from gross income, but the exclusion of municipal bond interest, life insurance proceeds, and distributions from Roth IRAs can provide meaningful tax planning opportunities for many taxpayers. The remaining exclusions provide more targeted or limited benefits.

Interest Income from Certain State and Local Government Obligations

Municipal bonds are debt instruments issued by states and their political subdivisions (counties, cities, school districts, and similar entities). Interest income on municipal bonds issued to finance government operations is generally excluded from federal gross income. This tax-exempt status of bonds allows state and local governments to issue bonds at lower interest rates than prevailing rates paid on taxable bonds of comparable quality because the net after-tax return is equivalent.

Municipal bonds are typically more appropriate for taxpayers with high marginal tax rates than for those in lower marginal tax rate brackets. A comparison of the after-tax interest rate available on taxable bonds to tax-free municipal bonds can be made using the following formulas:

$$\textbf{Equivalent Tax-Free Rate} = \textbf{Taxable Rate} \times (1 - \textbf{Marginal Tax Rate})$$

$$\textbf{Equivalent Taxable Rate} = \frac{\textbf{Tax-Free Rate}}{1 - \textbf{Marginal Tax Rate}}$$

Example 4.11

Saul's marginal tax rate is 35% and he is subject to the 3.8% additional Medicare tax on investment income (discussed in Chapter 3). He wants to invest in either a taxable bond with an interest rate of 6% or a tax-exempt municipal bond of comparable risk and quality, with an interest rate of 4%. The equivalent tax-free rate for the taxable bond is 3.67%.

$$\text{Equivalent Tax-Free Rate} = 0.06 \times (1 - 0.388) = 3.67\%$$

The equivalent taxable rate for the municipal bond is 6.54%.

$$\text{Equivalent Taxable Rate} = \frac{0.04}{1 - 0.388} = 6.54\%$$

Therefore, the municipal bond provides a higher after-tax return for Saul. The comparison can be after-tax (4% vs. 3.67%) or pre-tax (6.54% vs. 6%). Under both methods, the municipal bond is superior in terms of after-tax yield.

Example 4.12

Use the facts from **Example 4.11**. If Saul's marginal tax rate were 24% rather than 35%, indicting that he is not subject to the 3.8% additional Medicare tax since the top threshold of the 24% bracket is lower than the threshold for the additional Medicare tax, which bond would provide a better after-tax return? The equivalent tax-free rate for the taxable bond is 4.56% (6% x 0.76). The equivalent taxable rate for the municipal bond is 5.26% (4%/0.76). Therefore, the taxable bond would provide a higher after-tax return (4.56% vs. 4.0%, or alternatively 6% vs. 5.26%).

Interest income from municipal bonds is also excluded from gross income by many states. Some states exclude the interest earned from municipal bonds issued by entities within that state and tax the interest earned on bonds issued by state and local governments of other states. When comparing interest rates for taxable and tax-exempt bonds, the impact of state income tax laws should be included in the analysis.

The interest on some state and local bonds is taxable. Interest on some federally guaranteed bonds, some mortgage revenue bonds, some private activity bonds, and arbitrage bonds must be included in federal gross income.

The income tax exemption applies only to the interest on municipal bonds. Capital gains realized on the sale of municipal bonds must be included in gross income. Some interest from municipal bonds and private activity bonds is treated as a preference item for alternative minimum tax (AMT) purposes and may trigger additional tax liability. This is discussed further in Chapter 15.

Life Insurance Proceeds

Life insurance proceeds paid to a beneficiary because of the death of the insured person are normally excluded from gross income. The entire death benefit is excludable regardless of the amount received. A beneficiary of a life insurance policy may choose to receive the death benefit in periodic installment payments, in which case the insurance company will pay interest on the proceeds that it retains. If the periodic installment payment option is selected, the part of each payment representing the death benefit will be excluded from income, with the remaining portion of the payment included in income as interest income.

Example 4.13

Chachi died during the year. The $500,000 death benefit on his life insurance policy was payable to Joanie, his wife and sole beneficiary. Rather than receiving a lump-sum payment of $500,000, Joanie chose to receive $5,500 per month for a period of 120 months. The excludable portion of each payment is $4,166.67 ($500,000/120), the death benefit divided by the number of payments. The remaining $1,333.33 from each payment must be included in gross income as the interest component.

Life insurance death benefits must be included in gross income of a policy owner if the life insurance policy is sold ("transferred for value") by the original owner of the policy. This exception to the general rule that life insurance proceeds are exempt from income tax if received by reason of the death of the insured is known as the transfer for value rule.

Example 4.14

Roger owned a life insurance policy on his own life. Since he didn't need the policy any longer, he sold the policy to Don, his uncle, for $30,000. Don paid $20,000 in additional premiums over a period of years. When Roger died, Don received the death benefit of $400,000. Since the policy was transferred for value, Don must recognize $350,000 of ordinary income ($400,000 death benefit - $50,000 investment in the contract).

There are five exceptions to the transfer for value rule. The death benefit is received income tax free by the beneficiary if the policy is transferred for valuable consideration to:

1. the insured,
2. a corporation in which the insured is a shareholder,
3. a partnership in which the insured is a partner,
4. a partner of the insured, or
5. a transferee who takes the transferor's basis.

Example 4.15

Peggy is a key employee at a large international manufacturing company. The company purchased a life insurance policy on Peggy's life several years ago to provide compensation to the company for the loss of Peggy's services in the event of her early death. Peggy is retiring this month and the company no longer wants to maintain the life insurance policy on her life. Peggy, however, could use the policy in her estate plan. The value of the policy is $95,000. If Peggy purchases the policy from the company for $95,000 a transfer for value has occurred, but the death benefit will not be subject to income tax because the life insurance policy was transferred for valuable consideration to the insured.

Example 4.16

Bertram has a life insurance policy on his life that he purchased years ago, and does not really need it any longer. Last year, Bertram and two colleagues started a business in corporate form, and so far business has been booming. The shareholders would like to set up an entity type buy sell agreement whereby the corporation will purchase the shares of the deceased owner upon the owner's death. If Bertram sells his life insurance policy to the corporation to fund the buy-sell agreement, a transfer for value has occurred. The death benefit received by the corporation, however, will not be subject to tax since a transfer of a life insurance policy for valuable consideration to a corporation in which the insured is a shareholder is an exception to the transfer for value rule.

Example 4.17

Joan has a life insurance policy on her life that she purchased years ago, and does not really need it any longer. Last year, Joan and two colleagues started a business in partnership form, and so far business has been booming. The partners would like to set up an entity type buy sell agreement whereby the partnership will purchase the interest of the deceased owner upon the owner's death. If Joan sells her life insurance policy to the partnership to fund the buy-sell agreement, a transfer for value has occurred. The death benefit received by the partnership, however, will not be subject to tax since a transfer of a life insurance policy for valuable consideration to a partnership in which the insured is a partner is an exception to the transfer for value rule.

Example 4.18

Sergio has a life insurance policy on his life that he purchased years ago, and does not really need it any longer. Last year, Sergio and his golf buddy, Rory started a business in partnership form, and so far business has been booming. The partners would like to set up a cross-purchase type buy sell agreement whereby the surviving partner will purchase the interest of the deceased owner upon the owner's death. If Sergio sells his life insurance policy to Rory to fund the buy-sell agreement, a transfer for value has occurred. The death benefit received by Rory, however, will not be subject to tax since a transfer of a life insurance policy for valuable consideration to a partner of the insured is an exception to the transfer for value rule.

Example 4.19

Paulina sold a life insurance policy that she owned on her own life to a grantor trust that she created a few years ago. The sale of the life insurance policy is a transfer for value. The trust, however, will have a basis in the life insurance policy equal to Paulina's basis. The sale of the policy to the trust is disregarded for income tax purposes due to the trust's status as a grantor trust. Since, in this case, the transferee (the trust) will take the transferor's (Paulina's) basis, the last exception to the transfer for value rule has been met, and the death benefit will be received income tax free.

A taxpayer may borrow money (in the form of a loan or a series of periodic loans) from a life insurance policy without income tax consequences. Since the cash value in the policy secures the loan, the interest rates are normally very favorable for the borrower. Loans must be repaid and are therefore not considered income distributions to the borrower. Policy loans and any related accrued interest are often paid off with some of the tax-free proceeds of the policy upon the death of the insured owner of the policy. If the life insurance policy is classified as a modified endowment contract (MEC), a policy loan is treated as a distribution of income to the extent of all of the deferred income in the policy. When determining the tax nature of a distribution from a MEC, a last-in, first-out (LIFO) approach is used in which all income (the last money going into the policy) is deemed to be distributed before the invested premiums (the first dollars into the policy) are deemed to be distributed.

Quick Quiz 4.6

1. Municipal bonds are generally more appropriate for taxpayers with low marginal tax rates.
   a. True
   b. False
2. Life insurance proceeds are normally excludable from the gross income of the beneficiary.
   a. True
   b. False

False, True.

Accelerated Death Benefits

Accelerated death benefits are benefits paid to a person who is terminally ill when the policy has an accelerated death benefits rider. Accelerated death benefits paid by an insurance company under a life insurance policy before the death of the insured are excluded from gross income if the insured person is terminally ill. A person is deemed to be terminally ill if a physician certifies that he is reasonably expected to die from the illness or physical condition within 24 months. The same tax treatment applies if the policy is sold or assigned to a qualified viatical settlement provider.

Accelerated death benefits paid by an insurance company or a viatical settlement provider to a chronically ill individual are excluded from income to the extent that they are used to pay long-term care costs. Chronically ill individuals are people who are unable to perform two of the six activities of daily living (eating, bathing, dressing, toileting, transferring, and continence) that would qualify the individual for benefits under a long-term care policy. Accelerated death benefits in excess of these costs and the owner/insured's basis in the policy are includible in gross income.

Without the special rules excluding certain types of accelerated death benefits from income, these benefits would be taxable because the payments are not paid to a beneficiary upon the death of the insured person.

Roth IRAs

The tax treatment of Roth IRAs is very different from that for traditional IRAs. Distributions from Roth IRAs are normally excluded from gross income, while distributions from traditional IRAs are normally included in gross income. In order to avoid income tax on the distributions from a Roth IRA, the owner must contribute after-tax dollars to the Roth IRA account. In addition, distributions must be qualified distributions, which means that the taxpayer must leave the account open for at least five years from the beginning of the year for which the first contribution is made to the account, and receive a distribution:

1. after age 59½,
2. after the death of the owner,
3. after the disability of the owner, or
4. of up to $10,000 for a first-time home purchase.

In addition to qualified distributions, amounts contributed to the Roth IRA (on an after-tax basis) may be distributed at any time without including the distribution in gross income. Distributions from Roth IRAs are first deemed to come from the contributions to the plan rather than from income (a first-in, first-out or FIFO assumption). Part or all of any other distributions may be includible in gross income and may be subject to a ten percent penalty tax if they do not meet the requirements of a qualified distribution.

Since 2010, taxpayers have been able to convert traditional IRAs to Roth IRAs without regard to any adjusted gross income limitations. In the year of conversion, the taxpayer must normally include the entire value of the converted traditional IRA in gross income. Only part of the value of a converted traditional IRA will be included in gross income if nondeductible contributions have been made to traditional IRAs.

When a traditional IRA is converted to a Roth IRA, a special application of the ten percent penalty rule applies. Upon conversion, the taxpayer will pay income tax on the amount in excess of basis that is transferred to the Roth IRA. If a taxpayer under the age of 59½ takes a distribution from a converted Roth IRA within five years of the conversion, the ten percent penalty will apply to both the basis and income distributed from the Roth account. This 5-year rule applies in addition to the 5-year rule for contributions to a Roth IRA and each conversion has a separate 5-year period.

If a traditional IRA is converted to a Roth IRA, the amount converted is not eligible for recharacterization back to traditional IRA status. Prior to the enactment of TCJA 2017, traditional IRAs could be converted to Roth IRAs in one year, and, if the value of the account went down after the conversion, could be recharacterized back to a traditional IRA up to the due date of the tax return, plus extensions, to avoid income tax on the decline in value. After enactment of TCJA 2017, amounts converted from a traditional IRA to a Roth IRA are no longer eligible for recharacterization.

Distributions from a Roth IRA to an individual under age 59½ will be made in the following order:

1. the taxpayer's basis in Roth IRA contributions will be distributed first on a tax-free basis;
2. the taxpayer's basis in Roth IRA conversions will be distributed on a tax free basis, but will be subject to the ten percent penalty if the distribution is made within five years of the conversion; and
3. any remaining amounts will be considered a distribution of growth (income) from the Roth IRA and will be subject to both income tax and a ten percent penalty unless another exception to the ten percent penalty rule applies.

Example 4.20

In 2003, Enzo opened a Roth IRA account, and made annual contributions to the account until 2007, when his adjusted gross income exceeded the contribution limit for Roth IRAs. Enzo's total contributions to Roth IRAs over that period were $15,000. In 2019, Enzo's income was still too high to make a contribution to a Roth IRA, but he took advantage of the opportunity to convert his traditional IRAs to Roth IRAs, and included the converted amount, less his basis, in his income for 2019. The value of the Traditional IRA that Enzo converted was $40,000 of which $20,000 represented his basis (constituting after-tax contributions to the traditional IRA), requiring him to pay tax on the $20,000 difference. In 2021, Enzo needed some additional money to meet family obligations, and took a $20,000 distribution from his Roth IRA. The tax treatment of the distribution will be:

1. $15,000 will be considered a tax-free return of Enzo's Roth IRA contributions.
2. $5,000 will be considered a distribution from the basis of his converted Roth IRA. Since Enzo paid tax on the conversion, his basis in the converted Roth IRA is $40,000. Even though the converted Roth IRA had not been open for 5 years, Enzo is able to take his basis out without triggering an income tax, since the income tax was already paid.
3. Even though the $5,000 distribution from the basis of his converted Roth IRA is not subject to income tax, it will be subject to the 10% penalty, since Enzo took the distribution within 5 years of the conversion.

Enzo will, therefore, have a tax liability of $500 as a result of the distribution from the Roth IRA.

Educational Savings Bonds

Part or all of the interest income from the redemption of qualified U.S. savings bonds is excludable from gross income if the taxpayer pays for qualified higher educational expenses during the same year. The amount of interest that can be excluded is based on the following formula:

$$\frac{\text{Qualified Education Expenses}}{\text{Bond Redemption Proceeds}} \times \text{Interest Income} = \text{Excludable Interest}$$

To exclude interest from income, qualified savings bonds must meet the following requirements:

1. the bonds must be series EE bonds issued after December 31, 1989, or Series I bonds;
2. the bonds must be issued in the name of the taxpayer or the names of the taxpayer and the taxpayer's spouse; and
3. the bond owner(s) must be at least 24 years of age on the issue date of the bonds.

Qualified education expenses must be paid to an eligible institution. Qualified education expenses include tuition and fees paid for the taxpayer, spouse, or dependent, contributions to a qualified tuition program (discussion follows), or contributions to a Coverdell Education Savings Account (discussion follows). Qualified expenses do not include any expenses for room and board nor for courses related to sports, games, or hobbies that are not part of the student's degree or certificate program. Qualified expenses must be reduced by any scholarships or other tax-free sources of education funding and for expenses used to calculate either of the education tax credits discussed in Chapter 9.

Example 4.21

After 1989, Tatiana purchased series EE savings bonds for $2,500 at the age of 25. This year she redeemed the bonds for $5,000 and paid qualified higher educational expenses in the amount of $4,000 for her daughter. The $2,500 difference between the redemption proceeds of $5,000 and the cost of $2,500 would all be taxable as interest income this year if she had not paid for the qualified expenses during the year. Since she did pay for the education expenses, she is allowed to exclude $2,000 [($4,000/$5,000) x $2,500] of the interest income. She will be required to include only $500 of the interest in gross income. If she had paid $5,000 or more for qualified education expenses, she would have been able to exclude all of the interest income from the savings bonds.

The amount of interest that can be excluded from gross income may be reduced or completely eliminated if the taxpayer's modified adjusted gross income (MAGI) exceeds specified amounts.

Exhibit 4.11 | Phaseout Levels for Savings Bond Interest Exclusion

Filing Status	*2021*
Married Filing Jointly, Surviving Spouse	$124,800 - $154,800
All Other	$83,200 - $98,200

Qualified Tuition Programs/529 Plans

Qualified tuition programs, often called Section 529 plans, permit a taxpayer to save for post-secondary education of family members in a tax-favored manner. 529 plans come in two varieties: prepaid tuition programs and college savings plans. Prepaid tuition plans entitle a designated beneficiary (a student) to a waiver or a payment of qualified education expenses by the plan. No benefits or distributions are taxable unless the amounts distributed exceed the beneficiary's qualified education expenses. College savings plans allow taxpayers to earn income that will never be subject to income taxes if used to pay for future qualified education expenses for designated account beneficiaries.

Prepaid tuition plans allow parents to prepay future tuition at state educational institutions at today's rates. They are sometimes guaranteed by the sponsoring states. The states that sponsor prepaid tuition plans often allow the custodian of the account to transfer the value of a contract to an out-of-state or even a private school. Prepaid tuition plans can be sponsored by states, by a higher education institution, or by a group of such institutions.

College savings plans offer greater variety and flexibility than prepaid tuition plans, but they do not offer guarantees. To enjoy the tax benefits of a college savings plan, a donor (often a parent or grandparent) invests after-tax dollars in a college savings plan account for a family member (often the donor's child or grandchild) who is named as the account beneficiary. The donor selects from the available investments in the plan and the investment grows on a tax-deferred basis. When distributions are made by the donor to fund the beneficiary's education, each distribution consists of a nontaxable return of investment and income. The income portion of the distribution is excluded from the beneficiary's gross income if the entire distribution is less than or equal to the amount of qualified education expenses for the year. If the distribution exceeds the qualified education expenses for the year, the beneficiary (or account owner if funds are distributed to the account owner) will be required to include some of the distribution in gross income and will be required to pay a 10 percent penalty tax on the amount included in gross income unless one of several exceptions applies. In addition to this favorable treatment for federal income tax purposes, some states offer income tax breaks as well, often only for residents of the state.

Transfers to Section 529 plans are considered gifts for federal gift tax purposes. The federal gift tax exclusion of $15,000 (2021) per donee per year is allowed for a gift to a qualified tuition program. A special rule allows a taxpayer to transfer up to $75,000 (2021) to a qualified tuition program in one year without paying gift taxes if the taxpayer elects to treat the gift as an annual exclusion gift for the year of the gift and for each of the next four years.

The definition of qualified education expenses for a 529 plan is very broad. Eligible expenses include tuition, fees, books, supplies, and equipment required for enrollment at an eligible institution, the cost of computers, peripheral equipment, and internet services during the years the beneficiary is enrolled at an eligible institution, and the reasonable costs of room and board for a designated beneficiary who is at least a half-time student at an eligible institution. TCJA 2017 expanded the definition of higher education expenses to include up to $10,000 in expenses for tuition incurred during the taxable year in connection with enrollment or attendance at a public, private, or religious elementary or secondary school. The $10,000 limit for elementary or secondary school tuition applies on a per student, not on a per account, basis. For distributions made after December 31, 2018, the SECURE Act of 2019 further expanded qualified education expenses to include the costs of registered apprenticeship programs, and up to $10,000 (lifetime total per individual, not per 529 plan) of student loan payments of the designated beneficiary or a sibling of the designated beneficiary. Distributions made for qualified student loan payments for a sibling do not reduce the $10,000 limit for the beneficiary. When a distribution from a 529 plan is used to make a student loan payment, the interest portion of that payment will not qualify for the student loan interest deduction.

When determining the amount of qualified education expenses for the year, the total must be reduced for any scholarships, Pell Grants, other tax-free payments received as educational assistance, and for expenses used to generate either of the education tax credits discussed in Chapter 9.

College savings plans are operated primarily by states or agencies of state governments. Although each plan may have some unique provisions, all of the plans allow the donor to enjoy significant control over an account even though any gross income is normally taxed to the designated beneficiary rather than the donor. Each plan may specify limits on contributions, but the basic limitation is that contributions on behalf of a beneficiary cannot exceed the amount necessary to provide for the beneficiary's qualified education expenses. The donor may contribute a lump-sum payment or make regular periodic payments to the plan. Donors are not allowed to actively manage the investments in an account, but they are normally allowed to change to another available portfolio twice per year or move the account to another 529 plan once per year. The donor decides when distributions will be made and the donor is allowed to change the beneficiary to another family member at any time. Taxpayers may make contributions to both a qualified tuition program and a Coverdell Education Savings Account in the same year for the same beneficiary. Finally, and importantly, there are no income limitations on the right to contribute to a 529 plan.

Donors may make withdrawals from 529 plans for purposes other than paying qualified education expenses (those in excess of adjusted education expenses, tuition and related fees, minus costs covered by Pell Grants, tax-free scholarships, fellowships and tuition discounts). However, the donor must include any income distributed to them in gross income and must also pay a 10 percent penalty on any earnings included in gross income. Distributions may be made directly to an educational institution, or to the student. If excess distributions are paid from the 529 plan to a student, the student must include the excess distribution in his or her income The donor should be thoughtful as to who receives the funds. If the school is the payee, it could adversely affect financial aid from the institution.

TCJA 2017 permits amounts in 529 plans to be rolled over without penalty to an ABLE (Achieving a Better Life Experience) account, provided that the ABLE account is owned by the designated beneficiary of the 529 plan, or a member of the designated beneficiary's family. ABLE accounts are tax-advantaged savings accounts for individuals with disabilities. "Family," for this purpose, means a spouse, child or descendant of a child, brother, sister, stepbrother, stepsister, father, mother, ancestor of either a father or mother, stepfather, stepmother, niece, nephew, aunt, uncle, in-law, the spouse of any of these individuals and any first cousin of the designated beneficiary. Rolled-over amounts count towards the overall limitation on amounts that can be contributed to an ABLE account within a taxable year. The ability to roll over amounts from 529 plans to ABLE accounts is only available for tax years from 2018 to 2025.

Quick Quiz 4.7

1. Distributions from Roth IRAs are normally included in gross income.
   a. True
   b. False
2. For the purpose of redeeming a Series EE savings bond, qualified educational expenses do not include expenses for room and board.
   a. True
   b. False
3. 529 plans may be either prepaid tuition programs or college savings plans.
   a. True
   b. False
4. Up to $15,000 per year may be contributed to a Coverdell Education Savings Account.
   a. True
   b. False

False, True, True, False.

Coverdell Education Savings Account

As with a college savings plan, distributions from a **Coverdell Education Savings Account** are excluded from the gross income of the beneficiary if they are less than or equal to the qualified educational expenses of the beneficiary for the year. If the distributions for the year exceed the qualified educational expenses, some of the distribution will be recognized as gross income by the beneficiary.

In many other respects, a Coverdell Education Savings Account is similar to a college savings plan. Some of the features of a Coverdell Education Savings Account that are different from college savings plans are:

- The maximum contribution per year per beneficiary is $2,000.
- The definition of qualified educational expenses includes:
    1. qualified elementary and secondary school expenses and qualified higher education expenses
    2. certain special needs services
    3. contributions to a qualified tuition program (529 plan)
- Contributions must be completed by the time the beneficiary reaches age 18.
- Distributions from the account must be completed by the time the beneficiary reaches age 30.
- More investment options are available for a Coverdell Education Savings Account than for a Section 529 plan.
- The ability of the donor to contribute is phased out based on the modified adjusted gross income (MAGI) of the donor.

The following exhibit shows the beginning and ending phaseout thresholds for taxpayers contributing to a Coverdell Education Savings Account.

Exhibit 4.12 | Coverdell Education Savings Account Phaseouts (2021)*

Filing Status	*2021*
Married Filing Jointly, Surviving Spouse	$190,000 - $220,000
All Other	$95,000 - $110,000

** Does not adjust for inflation.*

When the taxpayer's MAGI exceeds the beginning of the phaseout range, the maximum allowable contribution is reduced ratably using the following formula:

$$\textbf{\$2,000(Maximum Contribution)} \times \frac{\textbf{AGI - Beginning Phaseout}}{\textbf{Ending Phaseout - Beginning Phaseout}} = \textbf{Reduction}$$

Example 4.22

Ziggy and his wife, Marley, would like to make a contribution to a Coverdell Education Savings Account for their son, Jethro. Ziggy and Marley are married filing jointly and their AGI is $200,500. Because they are in the phaseout range, Ziggy and Marley will not be able to make the maximum contribution of $2,000. Instead, their contribution limit will be reduced by $700. The contribution limit is therefore $1,300 ($2,000 - $700). The calculation of the reduction is below.

$$\$2,000 \times \left(\frac{\$200,500 - \$190,000}{\$220,000 - \$190,000}\right) = \$700 \text{ (Reduction)}$$

Improvements by Tenant to Landlord's Property

A lessee of real estate may build buildings on or make other improvements to the real property that is rented from the lessor. At the end of the lease term, the tenant gives up all rights to the leased buildings and other improvements. Therefore, the landlord or lessor may receive valuable property in the form of buildings or other improvements upon the termination of the lease. The landlord may exclude the value of these improvements from gross income. The reason that an improvement would not be taxable is that if there is any improvement of significance it will result in either higher rent or a higher sales price when the property is sold. Either way, the IRS will ultimately receive its share.

INCOME FROM PERSONAL ACTIVITIES

Personal Activity Items Included in Gross Income

Prizes and Awards

In most cases, prizes and awards received by a taxpayer must be included in gross income. Two exceptions to the general rule exist. If the prize, such as a Nobel Prize, is received and it is paid directly to a qualified charity or if the exclusion qualifies as an employee achievement award under IRC Section 74(c), the prize or award is excluded from gross income. In the first case, if at the request of the recipient, the prize is paid directly to the qualified charity, the recipient is allowed to exclude the prize from gross income if three requirements are met:

1. the prize or award must be given primarily in recognition of religious, charitable, scientific, educational, artistic, literary, or civic achievement;
2. the recipient must not apply for the award; and
3. the recipient must not be required to render substantial future services to receive the prize or award.

In the second exception, IRC Section 74(c) excludes from gross income the value of an employee achievement award received by the taxpayer, unless the cost to the employer exceeds the amount that can be deducted by the employer for the cost of the employee achievement award. Two limitations apply to the employer's deduction for the cost of an employee achievement award made to a particular employee:

1. awards to a single employee which are not qualified plan awards cannot exceed $400 during a year, and
2. the total awards to a single employee, under all plans, cannot exceed $1,600 for the year.

Qualified plan awards are employee achievement awards granted as part of an established written plan or program of the employer. The plan cannot discriminate in favor of highly compensated employees. TCJA 2017 clarified that awards must be in the form of tangible personal property. The exclusion does not apply for awards granted in the form of cash, cash equivalents, gift certificates (unless the certificate permits an employee to choose among pre-selected tangible items chosen by the employer), vacations, meals, lodging, tickets to artistic or sporting events, stocks, bonds, securities, or other forms of intangible property.

CASE STUDY 4.1

Prizes and Awards

Alejandra Conyers, Petitioner v. Commissioner of Internal Revenue, Respondent. Tax Court Docket No. 13969-18.

In 2016, Ms. Conyers was a high school senior in Columbia, TN and was awarded a car by a local dealership, Columbia Chrysler Dodge Jeep Ram, as a result of its annual "Strive to Drive" competition, an "academic initiative which encourages good grades and attendance" for local high school seniors. Students do not enter their names in the competition; rather, local high schools automatically enter students into the drawing. At the end of the school year, the dealership randomly chooses a name from amongst the qualifying entries. The winner gets a free car and insurance for one year.

The dealership drew Ms. Conyers' name for the grand prize in 2016. She won a 2016 Jeep Renegade. Ms. Conyers accepted the car and registered it in her name but did not include the fair market value of the Jeep in her gross income. On April 16, 2018, Ms. Conyers received a notice of deficiency from the IRS. The notice determined additional income of $23,780 and a deficiency of $3,267.20 The IRS determined this additional income from a Form 1099-MISC issued by the Columbia Chrysler Dodge Jeep Ram dealership that reported the value of the car as $23,780.

In July 2018, Ms. Conyers timely filed a petition with the Tax Court. She claimed the $23,780 should not be included in her taxable income and asserted the car was a gift under section 102 and thus should be excluded from taxable income. The Tax Court ruled that Ms. Conyers received a prize when the dealership gave her the car. The dealership gave her something of value as a reward for her goods grades and perfect attendance. Because Ms. Conyers received the car as a prize, she cannot exclude its value from income as a gift.

Ms. Conyers' receipt of the car does not fit under the section 74(b) exception because she accepted the car and transferred title to her name. The Tax Court acknowledged that the dealership awarded her the car in recognition of academic achievements; that Ms. Conyers did not enter herself into the contest, and that she had no service obligations. But Ms. Conyers did not ask the dealership to directly transfer the car to a governmental or charitable organization as required by section 74(b)(3). Because Ms. Conyers received a prize from the dealership and did not qualify for income exclusion under section 74, she was required to include the value of the car in her taxable income for 2016.

Alimony and Separate Maintenance Payments

Alimony sometimes referred to as separate maintenance payments) is intended to replace income lost by one spouse as a result of separation or divorce and is usually paid by the spouse with higher income. The payment of alimony may shift both income and tax liability from one former spouse to the other. It is often difficult to distinguish between alimony (payments incident to a divorce) and child support or property settlements. This distinction is significant because different tax treatments apply to these three types of payments.

Alimony Paid

> **Key Concepts**
>
> 1. Identify the types of income from personal activities that are included in gross income.
> 2. Describe the imputed interest rules for below-market loans.
> 3. Identify personal activity income that is excluded from gross income.

For divorce decrees entered on or before December 31, 2018, alimony payments are deducted from the income of the payor (as an adjustment to income, or above-the-line deduction), and included in the income of the former spouse receiving the payment (the payee). When treated in this manner, alimony receives pass-through tax treatment - the person who winds up with the cash has to pay the tax.

TCJA 2017 repealed the deduction by the payor for payment of alimony, and the inclusion in income by the payee for alimony payments received, for alimony decrees that are entered into after December 31, 2018. If alimony decrees entered into before January 1, 2019 are substantially modified and the modification specifically states that the rules set forth in TCJA 2017 apply, the income tax deduction for the payor and the income tax inclusion for the payee is also repealed.

After 2018, a financial professional may have some clients who follow the traditional alimony rules (deduction for the payor; inclusion for the payee), and others who are subject to the repeal of the traditional rules (no deduction for the payor; no inclusion for the payee). Those clients subject to the repeal of the rules have clear tax treatment - no deduction is permitted for the payor, and no inclusion is required for the payee. Clients who are not subject to the repeal of the traditional alimony rules under TCJA 2017 are subject to the tax treatment specified below.

To achieve pass-through tax treatment, the payments must actually constitute alimony. IRC Section 71(b) sets forth the requirements necessary to classify payments as alimony. These requirements include:

1. The payments must be in cash or a cash equivalent (such as a check or money order).
2. The payments must be required by a court decree.
3. The court decree must not specify that the payments are "not alimony."
4. The payments must cease at the death of the recipient.
5. The payments may not be disguised child support payments.
6. The former spouses may not be members of the same household.
7. The parties may not file a joint income tax return (married filing jointly).

Note that the word alimony need not appear in the written instrument for the payment to be alimony. Child support may or may not be called child support in the written instrument. If any amount in the written instrument will be reduced on the happening of a contingency related to a child, the amount is presumed to be child support.

Example 4.23

Under a provision of a divorce decree entered into before 2019, Hector is to pay his former spouse, Lydia, $5,000 per month. Lydia has custody of their only child, Tuco. When Tuco reaches age 18, the payments are to be reduced to $3,000 per month. The remaining $3,000 is to be paid to Lydia for as long as she lives or until she remarries. $2,000 of the $5,000 payment is child support because the payment is reduced when Tuco reaches age 18 (a contingency related to a child). The remaining $3,000 is alimony.

A property settlement involves the division of marital assets between the spouses. At times, it may appear that the payor of alimony is seeking to take tax deductions for a payment that is really part of a property settlement. If the amount of alimony paid is over $15,000 per year and the payments decrease significantly from year one to years two and three, a front-loading formula is used to determine the amount of excess alimony that must be recaptured. This recaptured amount must be added to the gross income of the payor and deducted from the gross income of the payee for the third year that such payments are made. The amount of alimony recaptured in Year 3 (R3) is equal to the amount of Year 2 (R2) recapture plus Year 1 (R1) recapture.

$$R3 = R2 + R1$$

The alimony recapture in Year 2 (R2) is calculated as follows:

$$R2 = P2 - (P3 + \$15{,}000)$$

The alimony recapture in Year 1 (R1) is calculated as follows:

$$R1 = P1 - \left(\frac{P2 - R2 + P3}{2} + \$15{,}000\right)$$

In the above calculations, P1 is the alimony payment in Year 1, P2 is the payment in Year 2 and P3 is the payment in Year 3.

Example 4.24

Homer pays alimony (not subject to the repeal of the traditional alimony rules specified in TCJA 2017) to his former spouse, Marge, in the following amounts: $120,000 in year 1; $30,000 in year 2; and $12,000 in year 3. Due to the significant decrease in the payments, it appears that part of the payment for the first and second years is actually a property settlement. In the third year, Homer will be required to include in gross income and Marge will be allowed to deduct $88,500 for excess alimony reported in years 1 and 2. "P" = payment in the calculations shown below.

$$R2 = P2 - (P3 + \$15{,}000)$$
$$R2 = \$30{,}000 - (\$12{,}000 + \$15{,}000)$$
$$R2 = \$3{,}000$$

$$R1 = P1 - \left(\frac{P2 - R2 + P3}{2} + \$15{,}000\right)$$

$$R1 = \$120{,}000 - \left(\frac{\$30{,}000 - \$3{,}000 + \$12{,}000}{2} + \$15{,}000\right)$$

$$R1 = \$120{,}000 - \$34{,}500$$

$$R1 = \$85{,}500$$

$$R3 = R2 + R1$$
$$R3 = \$3{,}000 + \$85{,}500$$
$$R3 = \$88{,}500$$

The amount of alimony recaptured in Year 3 may also be calculated by using the following formula if alimony payments decreased by more than $15,000 per year over the first three years. The formula is:

R3 = P1 + P2 - 2P3 - $37,500

where:
R3 = Recapture in year 3
P1 = Alimony payment in year 1
P2 = Alimony payment in year 2
P3 = Alimony payment in year 3

Please note that this shortcut formula will not work unless the alimony payments decline by $15,000 or more each year during the first three years of payments.

For instance, **Example 4.24** could have been calculated as follows:

R3 = $120,000 + $30,000 - (2 x $12,000) - $37,500 = $88,500

This formula was derived from the regulations and the $37,500 is a fixed amount to determine the total to recapture in Year 3. It is a shortcut when compared to the two previous formulas.

Income from Discharge of Indebtedness

When a taxpayer's debt is discharged or forgiven by a lender, the taxpayer must normally include the amount of the discharge of indebtedness in gross income. However, the amount of debt forgiven need not be included in gross income in certain circumstances, including the following:

- Certain forgiven student loans[6]
- Debts forgiven in a Title 11 bankruptcy
- Debts forgiven when a taxpayer is insolvent (up to the amount of a taxpayer's insolvency)
- Forgiveness of qualified farm indebtedness
- Forgiveness of qualified real property business indebtedness
- Forgiveness by a seller of a buyer's debt
- Forgiveness of debt as a gift
- Forgiveness of indebtedness for a qualified principal residence[7]

Although current gross income recognition is not required in these situations, the taxpayer is usually required to reduce specified "tax attributes" (such as net operating losses, the general business tax credit carryforward, the minimum tax credit, net capital losses, and the income tax basis of assets) in the amount of the debt forgiveness that is excluded from gross income.

Example 4.25

Karl owes $100,000 to Billy Bob Inc. Billy Bob Inc. agrees to discharge the debt in exchange for a cash value life insurance policy with a fair market value of $40,000. Karl has imputed income of $60,000 from the discharge of indebtedness. If Billy Bob Inc. holds the insurance policy until Karl's death and collects the proceeds, the death benefit

6. For loans forgiven in tax years 2021-2025, the American Rescue Plan Act of 2021 expanded the types of student qualifying for this exclusion to include any loans provided for postsecondary education expenses which are made, insured, or guaranteed by the U.S. government, a state government or an eligible education institution, as well as private education loans and loans from certain types of charitable organizations.
7. The Taxpayer Certainty and Disaster Tax Relief Act of 2020 extended this exclusion for qualified personal residence debts discharged after December 31, 2020 and before January 1, 2026, and reduced the maximum exclusion from $2 million to $750,000.

less Billy Bob Inc.'s basis in the policy will be subject to ordinary income tax, since Billy Bob Inc. acquired the life insurance policy in a transfer-for-valuable consideration.

Imputed Interest on Loans with Below-Market Interest Rates

When an interest-free or below-market rate loan is made to an individual, interest will be imputed to the lender for income tax purposes. The amount of **imputed interest** will equal the difference between the interest rate charged on the loan and the applicable federal rate, which is set by the IRS on a monthly basis. In addition to the phantom income from imputed interest that is included in the lender's gross income, the lender is deemed to make a gift of the imputed interest back to the borrower. If the imputed interest is less than $15,000 (2021), the gift may be shielded by the gift tax annual exclusion. This treatment must be applied to a variety of loans, including gift loans, compensation-related loans, and corporation to shareholder loans.

Example 4.26

Neil (lender) loans $600,000 to his daughter, Caroline (borrower) and does not charge any interest. The applicable federal rate is 5%. There are two consequences of this transaction:

First, the imputed interest rules will apply, and Neil will be deemed to receive interest from Caroline on the loan each year. The imputed interest payment of $30,000 (5% of $600,000) is phantom income for Neil and must be included on his income tax return. Caroline may be able to deduct the imputed interest payment if it is considered deductible interest (such as home mortgage or investment interest).

Second, because Caroline is not making the interest payment to Neil, Neil will be deemed to make a gift to Caroline of the imputed interest. Since Caroline has use of the property, the gift would be considered a present interest gift and would qualify for the gift tax annual exclusion of $15,000 (in 2021). Therefore, Neil will have made a taxable gift of $15,000 ($30,000 imputed interest, less the $15,000 annual exclusion) to Caroline, which will reduce his applicable credit for gift and estate tax purposes, or, if Neil has already fully used his applicable credit, will result in the payment of a gift tax on $15,000.

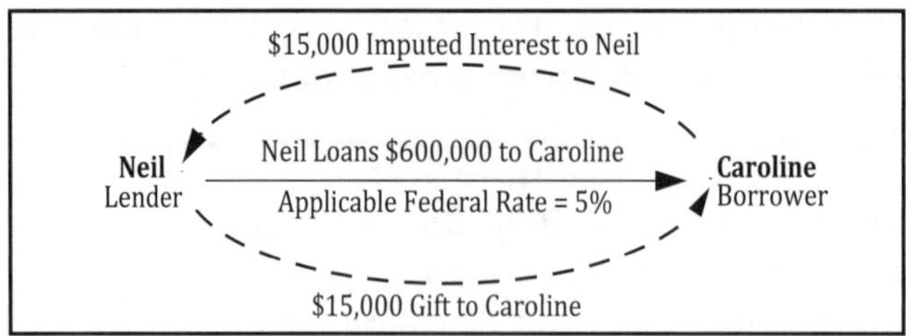

Example 4.27

Crandle Corporation (lender) loans $300,000 to an employee (borrower) and does not charge interest. The applicable federal rate is 5%. The employee is deemed to pay $15,000 (5% x $300,000) in annual interest to Crandle Corporation. This interest may be deductible by the employee if it otherwise meets the requirements for deductible interest. Crandle Corporation will report $15,000 of phantom interest income on it's tax return. In addition, Crandle Corporation will be deemed to pay compensation equal to the imputed interest amount to the employee. Crandle Corporation will be able to deduct this payment (provided that total compensation is deemed to be reasonable), and the employee will have to include the payment in his or her gross income as salary/wages (which is subject to both income and Social Security/Medicare taxes). When a below market loan is made from a corporation to an employee, both the corporation and the taxpayer will incur additional tax liability. Even though the corporation reports the imputed interest in income, and receives a deduction for the compensation payment made, it will have to pay ½ of the Social Security and Medicare taxes on the compensation payment. Even if the employee is able to deduct the imputed interest, he or she must pay Social Security tax on the deemed compensation payment received.

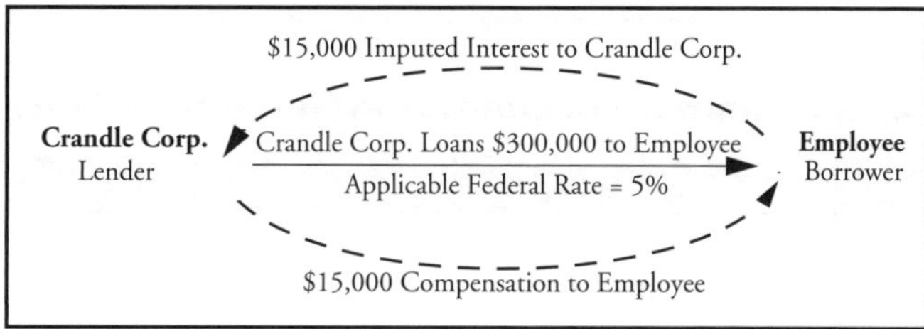

Example 4.28

Highland Corporation (a C Corporation) (lender) loans $300,000 to a shareholder (borrower) of Highland Corporation and doesn't charge any interest. The applicable federal rate is 5%. Highland Corporation is deemed to pay the shareholder dividends in the amount of $15,000. Highland Corporation is not allowed a tax deduction for the deemed dividend payment, but the shareholder must include the payment in gross income. The shareholder is then deemed to pay interest in the amount of $15,000 to Highland Corporation. Highland Corporation must include the deemed interest payment in gross income and the shareholder may be allowed to take a tax deduction for the deemed interest paid.

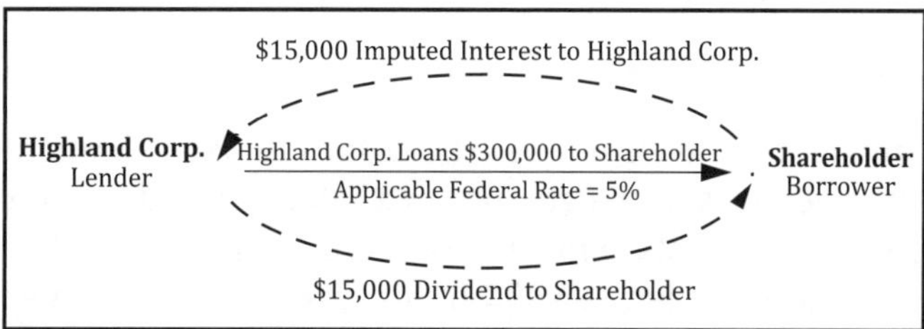

Limitations on Imputed Interest

While the imputed interest rules are designed to limit the planning opportunities associated with gift loans, compensation related loans, and shareholder loans, there are exceptions. First, there is a de minimis amount of $10,000 that applies. If the outstanding loan balance is $10,000 or less, no interest will be imputed on the loan.

A special exception applies to gift loans. The imputed interest rules will not apply if the total outstanding balance of the loan is $100,000 or less and the borrower has less than $1,000 in net investment income for the year. If the outstanding loan balance is $100,000 or less and the borrower's net investment income exceeds $1,000 per year, the interest imputed on the loan will be the lesser of:

- the borrower's net investment income, or
- the amount necessary to match the percentage interest paid on the loan with the applicable federal rate.

Example 4.29

Katy loans her daughter $30,000 for a down payment on a house. If her daughter has only $200 of investment income for the year and no investment deductions, no interest will be imputed. If the daughter has net investment income of $1,100 for the year, the amount of imputed interest will not exceed $1,100.

Exhibit 4.13 | Summary of Limitations on Imputed Interest

Loan Value	*Imputed Interest*
$0 ≤ $10,000	$0
$10,001 ≤ $100,000	The lesser of: • Net investment income, or • Interest calculated using AFR less interest calculated using stated rate of the loan If borrower's net investment income ≤ $1,000, $0 imputed interest.
> $100,000	Interest calculated using AFR less interest calculated using stated rate of the loan.

Tax Benefit Rule

If a taxpayer takes a tax deduction for an expenditure in one year and recovers (i.e., receives a refund) part or all of the expenditure in a later year, the recovered amount should be included in gross income in that later year. If he receives a limited or no tax benefit for his deduction, however, only part or possibly none of the recovered amount must be included in gross income.

Example 4.30

Perry itemizes his deductions in year one. His total itemized deductions, including a deduction for state income taxes in the amount of $3,000, exceed his standard deduction by $2,000. If he receives an $800 state income tax refund in year two for overpayment of his year one taxes, he must include the $800 in his gross income for year two. If Perry's itemized deductions for year one had exceeded his standard deduction by only $200, Perry would be required to include only $200 of the refund in his gross income because he received a tax benefit of only $200 for itemizing and deducting his state income taxes. If Perry had taken the standard deduction in year one, none of the refund would be includible in gross income because he received no tax benefit from deducting state income taxes in year one.

Other Income

Some other income items that must be included in gross income are:

- Gambling winnings
- Fees for jury duty
- Fees for being an executor, administrator, or personal representative of an estate (unless you are a professional)
- Income from a hobby

Personal Activity Items Excluded from Gross Income

Gifts

The value of property received as a gift is excludable from gross income by the recipient (the donee). This exclusion applies whether the gift is a birthday gift with a small value or a gift of a stock portfolio worth several million dollars. The value is irrelevant. The gift can be in cash, property, or even services. In order to qualify for the income tax exclusion, the transfer must be a gift, not a disguised form of compensation.

Income generated by gifted property must be included in gross income of the donee. A gift from an employer to an employee is not normally excludable from the employee's gross income, but there are exceptions (see the discussion of employee achievement awards and certain de minimis fringe benefits in Chapter 5).

Inheritances

The value of property received by bequest, devise, or inheritance is excludable from gross income by the recipient, regardless of the value of the inherited property.

Any income generated by inherited property must be included in the gross income of the heir. Generally, the receipt of property from a decedent's estate in lieu of compensation or fees receivable from the decedent or the decedent's estate must be included in gross income. The executor of an estate, however, may elect to waive the right to collect fees for the services performed, and therefore avoid a gross income inclusion.

Scholarships

The value of a scholarship or fellowship can be excluded from gross income by an individual who is a candidate for a degree at an eligible educational institution if the proceeds are used for qualified tuition and related expenses. An eligible educational institution must maintain a regular faculty and curriculum and have a regularly enrolled student body at the place where it carries on its educational activities. Most colleges and universities, as well as other schools, qualify as eligible educational institutions.

Qualified tuition and related expenses include required tuition and fees and course-related expenses such as required books, supplies, and equipment.

Scholarship proceeds used for purposes other than qualified tuition and related expenses must be included in gross income. Therefore, amounts used for room, board, research, travel, clerical help, equipment not required for the course of study, and other purposes are subject to income taxes. In addition, amounts received that represent payment for teaching, research, or other services by the student that are required as a condition for receiving the scholarship, fellowship, or tuition reduction must be included in gross income, even if used to pay tuition.

Qualified tuition reductions and need-based educational grants, such as Pell Grants, can also be excluded from gross income. A qualified tuition reduction allows the taxpayer (and sometimes the taxpayer's dependents) to study at an eligible educational institution for free or for a reduced rate of tuition.

Child Support and Property Settlements

When a divorce occurs, three different types of payments can be made by one former spouse to the other: alimony, child support, and property settlements. All of these topics were briefly covered under the discussion of alimony, above. As indicated in that discussion, for divorce decrees entered prior to December 31, 2018, alimony must be included in the gross income of the payee and is deductible (for AGI) by the payor. Child support payments are excluded from the gross income of the payee and are not deductible by the payor since these payments simply satisfy the legal obligation of the payor to support the children. Property settlements do not result in any immediate tax consequences for either party, but the recipient of a property settlement pursuant to a divorce has an income tax basis in the property equal to the basis of the property before the divorce. IRC Section 1041 requires all transfers between spouses during marriage or incident to a divorce to be treated as a gift for income tax purposes, resulting in a carryover basis (basis adjustments for losses, as discussed in the capital assets chapter, do not apply). Other tax attributes of the property may also influence the tax impact when the property is sold in subsequent years.

Quick Quiz 4.8

1. For divorce agreements entered into before 2019, alimony is deductible for AGI by the payor, but must be included in the gross income of the payee.
   a. True
   b. False
2. No interest is generally imputed on below-market rate loans of $10,000 or less.
   a. True
   b. False

True, True.

Example 4.31

Jack and Diane divorced in 2018. As part of a property settlement incident to that divorce, Diane received the personal residence that she had shared with Jack. The personal residence has a basis of $150,000 and a value of $250,000. Jack received a stock portfolio with a basis of $150,000 and a value of $250,000. Both properties had been owned for more than two years as joint tenants with rights of survivorship. At the time of the property settlement, neither party reports any gross income or deductions. If each property is sold shortly after the divorce for $250,000, Diane will be able to exclude all of the $100,000 gain on the sale of the principal residence under Section 121, but Jack will be required to recognize $100,000 of long-term capital gain on the sale of the stock. As this example illustrates, Jack and Diane receive the same pre-tax amount pursuant to the divorce decree. However, on an after-tax basis Jack received less than Diane. The tax consequences of property transfers should be considered when property settlement agreements pursuant to divorce are being negotiated.

Gain on the Sale of Residence (Section 121)

As explained in Chapter 13, a realized gain of up to $250,000 ($500,000 on a joint return) can be excluded from gross income on the sale of a residence that has been owned and occupied as the taxpayer's principal residence for two of the preceding five years.

Amounts Received Under Insurance Contracts for Certain Living Expenses

As a result of a fire, storm, or some other type of casualty, a taxpayer may be unable to occupy his residence. If these events seem imminent, government officials may not allow people to occupy their residences. Payments received from insurance companies to pay for additional temporary housing costs as a result of these events may be excluded from gross income.

Qualified Foster Care Payments

Certain qualified care payments received by a foster care provider can be excluded from gross income.

Destruction of Property

If compensatory damages are received for the destruction of the taxpayer's property, the recipient normally treats the payments received as payment received for the sale of the property. Therefore, a gain may need to be recognized. However, the gain may be deferred until a later date if the taxpayer meets the criteria for an involuntary conversion under IRC Section 1033 (discussed in more detail in Chapter 13).

Disaster Relief Payments

Qualified disaster relief payments received by a taxpayer can be excluded from gross income. A qualified disaster relief payment must be received for one of the following reasons:

- To pay for reasonable and necessary personal, family, living, or funeral expenses incurred as a result of a qualified disaster;
- To pay reasonable and necessary expenses to repair or rehabilitate a personal residence or its contents as a result of a qualified disaster;
- To promote the general welfare in connection with a qualified disaster and paid by a federal, state, or local government, or government agency; or
- It is paid by a person engaged in the furnishing or sale of transportation as a common carrier by reason of the death or personal physical injuries incurred as a result of a qualified disaster.

Quick Quiz 4.9

1. Income generated on inherited property is excluded from the gross income of the heir.
   a. True
   b. False
2. Punitive damages must be included in the gross income of the party that receives the damages.
   a. True
   b. False
3. Child support payments are included in the gross income of the payee.
   a. True
   b. False

False, True, False.

A qualified disaster includes a disaster resulting from a terrorist attack or military action, a Presidentially declared disaster, a disaster that results from an accident involving a common carrier, a disaster from any other event, which is determined by the Secretary of the Treasury to be of a catastrophic nature, or a disaster which is determined by an applicable federal, state, or local authority to warrant assistance from a federal, state, or local government, or government agency.

Most of the disaster relief payments received by taxpayers as a result of hurricanes Michael, Florence, Harvey, and Dorian would qualify for this exclusion. Under the tax benefit rule, however, disaster payments may be taxable if the recipient had previously deducted losses associated with the same disaster (at least to the extent of the deduction, according to the tax benefit rule).

Special Rules for Compensation for Injuries and Sickness

When one person (or entity) injures another person or damages another person's property, the injured party may seek and receive compensatory damages (compensation) for the losses and injuries suffered. The **compensatory damages** may be intended to compensate for damage to property, for recovery of expenses incurred, for income lost, or for personal injury. The injured person may also receive **punitive damages** (payments intended to punish the offending party). The tax treatment for the receipt of such payments, as addressed below, is the same whether the payments are received as a result of court action or not. The treatment is also the same whether the payment is received from the injuring party or from an insurance company.

Recovery of Expenses Incurred

Compensatory damage payments intended to reimburse the injured person for expenses incurred are excluded from gross income unless the taxpayer receives a tax benefit from the deduction of the expenses in a prior year.

Example 4.32

Katrina is injured by a hurricane. On this tax return, Katrina claimed and deducted medical expenses related to the injury. She was reimbursed for her losses in a later year by her health care insurer. She must include the reimbursement in gross income in the later year to the extent she received a tax benefit for the prior year's deduction.

Lost Income

If compensatory damage payments are received to compensate the injured person for lost income, the payments must normally be included in gross income because the income replaced would have been taxable if it had actually been earned. A major exception to this rule exists (see the discussion of physical personal injury below).

Example 4.33

A driver loses control of his truck and damages the front of Claudette's business building. She is required to shut down her business for two weeks while the building is repaired. She receives $12,000 from the driver's insurance company to compensate her for the lost income. Claudette must include the $12,000 in gross income.

Punitive Damages

Punitive damage payments to the injured party must be included in gross income.

Physical Personal Injury

If a person suffers physical personal injuries or physical sickness as a result of the actions of someone else, any compensatory damages received can be excluded from gross income. The compensatory payments are fully excludable even if the payments are intended to replace lost income. If punitive damages are received; however, they must be included in gross income.

Example 4.34

Antwon's car was hit by another driver who was intoxicated and Antwon was seriously injured. In addition to payment for the damage to his car, Antwon received compensatory payments of $30,000 to reimburse him for medical expenses, $2,000,000 for lost future income, and $100,000 for pain and suffering. He also received $300,000 in punitive damages. Antwon must include the punitive damages in gross income. The remaining $2,130,000 can be excluded from gross income.

Compensatory damages for physical injuries are intended to make the recipient "whole" and are therefore not taxable. In contrast, punitive damages are intended to "punish" the wrongdoer, and represent an accretion to wealth for the victim, and are fully taxable.

Other Personal Injuries

Compensatory damages can be received for personal injuries that are not due to physical injuries or sickness. Examples include damages for age discrimination and damage to the reputation of the injured party. Compensatory damage payments for non-physical personal injuries must be included in gross income.

Exhibit 4.14 | Inclusion/Exclusion of Compensation for Damages from Injuries

Injury Type	*Compensatory Damages*	*Punitive Damages*
Bodily injury	Excluded	Included
Personal injuries not including bodily injury	Included	Included
Lost income	Included	Included
Any other type of injury	Included	Included

CASE STUDY 4.2

DAMAGES FOR EMOTIONAL DISTRESS

Daniel R. Doyle and Lynn A. Doyle, Petitioners v. Commissioner of Internal Revenue, Respondent. T.C. Summary Opinion 2019-8 (February 6, 2019).

Daniel Doyle enjoyed a long and successful career in technology development, and in the mid-1990's began work on LCD touch screens, for which he owns multiple patents. In 2008 Doyle began a consulting business and was hired by Wacom, the company behind the pen-based technology that is used in Samsung smart phones. After the great recession in 2008, Doyle stepped away from his consulting business and became an employee of Wacom. Doyle was well compensated and used his contacts to bring in additional business. However, after seeing some high-profile cases in which several technology company executives were sentenced to prison time and large fines in an LCD price-fixing conspiracy, he feared that he may be in a similar situation and hired a lawyer. His lawyer advised him to either leave Wacom or take his concerns to the company's CEO. Doyle met with Wacom's CEO to raise his concerns and was fired a week later. Doyle, who described himself as "very, very healthy" prior to being fired from Wacom, began to experience insomnia, digestive problems, headaches, and neck, shoulder, and back pain as a result of the emotional distress he suffered from being fired by Wacom.

As a result, he threatened to sue Wacom for breach of contract, antitrust violations, civil conspiracy, failure to pay wages, and wrongful discharge. His complaint did not mention personal physical injury or emotional distress. Wacom and Doyle entered into a settlement agreement under which Wacom agreed to pay Doyle "$350,000 as settlement for his alleged unpaid wages" and "$250,000 as settlement for his alleged emotional distress damages." The payments were made in two installments, a partial payment in 2010 and the remainder in 2011. The payments for wages were issued on Form W-2 and the payments for emotional distress were issued on Form 1099-MISC for each year. Doyle, under the advice of his CPA, reported the $125,000 of Form 1099-MISC payments for emotional distress in 2010 as Schedule C income and then deducted $23,584 as an expense for attorney fees and deducted an additional $101,416 for "personal injury," netting out to $0. In 2011, the $125,000 payment for emotional distress was again reported on Schedule C and a deduction of $125,000 taken for "pain and suffering". In both years, the Doyle's paid no taxes on the payments received for emotional distress.

CASE STUDY 4.2 CONTINUED

While the tax court acknowledged that Section 104(a)(2) excludes from gross income "any damages (other than punitive damages) received (whether by suit or agreement and whether as lump sums or as periodic payments) on account of personal physical injuries or physical sickness," the Court also noted that, to fall within the exclusion, the taxpayer must show "a direct causal link between the damages and the personal injuries sustained." In Doyle's case the settlement agreement specifically states that the $250,000 payment is for his "alleged emotional distress." IRC Section 104(a) states that "emotional distress shall not be treated as a physical injury or physical sickness," and case law supports that symptoms such as headaches, stomach problems, and insomnia are symptoms resulting from emotional distress (Pettit v. Commissioner, T.C. Memo. 2008-87; H.R. Conf. Rept. No. 104-737).

Since the settlement agreement expressly stated that the payments were for emotional distress, the $125,000 per year payments made in 2010 and 2011 were not excludable and the deductions were properly denied. The 2010 deduction for attorney expenses was recharacterized as a miscellaneous itemized deduction, subject to the 2% floor, on Schedule A.

SUMMARY AND CONCLUSION

As you can see from our discussion so far, the definition of income is much broader than most people first anticipate. Income is any accretion to wealth that is realized, and unless an exclusion can be found in the IRC, the taxpayer must pay tax on that income. Thankfully, Congress has provided exclusions from the definition of gross income, many of which have been described in this chapter. While this chapter has focused on income and exclusions from personal and investment activities, Chapter 5 will continue our discussion of gross income and exclusions by reviewing the tax rules associated with income from employment.

KEY TERMS

Accrual Method - An accounting method under which income is reported when it is earned rather than when it is received in cash, and expenses are reported when they are incurred rather than when they are paid.

Alimony - A separate maintenance payment that is intended to replace income lost by one spouse as the result of a divorce and may be included in the gross income of the payee. Alimony will be included in income of the payee for divorce decrees signed prior to 2019.

Annuitized - When regular periodic payments on an annuity contract begin for life or for a specified period of time in excess of one year.

Bartering - An exchange of property and/or services for other property and/or services.

Cash Receipts and Disbursements Method - An accounting method under which income items are reported for the tax year in which they are received in cash and expenses are deducted in the year in which they are paid with cash.

Community Property - A regime in which married individuals own an equal, undivided interest in all of the property accumulated, using either spouse's earnings, during the marriage.

Compensatory Damages - Monetary award intended to compensate for damage to property, for recovery of expenses incurred, for income lost, or for personal injury.

Coverdell Education Savings Account - Plan similar to a college savings plan that allows taxpayers to contribute up to $2,000 per beneficiary per year to an account.

Dividend Income - A distribution of corporate earnings to shareholders, usually in cash.

Endowment Contract - A type of insurance contract that pays a specified death benefit to a beneficiary upon the death of the insured owner, but also pays a specified benefit (in lieu of the death benefit) to the owner of the policy if the insured person lives to a specified age or date.

Gross Income - All income from whatever source derived unless it is specifically excluded by some provision of the Internal Revenue Code.

Imputed Interest - A payment deemed to be made by the borrower to the lender when the interest rate on a loan is less than the applicable federal rate.

Interest Income - Gross income generated by a variety of debt instruments, including bank accounts, money market instruments, and bonds.

Municipal Bonds - Debt instruments issued by states and their political subdivisions, the interest income from which is generally excluded from federal gross income.

Original Issue Discount - The difference between the redemption price at maturity and the purchase price for debt instruments issued at a discount.

Punitive Damages - Payments intended to punish the offending party.

Qualified Dividends - Dividends subject to favorable tax rates.

Qualified Education Expenses - Educational expenses that receive favorable tax treatment. Such expenses may vary depending on the type of program or tax benefit.

Qualified Tuition Programs - Also known as 529 Plans, they permit taxpayers to save for elementary, secondary, and post-secondary education expenses of family members on a tax-favored basis through either a prepaid tuition program or a college savings plan.

DISCUSSION QUESTIONS

SOLUTIONS to the discussion questions can be found exclusively within the chapter. Once you have completed an initial reading of the chapter, go back and highlight the answers to these questions.

1. What is a barter transaction and how is income associated with such a transaction reported?
2. To whom is investment income normally taxable?
3. How do community property regimes affect the reporting of income?
4. What are the three types of relief provided by Section 66 to spouses?
5. Give several examples of income generated by investment activities that are included in gross income.
6. What types of investments generate interest income and how is interest income reported?
7. What are the requirements for a dividend to be a qualified dividend?
8. How is an annuity contract annuitized and how are the tax consequences of each annuity payment determined?
9. What are the tax consequences of taking distributions from an annuity without annuitizing?
10. What are the tax consequences of surrendering a life insurance contract?
11. Under what circumstances are life insurance proceeds excluded from gross income?
12. What are the requirements for a qualified savings bond?
13. Compare and contrast prepaid tuition programs and college savings plans.
14. Describe the characteristics of a Coverdell Educational Savings Account that make it different from a college savings plan.
15. Under what circumstances can a prize or award be excluded from the recipient's gross income?
16. What are the requirements for treating a payment made between divorcing spouses as alimony?
17. Summarize the limitations on imputed interest.
18. Compare and contrast compensatory damages and punitive damages.
19. Discuss the tax treatment of child support payments.
20. When is the amount of debt forgiven not included in gross income?

MULTIPLE CHOICE PROBLEMS

A sample of multiple choice problems is provided below. Additional multiple choice problems are available at money-education.com by accessing the Student Practice Portal.

1. Gianna has an account at First Maryland Bank. $10,000 of her account balance is invested in a certificate of deposit (CD). When must interest paid on the CD be included in Gianna's income?
   a. Interest on a CD is never included in income.
   b. The interest is included in Gianna's income when it is added to her account balance.
   c. The interest is included in Gianna's income when she withdraws it from the account.
   d. The interest is included in Gianna's income when she spends it.

2. Conway owns 100 shares of Darling Company stock. On December 29, 2021, Darling Company prepared the dividend checks for its shareholders. On December 31, 2021, Darling Company mailed dividend checks to all of its shareholders. Conway did not receive his dividend check until January 3, 2022. On what date must Conway include the dividends in his income?
   a. Conway is not required to include the dividends in his income.
   b. Conway must include the dividends in his income on December 29, 2021.
   c. Conway must include the dividends in his income on December 31, 2021.
   d. Conway must include the dividends in his income on January 3, 2022.

3. Jamie is awarded $55,000 in compensatory damages for harm to her reputation and $30,000 in compensatory damages for bodily injury. In addition, she is awarded $275,000 in punitive damages. How much of these awards must Jamie recognize in taxable income?
   a. $85,000.
   b. $275,000.
   c. $330,000.
   d. $360,000.

4. Brian had the following items of income this year.
   - Salary - $22,000
   - Child support received - $6,000
   - Alimony received - $10,000 (2006 divorce decree)
   - Personal injury award from an auto accident. He lost the use of his left hand and was awarded compensatory damages of $200,000. He also received $50,000 in punitive damages.

   Calculate Brian's gross income for the current year.
   a. $32,000.
   b. $38,000.
   c. $82,000.
   d. $288,000.

5. Which of the following must be included in Raven's income?
    1. Short-term capital gains of $10,000 from the sale of stock.
    2. Long-term capital gains of $80,000 from the sale of real property.
    3. Interest income from Raven's savings account.
    4. A gift from Raven's brother of $15,000.
        a. 1 and 2.
        b. 3 and 4.
        c. 1, 2, and 3.
        d. 1, 2, 3, and 4.

Additional multiple choice problems are available at *money-education.com* by accessing the Student Practice Portal. Access requires registration of the title using the unique code at the front of the book.

QUICK QUIZ EXPLANATIONS

Quick Quiz 4.1

1. True.
2. False. When barter transactions are made through a barter exchange, an organization established to facilitate the trading of goods and services, the transaction must be reported to the taxpayer and the Internal Revenue service by the barter exchange. Even if a barter transaction is not through a barter exchange, any gross income realized should be reported by the taxpayer on his tax return.

Quick Quiz 4.2

1. True.
2. False. There are three types of relief available under Section 66: separated spouse relief, innocent spouse relief, and equitable relief.

Quick Quiz 4.3

1. False. Interest income of $10 or more per year is normally reported to a taxpayer on Form 1099-INT by the payor of the interest, but the interest must be recognized by the taxpayer even when this form is not received or when the interest income is less than $10.
2. True.

Quick Quiz 4.4

1. False. In addition to being paid by a U.S. corporation (or qualified foreign corporation), qualified dividends must also meet the following requirements: (1) the dividend must not be a type of dividend excluded by law from the definition of a qualified dividend; and (2) the shareholder must meet a holding period requirement.
2. True.
3. True.

Quick Quiz 4.5

1. True.
2. True.

Quick Quiz 4.6

1. False. Municipal bonds are generally more appropriate for taxpayers with high marginal tax rates than for those with lower marginal rates.
2. True.

Quick Quiz 4.7

1. False. Distributions from Roth IRAs are normally excluded from gross income while distributions from traditional IRAs are normally included in gross income.
2. True.
3. True.
4. False. The maximum contribution per year per beneficiary to a Coverdell Education Savings Account is $2,000.

QUICK QUIZ EXPLANATIONS

Quick Quiz 4.8

1. True.
2. True.

Quick Quiz 4.9

1. False. Any income generated by inherited property must be included in the gross income of the heir.
2. True.
3. False. Child support payments are excluded from the gross income of the payee and are not deductible by the payor since these payments simply satisfy the legal obligation of the payor to support the children.

LEARNING OBJECTIVES

1. Identify the various sources of gross income from employment.*
2. Describe the tax consequences of self-employment income.*
3. Explain the difference between unemployment compensation and workers compensation, and the tax attributes of both forms of compensation.*
4. Explain the tax consequences of foreign earned income.*
5. Calculate the amount of income that can be excluded from a taxpayer's gross income under the foreign earned income exclusion.*
6. Explain why fringe benefits are valuable to employees.
7. Identify the nondiscrimination rules applicable to fringe benefits.
8. Identify the ways that an employer may provide health/medical benefits to employees as a fringe benefit.*
9. Define a highly compensated employee.
10. Define a key employee.
11. Describe how MSAs and HSAs are used in combination with health insurance benefits.*
12. Describe the taxation of contributions to, accumulations within, and distributions from HSAs and MSAs (including any penalty taxes that may apply).*
13. Identify the amount of group term life insurance that can be provided to employees as a fringe benefit.*
14. Explain the tax consequences of providing group term life insurance in excess of $50,000 to employees.*
15. Explain the tax consequences of employer provided disability insurance.*
16. Describe the purpose of, and the rules associated with cafeteria plans.*
17. Explain when employee death benefits can be excluded from income.*
18. Identify the advantages and disadvantages of FSAs.*
19. Explain the tax consequences of employer-provided long-term care insurance.*
20. Explain the differences between FSAs and HSAs/MSAs, and describe the planning opportunities that these techniques make available to taxpayers.*
21. Describe the rules regarding the provision of meals and lodging as a fringe benefit.*
22. Define no additional cost services, and explain the tax consequences of these services to taxpayers.*
23. Identify the requirements for qualified employee discounts.*
24. Describe working condition fringe benefits.*
25. Identify various types of de minimis fringe benefits.*
26. Explain the requirements for qualified transportation fringe benefits.
27. Describe the tax treatment of qualified moving expense reimbursements.*
28. Describe the tax consequences of qualified retirement planning services.*
29. Identify the limitations imposed on educational assistance programs.*

**Ties to CFP Certification Learning Objectives*

LEARNING OBJECTIVES

30. Describe the limitations associated with dependent care assistance, and the tax advantages available to the client.*
31. Describe the tax benefits associated with adoption assistance programs.*
32. Describe the tax advantages associated with employer-sponsored retirement plans.*
33. Identify the tax consequences of employer-sponsored retirement plan contributions and distributions.
34. Describe the tax consequences associated with nonqualified stock options (NQSOs).*
35. Describe the tax consequences of incentive stock options (ISOs).*
36. Explain the taxation of unemployment compensation.*
37. Explain how Social Security benefits may be taxable.*
38. List the items used to modify AGI when determining the portion of Social Security benefits subject to tax.*

**Ties to CFP Certification Learning Objectives*

INTRODUCTION

The primary source of income for most people is derived from employment, where an individual provides services to an employer in exchange for **compensation** in the form of salary or wages and various fringe benefits. Compensation received by an employee as salary or wages is normally includible in gross income. Fringe benefits are compensation for services, and therefore, meet the definition of income. They must be included in gross income unless they are excluded by some provision of the Internal Revenue Code (IRC). Fortunately for employees, many employer-provided fringe benefits are excluded from gross income if certain requirements are met.

Key Concepts

1. Identify the various sources of gross income from employment.
2. Describe the tax consequences of self-employment income.
3. Explain the tax consequences of foreign-earned income.

Some individuals are compensated for their services through self-employment rather than through working for a business owned by someone else. Although the self-employed may enjoy more freedom to control their work environment and work activities, they are required to pay taxes on their net earnings, bear the burden of various payroll taxes, and have more difficulty enjoying tax-free treatment of some fringe benefits when compared to traditional employees.

This chapter discusses gross income and exclusions related to employment and self-employment.

GROSS INCOME RELATED TO EMPLOYMENT

Compensation received for services must be included in gross income, regardless of the type of compensation received. Therefore, salary, wages, commissions, fees, tips, or any other type of compensation earned by an employee is subject to income taxation.

Although compensation is normally received in cash, it may be received in other forms. As discussed in Chapter 4, compensation may be received in the form of cash or a cash equivalent, including non-cash property, services, and benefits. If non-cash compensation is a substitute for salary, wages, or self-employment income, it must nevertheless be included in gross income unless it is specifically excluded by the IRC.

Gross income received for services provided to an employer is normally taxable to the person who performs the services. This rule is an application of the fruit and the tree doctrine. For example, income earned by a child actor is taxable to the child rather than to the parent of the child. Gross income cannot normally be assigned by the person who earns it to anyone else. In community property states, however, half of the income earned (wages, salaries, etc.) by a spouse is deemed to be earned by each spouse. See Chapter 4 for a discussion of community-property laws.

Gross income from compensation and taxable employee fringe benefits are treated as ordinary income and must be reported to the employee by the employer on Form W-2.

Exhibit 5.1 | Form W-2

22222 VOID ☐ | a Employee's social security number | For Official Use Only ▶ OMB No. 1545-0008

b Employer identification number (EIN)	1 Wages, tips, other compensation	2 Federal income tax withheld
c Employer's name, address, and ZIP code	3 Social security wages	4 Social security tax withheld
	5 Medicare wages and tips	6 Medicare tax withheld
	7 Social security tips	8 Allocated tips
d Control number	9	10 Dependent care benefits
e Employee's first name and initial / Last name / Suff.	11 Nonqualified plans	12a See instructions for box 12 Code
	13 Statutory employee ☐ Retirement plan ☐ Third-party sick pay ☐	12b Code
	14 Other	12c Code
		12d Code
f Employee's address and ZIP code		

15 State Employer's state ID number	16 State wages, tips, etc.	17 State income tax	18 Local wages, tips, etc.	19 Local income tax	20 Locality name

Form **W-2** **Wage and Tax Statement** 2020

Department of the Treasury—Internal Revenue Service

For Privacy Act and Paperwork Reduction Act Notice, see the separate instructions.

Cat. No. 10134D

Copy A—For Social Security Administration. Send this entire page with Form W-3 to the Social Security Administration; photocopies are **not** acceptable.

Do Not Cut, Fold, or Staple Forms on This Page

Income generated by an employer as a result of the services of an employee is included in the gross income of the employer. Only the compensation paid by the employer to the employee (or the employee's designee) must be included in the employee's gross income.

Income generated through self-employment in a sole proprietorship or in certain other forms of business is normally taxable to the self-employed person, but in some cases, the income is taxable to the business itself. The taxation of business income is discussed more fully in Chapter 16.

Compensation received by an independent contractor (a self-employed person) must normally be reported to that contractor as nonemployee compensation on Form 1099-NEC by a business that receives services from the independent contractor. All income (or revenue) received by an independent contractor, including revenue not reported on Form 1099-NEC must normally be reported as income on Schedule C (Profit or Loss from Business) if the business is conducted in the form of a sole proprietorship. The income and expenses of a self-employed person running an agricultural business are reported on Schedule F (Profit and Loss from Farming). Statutory employees (independent contractors classified as employees by statute) have their compensation reported to them on Form W-2 even though they report their income to the government on Schedule C.

Exhibit 5.2 | Form 1099-NEC

7171 ☐ VOID ☐ CORRECTED

PAYER'S name, street address, city or town, state or province, country, ZIP or foreign postal code, and telephone no.			OMB No. 1545-0116 **2020** Form **1099-NEC**		**Nonemployee Compensation**
		1 Nonemployee compensation $			**Copy A** **For Internal Revenue Service Center** **File with Form 1096.**
PAYER'S TIN	RECIPIENT'S TIN	2			
RECIPIENT'S name		3			For Privacy Act and Paperwork Reduction Act Notice, see the **2020 General Instructions for Certain Information Returns.**
Street address (including apt. no.)		4 Federal income tax withheld $			
City or town, state or province, country, and ZIP or foreign postal code					
	FATCA filing requirement ☐				
Account number (see instructions)	2nd TIN not. ☐	5 State tax withheld $ $	6 State/Payer's state no.	7 State income $ $	

Form **1099-NEC** Cat. No. 72590N www.irs.gov/Form1099NEC Department of the Treasury - Internal Revenue Service

Do Not Cut or Separate Forms on This Page — Do Not Cut or Separate Forms on This Page

A limited liability company (LLC) generally has more than one owner and is generally classified as a partnership, but most states permit an LLC to have just one owner. A single owner LLC will typically report income and deductions of the LLC on Schedule C in the same manner as a sole proprietor (the LLC is a disregarded entity for tax purposes). An LLC owner could, however, elect S or C Corp status for income tax purposes, although such an election is unusual and is often disadvantageous from an income tax standpoint. An LLC with multiple members usually files as a partnership.

A partnership files a partnership tax return (Form 1065). A partner receives a Schedule K-1 from the partnership each year, which allocates the distributive share of the partnership's income, deductions, tax credits and QBI or Section 199A deduction amount to the partners. Some of a general partner's income from a partnership may be classified as self-employment income (See line 14 of the Schedule K-1). General partnerships, limited partnerships, limited liability companies, and limited liability partnerships are normally taxed as partnerships for federal income tax purposes. If an LLC is treated as a partnership for income tax purposes, any active member (sometimes referred to as a managing member) is taxed as a general partner.

The owner of a proprietorship is not usually considered to be an employee of the entity for fringe benefit purposes. A partner in an entity taxed as a partnership is treated as an employee for some fringe benefit purposes, but not for others. A more than two percent owner of an S corporation is normally not considered to be an employee of the S corporation for fringe benefit purposes. Some of the special tax rules that apply to business owners will be addressed in later chapters.

While unemployment compensation, as the name indicates, is not employment related income, it is meant to replace employment income when a taxpayer is out of work. Unlike workers' compensation, which is designed to compensate a worker for physical injuries received at work (and is therefore excluded from the definition of income), unemployment income is included in gross income.[1] If, however, an employee made after-tax contributions to a government or private unemployment compensation fund, the benefits would be excluded from income. This treatment is consistent with the tax treatment of private disability insurance benefits, which are included in income if premiums are paid by the employee with pre-tax dollars or if premiums are paid by the employer, but are excluded from income if the premium payments are made with after-tax dollars by the employee.

Foreign Earned Income

Since the United States taxes its citizens on their global income, citizens and certain other residents of the United States who work in foreign countries may be subject to income tax on both their U.S. and foreign source income. In certain circumstances, taxpayers may be able to exclude some or all of their income earned in foreign countries from U.S. taxation under the foreign earned income exclusion. They may also be able to exclude a portion of their housing costs incurred in foreign countries.

Income earned by employees of the U.S. government and its agencies while they serve in foreign countries does not qualify for the foreign earned income exclusion. Typically, government employees are not subject to income tax in foreign countries, and therefore must pay U.S. income tax on their earnings.

For 2021, a qualifying citizen or resident of the United States may exclude from U.S. gross income up to $108,700 (less any foreign housing exclusion taken for the year) of income earned from personal services performed in foreign countries. To exclude **foreign earned income**, a qualified individual must have a tax home in a foreign country and must either:

1. qualify as a bona fide resident of a foreign country or countries for an uninterrupted period that includes an entire taxable year (bona fide resident test), or
2. qualify by being present in a foreign country or countries for at least 330 full days during any period of twelve consecutive months (physical presence test).

1. The American Rescue Plan Act (ARPA) of 2021 excludes from income up to $10,200 (per spouse if filing jointly) of unemployment income received during 2020 if the taxpayer's adjusted gross income.is less than $150,000.

A taxpayer's tax home consists of the general area of the taxpayer's business (for self-employed persons) or employment, regardless of the location of the taxpayer's home or principal residence. The tax home of an employee is the place where the employee is permanently or indefinitely engaged to work. An employee who is "temporarily" assigned to work in a foreign country would not be eligible for the foreign earned income exclusion.

To be considered a bona fide resident of a foreign country (or countries), an individual must intend to work there for an indefinite or extended period of time and must establish permanent quarters in the foreign country for himself and his family. The individual's intentions, purpose for travel, and length of stay in the foreign country are important factors in determining bona fide residency. The Internal Revenue Service must determine whether a person meets the bona fide residence test based on information submitted on Form 2555.

Treaties and agreements with specific foreign countries may impact a taxpayer's ability to be considered a bona fide resident of that country. Occasional trips back to the United States for vacation or other purposes will not prevent a taxpayer from meeting the bona fide resident test. If a bona fide resident of a foreign country fails to meet the full tax year requirement only because he must leave the country due to war or civil unrest, he will normally be deemed to have met the full tax year requirement. Once an individual has met the **bona fide resident test**, the taxpayer is considered to be a bona fide resident until he abandons his residence in that country, even for a year in which he is not a bona fide resident for the entire tax year.

Quick Quiz 5.1

1. A person may assign the gross income that he earns to any other person for tax purposes.
   a. True
   b. False
2. In 2021, a qualifying citizen or resident of the U.S. may exclude up to $108,700 of foreign-earned income from his U.S. gross income.
   a. True
   b. False

False, True.

In order to meet the **physical presence test**, an individual must be present in a foreign country or countries for at least 330 full days during any period of 12 consecutive months. The twelve month period can begin on any day of any month. The 330 days do not have to be consecutive and days spent in foreign countries for any purpose can be included. A person who is present in foreign countries for only 329 days completely fails the test unless the early departure is due to war or civil unrest.

Example 5.1

Dana is a U.S. citizen who works for a U.S. corporation in London. During the current tax year, she earned $70,000 and was present in London for the entire year. Even though the income was paid by a U.S. corporation, her income is considered to be foreign earned income and can be fully excluded from her U.S. gross income.

A person who meets the physical presence test, but is not present in foreign countries during every day of the year, is allowed to exclude only a prorated portion of the maximum exclusion amount.

Example 5.2

Connor lives and works in France during 340 days out of the 365 days during the 2021 calendar year. He meets the physical presence test. The maximum amount of foreign earned income that Connor can exclude from his gross income is $101,254.79 [(340/365) x $108,700].

CASE STUDY 5.1

Unemployment Compensation

Lisa A. Ferreira, Petitioners v. Commissioner of Internal Revenue, Respondent. T.C. Summary Opinion 2001-167 (October 17, 2001).

Respondent determined a deficiency of $720 in Lisa's federal income tax for 1997. The sole issue for decision is whether $4,809 of unemployment compensation Lisa received during 1997 is includible in her gross income. Lisa timely filed her 1997 federal income tax return upon which she reported wages of $11,370 and Social Security benefits in the amount of $4,809. During 1997 Lisa received $4,809 of unemployment compensation from the Commonwealth of Massachusetts. Lisa, however, reported the unemployment compensation on her 1997 Form 1040, U.S. Individual Income Tax Return, as Social Security benefits. She called the Internal Revenue Service (IRS) to check on the status of her $486 refund. The IRS employee informed her that she made a mistake on her return and that the Social Security benefits, as reported, were not taxable. Lisa then explained the amounts and sources of her income for 1997, including the unemployment compensation. The IRS employee said that the refund was a final determination and it was hers to enjoy. After the tax refund of $1,206 was deposited in Lisa's bank account, she did not spend the money for 7 or 8 months because she feared the IRS would ask for the money to be returned. After IRS employees repeatedly confirmed that the refund belonged to her, she spent the money only when she encountered severe financial difficulties. Two years later, the IRS determined a deficiency of $720 in Lisa's 1997 federal income tax. The deficiency is attributable solely to Lisa's mistake in reporting unemployment compensation of $4,809 as Social Security benefits.

Lisa testified that she received unemployment compensation and that she was aware it was includible in income when she filed her 1997 income tax return. Lisa, however, claims that she relied on erroneous tax advice she received from IRS employees. In sum, Lisa argues that the deficiency notice issued by the IRS in this case is invalid because she made a good faith effort to correctly report her income on her federal income tax return for 1997 and relied on the advice of IRS employees. This Court has held that the authoritative sources of federal tax law are statutes, regulations, and published court opinions, not informal IRS sources such as telephone conversations with IRS employees.While the court was sympathetic to Lisa's plight, the record indicates that she was aware of potential problems with her tax return, so much so that she was hesitant to rely on the assurances of IRS employees the first few times she called. Accordingly, the court concluded that petitioner failed to report $4,809 of unemployment compensation that should have been included in her gross income for 1997.

Exhibit 5.3 | Form 2555

Form **2555**

Department of the Treasury
Internal Revenue Service

Foreign Earned Income

▶ Attach to Form 1040 or 1040-SR.
▶ Go to *www.irs.gov/Form2555* for instructions and the latest information.

OMB No. 1545-0074
2020
Attachment Sequence No. **34**

For Use by U.S. Citizens and Resident Aliens Only

Name shown on Form 1040 or 1040-SR | **Your social security number**

Part I General Information

1 Your foreign address (including country) | 2 Your occupation

3 Employer's name ▶

4a Employer's U.S. address ▶

b Employer's foreign address ▶

5 Employer is (check any that apply): **a** ☐ A foreign entity **b** ☐ A U.S. company **c** ☐ Self **d** ☐ A foreign affiliate of a U.S. company **e** ☐ Other (specify) ▶

6a If you previously filed Form 2555 or Form 2555-EZ, enter the last year you filed the form. ▶

b If you didn't previously file Form 2555 or Form 2555-EZ to claim either of the exclusions, check here ▶ ☐ and go to line 7.

c Have you ever revoked either of the exclusions? . . . ☐ **Yes** ☐ **No**

d If you answered "Yes," enter the type of exclusion and the tax year for which the revocation was effective. ▶

7 Of what country are you a citizen/national? ▶

8a Did you maintain a separate foreign residence for your family because of adverse living conditions at your tax home? See ***Second foreign household*** in the instructions . . . ☐ **Yes** ☐ **No**

b If "Yes," enter city and country of the separate foreign residence. Also, enter the number of days during your tax year that you maintained a second household at that address. ▶

9 List your tax home(s) during your tax year and date(s) established. ▶

Next, complete either Part II or Part III. If an item doesn't apply, enter "N/A." If you don't give the information asked for, any exclusion or deduction you claim may be disallowed.

Part II Taxpayers Qualifying Under Bona Fide Residence Test

Note: Only U.S. citizens and resident aliens who are citizens or nationals of U.S. treaty countries can use this test. See instructions.

10 Date bona fide residence began ▶ ______, and ended ▶

11 Kind of living quarters in foreign country ▶ **a** ☐ Purchased house **b** ☐ Rented house or apartment **c** ☐ Rented room **d** ☐ Quarters furnished by employer

12a Did any of your family live with you abroad during any part of the tax year? . . . ☐ **Yes** ☐ **No**

b If "Yes," who and for what period? ▶

13a Have you submitted a statement to the authorities of the foreign country where you claim bona fide residence that you aren't a resident of that country? See instructions . . . ☐ **Yes** ☐ **No**

b Are you required to pay income tax to the country where you claim bona fide residence? See instructions . ☐ **Yes** ☐ **No**

If you answered "Yes" to 13a and "No" to 13b, you don't qualify as a bona fide resident. Don't complete the rest of this part.

14 If you were present in the United States or its possessions during the tax year, complete columns **(a)–(d)** below. **Don't** include the income from column **(d)** in Part IV, but report it on Form 1040 or 1040-SR.

(a) Date arrived in U.S.	**(b)** Date left U.S.	**(c)** Number of days in U.S. on business	**(d)** Income earned in U.S. on business (attach computation)	**(a)** Date arrived in U.S.	**(b)** Date left U.S.	**(c)** Number of days in U.S. on business	**(d)** Income earned in U.S. on business (attach computation)

15a List any contractual terms or other conditions relating to the length of your employment abroad. ▶

b Enter the type of visa under which you entered the foreign country. ▶

c Did your visa limit the length of your stay or employment in a foreign country? If "Yes," attach explanation . ☐ **Yes** ☐ **No**

d Did you maintain a home in the United States while living abroad? . . . ☐ **Yes** ☐ **No**

e If "Yes," enter address of your home, whether it was rented, the names of the occupants, and their relationship to you. ▶

For Paperwork Reduction Act Notice, see the Instructions for Forms 1040 and 1040-SR. Cat. No. 11900P Form **2555** (2020)

Page 1 of 3. See www.irs.gov/Forms-&-Pubs for the complete form.

When a taxpayer qualifies for the exclusion for only part of a tax year, the maximum amount that can be excluded is determined using the following formula:

$$\frac{\textbf{Qualifying Days in the Tax Year}}{\textbf{Total Days in Tax Year}} \times \textbf{Maximum Annual Exclusion Amount} = \textbf{Exclusion}$$

Example 5.3

Aleisha earned $40,000 from her employment in Singapore during 2021. She met the physical presence test during a period beginning in 2020 and ending in 2021. She lived and worked in Singapore for 80 days during 2021 and has not returned to the United States since she first arrived in Singapore in 2020. She will be allowed to exclude a maximum of $23,824.66 [(80/365) x $108,700] of foreign earned income for 2021.

An exclusion for foreign housing costs is available to employees for housing costs considered to be paid by an employer. The amount of the exclusion is limited to the total housing expenses of the employee's family less a base housing amount (16 percent of the maximum annual exclusion). Any housing amount excluded cannot exceed 30 percent of the maximum foreign earned income exclusion amount for the year and it reduces the maximum amount available for the foreign earned income exclusion. Therefore, the housing exclusion must be calculated before the foreign earned income exclusion.

An eligible taxpayer must elect (choose) to use the foreign earned income exclusion. Once the election is made, it remains in effect until it is revoked. If the election is made but foreign earned income exceeds the maximum exclusion amount or if the election is not made, the taxpayer may take a foreign tax credit (Chapter 9) for foreign taxes paid on foreign source income not excluded from gross income. The most beneficial tax treatment is the exclusion of foreign earned income.

Exhibit 5.4 | Foreign Income Options for U.S. Taxation Purposes

Options	*Foreign Earned Income Exclusion*	*Tax Credit for Foreign Taxes Paid*	*Deduction for Foreign Taxes Paid (for tax years before 2018 and after 2025)**
Benefit	Taxpayer can exclude up to $108,700 for 2021 of foreign earned income from gross income.	Taxpayer can claim a credit for some or all of the taxes paid to the foreign country, including taxes on foreign earned income that *exceeds* the amount ($108,700 for 2021) of foreign earned income exclusion taken.	Taxpayer's foreign taxes paid may be deducted as an itemized deduction on Schedule A to reduce adjusted gross income.

** TCJA 2017 suspended deductibility of foreign property taxes as itemized deductions for tax years 2018-2025.*

CASE STUDY 5.2

Foreign Income Exclusion

Philippe Antoine Brunet, Petitioners v. Commissioner of Internal Revenue, Respondent. T.C. Summary Opinion 2008-96 (August 5, 2008).

Philippe Antoine Brunet, an American Airlines pilot, excluded purported foreign earned income under Section 9111 during 2002, 2003, and 2004. The IRS disallowed the foreign earned income exclusion and determined a $15,863 deficiency for 2002, a $10,074 deficiency for 2003, and a $24,912 deficiency for 2004. Philippe began working for American Airlines in 1989. American Airlines assigned Philippe to base airports in the United States during the years at issue. Philippe was based at LaGuardia Airport in Queens, New York, in 2002, Miami International Airport in Miami, Florida in 2003, and at LaGuardia Airport in 2004. When Philippe's flight schedule prevented him from returning to his base airport, American Airlines paid him Time Away From Base compensation. Philippe is a naturalized United States citizen. He maintained a residence in St. Martin, French West Indies, from at least June 1999 to July 2003, and he has maintained a residence in Pau, France, since August 2003. Philippe claimed foreign earned income exclusions of $88,0402 in 2002, $80,000 in 2003 and $80,000 in 2004. Philippe claimed he resided in the French West Indies on the return for 2002 and in France on the returns for 2003 and 2004. A taxpayer's tax home is generally the vicinity of his or her employment, rather than the location of the taxpayer's personal residence. The place of employment for an airplane pilot has been interpreted as the employee's base airport. Because Philippe's place of employment was in the United States during the years at issue, his tax home was in the United States. Accordingly, he is not a qualified individual for purposes of the foreign earned income exclusion. Philippe is not eligible for the exclusion because he fails the tax home requirement.

MAJOR EMPLOYER-PROVIDED FRINGE BENEFITS

Introduction to Fringe Benefits

When an employee provides services to an employer in return for compensation, the employee often receives **fringe benefits** in addition to wages or salary. Most employees value these fringe benefits, especially insurance benefits such as medical, life, and disability insurance, and consider them to be part of their overall compensation package. With a large number of employees, employers may be able to negotiate lower group insurance rates and better coverage than an individual employee would be able to negotiate in the open market. Thus, where insurance coverage is desired by a large number of employees, the employer may adopt an insurance plan as part of an overall compensation package. Providing insurance and other fringe benefits may make employers more attractive to potential employees while providing valuable tax-advantaged benefits to employees and their family members.

Key Concepts

1. Explain why fringe benefits are valuable to employees.
2. Identify the nondiscrimination rules applicable to fringe benefits.
3. Identify the ways that an employer may provide health/medical benefits to employees as a fringe benefit.

Taxation of Fringe Benefits

Salary and wages paid to employees are income tax deductible by the employer and must be included in the gross income of the employees. Employers are also allowed to take income tax deductions for fringe benefits provided to employees. As specified in IRC Section 61, all fringe benefits provided to an employee must be included in gross income as wages unless a specific provision of the IRC excludes the benefit from taxation or unless the employee pays the fair value for the fringe benefit. Although a fringe benefit may not be specifically excluded, the value of the fringe benefit is not taxable if it is paid for by the employee.

The general rules of income taxation discussed in Chapter 1 indicate that when someone (such as the employer) claims an income tax deduction, there must be a corresponding income inclusion somewhere in the tax system.

Fortunately for employees, Congress has chosen to promote certain fringe benefits by allowing employers to deduct the cost of the benefits while allowing employees to exclude the value of the benefits from gross income. Through this favorable tax treatment for selected fringe benefits, Congress seeks to promote a variety of social, economic, health, fitness, child welfare, educational, and other purposes. For example, if employers provide medical insurance for employees, the citizens of the United States may enjoy better health care and the government may have less of a financial burden to provide health care to its citizenry. By allowing favorable income tax treatment to employees, the government is foregoing tax revenues and is indirectly funding part of the cost of employer-provided medical insurance.

The employer reports taxable fringe benefits as compensation on each employee's Form W-2. Taxable fringe benefits are also subject to Social Security, Medicare, and federal unemployment taxes. Excludable fringe benefits are not reported as taxable compensation on an employee's Form W-2 nor are they subject to payroll taxes. In order to receive favorable income tax benefits for both the employer and the employee, each type of excludable fringe benefit must meet specific requirements.

Nondiscrimination of Fringe Benefits

To achieve favorable income tax treatment, most, but not all, fringe benefits require the employer not to discriminate against different classes of employees, especially employees who are not highly compensated. If nondiscrimination requirements apply and the fringe benefit is provided primarily to **highly compensated (or key) employees**, and the benefit is not available on substantially the same terms to non-highly compensated (or non-key) employees, then the fringe benefit is deemed to be discriminatory.

Highly-compensated employees are those employees who:

- hold a greater than five percent ownership interest, or
- have compensation in excess of $130,000 for 2021.

A **key employee** is an employee who is:

- a greater than five percent owner,
- a greater than one percent owner with compensation in excess of $150,000 (not indexed), or
- an officer with compensation in excess of $185,000 for 2021.

If a fringe benefit is discriminatory, then the exclusion may be lost by all employees (or by the favored group of employees), resulting in the value of the fringe benefit being included in the recipient employee's gross income. As discussed below, some fringe benefits have nondiscrimination requirements while others do not.

Individuals Who May Enjoy Benefits

An employee performing services in return for a fringe benefit need not be the person who actually uses or enjoys the fringe benefit. For instance, the spouse and children of an employee normally receive benefits from employer-provided medical insurance. Retired employees, spouses of employees, dependent children of employees, spouses of deceased employees, partners, directors, and even independent contractors may be able to enjoy excludable fringe benefits. The provisions related to each fringe benefit normally indicate who is eligible to enjoy the benefit without causing inclusion in taxable income of the employee.

Health Insurance

There are several ways that an employer can provide an employee with benefits for medical care. The employer may:

- establish and pay part or all of the premiums for group medical insurance,
- pay part or all of the premiums for private medical insurance policies,
- contribute to a separate trust or fund that provides medical benefits to employees, or
- directly pay or reimburse employee for medical expenses.

Medical insurance plans are normally written, but they need not be written to enjoy favorable tax benefits.

Employer payments of insurance premiums or contributions to medical benefit trusts or funds under these plans are currently income tax deductible by the employer and excludable from the gross income of employees. Medical benefits received by employees, their spouses, and dependents are excludable from the gross income of employees.

Medical plans normally cover hospital expenses, physician expenses, prescription medications, and other medical costs. These medical plans may or may not provide for vision and dental benefits. Eligible medical benefits include the payment or reimbursement of expenses for medical care due to personal injury or sickness and payments for: (1) the permanent loss or loss of use of a member or function of the body, or (2) permanent disfigurement.

Example 5.4

Frankie was seriously injured in a motorcycle accident. His employer's group medical insurance plan paid approximately $85,000 for his hospital expenses, physician expenses, and prescription medications. It also paid him $10,000 for the loss of his left hand and $5,000 for permanent disfigurement. All of these payments from the insurance company are excluded from Frankie's gross income.

A group accident or health plan is an arrangement that provides benefits for employees, their spouses, and their dependents in the event of personal injury or sickness. The plan may be insured by an outside company or self-insured by the employer and does not need to be in writing. The premiums paid by the employer for health insurance are not includible in the gross income of employees, but they are deductible as business expenses for the employer under IRC Section 162.

If an employee pays part or all of the insurance premiums through a payroll withholding arrangement, it is possible to exclude the amount of such premiums from the employee's gross income under the provisions of IRC Section 125 (See the discussion of cafeteria plans that follows).

Health reimbursement arrangements (HRAs) are employer-funded plans that reimburse employees for medical expenses and allow employees to carry any unused balances forward to be used in future years. The taxation of employer contributions and employee benefits is the same as for other employer-sponsored medical plans.

Exhibit 5.5 | Summary of the Tax Treatment of Employer-Provided Medical Benefits

Medical Fringe Benefits	*Employer*	*Employee*
Health insurance premiums paid by employer	Deduct	Exclude
Employer contributions to a fund that provides medical benefits to employees	Deduct	Exclude
Payment of employee medical expenses:		
By the employer	Deduct	Exclude
By an insurance company	No Impact	Exclude
By a separate fund or trust	No Impact	Exclude
Reimbursement of employee medical expenses in the year paid by the employee:		
Reimbursed by the employer	Deduct	Exclude
Reimbursed by an insurance company	No Impact	Exclude
Reimbursed by a separate fund or trust	No Impact	Exclude
Reimbursement of employee medical expenses after the year paid by the employee:*		
Reimbursed by the employer	Deduct	Tax Benefit Rule
Reimbursed by an insurance company	No Impact	Tax Benefit Rule
Reimbursed by a separate fund or trust	No Impact	Tax Benefit Rule

**If the employee used the standard deduction in the year paid, the reimbursement is excluded. If the employee itemizes deductions in the year paid, some or all of the reimbursement may be included in gross income based on the tax benefit rule. The tax benefit rule is discussed in Chapter 4.*

Employees who do not enjoy the benefits of an employer-provided medical plan often purchase private medical insurance coverage. Under these circumstances, the employees must pay for insurance premiums and out-of-pocket medical costs with after-tax dollars unless they establish Health Savings Accounts (discussed below) or qualify to deduct some of their medical expenses as itemized deductions (discussed in Chapter 7).

2010 Health Care Law

The Patient Protection and Affordable Care Act of 2010, and the Health Care and Education Reconciliation Act of 2010, collectively referred to here as the 2010 Health Care Law, requires all U.S. citizens and legal residents to maintain health insurance beginning on January 1, 2014. The 2010 health care law exempts incarcerated individuals, individuals illegally residing in the United States, and individuals for whom a qualified religious exemption applies from the requirement of maintaining health insurance. Taxpayers who are not provided with employer sponsored health insurance, therefore, must obtain their own insurance. The health care law created several programs to assist low income individuals in meeting their newly imposed legal obligation of maintaining health insurance, imposed penalties on large employers (employers with over 50 employees) who do not provide health care coverage for their employees, and created a tax credit to encourage small employers to provide coverage for their employees.

Failure to comply with the coverage requirement of the new law resulted in a tax penalty for tax years prior to 2018, but the IRS was prohibited from using seizures for payment enforcement and could not seek to impose criminal penalties against offenders. The penalty prior to 2018 was the greater of:

- 2.5% of household income less the threshold amount of income required for filing a tax return, or
- $695 per uninsured adult in the household.

In 2012, the United States Supreme Court found that the tax penalty imposed by Congress under the Affordable Care Act of 2010 was a constitutional exercise of Congress' taxing power (National Federation of Independent Business et al. v. Sebelius, Secretary of Health and Human Services, et al.) TCJA 2017 eliminated the tax penalty for failure to comply with the coverage requirement under the Affordable Care Act for tax years after 2017.

Archer Medical Savings Accounts

The Health Insurance Portability and Accountability Act of 1996 (HIPAA) established tax-favored savings accounts for medical expenses called **Archer Medical Savings Accounts (MSAs)**. MSAs could be established for eligible employees after 1996 and before 2006 for employers with fifty or fewer employees and for self-employed individuals. Employees could not establish MSAs but could contribute (subject to the limitations discussed below) to the accounts if the employer established MSAs for their benefit. Beginning in 2005, new MSAs may not be established, and have been replaced by the Health Savings Account (HSA), which is discussed below. However, many of the MSAs that were established prior to 2006 are still in existence, may still be maintained, and retain their tax-favored status.

MSA participants may contribute to their MSA account if their employer provides them with a high-deductible health plan that includes a maximum out-of-pocket cost for employees. Under the MSA requirements, a high deductible plan is a major medical health insurance plan with a deductible between $2,400 and $3,600 for individual coverage and between $4,800 and $7,150 for family coverage (2021). The maximum out-of-pocket cost for the plan is $4,800 for individual coverage and $8,750 for family coverage (2021). These same limitations apply for self-employed individuals.

Exhibit 5.6 | Archer Medical Savings Accounts (MSAs)

	2021
Self-Only Coverage	
• Minimum annual deductible	$2,400
• Maximum annual deductible	$3,600
• Maximum annual out-of-pocket expenses	$4,800
Family Coverage	
• Minimum annual deductible	$4,800
• Maximum annual deductible	$7,150
• Maximum annual out-of-pocket expenses	$8,750

Contributions can be made to an MSA by the employee or the employer, subject to limits. Employee contributions are deductible above-the-line (for adjusted gross income). Contributions to MSAs are reported on Form 8853, which should be filed with Form 1040. The MSA deduction is reported on Schedule 1 of Form 1040. Employer contributions are tax deductible by the employer, are not subject to payroll taxes, and are excludable from gross income by the employee. The aggregate contributions to the plan by the employee and the employer cannot exceed 65 percent of the deductible for individual coverage and 75 percent of the deductible for family coverage.

The earnings on the assets within an MSA are tax deferred until a distribution is taken from the account. Distribution for qualified medical expenses are income tax free. If the distribution is not for qualified medical expenses, the entire distribution is taxable as ordinary income. Taxable distributions taken before the owner of the account is age 65 results in an additional 20 percent excise penalty tax. The only exception to the early distribution penalty tax applies if the taxpayer is disabled at the time of the distribution.

Health Savings Accounts

The Medicare Act of 2003 created **Health Savings Accounts (HSAs)**, which are very similar to MSAs but less restrictive. In comparison with an MSA, an HSA can be established by an eligible individual with a high deductible health insurance plan (as explained below), and HSAs allow a higher contribution amount. With a few exceptions, an individual and spouse (if the insurance covers the family) cannot have any medical coverage other than a high deductible health plan.

An HSA may be independently established by an employee or the establishment of the account may be facilitated by an employer; however, HSA accounts are always owned and controlled by the employee. An employee who does not enjoy the benefits of any type of medical plan through an employer may obtain a private high-deductible health plan and establish an HSA with a qualified HSA trustee. Qualified HSA trustees include banks, insurance companies or any other entity already approved to serve as trustee of an IRA or Archer MSA.

The money in an HSA can be invested in a variety of instruments, including bank accounts, money market instruments, mutual funds, or even individual stocks.

To qualify for an HSA, an individual must have a health or medical insurance plan with a deductible of at least $1,400 (2021) for single coverage and the annual out-of-pocket costs cannot exceed $7,000 (2021). For family coverage under an HSA, the health insurance plan deductible must be at least $2,800 (2021) and the annual out-of-pocket costs cannot exceed $14,000 (2021). The out-of-pocket costs include deductibles, co-payments, and other payments for medical benefits, but they do not include insurance premiums paid by the individual.

Exhibit 5.7 | Health Savings Accounts (HSAs)

	2021
Self-Only Coverage	
• Minimum annual deductible	$1,400
• Maximum annual out-of-pocket expenses	$7,000
• Maximum annual contribution	$3,600
Family Coverage	
• Minimum annual deductible	$2,800
• Maximum annual out-of-pocket expenses	$14,000
• Maximum annual contribution	$7,200

Contributions to the HSA can be made by the individual or by the individual's employer. In either case, the aggregate annual contributions cannot exceed $3,600 for individuals and $7,200 for families (2021). However, individuals who are at least 55 years of age and younger than 65 years of age can make additional catch-up contributions of $1,000 over these limits for 2021. In addition to these amounts, rollovers into the account are allowed from an existing Archer MSA and from other HSAs of the individual. It should also be noted that family members or any other person can make contributions to an HSA on behalf of the owner. The full amount of contributions, up to the maximum contribution limit, may be deducted regardless of the deductible or maximum out-of-pocket expenses of the qualifying policy.

Since the limitations on deductible contributions are greater for HSAs than for MSAs, clients may wish to roll over their MSA to an HSA if their contributions exceed the MSA limits. Before doing so, however, clients should consult with their employer to ensure that the employer will continue to make contributions that would have been made to the MSA to the newly established HSA.

Contributions to an employee's HSA by an employer are deductible by the employer and excludable by the employee. Contributions by an employee or any other person (other than the employer) to an HSA are deductible for AGI on the employee's individual income tax return. All contributions to HSAs are reported on Form 8889, which should be filed with Form 1040.

Earnings within the HSA are tax deferred (not currently taxable), and amounts distributed from an HSA are excludable from the owner's gross income provided the distributions are used to pay for qualified medical expenses. If a distribution is not for qualified medical expenses, the entire distribution is taxable as ordinary income. If a distribution is taken before the owner of the

Quick Quiz 5.2

1. Fringe benefits are valuable to employees because they are always nontaxable.
   a. True
   b. False
2. Some fringe benefits have nondiscrimination requirements, while others do not.
   a. True
   b. False
3. An HSA must be established by an employer.
   a. True
   b. False

False, True, False.

account is 65 years old and it is not used to pay for qualified medical expenses, the distribution is includible in gross income and it is also subject to an additional 20 percent excise penalty tax.

Qualified Medical Expenses

Qualified medical expenses for an HSA include medical expenses for the taxpayer, spouse, or dependents that are not reimbursed by a health insurance policy, COBRA health insurance premiums, long-term care insurance premiums, and health insurance premiums if the taxpayer is receiving unemployment compensation. Prescription drugs, over-the-counter drugs, and insulin meet the definition of qualified medical expenses.[2]

Exhibit 5.8 | Tax Planning Issues with HSAs

1. Annual contributions to an HSA are no longer limited to the high deductible health plan's deductible amount (after 2006).
2. An individual who is an eligible individual during the last month of the tax year is considered to be an eligible individual for the entire year. Therefore, in most cases, the annual contribution limit no longer needs to be prorated on a monthly basis for the first year of participation in an HSA.
3. An individual may make a one-time, tax-free IRA distribution to fund an HSA, as long as the HSA owner remains eligible for the HSA for 12 months following the IRA distribution.
4. An employee may be able to have the employer make a one-time transfer of the employee's balance in a health reimbursement arrangement (HRA) or flexible spending plan (discussed below) to the employee's HSA.

Life Insurance

If an employer provides group permanent (not term) life insurance coverage for employees, the employees must include in gross income the insurance premiums paid by the employer. Permanent life insurance provides a permanent death benefit by building a cash value inside the policy. If group term life insurance is provided to employees, however, a limited amount of coverage can be provided to an employee without any inclusion of the premiums in the employee's gross income.

Group Term Life Insurance

An employer can deduct the cost of up to $50,000 (face or death benefit amount) of group term life insurance for each employee, and the employee can exclude the premiums paid by the employer from gross income if certain requirements discussed below are met.

Key Concepts

1. Identify the amount of group term life insurance that can be provided to employees as a fringe benefit.
2. Explain the consequences of providing life insurance in excess $50,000.
3. Explain the tax consequences of employer-provided disability insurance.
4. Describe the purpose of and rules associated with cafeteria plans.

2. The 2010 Health Care legislation removed over-the-counter medication without a prescription from the definition of qualified expenses for MSAs, HSAs, and Flexible Spending Accounts (FSAs); however, the CARES Act of 2020 repealed this rule, once again allowing over-the-counter drugs to be purchased with MSA, HSA, and FSA funds without the need for a prescription after December 31, 2019.

The cost, as determined under the Uniform Premium Table provided by the IRS, of any death benefit coverage in excess of $50,000 is taxable to the employee. The monthly cost of the insurance to include in the employee's gross income is determined by multiplying the number of thousands of dollars of group term life insurance coverage over $50,000 (figured to the nearest $100) by the cost shown in the following table. The table corresponds with the employee's age as of the last day of the tax year and the includible amount is reduced by any contribution payments made by the employee.

Exhibit 5.9 | Uniform Premium Table
Cost for Group Term Life Insurance Per $1,000 of Protection for One Month

Age	*Cost*
Under 25	0.05
25 through 29	0.06
30 through 34	0.08
35 through 39	0.09
40 through 44	0.10
45 through 49	0.15
50 through 54	0.23
55 through 59	0.43
60 through 64	0.66
65 through 69	1.27
70 and older	2.06

Example 5.5

Khabib's employer provides him with $80,000 of group term life insurance for which Khabib pays none of the premiums. Khabib is 56 years old at the end of the year. He can exclude the cost of the first $50,000 of coverage. He must include $154.80 ($30,000 of coverage at $0.43 per $1,000 per month x 12 months) in his gross income. This amount is reported as part of Khabib's W-2 income. If Khabib pays any amount toward the cost of the insurance coverage, the taxable amount is reduced by the amount of the payment.

If the group term life insurance plan discriminates in favor of key employees, each key employee must include in gross income the cost of all of the group term life insurance provided to that key employee. The cost to be included in gross income is the greater of the cost determined using the Uniform Premium Table above or the actual premium cost of the life insurance coverage to the employer. Under these circumstances, key employees are not allowed to exclude the cost of any group term life insurance. Employees other than key employees are taxed the same as they would be taxed if the plan were not discriminatory.

Example 5.6

Ronda is provided with $100,000 of group term life insurance by her employer. Her employer's plan discriminates in favor of key employees and Ronda is a key employee. Ronda is 46 years old at the end of the year and the company actually paid a premium of $250 for her life insurance coverage. The cost of Ronda's coverage is $180 (100 x 0.15 x 12) according to the Uniform Premium Table. Ronda will be required to include $250 in her gross income as a result of her life insurance coverage. Employees who are not key employees will still be able to exclude the cost of up to $50,000 of coverage for the year.

The cost of up to $2,000 of group term life insurance coverage paid for by the employer for the spouse or a dependent of an employee is excludable from an employee's gross income as a de minimis fringe benefit.

Employee Death Benefits

Employers sometimes pay death benefits to the spouse or family of a deceased employee. The Internal Revenue Service generally considers these payments to be compensation for past services rendered by the deceased employee. Under certain circumstances, however, some courts have held that these payments are in the nature of gifts and can be excluded from the recipient's gross income. For example, when there is clearly no obligation on the part of the employer to pay and the facts and circumstances clearly imply a gratuitous payment to the surviving spouse and children following the death of an employee, the payment would be excluded from the recipient's gross income.

Disability Insurance

Disability insurance provides benefits in the form of periodic payments to a person who is unable to work due to sickness or accidental injury. The cost of disability insurance varies depending on occupation, age, and gender of the insured, as well as the benefit term, the amount of coverage, and the length of the waiting period (elimination period) provided under the policy.

Disability insurance can be provided under a group or individual plan and as either short-term (up to two years) or long-term coverage (over two years). In any case, the *premiums* paid by the employer are deductible by the employer as a business expense and are excluded from the employee's gross income. When an employer pays the premium and the premium is excluded from the employee's gross income, any *disability income benefit* received by the employee is taxable and must be included in the employee's gross income. If the employee pays the entire premium with after-tax income or the employer pays the premium and the employee includes the premium payment in gross income, any benefits received can be excluded from the employee's gross income. This exclusion of disability income benefits also applies if a person purchases a private disability insurance policy rather than obtaining it through his employer. If the employer and employee each pay part of the premium, the prorated part of the benefits associated with the employer's contribution is taxable to the employee.

Example 5.7

Miesha pays 20% of the premiums for disability insurance and her employer pays the remainder. Miesha became disabled and received disability income benefits under the policy for several years. She must include 80% of any disability income benefits in gross income. The remaining 20%, the portion for which she paid the premiums, is excluded from her gross income. The premiums paid by Miesha's employer can also be excluded from her gross income. If Miesha's employer had paid all of the premiums, 100% of the disability income benefits would be taxable to her. If Miesha had paid 100% of the premiums with after-tax income, none of the income benefits would have been taxable to her.

The reason for the inclusion of benefits in gross income is that the disability benefits received are in lieu of wages that would have been taxable. If an individual buys a private disability insurance policy, however, the premiums paid are not deductible, but any disability income benefits received are excluded from gross income.

Cafeteria Plans

A **cafeteria plan** is a written plan under which an employee may choose to receive either cash or taxable benefits as compensation or qualified fringe benefits that are excludable from wages. Provided the cafeteria plan meets the requirements explained below, the value of any qualified tax-free fringe benefit, if chosen by an employee, will generate a deductible expense for the employer and will be excludable from gross income by the employee. An employee who chooses cash or taxable benefits rather than excludable fringe benefits will be required to include the cash or taxable benefit in gross income as taxable compensation.

These plans are referred to as Section 125 plans because they are permitted by IRC Section 125, which requires a cafeteria plan to offer at least one taxable benefit, usually cash, and one qualified nontaxable benefit. Commonly included qualified benefits are group term life insurance, medical reimbursement or insurance plans, disability benefits, and dependent care assistance.

Quick Quiz 5.3

1. Any group life insurance benefit in excess of $50,000 is taxable to the employer.
   a. True
   b. False
2. Disability insurance premiums paid by the employer are deductible by the employer and are excluded from the employee's gross income.
   a. True
   b. False
3. A cafeteria plan is most appropriate when all of the employees need the same benefits.
   a. True
   b. False

False, True, False.

A cafeteria plan is appropriate when employee benefit needs vary within the employee group. The employee mix often includes young, unmarried people with minimal life insurance and medical benefits needs, as well as older employees with families who need maximum medical and life insurance benefits. A cafeteria plan is also appropriate when employees want to choose the benefit package most suited to their individual needs.

A cafeteria plan is a way of managing fringe benefit costs for the employer by individually pricing each benefit. Cafeteria plans help give employees an appreciation of the value of their benefit package by allowing them to choose the cash or purchase the benefit. Cafeteria plans can also help control employer costs of providing benefit packages because the employer does not pay for benefits that are not used by the employees. These plans can be complex and expensive to design and administer.

IRC Section 125 provides an exception to the constructive receipt rule, which would otherwise require an employee to include the value of qualified excludable benefits in gross income simply because the employee had an unrestricted right to elect cash compensation instead of nontaxable benefits. The cafeteria plan must meet all of the requirements of Section 125 to obtain exclusion treatment for employees who choose to receive the excludable fringe benefits.

A cafeteria plan meets the qualifications of the IRC if the benefits provided under the plan are qualified (as discussed above), the plan does not favor the highly compensated employees, and the nontaxable benefits provided to key employees is less than 25 percent of the total nontaxable benefits provided under the plan to all employees.

If the plan provides a benefit that is not qualified, the value of that benefit will be included in the employee's gross income. If the plan is deemed discriminatory by favoring the highly compensated or by providing more than 25 percent of the benefits to the key employees, the value of the nontaxable benefits chosen by the highly compensated or key employees will be included in their gross income.

Flexible Spending Accounts (FSAs)

A **flexible spending account (FSA)** is a type of cafeteria plan that is funded through employee salary reductions. The employee can elect to have a portion of his salary or wages retained by the employer to fund an FSA. Any amount so retained by the employer is excludable from the salary or wages of the employee. The money in the FSA account can then be used to pay for or reimburse the employee for deductibles, co-payments, and medical expenses (including vision and dental expenses) that are not covered by the employer's medical plan. The end result of this arrangement is that certain expenses can be paid with pre-tax rather than after-tax dollars.

The type of FSA introduced above is called a health or medical FSA. It is also possible to set up an FSA to pay for child care and qualified transportation expenses.

Key Concepts

1. Identify the advantages and disadvantages of FSAs.
2. Explain the tax consequences of employer-provided long-term care insurance.

The employee must elect the amount of compensation to be retained and placed in the FSA before each plan year begins. Amounts contributed to the FSA are not included in the employee's income for the year, and are exempt from Social Security and Medicare taxes. One disadvantage of an FSA is that amounts remaining in the account at the end of the year are forfeited back to the employer (a use it or lose it arrangement). However, the employer can allow employees to use the money in an FSA to pay for qualified expenses incurred up to two and one-half-months after the end of the year of the plan.[3] This extension of time, referred to as a grace period, must apply to all participants in the FSA cafeteria plan. The effect of the grace period is that the participant may have as long as 14 months and 15 days (the 12 months in the current cafeteria plan year plus the grace period) to use the benefits or contributions for a plan year before those amounts are "forfeited" under the "use-it-or-lose-it" rule. As an alternative, employers can choose to amend their plan to allow employees to carryover up to $500 to the following year to reimburse medical expense under the FSA.[4] A plan adopting this carryover provision is not permitted to also provide a grace period with respect to health FSAs. Since it is difficult to estimate the optimal amount to put into an FSA, many employees choose not to participate at all or to participate only modestly.

One advantage of an FSA to an employee (and a disadvantage to the employer) is that the entire annual amount that an employee elects to pay into an FSA is available for the employee's use at the beginning of the plan year. This is true even though the employee contributions to the FSA will take place throughout the year. The employer is therefore at risk for the total annual amount an employee elects to allocate to health benefits under an FSA even if the employee terminates employment before funding the amount used from the plan.

3. The Taxpayer Certainty and Disaster Tax Relief Act (TCDTRA) of 2020 allows health or dependent care FSA grace periods for plan years ending in 2020 or 2021 to be extended to twelve months from the end of the plan year if the employer elects to amend the plan to provide for the extension.
4. The Taxpayer Certainty and Disaster Tax Relief Act (TCDTRA) of 2020 allows an unlimited amount of unused health or dependent care FSA funds for plan years ending in 2020 to carryover to 2021, and unused funds for plan years ending in 2021 to carryover to 2022, if the employer elects to amend the plan to provide for the unlimited carryover.

Example 5.8

Claudia elects to pay $200 per month into an FSA for the plan year. During the first month of the year, Claudia has elective lasik eye surgery at a cost of $4,000. Since this type of surgery is not covered by her employer's medical plan, Claudia pays for part of the cost of her surgery with money from her FSA. After three months of the plan year have passed, she leaves her job to take other employment. Through the FSA, the employer must pay $2,400 for the surgery even though Claudia only paid $600 into the FSA for the year. The employer will not be allowed to recover the $1,800 shortfall from Claudia's last paycheck or through any other means.

A flexible spending account is appropriate in any of the following situations:

- An employer wants to expand employee benefit choices without significant employer out-of-pocket costs (or possibly realize some actual dollar savings);
- Many employees have employed spouses with duplicate medical coverage;
- An employer wants employees to contribute to health insurance costs;
- The employer's medical plans have large deductibles or coinsurance (co-pay) provisions;
- There is a need for benefits that are difficult to provide on a group basis, such as dependent care; and/or
- The costs of employee benefit plans, such as health insurance, have increased and the employer must impose additional employee cost sharing in the form of increased employee contributions and deductibles.

The FSA approach provides many potential advantages. It minimizes employee outlay since the FSA converts what would have been after-tax employee expenditures for the benefits selected to pre-tax expenditures. It provides employees a degree of choice to receive either cash as compensation or the cash to pay for the costs of certain benefits. Since an FSA is normally funded entirely through employee salary reductions, an employer is only required to bear the administrative costs. The administrative costs of the employer may be more than offset by payroll tax savings, since salary reductions elected by employees are not subject to payroll taxes.

The maximum amount of income that can be contributed to a health-care flexible spending account is $2,750 (2021).

Example 5.9

Urijah participates in a company sponsored FSA for medical expenses and contributes the maximum $2,750 (2021) to cover expenses for himself, his wife, Brooke, and their son, Dominick. Urijah is in the 32% income tax bracket, and his salary is currently $350,000. Contributing to the FSA will reduce Urijah's income taxes by $880 ($2,750 x 32%), and will reduce his Medicare Tax by $64.63 ($2,750 x 2.35%, since Urijah must pay both the FICA Medicare tax and the additional Medicare tax on earned income). Urijah's salary exceeds the Social Security wage base so no additional tax savings results based on the Social Security portion of the FICA tax.

Example 5.10

Royce currently makes $90,000 per year and contributes the maximum $2,750 to a flexible spending account to cover health care expenses for himself, his wife, Grace, and their three children. Royce is in the 22% marginal tax bracket. Contributing to the FSA will reduce Royce's income taxes by $605 ($2,750 x 22%), and will reduce his Social Security and Medicare taxes by $210.38 ($2,750 x 7.65%, Royce's share of the Social Security and Medicare taxes).

In some circumstances, HSAs may be preferable to FSAs. Unlike FSAs, HSAs permit unused amounts to be carried forward to future years, permitting the creation of an emergency fund for health care purposes. Furthermore, contributions to HSAs will permit higher income tax deductions than contributions to FSAs. In 2021, an employee contributing to a health care FSA will have the contribution capped at $2,750, while the allowable contributions for an HSA will be $3,600 (2021) for single coverage and $7,200 (2021) for family coverage. Employees with high deductible health plans may wish to switch to HSAs to avoid the lower contribution limitations imposed on FSAs.

An FSA must meet the nondiscrimination requirements as previously discussed for cafeteria plans. Although the Internal Revenue Code specifies the maximum amount that an employee may contribute to an FSA, the particular plan itself may further limit the maximum dollar amount or maximum percentage of compensation that can be contributed.

Qualified medical expenses do not include amounts paid for health insurance premiums, amounts paid for long-term care insurance or expenses, and amounts that are covered under another health plan of the employee.

Quick Quiz 5.4

1. Any funds remaining in an FSA are rolled over for use in future years.
   a. True
   b. False
2. FSAs must meet nondiscrimination requirements.
   a. True
   b. False
3. When long-term care premiums are paid by the employer, benefits received by the employee (up to the greater of $400/day for 2021 or the actual cost of the care) are excluded from gross income.
   a. True
   b. False

False, True, True.

Dependent Care FSA

A dependent care FSA allows the employee to contribute up to $5,000 ($2,500 if married filing separately) on a pre-tax basis.[5] Using a flexible spending account to pay for dependent care expenses (if provided) may provide more tax savings for higher income taxpayers than utilization of the Child and Dependent Care Credit discussed in Chapter 9. In general, an employee is better off using an FSA unless the employee's income (AGI) is less than $43,000.[6]

5. The American Rescue Plan Act (ARPA), signed into law on March 11, 2021, temporarily increased the dollar limit for dependent care FSAs to $10,500 ($5,250 for married filing separately) for 2021 only. The Taxpayer Certainty and Disaster Tax Relief Act (TCDTRA) of 2020, which became law on December 27, 2020, permits an FSA plan amendment allowing employees to modify their contribution amount prospectively for plan years ending in 2021 without a change in status; therefore, employees of plans with such an amendment will have the ability to increase their dependent care FSA contribution mid-year to take advantage of the increased limit. Typically, FSA contributions must be elected prior to the start of the plan year, with mid-year modifications permitted only due a change in status (such as the birth of a child).
6. Form 2441.

Long-Term Care

Long-term care insurance pays benefits when the insured person is unable to perform some of the activities of daily living. Long-term care policies normally identify five or six **activities of daily living** (ADLs), including eating, bathing, dressing, toileting, transferring, and continence. If the insured cannot perform two or more of these activities of daily living (ADLs), the policy normally pays benefits.

Premiums paid by an employer for qualified group long-term care insurance are tax deductible to the employer and excludable from gross income by the covered employee. Benefits received from a qualified long-term care insurance plan are excludable by the employee to the extent that they do not exceed the greater of $400 per day for 2021 or the actual cost of the care.

Premiums paid by an employee for group long-term coverage or for private long-term care coverage provide a tax benefit to the employee only if the individual itemizes deductions and has sufficient medical expenses to generate a medical expense deduction (see Chapter 7). In addition, there is a limit on the amount of premiums that can be deducted for long-term care insurance depending on the age of the insured individual. Benefits received under such policies are excludable subject to the limits in the preceding paragraph. Long-term care premiums cannot be paid for through a cafeteria plan or flexible spending account.

To be a qualified long-term care insurance plan, the plan must meet the following requirements:

- Does not duplicate benefits paid by Medicare,
- Must be guaranteed renewable,
- Does not have a cash surrender value,
- Only provides qualified long-term care insurance coverage, and
- Only pays benefits when the employee or beneficiary of the plan is certified by a licensed health care practitioner as chronically ill.

In addition to the tax advantages, group long-term care insurance generally also provides the following other advantages:

- Lower rates than individual policies (generally 30% - 60% less),
- Guaranteed coverage for all employees, even those who might not be insurable under an individual policy,
- Increased eligibility for extended family members, including parents, grandparents, and in-laws, and
- Must be guaranteed renewable.

OTHER EMPLOYEE FRINGE BENEFITS

In addition to the major employer-provided fringe benefits discussed above, a variety of other tax-favored fringe benefits can be provided by employers to employees.

Meals and Lodging

The provisions of IRC Section 119 permit an employee to exclude the value of meals and lodging provided by the employer if certain requirements are met. If the requirements are not met, the value of the meals and lodging must be included in the employee's gross income unless the meals can be excluded as a de minimis fringe benefit (discussed later in this chapter).

In general, an employee can exclude from gross income the value of meals provided in-kind (not as cash reimbursement) to the employee as long as the meals are furnished:

- on the employer's business premises
- for the convenience of the employer

The business premises of the employer is the place of employment of the employee. For example, meals provided in the employer's home to a domestic servant would constitute meals furnished on the business premises of the employer. Similarly, meals furnished to cowhands while herding their employer's cattle on leased land would be regarded as furnished on the business premises of the employer.

Key Concepts

1. Describe the rules regarding the provision of meals and lodging as a fringe benefit.
2. Define no-additional-cost services.
3. Identify the requirements for qualified employee discounts.

Meals furnished by an employer without charge to the employee will be regarded as furnished for the convenience of the employer if the meals are furnished for a substantial business reason of the employer, not just as a means of providing additional compensation to the employee. The determination of "for the convenience of the employer" is made based on the surrounding facts and circumstances.

Example 5.11

T.J. works as a waiter in a restaurant. He has only thirty minutes for a lunch break. He is provided with lunch at no charge by his employer because of the short lunch break and so that he will be readily available if the restaurant becomes busy. Since the meals are provided at the business premises and are clearly provided for the convenience of the employer, T.J. is allowed to exclude the value of the meals from his gross income. The owner of the restaurant will be able to deduct the cost of providing the meals to T.J. and the other employees.

An employee is allowed to exclude from gross income the value of lodging furnished by an employer to the employee if the lodging is furnished:

1. on the employer's business premises
2. for the convenience of the employer
3. the employee is required to accept the lodging as a condition of employment

The first two requirements are the same as for meals. The third requirement applies only to lodging.

The third requirement is normally met if the employee is required to accept the lodging in order to properly perform the duties of his employment. If an employee is required to be readily available at all times, this requirement is met.

Example 5.12

Chael and Sonia manage apartments and they are required to live in apartment 101, the managers' apartment, as a condition of their employment. If they had refused to live in the managers' apartment, they would not have been hired. The lodging meets all three IRC requirements, and Chael and Sonia will be able to exclude the value of the lodging from gross income. Even if Chael and Sonia were paid a housing allowance and then required to pay it back to the employer for rent, they would be able to exclude the housing allowance from gross income.

As indicated in **Example 5.12**, if all three requirements are satisfied, the exclusion applies regardless of whether the employee is charged a fee for the lodging.

Example 5.13

A construction worker is employed at a construction project at a remote job site in Alaska. Due to the inaccessibility of facilities for the employees who are working at the job site to obtain food and lodging in the prevailing weather conditions, the employer is required to furnish meals and lodging to the employee at the camp site in order to carry on the construction project. The employee is required to pay $40 a week for the meals and lodging. The weekly charge of $40 is not part of the compensation includible in the gross income of the employee, and the value of the meals and lodging is excludable from his gross income.

If an employee is given the choice of accepting the lodging or receiving additional pay instead, the employee is not allowed to exclude the value of the lodging if the lodging is accepted.

Example 5.14

An employee of an institution is given the choice of residing at the institution free of charge or of residing elsewhere and receiving a cash allowance in addition to his regular salary. If he elects to reside at the institution, the value to the employee of the lodging furnished by the employer will be includible in the employee's gross income because his residence at the institution is not required as a condition of employment.

Prior to 2018, the cost of providing meals and lodging to employees for the convenience of the employer was fully deductible by the employer. However, the TCJA 2017 changed the deductibility of meals provided for the convenience of the employer. After 2017 and before 2026, employers can only deduct 50 percent of these costs, while they can still deduct 100 percent of the cost of lodging provided for the convenience of the employer. After 2025, there is no deduction for the cost of providing meals. Under the Taxpayer Certainty and Disaster Tax Relief Act (TCDTRA) of 2020, an exception to the 50% deduction limit applies to food and beverages provided by a restaurant, allowing such meals to be fully deductible by the employer when paid or incurred after December 31, 2020 and before January 1, 2023.

There has been significant litigation concerning what constitutes the business premises of the employer. The courts have been somewhat flexible on this issue.

CASE STUDY 5.3

Lodging as an Excludable Fringe Benefit

Coyner v. Bingler, 344 F.2d 736, 738 (3rd Cir. 1965)

A park foreman for the City of Pittsburgh volunteered to become a resident caretaker at a community cultural center while still working and receiving his salary as a park foreman. Mr. Coyner lived free of charge at the cultural center where he acted as caretaker. The Tax Court ruled that the value of the lodging should have been included in gross income, but the United States Third Circuit Court of Appeals disagreed, overturning the Tax Court and finding that the value of the lodging was excludable from gross income because Mr. Coyner had to live there in proper performance of his duties as caretaker. Mr. Coyner's occupancy of the apartment was not simply for his convenience and benefit, but was of distinct benefit to the City and, therefore, "for the convenience of the employer" within the terms of the statute.

The Court recognized the facts that his presence was required to prevent vandalism, to perform certain janitorial services, to be present to admit persons entitled to use the facilities and to secure and lock the building at night. Because the cultural center was almost constantly in use, Mr. Coyner could exclude the lodging from his gross income because it related to the practical working necessity of performing his duties with any sort of efficiency.[1] The Court did acknowledge that, had the commissioner introduced any evidence that Mr. Coyner was not required to be available for duty at all times, a different result may have been in order.

1. Excluding the value of lodging for officers and employees of a family owned funeral business was allowed where the lodging was furnished as a matter of company policy and the nature of the business required that close personal contact be made available on a 24-hour per day basis. ***In the Matter of Harry Schwartz***, 22 T.C.M. 835 (1963).

No-Additional-Cost Services

An employee can exclude the value of any service provided to the employee by the employer if:

1. the service is offered for sale to customers
2. in the line of business in which the employee works
3. the employer incurs no substantial additional costs (including foregone revenue) in providing the service to the employee

Examples of **no-additional-cost services** include providing airline tickets, bus tickets, train tickets, hotel accommodations, or telephone services at no cost or at reduced prices to employees who work in those lines of business.

Example 5.15

Rose, a parking lot attendant, is allowed to park in the employer's parking lot for free. The cost of parking can be excluded from Rose's gross income for days when the parking lot has excess capacity. On days when the parking lot is full and customers must be turned away, the employer loses revenue in order to provide free parking for Rose; therefore one of the three requirements is not met and Rose must include the value of the free parking in her gross income for those days.

A service provided to an employee's spouse or dependent child is viewed as being provided to the employee individually. Use of air transportation by an employee's parents is considered to be use by the employee. Former employees and other specified individuals can also qualify for no-additional-cost services.

Services must be in the line of business in which the employee works. If an employer has several lines of business and an employee receives services from another line of business, those services must be included in the employee's gross income. If unrelated employers in the same line of business have reciprocal arrangements to provide each other's employees with services, each employee can treat any services received from the other employer as though they were provided by his own employer.

Airlines frequently provide personal flights at no charge for employees or family members of employees. Whether the no-additional-cost exclusion is available depends upon seat availability to other customers. The key issue is that the airline must not forgo revenue in order to provide the excludable fringe benefit.

Example 5.16

Commercial Airline permits its employees to enjoy personal travel on its scheduled flights at no charge and receive reserved seating. Because Commercial Airline foregos potential revenue by permitting the employees to reserve seats, employees receiving free flights are not eligible for the no-additional-cost exclusion and must include the value of the flight in their gross income. However, if the employees are not allowed to reserve seats and only board the flight if there is available capacity, then employees receiving those flights are eligible for the no-additional-cost exclusion and may exclude the value of the flight from their gross income.

If a no-additional-cost service discriminates in favor of highly-compensated employees, the highly-compensated employees must include the value of the service in gross income.

Qualified Employee Discounts

Qualified employee discounts on qualified property and services can be excluded from an employee's gross income. Qualified employee discounts on property cannot exceed the employer's gross profit percentage of the price at which the employer offers the property for sale to customers. Qualified employee discounts on services cannot exceed 20 percent of the price at which the employer offers the services for sale to customers. Qualified property means any property other than real property or personal property of a kind that is held for investment (such as stocks or bonds) which is offered for sale to customers in the line of business in which the employee works. Qualified services means any services offered by the employer to customers in the line of business in which the employee provides services.

Quick Quiz 5.5

1. An employee can exclude the value of meals provided in-kind from gross income even if the meals are not furnished on the employer's business premises.
   a. True
   b. False
2. Free guaranteed seats for airline employees are a no-additional-costs service.
   a. True
   b. False
3. Qualified employee discounts on services may not exceed 20%.
   a. True
   b. False

False, False, True.

Example 5.17

During the prior year, Forrest's employer sold property to customers at a gross profit percentage of 40%. For example, an item purchased for $60 was sold for $100, and the gross profit of $40 was 40% of the sales price. During the current year, Forrest paid $65 for a sleeping bag that was priced at $100 by his employer. His employee discount was 35% of the normal price. Since Forrest's discount of 35% is less than his employer's normal gross profit percentage of 40%, Forrest can exclude the discount from his gross income.

Example 5.18

Joanna worked for a carpet cleaning company. Her employer cleaned her carpets and charged only $140 for services that would cost $200 for regular customers. Her discount on the service is $60 or 30%. Joanna will be able to exclude $40 or 20% from her gross income, but the remaining $20 must be included in her gross income as compensation.

In addition to current employees, certain individuals (such as spouses and dependents) are permitted to exclude qualified employee discounts.

As with no-additional-cost services, if qualified employee discounts discriminate in favor of highly-compensated employees, the highly-compensated employees must include the discounts in gross income.

Working Condition Fringe Benefits

A **working condition fringe benefit** provided by an employer to an employee to help the employee perform his job better can be excluded from the employee's gross income. A working condition fringe benefit is defined as any property or service for which the employee could have taken a tax deduction as a business expense or as depreciation expense if the employee had personally paid for the benefit. Working condition fringe benefits might include such things as employer-paid subscriptions to professional journals, dues for professional organization memberships, payment or reimbursement for employment-related professional education, or business use of a company car.

The use of a company car is a common working condition fringe benefit. If the employee uses the car for both personal and business purposes, the business-use value is considered to be a working condition fringe benefit, but the personal use value of the car must normally be included in the employee's gross income. Use of a demonstration car by full-time automobile salespersons qualifies as a working condition fringe benefit if the demonstration car is predominately used to facilitate the services the salesperson provided to the employer and there are restrictions on personal use of the automobile.

All of an employee's use of a qualified non-personal use vehicle, such as a police car, fire vehicle, ambulance, hearse, farm tractor, or school bus, is treated as a qualified working condition fringe benefit.

In addition to employees, eligible recipients of excludable working condition fringe benefits might include a partner who performs services for a partnership, a member of the employer's board of directors, or an independent contractor who performs services for the employer.

Working condition fringe benefits are not subject to nondiscrimination requirements; therefore, they **can** be used by any employee **even** if the benefits favor highly compensated employees.

Key Concepts

1. Describe working condition fringe benefits.
2. Identify various types of de minimis fringe benefits.
3. Explain the requirements for qualified transportations fringe benefits.

De Minimis Fringe Benefits

An employee can exclude the value of de minimis fringe benefits from gross income. A **de minimis fringe benefit** is defined in Internal Revenue Code as "any property or service the value of which is (after taking into account the frequency with which similar fringes are provided by the employer to the employer's employees) so small as to make accounting for it unreasonable or administratively impracticable." De minimis fringes are considered to be minimal or small. A partial list of de minimis fringe benefits is presented in **Exhibit 5.10**.

Exhibit 5.10 | Some De Minimis Fringe Benefits From An Employer

- Occasional personal use of an employer's copy machine
- Occasional typing of a personal letter by a secretary hired by an employer
- Occasional cocktail parties, group meals, or picnics for employees and guests
- Birthday or holiday gifts (not cash) with a low value
- Occasional theater or sporting event tickets
- Coffee, donuts, or soft drinks
- Flowers, fruit, books and similar items provided to an employee because of illness or a family crisis

A cash de minimis fringe benefit is not usually excludable unless the cash is for reasonable, occasional meal money or local transportation fare. The furnishing of meal money or local transportation fare on a regular or routine basis is not considered to be "occasional." Further, the meal money (or actual meals) or local transportation fare must be provided due to overtime work necessitating an extension of the employee's normal work schedule.

Employer-operated eating facilities for employees qualify for this exclusion if the facility is located on or near the business premises of the employer and the annual revenue of the facility is equal to or greater than the direct operating costs of the facility.

Nondiscrimination rules do not normally apply in determining the amount of a de minimis fringe benefit. However, nondiscrimination rules do apply to employer-operated eating facilities. If access to such facilities discriminates in favor of highly compensated employees, highly compensated employees who use the facilities must include the value of meals received in gross income.

Qualified Transportation Fringe Benefits

The value of **qualified transportation fringe benefits** provided by an employer can be excluded from the gross income of employees if certain requirements and limitations are met. Qualified transportation fringe benefits include:

1. transportation between an employee's residence and the place of employment in a commuter highway vehicle
2. any transit pass
3. qualified parking

The amounts that can be excluded from gross income are limited to $270 per month for 2021 for commuter highway vehicle use (item 1) and transit passes (item 2) combined. The monthly limit for qualified parking is $270 per month for 2021. Any benefits received in excess of these amounts, less any amount paid by the employee for the benefits, must be included in an employee's gross income.

Example 5.19

Cris is provided with free parking at her employer's workplace. The value of the parking benefit is $300 per month during 2021. Cris does not pay any of the cost. The monthly parking benefit provided by the employer that can be excluded is $270 for 2021. Therefore, Cris can exclude $270 per month as qualified parking. However, she must report the remaining $30 per month in her gross income ($30 ($300-$270) for 2021). The $30 excess cannot be excluded as a de minimis fringe benefit.

Example 5.20

For 2021, Nate's employer provides him with a bus pass at a cost of $130 per month for work purposes. Nate can exclude the entire $130 of the monthly amount for 2021. He could also exclude the transit pass if it were for rail or ferry transportation.

TCJA 2017 eliminated the employer deduction for qualified mass transit and parking benefits, but did not eliminate the employee exclusion for those benefits. After the enactment of TCJA 2017, an employer may deduct qualified mass transit and parking benefits only if those benefits are necessary for ensuring the safety of an employee. The changes to qualified mass transit and parking benefits enacted by TCJA 2017 expire for tax years beginning after December 31, 2025.

From 2008 through 2017 (and for tax years beginning after December 31, 2025), an employee who did not receive any of the transportation fringe benefits explained above may exclude up to $20 per month of qualified bicycle commuting reimbursements from an employer. TCJA 2017 suspended the employer deduction and the employee exclusion from income for qualified bicycle commuting reimbursements from 2018 - 2025. Qualified bicycle commuting reimbursements are employer reimbursements for the purchase, improvement, repair, or storage of a bicycle that is regularly used for travel between the employee's residence and place of employment. The $20 per month limit is not adjusted for inflation.

Quick Quiz 5.6

1. Personal use of a company car is a working condition fringe benefit.
   a. True
   b. False
2. There is no limit on qualified transportation fringe benefits.
   a. True
   b. False

False, False.

Under appropriate circumstances, some transportation-related benefits may be excludable as de minimis or working condition fringe benefits.

Qualified Moving Expense Reimbursements

Before 2018, and for tax years beginning after December 31, 2025, qualified moving expense reimbursements from an employer are excluded from gross income by employees. TCJA 2017 eliminated both the deduction for qualified moving expenses and the exclusion from income of qualified moving expense reimbursements. TCJA 2017 provided only one exception to this rule - Members of the Armed Forces (or their spouse or dependents) on active duty who move pursuant to a military order and incident to a permanent change of station may deduction amounts attributable to in-kind moving and storage expenses, and may exclude from income any reimbursements or allowances received for these expenses.

Key Concepts

1. Identify the rules for qualified moving expense reimbursements.
2. Describe qualified retirement planning services.
3. Explain how employers can assist employees with educational costs, dependent care costs, and adoption costs.

For tax years before 2018 and after 2025, a **qualified moving expense reimbursement** includes direct or indirect payment by the employer to pay for the cost of moving an employee's family and belongings. In order to qualify for exclusion by the employee, the reimbursement must be for expenses that would be deductible (for AGI) by the employee as moving expenses under IRC Section 217 if paid by the employee. Expenses such as house hunting expenses and meals are not eligible to be deducted as moving expenses. The requirements for deducting moving expenses are discussed more fully in Chapter 6.

Example 5.21

Paige paid $3,800 to move her family and belongings to her new work location with the same employer. All $3,800 would be deductible under IRC Section 217. If her employer paid her $3,800 as reimbursement for her moving expenses, Paige can exclude the $3,800 from gross income (but she could not also deduct the $3,800). If Paige had deducted the moving expenses in one year and received the reimbursement in the next year, the tax benefit rule would prevent her from excluding the reimbursement from gross income. If the employer had reimbursed Paige for nondeductible expenses, the reimbursement would have to be included in her gross income as well. After 2017, aforementioned tax treatment for Paige would only be correct if she were an active member of the armed forces and moved pursuant to a military order.

Before 2018 and after 2025, both employees and leased employees qualify for the exclusion of qualified moving expense reimbursements. Moving expense reimbursements can discriminate in favor of highly compensated employees.

Qualified Retirement Planning Services

Qualified retirement planning services provided by an employer can be excluded from an employee's gross income. As defined in IRC Section 132(m)(1), **qualified retirement planning services** include "any retirement planning advice or information provided to an employee and his spouse by an employer maintaining a qualified employer plan." Qualified employer plan refers to an employer-sponsored retirement plan.

Excludable services may include advice and information about the employer's retirement plan as well as general advice and information on retirement. The exclusion does not apply to the value of services for tax preparation, accounting, legal, or brokerage services.

If qualified retirement planning services discriminate in favor of highly compensated employees, the highly compensated employees must include the value of such services in gross income.

Athletic Facilities

The value of the use of on-premises gyms and other athletic facilities can be excluded from an employee's income if:

1. the facilities are located on the premises of the employer
2. the employer operates the facilities
3. substantially all the use of the facilities is by employees of the employer, their spouses, and their dependent children

The facilities have to be on premises owned or leased by the employer; the facilities do not have to be on the business premises of the employer.

Example 5.22

Quinton uses tennis courts and other athletic facilities provided by his employer on their business property on a daily basis. He can exclude the value of using the facilities from his gross income if the facilities are used almost exclusively by employees and their immediate family members. If Quinton's employer had paid for his membership to a private gym, the cost of the membership would be includible in his gross income.

The athletic facilities fringe benefit can discriminate in favor of certain employees or groups of employees without jeopardizing the exclusion for any employees. A variety of individuals other than current employees are eligible to receive this benefit.

Educational Assistance Programs

The value of educational assistance provided by an employer through an **educational assistance program** to an employee can be excluded from the employee's gross income up to $5,250 per year. The program must be a separate written plan of the employer set forth in a separate document, must only provide educational assistance, and must meet several other requirements specified in IRC Section 127.

Qualifying educational assistance can be provided for tuition, fees, books, supplies, and equipment, but it cannot pay for lodging, meals, transportation, nor tools and supplies that are retained by the employee after the course of instruction. Qualifying assistance can pay for either undergraduate or graduate education, but it cannot pay for courses related to sports, games, or hobbies unless those courses are either required for the employee's degree program or have a reasonable relationship to the employer's business. The CARES Act of 2020 expanded the definition of qualifying educational assistance to include eligible student loan repayments made to either the employee or directly to the lender after March 27, 2020 and before January 1, 2021, subject to the overall $5,250 per year limitation. Eligible student loans are qualified higher education loans of the employee only; loans of spouses or dependents do not qualify. Interest paid by the employer under this provision does not qualify for the above-the-line deduction for student loan interest (discussed in Chapter 6). TCDRA of 2020 extended the exclusion for student loan payments made by the employer before January 1, 2026.

Nondiscrimination rules apply to educational assistance programs. Individuals other than current employees may be eligible for participation.

If an educational assistance program provides an employee with assistance in excess of $5,250 in a given year, the excess may or may not be excludable as a working condition fringe benefit, or as a training program for employees.

Dependent Care Assistance

Dependent care assistance provided or paid for by an employer through a dependent care assistance program can be excluded from the benefited employee's gross income up to $5,000 per year ($2,500 for a married employee filing separately).[7] The amount excluded cannot exceed the earned income of the employee or the earned income of the employee's spouse (if less than the employee's earned income). A spouse is deemed to earn income ($250 with one qualifying person or $500 for two or more) for each month that the spouse is a full-time student or is incapable of caring for himself. Any amount paid by the employer in excess of the above limits must be included in the gross income of the employee.

Household or dependent care assistance must be paid for the care of a qualifying person and must be paid to allow the employee to work. A qualifying person can be:

1. a dependent of the employee who has not attained the age of 13,
2. a dependent of the employee who is physically or mentally incapable of caring for himself and who has the same principal place of abode as the employee for more than one-half of the year, or
3. the employee's spouse who is physically or mentally incapable of caring for himself and who has the same principal place of abode as the employee for more than one-half of the year.

To qualify for exclusion treatment, the employer's dependent care assistance plan must be a separate written plan for the exclusive benefit of employees and must normally meet a variety of other requirements.

Nondiscrimination requirements apply to the dependent care assistance exclusion. If the plan discriminates in favor of highly compensated employees, the highly compensated employees are not allowed to exclude the benefits.

Tuition Reductions Granted to Employees of Educational Institutions

An employee of an educational institution can exclude from gross income the value of a qualified tuition reduction for himself, his spouse, or his dependent child. This exclusion normally applies to education below the graduate level. However, a tuition reduction for graduate education can be excluded if the graduate student performs teaching or research activities for the educational institution. For education below the graduate level, the educational institution can be an elementary school, a secondary school, a college, or a university.

7. Increased by ARPA of 2021 to $10,500 ($5,250 for married filing separately) for 2021 only.

Individuals other than current employees may also be eligible for this exclusion. If tuition reductions discriminate in favor of highly compensated employees, the highly compensated employees must include the tuition reduction in gross income.

Adoption Assistance Programs

Normally, the gross income of an employee does not include amounts paid by the employer for qualified adoption expenses in connection with the adoption of a child by the employee if such amounts are furnished pursuant to a written adoption assistance program of the employer. A maximum exclusion of $14,440 for 2021 applies to the adoption of a child with special needs, regardless of the actual qualified adoption expenses.[8] For other children, the maximum exclusion is equal to the amount of qualified adoption expenses up to $14,440 for 2021.

Example 5.23

Tito's employer pays for his qualifying adoption expenses in 2021 through its adoption assistance program. His actual qualifying expenses in 2021 are $9,000. If the adopted child is a child with special needs, Tito will be able to exclude up to $14,440 of adoption assistance payments from his employer. If the child is not a child with special needs, he will be able to exclude up to a maximum of $9,000 of adoption assistance payments from his employer.

There is a phaseout of the amount excludable by an employee when the employee's modified adjusted gross income exceeds $216,660 for 2021. The phaseout is complete when the employee's modified adjusted gross income reaches $256,600 for 2021.

The employer's **adoption assistance program** must meet a variety of requirements, and nondiscrimination rules apply. Qualified adoption expenses include reasonable and necessary adoption fees, court costs, attorney fees, and other expenses for the legal adoption of an eligible child. An eligible child is a child under 18 or a child who is physically or mentally incapable of caring for himself. Qualified adoption expenses do not include the costs of adopting a child of the employee's spouse.

Employee Achievement Awards

Awards and prizes are normally includible in an individual's gross income. Certain employee achievement awards, however, can be excluded from an employee's gross income. The exclusion is allowed for the value of tangible personal property (such as a watch) given to an employee for length of service or safety achievement. Eligible tangible personal property does not include cash, vacations, meals, lodging, tickets to theater and sporting events, and stocks, bonds, and other securities.

The maximum amount that an employee can exclude from gross income is $1,600 ($400 for awards that are not "qualified plan awards"). Amounts in excess of the limits must be included in the employee's gross income.

8. The definition of "children with special needs" for purposes of the adoption credit is not the same definitions of "children with special needs" for other purposes. Foreign children are not considered to have special needs for purposes of the adoption credit. Even U.S. children who have disabilities may not have special needs for purposes of the adoption credit. Generally, "special needs adoptions" are the adoptions of children whom the state's child welfare agency consider difficult to place for adoption.

Excludable awards must be made based on an employer's written plan that meets a variety of requirements. Nondiscrimination rules apply to employee achievement awards.

The TCJA 2017 modified these rules to include a provision that limits deductible achievement awards to tangible personal property. The new provision states that "tangible personal property" shall not include cash, cash equivalents, gift cards, gift coupons or gift certificates (other than arrangements conferring only the right to select and receive tangible personal property from a limited array of such items pre-selected or pre-approved by the employer), or vacations, meals, lodging, tickets to theater or sporting events, stocks, bonds, other securities, and other similar items. The purpose of this new rule is to ensure that awards are not compensation disguised as an achievement award.

Combat Pay and Other Benefits of Military Personnel

Military personnel can exclude combat zone pay from gross income. They can also exclude a variety of other fringe benefits and allowances, including basic allowances for housing, cost-of-living allowances abroad, overseas housing allowances, military base realignment and closure benefits (subject to limits), death gratuity payments to eligible survivors, and many others. IRS Publication 3, Armed Forces Tax Guide, contains a list of excludable items.

Rental Value of Parsonage

The rental value of a home furnished to a minister can be excluded from the minister's gross income. Alternatively, a rental allowance paid to a minister can be excluded from the minister's gross income to the extent that it is used to rent or provide a home.

Quick Quiz 5.7

1. The qualified retirement planning services exclusion does not apply to the value of tax preparation services.
   a. True
   b. False
2. The athletic facilities fringe benefit can discriminate without jeopardizing the exclusion.
   a. True
   b. False
3. Combat zone pay received by military personnel is included in gross income.
   a. True
   b. False

True, True, False.

Frequent Flyer Miles

The Internal Revenue Code does not contain a provision that specifically allows an employee to exclude from gross income the value of frequent flyer miles earned through employment activities. In Announcement 2002-18, however, the Internal Revenue Service announced that it "will not assert that any taxpayer has understated his . . . federal tax liability by reason of the receipt or personal use of airline frequent flyer miles or other in-kind promotional benefits attributable to the taxpayer's business or official travel." In other words, the value of frequent flyer miles can be excluded from gross income. The Announcement also indicates that any change in this policy will not be applied retroactively. This exclusion may be allowed by the IRS because of the associated enforcement challenges of including such amounts in gross income.

EMPLOYER-SPONSORED RETIREMENT PLAN CONTRIBUTIONS AND DISTRIBUTIONS

Employee Deferrals

When an employee elects to make contributions (salary deferrals) to an employer-sponsored retirement plan, those contributions can be excluded from the employee's current gross income (but are subject to payroll taxes). As the phrase "employee deferral" implies, the exclusion from income is temporary; the employee will pay tax on amounts contributed when those amounts are withdrawn during retirement.

Key Concepts

1. Identify the tax consequences of employer-sponsored retirement plan contributions and distributions.
2. Describe the tax consequences of employee stock options.

Employer Contributions

When an employer makes contributions to an employer-sponsored retirement plan, the employee can exclude the employer's contribution from current gross income. Unlike a pure exclusion to income, however, the employer contribution will be taxable to the employee when the employee withdraws the funds during retirement.

Retirement Plan Earnings

Any earnings (including interest, dividends and capital gains) on the amounts contributed to the plan are tax deferred until the employee receives distributions from the plan. This means that no one pays income taxes on the earnings until they are distributed to the employee.

Retirement Plan Distributions

When distributions are made from a retirement plan to an employee, the employee must generally report the distributions as ordinary income, but not as compensation subject to payroll taxes.

If after-tax contributions are made to a plan by the employee, then part of each periodic distribution from the plan is normally treated as a nontaxable return of investment (basis) and the remainder is included in gross income as ordinary income.

If a taxable distribution is made from a retirement plan before the employee reaches the age of 59½, a 10 percent penalty tax is also imposed (in addition to the income tax) on the taxable amount unless the distribution meets one of the exceptions provided in the Internal Revenue Code.

Income from Roth 401(k) and 403(b) Accounts

Since 2006, employees have been allowed to designate part or all of their contributions (elective deferrals) to a 401(k) or 403(b) retirement account as after-tax Roth contributions. While amounts contributed to a Roth 401(k) or 403(b) account are included in gross income, earnings are not subject to tax when withdrawn in a qualified distribution. The real benefit of making such after-tax contributions is that amounts distributed from the retirement plan, both contributions and earnings, can be fully excluded from gross income if:

1. the distributions are made at least five years from the beginning of the year for which the first contribution is made to the account, and
2. the distributions are made after the employee reaches age 59½, becomes disabled, or dies.

A distribution from a designated Roth account can be rolled over to another designated Roth account or to a Roth IRA.

Employee Stock Options: ISOs & NQSOs

An **incentive stock option (ISO)** is an option granted by a corporation (or a parent or subsidiary corporation) to an employee (or certain other individuals) to purchase the stock of that corporation (or a parent or subsidiary corporation) if numerous requirements are met by the ISO plan. Two of the most important plan requirements are that:

1. the option must be exercisable within 10 years of the date it is granted, and
2. the exercise price of the option (the purchase price of the stock) must not be less than the fair market value of the stock at the time the option is granted.

Quick Quiz 5.8

1. Employer contributions to employer-sponsored retirement plans are generally excluded from the employee's gross income.
   a. True
   b. False
2. No gross income for regular tax is recognized by the employee on the date an ISO is granted nor on the date an ISO is exercised.
   a. True
   b. False

True, True.

A **nonqualified stock option (NQSO)** is a type of stock option that does not meet the statutory requirements applicable to incentive stock options. If, at the date of grant of the option, the exercise price of the NQSO is greater than or equal to the fair market value of the stock, there is no income to the employee at that time. If the fair market value is more than the exercise price at the grant date, the employee has income as of the date of the grant for the difference.

The ordinary tax treatment of nonqualified stock options is relatively straightforward and follows the general rules of income taxation. At the date of exercise, if the fair market value of the stock exceeds the exercise price, the employee will have W-2 income to the extent of the difference. In addition, the employee will have a basis in the stock equal to the fair market value of the stock on the date of exercise. If the stock is later sold, any gain or loss will depend on the sale price of the stock.

The exercise of an incentive stock option (ISO), however, may have more favorable tax consequences because the simple exercise of the ISO does not ordinarily result in regular income. In addition, if certain requirements are met, more favorable capital gains rates will apply to a subsequent sale of the stock after exercise of the ISO. No gross income for regular tax purposes is recognized by the employee on the date the ISO is granted nor on the date the ISO is exercised. However, the exercise of an ISO will cause a positive adjustment in the calculation of alternative minimum taxable income (AMTI) and may result in the taxpayer having to pay alternative minimum tax (AMT). The AMT is discussed in Chapter 15. Upon exercise of the ISO, the employee will generate basis equal to the amount paid for the stock (the exercise price multiplied by the number of shares). When stock acquired through the exercise of an ISO is sold, any gain or loss on the sale is normally treated as a long-term capital gain or loss unless the employee sells the stock within two years from the day the ISO was granted or within one year from the day the ISO was exercised. If either holding period requirement is not met, any gain or loss on the sale is treated as an ordinary gain to the extent of the difference between the value of the stock and the option price on the day the option is exercised (this difference is referred to as the bargain element); any remaining gain is a capital gain. Any loss on the sale is a capital loss. The capital gain or loss may be either long-term or short-term depending on the length of the holding period between the date of exercise and the date of sale. A holding period of one year or less results in a short-term capital gain or loss while a holding period of longer than one year results in a long-term capital gain or loss.

Exhibit 5.11 | Tax Consequences of Stock Options

	NQSO	*ISO*
At Grant Date	If Strike Price ≥ FMV No Income Tax Consequence	No Income Tax Consequence
At Exercise Date	Ordinary (W-2) Income* = FMV - Exercise Price	No Ordinary Income AMT Preference = FMV - Strike Price
At Sale Date	Long-Term or Short-Term Capital Gain/Loss Depending on Holding Period Basis = FMV at Date of Exercise	If stock was held for 2 years from date of grant and 1 year from date of exercise: Gain = LTCG. If the holding period is not met, the difference between the fair market value on date of exercise and the strike price will be treated as ordinary (W-2) income, and the difference between the sale price and the price at the date of exercise will be treated as a capital gain.

**This result can be changed if the taxpayer makes an election under IRC Section 83(b). A Section 83(b) election permits the employee to include the value of property received as of the date of the grant in his or her income for the year of the grant. If a Section 83(b) election is made, the amount included in income will become the taxpayer's basis in the property, and subsequent gain or loss will be treated as capital gain.*

Example 5.24

On June 20, 2020, Valentina was granted an ISO to purchase 100 shares of her employer's stock at $10 per share, the value of the stock on the day the option was granted. When the stock had a value of $14 per share on February 20, 2021, Valentina exercised the option and purchased 100 shares for $1,000. On July 25, 2022, she sold the shares for $1,700. Valentina is not required to recognize any gross income on June 20, 2020 (the grant date) nor on February 20, 2021 (the exercise date). Since she met both of the holding period requirements, she can report her entire gain of $700 as a long-term capital gain. If she had sold the stock before both of the holding period requirements had been met, she would have reported $400 (the difference between the value of the stock and the exercise price on the exercise date) of the gain as ordinary wages and the remaining $300 of the gain as a capital gain in the year of the sale.

GOVERNMENT-REQUIRED BENEFITS

Unemployment Compensation

Unemployment compensation must be included in gross income unless the employee made after-tax contributions to a government or private unemployment compensation fund. Since unemployment compensation benefits are normally funded by employer contributions to government programs, benefits received by an employee are normally taxable.[9] Any unemployment taxes paid by the employer to fund the program can be deducted by the employer and excluded from gross income by the employee.

9. As a result of the coronavirus pandemic in 2020, the American Rescue Plan Act (ARPA) of 2021 excludes from income up to $10,200 of unemployment benefits received during 2020 for taxpayers whose adjusted gross income is below $150,000.

Workers' Compensation

An employee may receive workers' compensation benefits to pay for medical expenses, rehabilitation expenses, or lost income due to work-related injuries and sickness. Workers' compensation insurance premiums paid by an employer and any benefits received under workers' compensation insurance are excludable from an employee's gross income. Workers' compensation is intended to alleviate the conflict between employers and employees and attempts to make the employee whole when injured on the job.

Key Concepts

1. Explain the taxation of unemployment compensation.
2. Describe how Social Security is funded by employers and employees.
3. Explain how Social Security benefits may be taxable.

Social Security

The employer and the employee usually contribute equally to the funding of old age, survivors, and disability income (OASDI) benefits under the Social Security system of the United States. The employer pays a payroll tax of 6.2 percent of compensation up to an annual contribution base limit ($142,800 for 2021) for each employee. In addition, the employer pays 1.45 percent (no limit on compensation) for each employee for the Medicare portion of the Social Security tax. The employer is allowed to deduct this payroll tax, and the employee is allowed to exclude the employer paid portion from gross income. The employer also withholds an identical 6.2 percent for Social Security (up to $142,800 of compensation for 2021) and 1.45 percent for Medicare (with no limit on compensation) from each employee's compensation and remits it to the federal government. This half is included in the employee's gross income as taxable compensation and is withheld (along with federal income taxes) from the employee's gross pay and remitted to the federal government. In addition, high income taxpayers are subject to an additional 0.9 percent Medicare surtax on earnings imposed by the Affordable Care Act of 2010. Employers will withhold the additional tax for Individuals with income over the specified thresholds. The amount withheld from an employee's pay for OASDI and Medicare benefits is often referred to as **FICA (Federal Insurance Contributions Act)** on the employee's pay stub.

When an employee receives Social Security retirement or other benefits, up to 85 percent of the benefits may be included in the employee's gross income, depending on the employee's modified adjusted gross income (MAGI) for the year. If a retired taxpayer's only income is from Social Security retirement benefits, the benefits will generally be excludable. If a taxpayer receives Social Security benefits and has significant amounts of other income for the year as well, a portion of the Social Security benefits, up to a maximum of 85 percent of benefits received, must be included in gross income for the year.

If a taxpayer's MAGI plus one-half of the Social Security benefits received during the year do not exceed the base amount below, none of the Social Security benefits are includible in gross income.

Exhibit 5.12 | Social Security Base Amounts

	Married Filing Jointly	*All Others (Except MFS)*	*Married Filing Separately*
Base Amount	$32,000	$25,000	$0
Adjusted Base Amount	$44,000	$34,000	$0

The rules above also apply to tier 1 railroad retirement benefits, which serve as a substitute for Social Security retirement benefits.

Example 5.25

Chuck, an unmarried taxpayer using the single filing status, received $15,000 of Social Security retirement benefits this year. He also received $5,000 of interest income during the year. Since the total of Chuck's MAGI ($5,000) and one-half of his Social Security benefits (0.50 x $15,000 = $7,500) is less than his base amount ($25,000), none of his Social Security benefits are included in gross income.

If a taxpayer's MAGI plus one-half of Social Security benefits exceeds the relevant base amount but not the adjusted base amount, the amount of Social Security benefits that must be included in gross income is equal to the lesser of:

1. 50% of Social Security benefits,
   OR
2. 50% x [MAGI + (50% x Social Security Benefits) - Base Amount]

Example 5.26

Julianna, an unmarried taxpayer using the single filing status, received $15,000 of Social Security retirement benefits this year. She also received $5,000 of interest income, $3,000 of dividend income, and $18,000 of income from her retirement plan during the year. Since her MAGI ($26,000) plus one-half of her Social Security benefits (0.5 x $15,000 = $7,500) exceeds her base amount ($25,000) but not her adjusted base amount ($34,000), Julianna must calculate her includible Social Security benefits using the formulas above. Half of her Social Security benefits is $7,500. The second formula yields an inclusion amount of $4,250 [0.5 x ($26,000 + $7,500 - $25,000)]. Julianna must include the lesser of the two amounts ($4,250) in her gross income.

If a taxpayer's MAGI plus one-half of Social Security benefits exceeds the adjusted base amount, the amount of Social Security benefits that must be included in gross income is equal to the lesser of:

3. 85% of Social Security benefits,
   OR
4. 85% x [MAGI + (50% x Social Security Benefits) - Adjusted Base Amount]
   PLUS
   Lesser of: Amount included from formulas 1 and 2 OR $4,500 ($6,000 for married filing jointly; $0 for married filing separately).

Example 5.27

Andrea, an unmarried taxpayer using the single filing status, received $15,000 of Social Security retirement benefits this year. She also received $5,000 of interest income and $48,000 of income from her retirement plan during the year. Since her MAGI ($53,000) plus one-half of her Social Security benefits (0.5 x $15,000 = $7,500) exceeds her adjusted base amount ($34,000), she must calculate her includible Social Security benefits using the formula 3 or 4 above.

3. 0.85 x $15,000 = $12,750
4. 0.85 x [$53,000 + (0.50 x $15,000) - $34,000] = $22,525 plus the lesser of the amount calculated using 1 and 2 above:
    1. 0.50 x $15,000 = $7,500
    2. 0.50 x [$53,000 + (0.50 x $15,000) - $25,000] = $17,750

The lesser amount is $7,500.

The formula 4 total is $30,025 ($22,525 + $7,500) OR $27,025 ($22,525 + $4,500).

The lesser of the formula 3 or 4 amounts is $12,750. Therefore, $12,750 of the Social Security benefits must be included in Andrea's gross income.

Modified Adjusted Gross Income (MAGI) for Social Security Income Inclusion

Modified adjusted gross income is equal to adjusted gross income before any Social Security benefits plus excluded municipal bond interest, excluded foreign earned income and housing allowances, excluded U.S. Savings Bond interest, excluded adoption assistance benefits, deducted student loan interest expense, excluded income from Guam, American Samoa, the Northern Marianna Islands, and Puerto Rico.

Quick Quiz 5.9

1. Up to 85% of Social Security benefits may be taxable.
    a. True
    b. False
2. MAGI includes municipal bond interest.
    a. True
    b. False

True, True.

Impact of Roth IRAs and Roth Accounts on Taxation of Social Security Benefits

Distributions from retirement plans, including qualified plans and IRAs, increase MAGI to the extent that the distribution is taxable. Qualified distributions from Roth IRAs and Roth Accounts are not taxable and will therefore not increase the taxation of Social Security benefits.[10] However, conversions of traditional IRAs to Roth IRAs or in-plan Roth rollovers will increase MAGI and therefore could impact the taxation of Social Security benefits.

10. Qualified distributions from Roth IRAs and Roth Accounts require taxpayers to meet a two-pronged test. The first prong is a five-year holding period requirement. The second prong requires that the distribution occur as a result of death, disability or attainment of age 59½ by the taxpayer. Roth IRAs have an additional exception for distributions that qualify for first time home purchases up to $10,000.

SUMMARY AND CONCLUSION

The following two tables contain summary information about employment-related income and fringe benefit items that are commonly included in gross income and excluded from gross income, respectively.

Exhibit 5.13 | Summary of Gross Income Items

Item	*IRC Section*	*Category*	*Reported on Form*	*IRS Publication*
Wages, Salaries, Tips, Commissions, Fees, Etc.	61(a)(1)	Employment	1040	17
Fringe Benefits (Unless Specifically Excluded)	61	Employment	1040	15B
Self-Employment Income	61(a)(2)	Self-Employment	Sch. C or F	334
Disability Income Insurance Benefits (If Employer Pays Premiums)	105	Employment	1040	17
Retirement Plan Distributions	61(a)(11)	Employment	1040	575
Nonqualified Stock Options (NQSO)	422/83	Employment	1040	525/15B
Unemployment Compensation	85	Employment	1040	525
Social Security Benefits (0% to 85% Included in Gross Income)	86	Employment	1040	915

Exhibit 5.14 | Summary of Exclusions from Gross Income Items

Item	IRC Section	Category	IRS Publication
Foreign Earned Income Exclusion	911	Employment	54
Health Insurance Premiums and Benefits	105/106	Employment	15B
Medical Reimbursement Plans	105/106	Employment	15B
Loss or Loss of Use of a Member or Function of the Body	105/106	Employment	15B
Archer Medical Savings Accounts	106(b)/220	Employment	969
Health Savings Accounts	106(d)/223	Employment	969
Group Term Life Insurance	79	Employment	15B
Employee Death Benefits	102	Employment	*
Survivor Benefits for Public Safety Officer Killed in the Line of Duty	101(h)	Employment	17
Disability Insurance Premiums and Benefits	105/106	Employment	17
Cafeteria Plans	125	Employment	15B
Flexible Spending Plans	125	Employment	969
Long-term Care Premiums and Benefits	7702B	Employment	525
Meals and Lodging***	119	Employment	15B
No-additional-cost Services	132	Employment	15B
Qualified Discounts on Goods and Services	132	Employment	15B
Working Condition Fringe Benefits	132	Employment	15B
De minimis Fringe Benefits	132	Employment	15B
Qualified Transportation Fringe Benefits***	132	Employment	15B
Qualified Moving Expense Reimbursements (Armed Forces Only)***	132	Employment	15B
Qualified Retirement Planning Services	132	Employment	15B
Athletic Facilities Provided to Employees	132	Employment	15B
Educational Assistance Programs	127	Employment	15B
Dependent Care Assistance Programs	129	Employment	15B
Tuition Reductions Granted to Employees of Educational Institutions	117	Employment	15B
Adoption Assistance Program Payments	137	Employment	15B
Employee Achievement Awards***	74	Employment	15B
Combat Pay	112	Employment	3
Other Specified Military Fringe Benefits	134/132	Employment	3
Rental Value of Parsonage	107	Employment	517
Frequent Flyer Miles	An. 2002-18	Employment	**
Other Fringe Benefits		Employment	15B
Retirement Plan Contributions and Earnings	401/402	Employment	560
Incentive Stock Options	422	Employment	15B/525
Workers' Compensation Premiums & Benefits	104	Employment	907/525
Social Security Benefits (0% to 85% Included in Gross Income)	86	Employment	915

** Estate of Sydney J. Carter v. Comm, 29 AFTR2d 332*

*** Announcement 2002-18*

*** Announcement 2002-18, I.R.B. 2002-10, 621*

**** These benefits have been limited and/or suspended (for tax years 2018-2025) by TCJA 2017.*

KEY TERMS

Activities of Daily Living - Eating, bathing, dressing, toileting, transferring, and continence.

Adoption Assistance Program - An employer plan that assists employees with the cost of adoption and may not discriminate in favor of highly compensated or key employees.

Archer Medical Savings Accounts (MSAs) - Tax-favored savings accounts for medical expenses that were established by HIPAA in 1996, but cannot be established after 2005.

Bona Fide Resident Test - Requirement for the Foreign Earned Income exclusion that requires the taxpayer to generally intend to work and reside in the foreign country for an indefinite period of time.

Cafeteria Plan - A written plan under which an employee may choose to receive either cash or taxable benefits as compensation or qualified fringe benefits that are excludable from wages.

Compensation - Salary, wages, and fringe benefits received in exchange for providing services to an employer.

De Minimis Fringe Benefit - Fringe benefits that are so small or insignificant that accounting for them would be unreasonable or administratively impracticable.

Disability Insurance - Provides benefits in the form of periodic payments to a person who is unable to work due to sickness or accidental injury.

Educational Assistance Program - A separate written plan that establishes a program through which an employer provides educational assistance to employees.

Federal Insurance Contributions Act (FICA) - A law that dictates the amount to be withheld from an employee's pay for OASDI benefits.

Flexible Spending Account (FSA) - A type of cafeteria plan that is funded through employee salary reductions. The health care FSA limit is $2,750 (2021).

Foreign Earned Income - Income earned by a qualifying citizen or resident of the United States in exchange for personal services rendered in a foreign country. The foreign earned income limit is $108,700 (2021).

Fringe Benefits - Non-cash benefits provided to an employee by an employer in addition to wages and salary.

Health Reimbursement Arrangements (HRAs) - Employer-funded plans that reimburse employees for medical expenses and allow employees to carry any unused balance forward to be used in future years.

Health Savings Accounts (HSAs) - Accounts that allow individuals who have high deductible health insurance plans to save on a tax-free basis to fund their medical expenses.

Highly Compensated Employees - Those employees who are either a greater than five percent owner or have compensation in excess of $130,000 (2021).

Incentive Stock Option (ISO) - A tax-favored stock option that meets certain requirements and is granted by a corporation to an employee to purchase the stock of that corporation.

Key Employee - An employee who is (1) a greater than five percent owner, (2) a greater than one percent owner with compensation in excess of $150,000, or (3) an officer with compensation in excess of $185,000 (2021).

Long-Term Care Insurance - Provides benefits when the insured is unable to perform some of the activities of daily living.

No-Additional-Cost Services - A fringe benefit provided by employers that may be excluded from the employee's gross income if the service is (1) offered for sale to customers, (2) in the line of business in which the employee works, and (3) does not cause the employer to incur any substantial costs (including foregone revenue) in providing the service to the employee.

Nonqualified Stock Option (NQSO) – A right to purchase shares of company stock at a given strike price (generally set at the market price of the stock on the day the option is granted).

Physical Presence Test - Requirement for the Foreign Earned Income exclusion that requires the taxpayer to be present in a foreign country or countries for at least 330 full days during any period of 12 consecutive months.

Qualified Employee Discounts - Employer-provided discounts on qualified property and services that can be excluded from an employee's gross income.

Qualified Moving Expense Reimbursement - Direct or indirect payments by an employer to pay the cost of moving an employee's family and belongings (TCJA 2017 limited this provision to members of the Armed Forces after 2017).

Qualified Retirement Planning Services - Any retirement planning advice or information provided to an employee and his spouse by an employer maintaining a qualified employer-sponsored retirement plan.

Qualified Transportation Fringe Benefits - Benefits in the form of (1) transportation between an employee's residence and the place of employment in a commuter highway vehicle, (2) any transit pass, or (3) qualified parking. After 2017, employers are no longer permitted to take a deduction for qualified transportation fringe benefits, unless the benefit is provided for the safety of the employee.

Working Condition Fringe Benefit - Any property or service provided to an employee to help the employee perform his job better.

DISCUSSION QUESTIONS

SOLUTIONS to the discussion questions can be found exclusively within the chapter. Once you have completed an initial reading of the chapter, go back and highlight the answers to these questions.

1. Discuss the various types of compensation and whether they must be included in gross income.
2. How is compensation received by an independent contractor reported?
3. Under what circumstances can foreign earned income be excluded from gross income?
4. Explain the bona fide resident test and the physical presence test.
5. When are fringe benefits included in the gross income of employees?
6. How do nondiscrimination requirements affect the taxation of fringe benefits?
7. List the various ways that an employer can provide an employee with benefits for medical care.
8. How much group term life insurance can be provided to employees without causing inclusion in gross income?
9. Describe the circumstances under which disability insurance benefits are excludable from gross income.
10. How do cafeteria plans help manage the costs of fringe benefits?
11. In what situation would a flexible spending account be appropriate?
12. Under what circumstances are meals provided by an employer excludable from the employee's gross income?
13. Under what circumstances can the value of lodging furnished by an employer be excluded from the employee's gross income?
14. What are no-additional-cost services?
15. Describe the rules regarding qualified employee discounts.
16. What are de minimis fringe benefits?
17. Under what circumstances can the value of athletic facilities be excluded from an employee's income?
18. Describe the taxation of ISOs.
19. Describe the taxation of unemployment compensation.
20. What percentage of Social Security benefits are taxable?

MULTIPLE CHOICE PROBLEMS

A sample of multiple choice problems is provided below. Additional multiple choice problems are available at money-education.com by accessing the Student Practice Portal.

1. B.J. and Penny, a married couple, have income of $50,000 and Social Security benefits of $20,000. What amount of their Social Security benefits must be included in their gross income?
    a. $13,600.
    b. $14,000.
    c. $17,000.
    d. $19,600.

2. Dustin and Diamond are married and had the following income and expenses for this year.
    1. Dustin's salary of $60,000.
    2. Dustin's employer provides him with a group term life insurance policy for two times his salary. The policy premium paid by the employer is $150 per year. The Uniform Premium Table amount is $0.10.
    3. Diamond had salary of $10,000 and unemployment compensation of $9,000.
    4. Diamond won $1,500 on a game show.

    What is Dustin and Diamond's joint gross income?

    a. $71,584.
    b. $78,184.
    c. $78,250.
    d. $80,584.

3. Which of the following statements is correct regarding the taxation of fringe benefits?
    1. The value of the fringe benefit is included in the employee's gross income unless the IRC specifically excludes it from taxation.
    2. The value of the fringe benefit is excluded from the employee's gross income unless the IRC specifies otherwise.
    3. The value of the fringe benefit is taxable if the benefit is only provided to employees owning more than 5% of the company and the fringe benefit has a nondiscrimination requirement.
    4. The value of the fringe benefit is always taxable if someone other than the employee (e.g., the employee's spouse) benefits from the fringe benefit provided by the employer.

    a. 1 and 2.
    b. 1 and 3.
    c. 2 and 4.
    d. 3 and 4.

4. Which of the following is not a qualifying person for the purpose of employer-provided dependent care assistance?
    a. A child of the employee regardless of whether the child can be claimed as a dependent on the employee's tax return.
    b. A dependent of the employee who has not attained the age of 13.
    c. A dependent of the employee who is physically or mentally incapable of caring for himself and who has the same principal place of abode as the employee for more than one-half of the year.
    d. The employee's spouse who is physically or mentally incapable of caring for himself and who has the same principal place of abode as the employee for more than one-half of the year.

5. Brock receives stock options (ISOs) with an exercise price of $16 when the stock is trading at $16. Brock exercises these options two years after the date of the grant when the stock price is $37 per share. Which of the following statements is correct?
    a. Upon exercise, Brock will have no income for regular tax purposes.
    b. Brock will have W-2 income of $21 per share upon exercise.
    c. Brock will have $16 of AMT income upon exercise.
    d. Brock's adjusted basis for regular income tax will be $37 at exercise.

Additional multiple choice problems are available at *money-education.com* by accessing the Student Practice Portal. Access requires registration of the title using the unique code at the front of the book.

QUICK QUIZ EXPLANATIONS

Quick Quiz 5.1

1. False. Gross income cannot normally be assigned by the person who earns it to anyone else.
2. True.

Quick Quiz 5.2

1. False. Fringe benefits are not always nontaxable. However, fringe benefits may still be valuable to employees even if they are taxable. For example, with a large number of employees, employers can negotiate lower group insurance rates and better coverage than an individual employee would be able to negotiate in the open market.
2. True.
3. False. An HSA may be independently established by an employee, or it may be facilitated by an employer.

Quick Quiz 5.3

1. False. The cost, as determined under the Uniform Premium Table provided by the IRS, of any death benefit coverage in excess of $50,000 is taxable to the employee, not the employer.
2. True.
3. False. A cafeteria plan is appropriate when employee benefit needs vary within the employee group; the employee mix includes young, unmarried people with minimal life insurance and medical benefits needs, as well as older employees with families who need maximum medical and life insurance benefits.

Quick Quiz 5.4

1. False. One disadvantage of an FSA is that amounts remaining in the account at the end of the year are forfeited back to the employer (a use it or lose it arrangement).
2. True.
3. True.

Quick Quiz 5.5

1. False. In general, an employee can exclude from gross income the value of meals provided in-kind (not as cash reimbursement) to the employee as long as the meals (1) are furnished on the employer's business premises, and (2) are for the convenience of the employer. However, after 2017, the employer can only deduct 50% of the cost of providing these types of meals. Note: Under the Taxpayer Certainty and Disaster Tax Relief Act (TCDRA) of 2020, an exception to the 50% deduction limit applies to food and beverages provided by a restaurant, allowing such meals to be fully deductible when paid or incurred after December 31, 2020 and before January 1, 2023.
2. False. Guaranteed seats are not a no-additional-cost service because guaranteeing seats for an employee might cause the employer to forego revenue. Only standby seats, which depend on availability, are a no-additional cost service.
3. True.

QUICK QUIZ EXPLANATIONS

Quick Quiz 5.6

1. False. If the employee uses the car for both personal and business purposes, the business-use value is considered to be a working condition fringe benefit, but the personal use value of the car must normally be included in the employee's gross income.
2. False. The amounts that can be excluded from gross income are limited to $270 per month for 2021 for commuter highway vehicle use (item 1) and transit passes (item 2) combined. The monthly limit for qualified parking is $270 for 2021. Any benefits received in excess of these amounts, less any amount paid by the employee for the benefits, must be included in an employee's gross income. However, after 2017, the employer can no longer deduct expenses associated with providing any qualified transportation fringe to employees, except for ensuring the safety of an employee.

Quick Quiz 5.7

1. True.
2. True.
3. False. Military personnel can exclude combat zone pay from gross income.

Quick Quiz 5.8

1. True.
2. True.

Quick Quiz 5.9

1. True.
2. True.

6
INTRODUCTION TO DEDUCTIONS

LEARNING OBJECTIVES

1. Describe the different classifications of income tax deductions.*
2. Describe the tax treatment of business expense deductions for sole proprietors, partnerships, and corporations.*
3. Calculate a taxpayer's adjusted gross income (AGI) and taxable income (TI) taking into account tax deductions available to the taxpayer.*
4. Discuss the special deduction rules for self-employed individuals who pay self-employment tax, pay health insurance premiums, or make contributions to self-employed pension plans, and explain the tax impact on self-employed individuals.*
5. Describe the impact of taking above-the-line vs. below-the-line deductions.*
6. Discuss the tax treatment of qualified long term care insurance premiums for self-employed individuals, and for employees.*
7. Discuss the contribution and deduction rules for Medical Savings Accounts (MSAs) and Health Savings Accounts (HSAs).*
8. List the qualification requirements necessary for a taxpayer to use an HSA.*
9. Describe how contributions to an HSA affect a self-employed individual's self-employment (Social Security/Medicare) tax and pension plan contributions.*
10. Explain how HSAs/MSAs can minimize lifetime health insurance premium costs for a client.*
11. Describe the requirements for traditional and Roth IRA contributions, the tax benefits of using both types of IRAs, and the tax penalties that may apply to contributions and distributions from both types of IRAs.*
12. Discuss the spousal IRA rules and identify the benefit of these rules for taxpayers.*
13. Describe the tax treatment of penalties on early withdrawal of savings from certificates of deposit.*
14. Discuss the tax deductibility of student loan interest, including any applicable limitations that may apply.*
15. List the requirements for alimony to be deductible.*
16. Describe the tax deductibility of alimony and child support payments, and the circumstances under which alimony may be considered child support.*
17. Calculate alimony recapture, and describe the tax treatment for both the payor and payee.*
18. Discuss the differences between S-corporations and C corporations from an income tax perspective.*
19. Discuss the income tax treatment of partnership income and deductions.*
20. List and describe the requirements necessary for business expenses to be deductible.*
21. Identify and describe common business deductions.*
22. Describe the tax deductibility of investigation of business expenditures.
23. Discuss the requirements for the home office deduction.*
24. Describe typical tax planning techniques using deductions for employees, business owners, and investors.*

**Ties to CFP Certification Learning Objectives*

INTRODUCTION

The 16th Amendment to the U.S. Constitution gives Congress the power to tax income. Congress could, presumably, assess an income tax on gross income without taking into consideration any deductions, but for fairness and public policy reasons, deductions from income are made available to taxpayers. Deductions are not entitlements for taxpayers – they are based on legislative grace. Legitimate deductions from income must be specifically permitted by statute (the Internal Revenue Code).

In the U.S. tax system, the taxpayer, not the IRS, has the responsibility for substantiating deductions. To justify deductions taken for income tax purposes, taxpayers must maintain adequate records of their expenses. Receipts or proof of expenditures should be kept by taxpayers at least until the statute of limitations expires for the tax year in question. For some deductions, such as those for meals, more extensive recordkeeping is required. This chapter introduces deductions available to taxpayers.

CLASSIFICATION OF DEDUCTIBLE EXPENSES

Income tax deductions fall into two basic categories: **above-the-line deductions** (or deductions for AGI) which are sometimes referred to as adjustments, and **below-the-line deductions** (deductions from AGI) which are often referred to as Itemized Deductions. (Note that the "line," for income tax purposes, is adjusted gross income (AGI).) AGI is the basis for many of the phaseouts and thresholds that will have to be met to take advantage of certain deductions and tax planning opportunities. Understanding where deductions are taken in the tax formula, therefore, is important when considering tax planning alternatives for clients.

When considering income tax deductions and their planning implications for clients, it is helpful to recall the income tax formula.

Gross Income	**$xx,xxx**
Less: Deductions for Adjusted Gross Income *(above-the-line deductions)*	(x,xxx)
Adjusted Gross Income (AGI)	**$xx,xxx**
Less: Deductions from Adjusted Gross Income *(below-the-line deductions)* Greater of Standard or Itemized Deductions and the Qualified Business Income Deduction	(xx,xxx)
Taxable Income	**$xx,xxx**

As the tax formula illustrates, adjustments (above-the-line deductions) are subtracted from gross income to arrive at AGI, while below-the-line deductions (the greater of itemized deductions or the standard deduction, plus the QBI deduction) are subtracted from AGI and are not taken into account until after AGI is computed.

Exhibit 6.1 | Adjustments to Gross Income
(from Form 1040, Schedule 1)

	Part II Adjustments to Income		
10	Educator expenses	10	
11	Certain business expenses of reservists, performing artists, and fee-basis government officials. Attach Form 2106	11	
12	Health savings account deduction. Attach Form 8889	12	
13	Moving expenses for members of the Armed Forces. Attach Form 3903	13	
14	Deductible part of self-employment tax. Attach Schedule SE	14	
15	Self-employed SEP, SIMPLE, and qualified plans	15	
16	Self-employed health insurance deduction	16	
17	Penalty on early withdrawal of savings	17	
18a	Alimony paid	18a	
b	Recipient's SSN ▶		
c	Date of original divorce or separation agreement (see instructions) ▶		
19	IRA deduction	19	
20	Student loan interest deduction	20	
21	Tuition and fees deduction. Attach Form 8917	21	
22	Add lines 10 through 21. These are your **adjustments to income.** Enter here and on Form 1040, 1040-SR, or 1040-NR, line 10a	22	

Deductions for AGI (Above-the-Line Deductions)

Adjustments, or above-the-line deductions, reduce a taxpayer's adjusted gross income (AGI). Most above-the-line deductions relate to expenses for business and production of income activities (from investment activities) by taxpayers, but there are some deductions permitted for individual taxpayers as well (such as IRA deductions, student loan interest, and educator expenses, to name a few). Above-the-line deductions are listed in IRC Section 62, and they can be claimed by the taxpayer even if the taxpayer does not itemize deductions. See **Exhibit 6.1**.

> ### Key Concepts
>
> 1. Name the two categories of income tax deductions.
> 2. Describe an above-the-line deduction.
> 3. Describe a below-the-line deduction.
> 4. Explain which type of deduction is generally considered to be most favorable to taxpayers.

Expenses associated with a business activity are above-the-line deductions. Only the net income of the business (gross receipts from the business less expenses incurred in producing that income) is included in the taxpayer's gross income for the year. For example, if a taxpayer operates a sole proprietorship, the financial results will be reported on Schedule C of the taxpayer's individual tax return. If a taxpayer engages in rental real estate activities, the gross receipts from the rental activity less expenses associated with the rental activity will be reported on Schedule E of the income tax return, and only the net income from the activity will be reported in the taxpayer's gross income for the year. Schedules C and E are essentially income statements for the business and production of income activities, detailing the gross receipts and expenditures incurred in the activity. Similarly, capital losses on the sale of capital assets (e.g., investments such as stocks or bonds) offset capital gains on Schedule D and only the net amount of gain for the year is reported as income. Since business related and production of income related expenses directly reduce gross income, they are effectively treated as above-the-line deductions.

All other above-the-line deductions are found in the Adjustments to Income section (**Exhibit 6.1**) of Form 1040, Schedule 1.

Deductions from AGI (Below-the-Line Deductions)

When most taxpayers think of deductions, they usually think of itemized deductions. Itemized deductions, one of the two types of below-the-line deductions, are deductions that are allowed for personal expenses and losses that are not typically associated with the conduct of a business or with production of income activities. While there are fewer itemized deductions than above-the-line deductions (there are only six categories of itemized deductions), itemized deductions are sometimes more important when planning for individual clients.

Taxpayers may take the greater of their itemized deductions or the standard deduction in determining taxable income. In order to achieve a tax benefit, the taxpayer's itemized deductions must be greater than the allowable standard deduction.

The types of itemized deductions, and their associated limitations, are discussed in detail in Chapter 7.

TCJA 2017 introduced a new type of below-the-line deduction: the deduction for Qualified Business Income (QBI) (also known as the Section 199A deduction). The QBI deduction is a below-the-line deduction that is not affected by a taxpayer's standard deduction. A taxpayer who qualifies for the QBI deduction may take both the QBI deduction plus the greater of his or her itemized deductions or standard deduction when calculating taxable income.

Quick Quiz 6.1

1. Above-the-line deductions are also known as adjustments to income.
   a. True
   b. False
2. Whenever expenses are associated with a business activity, they are below-the-line deductions.
   a. True
   b. False
3. Taxpayers must deduct the lesser of their itemized deductions or the standard deduction.
   a. True
   b. False
4. Above-the-line deductions are usually considered to be more favorable than below-the-line deductions on a dollar-for-dollar basis.
   a. True
   b. False

True, False, False, True.

Which Type of Deduction is Better – Above- or Below-the-Line Deductions?

Due to the limitation imposed on itemized deductions by the standard deduction (since a taxpayer can only take the greater of the two), the various deduction floors and ceilings, as well as phaseouts associated with below-the-line deductions, above-the-line deductions are usually considered to be more favorable to the taxpayer on a dollar-for-dollar basis.

Example 6.1

William and Serena are single, and each of them has gross income of $75,000 and deductions of $15,000. Neither William nor Serena qualify for the QBI (or Sec. 199A) Deduction. Serena's deductions, however, can be taken above-the-line, while William will have to report his deductions as itemized deductions. Serena and William's taxable income for 2021 is calculated as follows:

	Serena	*William*	*Difference*
Gross Income	$75,000	$75,000	$0
- Adjustments (for AGI ded)	$15,000	$0	$15,000
= Adjusted Gross Income (AGI)	$60,000	$75,000	($15,000)
- Standard/Itemized Deductions	$12,550	$15,000	($2,450)
- Personal Exemption (Repealed TCJA)	$0	$0	$0
= Taxable Income	**$47,450**	**$60,000**	**($12,550)**

While both William and Serena have exactly the same gross income and the same out of pocket deductions, Serena's taxable income is less than William's. The difference between their incomes equals the standard deduction. Serena was able to take both the standard deduction and her above-the-line deductions, while William was only able to benefit from his below-the-line deductions and then only to the extent that they exceeded the standard deduction. Serena will pay a much lower tax than William, even though their income and out-of-pocket expenses were the same.

In the example above, Serena and William had modest income, and would not have been subject to phaseouts, floors, and ceilings that apply to some itemized deductions. If their income was higher, or their expenses were subject to the limitations imposed on itemized deductions, the difference in tax liability between the two parties would be even greater.

ABOVE-THE-LINE DEDUCTIONS FOR INDIVIDUALS

Trade or Business Expenses

Trade or business expenses are, by their very nature, above-the-line tax deductions. If a taxpayer owns an interest in a C corporation, S corporation or Partnership (including general and limited partnerships, LLCs, and LLPs), business expenses are deducted from income on the entity tax return, and only the net profit (in the case of S corporations and partnerships), or dividends distributed (in the case of C corporations) are included on an individual taxpayer's income tax return. Likewise, if the taxpayer conducts business as a sole proprietorship, business income and expenses are reported on Schedule C, and only the net income of the business (gross receipts less expenditures) is included in gross income on the income section of the taxpayer's income tax return.

For sole proprietors and partners, there are three additional above-the-line deductions related to business activities that may be available. These include:

1. one-half of self-employment tax paid
2. self-employed pension contributions (to Simplified Employee Pensions (SEPs), SIMPLEs, and other qualified retirement plans)
3. the self-employed health insurance deduction

Self-employed individuals must pay Social Security taxes, just like employees. Employees, however, have an advantage in that one-half of their Social Security taxes is paid by their employer. An employee pays 7.65 percent on income up to the Social Security wage base for Social Security and Medicare taxes, and 1.45 percent (the Medicare component) on income above the Social Security wage base ($142,800 for 2021). The employer matches these contributions. High income individuals, as defined in the Affordable Care Act, must also pay an additional 0.9 percent Medicare surtax on income over specified thresholds ($250,000 for married filing jointly status; $200,000 for single individuals). Self-employed individuals have a dual role, they are both the employer and the employee, so they must pay both the employer and employee portion of the tax. Employers who pay Social Security and Medicare taxes on behalf of an employee deduct their payment from business income in arriving at a net profit amount, so a self-employed person should be able to do the same. A deduction is not allowed on Schedule C for employment taxes paid, but an adjustment to income (an above-the-line deduction) is permitted for one-half of the self-employment taxes paid (not including the 0.9 percent Medicare surtax imposed by the Affordable Care Act on "high income individuals"). Allowing this deduction above the line ensures that it will not be subject to the limitations and phaseouts that apply to below-the-line (itemized) deductions.

Self-employed individuals are also permitted to set up qualified and nonqualified tax advantaged retirement plans, and are permitted to deduct contributions to those plans up to a specified amount. The deduction allowed depends on the type of plan established, as well as the coverage rules that apply to the plan. Plan contributions for employees of a business are deducted on the business tax return or on the Schedule C of a self-employed individual. Allowable retirement plan deductions for a self-employed person are treated as adjustments to income and are deducted above-the-line. By making the retirement plan contributions for self-employed individuals an adjustment to income as opposed to a business expense deduction, the IRC subjects the self-employed individual's retirement plan contributions to the self-employment tax.

Self-employed individuals are also permitted to deduct 100 percent of health insurance premiums paid on behalf of themselves and their dependents. The deduction for their own insurance is not permitted on Schedule C (for sole proprietors) or in determining business income on Form 1065 or 1120S (partnership/S Corporation tax return, but can be taken as an adjustment to income (above-the-line). Health care premiums paid on behalf of employees by the self-employed individual are deducted on the business tax return or on the Schedule C of a self-employed individual. These rules apply to self-employed individuals who file a Schedule C, partners, and more than two percent owners of S corporations.

One type of health insurance often overlooked by business owners is long-term care insurance. Self-employed individuals may deduct the cost of long-term care insurance on their lives up to specified amounts based on their age (**Exhibit 6.2**) as an adjustment to income (above-the-line). Long-term care can be provided as an employee benefit on a discriminatory basis, so business owners who wish to purchase long-term care coverage for themselves may do so without creating an obligation to purchase similar coverage for their employees.

In order to obtain the deduction, however, the contract must be a qualified long-term care contract. Most contracts currently being sold are qualified contracts. Qualified contracts cover only qualified long-term care expenses, are guaranteed renewable, do not provide cash surrender value, and do not reimburse expenses recovered under Medicare. Long-term care policies that have life insurance features and cash values will not generally meet the definition of a qualified long-term care contract.

Exhibit 6.2 | Deduction Limitation on Long-Term Care Insurance Premiums

Age	*2021 Deduction Limit*
40 or less	$450
41-50	$850
51-60	$1,690
61-70	$4,520
71 and over	$5,640

Medical Savings Accounts (MSAs) and Health Savings Accounts (HSAs)

As part of the Health Insurance Portability and Accountability Act (HIPAA) of 1996, Congress created **Medical Savings Accounts**. These accounts were available to self-employed individuals and small corporations, and allowed participants to contribute part of the annual deductible amount on their health insurance policies to the MSA, which could grow on a tax-free basis if funds distributed from the account were used to pay for medical expenses. MSAs were available on a pilot basis, and can no longer be set up due to legislation passed in 2003 authorizing the creation of **Health Savings Accounts (HSAs)**. MSAs that were in existence at the time of the HSA legislation may still be used, and are referred to as "Archer MSAs" in honor of their sponsor, Congressman Bill Archer of Texas. Subject to certain limits, contributions to an HSA or MSA allow the taxpayer to take an above-the-line deduction on their income tax returns.

Unlike MSAs, which were primarily for the self-employed, HSAs allow individuals to save on a tax-free basis to fund their medical expenses. To qualify for an HSA, a taxpayer must:

1. be covered by a high deductible health insurance plan (sometimes referred to as an HDHP)
2. have no other health insurance coverage except the HDHP
3. not be enrolled in Medicare
4. not be claimed as a dependent on someone else's tax return

A High Deductible Health Plan (HDHP) is any plan that had a deductible falling between the minimum and maximum annual amounts, shown in **Exhibit 6.3**.

Key Concepts

1. List those who qualify to participate in MSAs and HSAs.
2. Discuss the contribution rules for MSAs and HSAs.
3. Describe the deduction for contributions to an HSA or MSA.
4. Explain the circumstances under which long-term care insurance premiums are deductible.

Exhibit 6.3 | Deductible Limits for HDHPs (2021)

	Minimum Deductible	*Maximum Deductible and Out of Pocket Expenses*
Individual	$1,400	$7,000
Family	$2,800	$14,000

HSA contributions can be made at any time during the tax year and up to the due date of the tax return, plus extensions. Contributions may not be made in advance, however. If the HSA is offered through an employer, contributions may be made through the employer's cafeteria plan. For taxable years beginning after December 31, 2006, the maximum allowable contribution to an HSA is an indexed amount provided by the IRS. In addition, individuals age 55 or older are entitled to a catch-up contribution.

Exhibit 6.4 | Maximum HSA Contributions (2021)

	Maximum Contribution	*Age 55 or older Catch-Up*
Individual	$3,600	$1,000
Family	$7,200	$1,000

The maximum allowable contribution to a HSA is reduced by any contributions made to an MSA. An individual who qualifies for an HSA as of the first day of the last month of the year (December 1st for most taxpayers) is an eligible individual for the entire year.

If contributions exceed the allowable amount, they are not deductible if made by the individual, and are included in the gross income of employees who receive funding through a cafeteria plan at work. In addition, if the excess contribution is not distributed prior to the due date of the income tax return including extensions, a six percent penalty applies to the excess contribution (which is similar to the excess contribution penalty that applies to retirement plans).

If a self-employed individual makes a contribution to his own HSA, that contribution is not taken into account when calculating net earnings from self employment. Consequently, the contribution to the HSA is subject to employment tax, but will not reduce self-employment earnings for purposes of calculating the maximum self-employed pension contribution for the individual.

Once in the HSA, contributions are placed in available investment vehicles to generate a return on investment. Unlike Flexible Spending Accounts offered by employers, which allow employees to make an election to allocate part of their income on a pre-tax basis each year to the account but require the funds to be used or forfeited by the end of the calendar year, contributions to HSAs are not required to be spent or forfeited at the end of each year, allowing taxpayers to accumulate an emergency fund for future health care purposes.

Distributions from HSAs used to cover qualified medical expenses for the taxpayer, the taxpayer's spouse, or the taxpayer's dependents are excluded from income. "Qualified medical expenses" are the same as medical expenses eligible for deduction if a taxpayer itemizes deductions, with the exception of medical insurance premiums. Interestingly, distribution of amounts to cover long-term care insurance premiums, and health insurance premiums under COBRA are also excluded from income. Any distributions from an HSA or Archer MSA that are not used to pay for qualified medical expenses are subject to income tax plus a 20 percent penalty. Note that if a medical expense is reimbursed from an HSA, it is not a deductible qualified medical expense. See IRS Publication 502 for more information on this topic.

Once the taxpayer reaches age 65, he is eligible to receive Medicare health coverage from the government. Amounts in the HSA may continue to be used to cover medical expenses after age 65 (and will therefore be excluded from income), but if distributions are made for other purposes, the 20 percent penalty rule will no longer apply. Other exceptions to the 20 percent penalty rule include distributions caused by the account owner's death or disability. In the event the account owner dies when there are still funds in the HSA, the account is transferred to the person who is named as beneficiary, which is often the surviving spouse. A spousal beneficiary may treat the account as his own HSA, but a nonspouse beneficiary must include the HSA in his or her ordinary income.

HSAs are particularly valuable tools for younger individuals. Since young individuals tend to have few health problems, using a HDHP will help lower their annual insurance costs. If contributions are made to HSAs on an annual basis, but are not used each year (during the taxpayer's younger years) to fund health care expenses, the funds inside the HSA are permitted to grow, creating an emergency fund for medical expenses. This emergency fund can be drawn down without income tax consequences when needed, allowing the taxpayer to continue to use high deductible health plans when they are older since the funds needed to cover increased medical expenses incurred as the taxpayer ages can be drawn from the HSA. HSAs are tools that can be used to help minimize an individual's health insurance premiums over their lifetime by creating a tax-advantaged reserve of funds to pay health care expenses when necessary.

Quick Quiz 6.2

1. Individuals who are enrolled in Medicare qualify to establish an HSA.
   a. True
   b. False
2. The maximum allowable contribution to an HSA is reduced by any contributions made to an MSA.
   a. True
   b. False
3. Self-employed individuals may deduct 100% of health insurance premiums paid on behalf of themselves and their dependents.
   a. True
   b. False
4. The long-term care contract must be a qualified contract in order to receive an income tax deduction.
   a. True
   b. False

False, True, True, True.

Individual Retirement Accounts

Traditional IRAs

In addition to the use of company-sponsored retirement plans, taxpayers can also save for retirement by making contributions to Individual Retirement Accounts. Some taxpayers can make tax deductible contributions to traditional IRAs, while others may not. All taxpayers making traditional IRA contributions, however, receive the benefit of tax-deferred growth. The earnings generated on traditional IRA investments are not subject to income taxation until they are withdrawn from the account, which will presumably occur on or after the date of the taxpayer's retirement. Penalty free distributions may be made after the age of 59½. Furthermore, distributions must begin by April 1 of the year following the year the taxpayer attains age 70½ (for those who reached age 70½ by December 31, 2019), or a penalty tax will be assessed. Under the SECURE Act of 2019, Congress extended the age at which minimum distributions must begin to age 72 (from age 70½ under prior law). Individuals who had not reached the age of 70½ by December 31, 2019 will not have to begin taking distributions until April 1 of the year following the year they turn age 72. Individuals who had attained age 70½ by December 31, 2019 must continue to take required minimum distributions in order to avoid a tax penalty.

Contributions

Those taxpayers who qualify for an income tax deduction on contributions to a traditional IRA may take that deduction as an adjustment to income. The maximum allowable contribution to a traditional IRA is $6,000 for 2021. Taxpayers age 50 and older can make an additional $1,000 catch-up contribution. If the taxpayer has both a traditional and a Roth IRA, the maximum contributed to both accounts is aggregated and may not exceed these limits.

> ### Key Concepts
>
> 1. Describe the circumstances under which an individual can make a contribution to a traditional and Roth IRA.
> 2. Explain the limits on the deductibility of a contribution to a traditional IRA.
> 3. Discuss the active participant rules for contributions made to a deductible traditional IRA.
> 4. Explain under what circumstances a non-active participant spouse can contribute to a deductible traditional IRA.

To make a contribution to a traditional IRA, the taxpayer must have earned income. The maximum allowable contribution to a traditional IRA in any one tax year is the lesser of the taxpayer's earned income or the contribution limit (including the catch-up amount) set forth by law. If a taxpayer is married and has a non-working spouse, a spousal IRA can be set up and the same amounts can be contributed to the spousal IRA even if the spouse does not have any earned income and the working spouse has sufficient earned income to cover both contributions.

Contributions to traditional IRAs that are in excess of the allowable amount are subject to a six percent penalty. In addition, contributions must be made by the tax-filing deadline for the year, usually April 15, (not including extensions).

Deductibility of Contributions

Traditional IRA contributions are fully deductible each year for all individuals who are not active participants in qualified retirement plans. This rule is modified, however, when one spouse is an active participant while the other is not.

Active participants in retirement plans may still be able to make tax-deductible contributions to an IRA provided that their adjusted gross income does not exceed specified limits. An "active participant" in a defined contribution pension plan is any person who contributes to the plan (in a cash or deferred arrangement) or who receives an allocation from the employer for the plan year (including forfeitures). Any employee eligible to participate in a defined benefit plan is also considered to be an active participant, even if he or she declines to be covered by the plan.

Once an individual is considered an active participant in a retirement plan, deductible traditional IRA contributions are phased out over specified AGI ranges. The AGI ranges for 2021 are shown in **Exhibit 6.5**.

The deductibility threshold for a traditional IRA is increased for a non-active participant spouse. For purposes of determining the non-active participant spouse's IRA deduction, the AGI phaseout range is

$198,000 - $208,000 (2021). To qualify for this increased phaseout range, the spouses must be filing their income tax return jointly.

Those with an AGI below the lower limit can make a fully deductible traditional IRA contribution. The deductibility of the contribution is phased out for AGI between the noted limits, with a minimum deduction of $200.[1] Once the taxpayer has income equal to or in excess of the upper limit, no deductible IRA contribution can be made.

Exhibit 6.5 | Who Can Deduct Contributions to a Traditional IRA

<table>
<tr><th>Taxpayer is not an active participant</th><th colspan="2">Taxpayer(s) is an active participant</th><th>One spouse is an active participant, while the other spouse is not</th></tr>
<tr><td rowspan="4">No AGI Limit</td><td rowspan="2">Single</td><td>AGI Phaseout</td><td rowspan="4">The spouse who is not an active participant may have a deductible traditional IRA contribution as long as their joint AGI does not exceed $208,000 (2021). The deductible IRA contribution is phased out between $198,000 - $208,000 for 2021.</td></tr>
<tr><td>$66,000 - $76,000 (2021)</td></tr>
<tr><td rowspan="2">MFJ</td><td>AGI Phaseout</td></tr>
<tr><td>$105,000 - $125,000 (2021)</td></tr>
</table>

Example 6.2

Jackie, a recent college graduate, had AGI this year of $45,000. She is single, and has no dependents. If Jackie made a contribution of $6,000 to a traditional IRA this year, she would be able to deduct the entire contribution, since her AGI is below the phaseout threshold.

Example 6.3

Nolan, a single individual age 40, has AGI of $71,000. If Nolan makes a contribution to a traditional IRA in 2021, he will be able to deduct $3,000 (since his AGI is exactly half way through the phaseout range, he can only deduct 50% of the otherwise allowable amount, or $3,000). The first $3,000 of the IRA contribution could be made to a traditional IRA, but if Nolan wishes to make additional contributions, the additional amounts (up to another $3,000) should be made to a Roth IRA.

$$\text{Reduction} = \text{Contribution Limit} \times \frac{\text{AGI} - \text{Lower Limit}}{\text{Phaseout Range}}$$

$$2021 = \$6{,}000 \times \frac{(\$71{,}000 - \$66{,}000)}{\$10{,}000} = \$3{,}000$$

The phaseout range for tax deductibility of IRA contributions for married filing jointly taxpayers is twice the phaseout range for single individuals. Therefore, the phaseout reduction calculation for married filing jointly is as follows:

$$\text{MFJ Reduction} = \text{Contribution Limit} \times \frac{\text{AGI} - \text{Lower Limit}}{\$20{,}000}$$

1. IRC §219(g)(2)(B).

Example 6.4

Pete and Rose, both age 35, are married and filed a joint return for 2021. Pete earned a salary of $135,000 in 2021 and is covered by his employer's 401(k) plan. Pete and Rose earned interest of $15,000 in 2021 from a joint savings account. Rose is not employed, and the couple had no other income. On April 15, 2022, Pete contributed $6,000 to an IRA for himself and $6,000 to an IRA for Rose. The maximum allowable IRA deduction on the 2021 joint return is $6,000. Pete will not be permitted to make a tax deductible IRA contribution for the year, since he is an active participant in his employer's plan and the couple's AGI for the year exceeds the phaseout threshold of $125,000 for a married active participant spouse. Rose, however, will be permitted to make a tax-deductible traditional IRA contribution since she is not an active participant in a qualified plan, and the couple's AGI fell below the increased threshold (that applies to non-participant spouses) of $198,000 (2021). Since Pete cannot make a tax-deductible traditional IRA contribution, and the AGI on his tax return this year falls below $198,000 (the lower end of the Roth IRA phaseout range), Pete should place his IRA contribution in a Roth IRA because he will get tax-free compounding and tax-free distributions in the Roth. Rose should consider whether her IRA contribution should be made to a Roth IRA as well, but if they want the current income tax deduction they will make Rose's contribution to a traditional IRA.

Taxpayers who cannot make income tax-deductible contributions to a traditional IRA may still make nondeductible contributions to nondeductible IRAs to achieve the tax benefits of income tax deferral on the earnings growth. Those electing to do this should file Form 8606 each year to keep track of their adjusted basis in the IRA so that the basis can be distributed to them tax-free when distributions begin.

Roth IRAs

A better alternative than a nondeductible IRA for many taxpayers above the traditional IRA phaseout range but below the Roth IRA phaseout range (**Exhibit 6.6**) is to make IRA contributions to a Roth IRA. Contributions made to a Roth IRA are not deductible, but the growth and withdrawals are tax-free for qualified distributions made after the age of 59½. Roth IRAs do not have required mandatory distributions, therefore unlike traditional IRAs, there is no penalty tax on insufficient withdrawals after age 70½ (for those who reached age 70½ by the end of 2019) or age 72 (for those who turned 70½ after December 31, 2019).

Contributions

The maximum allowable contribution to a Roth IRA is $6,000 for 2021. Taxpayers age 50 and older can make an additional $1,000 catch-up contribution. As stated previously, if the

Quick Quiz 6.3

1. An unmarried taxpayer can make a contribution to an IRA, even if he does not have earned income.
   a. True
   b. False
2. Active participation in a retirement plan does not affect the deductibility of a traditional IRA.
   a. True
   b. False
3. The deductibility threshold for a traditional IRA is increased for a non-active participant spouse.
   a. True
   b. False
4. Contributions to traditional and Roth IRAs that are in excess of the allowable amount are subject to a 4% penalty.
   a. True
   b. False

False, False, True, False.

taxpayer has both a traditional and a Roth IRA, the maximum contributed to both accounts is aggregated and may not exceed these limits.

As is the case with a traditional IRA, in order to make a contribution to a Roth IRA, the taxpayer must have earned income. The maximum allowable contribution to a Roth IRA in any one tax year is the lesser of the taxpayer's earned income or the contribution limit (including catch-up amount) set forth by law. If a taxpayer is married and has a non-working spouse, a spousal IRA can be set up and the same amounts can be contributed to the spousal IRA even if the spouse does not have any earned income as long as the working spouse has sufficient earned income.

Contributions to Roth IRAs that are in excess of the allowable amount are subject to a six percent penalty. In addition, contributions must be made by the tax-filing deadline for the year (not including extensions).

The 2021 AGI phaseout ranges for Roth IRAs are identified in **Exhibit 6.6**.

The phaseout ranges for single taxpayers and for married taxpayers filing jointly are increasing each year, but the phaseout range for those married filing separately is static. Distributions from Roth IRAs will be tax-free if the account has been open for at least five years and the distribution occurs after the taxpayer reaches age 59½. Distributions meeting these two requirements are referred to as qualified distributions.

Exhibit 6.6 | Roth IRA Phaseouts

Filing Status	*2021*
Single	$125,000 - $140,000
Married Filing Jointly	$198,000 - $208,000
Married Filing Separately	$0 - $10,000

Moving Expenses

Moving expenses were deductible for tax years before 2018, and will be deductible for tax years after 2025. TCJA 2017 suspended the deduction for qualified moving expenses and the exclusion for qualified moving expense reimbursements for tax years beginning in 2018 and ending in 2025.

Under the provisions of TCJA 2017, there is only one exception to the suspension of the deduction/exclusion of moving expenses. Active duty members of the Armed Forces (or their spouse or dependents) who move pursuant to a military order and incident to a permanent change of duty station may deduct qualified moving expenses and may exclude from income amounts attributable to in-kind moving and storage expenses, including reimbursements or allowances for these expenses.

Moving expenses that can be deducted (before 2018 and after 2025, as well as for active duty members of the Armed Forces) include costs associated with moving household goods and personal effects, storage of these items while in transit, and travel expenses for one trip by the taxpayer and members of the household. Expenses that cannot be deducted include meals during travel (these are considered personal expenses), the expenses of buying or selling a home (these expenses are either added to basis or subtracted from the amount realized in a sale transaction), temporary living expenses, and house-hunting expenses. The deduction is available to those moving due to a change in employment with an existing or new employer, but in either case, it must involve full-time employment at the new location.

To qualify for a moving expense deduction, a **distance test** must be met. The distance between the old home and the new job location must be at least 50 miles greater than the distance between the old home and the old job location. Recognize that it is not important where a taxpayer moves to, only that the distance test is met.

Penalty on Early Withdrawal of Savings

Penalties paid on early withdrawal of savings are deductible as an adjustment to income. Typically, penalties are imposed when an individual who has a Certificate of Deposit with a bank cashes in that certificate early. The penalty constitutes a forfeiture of interest. Under the doctrine of constructive receipt, money set aside for a taxpayer is taxable to the taxpayer in the year it is credited to their account, not the year the taxpayer receives the interest payment. Often, a CD can be purchased for a greater than one year maturity, in which case the bank will send the taxpayer a Form 1099 at the end of each year indicating the amount of interest that has been credited to the taxpayer's account, and the taxpayer must include that amount in their income tax return for that year, and pay tax on the interest. The allowance of a deduction for a penalty on the early withdrawal of savings simply reverses the inclusion of interest income on the CD when it is cashed in early. The penalty must be reported as an adjustment to income, however, and cannot be used to directly offset interest income in the gross income section of the tax return (including the interest reported by the bank on a CD that was cashed in early).

Educator Expenses

Teachers in elementary and secondary schools (grades Kindergarten through 12th grade), principals, aides, and counselors may deduct up to $250 (2020 and 2021) of out-of-pocket expenses paid as an adjustment to gross income (on Schedule 1 of Form 1040).[2] In tax years before 2018 and after 2025, expenses that can be deducted include items such as books, supplies, computers, computer equipment, and materials used in the classroom. In response to the COVID-19 pandemic, TCDTRA of 2020 expanded the definition of qualified expenses to include the cost of personal protective equipment (PPE), disinfectant, and other supplies used for the prevention of the spread of COVID-19, effective for expenses incurred after March 12, 2020. To qualify for the deduction, an individual must have spent more than 900 hours during a school year as a K-12 educator. Expenses in excess of the $250 above-the-line maximum may be deducted below-the-line in tax years before 2018 and after 2025, as an unreimbursed employee business expense (a miscellaneous itemized deduction subject to the two percent floor, which will be discussed in the next chapter).

Key Concepts

1. Explain who is entitled to deduct student loan interest incurred on qualified student loans.
2. Describe the requirements for classifying a payment as alimony.
3. Explain the consequences of alimony recapture.

Student Loan Interest

Up to $2,500 of student loan interest incurred on qualified student loans may be deducted as an adjustment to gross income. The deduction is available for interest on loans for the benefit of the taxpayer, the taxpayer's spouse, or the taxpayer's dependent that were incurred while the student was either the taxpayer, a spouse, or a dependent. To be eligible for the deduction, the taxpayer must have a primary obligation to repay the debt, and must actually make interest payments during the year

2. The $250 is indexed.

(deferred interest payments are not deductible until they are paid, since all individuals are cash-basis taxpayers).

Exhibit 6.7 | Deductibility of Student Loan Interest

Loan Made By	*Loan Repaid By*	*Is it deductible?*
Parent	Parent	Yes
	Student	No
Student	Parent	No
	Student	Yes

The ability to deduct student loan interest is phased-out for higher income taxpayers, and the phaseout range is indexed for inflation. Individuals with modified adjusted gross income (MAGI) below the lower limit may take a deduction for student loan interest up to $2,500. The deduction is phased out ratably over the phaseout range, and once MAGI reaches the upper limit, no deduction for student loan interest is permitted. Modified adjusted gross income (MAGI) for purposes of determining the student loan interest deduction phaseout is calculated by taking the taxpayers AGI and adding back the foreign earned income exclusion plus the income exclusion for certain U.S. Possessions and Puerto Rico, as well as the deductions taken for tuition and fees. Qualified production activities include manufacturing, producing, growing, and extracting tangible personal property, computer software, and sound recordings, and the construction and substantial renovation of real property including infrastructure.

Exhibit 6.8 | Student Loan Interest Deductible Phaseout (2021)

Filing Status	*2021*
Single	$70,000 - $85,000
Married Filing Jointly	$140,000 - $170,000
Married Filing Separately	$0

Married individuals filing separately and dependents are not eligible to take the student loan interest deduction.

In order to be deductible, the interest must have been incurred on a qualified education loan. A qualified education loan is one that is taken out to cover qualified education expenses, which include tuition, fees, books, equipment, transportation and room and board incurred to attend a post-secondary school or college eligible to participate in the Department of Education student loan programs.

To the extent that educational expenses are paid with pre-tax or tax-free benefits, such as with distributions from Section 529 plans, series EE or I Savings Bonds, or employer provided and veterans educational benefits, qualified education expenses must first be reduced by these amounts before determining the amount of interest that is deductible under the Student Loan interest deduction. The SECURE Act of 2019 expanded the definition of qualified education expenses for 529 plan distributions to include up to $10,000 (lifetime maximum) to repay student loans. When tax-free distributions are made from a 529 plan to repay student loans, the otherwise deductible amount for student loan interest is reduced by the amount of interest paid from a tax-free distribution from a 529 plan. Likewise, when student loan payments are made by an employer under an educational assistance program, as permitted by the CARES Act and TCDTRA of 2020 (discussed in Chapter 5), the interest associated with those payments is not deductible.[3]

Furthermore, the loan must have been incurred for an individual who was at least a half-time student (a student who maintained a credit load of at least one-half of the normal full-time credit load).

Qualified Tuition and Related Expenses

Prior to 2021, an adjustment to income was permitted for qualified tuition and related expenses of up to $4,000. The Taxpayer Certainty and Disaster Tax Relief Act (TCDTRA) of 2020 repealed the tuition and fees deduction for tax years beginning after 2020, but increased the phaseout range for the Lifetime Learning tax credit for qualified education expenses (discussed in Chapter 9).

ABOVE THE LINE CHARITABLE DEDUCTIONS

The CARES Act of 2020 created a new adjustment to income for contributions of cash to public charities. In 2020, taxpayers who do not itemize deductions may deduct up to $300 of cash contributions to public charities as an adjustment to gross income. Cash contributions to donor advised funds or certain private foundations and non-cash contributions (such as donation of personal property to Goodwill or donation of appreciated securities) do not qualify for this deduction. Taxpayers who itemize deductions will not qualify for this deduction, since those taxpayers can claim their charitable deductions on Schedule A (Itemized deductions) as below-the-line deductions.

The Taxpayer Certainty and Disaster Tax Relief Act (TCDTRA) of 2020 (signed by President Trump on December 27, 2020 as part of the Consolidated Appropriations Act of 2021) extends to 2021 the deduction created under the CARES Act and modifies it by increasing the maximum amount that can be deducted by married couples filing jointly to $600. Individuals with filing statuses other than married filing jointly are subject to the $300 limitation imposed by the CARES Act.

In an effort to combat abuse of this new adjustment to income, the TCDTRA of 2020 also increased the accuracy related penalty under I.R.C. Sec. 6662 from 20 percent to 50 percent of the underpayment caused by a taxpayer who overstates this deduction.

Quick Quiz 6.4

1. If an employer reimburses an employee for moving expenses, the employee may not claim a deduction based on the same expenses.
   a. True
   b. False
2. Temporary living expenses may be deducted by an employee as moving expenses.
   a. True
   b. False
3. Educator expenses in excess of $250 are not deductible below the line for tax years 2018-2025.
   a. True
   b. False
4. Alimony recapture is only an issue if alimony payments increase during the first three post-separation years.
   a. True
   b. False

True, False, True, False.

Alimony Paid

For divorce decrees entered on or before December 31, 2018, alimony payments are deducted from the income of the payor (as an adjustment to income, or above-the-line deduction), and included in the

3. An employer is permitted to make student loan payments on behalf of an employee, which are excluded from the income of the employee, as part of an educational assistance program, effective for payments made after March 27, 2020 and before January 1, 2026.

income of the former spouse receiving the payment (the payee). When treated in this manner, Alimony receives pass-through tax treatment - the person who winds up with the cash has to pay the tax.

TCJA 2017 repealed the deduction by the payor for payment of alimony, and the inclusion in income by the payee, for alimony decrees that are entered into after December 31, 2018. If alimony decrees entered into before January 1, 2019 are substantially modified and the modification specifically states that the rules set forth in TCJA 2017 apply, the income tax deduction for the payor and the income tax inclusion for the payee is also repealed.

After 2018, a financial professional may have some clients who follow the traditional alimony rules (deduction for the payor; inclusion for the payee), and others who are subject to the repeal of the traditional rules (no deduction for the payor; no inclusion for the payee). Those clients subject to the repeal of the rules have clear tax treatment - no deduction is permitted for the payor, and no inclusion is required for the payee. Clients who are not subject to the repeal of the traditional alimony rules under TCJA 2017 are subject to the tax treatment specified below.

To achieve pass-through tax treatment, the payments must actually constitute alimony. IRC Section 71(b) sets forth the requirements necessary to classify payments as alimony. These requirements include:

1. the payments must be in cash or cash equivalent (such as a check or money order)
2. the payments must be required by a court decree
3. the court decree must not specify that the payments are "not alimony"
4. the payments must cease at the death of the recipient
5. the payments may not be disguised child support payments
6. the former spouses may not be members of the same household
7. the parties may not file a joint income tax return (married filing jointly)

Child support payments are not alimony – they are a right of the child to receive support from the parent, and are therefore not deductible as alimony even though the payments are typically made to the former spouse. If alimony payments are structured to decline when a child reaches the age of majority, the decline in the payment made to the former spouse will be assumed to be child-support and not deductible alimony, even if the court decree refers to the payment as alimony. Technically, if the payments are reduced within six months before or after the child attains the age of majority, that portion of the payment will be presumed to be child support and will not be treated as deductible alimony.[4]

Example 6.5

Willie and Maye were divorced on December 15, 2017. The divorce decree required Willie to pay alimony. They had been married for 15 years, and had two children, Erin (14 years old) and Hank (12 years old). Under the terms of the divorce decree, Willie is required to pay Maye $2,000 per month in alimony for four years, $1,500 for the next two years, and $1,000 per month for the following two years. Willie's alimony deduction each month will be $1,000. Even though the divorce decree classified the payment as alimony, the payment was reduced by $500 when each child reached the age of 18, so $1,000 of the payment ($500 x 2) will be reclassified as child support for income tax purposes.

4. See Treasury Regulation 1.71-1T(c)Q-A18 for more information.

IRC Section 1041 states that all property transfers between spouses and incident to a divorce are considered to be nontaxable exchanges for income tax purposes, and therefore result in a carry-over basis. Property settlements of divorcing spouses fit into this rule, and do not result in income tax benefits. Due to the pass-through nature of alimony payments, some individuals may be encouraged to re-characterize property settlements related to divorce as alimony payments. This is especially true when one spouse (payor) is in a high income tax bracket (and can use the tax deduction), and the other spouse (payee) is in a low income tax bracket. Characterizing a property settlement as deductible alimony would permit the divorcing spouses to achieve a tax-arbitrage due to the different tax rates paid by each spouse.

While the temporary regulations covering alimony payments have indicated that it is possible to classify a single payment from one divorcing spouse to another as alimony, several tax court decisions have come to the conclusion that a single alimony payment is "in the nature of a property settlement," and have denied an alimony deduction in such cases. For divorce decrees requiring the payment of alimony that were entered into after December 31, 2018, or divorce decrees entered at other times that were modified and specifically opted in to the TCJA 2017 tax treatment of alimony, no deduction is permitted to the payor, making the "alimony" payment akin to a property settlement whether it is a single payment or a series of payments during that period.

CASE STUDY 6.1

Deductibility of Alimony

Brendon James DeLong v. Commissioner., U.S. Tax Court, CCH Dec. 59,475(m), T.C. Memo. 2013-70, T.C.M., (March 11, 2013).

Family support payments made by a husband to his wife under two support orders by a state (California) court were alimony rather than child support. The husband was entitled to deduct the entire amount of the payments for the year at issue. The husband was required to make the family support payments to his legally separated spouse both for spousal and child support. Even though the support orders were silent as to an allocation of the payments between spousal support and child support and as to whether the payments were to continue despite the death of his spouse, the husband was determined to have no continuing liability to make the payments past the death of the spouse; therefore, IRC Sec. 71(b)(1)(D) requirements were met with respect to the definition of alimony.

The **alimony recapture** rules are designed to prevent taxpayers from transforming property settlements into deductible alimony. The alimony recapture rules, therefore, apply only to alimony payments that would qualify as a tax deduction for the payor. Under the alimony recapture rules, the first three post-separation years are examined to determine if the alimony payments claimed as deductions on the payor's tax return are really disguised property settlements. A mathematical test is employed to make this determination. Alimony recapture will only be an issue if:

- alimony payments decline during the first three post-separation years, and
- the alimony payment in years two and three decrease by more than $15,000 per year.

The mathematical test will determine the amount of excess alimony in the first and second post-separation years. Any excess alimony is added to the payor's income in the third post-separation year, and is deducted from the payee's income in the third post-separation year. Prior year tax returns are not amended and refiled to take excess alimony into account.

An amount for excess alimony is determined for the first and second post-separation years (the third post-separation year serves as the base for the calculation). The sum of these amounts is added to the payor's income in the third post-separation year, and subtracted from the payee's income for the third post-separation year. The calculation of excess alimony is determined as follows:

1. For the second post-separation year, excess alimony (R2) equals the amount of year 2 alimony (P2) in excess of year 3 alimony (P3) plus $15,000. If the result is zero or negative, it is not taken into account in determining the total amount of excess alimony. Stated mathematically, the formula is:

$$R2 = P2 - (P3 + 15{,}000)$$

2. For the first-post separation year, excess alimony (R1) takes into account the alimony payments in years 1 and 2, as well as the excess alimony from year 2. If the result is zero or negative, it is not taken into account in determining the total amount of excess alimony. Stated mathematically, the formula is:

$$R1 = P1 - \left(\frac{P2 - R2 + P3}{2} + \$15{,}000\right)$$

3. Add the results from steps 1 and 2. This equals the total amount of excess alimony.

Example 6.6

Barry and Ruth were recently divorced and the divorce decree requiring the payment of alimony was entered on November 15, 2018. In the first year after their divorce, Barry pays Ruth $80,000; in the second year, he pays her $50,000; and in the third year, he pays her $20,000. The excess alimony in Year 2 (R2) is equal to $15,000.

$50,000 – ($20,000 + $15,000) = $15,000.
The excess alimony in Year 1 (R1) is equal to $37,500.

$$\$80{,}000 - \left(\frac{\$50{,}000 - \$15{,}000 + \$20{,}000}{2} + \$15{,}000\right) = \$37{,}500$$

The total excess alimony is $52,500.

Remember, the purpose of alimony is to provide support. If a payment is made for support, it probably should not decrease substantially in future years, and cannot be paid to the payee or the payee's estate after the payee's death.

If alimony payments decreased by more than $15,000 per year over the first three years of payments, a shortcut formula can be used. The formula is:

$$R3 = P1 + P2 - 2P3 - \$37{,}500$$

where:
R3 = Recapture in year 3
P1 = Alimony payment in year 1
P2 = Alimony payment in year 2
P3 = Alimony payment in year 3

Please note that this shortcut formula will not work unless the alimony payments decline by $15,000 or more each year during the first three years of payments.

Example 6.7

Using the same facts as presented in **Example 6.6** along with the shortcut formula presented above, excess alimony is calculated as:

R3 = $80,000 + $50,000 - 2($20,000) - $37,500
R3 = $52,500

Note that this answer is the same as the answer derived using the long-method since the alimony payments declined by more than $15,000 per year.

The alimony recapture rules will only be effective for tax years 2019, 2020, and 2021. For tax years after 2021, no taxpayer will be subject to alimony recapture. Since the alimony recapture rules only apply to the first three years of post-separation alimony payments, all pre-2019 divorce decrees requiring alimony payments will have been subject to recapture by the end of 2021. For tax years after 2021, no taxpayer will be subject to alimony recapture.

Exhibit 6.9 | Summary of Above-The-Line Deductions for Individuals

- MSAs
- HSAs
- Trade or Business Expenses
- IRAs
- Moving Expenses*
- Penalty on Early Withdrawal of Savings
- Educator Expenses
- Student Loan Interest
- Alimony Paid*

** The deduction for moving expenses (for tax years 2018-2025) was suspended by, and the deduction for alimony paid pursuant to a divorce decree entered into after December 31, 2018 was repealed by TCJA 2017.*

DEDUCTION ISSUES FOR EMPLOYERS AND EMPLOYEES

Types of Businesses and General Deduction Rules

Federal tax law classifies all business entities into one of three types:

- Corporations
- Partnerships
- Sole Proprietorships

Regardless of what state law calls a particular business organization, it must fit into one of these categories for federal income tax purposes.

Key Concepts

1. Describe the limitations on an S corporation's ability to deduct expenses incurred in generating corporate income.
2. Describe common above-the-line deductions for self-employed taxpayers.
3. Explain the requirements for deducting home office expenses for business owners.

Corporations are created under state law, and give the business owner the advantage of limited liability protection. The creation of a corporation involves a formal process, and, once in existence, a corporation is treated as a person in the eyes of the law. Regular corporations are taxed under Subchapter C of the Internal Revenue Code, and are therefore referred to as C corporations. Since a C corporation is separate and distinct from its owners (it is treated as a separate entity), it is subject to tax on its income, and must file its own income tax return (Form 1120). When a C corporation distributes some of its earnings to its shareholders (the owners of the corporation), the distribution is referred to as a dividend. Dividends are taxable to the shareholder when received. Qualified dividends are taxed as follows:

- **Zero percent:** For single taxpayers and married taxpayers filing separately with taxable income up to $40,400; for married taxpayers filing jointly with taxable income up to $80,800; and for taxpayers claiming head of household status with taxable income up to $54,100),
- **15 percent:** For single taxpayers with taxable income up to $445,850; married taxpayers filing jointly with taxable income up to $501,600; married taxpayers filing separately with taxable income up to $250,800; and taxpayers claiming head of household status with taxable income up to $473,750), or
- **20 percent:** For single individuals with taxable income over $445,850; married individuals filing jointly with taxable income over $501,600; married individuals filing separately with taxable income over $250,800; and for taxpayers claiming head of household states with taxable income over $473,750).

Exhibit 6.10 | Qualified Dividend Tax Rates*

Dividend	*Single Taxpayers*	*Married Filing Jointly*	*Head of Household*	*Married Filing Separately*
0%	Up to $40,400	Up to $80,800	Up to $54,100	Up to $40,400
15%	$40,001 - $445,850	$80,001 - $501,600	$53,601 - $473,750	$40,001 - $250,800
20%	Over $445,850	Over $501,600	Over $473,750	Over $250,800

** Income Thresholds in this Table are Based on Taxable Income*

C corporations, as separate taxable entities, will deduct all ordinary, necessary, and reasonable expenses incurred in the production of income for the company on its own income tax return. The deductions for these expenses do not pass through to the owners of the corporation.

Once organized, the owners of a corporation can make an election under Subchapter S of the Internal Revenue Code to have the corporation taxed as a pass-through entity. When this election has been made, the corporation is referred to as an S corporation. S corporations are still corporations, and are treated as entities distinct and separate from their owners, and must still file a separate income tax return (Form 1120-S), but the incidence of federal income tax changes. Instead of having the corporation pay tax on its operating income, the operating income is "passed through" to the owners the year it is earned, and the shareholders will report their proportionate share of corporate operating income on their individual income tax returns. This does not mean that the owners actually receive a cash distribution from the corporation – whether or not the corporation distributes anything to the owners, the owners must pay tax on their pro-rata share of the corporate income in the year it is earned.

The advantage of S corporation status is that corporate income is taxed only once – on the individual tax returns of the owners. Distributions issued from S corporations are not subject to tax, since the owners paid tax on the corporate operating income when it was earned (whether or not the operating income was distributed). From an operating standpoint, S corporations look a lot like partnerships, which pass through all of their income to their owners, but some attributes of corporate taxation still apply to S corporations.

Like C corporations, S corporations deduct all the ordinary, necessary, and reasonable expenses incurred in generating corporate income on the S corporation tax return. Only the net profit or loss flows through to the owners to report on their individual income tax return. There is one major exception to this rule, however. An S corporation cannot deduct medical insurance costs for greater than two percent owners of the corporation. These amounts are passed through to the individual shareholder as additional gross wages and are deducted as adjustments to income (above-the-line deductions) on the individual shareholder's personal income tax return. The increase in gross wages, however, does not increase income subject to Social Security and Medicare (FICA) taxes. Medical insurance costs for employees and less than two percent shareholders are deducted on the S corporation income tax return.

Any organization created under state law that is not a corporation or a trust, and that has two or more owners, is classified as a partnership for federal income tax purposes.A partnership for federal income tax purposes includes general partnerships, limited partnerships (LPs), family limited partnerships (FLPs), limited liability partnerships (LLPs), limited liability companies (LLCs), Limited Liability Limited Partnerships (LLLPs), and any other organization that meets the above criteria. Partnerships must file informational tax returns (Form 1065), but are not responsible for paying any federal income tax. All of the ordinary, necessary, and reasonable expenses of partnerships are deducted on the partnership tax return, and it is only the net income of the partnership that flows through to, and is subject to tax in, the hands of the owners. Partners may not be treated as employees of the partnership. Medical insurance costs and pension contributions cannot be deducted as business expenses on the partnership's income tax return, but are separately reported to the partners, who may deduct them as an adjustment to income (above-the-line). Furthermore, partners are not classified as employees of the business, so payments for their services are not deducted on the partnership tax return. Instead, they are classified as guaranteed payments and are passed through to the owners to be individually reported on the owner's tax return.

Any organization created under state law that is not a corporation or a trust, and that has only one owner, is classified as a sole-proprietorship for federal income tax purposes. Sole proprietorships, therefore, include traditional sole proprietorships and single-member LLCs. A sole proprietor files Schedule C with his personal income tax return to report the net income associated with business operations. All necessary, reasonable, and ordinary business expenses incurred in the production of the sole proprietorship's income are deducted on Schedule C, and only the net income or loss from the activity is included in the gross income on the owner's personal income tax return. As is the case with all other business entities, business expense deductions for sole proprietors are above-the-line deductions, since they directly offset the income generated through the conduct of the trade or business activity. Sole proprietors are not permitted, however, to deduct medical insurance costs or pension contributions against business income, but must report those amounts separately as adjustments to income (above-the-line deductions).

Common Deductions for Employers and the Self-Employed

To qualify as deductions for federal income tax purposes, a business related expense must be ordinary, necessary, and reasonable. If the expenditure fails to meet all three of these requirements, it will be disallowed by the IRS.

An **ordinary expense** is one that is typically incurred in the normal, usual, or customary conduct of businesses in the same line of operations. As discussed in other areas of this textbook, expenses usually cannot be capital in nature. Capital expenditures typically must be capitalized, and can be deducted (through the use of cost recovery methods, such as depreciation, depletion, or amortization) over the useful life of the asset. There are some special rules that enable a small business owner to deduct an expense that would otherwise be capitalized. These rules are covered in detail in Chapter 10. Only expenses that are ordinarily incurred in the conduct of the given trade or business will qualify as a current deduction.

Assuming that an expense is considered to be ordinarily incurred in the conduct of a trade or business, the taxpayer must demonstrate that the expense is necessary. A **necessary expense** is one that a prudent business person would incur in the conduct of business. For example, lavish travel expenses are rarely considered to be necessary expenses associated with the conduct of business. Only those travel expenses that are both ordinary and necessary will qualify for a deduction.

If both the ordinary and necessary requirements have been met, the taxpayer must still demonstrate that the expense in question is reasonable. Reasonableness is a question of fact, and overlaps with the ordinary and necessary requirements. An expense that may be ordinary and necessary in the conduct of business may not be reasonable if it does not contribute to the goal of generating income for the business activity.

Fringe Benefits

Fringe benefits include non-cash compensation provided by an employer to an employee. An employer can deduct the costs of providing qualified fringe benefits to employees without causing the value received by the employee to be included in the employee's income.

Perhaps the most well-known fringe benefit provided by employers is insurance coverage for the employees, including accident and health plans, Health Savings Accounts and Medical Savings accounts, most long-term care plans, and life insurance.

For health insurance and long-term care plans, the employer can pay the premium on behalf of the employee, and the employee will not have to include the benefit received in his taxable income. Recall that one of the general rules of income taxation states that when someone takes a tax deduction, someone else must include the same amount in income. This rule does not apply to employer provided health insurance. Furthermore, the Economic Benefit doctrine, which normally requires economic benefits conferred on an employee to be included in taxable income, does not apply to medical insurance coverage provided as an employee benefit. Congress has provided a specific exemption for the inclusion of the economic benefit received by an employee from employer payments of health insurance premiums in IRC Section 106. Benefits received under these plans by employees are not included in taxable income provided that the benefit received does not exceed the cost of the health services provided.

When group term life insurance is provided to employees, the employer can deduct the premium paid for the coverage. The first $50,000 of coverage will not be taxable to the employee provided that the benefit is nondiscriminatory, but any coverage in excess of $50,000 will be considered an economic benefit received by the employee and the imputed premium cost will be included in the employee's income. This exception only applies to employees and is not available to sole proprietors, partners in a partnership, or greater than two percent owners of S corporations.

Other examples of fringe benefits that can be provided by an employer without requiring the employees to recognize income include qualified transportation expenses (as discussed in Chapter 5), meals and lodging furnished on the employer's premises for the convenience of the employer, qualified educational assistance plans (providing benefits of up to $5,250 per year), qualified adoption assistance and retirement planning services.

Self-Employed Retirement Contributions and Health Insurance Costs

Sole proprietors, partners, and more than two percent owners of S corporations are considered to be self-employed individuals for fringe benefit purposes. As noted earlier, the costs of providing retirement planning benefits or medical insurance cannot be deducted from business income for the self-employed. Instead, medical insurance premiums and retirement plan contributions are deducted as an adjustment to income (above-the-line) on the personal tax return of the self-employed individual. An exception applies to retirement plan contributions made on behalf of a more than two percent S corporation owner who is an employee of the business. While medical insurance premiums increase the more than two percent S corporation owner's gross income reported on Form W-2, retirement plan contributions made by the S corporation do not; retirement plan contributions made by the S corporation are deducted on the S corporation's tax return.

Self-employed retirement contributions made to qualified defined benefit or defined contribution pension plans, or simplified employee pension plans (SEPs) and Simplified Incentive Match Plans for Employees (SIMPLE plans) are deductible as an adjustment to income on the sole proprietor or partner's personal income tax return.

Medical insurance premiums are deducted as an adjustment to income on the sole proprietor's, partner's, or more than two percent S corporation owner's personal tax return. Under current law, the deduction for medical insurance premiums is not limited, but long-term care insurance premium deductions are limited based on the age of the individual as of the end of the tax year.

Social Security and Self-Employment Tax Costs

Self-employed individuals, like all employees, must pay Social Security taxes. Unlike employees, who only pay half of the applicable Social Security and Medicare taxes (the other half is paid by the employer), a self-employed individual must pay both the employee and the employer portions of Social Security and Medicare taxes. The tax equals 15.3 percent (12.4 percent for Social Security, and 2.9 percent for Medicare) of income up to the Social Security wage base ($142,800 for 2021), and 2.9 percent on income over the Social Security wage base. Since 2013, an additional Medicare surtax is imposed on high income taxpayers, as defined in the Affordable Care Act (married filing jointly with modified adjusted gross income over $250,000 and single individuals with modified adjusted gross income over $200,000) that is equal to 0.9 percent on income above the "high income" thresholds.

When a business pays half of the Social Security taxes on behalf of an employee, the business is entitled to deduct that expense since it constitutes an ordinary, necessary, and reasonable expense in the conduct of the trade or business. To give equal treatment to self-employed individuals, the IRC allows self-employed individuals to deduct one half of self-employment taxes paid as an adjustment to income (above-the-line) deduction. Since the 0.9 percent Medicare surtax on high income taxpayers only applies to the employee portion of the Medicare tax, it is excluded from self-employment taxes when determining the amount that a self-employed person may claim as an above-the-line deduction.

Investigation of Business Expenditures

The deductibility of costs incurred to investigate or acquire a new line of business depends on two factors:

1. whether the expenses are incurred in the investigation of purchasing a business in the same line of business
2. whether the new business is actually acquired

If the new business is not acquired, and the potential acquirer was not already in the business, no deduction is allowed. However, if an existing business incurs investigation costs to expand, protect, or grow that existing business, these costs are deductible as ordinary and necessary, even if the new business line is not acquired.

If the new business is acquired, the deduction depends on whether or not the business acquired is in the same line of business as the current trade or business operation. If a new, similar type of business is acquired, all of the investigation of business expenses are fully deductible. If a new, but different line of business is acquired, the expenses are subject to the same capitalization and amortization rules as a new line of business. In the case of a new (and unrelated) line of business, up to $5,000 of start up costs (reduced (but not below zero) by the amount the start up expenditures exceed $50,000) can be deducted in the year that the new active trade or business begins its operations. Start up organizational costs in excess of $5,000 are amortized over 180 months beginning with the month the new business begins its operations.

Home Office Deduction for Business Owners

In some cases, a taxpayer who uses part of his home for the conduct of a trade or business is entitled to take a deduction for costs associated with business use of the home. Expenses must be prorated between personal and business use based on the percentage of the home that qualifies for the home office deduction, and only those expenses allocated to the business use of the home are deductible as a business expense. A further limitation on the home office expense deduction states that a taxpayer claiming a home office expense cannot generate a loss on the business activity as a result of taking the deduction. Home office expense deductions may only be claimed to the extent that there is net income from the business activity. Some of the expenses that can be claimed for the home office include mortgage interest, real estate taxes, utilities (such as electric, oil or gas, and security costs), homeowners insurance, casualty losses, maintenance and repairs, and depreciation. Any expenses incurred by a taxpayer that benefit only the portion of the home used for business purposes are deductible in full (they do not have to be prorated between business and personal use).

The ability to take a home office deduction depends on whether the taxpayer is a business owner or an employee. If the taxpayer owns a business, a portion of the home must be used regularly and exclusively as a principal place of business, as a place to meet clients in the normal course of business, or in connection with the business if the home office is not included in a separate structure that is detached from the taxpayer's principal residence. If one of these use tests is met, a self-employed business owner may deduct home office expenses against income generated by the business, but the deduction of home office expenses cannot cause the business to show a loss for the tax year.

If the taxpayer is an employee rather than a business owner, TCJA 2017 suspended the home office deduction for tax years 2018-2025 (all miscellaneous itemized deductions subject to the 2% floor are suspended during this period). For tax years prior to 2018, and after 2025, the taxpayer must meet an additional use test to take a deduction for a home office. The use of the home office must be for the "convenience of the employer," not just helpful and appropriate for the taxpayer.

Quick Quiz 6.5

1. An S corporation cannot deduct medical insurance costs for greater than 2% owners of the corporation.
   a. True
   b. False
2. An ordinary expense is one that is typically incurred in the normal conduct of businesses in the same line of operations.
   a. True
   b. False
3. The costs of investigating the purchase of a new business line are deductible regardless of whether the new line of business is actually acquired.
   a. True
   b. False

True, True, False.

A key to the availability of the home office deduction is use of a portion of the home *exclusively* for business purposes. If the space is used for both business and personal purposes, no deduction is permitted. There are two exceptions to the exclusivity requirement. The first exception deals with storage of inventory or product samples. Provided that storage space or inventory is used regularly for business purposes, and the home is the only fixed location for a retail or wholesale business, a deduction is permitted as long as the space used is identifiable as space separate from areas used for personal use. The second exception deals with day care facilities run from the home of a taxpayer. Taxpayers who run day care facilities may deduct costs associated with the business use of the home even if the same space is used for personal purposes during nonbusiness hours.

When a taxpayer claims a home office deduction, depreciation is taken on the portion of the home used for business purposes. The depreciation method that must be used is 39 year straight-line depreciation (since that portion of the home is being used for commercial purposes). As depreciation deductions are taken, the taxpayer's basis in their home decreases, and, upon sale, gain on the home to the extent of depreciation taken is considered to be unrecaptured Section 1250 depreciation subject to a special tax rate of 25 percent. Individuals meeting the definition of high income taxpayers under the Affordable Care Act are also subject to the 3.8 percent Medicare surtax on unrecaptured Section 1250 depreciation.

The Section 121 exclusion on the sale of a principal residence cannot be used to offset the portion of the gain that is classified as Unrecaptured Section 1250 gain. Gain in excess of depreciation taken will be capital gain, and may be offset by the Section 121 exclusion on the sale of a principal residence (allowing a taxpayer to exclude up to $250,000 in gain, if single, or $500,000 in gain, if married on the sale of the home, provided some additional requirements are met). The depreciation recapture rules will be covered in detail later in text.

In IRS Revenue Procedure 2013-13, the Internal Revenue Service states that the calculation, allocation, and substantiation of allowable deductions attributable to the use of a portion of the taxpayer's residence for business purposes can be complex and burdensome for small business owners. It is for this reason that this optional safe harbor method is being offered to taxpayers. Under this safe harbor method, taxpayers determine their allowable deduction for business use of a residence by multiplying a prescribed rate by the square footage of the portion of the taxpayer's residence that is used for business purposes. The allowable square footage is the portion of a home used in a qualified business use of the home, but not to exceed 300 square feet. The prescribed rate is $5.00 per square foot.

CASE STUDY 6.2

Deduction Substantiation Requirements

Edwina S. Etchinson, Petitioner v. Commissioner of Internal Revenue, Respondent.
T.C. Summary Opinion 2011-30 (March 16, 2011).

From 1994 to April of 2005, Edwina lived in California, and was employed by Federal Express. In April 2005 she moved to her mother's house in Georgia to care for her ailing parent, and she began to make the mortgage payments on the home owned by her mom. Her tax returns for 2004, 2005, and 2006 were prepared by a professional tax preparer. The IRS audited each of these returns, and denied certain itemized deductions and moving expenses that were claimed on her return. In 2004, she claimed itemized deductions of $9,856 for unreimbursed employee business expenses, $2,895 for charitable contributions, and $6,652 for home mortgage interest. The IRS disallowed all of the itemized deductions claimed in 2004, with the exception of $400 for charitable contributions. Edwina challenged the IRS' action, but failed to produce any substantiating documents to support any of the deductions in dispute. Edwina claimed that her records were stolen from a storage facility in December 2005, but that her tax preparer had access to the records when he completed her return.

Citing **Gizzi v. Commissioner, 65 T.C. 342 (1975),** the tax court noted that in cases where a taxpayers records are unavailable through no fault of the taxpayer, the Court expects the taxpayer to make some attempt to reconstruct those records. Edwina had not done so. Furthermore, the court deduced that Edwina's records for 2005 could not have been available to her return preparer when her 2005 return was prepared in 2006 if, in fact, they had been stolen from her storage unit in December of 2005. Since Edwina could not substantiate the deductions, the court concluded that "she is not entitled to itemized deductions in excess of the amounts ... already allowed."

DEDUCTIONS AND TAX PLANNING

In order to deduct an expense for income tax purposes, the expense must be incurred in the conduct of an individual's trade or business, or in a transaction entered into for profit. Personal expenses are generally not deductible (although some exceptions have been made for public policy reasons, such as the mortgage interest deduction, deduction for taxes paid to state and local governments, medical expenses, and casualty losses).

Key Concepts

1. Explain why it is more advantageous to classify expenses as business expenses rather than employee-related business expenses.
2. Describe the deductibility of investor expenses.

For Employees

As a review of this chapter indicates, deductions available to those workers classified as employees are relatively limited. An employee is permitted to take an above-the-line deduction for unreimbursed moving expenses (for active duty members of the Armed Forces only, for tax years 2018-2025) and educator expenses up to $250, but other unreimbursed business expenses are deducted as a miscellaneous itemized deduction subject to the two percent floor. For tax years 2018 through 2025, TCJA 2017 suspended all miscellaneous itemized deductions subject to the two percent floor. Therefore, employees who would have otherwise been able to deduct unreimbursed business expenses as a miscellaneous itemized deduction will not be able to do so until 2026.

For tax years beginning after December 31, 2025, the timing of some of these business related expenses can be controlled by an employee taking advantage of the cash basis reporting requirements imposed by the IRS. From a planning perspective, assuming that expenses will be incurred for business related purposes, an employee should attempt to incur those expenses in one tax year if possible, since it will be more likely that he or she will exceed the two percent of AGI floor that applies to miscellaneous itemized deductions.

Example 6.8

Clayton is an employee at JarvCo, Inc. and he regularly incurs business related expenses that are not fully reimbursed by his employer. His AGI for 2026 is $100,000. In 2026, his employer did not reimburse him for $800 in travel expenses, $500 in professional dues and fees, and $500 for periodicals and books relating to Clayton's business activities, for a total of $1,800 in unreimbursed employee business expenses. If Clayton does not incur additional expenses, he will not receive any deduction since this amount does not exceed $2,000 (two percent of his AGI).

Beginning in January of 2027, Clayton plans on taking three classes toward his MBA at a cost of $6,000 (for all three classes). Clayton can also prepay his professional dues and fees, and renew his periodical and book subscriptions early if he would like to. If Clayton pays the tuition by December 31, 2026 (instead of January 20, 2027 the due date for tuition for the next term), and prepays $1,000 in professional dues, fees, and periodical and book subscriptions, he will increase his business related expense deduction to $8,800. Clayton will be able to take a Tier II miscellaneous itemized deduction for business related expenses of $6,800 in 2026 (the portion that exceed two percent of his AGI).

Miscellaneous itemized deductions subject to the 2% floor are suspended for tax years 2018-2025 by TCJA 2017.

For Business Owners

Business owners have the advantage of being able to classify expenses related to the trade or business as above-the-line deductions. All ordinary, necessary, and reasonable expenses associated with the active conduct of a trade or business directly offset the income generated from that activity.

To the extent possible, individuals who own businesses should classify as many of their expenses as they can as business expenses instead of as employee related business expenses. This achieves two things:

1. it avoids the 2% floor on miscellaneous itemized deductions (and the suspension of miscellaneous itemized deductions subject to the 2% floor for tax years 2018-2025 by TCJA 2017) – there is no floor imposed on the business expenses incurred by owners of businesses, and
2. the expenses directly offset income from business operations, which has the impact of reducing AGI.

Example 6.9

Gerri is principal of her town's middle school, but also has a consulting practice in which she confers with boards of education and schools within the state on educational programs and functions. Her consulting business is set up as a single-member LLC filing a Form 1040 Schedule C. Gerri subscribes to several journals, and purchases several timely books covering topics that apply to both her job as a principal and her consulting practice. Each year, she spends approximately $1,500 on these materials. Assuming that Gerri's AGI is $100,000 for the current year, if she tried to take a deduction for these materials as an employee related unreimbursed business expense, she would receive no tax benefit. Since these expenditures represent ordinary, necessary, and reasonable expenses for the conduct of her consulting practice, however, Gerri can deduct the cost against her consulting income. This deduction directly offsets income, and is therefore an above-the-line deduction that reduces Gerri's AGI on a dollar-for-dollar basis. Furthermore, there is no floor that applies to business expense deductions, so Gerri can deduct the full $1,500 from her income this year on her Schedule C.

Remember that only those expenses that are ordinary, necessary, and reasonable may be deducted as business expenses. To the extent that a business owner can satisfy these requirements for an expenditure, he or she should deduct those expenses from the income of the business, and should not deduct them as an itemized deduction on his tax return.

Exhibit 6.11 | Summary of Above-The-Line Business Deductions

• Ordinary	• Self-Employed Retirement and Health Costs
• Necessary	• Social Security Tax Costs
• Reasonable	• Investigation of a Business
• Fringe Benefits	• Home Office Deduction*

** Home Office Deductions are available for business owners, but due to the enactment of TCJA 2017, employees will be unable to claim home office deductions as miscellaneous itemized deductions subject to the 2% floor for tax years 2018 through 2025.*

For Investors

Like business owners, investors may deduct expenses that are necessary to generate profits. When the expenses are directly related to the production of income, such as when a taxpayer operates a rental real estate activity, those expenses are claimed directly against the income generated by the activity and therefore are above-the-line deductions that reduce the taxpayer's gross income.

As noted earlier, some investment expenses, such as those associated with ownership of a portfolio of intangible investment assets (such as stocks and bonds) are miscellaneous itemized deductions. Due to the enactment of TCJA 2017, all miscellaneous itemized deductions are suspended for tax years 2018-2025. After 2025, taxpayers will again be able to deduct these expenses. Expenses in this category include investment advisory and custodial fees, the cost of preparing income tax returns, safe deposit rental fees, and the cost of receiving investment and tax advice. Itemized deductions are only advantageous, however, if the total deductions exceed the standard deduction. To the extent possible, investors should keep track of their investment expenses and claim them as expenses on their tax returns. This is an area that is often overlooked by individual taxpayers.

SUMMARY AND CONCLUSION

This chapter introduced the classification of deductions available to taxpayers (above-the-line and below-the-line), and reviewed the rules associated with the above-the-line deductions that are important from a tax planning perspective. Generally, above-the-line deductions are more valuable to the taxpayer than below-the-line deductions since above-the-line deductions result in a decrease in adjusted gross income (AGI). Typically, above-the-line deductions result from business activity, production of income activities, and personal activities that have the potential of increasing future income that will be subject to tax.

The next chapter reviews the rules associated with below-the-line deductions (itemized deductions and the QBI (Section 199A) deduction), many of which are limited by the taxpayer's AGI. Unlike above-the-line deductions, itemized deductions tend to allow taxpayers to deduct some personal expenses that are not necessarily associated with the production of income but are deductible because they tend to promote social objectives (such as encouraging home ownership and contributions to charitable organizations). Tax advisors need to be aware of the rules concerning itemized deductions, since it is likely that more of their clients will qualify for itemized deductions than above-the-line deductions.

Quick Quiz 6.6

1. Businesses owners should classify as many of their expenses as they can as business expenses.
   a. True
   b. False

2. Investor expenses such as investment advisory and custodial fees and tax advice are miscellaneous itemized deductions subject to the 2% floor, and have been suspended for tax years 2018-2025 by TCJA 2017.
   a. True
   b. False

True, True.

KEY TERMS

Above-the-Line Deductions – Deduction for adjusted gross income, also known as adjustments to income.

Alimony Recapture – Rules designed to prevent taxpayers from transforming property settlements into deductible alimony payments.

Below-the-Line Deductions – Deductions from adjusted gross income. Also known as itemized deductions. Personal and dependency exemption amounts are also deducted below-the-line. However, they have been suspended by the TCJA 2017 until 2026. In addition, the new 20% deduction for flow-through entities (commonly referred to as the Qualified Business Income (QBI) or Section 199A deduction) introduced in the TCJA 2017 is also a below-the-line deduction.

Distance Test – In order to qualify for a moving expense deduction for tax years before 2018 and after 2025, the distance between the taxpayer's old home and new job location must be at least 50 miles greater than the distance between the old home and the old job location.

Fringe Benefits – Non-cash benefits provided to an employee by an employer in addition to wages and salary.

Health Savings Account (HSA) – Accounts that allow individuals who have high deductible health insurance plans to save on a tax-free basis to fund their medical expenses.

Medical Savings Account (MSA) – Accounts authorized by HIPAA 1996 which allowed contributions to the account to grow tax-free if funds distributed from the account were used to pay for medical expenses.

Necessary Expense – An expense that a prudent business person would incur in the conduct of business.

Ordinary Expense – An expense that is typically incurred in the normal, usual, or customary conduct of businesses in the same line of operations.

Reasonable Expense – An expense that is incurred in a trade or business that is considered by the IRS to be reasonable based on the facts and circumstances surrounding the expense.

DISCUSSION QUESTIONS

SOLUTIONS to the discussion questions can be found exclusively within the chapter. Once you have completed an initial reading of the chapter, go back and highlight the answers to these questions.

1. Who is responsible for substantiating income tax deductions and how are income tax deductions substantiated?
2. Name and describe the two basic categories of deductions.
3. Explain why taxpayers generally prefer above-the-line deductions to below-the-line deductions.
4. Describe the consequences of contributing too much to an HSA.
5. In addition to general business expenses, what above-the-line deductions may be available to sole proprietors, partners, and greater than two percent owners of S corporations?
6. What are the requirements for making a deductible contribution to a traditional IRA?
7. Describe what does and does not qualify as a deductible moving expense.
8. Explain the distance test and the time test that applies to moving expenses claimed after 2025.
9. Describe how the deduction for a penalty on the early withdrawal of savings would affect a taxpayer who cashed in a CD before its maturity.
10. Explain the above-the-line deduction for educator expenses.
11. What are the requirements for deducting student loan interest?
12. Why do some divorcing spouses try to characterize property settlements as alimony?
13. What is the purpose of alimony recapture and how does it work?
14. Under what circumstances is a business-related expense considered “ordinary?”
15. Under what circumstances is a business-related expense considered “necessary?”
16. Under what circumstances will a business-related expense be considered “reasonable?”
17. Describe the deduction for the cost of investigating the purchase of a new business line.
18. If a taxpayer owns a business, what are the three circumstances under which expenses related to a home office can be deducted?
19. Describe the exceptions to the exclusivity requirements associated with the home office deduction.
20. How does timing affect the deduction of business-related expenses by an employee?

MULTIPLE CHOICE PROBLEMS

A sample of multiple choice problems is provided below. Additional multiple choice problems are available at money-education.com by accessing the Student Practice Portal.

1. In 2021, Dottie, a single individual who is not in the Armed Forces, received a salary of $85,000 after making a contribution to her 401(k) plan. Dottie had the following expenditures:

Moving expenses (due to change in employment)	$5,000
Individual retirement account contribution	$6,000
Mortgage interest	$6,500
Charitable gifts of cash to public charities	$2,000

What is Dottie's adjusted gross income for 2021?

   a. $68,500.
   b. $75,000.
   c. $84,700.
   d. $85,000.

2. All of the following requirements must be met for a payment to be treated as alimony EXCEPT:
   a. The payment must be required by a court decree.
   b. The payment must cease at the death of the payor.
   c. The parties may not live in the same household.
   d. The payment must not be a form of disguised child support.

3. All of the following individuals are considered to be self-employed individuals EXCEPT:
   a. Sole Proprietors.
   b. Partners.
   c. Greater than 2% owners of S corporations.
   d. Greater than 5% owners of C corporations.

4. Reggie is the three year old son of Jackson. Since he was born, Reggie has received large gifts from family members, which have been invested for his benefit, and are now beginning to generate some investment income even though a majority of the funds are invested in growth-type investments. This year, Reggie will earn $2,000 in investment income, but due to his age, he does not have any earnings from employment. Jackson recently attended a tax planning seminar sponsored by Fly-By-Nite Financial Services, and, based on advice he received at the seminar, has decided to take Reggie's income and contribute it to an IRA for Reggie's benefit. Jackson feels that the additional deferral of tax on the income would be beneficial from an income tax standpoint. How much can Reggie contribute to his IRA this year?
   a. $0.
   b. $2,000.
   c. $4,000.
   d. $5,000.

5. Which of the following expenses can a taxpayer deduct as an adjustment to gross income (above-the-line)?
   a. Expenses incurred in conducting a sole proprietorship.
   b. Real estate taxes paid on the taxpayer's principal residence.
   c. Charitable gifts of property made to the taxpayer's church.
   d. Employee business expenses that are not reimbursed by the taxpayer's employer.

Additional multiple choice problems are available at *money-education.com* by accessing the Student Practice Portal. Access requires registration of the title using the unique code at the front of the book.

QUICK QUIZ EXPLANATIONS

Quick Quiz 6.1

1. True.
2. False. Whenever expenses are associated with a business activity, they are above-the-line deductions.
3. False. Taxpayers may deduct the greater of their itemized deductions or the standard deduction.
4. True.

Quick Quiz 6.2

1. False. Individuals who are enrolled in Medicare do not qualify for an HSA.
2. True.
3. True.
4. True.

Quick Quiz 6.3

1. False. To make a contribution to an IRA, the taxpayer must have earned income.
2. False. Deductible traditional IRA contributions are phased out over specified AGI ranges for active participants.
3. True.
4. False. Contributions to traditional and Roth IRAs that are in excess of the allowable amount are subject to a 6% penalty.

Quick Quiz 6.4

1. True.
2. False. Temporary living expenses cannot be deducted as moving expenses (no moving expense deduction following TCJA 2017).
3. True. TCJA 2017 suspended deductibility of miscellaneous itemized deductions subject to the 2% floor for tax years 2018 - 2025. Educator expenses in excess of the $250 permitted as an adjustment to income are treated as unreimbursed employee business expenses, which are miscellaneous itemized deductions subject to the 2 percent floor. Therefore, educator expenses in excess of $250 are not deductible for tax years 2018-2025.
4. False. Alimony recapture is only an issue if alimony payments decrease during the first three post-separation years.

Quick Quiz 6.5

1. True.
2. True.
3. False. The cost of investigating the purchase of a new business line are only deductible if the new line of business is actually acquired.

Quick Quiz 6.6

1. True.
2. True.

7

BELOW-THE-LINE DEDUCTIONS (DEDUCTIONS FROM AGI)

LEARNING OBJECTIVES

1. List the six categories of itemized deductions.*
2. Explain the rules and limitations associated with the deduction for medical expenses.*
3. Explain the rules and limitations associated with the deduction for state, local and foreign taxes.*
4. Describe how the tax benefit rule affects the deduction of taxes paid to state, local, and foreign governments.*
5. Identify the three categories of interest expense that qualify for an income tax deduction.*
6. Distinguish between acquisition indebtedness and home equity indebtedness and describe how these classifications limit the mortgage interest deduction for the taxpayer.*
7. Calculate the allowable mortgage interest deduction for a taxpayer.*
8. Describe the income tax treatment of points and late payment fees paid on loans to acquire a personal residence.*
9. Describe the rules associated with the investment interest deduction and calculate the allowable amount of the investment interest deduction for a taxpayer.*
10. Describe the rules governing the deduction of contributions to charities.*
11. Identify the types of contributions to charities that qualify for an income tax deduction.*
12. Calculate the charitable deduction available for a taxpayer in any given tax year.*
13. Describe the advantages and limitations associated with gifts of long-term capital gain property to charity.*
14. Calculate the charitable deduction available for a gift of tangible personal property made to a charity.*
15. Describe how corporations can be used to generate above-the-line charitable income tax deductions for taxpayers.*
16. Calculate the charitable deduction available (if any) when making contributions to universities for sporting event tickets.*
17. Describe the gifts of partial interests in property that qualify for an income tax charitable contribution deduction.*
18. Calculate the permissible deduction for personal and business casualty losses.*
19. Identify miscellaneous itemized deductions not subject to the two percent floor limitation..
20. Calculate a taxpayer's allowable miscellaneous itemized deductions.*
21. Determine the permissible deduction for losses incurred by a taxpayer in IRAs.*
22. Explain how deduction clustering results in a lower tax liability.*

**Ties to CFP Certification Learning Objectives*

INTRODUCTION

Below-the-line deductions can provide a significant benefit to taxpayers. Below-the-line deductions come in two forms: (1) itemized deductions; and (2) the QBI (or Section 199A) deduction. Although above-the-line deductions are usually considered to be more favorable to the taxpayer because they are typically not subject to phaseout, and they reduce the taxpayer's AGI, itemized deductions can allow a taxpayer to take a below-the-line deduction in excess of the standard deduction. If the taxpayer also qualifies for the QBI deduction, the QBI deduction can be taken below the line in addition to the greater of the taxpayer's itemized deductions or standard deduction.

GENERAL CLASSIFICATION OF EXPENSES

Expenses related to the conduct of a trade or business or those related to the production of income are allowed to be deducted "above-the-line" and are often obtained by offsetting gross income from the business or production of income activity. Since the taxpayer is generating income that can be shared with the government through the tax system, the costs of producing that income can be directly offset against income.

Personal expenses are generally not deductible. Congress does, however, allow deductions for personal expenses when it desires to encourage certain behavior or wishes to encourage investment in specific types of property. Some personal deductions are adjustments to income (above-the-line deductions), such as contributions to HSAs (Health Care Savings Accounts), IRAs, alimony (pre-2019 divorce), educator expenses, and student loan interest. Personal deductions taken above the line often serve specified public policy objectives (such as contributions to HSAs and MSAs, contributions to IRAs, and educator expenses), or are related to increasing the taxpayer's intellectual capital, and, thus, the taxpayer's future earnings subject to tax (such as the student loan interest deduction). Most personal deductions that can be taken by taxpayers are taken "below-the-line" and are referred to as itemized deductions. These deductions reduce adjusted gross income in arriving at taxable income. Itemized deductions are reported on Schedule A of the tax return, and include:

- Medical Expenses
- Taxes
- Interest
- Charitable Contributions
- Casualty Losses
- Miscellaneous Itemized Deductions

Exhibit 7.1 | Form 1040 Schedule A

SCHEDULE A (Form 1040)
Department of the Treasury Internal Revenue Service (99)

Itemized Deductions

▶ Go to *www.irs.gov/ScheduleA* for instructions and the latest information.
▶ Attach to Form 1040 or 1040-SR.
Caution: If you are claiming a net qualified disaster loss on Form 4684, see the instructions for line 16.

OMB No. 1545-0074
2020
Attachment Sequence No. **07**

Name(s) shown on Form 1040 or 1040-SR | **Your social security number**

Medical and Dental Expenses		**Caution:** Do not include expenses reimbursed or paid by others.			
	1	Medical and dental expenses (see instructions)	1		
	2	Enter amount from Form 1040 or 1040-SR, line 11 [2]			
	3	Multiply line 2 by 7.5% (0.075)	3		
	4	Subtract line 3 from line 1. If line 3 is more than line 1, enter -0-			4
Taxes You Paid	5	State and local taxes.			
	a	State and local income taxes or general sales taxes. You may include either income taxes or general sales taxes on line 5a, but not both. If you elect to include general sales taxes instead of income taxes, check this box ▶ ☐	5a		
	b	State and local real estate taxes (see instructions)	5b		
	c	State and local personal property taxes	5c		
	d	Add lines 5a through 5c	5d		
	e	Enter the smaller of line 5d or $10,000 ($5,000 if married filing separately)	5e		
	6	Other taxes. List type and amount ▶	6		
	7	Add lines 5e and 6			7
Interest You Paid **Caution:** Your mortgage interest deduction may be limited (see instructions).	8	Home mortgage interest and points. If you didn't use all of your home mortgage loan(s) to buy, build, or improve your home, see instructions and check this box ▶ ☐			
	a	Home mortgage interest and points reported to you on Form 1098. See instructions if limited	8a		
	b	Home mortgage interest not reported to you on Form 1098. See instructions if limited. If paid to the person from whom you bought the home, see instructions and show that person's name, identifying no., and address ▶	8b		
	c	Points not reported to you on Form 1098. See instructions for special rules	8c		
	d	Mortgage insurance premiums (see instructions)	8d		
	e	Add lines 8a through 8d	8e		
	9	Investment interest. Attach Form 4952 if required. See instructions	9		
	10	Add lines 8e and 9			10
Gifts to Charity **Caution:** If you made a gift and got a benefit for it, see instructions.	11	Gifts by cash or check. If you made any gift of $250 or more, see instructions	11		
	12	Other than by cash or check. If you made any gift of $250 or more, see instructions. You **must** attach Form 8283 if over $500	12		
	13	Carryover from prior year	13		
	14	Add lines 11 through 13			14
Casualty and Theft Losses	15	Casualty and theft loss(es) from a federally declared disaster (other than net qualified disaster losses). Attach Form 4684 and enter the amount from line 18 of that form. See instructions			15
Other Itemized Deductions	16	Other—from list in instructions. List type and amount ▶			16
Total Itemized Deductions	17	Add the amounts in the far right column for lines 4 through 16. Also, enter this amount on Form 1040 or 1040-SR, line 12			17
	18	If you elect to itemize deductions even though they are less than your standard deduction, check this box ▶ ☐			

For Paperwork Reduction Act Notice, see the Instructions for Forms 1040 and 1040-SR. Cat. No. 17145C **Schedule A (Form 1040) 2020**

Key Concepts

1. Describe the function of below-the-line deductions.
2. Explain the IRS' interest in reducing the number of individuals who itemize their deductions.
3. Explain the circumstances under which medical expenditures are deductible.
4. Describe the circumstances under which a medical expenditure might be an above-the-line deduction.

Taxpayers can deduct the greater of their itemized deductions or the standard deduction when computing taxable income. A tax benefit is only achieved by itemizing deductions if the taxpayer's total itemized deductions exceed the standard deduction. As **Example 6.1** in the previous chapter illustrates, below-the-line itemized deductions are not as beneficial to the taxpayer as above-the-line adjustments to income.

Many expenses that qualify as itemized deductions such as interest on a home mortgage and property taxes are reported to the IRS by the recipient institution, but medical expenses, charitable contributions, casualty losses, and miscellaneous itemized deductions are only verifiable by the IRS by using an audit. Therefore, it should be obvious that the IRS has a vested interest in reducing the number of itemizers, reducing the number of audits, and making the IRS audit process more effective. The annual increase in the standard deduction due to inflation adjustments helps reduce the number of taxpayers who benefit from claiming itemized deductions. For tax years 2017 and earlier, the IRS estimated that approximately 30 percent of taxpayers itemized deductions. Due to the enactment of TCJA 2017, the number of taxpayers itemizing deductions is expected to decline to approximately ten percent in tax years 2018-2025. For tax year 2018, the first tax year that TCJA 2017 provisions were effective, 12.7 percent of taxpayers itemized deductions.

Financial professionals need to know about itemized deductions because they impact a large number of clients. Some itemized deductions will be routinely used in the planning process (such as the deduction for taxes, interest, and charitable contributions), while other itemized deductions are best avoided through the use of insurance products (such as the medical expense deduction and the casualty loss deduction). In either case, a working knowledge of itemized deductions and their limitations is important for anyone offering tax advice to a client.

MEDICAL EXPENSES

Amounts spent for the diagnosis, cure, treatment or prevention of disease or for treatment of conditions affecting any structure or function of the body are deductible if incurred by the taxpayer, the taxpayer's spouse, or the taxpayer's dependent. These items are not deductible if the taxpayer has been reimbursed through insurance or other means, since this would provide a double benefit to the taxpayer.

Timing of Deduction

Medical expenditures are deductible in the year paid, since individuals are cash-basis taxpayers. To receive a tax benefit for medical expenses, medical expenses must exceed 7.5 percent of the taxpayer's AGI.Only those expenses in excess of this threshold are deductible. This type of limitation is referred to as a "floor," since no deduction is allowed until the allowable expenses exceed the threshold. Medical expenses within the first 7.5 percent of AGI are nondeductible.

Example 7.1

Garth, age 50, has an AGI of $40,000 and medical expenses of $5,000 in 2021. Garth's medical expense deduction will equal $2,000 [$5,000 - 0.075($40,000)]. The first $3,000 of medical expenses are not deductible.

Itemized Deductible Medical Expenses Overview

Medical expenses that are deductible include: prescription drugs and insulin, acupuncture, treatment for alcoholism, artificial limbs and teeth, diagnostic fees, drug addiction treatment, hearing aids and batteries, health insurance premiums (including Medicare and long-term care insurance premiums), laser eye surgery, nursing care, medical aids, and x-ray services. Deductible medical expenses generally require doctor's orders.

Capital Expenses

Capital expenses incurred to improve the taxpayer's home are deductible in an amount equal to the difference between the cost of the improvements and the increase in the value of the taxpayer's home provided that the expenditures are made primarily to provide medical benefits.[1] To be deductible, capital medical expenses must be medically necessary, advised by a physician, used primarily by the patient, and reasonable given the health status of the patient. Examples of capital improvements to homes that are deductible include installation of air conditioning for taxpayers who have respiratory ailments, installation and maintenance of a swimming pool for taxpayers with severe arthritis or asthma, and elevators to allow individuals to access all floors of their home. Improvements made for accessibility are fully deductible, and include handicapped entrance and exit ramps, and modifications to bathrooms and kitchens for the physically handicapped.

Quick Quiz 7.1

1. Personal expenses are always deductible.
   a. True
   b. False
2. The standard deduction is not adjusted for inflation.
   a. True
   b. False
3. Qualified medical expenses in excess of 7.5% of AGI are deductible as an itemized deduction.
   a. True
   b. False
4. Capital medical expenses must be medically necessary and advised by a physician in order to be deductible.
   a. True
   b. False

False, False, True, True.

CASE STUDY 7.1

Medical Expenses

Estate of Lillian Baral, Deceased, David H. Baral, Administrator, Petitioner v. Commissioner of Internal Revenue, Respondent.137 T.C. No. 1 (July 5, 2011).

Lillian was diagnosed by her physician as suffering from dementia. The physician determined that, because of her diminished capacity, Lillian required assistance and supervision 24 hours a day for medical reasons, as well as for her safety. Lillian's brother, David, acting as her attorney-in-fact, hired caregivers to provide the necessary assistance for Lillian. During 2007, $760 was paid on Lillian's behalf to physicians and to the New York University Hospital Center (which was not reimbursed by insurance), $5,566 was paid to caregivers for supplies, and $49,580 was paid to caregivers for their services. The caregivers were not licensed healthcare providers.

1.Treas. Reg. §1.213-1(e)(1)(iii).

CASE STUDY 7.1 CONTINUED

Neither Lillian nor her attorney in fact filed an income tax return for 2007. Consequently, the IRS filed a substitute return claiming $94,229 of income and assessed an income tax deficiency of $17,681. The IRS refused to permit the medical expenses as a deduction on Lillian's tax return, asserting that the expenses paid to caregivers were incurred for custodial, not medical, purposes. Without these amounts classified as medical expenses, Lillian's medical expenses would not have exceeded 7.5% of her adjusted gross income, and would therefore not qualify as an income tax deduction (Effective for years after 2012, the 7.5% limit is increased to 10 percent for most taxpayers. TCJA 2017 reduced it back to 7.5% for 2017 and 2018.).

The court came to the obvious conclusion that the amounts paid directly to physicians and hospitals, totaling $760 were medical expenses incurred for the diagnosis, cure, mitigation, treatment, or prevention of disease, and were therefore deductible. The payment of $5,566 for supplies, however, was not classified as a medical expense by the court because Lillian's attorney in fact did not provide receipts indicating that the expenses were incurred for medical purposes. The court raised the possibility that those expenses may have been used for purposes other than medical care (such as for food, clothing, entertainment, etc.), and cannot be claimed as a medical expense without substantiation.

The IRS denied a medical expense deduction for amounts paid to Lillian's caregivers because the caregivers were not licensed healthcare providers, and the expenses were not used to diagnose, cure, mitigate, treat, or prevent the decedent's disease. The court concluded, however, that these payments were qualified long-term care services, and were deductible. In this case, Lillian was certified by a licensed healthcare provider (her physician) that she had a cognitive impairment that prevented her from performing all of the activities of daily living, and concluded that she required substantial supervision to protect her from threats to her health and safety due to that cognitive impairment.

As such, the court found that Lillian met the definition of a chronically ill individual. The fact that the individuals who provided Lillian with daily supervision were not licensed healthcare professionals is not a reason to deny a medical expense deduction. As the court concluded, "the services provided... by her caregivers were necessary maintenance and personal care services she required because of her diminished capacity and they were provided pursuant to a plan of care prescribed by a licensed health care practitioner. Therefore, they are qualified long-term care services" and are deductible as a medical expense on Lillian's Schedule A.

Nursing Homes and Special Schools

Nursing home and special school expenses are also deductible as medical expenses if the primary purpose of the service is to provide medical treatment. If the primary purpose is personal (for example, custodial care in the case of nursing homes, or attainment of educational degrees in the case of special schools), only those costs specifically allocable to medical treatment are deductible.

Travel and Lodging Expenses

Travel and lodging expenses incurred to acquire medical care are also deductible up to specified limits. The mileage allowance is $0.16 per mile (2021) and the maximum deductible lodging expense is $50 per night per person (this amount is not indexed for inflation). If it would be prudent to have another individual accompany the patient while the patient is receiving care (such as a parent accompanying a child receiving care in a specialized medical facility), that person's travel and lodging expenses (up to the specified maximums) are also considered to be deductible medical expenses.

Nondeductible Medical Expenses

Medical expenses that do not qualify for a deduction include elective cosmetic surgery (including face lifts, hair transplants, hair removal, teeth whitening even when performed by a dentist),[2] dancing lessons even if recommended by a doctor, funeral expenses (these are deductible on the decedent's estate tax return), health club dues (unless related to a specific medical condition), marijuana (even if prescribed legally by a physician in the state of the taxpayer's domicile),[3] over-the counter drug purchases without a prescription, and general health items.

Above-the-Line Medical Expenses

Not all medical expenses must be deducted as a below-the-line deduction and some medical expenses that are disallowed below the line may be permitted to be deducted elsewhere. For example, consider an actress who undergoes elective cosmetic surgery to reverse signs of aging, thereby allowing her to star in more movies or television shows. In this case, the cosmetic surgery will be considered a trade or business expense and may be deducted above-the-line (the expenses can be deducted on the taxpayer's Schedule C to offset income received from the acting trade or business). If given a choice of taking the medical expenses as a trade or business expense or as an itemized deduction, a taxpayer should deduct the expenses as a trade or business expenses. Trade or business expenses result in a reduction of AGI and are not subject to the medical expense floor that applies to itemized medical expenses. Above-the-line deductions also reduce the floor associated with other itemized deductions by reducing the taxpayer's AGI.

Exhibit 7.2 | Summary of Deductible and Nondeductible Medical Expenses

Deductible	*Nondeductible*
• Prescription Drugs	• Elective Cosmetic Surgery
• Health Insurance Premiums	• Dance Lessons
• Capital Expenditures	• Health Club Dues
• Nursing Home and Special Schools	• Marijuana
• Premiums for Long-Term Care Insurance	• Over-the-Counter Drugs
• Travel and Lodging	• General Health Items (e.g., vitamins)
• Expenses Related to Diagnosis, Cure, & Treatment	

2.Revenue Ruling 2003-57.
3.Treas. Reg. §1.213-1(e)(2); Revenue Ruling 97-9.

TAXES

The Tax Cuts and Jobs Act of 2017 (TCJA 2017) limited the deduction for state and local property and sales taxes, and state and local income taxes, paid by a taxpayer to $10,000 ($5,000 for married taxpayers filing separately) for tax years 2018 through 2025. Foreign property taxes, and prepayments of state or local income and property taxes are not deductible during this period. Excise taxes, gift taxes, and estate taxes are also not deductible. Note that the $10,000 limitation imposes a significant marriage penalty - both single taxpayers, and married taxpayers are subject to the $10,000 tax deduction cap. If a married couple attempts to file separately, each will be subject to a $5,000 cap on the deduction for taxes, but if the couple divorced and were single by the end of the year, each would be subject to the higher $10,000 tax deduction cap.

Taxes paid to state, local, and foreign governments are normally deductible as itemized deductions. Excise taxes, gift taxes, and estate taxes are not deductible.

Key Concepts

1. Describe how the tax benefit rule affects the deduction of taxes paid to state, local, and foreign governments.
2. Explain the general rule concerning the deductibility of interest for income tax purposes.
3. List the limitations on deducting qualified personal residence interest.
4. Describe the extent to which investment interest is deductible.

Timing of Deduction

State and local income taxes are deducted in the year paid. A deduction is available, therefore, for all amounts withheld, made as estimated payments, and paid to satisfy a prior year income tax liability subject to the $10,000 ($5,000 for MFS) limit imposed by TCJA 2017 for tax years 2018-2025. When a taxpayer receives a state income tax refund in a subsequent year, the tax benefit rule applies and requires the taxpayer to include the state income tax refund in his or her taxable income to the extent that a deduction was taken for state income taxes paid in a prior tax year (the tax benefit rule).

Example 7.2

In 2021, Kenny had withholding for Connecticut Income Tax of $4,000 and had made estimated tax payments to Connecticut totaling $2,000. Kenny itemizes deductions on his tax return, and includes all $6,000 as a deduction on his 2021 federal income tax return. When he completed his 2021 state income tax return (which he filed on April 15, 2022), Kenny found out that he had overpaid state income taxes for the year, and was entitled to a $500 state income tax refund, which he received in June of 2022. When Kenny files his 2022 income tax return, he must include the $500 state income tax refund in his income (due to the imposition of the tax benefit rule, which states that when a deduction has been taken, and the amount deducted was later refunded, the refund must be included in income).

Example 7.3

Assume the same facts as **Example 7.2**, except that Kenny did not itemize deductions on his 2021 federal income tax return. In this case, since Kenny took the standard deduction and did not deduct his state income tax, he will not have to include any state income tax refund in his taxable income for the next year.

Example 7.4

Dolly has a primary residence in New Orleans and a vacation home in Destin with associated property taxes of $12,000 and $7,000, respectively. She also pays $8,000 in Louisiana state income tax. Dolly and her husband, Willie, are limited to a deduction for taxes of $10,000 in 2018 or after, even though they spend $27,000 in property and income taxes. For 2017, they would have been able to deduct the full $27,000.

The IRS provided additional guidance in Revenue Ruling 2019-11 regarding the interaction of the tax benefit rule with the $10,000 limit on deductions for state and local taxes for tax years 2018-2025. The tax benefit rule applies only to the extent that the overpayment causing the refund actually resulted in a tax benefit. To make that determination, the overpayment must be viewed in relation to the amount of itemized deductions or standard deduction the taxpayer would have claimed had the correct amount been paid.

Example 7.5

Hank paid local real property taxes of $4,000 and state income taxes of $5,000 in 2021. His deduction for state and local taxes was not limited by the $10,000 maximum. His total itemized deductions for the year were $16,000. In 2022, Hank received a refund of $1,500 due to overpayment of state income taxes in 2021. Had Hank paid the correct amount of state income taxes in 2021, his itemized deductions would have been $14,500 instead of $16,000. His tax benefit from the overpayment was $1,500, therefore, he is required to include the entire $1,500 as income in 2022.

Example 7.6

Reba paid local real property taxes of $5,000 and state income taxes of $7,000 in 2021. Her deduction for state and local taxes was limited by the $10,000 maximum, so she could not deduct $2,000 of the $12,000 paid. Her total itemized deductions for the year were $15,000. In 2022 Reba received a refund of $750 due to overpayment of state income taxes in 2021. Had Reba paid the correct amount of state income taxes in 2021, her state and local tax deduction would have remained the same and her itemized deductions would still have been $15,000. She received no tax benefit from the overpayment of $750, therefore, she is not required to include the $750 as income in 2022.

Example 7.7

Carrie paid local real property taxes of $5,000 and state income taxes of $6,000 in 2021. Her deduction for state and local taxes was limited by the $10,000 maximum, so she could not deduct $1,000 of the $11,000 paid. Her total itemized deductions for the year were $15,000. In 2022 Carrie received a refund of $1,500 due to overpayment of state income taxes in 2021. Had Carrie paid the correct amount of state income taxes in 2021, her state and local tax deduction would have been $9,500 (instead of $10,000) and her itemized deductions would have been $14,500. She realized a $500 tax benefit from the overpayment, therefore, she is required to include $500 as income in 2022.

Example 7.8

George paid local real property taxes of $4,250 and state income taxes of $6,000 in 2021. His deduction for state and local taxes was limited by the $10,000 maximum, so he could not deduct $250 of the $10,250 paid. His total itemized deductions for the year were $12,800. In 2022 George received a refund of $1,000 due to overpayment of state income taxes in 2021. Had George paid the correct amount of state income taxes in 2021, his deduction for state and local taxes would have been $9,250, his itemized deductions would have been $12,050 instead of $12,800, and he would have used the standard deduction of $12,550. His tax benefit from the overpayment was $250 ($12,800 - $$12,550 = $250), therefore, he is required to include $250 as income in 2022.

As an alternative to deducting state income taxes, a taxpayer may deduct state sales taxes. Those taxpayers who live in states with no income tax, or those taxpayers who have made large purchases during the year and whose sales taxes exceed their state income taxes will benefit by using the sales tax deduction. A taxpayer may deduct either state sales taxes or state income taxes, but not both. The deduction for sales taxes can be either the actual sales taxes paid (which requires the taxpayer to keep records showing the total sales taxes paid throughout the year), or a predetermined deduction amount provided by the IRS that is based on the taxpayer's AGI plus nontaxable income for the year. The ability to deduct sales taxes in lieu of income taxes was made permanent by the PATH Act of 2015.

After enactment of TCJA 2017, foreign property taxes are not deductible for tax years 2018 through 2025. Those paying foreign income taxes may, however, claim a Foreign Tax Credit. Generally, the foreign tax credit will give the taxpayer a greater tax benefit than a tax deduction for foreign income taxes since a credit is a dollar for dollar reduction in tax liability while a deduction simply reduces the amount subject to income tax.

Property taxes paid to state and local governments are also deductible, provided that the taxes are based on the value of the property (when a tax is based on the value of property, it is referred to as an *ad valorem* tax). While the federal government is constitutionally prohibited from taxing property, state and local governments may tax property, and these taxes often provide a significant source of revenue for the operation of state and local governments. Property taxes are deducted in the year paid to the taxing authority. If a taxpayer makes monthly payments into an escrow account with a mortgage lender, no deduction is permitted until the funds are disbursed from the escrow account to the taxing authority.

There is no limitation on the number of properties that can be claimed as a deduction for property taxes for regular tax purposes; if that taxpayer has multiple properties, he or she may claim all of the property taxes paid (subject, of course, to the overall limitation of $10,000 for tax years 2018-2025). When a taxpayer becomes liable for the Alternative Minimum Tax (AMT), however, some or all of the tax benefit of this deduction is lost. The AMT is covered in detail later in this textbook.

When property is sold, the property taxes will be prorated between the buyer and seller of the property based on the date ownership of the property changed hands. Adjustments can be found on the closing statements of the property that is sold, and should be reflected on the taxpayer's Schedule A. One special rule applies when the seller of real estate pays property taxes that are considered to be the obligation of the purchaser. The purchaser is deemed to have paid the property taxes and can take an income tax deduction for the taxes paid, which results in a reduction in basis in the property. The seller is treated as receiving a reduced price for the real estate, thereby reducing the amount realized, and any gain realized, on the transaction and cannot deduct the portion paid for the purchaser.

Nondeductible Fines and Fees

Taxes do not include fines and fees, even if paid to a state or local government. Fines are intended to be punitive in nature and are therefore nondeductible.

Example 7.9

Toby has an appointment with an important client at the client's home in Manhattan, and is having a difficult time finding a parking spot. Believing that his time is valuable, he parks in a no-parking zone and visits the client. When he returns, he finds a $200 parking ticket on his windshield. Toby will not be able to deduct the parking ticket as a local tax, since it was a fine for violating local law.

Exhibit 7.3 | Summary of Deductible and Nondeductible Taxes

Deductible	*Nondeductible*
• State and Local Income Taxes	• Fines or Fees
• State Sales Tax (Alternative)	• Excise Taxes
• Foreign Property Taxes (before 2018 and after 2025)	• Gift Taxes
• Property Taxes	• Estate Taxes

INTEREST

The general rule concerning the deductibility of interest for income tax purposes may come as a surprise to most people. It states that all interest paid or accrued within the taxable year on indebtedness is deductible. Of course, many exceptions apply, resulting in interest being deductible only when it is:

- qualified residence interest;
- interest incurred in a trade or business; or
- interest incurred for the production of income (investment interest).

Interest incurred in the conduct of an active trade or business is deductible against business income above-the-line. It is not treated as a Schedule A below-the-line itemized deduction.

Personal interest, which includes all interest other than qualified residence interest, investment interest, and trade or business interest, is not deductible for income tax purposes. Examples of personal interest include interest incurred on personal credit cards, personal car loans, personal obligations and bills, and finance charges for personal transactions.

For interest to be deductible, it must be incurred on a valid obligation to pay a fixed or determinable sum of money in return for the use of money. The amount of interest must be within limits set by the state. If interest is charged on an obligation at a rate higher than the maximum rate permitted by law, collection of the interest is not legally permissible, and is therefore not deductible for income tax purposes, even if paid.

Another requirement necessary for the interest deduction to apply is that the obligation to pay the interest must be the taxpayer's obligation. Payment of the interest obligation of another person does not give rise to an interest expense deduction for the payor.

Example 7.10

Years ago, Miranda set up a business called Sports Fanatic, Inc., a C corporation. The business had been successful, but has recently fallen on hard times and does not have the cash flow necessary to make the required interest payments on its outstanding loans. Since Miranda anticipates that the business problems are temporary and she does not want to jeopardize the company's credit rating, she personally makes the payments on the loans. While Miranda has paid the interest, she may not deduct those payments as an interest expense on her personal tax return since she was not obligated to make the loan payments – the corporation had the obligation. Instead, Miranda will treat the payments as a capital contribution to the corporation, which will increase her basis in her interest in the corporation. The corporation will be permitted to take an interest expense deduction, which may increase its tax loss, and may carry that loss forward to offset future income generated by the company.

Qualified Residence Interest Deduction

Perhaps one of the most frequently used and most important income tax deductions by individuals is the home mortgage interest deduction, referred to in tax parlance as the **qualified residence interest deduction**. Taxpayers are permitted to deduct interest on up to $750,000 of home indebtedness (referred to as acquisition indebtedness).[4] Subsequent to the enactment of TCJA 2017, interest on home equity indebtedness not used for buying, building or making capital improvements to the taxpayers residence is no longer deductible (for tax years 2018-2025). Interest expense incurred on amounts in excess of $750,000 of acquisition indebtedness is not deductible.

Despite the restrictions on home mortgages under TCJA, taxpayers can still deduct interest on a home equity loan, home equity line of credit or second mortgage, if the loan is used for buying, building, or making capital improvements to the taxpayer's residence regardless of how the loan is labeled. The TCJA of 2017 suspends from 2018 until 2026 the deduction for interest paid on home equity loans and lines of credit, unless they are used to buy, build or substantially improve the taxpayer's home that secures the loan and the total of all loans is no greater than $750,000. Interest attributable to these types of home equity loans are deductible because these loans are classified as acquisition indebtedness, which is defined below.

Acquisition Indebtedness

Acquisition indebtedness is indebtedness used to acquire, construct, or substantially improve the taxpayer's primary residence and one additional residence (third, fourth, and fifth residences do not qualify for the interest deduction). To meet the definition of qualified residence interest, the indebtedness must be secured by the home. The interest expense on the first $750,000 of acquisition indebtedness (a combined limit for both the primary and secondary residence - not $750,000 of indebtedness for each residence) is deductible as an itemized deduction. Since most home loans are amortized, acquisition indebtedness is reduced as payments of principal are made and the acquisition

4.Prior to 2018, the limit was $1,000,000 plus up to $100,000 of home equity indebtedness.

indebtedness cannot be increased (e.g., by refinancing) unless a new home is acquired. Interest-only loans do not result in amortization of acquisition indebtedness.

Loans incurred by the taxpayer to add an addition to an existing primary or secondary residence are considered to be acquisition indebtedness, and are subject to the $750,000 cap for deductibility of interest. Loans incurred by a taxpayer to repair an existing primary or secondary residence are not considered to be acquisition indebtedness, but may be classified as home equity indebtedness (discussed below).

Refinancing is the process of replacing an existing mortgage with a new mortgage, generally for the purpose of reducing the interest rate on the mortgage. Acquisition indebtedness also includes any indebtedness secured by the taxpayer's residence resulting from the refinancing of indebtedness. However, the interest on the refinanced debt is only deductible to the extent the amount of the indebtedness is not increased from the prior mortgage, unless such an increase is used to substantially improve the property.

Example 7.11

Jason recently borrowed $150,000 from his bank to put an addition on his home to accommodate his growing family. Jason is required to treat the loan as acquisition indebtedness when calculating his mortgage interest deduction.

Example 7.12

Faith borrowed $15,000 from her bank to repair the roof on her home. She cannot treat this loan as acquisition indebtedness since it was used to repair an existing primary residence, and the interest on this loan will not be deductible.

Example 7.13

In January 2021, Waylon takes out a $500,000 mortgage to purchase a main home with a fair market value of $800,000. In February 2021, Waylon takes out a $250,000 home equity loan to put an addition on the main home. Both loans are secured by the main home and the total does not exceed the cost of the home. Because the total amount of both loans does not exceed $750,000, all of the interest paid on the loan is deductible. However, if Waylon uses the home equity loan proceeds for personal expenses, such as paying off student loans and credit cards, then the interest on the home equity loan would not be deductible.

Example 7.14

In January 2021, Patsy takes out a $500,000 mortgage to purchase a main home. The loan is secured by the main home. In February 2021, Patsy takes out a $250,000 loan to purchase a vacation home. The loan is secured by the vacation home. Because the total amount of both mortgages does not exceed $750,000, all of the interest paid on both mortgages is deductible. However, if Patsy took out a $250,000 home equity loan on the main home to purchase the vacation home, then the interest on the home equity loan would not be deductible.

Example 7.15

In January 2021, Conway takes out a $500,000 mortgage to purchase a main home. The loan is secured by the main home. In February 2021, Conway takes out a $500,000 loan to purchase a vacation home. The loan is secured by the vacation home. Because the total amount of both mortgages exceeds $750,000, not all of the interest paid on both mortgages is deductible.

Example 7.16

Shania's home is worth $200,000 and she has a balance on her mortgage of $120,000. Because her mortgage has an interest rate of 6% and the prevailing rates are 4%, she wants to refinance her mortgage to lower her payment. The interest on Shania's refinanced loan is fully deductible as long as the total amount of debt on the property does not increase, or as long as any increase is used to substantially improve the property.

Home Equity Indebtedness

Home equity indebtedness is additional debt secured by the home that exceeds the amount of acquisition indebtedness. The interest on home equity indebtedness is no longer deductible after 2017 as a result of TCJA, unless the home equity indebtedness is used to substantially improve the home and the taxpayer's total acquisition and home equity indebtedness used for substantial improvements is equal to or below the acquisition indebtedness limitation.

Example 7.17

Five years ago, Kane purchased a home for $400,000, paying $80,000 in cash and taking out a $320,000 mortgage. The outstanding balance of the mortgage is now $270,000, but the value of the home has risen to $800,000. Kane needs some additional cash to pay for his children's education and to cover some personal expenditures, so he refinances the home, taking out an additional $210,000. His mortgage balance is now $480,000. Kane will be able to deduct the interest on $270,000 of the mortgage, but will not be permitted to deduct the interest on the remaining $210,000. $270,000 of the refinanced amount continues to be treated as acquisition indebtedness. The interest on the additional $210,000 is not deductible.

Example 7.18

Five years ago, Loretta purchased a home for $400,000 paying $80,000 in cash and taking out a $320,000 mortgage. Loretta recently was appointed CEO of The Amazing Company, and is drawing a salary far in excess of what she thought she would make. About six months ago, Loretta was watching television when Lynn, a nationally known self-proclaimed expert on personal finance, gave advice to pay off existing home mortgages. Loretta took Lynn's advice and paid off her mortgage, which used up most of her available cash. Last week, Loretta was presented with a business opportunity that would require a $300,000 investment on her part, and she would like to participate. Since she does not have any spare cash, she takes out a $300,000 home equity loan on her home. Loretta will not be able to deduct any interest on the loan. When she paid off her mortgage, she retired her acquisition indebtedness, which cannot be resurrected with a home equity loan. If Loretta had not taken Lynn's advice, and had not paid off the mortgage, she would have been able to deduct all of the interest on her loan as qualified residence interest and use her cash to make the investment.

Acquisition Indebtedness Incurred On or Prior to December 15, 2017

While the TCJA 2017 reduced the maximum amount of acquisition debt on which interest is deductible to $750,000, an exception was allowed for acquisition debt incurred on or before December 15, 2017 which allows for the deduction of interest on up to $1,000,000 of such acquisition debt. Thus, a taxpayer whose mortgage was incurred prior to December 16, 2017 can continue to use to the previous, higher, limit.

As discussed above, mortgage interest on refinanced acquisition loans is deductible up to the loan balance that was outstanding at the time of the refinance. If the original acquisition debt was incurred on or before December 15, 2017, and the new mortgage does not exceed the remaining balance on the refinanced debt, the $1 million limit will continue to apply. However, if the total new mortgage balance exceeds the amount of the remaining acquisition debt on the refinanced mortgage, the taxpayer will be subject to the reduced limit of $750,000. Taxpayers with mortgage balances over $750,000 who are refinancing a mortgage incurred on or prior to December 15, 2017 should be cautious regarding the decision to refinance other debt or expenses into the new mortgage as it will result in a reduction of the total interest that may be deducted.

Exhibit 7.4 | Deductible Mortgage Interest

		Deduct Interest on Debt of Up To	*Deduct Interest on Refinanced Debt of Up To*
Prior to 2018	Acquisition Debt	$1,000,000	$1,000,000
	Home Equity Debt (for any purpose)	$100,000	$100,000
TCJA for 2018 - 2025	Acquisition Debt Incurred on or Before 12-15-17	$1,000,000	$1,000,000 (but no greater than the refinanced prior loan balance)
	Acquisition Debt Incurred After 12-15-17; Including Home Equity Debt Used to Improve the Property*	$750,000	$750,000
	Home Equity Debt (not used to improve the property)	$0	$0
2026 and Beyond	Acquisition Debt (regardless of when incurred)	$1,000,000	$1,000,000
	Home Equity Debt (for any purpose)	$100,000	$100,000

* For the years 2018–2025, the interest on home equity debt generally is not deductible; however, the interest on home equity debt used for improvements to the home remains deductible as acquisition debt, subject to the dollar limits for total acquisition debts.

Points

When taxpayers acquire or refinance homes, they often pay "points" (a form of pre-paid interest) to get a lower rate on the mortgage loan. When points are paid to acquire a new personal residence or vacation home, or to improve a personal residence or vacation home, the points paid are fully deductible as qualified residence interest expense in the current tax year provided that they are clearly identified, that they represent a percentage of the principal amount of the mortgage, and they are paid from the taxpayers' own funds.[5] Only the points paid on the first $750,000 of acquisition indebtedness qualify for a tax deduction. Points paid to refinance an existing loan are amortized over the life of the loan.

Late payment fees on mortgage loans are also deductible as mortgage interest, since they represent an additional interest charge on the loan. If the late payment fees are reimbursements for specific services such as collection of the amount due, then they are not deductible.

Quick Quiz 7.2

1. Taxpayers must include state income tax refunds in taxable income to the extent that a deduction was previously taken, and a tax benefit realized, for state income taxes paid in a prior tax year.
   a. True
   b. False
2. Only property taxes paid on the taxpayer's primary residence are deductible.
   a. True
   b. False
3. Interest is only deductible if it is incurred on a valid obligation to pay a fixed or determinable sum of money in return for the use of the money.
   a. True
   b. False
4. Taxpayers are permitted to deduct the interest on an unlimited amount of home indebtedness.
   a. True
   b. False

True, False, True, False.

Mortgage Insurance Premiums

For tax years beginning after December 31, 2020 and before January 1, 2022, the Taxpayer Certainty and Disaster Tax Relief Act of 2020 allows a deduction as qualified residence interest for mortgage insurance premiums paid in connection with acquisition indebtedness. The amount of mortgage insurance premiums which can be deducted is reduced by 10 percent for each $1,000 ($500 for married filing separately) that the taxpayer's AGI exceeds $100,000 ($50,000 for married filing separately).

Qualified Residence

For purpose of the qualified residence interest deduction, a "home" includes not only a traditional residence, but also mobile homes, trailers, boats, and timeshares. Provided that the "residence" has cooking, toileting, and sleeping facilities, it can be considered a residence for purposes of the qualified residence interest deduction.

Reporting

The Highway and Transportation Funding Act of 2015 (PL 114-21) imposed new requirements on mortgage interest reporting for tax years beginning in 2016. Under prior law, lenders were required to report mortgage interest paid by a borrower on Form 1098. Since 2016, lenders must also report on form 1098 the amount of outstanding principal on the mortgage at the beginning of the calendar year, the date of origination of the mortgage, and the address of the property on which mortgage interest was paid. This information will make it easier for the IRS to ascertain if mortgage interest deductions in excess of the amounts specified by the rules discussed above. As a consequence, those with large

5.Rev. Proc. 94-27.

mortgages, or those who are attempting to deduct interest on mortgages not associated with their residential address on Schedule A or with their rental properties on Schedule E should anticipate increased IRS inquiry and scrutiny.

Investment Interest Deduction

An itemized deduction is also allowed for investment interest expense, which is interest incurred to purchase or hold securities and income-producing instruments. Investment interest is typically associated with margin accounts used to purchase stocks, bonds, and mutual funds.

Investment interest is deductible but only to the extent of net investment income. Net investment income equals investment income less investment expenses other than investment interest expense. Investment expenses include any expenses that were directly connected with the production of investment income without regard to any disallowance caused by the two percent floor on miscellaneous itemized deductions. Investment income includes gross income from property held for investment (interest and dividends) and gains on the sale of property in excess of net capital gain (i.e., gains on the sale of property that are taxed at ordinary income tax rates due to the imposition of the depreciation recapture rules). Investment income can include short-term capital gains and nonqualified dividends. Qualified dividends and net long-term capital gains, however, are excluded unless the taxpayer makes a special election as discussed below.

Any investment interest expense not used in the current year due to the net investment income limitation may be carried forward indefinitely.

Investors with growth-oriented investment portfolios may have little investment income to offset their investment interest expenses due to the exclusion of capital gains from the definition of net investment income. Taxpayers may elect to include qualified dividends and net capital gains in their net investment income, but there is a cost to making the election – the taxpayer will lose the preferential capital gains tax rate (currently, the maximum capital gains tax rate is 20 percent) that applies to qualified dividends and long-term capital gains. This election would most likely be made by a taxpayer who has a significant amount of investment interest expense which would offset tax liability on the identical amount of net investment income. A taxpayer can make the election to include capital gains in net investment income on Form 4952.

Two additional rules concerning the investment interest expense deduction are important – one deals with interest paid on the acquisition of investments that generate tax-free income, and the second deals with interest paid on the acquisition of passive investments. The deduction of investment interest is allowed because the taxpayer is purchasing assets that will generate taxable income in the future, which will be shared with the government through the tax system. Loans used to acquire assets that will generate tax-free income will not qualify for the investment interest deduction and interest paid on loans to acquire passive investments will be subject to the passive loss limitation rules. The passive loss limitation rules are explained in Chapter 14.

If interest is paid on a loan used to purchase assets that will not generate taxable income in the future, such as a portfolio of municipal bonds, investment interest itemized deduction will not be permitted. If, however, the taxpayer purchases municipal bonds that are not public purpose municipal bonds, and the taxpayer becomes an alternative minimum tax (AMT) taxpayer, the interest on those bonds will become taxable in the AMT tax system (even though the interest is exempt for regular tax purposes), and the taxpayer will receive an investment interest expense deduction in the AMT tax system (but not the regular tax system). Special rules apply to income subject to the alternative minimum tax and will be addressed in more detail in Chapter 15.

When interest is paid on loans used to acquire passive assets, such as investment real estate and limited partnership interests, the interest will be deductible to the extent that the passive investment generates investment income. The interest deduction is suspended and will be carried forward in the taxpayer's passive income bucket until passive income is generated to deduct the loss generated by the interest charges. In this respect, the passive activity loss rules are similar to the investment interest deduction rules. Investment interest expense used to acquire either portfolio assets or passive investments may only be deducted to the extent that the taxpayer has either net investment income (in the case of portfolio investment interest expense) or passive income (in the case of passive investment interest expense).

Exhibit 7.5 | Summary of Deductible and Nondeductible Interest Expense as Itemized Deduction

Deductible	*Nondeductible*
• Qualified Residence Interest (Limit of two houses and $750,000 debt) • Investment Interest Expense (to extent of investment interest income) • After 2017, Home Equity Indebtedness used for buying, building, or making capital improvements	• Personal Interest Including Credit Cards, Bank Loans, etc. • Interest Used to Buy Tax-Free Municipal Bonds • After 2017, Home Equity Indebtedness used for non-home improvement purposes

CHARITABLE CONTRIBUTIONS AND DEDUCTIONS

Americans are among the most charitably inclined individuals in the world. Studies consistently show that Americans, as a whole, give a greater percentage of their income to charitable causes than citizens of many other countries. In the United States, individuals who give to qualified charitable organizations qualify for an income tax charitable deduction. In 2020 and 2021, taxpayers who do not itemize deductions may take $300 in cash contributions to charity ($600 for those married filing jointly in 2021) as an adjustment to income. Taxpayers who itemize deductions claim all of their charitable contributions on Schedule A of Form 1040. The rules concerning charitable deductions described in this chapter apply to itemized charitable deductions claimed on Schedule A of Form 1040.

Key Concepts

1. List the requirements that must be met in order to qualify a charitable contribution for an income tax charitable deduction.
2. Name the exceptions to the partial interest rule.
3. Describe how the type of charity and type of property donated impact the limits on charitable contribution deductions.
4. Explain how the special election impacts the charitable contribution deduction.

Qualified Charitable Organizations

Not all donations made for charitable purposes are deductible on the donor's income tax return, however. Only contributions made to qualified charitable organizations qualify for an income tax deduction. A **qualified charitable organization** is operated exclusively for religious, charitable, scientific, literary, or educational purposes, or for the prevention of cruelty to animals or children (the charitable purposes listed here are sometimes referred to as the charitable purpose test).

Qualified charitable organizations may not allow any part of the earnings of the charity to be used for the private benefit of an individual, an event called "private inurement" in tax parlance, and are prohibited from engaging in propaganda or lobbying at the federal level, although they are allowed to influence state and local legislation. To ensure that deductions to a charitable organization are deductible for income tax purposes, a taxpayer should make sure that the charity has received an exempt determination letter from the IRS. A list of charities that have received exempt determination letters may be obtained from the Internal Revenue Service, or may be accessed on the IRS website at www.irs.gov.

For income tax purposes, only gifts to U.S. based charities are eligible for a charitable income tax deduction; gifts to foreign charities do not qualify. When an individual dies and makes charitable gifts through his or her estate, the estate tax charitable deduction applies to both U.S. based and foreign charities, provided that the charitable purpose test is met.

There are two primary ways a taxpayer can avoid the income tax rule limiting the income tax charitable deduction for donations to domestic charities. The first method involves a transfer from the taxpayer to a U.S. based charity that will subsequently transfer the funds oversees for the use of a foreign charity. Common examples of this approach include Save the Children type funds (which sponsor economically disadvantaged children in third world countries), or "friends of organizations," such as The Friends of Oxford University (a U.S. based charity that transfers donated funds from the United States to Oxford University in England). The second method a taxpayer could use to obtain an income tax deduction for foreign charitable gifts is to form a private foundation in the United States and make tax-deductible contributions to the foundation. The private foundation may then transfer the funds to a foreign charity or charitable cause.

Additional Requirements for Deduction

Three additional requirements must be met to qualify for an income tax charitable deduction.

1. The subject of the charitable gift must be property, not services.
2. The deductible portion of the gift must not exceed the value received by the charity.
3. The charitable gift must be paid in cash or property by the close of the taxable year.

Gifts that Qualify for the Deduction

Only gifts of cash or property will qualify for a charitable income tax deduction. Volunteering time for a charity by donating services is a great way to make a charitable gift, but the value of the time donated will not qualify for the income tax charitable deduction. This rule is consistent with the matching principal of income taxation, which states that for every deduction, there must be an inclusion. Since the value of the taxpayers services have never been brought into income and the charity will not report income due to receipt of the gift, the value of services cannot be deducted as a charitable gift. A taxpayer could elect to include the value of services in income to generate a charitable deduction, but for reasons that will be discussed in detail later, this will rarely be beneficial for the taxpayer (due to the limitation imposed on charitable deductions). Consequently, only gifts of cash or property will be eligible for the income tax charitable deduction.

Individuals who volunteer time for charitable causes often incur expenses in completing their charitable service. To the extent that these expenses are not reimbursed, they qualify as a charitable income tax deduction. Examples may include mileage (at $0.14 per mile) and travel expenses, parking costs, and incidental expenses (for supplies and materials) incurred when performing charitable services.

Example 7.19

Rhett, a tax attorney, volunteered to create a private operating foundation for a local group that was forming a new charitable organization. Usually, Rhett charges $5,000 to draft the documents and obtain the IRS exempt determination letter for the operating foundation. Rhett may not deduct the value of his services as a charitable deduction, since he never recognized the $5,000 as income. Rhett will be able to deduct the actual costs he incurred in setting up the operating foundation, such as the cost of obtaining the exempt determination letter for the organization.

Likewise, giving a charity the right to use property will generally not qualify the donor for an income tax charitable deduction. To be deductible for income tax purposes, a gift of property must be a gift of the donor's entire interest in the property. Since the donor does not transfer control of the asset to a charity when he or she gives the charity the right to use the asset, no tax deduction is available.

Example 7.20

Bentley is a board member of Friends of Foley, a charitable organization dedicated to the prevention of cruelty to animals. Friends of Foley is embarking on a fundraising campaign to expand their animal shelter facilities and Bentley has an office building with vacant office space. Bentley allows Friends of Foley to use the vacant office space to run their fundraising campaign. While Bentley has made a significant contribution to the charity, she may not take an income tax charitable deduction for the value of the rental use of the office since she did not donate her entire interest in the property (the entire building) to the charity.

Similar to the donation of services to charitable organizations, this donation is a variation on the matching principal of income taxation. Since Bentley never included the rental income value of the office in her income, she may not take a charitable deduction for the value given to charity.

Example 7.21

Dierk owns an original sculpture created by the late artist, Frederick Hart. The Wadsworth Athenaeum, a local art museum, is sponsoring a special exhibit on the work of Frederick Hart and Dierk allowed the museum to display his sculpture at the museum during the exhibit. While the donation of the use of the sculpture made the exhibit more complete and attracted more patrons to visit the exhibit and pay the entrance fee to the museum, Dierk may not deduct the value of the use of the sculpture by the museum as an income tax charitable deduction, since he did not give his entire interest in the property (a fee simple ownership interest) to the museum.

There are some exceptions to the partial interest rule. As noted above, a gift of a partial interest in property (something less than the donor's entire interest) is not deductible for income tax purposes unless an exception applies. The primary exceptions (which will be covered later in this section) include:

- A gift of an undivided portion of the donor's entire interest in the property;
- A gift of a remainder interest in a personal residence or farm;
- A gift of a partial interest if transferred in trust (a charitable remainder trust, a charitable lead trust, or a pooled income fund); and
- Purchase of a charitable gift annuity.

When a donor makes a charitable gift, the charitable income tax deduction must not exceed the value received by the charitable organization. When a taxpayer makes a gift and receives something from the charity in return, the value of the charitable deduction is reduced by the fair market value of the property received by the donor. Small gifts, however, do not reduce the value of the income tax deduction.

Example 7.22

Tanya, a fan of the Britcom Keeping Up Appearances, donated $100 to her local public television station (a qualified charity) to encourage them to keep the show on the air. In return for her donation, the television station sent her a coffee mug with the name of the station and its logo prominently displayed on the mug. Tanya's charitable deduction is $100, since the mug is a de-minimus item (a small gift).

Example 7.23

Charley, a fan of the Britcom Father Ted, makes a $500 donation to his public television station. In return for the donation, the public television station gives Charley front-row tickets to the Irish Tenors concert coming up later in the month, as well as a backstage pass and reception, and a CD of the performance. The fair market value of this package is $175. Charley is entitled to take a charitable deduction for the difference between what he donated to the charity, and what he received from the charity or a total of $325.

In response to high-tax states' attempts to work around the $10,000 deduction limit on state taxes by offering state tax credits in exchange for contributions to charities established by the states, the IRS has issued regulations requiring that if a taxpayer makes a gift to a charity and receives a state or local tax credit in return, the charitable contribution deduction is reduced by the amount of the tax credit received. An exception to the dollar-for-dollar reduction applies if the tax credit is no more than 15 percent of the contribution amount.[6] Taxpayers are permitted to treat these credits as state or local tax payments, allowing some taxpayers a deduction, as taxes paid, for the denied contributions.[7] The reduction rule does not apply to businesses making contributions to charities or government entities and taking the deduction as an ordinary and necessary business expense.[8]

6. Treas. Reg. §1.170A-1(h)(3)
7. Notice 2019-12
8. Rev. Proc. 2019-12

Example 7.24

Blake makes a $1,000 charitable contribution to a qualified public charity for which he will receive a state tax credit equal to 80% of the contribution amount. Blake must reduce his charitable contribution deduction by $800 (80% x $1,000); therefore, his charitable contribution is $200. This reduction applies regardless of whether he is able to claim the state tax credit for that year.

Example 7.25

Assume the same facts as in the previous example, but that the state tax credit is equal to 10% of the contribution to the charity. Blake's charitable deduction is not reduced by the $100 tax credit since the credit is less than 15% of the value of the property donated to the charity. Blake's charitable deduction is $1,000.

The final general requirement for the income tax charitable deduction is that the gift must be made in cash or property by the close of the taxable year. As cash basis taxpayers, individuals must make the charitable gift prior to the close of the taxable year in order for the gift to be deductible. Gifts made on or before December 31 may be deducted by the taxpayer.

Assuming that the requirements for the charitable deduction have been met, our attention turns to the amount of the charitable deduction that may be taken. The amount of the deduction depends on:

1. The type of property given away
2. The identity of the donee/charity
3. The identity of the contributor
4. The amount of property given away

The starting point for determining the amount of the charitable deduction allowed in any one year is the amount of cash given or the fair market value of property that is transferred to charity.

CASE STUDY 7.2

Charitable Deduction

Jan Elizabeth Van Dusen, Petitioner v. Commissioner of Internal Revenue, Respondent, 136 T.C. No. 25 (June 2, 2011).

Jan incurred expenses as a volunteer while caring for 70-80 foster cats in her private residence. In addition to her foster cats, she had an additional seven cats that she considered her pets. The expenses Jan incurred included costs for veterinary services, pet supplies, and a portion of cleaning supplies, and household utilities. In 2004, Jan claimed a $12,068 charitable contribution deduction.

The IRS denied the entire charitable deduction, claiming that Jan was an independent cat rescue worker whose services were unrelated to a charitable organization, and that she failed to substantiate her expenses. The IRS also claimed that the expenses claimed by Jan had an indistinguishable personal component, and therefore did not qualify for a tax deduction. To substantiate her deduction, Jan produced check copies, bank account statements, credit card statements, a Thornhill Pet Hospital client account history, and several utility statements and invoices. These documents did not soften the IRS perspective, and Jan took the IRS to Tax Court in an attempt to salvage her charitable deduction.

The court determined that Jan had demonstrated a strong connection with Fix Our Ferals (a 501(c)(3) organization that specializes in the neutering of wild cats), and had therefore rendered volunteer services to that charitable organization, by caring for foster cats in her home. As such, Jan was permitted to claim her volunteer expenses as charitable deductions, including 90% of her veterinary expenses, pet supplies, and cleaning supplies, and 50% of her laundry detergent, utility, and Costco membership fees. Some expenses that Jan claimed on her tax return, however, were disallowed (such as the cost of cremating a pet cat, bar association dues, and DVM fees) because they were insufficiently related to foster-cat care or could not be determined with precision.

The court noted that the record keeping requirements govern unreimbursed volunteer expenses of less than $250, and that Jan's records, while not as precise as they could be, substantially met these requirements. Foster-cat expenses of $250 or more, however, were not deductible since Jan did not obtain a contemporaneous written acknowledgment from the charitable organization.

As this case illustrates, compliance with the record keeping requirements for charitable contributions is essential in order to substantiate income tax deductions. While unreimbursed volunteer expenses are deductible, the taxpayer must demonstrate a strong connection with a charitable organization for which the expenses are incurred, or risk losing the charitable income tax deduction. Keeping records of involvement with a charitable organization may be necessary to overcome IRS assertions that the taxpayer was acting in an independent capacity. Recall that, for income tax purposes, only contributions made to or on behalf of a qualified charitable organization qualify for the charitable income tax deduction.

Itemized Deduction Limitations

Unlike other itemized deductions, which are limited by the imposition of "floors" that must be exceeded by the taxpayer in order to receive a deduction, the charitable deduction is limited by a "ceiling." The maximum amount that may be deducted in any one year equals 60 percent of the taxpayer's contribution base. Contribution base is the taxpayer's adjusted gross income. By imposing a ceiling limitation on charitable gifts, Congress has made it impossible to completely eliminate taxable income by making contributions to charity. An exception applies to contributions made during calendar years 2020 and 2021. The CARES Act and TCDTRA of 2020 increase to 100 percent the ceiling for cash contributions to a qualified charity (donations to donor advised funds and certain private foundations are excluded) if the provision is elected by the taxpayer, allowing a taxpayer to fully eliminate taxable income by making cash contributions to charity.

The first characteristic that determines the amount of the allowable charitable deduction is the type of property given away. There are two classifications of property for this purpose:

1. Gifts of cash and non-long-term capital gain property
2. Gifts of long-term capital gain property

When a taxpayer makes a gift of cash, the amount of cash given is the value of the charitable gift. If non-long-term capital gain property is given instead of cash, the taxpayer is only permitted to deduct his or her cost basis in the property. When a taxpayer makes a gift of long-term capital gain property to a charity, however, the value for charitable deduction purposes is the fair market value of the property on the date of the gift.

Gifts of long-term capital gain property offer the taxpayer a significant planning opportunity. If the property was sold and the proceeds were given to charity, the taxpayer would have to recognize gain on the sale of the asset and subject that gain to capital gains tax. When the property is given directly to the charity, however, the taxpayer can deduct the entire fair market value of the property even though he or she did not bring the gain into taxable income. This is a major exception to the matching principal of income taxation. When making gifts of long-term capital gains property to a charitable organization, the taxpayer can avoid paying tax on the gain, but get a fair market value deduction for the gift. Further information about making an election on contributions of long-term capital gain property is available under the Special Election section in this chapter.

The second characteristic that determines the amount of the allowable charitable deduction is the type of charity that receives the donation. For income tax purposes, all charities are classified as either public charities or private charities. **Public charities** are organizations that receive support from a wide cross-section of the population. Public charities include organizations such as the Red Cross, universities, hospitals, animal shelters, and the YMCA. **Private charities** are corporations or trusts structured to further the charitable intentions of a donor or the donors' family. Private charities include private foundations and charitable lead trusts.

The deduction limitations for charitable gifts are determined based on the type of charity receiving the contribution and the type of property contributed. The deduction limitations are described in the following table.

Exhibit 7.6 | Charitable Contribution Deductions (Percent of Taxpayer's AGI)

<table>
<tr><th>Type of Property Donated</th><th>Valuation for Purposes of Charitable Deduction</th><th>Ceiling for Public Charities, Private Operating Foundations and Certain Private Nonoperating Foundations</th><th colspan="2">Ceiling for Other Private Nonoperating Foundations (PNOF) and Charitable Lead Trusts (CLTs)</th></tr>
<tr><td>Cash</td><td>Fair market value</td><td>60%***</td><td colspan="2">30%</td></tr>
<tr><td>Ordinary Income Property and Short-Term Capital Gain Property</td><td>Lesser of the adjusted basis or the fair market value</td><td>50%</td><td colspan="2">30%</td></tr>
<tr><td>Long-Term Capital Gain Property:
- Intangible</td><td>Fair market value</td><td>30%*</td><td rowspan="3">Adjusted Basis</td><td>20%**</td></tr>
<tr><td>- Tangible Personalty</td><td>(a) Fair market value -- if related use
(b) Lesser of the adjusted basis of fair market value -- if unrelated use</td><td>30%*
50%</td><td>20%</td></tr>
<tr><td>- Real Property</td><td>Fair market value</td><td>30%*</td><td>20%</td></tr>
</table>

**Taxpayer has the option to use the adjusted basis and the 50% of AGI ceiling for regular charities.*

***Certain contributions of Qualified Appreciated Stock may use the fair market value.*

****Cash contributions made in calendar year 2020 or 2021 to a public charity are subject to a 100% of AGI ceiling if the taxpayer elects to utilize the provision allowing the increased limit.*

The CARES Act and the TCDTRA of 2020 suspended the deduction cap on cash contributions to public charities (excluding donor advised funds and certain private charities) in calendar year 2020 or 2021. When the taxpayer elects to apply this provision to "qualified cash contributions for 2020 or 2021,"[9] the maximum that can be deducted is 100 percent of the taxpayer's contribution base less other charitable deductions, as described below. Any excess contributions above this amount may be carried forward up to five years.

Gifts of cash to a public charity that do not qualify for, or that the taxpayer does not elect to receive, the 100 percent deduction permitted by the CARES Act and TCDTRA of 2020 are deductible to the extent that they do not exceed 60 percent of the taxpayer's contribution base (referred to as 60 percent gifts). Recall that the value of gifts of non-long-term capital gains property for income tax purposes is the donor's cost basis in the property. The deduction for these gifts is limited to 50 percent of the taxpayer's contribution base.

9. The term "qualified cash contribution for 2020" is the terminology utilized by the IRS on Worksheet 2 of Publication 526, which is used to calculate a taxpayer's charitable contribution deduction in 2020, to denote the election for the 100% limit. The taxpayer can choose for each cash contribution whether the increased limit will be applied.

Long-term capital gains property donated to a charity may only be deducted to the extent of 30 percent of the donor's contribution base (referred to as 30 percent gifts). The donor will not be required to recognize gain on the asset donated, even though the value of the deduction is the fair market value of the property. The lower percentage limitation reflects the benefit of avoiding income inclusion on the gain.

Private foundations do not receive funding from the general public, but instead receive funding through private contributions, investments, and endowments. There are two types of private foundations: operating and nonoperating. An operating foundation spends substantially all of its income each year in fulfillment of its charitable mission (i.e., its tax exempt purpose). When determining the limitations that apply to charitable contributions, operating foundations are treated as public charities. Nonoperating foundations typically make grants to other organizations and can receive operating foundation treatment (the same as public charity treatments) if the nonoperating foundation distributes its income by the 15th day of the 3rd month after the close of its tax year.

When gifts are made to private non-operating foundations or to charitable lead trusts (CLT), the deduction limitations are further reduced to 30 percent for gifts of cash and non-long-term capital gain property (referred to as 30 percent gifts) and to 20 percent for gifts of long-term capital gain property (referred to as 20 percent gifts). The lower deduction limitations in this instance are a reflection of the increased control that the donor has over the private foundation or CLT as compared to a public charity.

If an individual makes a contribution that exceeds the allowable contribution, the excess amount can be carried forward for up to five years. In each of those carryforward years, however, the taxpayer must otherwise be able to deduct the charitable gift based on the limitations on charitable deductions calculated for those years.

Example 7.26

Maren has AGI of $100,000 for the current tax year. She made a cash gift of $70,000 to her university to assist in the construction of a new building on campus. Maren is permitted to deduct up to 60% of her contribution base as a charitable contribution. Since she made a charitable gift of cash to a public charity, the 60% limit applies and she will be able to deduct $60,000 in the current year. The remaining $10,000 will be carried forward for up to five years and deducted against future income, subject to the limitations on charitable gifts imposed in those years.

Example 7.27

Assume the same facts as **Example 7.26**, except that Maren's gift was stock with a fair market value of $60,000. She paid $40,000 for the stock 3 years ago. Maren will be able to deduct $30,000 this year (30% of her contribution base) and will be able to carry over the remaining $30,000 for use over the next five tax years. By making the gift with appreciated long-term gain property, Maren will not be required to recognize the gain on the stock in her income.

Special Election

A special election is available for taxpayers who wish to make contributions of long-term capital gain property. Instead of subjecting the gift to the 30 percent (for public charities) or 20 percent (for private charities) contribution limitations, the taxpayer can elect to treat the gift as a 50 percent contribution, thereby allowing a greater portion of the gift to be deducted as a charitable deduction in the current year. However, there is a cost to making this election. Instead of taking a deduction for the fair market value of the property donated, the deduction is limited to the donor's cost basis.

Example 7.28

Continuing with **Example 7.27**, concerning Maren's gift of $60,000 of long-term capital gain stock to his university, if Maren elects to treat the contribution as a 50% contribution, her charitable deduction for the current year will be $40,000, her cost basis in the property. By making the election, Maren is able to deduct $10,000 more this year, but loses the ability to deduct the appreciation in the stock of $20,000.

The overall limitation on non-cash charitable contributions (contributions of property) for a given tax year is 50 percent of the taxpayer's contribution base. When applying the overall limitation, allowable deductions first come from 50 percent gifts, then from 30 percent gifts, and finally from 20 percent gifts. However, if cash contributions are also made during the year, the overall 50 percent limit is first reduced by the amount of the cash contribution.

Example 7.29

Morris has AGI in 2022 of $200,000. He contributed $80,000 of cash, and $70,000 of long-term capital gain property (stock with a basis of $20,000) to the Irish Heritage Museum, a qualified charity. Morris's limit for cash contributions is 60% x $200,000 = $120,000. Under the 50% overall limit on property contributions, Morris's contribution limit is $100,000, and under the 30% limit, his maximum contribution is $60,000. Since Morris made contributions of property to a charity, the overall limit of 50% of the contribution base applies, and is reduced by the amount of the cash contributions. For 2022, Morris will be able to deduct the full amount of his cash contribution ($80,000), plus $20,000 of his property contribution, for a total of $100,000 (which equals 50% of his adjusted gross income). The remaining $50,000 of the property contribution will be carried forward for up to five tax years.

Example 7.30

Shay has AGI in 2021 of $100,000, and has no itemized deductions other than the following charitable contributions. She contributed $5,000 of cash to her church and did <u>not</u> elect to treat this as a qualified cash contribution for 2021 (under TCDTRA 2020). Shay also donated $35,000 of long-term capital gain property (stock with a basis of $15,000) and $60,000 cash to the local animal shelter, a public charity. Shay elected to treat the $60,000 cash contribution to the animal shelter as a qualified cash contribution for 2021 (under TCDTRA 2020). Under the 50% limit on property contributions, Shay's limit is $50,000 ($100,000 AGI x 50% = $50,000), allowing a full deduction for the fair market value of the stock. She is also subject to the overall 50% limitation. The $5,000 cash contribution to the church is applied first, followed by the $35,000 of property, for a total of $40,000 which is below the overall 50% limit. The $60,000 qualified cash contribution for 2021 is applied last, and without limit under TCDTRA 2020, bringing her total deductions for charitable contributions to $100,000 and her taxable income to zero.

Special Rule for Tangible Personal Property (Tangible Personalty)

Another special rule applies to donations of tangible personal property to charitable organizations. Normally when charitable contributions are made they are either paid in cash or marketable securities that can be easily transformed into cash. Securities and cash equivalents are intangible forms of property interests. Sometimes a donor may wish to give tangible personal property to a charity. When tangible personal property is donated to a charity, the amount and type of deduction that applies will depend on whether or not the charity uses the tangible personal property in its tax exempt function.

If tangible personal property donated to a charity is used by the charity to carry out its tax exempt purpose, the donor may take a deduction equal to the fair market value of the property on the date of the gift and the donation will be subject to the 30 percent limitation as long as the property had a long-term holding period in the hands of the donor. If the tangible property donated did not have a long-term holding period, the donor would be required to reduce the fair market value by 100 percent of the gain, resulting in a cost basis deduction, subject to the 50 percent limitation.

When tangible personal property donated to a charity will not be used by the charity to carry out its tax-exempt purpose, the deduction available to the donor is the fair market value of the property reduced by 100 percent of the gain (a cost basis deduction) and will be subject to the 50 percent limitation.

Example 7.31

Davis is redecorating his manor house and decides to donate to his local YMCA an original Rembrant sketch that had been purchased 20 years ago and was hanging in his study. Since the YMCA does not display fine art in fulfilling its tax exempt function, the YMCA will sell the painting and use the proceeds to support their activities. Davis will be able to take a charitable income tax deduction for the cost basis of the sketch, and the donation will be subject to the 50% limit.

Example 7.32

Assume the same facts as the previous example except that Davis donates the Rembrant sketch to the Smithsonian Museum of Fine Art in Washington, D.C. Since one of the charitable purposes of the Smithsonian is to acquire and display fine art, Davis will be entitled to take a charitable income tax deduction equal to the fair market value of the sketch at the time of the gift. The contribution will be subject to the 30% limitation because it was a gift of long-term capital gain property to a public charity.

Example 7.33

Gabby donates a painting of a religious theme that she has owned for several years to her church. The church will include the painting in a silent auction coming up later in the year and the proceeds of the auction will be dedicated to restoration of the church. Since the church will sell the property (in this case, by silent charitable auction) and will not use it in its tax-exempt purpose, Gabby is entitled to receive a cost basis deduction for the gift.

Ordinary Income Property

When a taxpayer donates ordinary income property to a charity, the donation will be valued at cost basis and will be subject to the 50 percent limitation. As discussed later in the property transactions section of this text, there are only three types of assets in the tax world – capital assets, ordinary income assets, and Section 1231 assets. Ordinary income assets include accounts/notes receivable, inventory, and copyrights or creative works held by the creator. Ordinary income assets, when sold, generate income subject to ordinary tax rates; they do not qualify for capital gains tax rates. As a result, ordinary income assets will always be subject to the 50 percent limitation (or 30 percent limitation for private charities) and will generate a cost basis tax deduction for the donor. Ordinary income assets receive the same tax treatment as short-term capital gains assets for purposes of the income tax charitable deduction.

One of the most common types of ordinary income assets donated to charity is a creative work in the hands of the author. Works of art, books and writings, letters, musical compositions and other creative works donated by the creator of the work to charity will qualify for a cost basis deduction. In most cases, the cost basis will be very low if it is a creative work. The tax treatment should make sense in that if the work was sold, the creator would recognize the sale price as ordinary income. Remember that if a creative work is held by someone other than the author, it may be classified as a capital asset and may qualify for a full fair market value deduction if the asset is held for a long-term holding period.

Example 7.34

Martina, a renowned author of children's novels and professor of literature, wrote all of her manuscripts by hand. Martina's novels have been widely acclaimed as the best children's literature of the era. She kept the original drafts of each of her novels for her own purposes, but recently decided to get rid of the growing mass of paper in her home. Martina donated all of the original manuscripts to the museum/archive of her university. Martina's charitable deduction is limited to her cost basis in the property – the cost of the paper and the ink that was used to write the novels.

From a tax perspective, authors of creative works should consider holding those works until death, and leaving those items to family members. At death, the basis of the asset in the hands of a beneficiary will be the fair market value of the asset as of the date of the decedent's death and a subsequent transfer of the property to a charity by the family member will qualify for a full fair market value deduction. The fair market value deduction applies since all property transferred through the estate of a decedent is deemed to have a long-term holding period.

Example 7.35

In the previous example, if Martina held the drafts of her literary works until her death, and left them to her children, the papers would have a basis equal to their fair market value at the date of her death, significantly more than the cost of the paper and the ink. When her children donate the documents to the university museum, they will be entitled to a full fair market value charitable deduction on their income tax returns.

One special exception to the charitable deduction rules covering ordinary income property involves a contribution of tangible personal property for scientific research. The charitable deduction for such property is the lesser of: (1) the cost of the property plus half of the gain; or (2) two times the cost basis of the property. To receive this increased deduction for scientific research property, two additional requirements must be met: (1) the property must be new inventory-type scientific equipment manufactured by the donor; and (2) the property must be donated to the charity within two years of its purchase, or, in the case of a manufacturer, when the equipment was fully constructed.

Applications

Three final charitable deduction rules are important for tax planning purposes:

1. charitable deductions by corporations
2. contributions made to purchase sporting tickets from universities
3. raffle tickets sold by charitable organizations

Charitable Deductions by Corporations

Unlike individuals, who can deduct up to 50 percent (60 percent for cash gifts) of their contribution base for gifts made to charitable organizations, regular corporations (C corporations) are only permitted to deduct up to 10 percent of their taxable income (after adjustments) for charitable gifts. The CARES Act and TCDTRA of 2020 temporarily increased the deduction limitation from 10 percent to 25 percent (in combination with all other deductible contributions) for tax years 2020 and 2021. When a contribution exceeds the limitation, the excess may be carried forward for up to 5 years. Subchapter S corporations must pass through the charitable gifts to the owners on Form K-1 and the owners will include their portion of the charitable contribution on their personal income tax return as an itemized deduction (below-the-line deduction).

Closely-held and family business owners who have business interests in corporate form (C corporations, not S corporations) may wish to use the corporation as a means of achieving an above-the-line charitable deduction. While C corporation charitable deductions are limited to 10 percent (25 percent for tax years 2020-2021) of their taxable income, gifts of corporate income to charity avoid tax at both the corporate and owner levels. Normally, corporate earnings are taxed to the corporation and are again taxed to the owners when they are distributed in the form of dividends. An owner who receives a dividend distribution could use the distribution to make a charitable gift, but that gift will be a below-the-line itemized deduction subject to limitations (based on the contribution base test). A more efficient way of making the transfer to charity is to have the corporation, to the extent it can achieve a charitable income tax deduction, make the gift directly to the charity. This planning tool can be particularly useful as a method of funding a private foundation.

Example 7.36

Lee is the 100% shareholder of RKLJ, Inc., a C corporation. Lee is also charitably inclined, and created the Jarvis Foundation earlier this year. RKLJ, Inc. expects to have net profits of $200,000 for the year, and Lee would like to take some money out of the corporation to begin to fund his foundation. The corporation will have to pay tax on its income for the year, and any amount remaining will be available for distribution as a dividend. Assume, for purposes of this example, that the corporation's combined federal and state income tax is $40,000. This leaves $160,000 of income available for distribution this year. If Lee distributes $20,000 to himself in the form of a dividend, he will have to pay tax on the dividend (which will most likely be classified as a qualified dividend and be subject to the appropriate dividend tax rate) of $3,000. The tax on the dividend will be offset by Lee's charitable deduction, but if Lee is in a high personal income tax bracket, or if he has made other significant charitable gifts for the current tax year, the limitations that apply to charitable deductions may limit his ability to deduct those charitable gifts for income tax purposes.

Example 7.37

Continuing with **Example 7.36**, assume that instead of distributing a dividend to himself and making a charitable gift, Lee has his corporation make a gift of $20,000 directly to the Jarvis Foundation. In this case, the corporation's income will be reduced from $200,000 to $180,000, lowering corporate income tax liability from $40,000 to $36,000 (a $4,000 corporate tax savings). Since the gift was made directly to the Foundation, there is no need for Lee to declare a $20,000 dividend to make the charitable gift, further saving $3,000 in income taxes on Lee's personal income tax return. Lee will not be able to deduct the charitable gift on his own tax return, but he does not have to include income in his return in order to make the charitable gift, either. In a sense, Lee has taken an above-the-line charitable deduction for the $20,000 contribution to the Foundation since he did not include any incremental income in his tax return. Avoiding inclusion of incremental income in his tax return lowers Lee's AGI, which has a positive effect on other personal tax planning options that are phased-out as AGI increases. This may be particularly valuable for taxpayers who also have to pay the additional 3.8% Medicare surtax on investment income that was imposed by the Affordable Care Act. Furthermore, corporate taxes were reduced, allowing Lee to donate pre-tax income to the Foundation as opposed to after-tax income. Since the charitable gift is not being deducted as an itemized deduction on Lee's personal tax return, the percentage limitations on charitable gifts are not an issue, although the overall deductibility limit for corporate donations does impose a limitation on the total amount that can be given to charity using this technique.

Exhibit 7.7 | Summary of Example 7.36 and Example 7.37

Dividend by C Corporation		*Charitable Donation by C Corporation*	
C Corporation Income	$200,000	C Corporation Income	$200,000
Less: Tax	<$40,000>	Less: Charitable Deduction	<$20,000>
Less: Dividend Paid	<$20,000>	Taxable Income	$180,000
Net Income	**$140,000***	Tax @ 20%	<$36,000>
		Net Income	**$144,000**

**Note that the $20,000 dividend is offset by the $20,000 charitable contribution.*

Particularly for high income taxpayers who wish to make large charitable gifts as a percentage of their income, using corporate earnings to make all or some of those charitable gifts may be a very effective planning technique.

Contributions to Universities for Sporting Tickets

When reviewing the general rules for charitable deductions, we noted that a taxpayer can only get a charitable deduction for the difference between the amount that he or she gives to a charity and the fair market value of what the taxpayer receives in return. In some cases, however, the value of what the taxpayer receives in return for a charitable gift is difficult to determine. One example is a charitable gift made to a university so that the donor can be placed on a waiting list to purchase basketball or football tickets. Due to the popularity of collegiate sports, and, in particular, basketball and football, some colleges and universities have conditioned purchase of game tickets on a donation to the school. Once the donation is made, the donor may then purchase tickets to the sporting event. It is clear that the purchase of the game tickets is not a charitable gift, but what about the original donation to the charity? Was the entire donation a charitable gift, or did the taxpayer receive something in return that reduces the value of that charitable gift?

The answer to this question was resolved by enactment of TCJA 2017. The Tax Cuts and Jobs Act of 2017 denies any charitable deduction for tax years 2018 through 2025 for a contribution made to an institution of higher learning if that donation qualifies the donor to purchase tickets to an athletic event. If a donor is not interested in purchasing athletic tickets, and wishes to preserve the ability to deduct his or her donation, the donor should make it clear at the time of the donation that he/she waives any option to purchase athletic tickets as a result of making the contribution.

Quick Quiz 7.3

1. Gifts of services qualify for a charitable income tax deduction.
   a. True
   b. False
2. Gifts of cash or property must be made by the close of the taxable year in order to be deductible.
   a. True
   b. False
3. Gifts of cash and non-long-term capital gains property to a public charity are deductible to the extent that they do not exceed 30% of the taxpayer's AGI.
   a. True
   b. False
4. Whether a charity uses donated property in a way that is related to its tax-exempt function may affect the amount and type of deduction to which a taxpayer is entitled.
   a. True
   b. False

False, True, False, True.

Raffle Tickets Sold by Charitable Organizations

Purchase of raffle tickets from a charitable organization is not a tax-deductible donation – it is the purchase of a chance to win the prize offered in the raffle. Taxpayers who wish to generate a charitable deduction for purchasing raffle tickets from a charity may do so by agreeing in advance that if they win the prize, it will be donated back to the charity.

Partial Interest Gifts

One of the general rules for charitable giving states that a donor must give his or her entire interest in the property to qualify for an income tax charitable deduction (known as the partial interest rule). As noted earlier in the chapter, there are several exceptions to the partial interest rule, including:

- A gift of an undivided portion of the donor's entire interest in the property
- A gift of a remainder interest in a personal residence or farm
- A gift of a partial interest if transferred in trust (a charitable remainder trust, a charitable lead trust, or a pooled income fund)
- Purchase of a charitable gift annuity

When a donor owns only a portion of a property, a charitable income tax deduction is available provided that the donor gives away his or her entire interest in the property. These types of charitable gifts are often seen when a taxpayer holds property jointly with another taxpayer.

Example 7.38

Kelsea, Luke, and Bryan own Greenacre as tenants in common. Each has a 1/3 interest in the property. A tenancy in common interest is an undivided interest in property. Kelsea no longer wants to deal with her co-tenants, and would like to make a charitable gift. She gives her 1/3 tenancy in common interest to her private foundation, which will then sell the interest (probably to Luke and Bryan). Since Kelsea gave away her entire interest in the property to a charitable entity, she will be entitled to a charitable income tax deduction. In this case, Kelsea's charitable income tax deduction will be limited to her cost basis in the asset, since it was donated to her private foundation.

Another method of making a partial gift in property to a charitable organization in a way that will qualify for the income tax charitable deduction is to give a remainder interest in a personal residence or farm. This technique can be useful when a taxpayer has a residence or farm that he or she would like to use until death, but the taxpayers heirs do not want to use the property and would likely sell it shortly after the taxpayer dies. Administering unwanted real property in the estate of a decedent increases costs and lengthens the estate settlement process. Assuming that the taxpayer is interested in making a charitable gift, donating a remainder interest in the property to a charitable organization would achieve two objectives: (1) the present value of the remainder interest will qualify for an income tax charitable deduction; and (2) at death, title immediately vests in the charity, removing the expense and hassle of dealing with unwanted real property in the decedent's estate.[10]

A charitable gift annuity is an arrangement where a taxpayer transfers an asset to charity in return for annuity payments over the taxpayer's lifetime. Charitable gift annuities are typically structured so that 50 percent of the transaction involves purchase of an annuity contract and 50 percent represents a charitable gift. Consequently, 50 percent of the value of the property transferred will qualify for the charitable income tax deduction. If the asset transferred has a value in excess of basis, there may be additional income tax consequences, but these are beyond the scope of this book.

CASUALTY LOSSES

The Tax Cuts and Jobs Act of 2017 (TCJA 2017) eliminated the deduction for casualty losses for tax years 2018 through 2025, with one exception. **Casualty losses** may be claimed, subject to the limitations specified below, only for losses attributable to a disaster declared by the President under Section 401 of the Robert T. Stafford Disaster Relief and Emergency Assistance Act.

As a threshold matter, only personal casualty losses will be deducted as an itemized deduction on the taxpayer's Schedule A. If the casualty loss is associated with a trade or business, the

Key Concepts

1. Describe the types of casualty losses that may be deducted as an itemized deduction.
2. Explain the restrictions on the deduction of personal casualty and theft losses.

10. The rules associated with the use of charitable remainder trusts and pooled income funds are typically covered in estate planning courses, and may be found in the textbook *Estate Planning* by Michael A. Dalton and Thomas P. Langdon.

loss will be deducted above-the-line as a business expense. If personal risks are properly insured, it is unlikely that the taxpayer will be able to generate a tax deduction for casualty losses, since the insurance proceeds received offset the taxpayer's loss. A client's ability to take a casualty loss deduction is probably evidence of a failure to identify and properly insure the risks that were facing the taxpayer. As you will see when we review the limitations on the casualty loss deduction, the tax deduction is not a good substitute for adequate insurance coverage.

A casualty loss deduction is available for losses or damages to a taxpayer's property resulting from a presidentially declared disaster caused by a sudden or unexpected event, such as a fire, storm, or shipwreck.

Casualty Loss Limitations

For personal casualty and theft losses, the amount of the loss is the lower of:

1. the difference between the fair market value of the property before the event and the fair market value of the property after the event, less insurance proceeds received, or
2. the taxpayer's adjusted basis in the property less insurance proceeds received.

This valuation rule prevents a taxpayer from taking a casualty loss on the gain attached to property that had not been brought into the taxpayer's income.

Example 7.39

Dwight owned a home in New Orleans that was severely damaged by a hurricane in a presidentially declared disaster zone. Dwight had purchased the home for $200,000, and the fair market value of the home prior to the hurricane was $400,000. His homeowners insurance policy had lapsed one month before the hurricane hit and Dwight had not obtained any other insurance. After the hurricane, the property had a fair market value of $90,000. Dwight's casualty loss is valued at $200,000 which is his adjusted basis less insurance proceeds received (insurance proceeds in this case are zero). The decline in the fair market value of the property is equal to $310,000, but Dwight's casualty loss is limited to his adjusted basis because his adjusted basis is less than the decline in the fair market value of the property.

The limitations on the deduction for personal casualty and theft losses do not end there. Two additional restrictions apply. First, $100 must be deducted from each occurrence. An occurrence is treated as one event, such as a hurricane. If a hurricane caused damage to a taxpayer's house and car, $100 in total would be deducted from both losses (not $200, or $100 for each separate loss). Second, to be deductible, the taxpayer's aggregate casualty and theft losses must exceed 10 percent of the taxpayer's adjusted gross income.

Example 7.40

Using the facts from **Example 7.39**, assume that Dwight's AGI for the year is $100,000. Dwight's casualty loss of $200,000 must be reduced by $100 and the result is only deductible to the extent it exceeds 10% of AGI. The deductible portion of Dwight's casualty loss is $189,900 ($200,000 - $100 - $10,000 [10% of AGI]).

There is one further limitation that applies to personal casualty and theft losses. To the extent that the taxpayer has a casualty gain, that casualty gain offsets any casualty losses suffered in the same year. For example, assume a taxpayer experienced two events causing complete losses to two assets and one of the assets was insured. Also assume the insurance company paid the taxpayer more than his or her basis in the property (which could happen when the property is insured for its replacement value), and the property for which the insurance proceeds were received will not be replaced. In this situation, the casualty gain on the insured asset will offset the casualty loss on the uninsured asset, and the net loss will then be subject to the $100 and 10 percent of AGI limitations.

Quick Quiz 7.4

1. Casualty losses are only deductible if they result from sudden or unexpected events and are declared a disaster by the President.
   a. True
   b. False

2. Casualty losses must exceed the lesser of $100 or 10% of the taxpayer's AGI in order to be deductible on Schedule A.
   a. True
   b. False

True, False.

Business Casualty Losses

As mentioned earlier, business casualty losses are deducted above the line against the income from the business activity. Unlike the case with personal casualty losses, business casualty losses do not require a disaster declaration by the President. The amount of the business casualty loss is the lower of:

1. the difference between the fair market value of the property before the loss and the fair market value of the property after the loss, or
2. the adjusted basis of the property in the case of a partial loss.

If a business related casualty causes a complete loss of the property, the amount of the casualty loss is the taxpayer's adjusted basis in the property. A casualty loss is reduced by insurance or any other type of reimbursement.

Example 7.41

In a fire that swept through her factory recently, LeAnn lost several pieces of business property. One item, a machine that made Roman Widgets, had an adjusted basis of $3,000 and was completely worthless after the fire. The fair market value of the machine before the loss was $1,300. LeAnn's business casualty loss deduction is $3,000. Since the machine was used in a trade or business, LeAnn is entitled to recoup her entire basis in the property even though the fair market value of the machine was lower at the time of the loss. The entire loss will be deductible against the income of LeAnn's business, and no limitations or phaseouts apply since the loss was incurred on a business asset.

Note that this result differs substantially from a personal loss situation. If the property was not a business machine, but rather a personal use asset that had an adjusted basis of $3,000 and a fair market value of $1,300, only $1,300 (the lower of the difference in fair market value before and after the casualty event, or the taxpayer's adjusted basis) would be deductible (before the imposition of limitations and phaseouts). Since the remaining part of the property ($1,700 = $3,000 - $1,300) was used for personal purposes (not in a trade or business or for the production of income), it does not qualify for a deduction.

Example 7.42

The fire that swept through LeAnn's factory also damaged the factory building. The fair market value of the building was $800,000 before the fire, and $650,000 after the fire. LeAnn's basis in the factory is $500,000. In this case, the deductible casualty loss is $150,000 (the difference in value before and after the loss). This was not a complete loss, so LeAnn can still use the remaining property and recoup the remaining capital investment over the property's useful life. Since the loss was sustained on a business asset, the entire loss is deductible against business income, and no limitations or phaseouts apply.

MISCELLANEOUS ITEMIZED DEDUCTIONS

Miscellaneous itemized deductions include all of the remaining deductions that individual taxpayers can take on their income tax return. Miscellaneous itemized deductions fall into two categories:

1. those that are deductible without limitation
2. those that are subject to the two percent floor

Almost all of the miscellaneous itemized deductions are subject to the two percent floor.

Deductions Not Subject to the Two Percent Floor (Tier I)

The deductions not subject to the two percent floor typically involve transactions where Congress deems it unfair to subject taxpayers to taxation on transactions where income is required to be included above the line, while deductions are taken below the line.

The most important miscellaneous itemized deductions not subject to the two percent floor are:

1. Gambling losses (to the extent of gambling income)
2. Credit for estate taxes imposed on IRD (income in respect of a decedent's assets)
3. Loss on the disposition of an annuity contract
4. Repayments of income (such as repayments of Social Security income when the taxpayer fails the earnings test)

Each of these instances requires income inclusion. Gambling winnings must be included in gross income, but losses to the extent of winnings can be used to offset the income. When IRD assets (such as pension plans, IRAs, and annuity contracts) are taxed in the estate of a decedent, the additional estate tax paid by reason of including the IRD asset becomes an income tax deduction for the person who receives the asset. Like the case with gambling winnings, distributions from inherited IRD assets must be included in income, so offsetting deductions should be allowed without being subject to the two percent floor. If a taxpayer purchased an annuity, and later surrenders the annuity suffering a loss, a full deduction should likewise be afforded to allow the taxpayer to recoup his or her full investment in the contract. Finally, if an individual under normal retirement age is receiving Social Security and has wage income above specified

Key Concepts

1. List the miscellaneous itemized deductions that are not subject to a 2% floor.
2. Name the major categories of miscellaneous itemized deductions subject to a 2% floor.
3. Describe the rules regarding the most common types of unreimbursed employee business expenses.

thresholds, the worker must pay back part of the Social Security benefit. The full amount received is included in income, so the taxpayer should be able to deduct the amount paid back without being subject to the two percent floor. Repayments of income (such as the repayment of excess social security benefits due to the imposition of the earnings limitation) are only deductible as a miscellaneous itemized deduction not subject to the 2 percent floor to the extent that they exceed $3,000. If the repayment of income is less than $3,000, no deduction is allowed for tax years 2018 through 2025.

Example 7.43

Darius started collecting Social Security Benefits when he retired at age 62. After six months of playing two rounds of golf each day, Darius decided he needed some mental stimulation and went back to work part-time. His work related income exceeded the threshold for avoiding the Social Security Earnings Limitation, and Darius was required to repay $2,500 of the Social Security benefits he received. Since the repayment is less than $3,000, Darius will not be able to claim the repayment as a miscellaneous itemized deduction not subject to the 2 percent floor. This results in $2,500 of phantom income for Darius, since the full amount of the Social Security payments he received will be included in income and he will not be able to deduct the $2,500 he had to pay back to the government.

Example 7.44

Assume the same facts as **Example 7.43**, except that as a result of the earning limitation, Darius has to repay $3,100 of his Social Security income to the government. Darius will be able to claim the $3,100 payment as a miscellaneous itemized deduction not subject to the 2 percent floor. Provided Darius can itemize deductions already (his itemized deductions exceed his standard deduction), Darius will not have to worry about paying tax on phantom income, as in the prior example. If his itemized deductions, however, are less than his standard deduction, Darius will not receive a tax benefit for the repayment of part of his Social Security Income, and will have, in this case, $3,100 in phantom income.

As the prior example shows, even though these miscellaneous itemized deductions are not subject to the two percent floor, a taxpayer only gets the benefit of these deductions if he or she is able to itemize deductions. To itemize deductions, total deductions must exceed the standard deduction amount (including any additional standard deduction for age or blindness).

Example 7.45

Carly, a 78 year old retired individual, enjoys going to the casino. Her income consists of Social Security, a small pension, and a bit of interest. She lives in an apartment and does not have any itemized deductions for the current year. Last week, Carly hit the jackpot on the slot machines at the casino and won $2,000, which must be included in her gross income. If she has $2,000 in gambling losses for the year, she can offset the gambling income with a miscellaneous itemized deduction for the gambling losses that will not be subject to the two percent floor. Since her total itemized deductions do not exceed the standard deduction, however, Carly will not receive a tax deduction for incurring the gambling losses, her gambling income will still be subject to income tax, and the additional income from gambling may also increase the amount of her Social Security payments that are subject to tax.

One additional miscellaneous itemized deduction not subject to the two percent floor applies to job related expenses for handicapped workers. Specified expenses, such as the cost of purchasing readers or retaining aids to help the handicapped person perform his or her job function will not be limited by the two percent floor.

Deductions Subject to the Two Percent Floor (Tier II)

The remaining expenses that are classified as miscellaneous itemized deductions are subject to the two percent floor. There are many items that fall into this category. The major categories of miscellaneous itemized deductions subject to the two percent floor that affect tax planning decisions are:

- Employee business expenses
- Hobby expenses (to the extent of hobby income)
- Investment expenses and tax advice, including research materials for investments
- Losses on IRAs (when the IRA has been terminated)

Hobby expenses will be considered in the next chapter, and therefore will not be covered here.

For tax years 2018 through 2025, Tier II miscellaneous itemized deductions (those subject to the 2 percent floor), are not deductible. For tax years beginning after 2025, the deduction will again be permitted. The discussion, below, concerning Tier II miscellaneous itemized deductions, therefore, only applies to tax years prior to 2018 and after 2025. From a tax planning perspective, it is helpful for a tax planner to be aware of these deductions, since it may be advisable for taxpayers, to the extent possible to incur these deductions after they are reinstated in 2026. For example, taxpayers that incur Tier II miscellaneous itemized deductions in December 2025 will not be permitted to claim the deductions, but had they deferred those expenses to January 2026, a deduction would be permissible.

Employee Business Expenses

Unreimbursed employee business expenses are deductible as a miscellaneous itemized deduction subject to the two percent floor. **Employee business expenses** include professional and union dues of employees, travel, supplies and services, professional books and journals, job-related educational expenses, work clothes and uniforms, and job hunting expenses in the same line of work. Business mileage is deductible at $0.56 per mile (2021).

Professional fees (such as licensing fees for lawyers, physicians, and accountants) or union dues are deductible as an employee business expense if they are not reimbursed by the employer. Recall that self-employed individuals will deduct these costs against business income (above the line) on a form, such as Schedule C. Only professionals and union members who are employees will claim professional and union dues as below-the-line itemized deductions.

Travel expenses include costs for transportation, lodging, incidental expenses and 50 percent of meals when a taxpayer is away from his or her tax home. The taxpayer's tax home is the general area where the taxpayer regularly conducts business. To be deductible as travel expenses, the expenses must be incurred when the taxpayer must be away from his or her tax home for work related reasons and it is reasonable for the taxpayer to require rest and lodging away from their tax home. Generally, domestic transportation expenses are fully deductible if the primary purpose of the trip is business related. The cost of lodging, dry cleaning and laundry, telephone, tips, and local transportation are fully deductible for the days that the taxpayer is conducting business. Meals for those days are deductible, but are limited to 50 percent of the cost incurred. Expenses incurred (with the exception of transportation expenses when the primary purpose of the trip is business-related) on days when the taxpayer is not conducting business are not deductible.

Example 7.46

Gilbert normally works in Connecticut. He traveled to San Diego, California for a business conference, and was not reimbursed by his employer. Since he enjoys sailing, Gilbert decided to stay an extra two days to sail around San Diego Bay after the 3-day conference ended. Since the primary purpose of the trip was business related (he spent 2 days on personal matters, and 3 days on business matters), Gilbert will be able to deduct the full cost of the airfare to and from San Diego. For the three days that Gilbert is attending the conference, he can also deduct the cost of lodging, dry cleaning, telephone, local transportation, incidental expenses, and 50% of the cost of his meals. The travel expenses for the two days that Gilbert spends sailing on San Diego Bay, however, are not deductible since they are personal expenses.

For travel outside the United States, the rule is a bit different. Expenses associated with trips purely for business will be fully deductible. When the trip is primarily for business, the travel expenses must be prorated between the personal and business days, and only the expense associated with the business days may be deducted. If the trip is primarily for personal purposes, none of the transportation expenses are deductible. Some exceptions do apply. A trip outside the United States will be considered to be purely business related when one of the following conditions exists:

1. The taxpayer does not have control over the timing or arrangements for the trip.
2. The trip outside the United States lasted for seven days or less.
3. Less than 25 percent of the time spent on the trip was for personal activities.
4. Vacation was not a primary consideration for the trip.

When counting days used for personal and business travel while on a foreign trip, all of the following are considered to be business days:

- Days during which business is conducted
- Travel days to and from the location
- Weekends and holidays provided that they fall between business days

Example 7.47

Thomas traveled to London for a business meeting. He left on Wednesday evening, and returned the following Saturday. The meeting began on Thursday, broke for the long weekend (Monday was Queen Elizabeth's official birthday), and resumed on Tuesday. On the weekend, Thomas spent time touring Southern England. The business meetings were concluded on Thursday, and Thomas resumed his tour of Southern England until his departure flight on Saturday evening. In this case, the travel covered a period of 11 days. The two travel days were business days, as were the 5 days actually spent at the business meeting. The three day weekend (including the holiday) were also business days, since business was conducted both before and after the holiday weekend. Out of the 11 day trip, 10 days were classified as business days, and one day was classified as a personal day. Since Thomas spent less than 25% of the trip on personal travel, the trip is deemed to be solely for business, and the full cost of the airfare is a deductible travel expense. The cost of lodging, incidentals, and 50% of meals on the one day that Thomas was not deemed to be conducting business will not be deductible, but those costs for the three-day weekend that were presumed to be business days are deductible.

There are also limitations imposed on water travel and conventions due to taxpayer abuse in the past. A deduction of up to $2,000 is permitted for conventions on cruise ships provided that the following conditions are met:

1. The convention is directly related to the taxpayer's trade or business.
2. The cruise ship is registered in the United States (has a U.S. Flag).
3. During the convention cruise, the ship only docks at ports within the United States or its possessions.

If any of these conditions are not met, no deduction for cruise-ship conventions is permissible. For conventions on land within the United States, travel expenses are deductible provided that the convention is directly related to the taxpayer's trade or business. For a convention outside of the United States, travel expenses are deductible provided that the meeting is directly related to the taxpayer's trade or business, and it is as reasonable to hold the meeting outside of North America as it is inside North America.

Example 7.48

Crystal paid $3,500 for a convention on board a cruise ship. The convention was directly related to her trade or business. The ship left San Diego and sailed north, stopping in San Francisco, Seattle, one or two Canadian ports and finally arriving in Alaska. Crystal will not be permitted to deduct any portion of the cost of this trip, since the cruise ship docked in a foreign port.

Example 7.49

Gayle, a neurosurgeon, decided she needed to learn how to invest all of the money that she had been making in her capacity as a surgeon. She paid $4,000 to attend an Investment Convention in Palm Springs this year. Gayle will not be able to deduct any of the cost associated with the convention as a business expense, since the convention is not directly related to Gayle's trade or business activity (medicine).

Travel related expenses are deductible only if the taxpayer's absence from their work-home is temporary. Temporary means that the work assignment is for one year or less. If the assignment exceeds one year, then none of the travel expenses are deductible, since the taxpayer is deemed to have changed his or her tax home. For taxpayers who have long work assignments away from their tax home, travel between their tax home and the work location (provided that they do not exceed the one year limitation) is deductible to the extent that the travel does not exceed the cost of remaining at the temporary workplace.

Example 7.50

Shelton has spent the last three months working on a contract in Arizona. His regular tax home is Connecticut. On weekends, Shelton flies home to spend time with his wife and children. The cost of the flight home (round-trip) is $350. If Shelton had remained at his work location, he would have incurred three additional nights of hotel bills per week (at $125 per night), plus meal and incidental costs. Since the cost to return home is less than the cost of remaining in the temporary work location, Shelton may deduct the full cost of the travel between his tax-home and temporary work location.

The cost of supplies and services incurred for work purposes while working at home are also deductible as work related expenses. If a home phone is used for both personal and work purposes, however, a special limitation applies. The cost of the first phone line into the home is not deductible as a business expense. Additional costs, such as long-distance calls for business, a second phone line installed for business use, a dedicated fax line, or telephone features such as call forwarding are deductible provided that those expenses are work related.

Likewise, the cost of professional books and journals necessary for the taxpayer to maintain his or her skills in a current trade or profession are deducted as employee related business expenses.

Educational expenses are deductible as employee business expenses provided that the purpose of the expense is to maintain or expand the taxpayer's competency in his or her current trade or profession. Tuition costs, books, supplies, transportation to and from class, meals and lodging while attending school away from home, and fees are deductible. Educational expenses incurred to meet the minimal requirements for a trade or business, to qualify the taxpayer for a new trade or business, or to help the taxpayer return to a former trade or business are not deductible.

Example 7.51

Morgan worked as a law librarian for Hogwarts University School of Law. In performing her duties as law librarian, Morgan assisted law professors with legal research and oversaw the administration of the library. While serving as Law Librarian, Morgan began to take law school classes and ultimately received a law degree. Despite the fact that the law school classes maintained or further expanded her skills in her current trade or profession (as law librarian), the classes qualified her to enter a new trade or profession (the practice of law) and are therefore nondeductible (Gilligan, T.C.M. 2002-150).

Example 7.52

Brantley, a financial planner, began taking classes to prepare him for the CFP® Certification Examination at a prestigious east-coast university. The classes were conducted every other weekend on Friday nights and Saturdays. Every other week, Brantley flew in to take the course and stayed at a hotel on Friday and Saturday night (there were no flights that could get him back home on Saturday night). Since Brantley is taking classes that further expand and enhance his knowledge in his current trade or profession, the tuition and fees for the program are deductible. Likewise, the cost of airfare, hotel, incidentals, and half of the cost of meals are also deductible as a business related education expense. Since completing the program (and the CFP® Exam) does not qualify Brantley to enter a new trade or profession, all of the costs are deductible.

Work clothes and uniforms are also deductible as a business related expense provided that they are purchased as a condition of employment and they are not items that could be worn outside of work. The cost of items suitable for wear outside of work will not qualify for a deduction.

Example 7.53

Billy, an employee of The Amazing Company, makes most of his money performing as a clown at childrens' birthday parties and corporate events. The cost of clown clothing is deductible as an employee related business expense, since the clothing is not suitable to be worn outside of a work setting.

An often overlooked group of work-related expenses that may be deducted as a business expense are job-hunting expenses. To be deductible, the expenses must be incurred in finding a new job in the taxpayer's current trade or profession. Provided that this condition is met, the expenses are deductible even if the taxpayer does not find or is not selected to fill a new job. Deductible expenses include travel costs, costs of printing resumes and assembling portfolios of work, phone calls, and fees paid to employment agencies or recruiters. Generally, the IRS will disallow a deduction if the primary purpose of a trip is personal as opposed to job-related, so it is wise to keep a log of job-hunting activities if the taxpayer would like to claim the costs as a deduction.

Example 7.54

Riley just graduated from law school, and passed the bar exam. She would like to try to find a job in California, so she flew to San Diego and San Francisco for a series of interviews with law firms. The primary purpose of the trip was to find a job, and her activities were substantiated with a detailed log that was kept by Riley. She will not be able to claim any deduction for job hunting expenses, since she is not already in the trade or business of practicing law. She is seeking admission to practice, not seeking a new job in her current trade or profession, so no deduction will be allowed.

The discussion relating to business-related expenses above applies to unreimbursed employee business expenses. If an employer reimburses an employee for business related expenses, the tax result will be dictated by whether or not the employer has an accountable expense reimbursement plan.

An **accountable plan** is a reimbursement plan that reimburses employees only for actual expenses incurred, and requires the employees to provide proof of, or "account for" their expenditures (usually, receipts are sufficient). When an employer has an accountable plan in place, there will be no tax impact for the employee. The reimbursement will not be included in the employee's income and the employee will not be entitled to take a deduction for the expenses incurred, since he or she has been fully reimbursed for those payments.

Some employers have **non-accountable reimbursement plans**. In this type of plan, the employer gives the employee a specified sum of money out of which the employee will cover all of the business related expenses. If the employee spends more than the amount given, he or she will be out of pocket for that amount. If the employee spends less, the excess does not have to be returned to the employer. When this type of plan is in place, the entire amount given to the employee will be included in the employee's W-2 income, thereby increasing AGI. The employee can claim an employee business expense deduction for amounts actually spent in the employee's itemized deductions to offset the income in the W-2. This treatment hurts the employee in two ways. First, the inclusion of the entire amount paid to the employee is included in income, thereby increasing AGI and subjecting the employee to higher expense deduction floors and possible phaseouts. Second, only miscellaneous itemized deductions in excess of the two percent floor are deductible, so if the employee does not have any other miscellaneous itemized deductions, the business expenses up to two percent of the employees AGI are out of pocket expenses that are not deductible. An accountable plan, which would exclude reimbursements from taxable income, would have put the employee in a much better tax position by reducing AGI and eliminating the need to claim an employee business expense deduction.

After 2025, employees can claim a home office deduction if a portion of the home is being used regularly and exclusively:

1. as a principal place of business,
2. as a place to meet clients in the normal course of business, or
3. in connection with the business if the home office is not included in a separate structure that is detached from the taxpayer's principal residence.

In addition, the home office must be for the convenience of the employee's employer. In other words, an employee must be required by the employer to maintain a home office in order to claim the deduction. Employees deduct home office expenses as a miscellaneous itemized deduction (an employee business expense), which is subject to the two percent floor.

Investment Expenses and Tax Advice

Taxpayers are also permitted to deduct investment expenses as a miscellaneous itemized deduction subject to the two percent floor. Allowing investment expense deductions is consistent with the partnership concept discussed earlier in the text – when a taxpayer engages in trade or business or investment activity, he or she is in partnership with the government, since the government will share in the gains through the tax system. Consequently, it is only fair to allow investment expenses incurred in producing that income to be deducted for income tax purposes. Under IRC Section 212, any ordinary and necessary expenses incurred for the production of income or for the management of assets held for the production of income are deductible. Examples of deductible investment expenses include:

- Custodial fees paid on Retirement Plans or IRAs with funds outside of the plan
- Cost of investment and tax advice (including legal fees and the cost of preparing tax returns)
- Cost of materials for researching investments (books, magazines, periodicals)
- Investment expenses allocated from partnerships and S corporation
- Safe deposit box fees

Quick Quiz 7.5

1. Gambling losses are a miscellaneous itemized deduction subject to the 2% floor.
   a. True
   b. False
2. Professional fees or union dues are deductible as an employee business expense after 2017 if they are not reimbursed by the employer.
   a. True
   b. False
3. The cost of materials for researching investments is deductible as a miscellaneous itemized deduction after 2017.
   a. True
   b. False

False, False, False.

Losses on IRAs

An investment related deduction often overlooked by taxpayers and advisors is the ability to claim a loss on IRAs that have been surrendered. This loss may only be claimed when all amounts have been withdrawn from the IRA and the taxpayer's basis in the IRA exceeded his or her recovery. To meet the "all amounts withdrawn" test, all funds in IRAs of the same type must be withdrawn. For example, to claim the deduction for traditional IRAs, the taxpayer must distribute all of the funds remaining in all of his or her traditional IRAs (a similar rule applies for Roth IRAs). Note that for this provision to apply, the taxpayer must have basis in the IRA. Usually, this means that he or she has made non-tax-deductible contributions to the IRA in previous years. Like any other investor, a taxpayer who loses money on a retirement account (i.e., receives less than his or her basis in the contract) should be permitted to recoup his or her capital through a loss deduction. Note that in the case of an IRA, though, the deduction is subject to the two percent floor. Unless the taxpayer has already met the two percent floor with his or her other deductions, the taxpayer will not be able to recoup all of his/her capital. This requirement is somewhat bizarre, especially considering the fact that a loss associated with an annuity contract (another type of retirement savings vehicle) can be deducted as a miscellaneous itemized deduction without regard to the two percent floor.

Exhibit 7.8 | Deductible Miscellaneous Itemized Deductions

Fully Deductible (Tier I) *(Not Subject to 2% Hurdle)*	*Deductible (Tier II)* *(Subject to 2% Hurdle)*
• Gambling Losses to Extent of Gains • Credit for Estate Tax on IRD Assets • Loss on Disposition of Annuity Contract • Repayment of Income	• Unreimbursed Employee Business Expenses (Travel, Journals, Uniforms, Union Dues) • Hobby Expenses to Extent of Hobby Income • Investment Expenses (e.g., Fees) • Tax Advice and Preparation • Losses on Terminated IRAs • Educational Expenses to Maintain or Improve Taxpayer Competency • Home Office Deduction

NOTE: After the enactment of TCJA 2017, Tier II Miscellaneous Itemized Deductions are not deductible for tax years 2018 - 2025, but will be available for tax years beginning after 2025.

Deduction Clustering

One of the objectives of TCJA 2017 was to simplify the tax filing process for many Americans. The new law significantly increased the standard deduction, which results in a larger number of taxpayers using the standard deduction on their income tax return, rather than itemizing deductions. Taxpayers who previously benefited from itemized deductions, but who will now take the standard deduction, may find a deduction clustering, or bunching, strategy to be attractive.

With a deduction clustering strategy, the taxpayer will "cluster" itemized deductions together in one year and take the standard deduction the following year, allowing for a higher amount of deductions overall. State taxes, mortgage interest, medical expenses, and charitable donations are four categories of itemized deductions that might be able to be bunched in a single year.

Early Payment of State Income or Property Taxes

Estimated state and local tax payments are typically due the 15th day of the month after the tax year, but if this payment is made prior to the end of the tax year it will increase itemized deductions. TCJA 2017 limits the deduction for state and local taxes to $10,000 per year (for tax years 2018 – 2025), so the tax savings from this strategy will be somewhat limited by that ceiling amount.

Early Payment of Mortgage Interest

The first mortgage payment of the next tax year can be paid in the current year, thereby, accelerating the mortgage interest deduction in a year when deductions are itemized.

Medical Expenses

Discretionary medical expenses can be bunched into tax years where the taxpayer is also bunching other itemized deductions. However, these expenses have to exceed 7.5% of AGI to be deductible.

Charitable Donations

Larger charitable contributions can be made before the end of the year in which taxes are to be itemized and small, or no, charitable contributions made in the year the standard deduction is taken. Alternatively, a donor-advised fund may be utilized to assist with bunching charitable contributions.

If a donor wants to donate funds to charitable causes but has not yet selected the specific charities, the taxpayer can contribute the funds to a donor-advised fund set up with a charity or brokerage firm. Contributions made to a donor-advised fund allow the contributing taxpayer an immediate tax deduction while deferring the distribution to the qualified charity of the taxpayer's choice to a later time, as directed by the taxpayer. As a result, the donor-advised fund provides the taxpayer with the up-front charitable deduction and the ability to spread charitable gifts over many years and over several different charities.

Example 7.55

Kacey, a single taxpayer typically makes annual charitable gifts of $7,000, and her total itemized deductions, including the charitable gifts, are expected to be $11,000 in 2021 and $11,000 in 2022. Since this amount is below the standard deduction, she will take the standard deduction in both years and receive no tax benefit from her charitable contributions (excluding the $300 above-the line deduction permitted for those who take the standard deduction in 2021). However, if Kacey makes 2 years of charitable gifts in 2021 (totaling $14,000), her total itemized deductions for 2021 will increase to $18,000. Kacey will take itemized deductions of $18,000 in 2021, and will still take the standard deduction in 2022, increasing her total deductions over the 2-year period by $5,450. Alternatively, Kacey could make a charitable gift of $21,000 to a donor-advised fund in 2021 (increasing her itemized deductions to $25,000), and distributions can be made from the donor-advised fund to Kacey's selected charities in 2022 and 2023 while Kacey takes the standard deduction in those years.

THE QUALIFIED BUSINESS INCOME (QBI OR SECTION 199A) DEDUCTION

Introduction

One of the primary objectives of TCJA 2017 was to lower tax rates on businesses. For the years leading up to its enactment, many businesses were discontinuing operations in the United States and moving those operations overseas due to tax and cost considerations. Many businesses also engaged in corporate inversions, which were designed to remove the business entity itself outside of the U.S. to avoid high taxes on corporate income. In the years before 2018, U.S. Corporate tax rates, especially when combined with the taxes imposed on dividend distributions from corporations to their shareholders, were among the highest in the world.

TCJA 2017 achieved its objective of reducing tax burdens on corporations by lowering the corporate tax rate from a marginal rate structure with rates as high as 35 percent to a flat 21 percent tax rate. Many members of Congress were concerned about the potential disparity this would cause between corporate and pass-through business entities which would have been subjected to tax on business income at personal tax rates (up to 37%), and sought to make sure that pass-through business entities enjoyed similar tax rates to corporations. The result was the **Qualified Business Income** (QBI, or Section 199A) deduction, which permits sole proprietors and owners of pass-through business entities (as described in Chapter 16) up to a 20 percent deduction on qualified business income. The QBI deduction does not lower AGI, which means it is not an above-the-line deduction, and can be taken regardless of whether a taxpayer itemizes deductions. By enacting the QBI deduction, TCJA created a new form of below-the-line deduction – a below-the-line deduction that can be taken in addition to the greater of the taxpayer's itemized or standard deduction.

While an exhaustive review of the QBI deduction is beyond the scope of this text, a basic understanding of its application is important for financial professionals.

Qualified Business Income

Section 199A defines qualified business income (QBI) as the net amount of qualified items of income, gain, deduction, and loss with respect to any trade or business (sole proprietorships, partnerships, limited partnerships, limited liability companies, limited liability partnerships, and S corporations) within the United States that is included or allowed to be included in determining taxable income for the year. The taxpayer is not required to materially participate in the business to qualify for the QBI deduction.

Since the purpose of the new deduction was to lower the tax rate on business income, certain types of income are excluded from the definition of QBI, including:

- Capital gains and losses
- Dividends
- Interest not allocable to a trade or business
- Commodities transactions
- Reasonable compensation for S corporation owners
- Guaranteed payments to partners for services rendered

Special rules concerning the determination of QBI also clarify that guaranteed payments for the use of capital, net operating losses, and income associated with a trade or business of performing services as an employee are not attributable to the trade or business for the purposes of calculating the deduction.

The QBI Deduction General Rule

For a taxpayer owning an interest in only one pass-through business entity,[11] the QBI deduction equals the lesser of:

- 20 percent of the qualified business income of the taxpayer, or
- 20 percent of the taxpayer's adjusted taxable income.

The taxpayer's adjusted taxable income equals taxable income from all sources (after taking above-the-line deductions – excluding the deductions related to the business for self-employment tax, self-employed health insurance premiums, and self-employed retirement plan contributions, and taking either the standard or itemized deductions), including the spouse's income if married filing jointly, reduced by net capital gains.[12]

Example 7.56

Jana's share of qualified business income from a partnership is $90,000, and her total adjusted taxable income from all sources (after taking above-the-line deductions not related to the business, and either the standard or itemized deduction, but before taking the 20% deduction for QBI) is $70,000, the deduction is the lesser of:

- 20% x $90,000, or
- 20% x 70,000; which limits the deduction to $14,000.

On the other hand, if Jana's share of qualified business income from a partnership is $90,000, and her total adjusted taxable income from all sources (after taking above-the-line deductions not relating to the business and either the standard or itemized deduction, but before taking the 20% deduction for QBI) is $110,000, the deduction is the lesser of:

- 20% x $90,000, or
- 20% x 110,000; which limits the deduction to $18,000.

The QBI deduction is phased down for taxpayers with taxable income above specified levels, and, in some cases, for businesses that are classified as specified service trades or businesses (SSTBs).

11. The QBI deduction for taxpayers owning an interest in two or more businesses is covered in Chapter 16.

12. Treas. Reg.§1.199A-1 defines "net capital gain" as the excess of net long-term capital gain for the taxable year over the net short-term capital loss for such year, plus any qualified dividend income for the taxable year.

Specified Service Trade or Business (SSTB)

Specified Service Trade or Business (SSTB), sometimes referred to as "out of favor" service businesses, will be subject to a phase-down of the QBI deduction once the taxable income of the business owner reaches certain amounts.

The IRC specifies that trades or business involving performance of services in the fields of health, law, accounting, actuarial services, consulting, performing arts, athletics, financial services, investing, investment management, trading or dealing in securities (including partnership interests and commodities) and any trade or business where the principal asset of the business is the reputation or skill of one or more of its owners are SSTBs.

Specifically excluded from the definition of SSTBs are businesses that provide engineering and architectural services.

Deduction Phase-Down and Transition

Taxpayers who qualify to claim the QBI deduction are subject to either a phase-down or transition of the deduction amount depending upon their taxable income from all sources (without regard to the Sec. 199A deduction, but including the spouse's income if MFJ). There are two taxable income tiers which will determine the amount of the deduction: The threshold amount and the phaseout amount.

Exhibit 7.9 | QBI Threshold & Phaseout Amounts (2021)

Filing Status	*Threshold Amount*	*Phaseout Amount*
MFJ	$329,800	$429,800
All Others	$164,900	$214,900

All taxpayers with taxable income below the threshold amount are eligible to claim a QBI deduction for business income regardless of whether or not that income was derived from a SSTB. Once the taxpayer's income exceeds the threshold amount, the deduction is phased-down until the taxpayer's taxable income reaches the phase-out amount. Once taxable income reaches the phase-out amount, income from SSTBs no longer qualifies for the QBI deduction, and income from businesses which are not SSTBs are subject to an alternate calculation that takes into consideration the wages paid by the business and the business' unadjusted basis in its depreciable property to determine the amount of the deduction.

The 3 Tiers of Section 199A

The impact of these rules implies that there are three tiers associated with the QBI deduction, illustrated in **Exhibit 7.10**.

Exhibit 7.10 | 3 Tiers of Section 199A

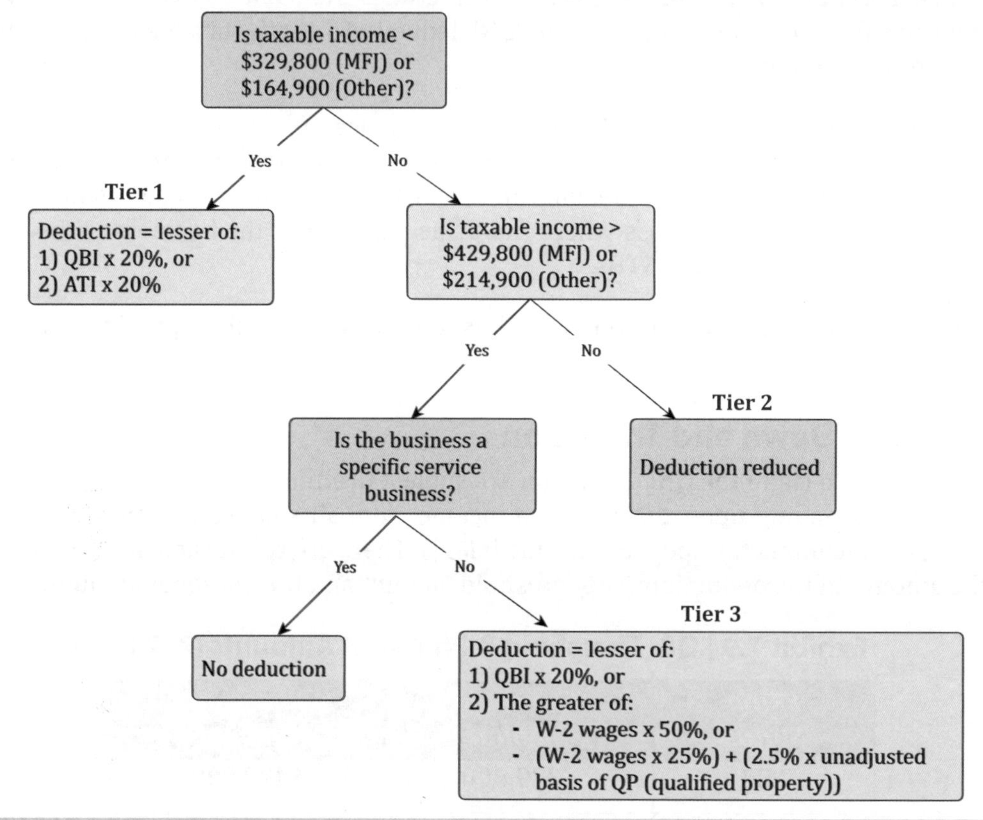

Tier 1

As described above, the Sec. 199A deduction for a taxpayer with taxable income below the threshold amount is the lower of:

- Qualified Business Income x 20%, or
- Adjusted Taxable Income x 20%.

When Tier 1 applies, the status of a SSTB does not impact the tax results.

Tier 2

Once the taxpayer's taxable income exceeds the threshold amount, the Section 199A deduction equals 20 percent of QBI less the "reduction amount." The reduction amount equals the "excess amount" times the phaseout percentage. The excess amount equals qualified business income times 20 percent minus the greater of:

- 50% of W-2 wages paid by the business, or
- 25% of W-2 wages paid by the business + 2.5% of the unadjusted basis of qualified assets used in the trade or business.

When a taxpayer is in Tier 2, a QBI deduction will be at least partially allowed regardless of whether or not the business income is generated by a SSBT.

Tier 3

Once a taxpayer's taxable income exceeds the phase-out amount, Tier 3 rules apply.

Income generated by an SSTB will not generate a tax deduction for a taxpayer in Tier 3.

If the business generating the qualified business income is not a SSTB, however, the QBI deduction will equal the lesser of:

1. Qualified Business Income x 20%
2. Adjusted taxable income x 20%
3. The greater of:
   - W-2 wages x 50%, or
   - W-2 wages x 25% plus 2.5% of the Unadjusted Basis of Qualified Property.

Planning Applications

While detailed calculations of the QBI (or Section 199A) deduction are beyond the scope of this text, financial professionals should be aware of the threshold and phase-out amounts that qualify or deny a taxpayer this deduction. Generally speaking, all taxpayers with taxable income less than $329,800 (MFJ) or $164,900 (all other filing statuses) in 2021 will qualify for the QBI (Section 199A) below-the-line deduction. The deduction begins to phase out above these amounts, and is completely phased out above the phase-out thresholds discussed above for SSTBs. Taxpayers who have income close to the threshold and phase-in amounts may wish to engage in tax planning to make sure they can qualify for this deduction.

QBI Deduction for Qualified REIT Dividends and Publicly Traded Partnership Income

In addition to the QBI deduction for flow-through business entities discussed above, the TCJA also allows a 20 percent QBI deduction for qualified Real Estate Investment Trust (REIT) dividends and publicly traded partnership (PTP) income. This component of the QBI deduction is not limited by W-2 wages or the unadjusted basis of qualified property unless the PTP operates an SSTB (as described previously). When a taxpayer has both qualified business income from a flow-through entity and qualified REIT or PTP income, the deduction is the lesser of:

- 20 percent of the qualified business income of the taxpayer, plus 20 percent of the taxpayer's qualified REIT dividends and qualified PTP income, or
- 20 percent of the taxpayer's adjusted taxable income (net of capital gains, as described previously).

REIT dividends that qualify for the QBI deduction are reported to the taxpayer in box 5 of Form 1099-DIV.

Exhibit 7.11 | Form 1099-DIV

9191 ☐ VOID ☐ CORRECTED

PAYER'S name, street address, city or town, state or province, country, ZIP or foreign postal code, and telephone no.		1a Total ordinary dividends $	OMB No. 1545-0110 2020 Form 1099-DIV	Dividends and Distributions
		1b Qualified dividends $		
		2a Total capital gain distr. $	2b Unrecap. Sec. 1250 gain $	Copy A For Internal Revenue Service Center
PAYER'S TIN	RECIPIENT'S TIN	2c Section 1202 gain $	2d Collectibles (28%) gain $	File with Form 1096.
RECIPIENT'S name		3 Nondividend distributions $	4 Federal income tax withheld $	For Privacy Act and Paperwork Reduction Act Notice, see the **2020 General Instructions for Certain Information Returns.**
		5 Section 199A dividends $	6 Investment expenses $	
Street address (including apt. no.)		7 Foreign tax paid $	8 Foreign country or U.S. possession	
City or town, state or province, country, and ZIP or foreign postal code		9 Cash liquidation distributions $	10 Noncash liquidation distributions $	
	FATCA filing requirement ☐	11 Exempt-interest dividends $	12 Specified private activity bond interest dividends $	
Account number (see instructions)	2nd TIN not. ☐	13 State / 14 State identification no.	15 State tax withheld $ $	

Form **1099-DIV** Cat. No. 14415N www.irs.gov/Form1099DIV Department of the Treasury - Internal Revenue Service

Do Not Cut or Separate Forms on This Page — Do Not Cut or Separate Forms on This Page

A simplified calculation method for QBI is provided by the IRS on Form 8995, and the full calculation including phase in on Form 8995-A.

Exhibit 7.12 | Form 8995

Form **8995**

Department of the Treasury
Internal Revenue Service

Qualified Business Income Deduction Simplified Computation

▶ Attach to your tax return.

▶ Go to *www.irs.gov/Form8995* for instructions and the latest information.

OMB No. 1545-2294

2020

Attachment Sequence No. 55

Name(s) shown on return	**Your taxpayer identification number**

Note. *You can claim the qualified business income deduction* ***only*** *if you have qualified business income from a qualified trade or business, real estate investment trust dividends, publicly traded partnership income, or a domestic production activities deduction passed through from an agricultural or horticultural cooperative. See instructions.*
Use this form if your taxable income, before your qualified business income deduction, is at or below $163,300 ($326,600 if married filing jointly), and you aren't a patron of an agricultural or horticultural cooperative.

1	**(a)** Trade, business, or aggregation name	**(b)** Taxpayer identification number	**(c)** Qualified business income or (loss)
i			
ii			
iii			
iv			
v			

2	Total qualified business income or (loss). Combine lines 1i through 1v, column (c)	2			
3	Qualified business net (loss) carryforward from the prior year	3	( )		
4	Total qualified business income. Combine lines 2 and 3. If zero or less, enter -0-	4			
5	Qualified business income component. Multiply line 4 by 20% (0.20)			5	
6	Qualified REIT dividends and publicly traded partnership (PTP) income or (loss) (see instructions)	6			
7	Qualified REIT dividends and qualified PTP (loss) carryforward from the prior year	7	( )		
8	Total qualified REIT dividends and PTP income. Combine lines 6 and 7. If zero or less, enter -0-	8			
9	REIT and PTP component. Multiply line 8 by 20% (0.20)			9	
10	Qualified business income deduction before the income limitation. Add lines 5 and 9			10	
11	Taxable income before qualified business income deduction	11			
12	Net capital gain (see instructions)	12			
13	Subtract line 12 from line 11. If zero or less, enter -0-	13			
14	Income limitation. Multiply line 13 by 20% (0.20)			14	
15	Qualified business income deduction. Enter the lesser of line 10 or line 14. Also enter this amount on the applicable line of your return ▶			15	
16	Total qualified business (loss) carryforward. Combine lines 2 and 3. If greater than zero, enter -0-			16	( )
17	Total qualified REIT dividends and PTP (loss) carryforward. Combine lines 6 and 7. If greater than zero, enter -0-			17	( )

For Privacy Act and Paperwork Reduction Act Notice, see instructions. Cat. No. 37806C Form **8995** (2020)

SUMMARY AND CONCLUSION

Chapter 7 focused on the deductions that are commonly used by taxpayers to help reduce their tax liability – itemized deductions and the QBI or Section 199A deduction. Itemized deductions permit taxpayers to deduct certain personal expenses (which, under normal tax rules, should not be deductible) that contribute toward various social goals. Perhaps the most commonly used itemized deductions are the deductions for taxes, interest (mortgage interest, in particular), and charitable donations. Due to the floor limitations, however, relatively few taxpayers are able to take advantage of medical expense, casualty, and miscellaneous itemized deductions. A thorough understanding of itemized deduction rules is necessary for a financial advisor to provide competent advice to his or her clients.

TCJA 2017 added a new below-the-line deduction, called the Qualified Business Income (QBI) or Section 199A deduction, which permits sole proprietors and pass-through business owners to claim a deduction (in addition to the greater of their itemized or standard deduction) of up to 20 percent of the qualified business income from the sole proprietorship or pass through entity. The QBI deduction was designed to bring some parity to the taxation of business income after TCJA lowered the corporate tax rate to 21 percent, and will be an important deduction for tax years 2018-2025 for business owners who qualify to claim it.

The next chapter concludes our discussion of deductions, and focuses on special deduction rules, some tax penalties, and the circumstances under which losses suffered by a taxpayer are not deductible for tax purposes.

KEY TERMS

Accountable Plan - A reimbursement plan that reimburses employees only for actual expenses incurred, and requires the employees to provide proof of, or "account for" their expenditures.

Acquisition Indebtedness – Indebtedness that is secured by the home and is used to acquire, construct, or improve the taxpayer's primary residence and one additional residence.

Casualty Loss Deduction – Deduction allowed for losses or damages to a taxpayer's property resulting from a sudden or unexpected event, such as fire, storm, shipwreck, or theft.

Employee Business Expenses – Expenses that include professional and union dues of employees, travel, supplies and services, professional books and journals, job related educational expenses, work clothes and uniforms, and job hunting expenses in the same line of work, which may be deductible as a miscellaneous itemized deduction subject to the two percent floor if they are not reimbursed by the employer.

Home Equity Indebtedness – Additional debt secured by the home that exceeds the amount of acquisition indebtedness.

Non-accountable Reimbursement Plans – Plans in which the employer gives the employee a specified sum of money out of which the employee will cover all of the business related expenses.

Private Charities – Corporations or trusts structured to further the charitable intentions of a donor or the donor's family.

Public Charities – Charitable organizations that receive support from a wide cross-section of the population, such as the Red Cross or the YMCA.

Qualified Business Income (QBI) - The net amount of income, gain, deductions, and losses with respect to a pass-through trade or business, which is used in determining the below-the-line deduction of 20% of QBI.

Qualified Charitable Organization – An organization that is operated exclusively for religious, charitable, scientific, literary, or educational purposes, or for the prevention of cruelty to animals or children.

Qualified Residence Interest Deduction – Tax deduction that permits taxpayers to deduct the interest on up to $750,000 of home indebtedness.

Specified Service Trade or Business (SSTB) - A trade or business involving performance of services in the fields of health, law, accounting, actuarial services, consulting, performing arts, athletics, financial services, investing, investment management, trading or dealing in securities, and any trade or business where the principal asset of the business is the reputation or skill of one or more of its owners. SSTBs are permitted only limited use of the QBI deduction.

DISCUSSION QUESTIONS

SOLUTIONS to the discussion questions can be found exclusively within the chapter. Once you have completed an initial reading of the chapter, go back and highlight the answers to these questions.

1. Why does Congress sometimes allow deductions for personal expenses?
2. How can a taxpayer achieve a tax benefit by itemizing his deductions?
3. Under what circumstances are capital expenses a deductible medical expense?
4. How does the tax benefit rule affect the deduction of state and local taxes?
5. Describe the deduction for state sales tax.
6. Under what circumstances is interest deductible?
7. What are the limits on the qualified residence interest deduction?
8. To what extent is investment interest deductible?
9. Describe the rules regarding interest paid on the acquisition of investments that generate tax-free income.
10. What is a qualified charitable organization?
11. What are the requirements for an income tax charitable deduction?
12. What is the partial interest rule and what are the exceptions to this rule?
13. Name the factors that affect the amount of an income tax charitable deduction.
14. What are the limits on the charitable contribution deduction?
15. Describe the special election available to taxpayers making contributions of long-term capital gain property.
16. What are the limits on charitable deductions by corporations?
17. What are the limits on deducting personal casualty losses?
18. Name several miscellaneous Tier I itemized deductions that are not subject to the two percent floor.
19. What are the major categories of Tier II miscellaneous itemized deductions that are subject to the two percent floor?
20. Describe how a taxpayer can deduct job-hunting expenses.

MULTIPLE CHOICE PROBLEMS

A sample of multiple choice problems is provided below. Additional multiple choice problems are available at money-education.com by accessing the Student Practice Portal.

1. Trisha, age 66, has a severe asthmatic condition, and her physician recommended that she install a lap pool in her home so that she can swim regularly, which should help control her condition. Trisha has a friend who is a real estate agent, and strongly advised her not to install the pool, since pools depress the market value of homes in the area. If Trisha's AGI for the year is $100,000 how much of the cost of the lap pool can Trisha actually deduct as a medical expense if it cost her $12,000 to install the pool and all of her other health insurance costs were covered by her health insurance policy? The value of the house did not change due to the pool.
    a. $0.
    b. $4,500 as an itemized deduction.
    c. $7,500 as an itemized deduction.
    d. $12,000 as an adjustment to income.

2. All of the following statements regarding the Section 199A qualified business income deduction are correct, EXCEPT:
    a. The deduction is generally 20% of qualified business income.
    b. The deduction is not available for service businesses such as health and accounting.
    c. The deduction may be limited based on taxable income.
    d. The deduction may be phased out for high income taxpayers.

3. In June of this year, Wynonna purchased her first home. The price of the house was $260,000, and she financed the purchase with a 30-year, $200,000 mortgage. Since she plans on staying in the home for quite a while, and she expects interest rates to rise in the future, she paid $4,000 in points to receive a lower interest rate on the loan. As of the end of the year, Wynonna had paid $7,614 in interest on the loan by making her monthly installment payments. How much should she claim as mortgage interest on her itemized deductions this year?
    a. $7,614.
    b. $7,747.
    c. $9,614.
    d. $11,614.

4. Jake's AGI for 2022 is $100,000. He inherited a large amount of money from the estate of his grandfather, and is very charitably inclined. A recent earthquake devastated several cities on the West Coast, and Jake wanted to assist in getting the people affected back on their feet. He gave a $75,000 donation to the Red Cross, which is spearheading relief efforts in the region. How much of the contribution can Jake deduct on his income tax return in 2022?
    a. $20,000.
    b. $30,000.
    c. $60,000.
    d. $75,000.

5. Owen is a tax attorney who specializes in intergenerational wealth transfer planning. He is also very charitably inclined, and sits on several charitable boards. A local animal shelter and Friends of Animals group recently decided to work together on joint goals, and decided to form a new charitable organization, which meets the definition of a public charity. Owen created the organization and received exempt determination status from the IRS. He usually charges $5,000 to perform this service, plus the exempt determination letter fee charged by the IRS of $500, but he volunteered for this activity since his wife will be on the board. Owen was not reimbursed for the expenses he incurred. Assuming that his AGI and contribution base is $150,000, how much can Owen deduct for income tax purposes?
   a. $0.
   b. $500.
   c. $2,750.
   d. $5,500.

Additional multiple choice problems are available at *money-education.com* by accessing the Student Practice Portal. Access requires registration of the title using the unique code at the front of the book.

QUICK QUIZ EXPLANATIONS

Quick Quiz 7.1

1. False. Personal expenses are generally not deductible.
2. False. The standard deduction is adjusted annually for inflation.
3. True.
4. True.

Quick Quiz 7.2

1. True.
2. False. There is no limitation on the amount that can be claimed as a deduction for property taxes; if the taxpayer has multiple residences, he or she may claim all of the property taxes paid.
3. True.
4. False. Taxpayers are permitted to deduct the interest on up to $750,000 of home indebtedness incurred after December 15, 2017.

Quick Quiz 7.3

1. False. Only gifts of cash or property will qualify for a charitable income tax deduction.
2. True.
3. False. Gifts of cash are limited to 60% (or 100% in 2020 and 2021, if the taxpayer elects to treat the cash contributions as qualified cash contributions under the CARES Act and TCDTRA of 2020), and gifts of non-long-term capital gains property are limited to 50%, of the taxpayer's AGI when made to a public charity.
4. True.

Quick Quiz 7.4

1. True.
2. False. The first step in calculating a casualty loss on Schedule A is to deduct $100 from each occurrence. Second, a taxpayer's aggregate casualty and theft losses must exceed 10% of the taxpayer's AGI in order to be deductible.

Quick Quiz 7.5

1. False. Gambling losses, to the extent of gambling income, are a miscellaneous itemized deduction not subject to the 2% floor.
2. False. Professional fees or union dues are a Tier II miscellaneous itemized deduction subject to the 2% floor and are no longer deductible after TCJA 2017.
3. False. The cost of research materials for investments are a Tier II miscellaneous itemized deduction subject to the 2% floor and are no longer deductible after TCJA 2017.

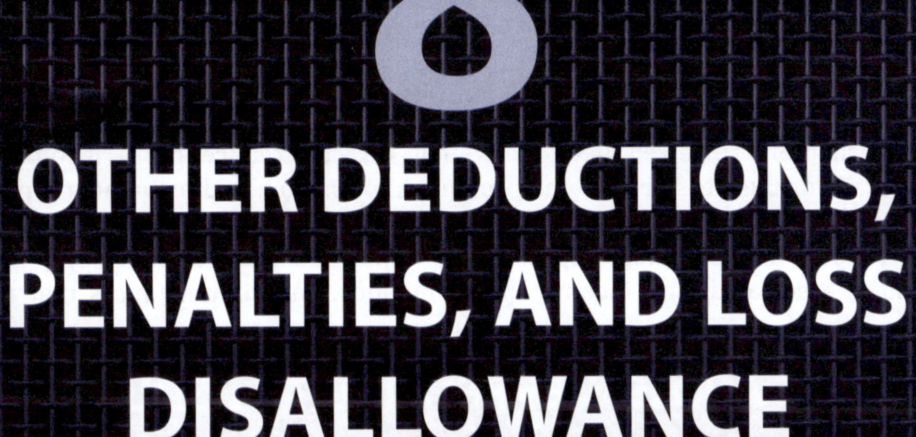

8

OTHER DEDUCTIONS, PENALTIES, AND LOSS DISALLOWANCE

LEARNING OBJECTIVES

1. Discuss the limitations imposed on deductions by public policy concerns.
2. Identify the types of political contributions that are deductible for income tax purposes.*
3. Explain the limitations imposed on the deduction of excessive compensation.*
4. Differentiate the tax treatment of a business activity with that of a hobby activity.*
5. Determine whether or not an activity should be classified as a hobby given information about the activity and the financial results of engaging in the activity over the past several years.*
6. Explain the three ways that a rental real estate activity can be classified for income tax purposes and the tax rules for each category of rental real estate activities.*
7. Identify exceptions to the general rule that personal expenses are not deductible when determining taxable income.*
8. Describe the circumstances under which bad debts are deductible.*
9. Calculate the permissible bad debt deduction for a taxpayer.*
10. Explain the rules for taking a loss on a worthless security.*
11. Describe the special tax treatment available for Sec. 1244 stock.*
12. Explain the net operating loss rules.*
13. Describe the tax penalties applicable to pension plan and IRA contributions and distributions.*
14. Describe two types of temporary loss disallowances.*
15. Describe three types of permanent loss disallowances.*

**Ties to CFP Certification Learning Objectives*

INTRODUCTION

The two previous chapters reviewed deductions that directly reduce gross income (deductions associated with a trade or business or with the production of income), adjustments to income (above-the-line deductions), and below-the-line deductions (itemized deductions and the QBI/Section 199A Deduction). This chapter discusses some special rules and circumstances that apply to income tax deductions, penalties associated with income and deductions, and circumstances that result in loss disallowance.

GENERAL RULES AND ISSUES RELATED TO DEDUCTIONS AND LOSS DISALLOWANCE

For a variety of reasons, Congress has chosen to place limitations on the ability of taxpayers to take certain deductions and losses. Some of the most common of these limitations will be discussed in this chapter and include:

- Public policy limitations
- Political contributions
- Excessive compensation
- Hobby losses
- Rental of vacation homes
- Personal expenditures

Public Policy Limitations

Public policy concerns impose some limitations on taxpayers' ability to take deductions. Deductions for activities that violate public policy are not permitted for income tax purposes. Some examples of items that are not deductible due to public policy considerations include penalties, fines, illegal bribes, and kickbacks.

Penalties and fines are intended to be a form of punishment for legal violations. Allowing a taxpayer to deduct penalties or fines assessed, even those incurred when in the conduct of a trade or business, would provide individuals with an incentive to engage in the action that the penalty was designed to discourage. It does not make sense from a public policy standpoint to discourage behavior by imposing a penalty while creating tax rules that reward individuals who engage in the prohibited behavior.

Example 8.1

When Lamont left his office to go to visit a client at the client's home, he was already running late. To make matters worse, he ran into a traffic jam caused by an accident, and by the time he arrived at the client's home he was approximately one hour late. There was no room in the client's driveway, and despite the presence of no parking signs all along the street, Lamont parked in front of the client's house and ran to the door to apologize for his tardiness. After the meeting, and upon return to his car, Lamont was greeted by a parking ticket prominently displayed on his windshield. Despite the fact that Lamont was conducting business at the time he incurred the parking fine, he cannot deduct the cost of the ticket as a business expense, since this would violate public policy.

Bribes and kickbacks are illegal acts themselves, and are never deductible for income tax purposes. This rule applies even when it is customary to provide bribes to facilitate the conduct of business. Individuals engaged in international business transactions in some parts of the world may be faced with such a situation. Giving or receiving a bribe, even in those jurisdictions, is an illegal act in the United States (and may also be a violation of the Foreign Corrupt Practices Act). These payments may never be deducted on a taxpayer's income tax return, even if they are considered reasonable, ordinary, and necessary expenses in that jurisdiction.

There are some illegal activities that generate permissible income tax deductions. If a taxpayer is involved in the operation of an illegal trade or business, the taxpayer is permitted to take all ordinary, necessary, and reasonable expenses associated with the production of that income as if the business activity was a legal business. As noted above, fines, penalties, bribes, and kickbacks may not be deducted, and are not considered to be ordinary, necessary, or reasonable business expenses. This rule appears to be a strange policy, but remember that the 16th Amendment grants Congress the power to collect tax on income from whatever source derived. "Income" constitutes the gross receipts of a business enterprise reduced by all ordinary, reasonable, and necessary expenses to generate that income.

Example 8.2

Edna runs an illegal gambling operation in the back room of her meat packing firm. This year, Edna received $750,000 in gross receipts from the gambling operation. The pro-rata portion of rent Edna paid for the space used for the gambling operation was $40,000. She paid her employees $250,000 to run the operation, and incurred $20,000 in product costs (cards, chips, dice, etc.). Edna's income from the gambling operation is $440,000 ($750,000 in gross receipts less $250,000 in salaries, $40,000 for rent, and $20,000 for product costs).

It may seem odd to calculate the income from an illegal operation, since it seems that a competent criminal would not be careless enough to tell the government that he was running an illegal business by reporting the income on his tax return. Smart criminals however, do report their illegal source income as "other income" on their tax return. Failure to do so would constitute fraud, which would allow the IRS to reopen the tax return for that year at will. By declaring the income, the statute of limitations begins to run, and, as discussed earlier, the IRS typically has three years to challenge the income and expenses reported on the return. Furthermore, due to the imposition of privacy rules on the IRS, the IRS cannot inform the Department of Justice, or other law enforcement agencies, that the taxpayer is conducting an illegal business activity. If the IRS provides this information to law enforcement, it may be possible for the criminal to have all evidence obtained from that tip classified as inadmissible for trial. This policy provides a fair degree of protection to the criminal, and encourages reporting of illegal source income. By structuring the system in this way, Congress is clearly indicating that it wants to tax ALL income from whatever source derived, even if that income is generated by illegal activities.

Key Concepts

1. Explain why penalties and fines are not deductible.
2. Describe the circumstances under which an illegal activity may give rise to an income tax deduction.
3. Explain the rules regarding the deductibility of political contributions and money spent monitoring legislation.
4. Describe the limits on the ability of publicly held corporations to deduct executive compensation.

All tax rules have exceptions, and the rules governing illegal source income do not deviate from this reality. If the illegal activity generating income involves trafficking in controlled substances (drugs), the only deduction the taxpayer is permitted to take is the cost of goods sold (the cost of the drugs).

Example 8.3

Fred supplements his income by running an illegal drug procurement and distribution business. This year, Fred received $750,000 in gross receipts from the illegal drug business. Fred paid $40,000 in rent for the space used to store and package the drugs. He also paid his employees and street pushers $250,000 to run the operation, and incurred $150,000 in product costs (costs of drugs sold) plus incidental expenses of $20,000. Fred's taxable income from the drug operation is $600,000 ($750,000 in gross receipts less the $150,000 for the cost of goods sold).

Some states have legalized the use of marijuana for medicinal purposes, recreational purposes, or both. While state law may permit the sale and distribution of marijuana within the state, the act of selling or distributing marijuana violates federal law. A company that has received a license from a state government to distribute marijuana within the state may only deduct the cost of goods sold from gross income when calculating taxable income for federal income tax purposes. All other expenses incurred in the business of selling and distributing marijuana (other than cost of goods sold) may not be deducted on the business' federal income tax return.

Political Contributions

Generally, businesses and individuals are not permitted to deduct political contributions or lobbying expenses. While, prior to 2018, expenses incurred to influence local legislation were deductible, TCJA 2017 repealed the deduction for local lobbying expenses.

Businesses can also deduct expenses associated with the monitoring of legislation. Many large businesses may be affected by pending legislation, and need to know if that legislation becomes law due to the added compliance responsibilities that must be performed. These types of expenditures do not attempt to influence legislation, and are considered ordinary, necessary, and reasonable business expenses.

Finally, businesses may deduct de minimis in-house expenses associated with lobbying, provided that the total expenses incurred do not exceed $2,000. If the expenses do exceed $2,000, none of the expenses are deductible.

Quick Quiz 8.1

1. Penalties and fines are intended to be a form of punishment for legal violations, and are therefore not deductible.
   a. True
   b. False
2. The IRS can inform a law enforcement agency if a taxpayer is conducting an illegal business activity.
   a. True
   b. False
3. Lobbying expenses for influencing legislation at both the federal and state level are deductible.
   a. True
   b. False
4. The $1 million limit on deductible executive compensation does not apply to performance-based compensation.
   a. True
   b. False

True, False, False, False.

Excessive Compensation

Publicly held corporations are subject to a deduction limitation on executive compensation. The maximum deduction that can be taken for compensation paid to the chief executive officer the chief financial officer, and the three highest compensated executives (covered employees) is $1 million each. Regular compensation of these top five officers in excess of $1 million is not deductible by the corporation. Once an employee becomes a covered employee, they will remain a covered employee even when no longer working for the company. For example, if a covered employee retires and receives income during retirement under a salary continuation plan, the employer's deduction for compensation paid to the former employee will continue to be capped at $1 million. There is no compensation cap placed on the deductibility of the salaries of corporate employees other than the top five executives.[1] Beginning in 2018, TCJA expanded the definition of publicly held corporation to include all foreign companies traded through ADRs (American Depository Receipts).

1. Under ARPA 2021, the disallowance of deduction for excess remuneration for tax years beginning after December 31, 2026 will apply to a third category of employees, which includes the next five highest paid employees (a total of ten: CEO, CFO, next three highest paid officers, and next five highest paid employees). The rule requiring covered employees to remain covered employees indefinitely, however, will not apply to those who become covered employees only as a result of this change.

The $1 million compensation limitation does not apply, however, to payments to qualified retirement plans or payments that are otherwise excludable from gross income. Prior to 2018, the limitation did not apply to performance-based compensation and commissions, but these exceptions were repealed by TCJA 2017.

Hobby Losses

All ordinary, necessary, and reasonable business expenses are deductible against income. To be classified as a business activity, the taxpayer must have a profit motive. Some individuals attempt to classify their hobbies as business activities so that they can deduct the expenses incurred in engaging in the activity.

Under IRC Section 183, a **hobby activity** is defined as any activity that the taxpayer engages in without a profit motive. Hobby activities are usually activities that involve personal pleasure, such as collecting exotic cars, raising horses, gardening, racing sailboats, and collecting and/or trading stamps or coins. Often, it is difficult to determine whether an activity is a hobby or a trade or business. The distinction between the two centers on the presence or absence of a profit motive. Profit motive does not imply that the activity must generate a profit each year. Most profit-motivated business activities generate losses in the early years of operation, turning profits as the business matures. Treas. Reg. §1.183-2(a) defines **profit motive** as "an actual and honest, even though unreasonable or unrealistic, profit objective in engaging in the activity."

CASE STUDY 8.1

Travel Expenses, Hobby Loss Rules & Timeshares

Douglas and Gina Rundlett, Petitioners v. Commissioner of Internal Revenue, Respondent, T.C. Memo 2011-229 (September 26, 2011).

Doug (an insurance agent) and Gina (who works in the construction industry), resided in California. In 2005, Doug and Gina purchased their first timeshare in Laguna Beach, California, and by the end of the year, owned four units. By the end of 2006, they owned a total of 11 timeshare units. Gina's goal was to own 52 timeshare units, and to use the income they generated to supplement the family's retirement income.

In 2005 and 2006, Doug and Gina reported net losses from the rental of their timeshare units on Schedule C (Profit or Loss from a Sole Proprietorship). The IRS issued a notice of deficiency for those tax years, claiming that the losses cannot be claimed on Schedule C because the expenses incurred were not paid in carrying on a trade or business engaged in for profit. The dwelling units were used by Doug and Gina or other owners as residences, and timeshare activity losses are considered passive, not active, losses.

Among the expenses claimed for the timeshare activity were travel expenses. Citing the rules set forth in §274(d), the court stated that in order to deduct travel expenses, the taxpayer must substantiate "by adequate records or by sufficient evidence corroborating the taxpayer's own statement:" (1) the amount of the expense, (2) the time and place of travel, (3) the business purpose of the expense, and (4) the business relationship to the taxpayer of the persons entertained.

CASE STUDY 8.1 CONTINUED

Although Doug and Gina submitted credit card bills and certain receipts, at trial they had difficulty identifying which of the charges were incurred in connection with the timeshare activity. Section 162 of the IRC requires business expenses to be ordinary and necessary. At trial, Doug and Gina testified that she would "bribe her family to tour a timeshare by staying the night, usually at a lavish resort, and then going to the beach the next day." Due to their failure to substantiate expenses, and, apparently, the violation of the ordinary and necessary expense rule, the travel expenses were disallowed.

The IRS also contended that the timeshare activity was not engaged in for profit, implying that the hobby loss rules should apply. When an activity is classified as a hobby, losses can only be claimed to the extent of income generated by the activity.

The court considered the factors specified in the Treasury Regulations to determine whether the activity was a for-profit business enterprise, or a hobby. While Gina explained that she had been updating her business plan from the beginning by maintaining a spreadsheet of business activity, none of these documents were presented at trial.

The court referred to the business plan as "a fly-by-the-seat-of-the-pants experiment beginning when she decided to give 'it a whirl' and purchase one timeshare to see how the activity went." The court found that there was no evidence that petitioners ever studied the business of renting timeshare units or consulted with experts, that they did not devote a substantial amount of time to the timeshare activity (they were both employed full time in other businesses), there was no evidence submitted at trial that the activity was expected to appreciate in value, there was no evidence that they carried on any successful businesses similar to the timeshare activity, and that they had a series of losses associated with the activity. Consequently, the tax court classified the timeshare activity as a hobby activity, thereby limiting expenses to the extent of income produced by the activity.

Taxpayers who wish to be able to deduct losses associated with trade or business activity need to make sure they treat the activity in a businesslike manner, and should document their compliance with the factors specified in the Treasury Regulations that would classify the activity as a business. As Doug and Gina found out, successfully claiming losses associated with a "business" requires the activity to be classified as a business to begin with.

Treas. Reg. §1.183-2(b) provides nine factors that should be considered in determining whether or not a taxpayer has a profit motive, including:

1. The manner in which the taxpayer manages the activity
2. The time and effort spent in running the activity
3. The expertise of the taxpayer and the taxpayer's advisors
4. The taxpayer's success in similar activities
5. The taxpayer's history of profit/loss associated with the activity
6. The amount of occasional profits generated by the activity
7. The expectation that assets used in the business will increase in value
8. The financial status of the taxpayer
9. The extent to which personal pleasure or recreation dictates the taxpayer's involvement in the activity

IRC Section 183 sets forth a rebuttable presumption that an activity is engaged in for profit if the activity has generated a profit in three out of the last five years (two out of seven years for horse breeding, racing, or training). If the activity generates a profit for the required number of years, the burden of proof shifts to the IRS to show that the taxpayer did not have a profit motive. If the activity does not generate a profit for the required number of years, the taxpayer has the burden of proving that he or she has a profit motive for the activity.

Example 8.4

Blair, an avid baseball fan, started a baseball card trading activity. Blair's profit or loss for the activity for the past seven years is shown in the following table. Using the three out of five year "for profit activity" presumption, the third column indicates whether or not the burden of proof has shifted to the IRS to show the taxpayer does not have a profit motive.

Year	*Profit (loss)*	*Profit Motive Presumed*
1	$500	No
2	(1,500)	No
3	700	No
4	(1,000)	No
5	900	Yes, profit 3 of 5 years
6	(500)	No, profit only 2 of 5 years
7	1,200	Yes, profit 3 of 5 years

In Years 5 and 7, there is a rebuttable presumption that the activity has a profit motive. If the IRS can prove that Blair does not have a profit motive despite the presence of a profit in three out of the last five years, the activity will be classified as a hobby activity for Years 5 and 7.

When a taxpayer operating an activity has a profit motive, the activity is classified as a trade or business. Business expenses are deductible against the income of the business (above the line) even if the expenses exceed the income from the business (generating a loss). If the business is a passive activity, however, the loss may be suspended under the at-risk or passive activity loss rules, as discussed in Chapter 14.

When there is no profit motive and the activity is classified as a hobby, all of the hobby income must be included in gross income, and expenses associated with the activity cannot be deducted after 2017 (TCJA 2017).

Prior to TCJA 2017, many hobby activity expenses were deductible as miscellaneous itemized deductions subject to a two percent hurdle and only up to the extent of hobby income. Other hobby expenses, such as mortgage expense or property taxes were not subject to the two percent hurdle.

Key Concepts

1. Name the factors to be considered in determining whether a taxpayer has a profit motive.
2. Describe the rules for including hobby income related to a hobby activity.
3. Explain the three ways that a rental real estate activity can be classified for income tax purposes.
4. Describe the tax rules for each category of rental real estate activities.

Example 8.5

In 2021, Julio raises and sells toy poodles. This activity is motivated primarily by Julio's love of dogs, and has been classified as a hobby activity for income tax purposes. This year, the gross income from the activity was $20,000. Julio incurred the following expenses:

Interest	$6,000
Taxes	$3,000
Vet Bills	$6,000
Food & Treats	$5,000
Advertising	$2,000
Depreciation	$1,000
Total Expenses	**$23,000**

Since the activity has been classified as a hobby activity, Julio will not be able to deduct any of the $23,000 in expenses as hobby expenses. However, Julio may still be able to deduct taxes and interest as an itemized deduction. (TCJA 2017).

CASE STUDY 8.2

Hobby Losses

Alton F. Emerson, Petitioner v. Commissioner of Internal Revenue, Respondent. T.C. Memo 2000-137 (April 12, 2000).

The primary issue for decision in this case is whether petitioner's automobile drag racing activity was engaged in with the intent to make a profit.

At the time the petition was filed, Alton resided in Orlando, Florida. Alton timely filed his federal income tax returns in 1992, 1995, and 1996. On Schedule C, Profit and Loss From Business, of his 1995 tax return, Alton reported deductions of $70,428.52 from his automobile drag racing activity named Emerson Racing Enterprises. Alton reported no income from this activity, resulting in a $70,428.52 loss. Related to this loss in 1995, Alton carried back a $63,095 net operating loss deduction to taxable year 1992, which resulted in a refund to him of $11,579. At the end of 1995, Alton was age 57. In 1996, Alton reported nontaxable income of $50,628 as sick pay, $29,500 in total IRA distributions, and $39,506 in total pensions and annuities. Respondent determined that the $39,506 in total pensions and annuities was attributable to Alton's disability. Alton reported zero income or loss from the automobile drag racing activity in 1996.

On his 1996 return, Alton stated: This [automobile drag racing] activity, [sic] still in existence, is operating at a loss, but since there were no winnings, all expenses are being absorbed as if they were "hobby losses" and, as such, have no effect on Adjusted Gross Income. (Schedule 1). At the end of 1996, Alton was age 58.

CASE STUDY 8.2 CONTINUED

During the years in issue, Alton engaged in an automobile drag racing activity named Emerson Enterprise Racing. The only asset of Emerson Enterprise Racing was a race car purchased by Alton in 1994. Alton located his race car, a two-door batwing 1959 Chevy El Camino, by placing an advertisement in an Orlando, Florida, newspaper.

The previous owner of the car was a farmer who had stored the car in a barn. When Alton went to look at the car in the farmer's barn, it could barely run, but he decided to purchase it. By spending over $100,000 on the car during the years he engaged in this activity, Alton revamped the car into a bright red dragster that could legally be driven on streets as well as for racing. The car was featured on the front cover of two magazines in 1997, Hot Street Cars and Bracket Racing USA.

Alton raced automobiles when he was younger, but he had to discontinue the activity because it was too costly. Between 1992 and 1997, Alton lost over $150,000 on the automobile drag racing activity in this case. Alton did receive a small number of cash prize awards in the hundreds of dollars from the activity.

However, except for reporting $200 of winnings in 1994, Alton never reported any income from this activity on his tax returns. Alton maintained no written records related to races or how he had placed in any races. Alton did not maintain a separate checking account for this activity.

Alton had no business plan for his automobile drag racing activity and made no forecasts of income or expenses. Although he tried to find one, Alton had no sponsor or other financial backers to finance his activity. Alton stopped the racing activity in 1997 or 1998. Since his departure from racing, Alton has tried to sell his race car. Although Alton has over $100,000 invested in the race car, the highest offer he has received for the car is $20,000, which he rejected. Alton devoted about 40 hours per week to the automobile drag racing activity, which included working on the race car and racing the car two to three nights a week at a race track. Alton employed a mechanic on a contract labor basis to do some of the work on the race car.

During 1995 and 1996, Alton was retired/disabled and did not have any other employment. The only type of business or operating license required for racing was a drag strip license (NHRA license), which Alton does have. However, because of Alton's heart condition, his NHRA license has speed restrictions which limit his ability to drive his race car competitively. Because of the restrictions placed on Alton's NHRA license and his health condition, to have any chance of winning "the money races," Alton's son has had to drive petitioner's car.

Section 162(a) allows deductions for all the ordinary and necessary expenses paid or incurred during the taxable year in carrying on any trade or business. In the case of an activity not engaged in for profit, prior to 2018, Section 183 generally limited allowable deductions attributable to the activity to the extent of gross income generated by the activity. The test for determining whether an individual is carrying on an activity for profit is whether the taxpayer's actual and honest objective in engaging in the activity is to make a profit.

CASE STUDY 8.2 CONTINUED

While a taxpayer's expectation of profit need not be reasonable, there must be a good-faith expectation of making a profit.

Those factors include:

1. the manner in which the taxpayer carried on the activity
2. the expertise of the taxpayer or his advisors
3. the time and effort expended by the taxpayer in carrying on the activity
4. the expectation that assets used in the activity may appreciate in value
5. the success of the taxpayer in carrying on other similar or dissimilar activities
6. the taxpayer's history of income or loss with respect to the activity
7. the amount of occasional profit, if any, which is earned
8. the financial status of the taxpayer
9. whether elements of personal pleasure or recreation are involved

No single factor controls. The manner in which the taxpayer carries on the activity is one indication of a profit objective. Elements relevant to this factor include whether the taxpayer maintained complete and accurate books and records, whether the activity was conducted in a manner substantially similar to comparable businesses that are profitable, and whether changes were attempted in order to improve profitability. Alton maintained no written records. He had no business plan for his activity, and he made no predictions of income or expenses. Alton had no sponsor for the activity.

The court found that Alton did not operate the activity in a businesslike manner. Preparation for the start of an activity through extensive study of its accepted business, economic, and scientific practices, or consultation with those who are experts therein, indicates that a taxpayer has entered into an activity for profit. There is no evidence that the persons with whom petitioner consulted had made a profit in car racing or advised petitioner on how to make one, or that they were other than racing fans or hobbyists. Accordingly, the court found this factor did not help petitioner.

The time and effort expended by the taxpayer in carrying on the activity is an indication of whether a profit objective existed, petitioner devoted 40 hours a week to the activity. In spite of a serious heart condition, petitioner described competitively driving the race car as a stressful, exhilarating experience that he enjoyed repeating. Therefore, on balance, this factor neither supports nor detracts from Alton's position.

An expectation that assets used in the activity may appreciate in value may be an indication of a profit objective. During his involvement in the automobile drag racing activity, Alton spent over $100,000 on the sole asset of the activity. Petitioner thought that he might be able to sell the race car for $40,000 to $50,000. Therefore, Alton had no expectation that the race car would appreciate in value. Accordingly, this factor weighs against Alton.

CASE STUDY 8.2 CONTINUED

The success of the taxpayer in carrying on other activities can be some indication of whether the taxpayer had a profit. Alton raced automobiles when he was younger but had to discontinue the activity because it was too costly. Accordingly, this factor suggests that Alton did not engage in the activity for profit.

A history of income, losses, and occasional profits with respect to an activity can be indicative of whether a profit motive exists. During the years he operated the activity, Alton received only small cash awards; however, he spent over $150,000 on the activity, generating losses in each year, including the $70,428.52 loss Alton reported in 1995. Given Alton's record of losses, the court saw no possibility that he could recoup his expenditures. Therefore, the court found this factor weighed against him.

The lack of substantial income from sources other than the activity in question may indicate the existence of a profit objective. At trial, Alton stated that the automobile racing activity is "almost like gambling." To support his addiction to this activity, he withdrew $37,500 in IRA distributions prematurely. Alton had substantial income unrelated to the automobile racing activity. Accordingly, this factor does not favor him.

The absence of personal pleasure or recreation relating to the activity indicates the presence of a profit objective. There is no question that Alton enjoyed and obtained pleasure from his automobile drag racing activity. Although this factor standing alone does not indicate that he did not engage in this activity for profit, the combination of factors is fatal to Alton's case. On the basis of the record, the court found that Alton did not engage in the automobile drag racing activity for a profit. Accordingly, the IRS is sustained on this issue, and Alton is not allowed to deduct Schedule C expenses associated with this activity in 1995.

Rental of Vacation Homes

Many individuals accumulate wealth by investing in rental real estate. While the investment often does not produce immediate cash returns, the use of rent received to reduce mortgage balances plus appreciation on the real estate over time assist in the wealth accumulation process. Almost all rental real estate activities are passive activities and are subject to the passive activity loss rules covered in Chapter 14.

There are three ways that a rental real estate activity can be classified for income tax purposes:

1. as a nontaxable rental activity
2. as a "primarily rental use" activity
3. as a mixed-use rental activity

To determine whether a rental activity will be treated as a nontaxable rental activity, primarily rental use, or as mixed-use activity, a two part test is applied. The first test addresses the question of whether the real estate was rented for less than 15 days. If the property is rented for 14 days or less, the activity will be a **nontaxable rental activity** for income tax purposes. None of the income received from the rental activity will be included in income, and none of the expenses associated with the rental may be deducted. Note that this rule follows the general tax principal that states deductions are only permitted for items that have already been brought into a taxpayer's income. If no income is reported, no deductions should be allowed.

Example 8.6

Jasmine owns a vacation home on a famous golf course where a national tournament is played each year. The prize for winning is so large that the tournament attracts the world's best golfers on an annual basis. The tournament is sponsored by corporations, which use their sponsorship as a way to advertise their product or service and entertain potentially large clients. Each year, Jasmine rents her home on the golf course to Monopoly, Inc. for a 10-day period, and the rest of the time uses the house as a personal vacation residence. Monopoly, Inc. pays Jasmine $120,000 in rent for the use of the home. Since Jasmine rents the home for less than 15 days each year, she is not required to report the $120,000 in rental income received, but is not permitted to claim any expenses associated with the rental.

If real estate is rented for 15 days or more, a second test will determine the classification of the activity for federal income tax purposes. This question focuses on the personal use of the property by the owner. If the owner's personal use of the property does not exceed the greater of 14 days or 10 percent of the rental days, the activity will be classified as a **primarily rental use activity**. If the owner's personal use exceeds this threshold, then the activity is considered to be a **mixed-use rental activity**. When determining the number of days of personal use, use by family members who do not pay fair rental value are treated as personal use days. Family members include the spouse, ancestors, lineal descendants, and siblings of the owner.

Exhibit 8.1 | Classification of Rental Real Estate Activities

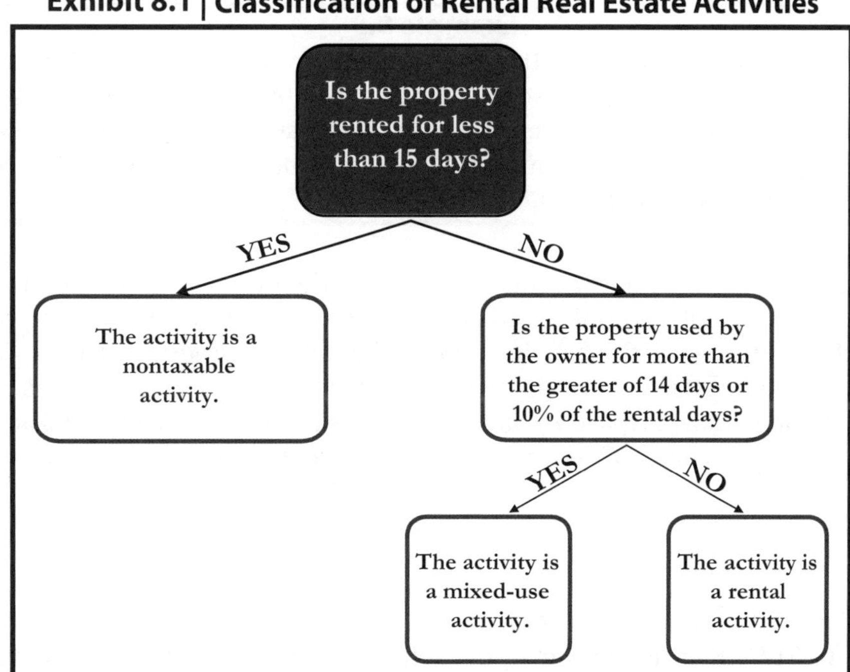

Example 8.7

Grady has a beach home that he rents for 180 days a year. Whether the activity is classified primarily as a rental activity or as a mixed-use activity will depend on Grady's personal use of the property. To be classified as a rental activity, Grady's personal use of the property cannot exceed the greater of 14 days or 10 percent of the rental days. Ten percent of the rental days in this example would be 18 days.

If Grady uses the property personally for 10 days during the year, the activity will be classified as a primarily rental activity.

If Grady uses the property personally for 18 days during the year, the activity is still classified primarily as a rental activity. While Grady's use exceeds the 14 day mark, it does not exceed 10 percent of the rental days, or 18 days.

If Grady uses the property personally for 25 days during the year, the activity will be classified as a mixed-use activity.

If the activity is classified as a nontaxable activity, the income is not reported but expenses may not be claimed. To the extent that the taxpayer makes mortgage interest or property tax payments on the property, however, those amounts can be claimed as personal expenses as itemized deductions. The taxpayer is not required to prorate mortgage interest and taxes between personal use and nondeductible rental use when the activity is classified as a nontaxable activity.

Example 8.8

Natalie owns a condo at the beach that is classified as a nontaxable activity. Natalie has mortgage interest of $15,000 and property taxes of $7,000 on the property this year. She can deduct the $15,000 as qualified mortgage interest, provided that she otherwise meets the requirements to deduct mortgage interest, and she will be allowed to deduct the full $7,000 of property taxes paid.

If the activity is classified as a primarily rental use activity, the taxpayer must report all of the income generated from the activity, but is permitted to deduct all ordinary, necessary, and reasonable expenses associated with the operation of the activity even if the activity produces a loss. The expenses for primarily rental use activities are above-the-line deductions, and directly offset the income from the activity. Typically (for individual taxpayers) the profit or loss from this type of rental activity is reported on Schedule E of Form 1040, and only the net profit or loss enters the taxpayer's gross income. While losses can be generated on a primarily rental use activity, they may not be currently deductible by the taxpayer due to the application of the at-risk rules and passive activity loss rules (covered in Chapter 14).

If the activity is classified as a mixed-use activity, the tax rules that apply are similar to the hobby loss rules prior to TCJA 2017. All of the income of the activity must be reported, but the taxpayer can only claim expenses in the current year to the extent of the income from the activity (stated differently, the activity cannot generate a loss above the line). The order in which deductions are taken matches the prior rules that applied to hobby losses. Expenses that are otherwise deductible ("Tier 1 expenses" such as mortgage interest and taxes) are claimed first, followed by other non-depreciation expenses ("Tier 2 expenses"), and finally depreciation or cost-recovery expenses ("Tier 3 expenses"). While the taxpayer may not be able to claim all of the expenses associated with the activity, mixed-use property is never subject to the passive loss limitations or the at-risk rules because it cannot generate a loss. However, if only a portion of the expenses that are otherwise deductible on schedule A (such as mortgage interest and taxes) can be taken against the income from the mixed-use property, then the remainder of those expenses, with some limitations, can be taken as itemized deductions, assuming the taxpayer itemizes. In such a case, total deductible expenses associated with the property may in fact exceed the income from the mixed-use property.

Mixed-use rental real estate activities differ from the old hobby loss rules in two ways. First, any disallowed rental expenses can be carried forward and deducted against income in future years (to the extent that the deduction of those expenses will not cause the activity to show a loss). Second, the expenses that are deductible are deducted directly against the income of the property, and are therefore above-the-line deductions. Other than itemized deductions such as mortgage interest or property taxes that would otherwise be deductible, hobby expenses are no longer deductible after 2017.

Expenses incurred in the operation of both mixed-use activities and primarily rental use activities must be allocated between personal and rental expenses. Only the rental expense portion is deductible.

The method of allocating mortgage interest and taxes is currently in dispute and has been for decades. The IRS requires the allocation of expenses to be based on the total days the property is used. For example, if the property is rented for 60 days, and personally used by the owner for 30 days, two thirds of mortgage interest and taxes must be allocated to the rental portion of the activity, and one third is allocated to the personal portion of the activity. By requiring this treatment, the IRS is attempting to skew the expenses into the rental portion, which may not give the taxpayer a current income tax benefit, since expenses can only be deducted to the extent of the income from the property. The courts, however, have allowed taxpayers to allocate certain expenses (such as real estate taxes and mortgage interest expenses) on a daily basis (with 365 days in the year). This approach tends to skew the expenses toward the personal use portion of the activity, which potentially allows the taxpayer to deduct the remaining portion of those expenses as itemized deductions. The taxpayer has the right to follow the court's ruling.

All other expenses (other than mortgage interest and taxes) associated with the mixed-use activity are allocated based on the total number of days that the property was used (the IRS approach). To the extent that expenses other than mortgage interest and taxes are allocated to the personal use portion of the activity, they are not deductible by the taxpayer.

Quick Quiz 8.2

1. Raising horses is not generally considered to be a hobby activity.
   a. True
   b. False
2. Hobby expenses are not deductible after 2017.
   a. True
   b. False
3. Real estate that is rented for 15 days per year is always a nontaxable activity.
   a. True
   b. False
4. Mixed-use rental activities are not subject to the passive loss limitations or the at-risk rules.
   a. True
   b. False

False, True, False, True.

Example 8.9

Garette rents his beach condo 60 days and uses the condo personally for 30 days. The income and expenses are as follows:

Rental Income	$8,000
Mortgage Interest	$5,000
Taxes	$10,000
Utilities	$1,200
Condo Association Fees	$6,000
Depreciation	$2,000

The IRS Position on Mixed-Use Property

Form 1040 Schedule E for Rental Property		
*Rental Income & Expenses**		
Rental Income	$8,000	
Expenses		
Mortgage Interest	$3,333	(60/90) x $5,000
Taxes	$6,667	(60/90) x $10,000
Utilities	$800	(60/90) x $1,200
Association Fees	$4,000	(60/90) x $6,000

** Interest and taxes would be limited to $8,000, the total income. Utilities and Association fees would not be deductible, nor would any depreciation. The remaining mortgage interest and taxes may be deductible on Schedule A, if itemized.*

Personal Expenses Deductible as Itemized Deductions		
Mortgage Interest	$1,667	Possible Deduction as Itemized Deduction
Taxes	$3,333	Possible Deduction as Itemized Deduction
Utilities	$1,003	Not Deductible
Condo Association Fees	$4,014	Not Deductible

* * *

The Current Tax Court's Position on Mixed-Use Property

Rental Income & Expenses		
Rental Income	$8,000	
Expenses		
Mortgage Interest	$822	60/365 x $5,000
Taxes	$1,644	60/365 x $10,000
Utilities	$800	60/90 x $1,200
Association Fees	$4,000	60/90 x $6,000
Depreciation	$1,333	60/90 x $2,000
Net Income	**($599)***	

** Expenses would be limited to $8,000. Therefore, $599 of depreciation expenses would not be deductible.*

Personal Expenses Deductible as Itemized Deductions		
Mortgage Interest (Balance)	$4,178	Possible Deduction as Itemized Deduction
Taxes (Balance)	$8,356	Possible Deduction as Itemized Deduction
Utilities		Not Deductible
Condo Association Fees		Not Deductible

Comparing the IRS method and the courts' method of allowing rental real estate income and expenses, the IRS method results in the taxpayer having no net rental income. In addition, the IRS method results in personal itemized deductions of $5,000.

Using the courts' method, the taxpayer has no net rental income and personal itemized deductions of $12,534. Clearly, the courts' position is more favorable to the taxpayer in this instance.

Recall from Chapter 7 that the TCJA 2017 limits the deduction for state and local property and sales taxes, and state and local income taxes, paid by a taxpayer to a total of $10,000 ($5,000 for married taxpayers filing separately) for tax years 2018 through 2025. This limitation could impact the deductibility of real estate taxes for mixed use property or property not used in the production of income.

Exhibit 8.2 | Home Ownership Classification for Income Tax Purposes

- Personal residence
- Second home
- Vacation home (rental less than 15 days) or non-taxable rental activity
- Mixed-use vacation home (>14 days of rental; personal use more than the greater of 14 days or 10% of rental days)
- Rental homes (>14 days of rental; personal use less than the greater of 14 days or 10% rental days)

Expenditures

Unless otherwise provided in the IRC, personal expenses are not deductible. Most itemized deductions, and some adjustments to income (such as student loan interest), are personal expenses that Congress has permitted taxpayers to deduct to further policy goals. For example, Congress considers home ownership to be a worthy goal, so it allows taxpayers to deduct mortgage interest and real estate taxes paid on their personal residence and one vacation home. Ownership of a personal residence is not active conduct of a trade or business or an activity entered into for profit, so without the special exception in the IRC, expenses associated with home ownership would not be deductible.

SPECIFIC DEDUCTIONS

This section of the chapter will address limitations on the following specific deductions:

- Bad debts
- Worthless securities
- Section 1244 stock
- Losses of individuals
- Research and experimental expenditures
- Net operating losses
- Depreciation

Bad Debts

The tax benefits and classification of bad debts depends on whether the bad debt is a business or personal bad debt.

Business bad debts are only deducted if the taxpayer uses the accrual method of accounting. If the business is a cash-basis taxpayer, income would not have been reported if it was not received. One of the general rules of income taxation is that deductions can only be taken for amounts brought into income, so if the taxpayer is a cash-basis taxpayer, no income would have been reported and no deduction will be permitted.

Example 8.10

Sondra is a CPA. She prepared Elvin's tax return and sent him a $2,000 bill for the work. Elvin refused to pay because it took Sondra eight months to complete the return. Elvin has since disappeared. If Sondra is an accrual-basis taxpayer, she includes the $2,000 in income upon the completion of the tax return then writes it off when she discovers that she cannot collect. If Sondra is a cash-basis taxpayer, she does nothing because she has not yet recognized the $2,000 as income.

CASE STUDY 8.3

Bad Debt Expenses

Todd A. and Carolyn D. Dagres, Petitioners v. Commissioner of Internal Revenue, Respondent, 136 T.C. No. 12 (March 28, 2011).

Todd is a manager of Venture Capital Funds. In 2000, he made a loan of $5 million to Mr. Schrader, a business associate, who provided leads on companies in which the Venture Capital funds might invest. The loan was re-negotiated in 2002, and Mr. Schrader stopped making payments in 2003. In settlement of the debt, Mr. Schrader transferred some securities to Todd in 2003. Todd claimed a $3,635,218 business bad debt deduction on his 2003 income tax return. The IRS issued a notice of deficiency for 2003, disallowing the deduction as a business bad debt, and assessing $981,980 in income tax plus an accuracy related penalty of $196,369. The IRS claimed that "the debt was a non-business bad debt because it was a personal loan and not created in connection with your trade or business... accordingly, taxable income is increased by $3,635,218." While the IRS did not completely disallow the loss, the notice of deficiency attempted to classify it as a personal bad debt, which would be treated as a short term capital loss, resulting in no tax benefit to Todd in 2003.

The court held that since Todd was in the trade or business of managing Venture Capital Funds, his bad debt loss was proximately related to that trade or business, and therefore the loss on the loan qualifies as a business bad debt deduction under IRC §166(a). The court considered the loan proximately related to Todd's trade or business because his "dominant motivation for lending $5 million to Mr. Shrader was to gain preferential access to companies and deals to which Mr. Schrader might refer him, so that ... [Todd] could use that information in the Venture Capital activities." Since the dominant motivation for the loan was business related, the debt could be classified as a business bad debt (and, therefore, could be deducted in full against other income) as opposed to a personal bad debt (which is required to be treated as a short term capital loss, subject to the $3,000 loss limitation rule for a given tax year).

Example 8.11

MedCare Clinic is an accrual basis taxpayer and has a $10,000 receivable from a drug company. The drug company files for bankruptcy and the clinic now expects to recover only $1,000 of the outstanding balance ($0.10 on the dollar) next year. The clinic can deduct $9,000 this year. If they only collect $500 next year instead of the expected $1,000 then they can deduct the additional $500 next year.

Businesses that use the accrual method of accounting report income when it is earned (when all events necessary to earn the income have been performed), not when it is received. Accrual method taxpayers may deduct bad debts to offset income reported but not received.

Most businesses are required to use the specific charge-off method, which allows the business to deduct the bad debt as an ordinary loss in the year in which the debt becomes partially or wholly worthless. An ordinary loss deduction is allowed, since accrual accounting subjected the income earned but not received to ordinary income tax in the year in which the income was reported. The only way to offset this ordinary income inclusion is to allow an ordinary loss deduction.

Some businesses (such as financial institutions) are permitted to use the **reserve method** of bad debt deductions, allowing them to take a bad debt deduction based on a percentage of accounts receivable representing the historical percentage of accounts that go bad. Naturally, any difference between actual bad debts and the bad debt reserve are reconciled.

If the bad debt is classified as a nonbusiness bad debt, the **specific charge-off method** must be used. A nonbusiness bad debt deduction is allowed only when the debt becomes wholly worthless, and is always treated as a short-term capital loss. No deduction is permitted for partial worthlessness when the debt is a nonbusiness bad debt.

Key Concepts

1. Describe the circumstances under which bad debts are deductible.
2. Explain the rules for taking a loss on a worthless security.
3. Describe the special tax treatment available for Section 1244 stock.
4. Explain the net operating loss rules.

Worthless Securities

On occasion (hopefully not too often), an investor will purchase a security that later becomes worthless. Taxpayers are entitled to take a loss on a security that becomes worthless during the taxable year. IRC Section 165 creates an artificial sale date on the last day of the taxable year in which the security becomes worthless. For most taxpayers, since they are cash basis taxpayers, the artificial sale date will be December 31. Fiscal year taxpayers may have a different artificial sale date.

The impact of the artificial sale date is to classify the loss as a long-term loss unless the taxpayer either purchased the investment in the same year that it became worthless, or purchased it on the last day of the tax year preceding the security becoming worthless (a holding period of exactly one year is not considered long-term).

Example 8.12

Theo, an avid reader, purchased common stock in Jane Austin Industries, Inc. on February 1 of this year. On August 30 of this year, the company announces that it is filing Chapter 7 bankruptcy and that the common shareholders should not expect to receive anything on liquidation of the corporation. Since the stock became worthless during the year, there will be a constructive sale of the stock on December 31, and Theo will be able to claim the amount he invested (his basis) as a loss deduction this year. The loss will be a short-term capital loss, since he held the stock for less than a year as of the artificial sale date.

Example 8.13

Vanessa purchased common stock in Satellite Television, Inc. on December 31 of last year. On August 30 of this year, the stock became worthless. A constructive sale will occur on December 31 of this year, and Vanessa will be able to claim the amount she invested (her basis) as a loss deduction this year. The loss will be a short-term capital loss, since she held the stock for exactly one year (not more than one year) on the date of the artificial sale.

Example 8.14

Rashad purchased 100 shares of Yankees Inc. on October 1 of last year. Unfortunately, Yankees Inc. has had some trouble, and became worthless on March 1 of this year. A constructive sale will occur on December 31 of this year, and Rashad will be able to claim the amount he invested (his basis) as a loss deduction this year. The loss will be a long-term capital loss, since he is deemed to have held the stock for more than one year as of the artificial valuation date. If Rashad was able to take the loss based on the day that Yankees Inc. shares became worthless, he would have been able to classify the loss as a short-term capital loss, which would potentially offset higher taxed income (recall that short-term capital gains are taxed at ordinary income tax rates, while the maximum long-term capital gains rate is 20%).

In the Yankees, Inc. example above, note that the tax benefits of the transaction may be affected by the creation of an artificial sales date. As a practical matter, some brokers will allow clients to sell worthless securities for a penny to book the transaction as a sale. While the client will not receive any cash from the transaction, the sale occurs on the actual trade date instead of on the artificial trade date presumed under IRC Section 165. Selling the worthless security in a book transaction can, in certain circumstances, allow the taxpayer to categorize the loss as a short-term capital loss.

Example 8.15

Use the same facts as the prior example, with the exception that, on September 15, Rashad sold the shares of Yankees, Inc. for a penny through his broker. When Rashad completes his tax return, he will show a short-term capital loss for Yankees, Inc. since he did not hold the shares for more than one year as of the sale date, September 15 of this year. If Rashad had other short-term capital gains this year, the loss of Yankees, Inc. would offset those short-term capital gains taxed at ordinary tax rates, generating a larger tax benefit for Rashad compared to using the loss to offset long-term capital gains taxed at the 20% rate.

CASE STUDY 8.4

Wash Sale and Worthless Securities

Stephen and Ann Schwalbach, Petitioners v. Commissioner of Internal Revenue, Respondent. 111 T.C. No. 9 (September 8, 1998).

Stephen Schwalbach (Dr. Schwalbach) practiced dentistry in River Falls. He was employed full time by Associated Dentists of River Falls, f.k.a. River Falls Dental Association (Associated Dentists), a personal service corporation that he owned equally with another dentist named Timothy Knotek.

On June 21, 1993, Dr. Schwalbach paid $16,050 for a 5/6 interest in 6,000 shares of stock in a corporation named Impression Delivery Corp. (Impression); the total purchase price was $19,266. Approximately three weeks later, the 6,000 shares were sold for $7,374, and six days after the sale, Dr. Schwalbach purchased an interest in another 4,100 shares of Impression. The Schwalbachs did not recognize a loss in 1993 on the sale of the stock because his CPA considered the purchase-sale-purchase as a "wash sale" under §1091. In 1994, the Schwalbachs, upon the advice of the CPA, reported a short-term capital loss of $16,050 on their 1994 Schedule D, Capital Gains and Losses, with respect to Impression's stock. The CPA rendered his advice after ascertaining that Impression had ceased operations and was facing litigation over allegedly fraudulent practices.

The IRS disallowed the $16,050 loss reported by the Schwalbachs. According to the notice of deficiency, "It has not been established that the company known as Impression Delivery Corp. was insolvent or out of business in the year 1994.

Further, it has not been established that you had an adjusted basis in this company in order to claim this loss." The Schwalbachs ultimately conceded that they may not deduct this loss for 1994.

The burden of proving that a security is worthless falls on the taxpayer. Generally, a taxpayer must establish that the securities had value at the beginning of the tax year, that the securities became worthless during the year and that there was an identifiable event that caused the worthlessness.

Section 1244 Stock

Much of the economic growth experienced in the United States is due to the operation of small businesses. Small businesses are riskier than larger businesses from an investment perspective, since they are often subject to strict competition and have an unproven business track record.

To encourage investment in small business enterprises, Congress enacted Section 1244 of the IRC, which allows the first $50,000 of losses ($100,000 for taxpayers who are married filing jointly), per year, on Section 1244 stock to be classified as an ordinary loss instead of a capital loss. Any additional loss incurred on the stock would still qualify as a capital loss. Section 1244 only applies to losses, not gains, so any gains on the sale of the stock will still be taxed at the favorable capital gains tax rate.

To qualify for this special tax treatment, the loss must be incurred by a shareholder who purchased the stock directly from the company when the company had $1 million or less in capitalization (money and other property received in exchange for its stock).

Example 8.16

Rudy purchased a 20% interest in Advertising Specialty Products, Inc. (ASP) for $150,000 when the company was first formed, which was held in a joint account with her husband. Rudy is married to Kenny, and they file a joint income tax return. Things have not been going well for ASP, and Rudy decides to sell her stock. She is able to find a buyer who pays her $25,000 for the stock. Upon sale of the stock, Rudy realizes a $125,000 loss. $100,000 of this loss can be deducted directly against ordinary income, and the remaining $25,000 will be treated as a capital loss. Assuming that Rudy has no other capital gains or losses in the current year, her AGI is reduced by $103,000 (comprised of the $100,000 deduction from ordinary income, plus the $3,000 loss deduction from the capital loss). The remaining $22,000 of capital loss must be carried forward and deducted against income in future years.

Losses of Individuals

The only losses that an individual can deduct are those incurred in a trade or business, incurred in a transaction entered into for profit, or specifically allowed by the IRC (i.e., casualty losses).

Personal losses are typically not deductible. Since personal losses are incurred in a transaction where the government is not intended to be a partner (due to the revenue sharing that occurs through the income tax system), those losses are usually disallowed (the exception is casualty losses). Losses are usually allowed only when a taxpayer engages in an activity designed to generate taxable income.

Example 8.17

At the peak of the real estate market, Cliff purchased a large personal residence with a jumbo mortgage. To afford the home, he took out a variable interest-only loan, with a balloon payment due in seven years (he had planned to refinance the loan at that time). Unfortunately, real estate prices have dropped, mortgage interest rates have climbed, and Cliff can no longer afford to make the mortgage payments. The bank foreclosed on the home, and Cliff suffered a $200,000 loss. Despite the loss of $200,000 in capital, Cliff is not entitled to a tax deduction, since the loss was incurred on the sale (or, in this case, other disposition) of a personal asset.

When an individual taxpayer experiences a personal loss on real estate, the taxpayer will often seek to find a way to transform that personal loss (which would not be deductible) into a tax deductible loss. For example, the taxpayer may attempt to turn a personal residence into a rental property, hoping that when the rental property is sold, the loss on the property will be deductible against other income on the taxpayer's tax return. Unfortunately, Congress and the IRS anticipated this type of loss planning, and imposed a special rule that may limit the deductible loss available when personal property is converted to rental property. At the time of conversion, the lesser of (1) the taxpayer's basis in the property, or (2) the fair market value of the property on the date of conversion will be the value upon which depreciation deductions may be taken, and will be the value that is used to determine the tax deductible loss upon sale of the property. [2]

Example 8.18

At the height of the real estate market, Claire changed jobs and purchased a home for $1,500,000 in a new state. Two years later, Claire lost her job and will have to relocate again, out of state, requiring her to sell her home. Unfortunately, the fair market value of Claire's home (based on comparable home sales in the area) is now $1,100,000. Claire realizes that if she sells the home, which was a personal use asset, she will not be able to deduct the $400,000 loss. Claire thought long and hard about her predicament, and decides to move out immediately and rent the home for a few months before selling it so that she can transform the $400,000 loss she experienced into a tax deductible loss (a loss on a production of income property).

Unfortunately, Claire cannot transform the loss that occurred during her personal use of the home into a tax-deductible loss. The starting point for calculating depreciation deductions on the rental activity, and calculating loss on the sale of the converted home, will be the lower of her cost basis ($1,500,000) or the fair market value of the home at the time of conversion ($1,100,000). Therefore, the starting point for Claire is $1,100,000.

If she rents the home for six months, and then sells it for $1 million, Claire's loss will be equal to $100,000 (calculated by subtracting the sale price of $1 million from the starting point of $1,100,000 and ignoring any adjustments necessary for depreciation taken and depreciation recapture). The $400,000 loss that occurred before Claire transformed the home into a rental activity was incurred during her personal use of the home, and is therefore not deductible for income tax purposes. The additional loss that Claire suffered after converting the home into a rental activity is deductible, since that loss was incurred while the property was being used for the production of income.

---

2. Treas. Reg. §1.165-9(b)(2) and 1.167(g)-1.

CASE STUDY 8.5

Car Accidents & Casualty Losses

Robert K.K. and Doris K. Pang, Petitioners v. Commissioner of Internal Revenue, Respondent, T.C. Memo 2011-55 (March 9, 2011).

In 2002, Robert struck and killed a pedestrian with his car. In 2004, he paid the pedestrian's estate $250,000 (above and beyond the amount paid by his insurance company) in settlement of a wrongful death lawsuit, and claimed the settlement payment (in excess of 10% of his adjusted gross income plus the $100 co-insurance amount) as a casualty loss on his 2004 Income Tax Return. The IRS disallowed the casualty loss deduction, and assessed a deficiency of $64,969.

Citing prior precedent, the Tax Court stated that "this court has consistently held that settlement payments which result from automobile accidents do not constitute deductible casualty losses." Robert asserted at trial that the payment is deductible as a casualty loss because Webster's Dictionary defines "casualty" as "[l]osses caused by death, wound" and the accident victim's death, therefore, was certainly a casualty. Unfortunately for Robert, the tax court determined that Webster's definition of casualty was not determinative; rather, it was the definition of casualty provided for in the IRC. Referring to other cases, the tax court stated that "the term 'losses of property' does not include a taxpayer's monetary payment to a third party or a decrease in the taxpayer's net worth."

Research and Experimental Expenditures

Businesses often incur costs for the development of products, processes, and formulas that can be used to generate a profit. These expenses are incurred to increase future profit or produce income, and are considered to be ordinary, necessary, and reasonable business expenses.

In tax years prior to 2022, there are three methods that can be used to deduct research and experimental costs. First, the expenses can be deducted in the year paid or incurred. Often, this is the most favorable choice, since it gives the company an immediate tax deduction for research costs. Second, the expenses can be amortized over a five year (60 month) period. Finally, the expenses can be capitalized (added to basis), and can be deducted when the project is abandoned or becomes worthless.

Alternatively, a tax credit of up to 20 percent of certain research and experimental costs may be available.

Specified Research and Experimental Expenses After 2021

For tax years beginning on or after January 1, 2022, specified research and experimental (R&E) expenses can no longer be deducted in the year paid or incurred. Instead, research and development expenses must be amortized over 60 months (5 years) if the research and development is conducted in the United States. For research and development costs conducted outside the United States, the amortization period will be 15 years. Any remaining basis when the property is retired, abandoned, or disposed of will not be recovered in that year; however, amortization will continue through the remaining amortization period.

Specified R&E expenses include any expenses for the development of computer software. Expenses incurred for the acquisition or improvement of land and exploration expenses for ore, oil, gas, or other minerals continue to be excluded from the definition of R&E expenses.

Net Operating Losses

When trade or business activities generate higher expenses than income in a given year, a **net operating loss** (NOL) results. A taxpayer can trigger NOLs by generating deductions for his or her trade or business or production of income activities (such as rental real estate), employee-related business expenses, personal casualty or theft losses, moving expenses, or foreign government confiscations of property.

Prior to 2018, NOLs for one tax year would be taken as a deduction (for AGI, or above-the-line) against income from prior and future tax years. NOLs incurred prior to 2018 could be carried back two years and forward 20 years. The TCJA eliminated the ability to carry back NOLs, except for a narrow provision for farmers. After 2017, NOLs can generally only be carried forward, but they there is no longer a 20-year limitation. Instead, NOLs can be carried forward indefinitely, but the use of NOL deduction is limited to 80 percent of the taxpayer's taxable income for any one year.

Prior to 2018, taxpayers could elect to waive the carryback period and simply carry forward a NOL. This election remains an option for farmers. However, after 2017, most taxpayers are no longer permitted to carryback NOLs.

When NOLs were able to be carried back to prior tax years, there would be a change in the AGI for those years. This change in the taxpayer's AGI would often impact the available credits or deductions available to the taxpayer. For example, a taxpayer might be able to take an IRA deduction after the NOL carryback, where as it may not have been available prior to the NOL carryback. NOLs carried forward to future years also impact the availability of credits and deductions for taxpayers.

The CARES Act temporarily reinstated a 5-year Net Operating Loss Carryback provision and eliminated the 80 percent of taxable income limitation for tax years beginning after December 31, 2017 and before January 1, 2021 (covering tax years 2018-2020). While the carryback provision will not apply for tax years beginning on or after January 1, 2021, taxpayers who experienced net operating losses in tax years 2018 through 2020 may wish to consider carrying back those losses by amending prior year tax returns. This may be particularly useful to the taxpayer if their marginal income tax rate in prior years covered by the NOL carryback exceeds their marginal income tax rate in the current year. The temporary extension of the NOL carryback rules by the CARES Act does not apply to Net Operating Losses incurred by real estate investment trusts (REITs).

Quick Quiz 8.3

1. If a debt is a nonbusiness debt, a bad debt deduction will only be allowed when the debt becomes wholly worthless.
   a. True
   b. False

2. IRC Section 165 creates an artificial sale date for worthless securities.
   a. True
   b. False

3. Section 1244 is intended to discourage investment in small businesses.
   a. True
   b. False

4. After 2020, net operating losses can be carried forward, but cannot generally be carried back.
   a. True
   b. False

True, True, False, True.

Loss Limitation for Individuals

In addition to providing a deduction for flow-through entities, TCJA 2017 limits certain taxpayer losses after 2017. For taxable years beginning after December 31, 2017 and before January 1, 2026, excess business losses of a taxpayer other than a corporation are not allowed for the taxable year. Such losses must be carried forward and treated as part of the taxpayer's net operating loss ("NOL") carryforward in subsequent taxable years.

An excess business loss for the taxable year is the excess of aggregate deductions of the taxpayer attributable to trades or businesses of the taxpayer, over the sum of aggregate gross income or gain of the taxpayer plus a threshold amount. The threshold amount for a taxable year is $262,000 (or $524,000 in the case of a joint return). The threshold amount is indexed for inflation and applies after the application of the passive loss rules.

Example 8.19

Malcolm, who is single, has $1 million of income from XYZ partnership. The same year, he starts a boat business (BB), in which he is an active participant. The only activity for BB is the purchase of a boat for $1 million, for which 100% bonus deprecation is taken. As a result, he has $1 million of income from XYZ and $1 million of loss from BB. The income and loss offset one another under these rules.

Example 8.20

In 2021, Malcolm, who is single, has $1 million of W-2 income from ABC Inc., where he works as an engineer. The same year, he starts a boat business (BB), in which he is an active participant. The only activity for BB is the purchase of a boat for $1 million, for which 100% bonus deprecation is taken. As a result, he has $1 million of W-2 income from ABC and $1 million of loss from BB. The loss limitation rules limit the loss from BB to $262,000, which means that Malcolm will have $738,000 ($1,000,000 less $262,000) of income for the year. The remainder of the loss from BB will be treated as part of his NOL and carried forward to subsequent years. However, the NOL can only offset up to 80% of taxable income.

The CARES Act suspended the limitation on excess business losses for tax years 2018 through 2020, allowing losses incurred during those years to be deducted without limitation. For tax years beginning after December 31, 2020 and before January 1, 2026, excess business losses are not allowed and are instead treated as a net operating loss carryforward.

Depreciation

Depreciation represents the portion of an asset placed in service in a trade or business that is used up in the conduct of business for that year. When assets are purchased for business or production of income purposes, the taxpayer is entitled to recoup the cost of that asset over its useful life, so that the cost can presumably be reinvested in replacement assets that will generate more income for the company. Depreciation, therefore, is a form of cost recovery.

The method of depreciation used depends on the type of asset purchased, as well as elections that the taxpayer is entitled to make. When a depreciable asset is sold, the depreciation deductions taken may be subject to recapture to the extent that the asset was depreciated for tax purposes at a rate greater than the actual decline in the value of the asset. More detailed information on depreciation and depreciation recapture is covered in Chapters 10 and 12.

Exhibit 8.3 | Summary of Specific Deductions

Bad Debts	If business debt and accrual method taxpayer, ordinary loss. If personal, specific write off and short-term capital loss.
Worthless Securities	Assumed worthless at year-end of realization.
Section 1244 Stock	$100,000 ordinary loss for married filing jointly, excess is capital loss ($50,000 for single filers).
Losses of Individuals	Not deductible except as casualty loss.
Research and Experimental Expenditures	For tax years prior to 2022, expenses can be deducted in year paid, amortized over 60 months, or capitalized. Beginning in 2022, expenses can no longer be deducted in year paid; R&D conducted in the U.S. must be amortized over 60 months; R&D conducted outside the U.S. must be amortized over 15 years.
Net Operating Losses	Generally, carry forward indefinitely (after 2020).
Depreciation	Ratably written off.

PENALTIES

In addition to the penalties that may be incurred for failure to file an income tax return, failure to pay the tax due, and taking unreasonable positions on returns or in tax court actions, three additional penalties apply directly to pension plan and IRA contributions and accumulations: the excess contributions penalty, the early distribution penalty, and the late distribution penalty.

Exhibit 8.4 | Retirement Plan Penalties

- Excess Contributions
- Early Distributions
- Late Distributions

Excess Contributions Penalty

While Congress views saving for retirement as a worthy goal, contributing too much to retirement plans can generate a tax penalty. Retirement plans and IRAs give the taxpayer the ability to make tax-deductible contributions to the plan that directly reduces the taxpayer's taxable income in the current tax year. To prevent taxpayers from contributing excessive amounts to pension plans and IRAs in an effort to avoid current tax liability, Congress has set contribution limits that vary based on the type of pension plan or IRA being used. Under IRC Section 4973(a), excess contributions made to IRAs will be subject to a six percent excise tax, and the excess contribution must be distributed from the plan.

Typically, the excess contribution amount is applied to the subsequent year contribution instead of forcing a distribution from the plan. To avoid the imposition of the six percent excise tax, the taxpayer should withdraw the excess (or allocate it to the contribution for the next tax year) by the due date of their income tax return, including extensions. Any withdrawal to reverse out an excess contribution must include the income earned on the excess contribution while inside the IRA, so taxpayers should take action quickly to avoid potential income taxation on additional growth.

Employers sponsoring certain types of retirement plans, such as SEPs, SIMPLEs, 401(k) plans, 403(b) plans, defined contribution profit sharing plans and defined benefit plans, are subject to a ten percent excess contributions penalty unless exceptions apply.

Early Distribution Penalty

Due to the tax benefits (a tax deduction and tax-deferral) received for contributions to pension plans and IRAs, Congress wants to encourage taxpayers to use the plan for its intended purpose – funding retirement. If the taxpayer takes a distribution from a qualified retirement plan or IRA prior to age 59½, a 10 percent excise tax applies to the taxable amount of the distribution (the entire amount is usually taxable). The 10 percent excise tax is imposed in addition to any tax incurred due to the inclusion of the distribution in the taxable income of the taxpayer. A special early distribution penalty applies to SIMPLE plans. If an early distribution is taken from a SIMPLE plan within two years of the date the taxpayer first participated in the plan, a 25 percent penalty applies to the distribution in addition to the regular income tax liability incurred as a result of the distribution.

Key Concepts

1. Describe the penalties applicable to pension plan and IRA contributions and distributions.
2. Describe the two types of temporary loss disallowance.
3. Describe the three types of permanent loss disallowance.

There are several exceptions to the 10 percent early distribution penalty. Whether or not a particular exception applies depends on the type of plan from which the distribution is made. Some exceptions apply to qualified plans only, some to qualified plans and IRAs, and some to IRAs only.

There are three exceptions to the early distribution penalty that apply only to qualified plans:

1. Distributions to an employee who separates from service after age 55.
2. Public safety employee separated from service after age 50.
3. Distributions made in accordance with a Qualified Domestic Relations Order (QDRO) or state order distribution under divorce (which splits plan benefits in the event of a divorce).

Qualified plan participants who take advantage of early retirement can begin to take distributions from the plan (on separation from service) at age 55 (or at age 50 if they are qualified public safety employees) without fear of the early distributions penalty.

Three exceptions to the early distribution penalty apply only to IRAs. These include:

1. Distributions to pay for health insurance for unemployed taxpayers.
2. Distributions to pay for qualified higher education expenses of the taxpayer, spouse, or dependents.
3. Distributions of up to $10,000 (lifetime maximum) for the first-time purchase of a home. A first-time home buyer is defined as a person who had not owned a home in the prior two tax years.

The remaining exceptions apply to both qualified plans and IRAs. These exceptions include:

1. Substantially equal periodic distributions under IRC Section 72(t).
2. Distributions made as a result of the disability of the taxpayer.
3. Distributions made by reason of the death of the taxpayer.
4. Distributions necessary to cover unreimbursed medical expenses that exceed 7.5 percent of the taxpayer's AGI.
5. Distributions due to an IRS levy to collect taxes due.
6. Qualified distributions of up to $5,000 for a birth or adoption. A distribution for birth or adoption is qualified if it is made within one year following the birth or date of adoption of an individual who has not attained age 18 or who is physically or mentally incapable of supporting him/herself.
7. Distributions to military reservists while serving on active duty for at least 180 days.

The 10 percent early distribution penalty also applies to distributions from non-qualified annuity contracts that are made before the annuitant reaches age 59½.

Exhibit 8.5 | Summary of 10 Percent Penalty Exceptions for Qualified Plans and IRAs

Applies to Distributions from:	*Exception to 10% Early Withdrawal Penalty*
Both Qualified Plans & IRAs	Death
Both Qualified Plans & IRAs	Attainment of age 59½
Both Qualified Plans & IRAs	Disability
Both Qualified Plans & IRAs	Substantially equal periodic payments (§72(t))
Both Qualified Plans & IRAs	Medical expenses that exceed 10% of AGI (7.5% for 2020 and 2021)
Both Qualified Plans & IRAs	Tax levy
Both Qualified Plans & IRAs	Qualified distribution of up to $5,000 for a birth or adoption
Both Qualified Plans & IRAs	Distributions to reservists while serving on active duty for at least 180 days.
Only Qualified Plans	QDRO or state order under divorce*
Only Qualified Plans	Attainment of age 55 and separation from service
Only Qualified Plans	Public safety employee separated from service after age 50
Only IRAs	Higher education expenses
Only IRAs	First time home purchase (up to $10,000)
Only IRAs	Health insurance for unemployed

**Where there is a distribution at divorce and the payee is under 59½, the use of a QDRO directed distribution will result in a taxable event but will not incur the 10% early withdrawal penalty. Under the same circumstances, except that the distribution is from an IRA, the result is both a taxable event and the application of the 10% early withdrawal penalty. However, the payee in any case can choose to rollover the distribution in which case, the rollover rules would apply or the payee can take substantially equal periodic payments under §72(t).*

Late Distribution Penalty

Congress views late distributions from pension plans and IRAs as a more serious problem than early distributions or excess contributions to plans, since late distributions defer the taxation of plan benefits. Individuals who are required to take distributions from retirement plans and IRAs (due to the imposition of the required minimum distribution rules) but fail to do so are subject to a 50 percent penalty. The required minimum distribution rules (RMDs) are found in Treas. Reg. §§1.401(a)(9) and 1.408-8. Additional information on RMDs may also be obtained in IRS Publication 590, available at www.irs.gov and in Retirement Planning and Employee Benefits.[3] Minimum distributions are required by April 1 of the year following the year in which the taxpayer reaches age 70½ (for taxpayers who attain the age of 70½ by December 31, 2019) or 72 (for taxpayers who attain the age of 70½ after December 31, 2019). The minimum distribution penalty may be waived if the taxpayer received erroneous advice from an advisor to the pension plan, or if the taxpayer can demonstrate that he or she acted in good faith when attempting to apply the RMD rules.

OTHER LOSS DISALLOWANCES – TEMPORARY AND PERMANENT

There are a number of other types of losses that may be either temporarily or permanently disallowed. Each of the following types of losses is discussed more extensively later in this text, but it is appropriate to mention them briefly in this chapter. The following chart references the chapter in which a full discussion of each of these topics can be found.

Exhibit 8.6 | Loss Disallowance Cross References

Section 1031 Exchanges	Chapter 13
Wash Sales	Chapter 11
Related Party Transactions	Chapter 11
Gifts Below FMV	Chapter 11
Sale of Personal Assets	Chapter 11

Section 1031 Exchanges Resulting in a Loss are Not Immediately Deductible

When like-kind assets are exchanged under Section 1031, no gain or loss is recognized in the transaction. The loss is not permanently disallowed; it is deferred and increases the basis of the new asset.

Example 8.21

Mel and Alice exchange like-kind parcels of land in a transaction that qualifies for nonrecognition under Section 1031. Mel's parcels of land is worth $17,000 and he has an adjusted basis of $18,000. Alice's parcels of land has a fair market value of $14,000 and she pays Mel cash of $3,000 in the exchange. Mel's realized loss is $1,000 ($17,000 amount realized - $18,000 adjusted basis). The loss is not deductible but Mel's new basis in Alice's parcels of land is $15,000 ($18,000 - $3,000 cash = $15,000) and the fair market value of the new asset is $14,000. If Mel sells the new asset immediately he will have a $1,000 loss.

For years after 2017, TCJA 2017 limits like-kind exchanges under Section 1031 to exchanges of real property. The new law eliminates the availability of the deferral of income for exchanges of tangible personal property.

3. James F. Dalton, Michael A. Dalton (www.money-education.com)

Wash Sales

When a taxpayer sells stock at a loss, and purchases substantially identical securities within 30 days before or after the sale, the taxpayer has participated in a wash sale and cannot recognize any loss from the sale of the stock. Note that this loss disallowance is temporary and the full benefit of the loss may still be recognized at a future date.

Example 8.22

Five years ago, Vera bought 80 shares of Bicycle Corp. at $50 per share. The stock has declined to $30, and Vera decides to sell it to take the loss deduction. Soon after, Vera sees some good news on Bicycle Corp. and buys it back for $32 approximately two weeks after she sold her original stock. Vera cannot deduct her loss of $20 per share. However, Vera does add $20 per share to the basis of her replacement shares. Those shares have a basis of $52 per share: the $32 Vera paid, plus the $20 wash sale adjustment. In other words, Vera is treated as if she bought the shares for $52. If Vera ends up selling the shares for $55, she will only report $3 per share of gain. In the alternative, if Vera later sells the shares for $32 (the same price she paid to buy them), she will report a loss of $20 per share.

Related Party Transactions

Unlike the losses from Section 1031 exchanges and wash sales (which defer the recognition of a loss), losses incurred in related party transactions are permanently disallowed. When property is sold at a loss to a related party, the seller may not recognize any loss on the sale.

A related party includes the taxpayer's spouse, lineal descendants and ascendants, and siblings (both whole and half bloods). Therefore, related parties does not include: nieces, nephews, aunts, uncles, cousins, step-children, parents-in-law, step-parents, or step-parents-in-law.

Example 8.23

Sanford owns 100 shares of CityCo stock, which have a fair market value of $20 per share. Sanford sells all 100 shares to his sister, Esther, for $15 per share. Although Sanford has realized a loss of $5 per share, he is not allowed to recognize this loss and it is permanently disallowed.

A **double basis rule** is applied when property subject to a loss is sold to a related party, or is gifted. The purpose of the rule is to discourage the transfer by sale or gift to related parties or those to whom the taxpayer would make gifts of property, which at the time of the transfer has a fair market value less than the transferors adjusted taxable basis.

Quick Quiz 8.4

1. If a taxpayer takes a distribution from a qualified retirement plan or IRA prior to age 59½, a 25% excise tax applies to the distribution.
   a. True
   b. False
2. Losses related to wash sales are temporarily disallowed.
   a. True
   b. False
3. Losses incurred in related party transactions are permanently disallowed.
   a. True
   b. False

False, True, True.

In the above example, Esther will have a basis of $15 for future losses but a second (thus, double) basis of $20 for gains. If Esther later sells the stock for $21, she will have a gain of $1. If instead, she were to sell the stock for $13, she would have a $2 loss. If she sold the stock at a price between the gain basis and the loss basis, she would have no gain or loss. In addition, the double basis rule applies to gifts where the fair market value of the gift is below the donor's (transferor) adjusted taxable basis. The holding period will be discussed in Chapter 11.

Gifts Below Fair Market Value

Like related party transactions, certain gifts will result in the permanent disallowance of a loss. When gifted property has a fair market value that is less than the donor's adjusted basis, the double basis rule applies, meaning that the donee has one basis for gains (the donor's original basis) and another basis for losses (the value of the property on the date of the gift). If the gifted property is subsequently sold by the donee for less than the fair market value on the date of the gift, part of the loss is permanently disallowed.

Example 8.24

Lilly purchased McLaurel stock several years ago for $40 per share. When the stock price fell to $30 per share, Lilly decided to gift the stock to her friend, Marshall. Under the double basis rule, Marshall's basis will be $30 for losses and $40 for gains. If Marshall subsequently sells the stock for $25 per share, he will recognize a loss of $5 per share. However, the loss that occurred while Lilly owned the stock ($40 - $30 = $10 per share) will be permanently disallowed.

Sale of Personal Assets for Loss

When personal assets are sold at a loss, that loss may not be recognized. Rather, in order for a loss on the sale of an asset to be recognizable, that asset must be used for the production of income in a trade or business. If a loss is disallowed because the asset is a personal asset, the loss is permanently disallowed and the taxpayer may not recognize it at any point in the future.

Exhibit 8.7 | Summary of Disallowed Losses

Temporarily Disallowed	*Permanently Disallowed*
• Section 1031 exchanges	• Related party transactions
• Wash sales	• Gifts below fair market value
	• Sale of personal assets at a loss

CONCLUSION

This chapter completes our discussion of deductions, with particular emphasis on various special rules and planning applications that are relevant in personal tax planning situations. The most commonly encountered situations in tax planning covered in this chapter center around rental of vacation homes, hobby losses, worthless securities, losses of individuals, Section 1244 stock, bad debts, wash sales, related party transactions, and gifts below fair market value. A thorough understanding of the application of these rules is necessary to provide competent advice to clients.

KEY TERMS

Double Basis Rule - A rule that applies to gifts and related party transactions where the transferee has a basis of the fair market value for losses and the transferor's basis for gains. The rule applies when the asset that is transferred has a fair market value less than the transferor's basis at the time of the transfer. This rule does not apply to arm's-length unrelated party transactions. This rule may also be referred to as the split basis rule, dual basis rule, or bifurcated basis rule.

Hobby Activity - Any activity that a taxpayer engages in without a profit motive. No deductions are permitted for hobbies after 2017.

Mixed-Use Rental Activity - Rental activity in which the real estate is rented for 15 days or more per year and the owner's personal use of the property is more than the greater of 14 days per year or 10 percent of the rental days.

Net Operating Loss - Occurs when trade or business activities generate higher expenses than income in a given year. After 2020, NOLs can generally only be carried forward and can only offset up to 80 percent of income for any one year.

Nontaxable Rental Activity - Rental activity in which the real estate is rented for less than 15 days per year.

Primarily Rental Use Activity - Rental activity in which the real estate is rented for 15 days or more per year and the owner's personal use of the property is less than the greater of 14 days per year or 10 percent of the rental days.

Profit Motive - An actual and honest, even though unreasonable or unrealistic, profit objective in engaging in an activity.

Reserve Method - A method of deducting bad debts used by some businesses in which bad debt deductions are taken based on a percentage of accounts receivable representing the historical percentage of accounts that go bad.

Specific Charge-Off Method - Allows businesses to deduct bad debts as an ordinary loss in the year in which the debt becomes partially or wholly worthless.

DISCUSSION QUESTIONS

SOLUTIONS to the discussion questions can be found exclusively within the chapter. Once you have completed an initial reading of the chapter, go back and highlight the answers to these questions.

1. Explain why penalties and fines are not deductible.
2. Under what circumstances do illegal activities give rise to income tax deductions?
3. Why are businesses allowed to deduct the costs of monitoring legislation?
4. What are the limits on deducting executive compensation?
5. How does the IRS determine whether an activity is a hobby or a trade or business?
6. What presumption regarding hobby activities is provided for under IRC Section 183?
7. What are the consequences of an activity being classified as a hobby instead of a trade or business?
8. What are the three ways that a rental activity can be classified for income tax purposes?
9. What are the requirements for the different ways that a rental activity can be classified?
10. Describe the taxation of mixed-use rental activities.
11. Describe the specific charge-off method used to deduct bad debts.
12. When can a taxpayer take a deduction for worthless stock?
13. How does Section 1244 encourage investment in small businesses?
14. What are the three methods for deducting research and experimental costs (for tax years prior to 2022)?
15. For how many years can a net operating loss be carried back or forward?
16. What is the excess contribution penalty?
17. What is the early distribution penalty?
18. What is the late distribution penalty?
19. List two types of temporarily disallowed losses and three types of permanently disallowed losses.

MULTIPLE CHOICE PROBLEMS

A sample of multiple choice problems is provided below. Additional multiple choice problems are available at money-education.com by accessing the Student Practice Portal.

1. All of the following expenses incurred when an individual travels from his office to a client's place of business to discuss business matters will qualify as a business deduction, EXCEPT:
    a. A $6 toll to cross the commerce bridge.
    b. Mileage expense for the round trip to visit the client.
    c. A $30 parking ticket for parking in a no-parking zone since no other parking spaces were available.
    d. Cost of printing material for the client meeting.

2. Barney not only uses drugs, he also sells them to a circle of friends and associates. This year, Barney grossed $650,000 from drug sales. He paid $125,000 to his street pushers to compensate them for their services, $200,000 for the raw drugs, $30,000 for rent for the drug processing and packaging plant, and $30,000 in supplies and equipment leasing costs. How much income will be subject to tax on Barney's income tax return?
    a. $275,000.
    b. $325,000.
    c. $450,000.
    d. $650,000.

3. Cobie, a single individual, is an avid coin collector. To raise some money to support her hobby, Cobie began to occasionally buy and sell coins about 10 years ago, incurring business-related expenses in those transactions. Cobie does not consider herself to be in the business of dealing in coins, and over the time she has been selling coins, she has never made a profit. This year, Cobie grossed $4,000 in sales, and had $4,500 in expenses associated with the activity. Cobie's AGI for the year (including any inclusion due to the coin trading activity) is $50,000, and aside from the coin trading loss, her only other permissible itemized deductions are mortgage interest of $8,000 and real estate taxes of $2,500. Which of the following statements concerning this situation is correct?
    a. Cobie will take the $500 loss from the coin business into her gross income.
    b. Since she has never made money from the activity, she is not required to report the purchase and sale transactions on her return.
    c. Cobie can offset the $4,000 in income with $4,000 of her expenses, so the coin trading activity will have no impact on her AGI.
    d. The increase in Cobie's taxable income as a result of the coin trading activity is equal to the income of $4,000.

4. Ted owns a mansion built on the cliff of a large island overlooking the Atlantic ocean. Each year, an international sailing race takes place around the Island, and large corporations descend on the town, inviting clients and business associates to entertain them. Carman Corporation, a custom designer of racing sailboats, is particularly interested in this event each year, and for the week and a half of the race, they rent Ted's mansion, paying him $200,000. At first, Ted was hesitant to rent the home, but decided that since it would only be a week and a half, he could go on vacation himself at that time. Ted incurs some costs associated with the rental, including storage charges for his valuables of $10,000, cleaning expenses before and after the rental of $8,000 and he estimates that the pro-rata portion of real estate taxes for the period of the rental is $1,000. How much income from this rental activity will be included in Ted's AGI?
   a. $0.
   b. $181,000.
   c. $190,000.
   d. $200,000.

5. Robin owns and operates an engineering consulting business as a sole proprietorship. For tax reporting, Robin uses the cash method. Last year, she provided services to a local builder, and upon completing the task she was asked to do, she sent an invoice to the builder for $5,000. The builder never paid the bill, and recently filed for bankruptcy, so Robin will not be able to collect the amount due. How should this bad debt be treated for income tax purposes?
   a. No bad debt deduction is permitted.
   b. Robin may deduct $5,000 from her business income.
   c. Robin may deduct $5,000 as a short-term capital loss.
   d. Robin may deduct $5,000 as a long-term capital loss.

Additional multiple choice problems are available at *money-education.com* by accessing the Student Practice Portal. Access requires registration of the title using the unique code at the front of the book.

QUICK QUIZ EXPLANATIONS

Quick Quiz 8.1

1. True.
2. False. Due to privacy laws, the IRS cannot inform a law enforcement agency if a taxpayer is conducting an illegal business activity.
3. False. Expenses incurred to influence local legislation or federal legislation are not deductible.
4. False. TCJA 2017 repealed the exemption for performance based compensation.

Quick Quiz 8.2

1. False. Raising horses is generally considered to be a hobby activity.
2. True.
3. False. Real estate that is rented for 15 days per year may or may not be a nontaxable activity, depending on the personal use of the property by the owner.
4. True.

Quick Quiz 8.3

1. True.
2. True.
3. False. Section 1244 is intended to encourage investment in small businesses.
4. True. NOLs can be carried forward but generally not back (after 2020).

Quick Quiz 8.4

1. False. If a taxpayer takes a distribution from a qualified retirement plan or IRA prior to age 59½, a 10% excise tax applies to the distribution, unless the taxpayer is covered by one of the exceptions to the 10% penalty.
2. True.
3. True.

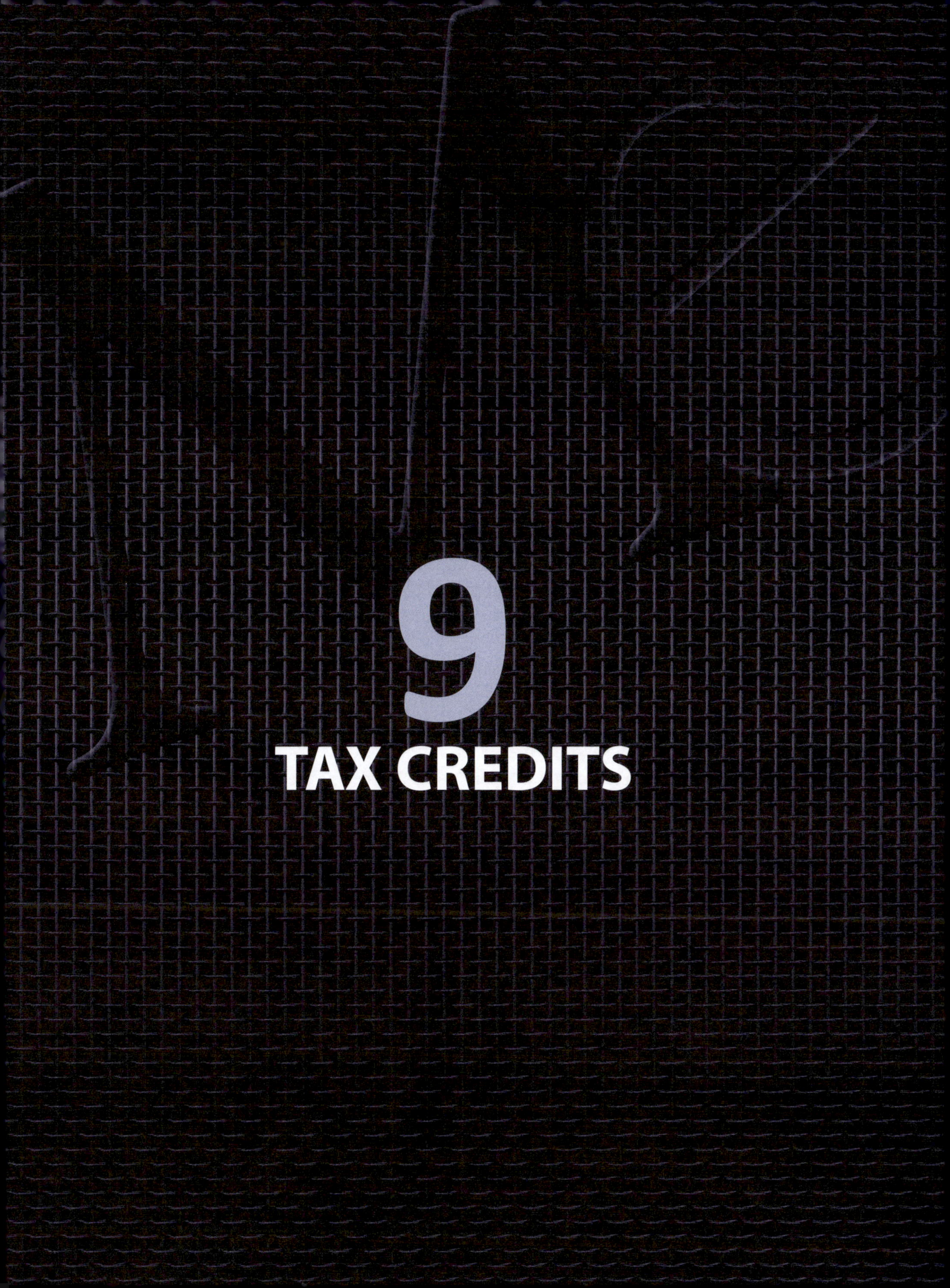

9
TAX CREDITS

LEARNING OBJECTIVES

1. Define "tax credit."*
2. Compare refundable and non-refundable tax credits.*
3. Describe the difference between a tax credit and a tax deduction.*
4. List the general requirements for claiming a tax credit.*
5. Describe the requirements for claiming the foreign tax credit.*
6. Calculate the allowable foreign tax credit for a given taxpayer.*
7. Explain the purpose and requirements of the credit for child and dependent care expenses.*
8. Define employment-related dependent care expenses.*
9. Describe the requirements for the credit for the elderly or disabled.*
10. Explain the "no double benefit" rule as it applies to education tax credits.*
11. Describe who can claim an education credit.*
12. Explain the "eligible student" requirement of the American Opportunity Tax Credit.*
13. Define the amounts of credit available under the American Opportunity Tax Credit and the Lifetime Learning Credit.*
14. Describe the benefits associated with the Retirement Savings Contribution Credit.*
15. Describe the qualifying child requirements for the child tax credit.*
16. Explain how income limitations impact the child tax credit.*
17. Describe the circumstances under which the child tax credit becomes a refundable credit.
18. Define qualified adoption expenses.*
19. Explain the standards for considering a child to be a child with special needs.*
20. Describe the phaseout range for the qualified adoption expenses credit.*
21. Describe the available credits for taxes paid.*
22. Explain the purpose of the earned income credit.*
23. Define "eligible individual" for purposes of the earned income credit.*
24. Describe the other available refundable tax credits.*
25. Describe the carryforward and carry-back rules for the general business credit.
26. List the components of the general business credit.

**Ties to CFP Certification Learning Objectives*

INTRODUCTION

Tax deductions (the topic of several prior chapters) reduce the amount of income that is subject to tax. In contrast, a **tax credit** reduces the calculated tax liability of the taxpayer. Income tax credits are subtracted from the tax on taxable income. As explained in Chapter 3, a taxpayer's income tax is determined by multiplying taxable income by the appropriate income tax rates (or by using the appropriate tax table).

Taxable Income x Tax Rate(s) = Tax on Taxable Income

As illustrated by the following formula, tax credits reduce the tax on taxable income.

Tax on Taxable Income – Credits = Tax Due

Tax credits come in two forms: nonrefundable or refundable. Nonrefundable credits may only apply to the current year or, in some cases, they may be carried back to an earlier year, carried forward to future years, or both. Refundable tax credits can be used to reduce or eliminate the current year's tax, but can also generate a refund.

Key Concepts

1. Define "tax credit."
2. Compare refundable and nonrefundable tax credits.
3. Describe the difference between a tax credit and a tax deduction.
4. List the general requirements for claiming a tax credit.

Nonrefundable Tax Credits

Nonrefundable tax credits can reduce the tax on taxable income to zero, but they cannot generate a tax refund. Nonrefundable tax credits include:

- Foreign Tax Credit
- Credit for Child and Dependent Care (refundable for the 2021 tax year only (ARPA 2021))
- Credit for the Elderly or Disabled
- Education Credits: Lifetime Learning, and part or all of the American Opportunity Tax Credit
- Retirement Savings Contributions Credit
- Child Tax Credit (up to $1,400 refundable; fully refundable in the 2021 tax year only (ARPA 2021))
- Residential Energy Efficient Property Credit
- Nonbusiness Alternative Motor Vehicle Credit
- Nonbusiness Alternative Fuel Vehicle Refueling Property Credit
- General Business Credit
- Qualified Adoption Credit

Example 9.1

Pearl's tax on her taxable income is $600. She is eligible for a nonrefundable tax credit of $700. Pearl is allowed to use the credit to reduce her tax to $0 for the year, but she is not allowed to use the remaining $100 of the credit to generate a refund.

Carryback or Carryforward of a Credit

If a nonrefundable credit exceeds the tax on taxable income for the tax year for which it can be claimed, the excess credit is normally lost. Some credits, however, allow the excess to be carried back and/or carried forward to offset income tax in past and future years. (See **Exhibit 9.1**.)

Example 9.2

Arnold's tax on his taxable income for the year is $1,200. He is eligible to claim a nonrefundable tax credit of $1,500. Arnold is allowed to offset his tax with $1,200 of the credit to reduce his tax for the current year to $0. Since the credit is of a type that can be carried back to the preceding year, he is allowed to carryback the remaining $300 of the credit to be offset against his tax for that year. He will carry the credit back by filing an amended income tax return and claiming a $300 refund of taxes for the preceding year. If he owed no tax for the preceding year, the excess credit for the current year may be lost.

Example 9.3

Use the facts from **Example 9.2**, but assume that the credit is of a type that can be carried forward to the following five years (but not carried back). Arnold can claim the $300 excess credit from the current year (Year 1) on the following year's tax return. If he is only able to use $200 of the excess on the tax return for the following year (Year 2), he will be able to use the remainder of $100 as a credit on his tax return for Year 3. If he is unable to use the excess in the five years following the current year, the unused credit will be lost.

Sequence of Nonrefundable Credits

Nonrefundable credits must be used in a specified sequence. Credits listed first in the sequence must be used up before the subsequent credits can be claimed. A partial list of nonrefundable credits, including sequence numbers, is presented in **Exhibit 9.1**. All of the credits in the exhibit are personal credits except for the second to last one (General Business Credit) and the first one (Foreign Tax Credit). The foreign tax credit can be generated by foreign source income from investment, employment, self-employment, or other business activity.

Exhibit 9.1 | Nonrefundable Tax Credits

Item	*Nonrefundable Credit Sequence*	*IRC Section*	*IRS Publication*	*Reported on Form*	*Category*	*Additional Information*
Foreign Tax Credit	1	27/901	514	1116 or 1118	Various	Carryback 1/ Carryforward 10
Credit for Child and Dependent Care[1]	2	21	503	2441	Personal	
Credit for the Elderly or Disabled	3	22	524	Schedule R	Personal	
Education Credits:[2] American Opportunity and Lifetime Learning	4	25A	970	8863	Personal	
Retirement Savings Contributions Credit	5	25B	17/590	8880	Investing	
Child Tax Credit (partially refundable)[3]	7	24	972	1040	Personal	
Residential Energy Efficient Property Credit	11	25D	17/523	5695	Personal	Carryforward to next year
Non-business Alternative Motor Vehicle Credit	13	30B	17/334	8910	Various	
Non-business Alternative Fuel Vehicle Refueling Property Credit	14	30C	17/334	8911	Various	
General Business Credit	15	38	334	3800	Business	Carryback 1/ Carryforward 20
Qualified Adoption Expense Credit	16	23	17	8839	Personal	Carryforward 5 years

1. The Credit for Child and Dependent Care is refundable in 2021 only (ARPA) 2021.
2. The American Opportunity Credit is partially refundable.
3. The Child Tax Credit is fully refundable in 2021 only (ARPA 2021).

Notice the Additional Information column in **Exhibit 9.1**. For many of these credits, there is no carryback or carryforward of the unused portion of the credit; any portion of the credit that cannot be used in the current year is lost. For the foreign tax credit and the general business credit, however, any portion of the credit that cannot be used in the current year can be carried back to the preceding year to generate a tax refund for that year. Any remaining credit after the carryback is then carried forward to be used in future years. A residential energy efficient property credit that cannot be used in the current year can be carried forward only to the following year. Any unused adoption expenses credit can be carried forward for up to five years. If a taxpayer is unable to use all of the available child tax credit in the current year, some or all of the unused child tax credit can be used to generate a refundable credit called the additional child tax credit.

Refundable Tax Credits

Refundable tax credits can be used not only to reduce or eliminate the current year's tax, but also to generate a tax refund in excess of estimated tax payments and withholdings.

Tax on Taxable Income – Refundable Credits = Tax Due (or Refund Due)

For federal income tax purposes, nonrefundable credits are used before refundable credits. A more complete presentation of the use of tax credits is presented by the following formula:

Tax on Taxable Income – Nonrefundable Credits – Refundable Credits = Tax Due (or Refund Due)

Example 9.4

The tax calculated on the taxable income of Willis and Kimberly Johnson is $3,000. They are eligible to claim a $1,000 nonrefundable credit and a refundable credit of $2,800. They can claim a tax refund of $800 ($3,000 - $1,000 - $2,800) even if they had no withholding or other tax prepayments for the year.

Example 9.5

Continuing with **Example 9.4**, assume that the Johnsons' calculated tax for the year is only $600. They can claim a refund of $2,800 ($600 - $600 - $2,800). Only $600 of the nonrefundable credit can be used, but all $2,800 of the refundable credit can be used. Unless the remaining $400 of the nonrefundable credit can be carried back or forward, it will be lost. Note that all of the nonrefundable credit would have been lost if refundable credits had to be used before nonrefundable credits [$600 - $2,800 - $0 = -$2,200 (refund)].

A list of refundable credits is presented in **Exhibit 9.2**. Refundable credits are far fewer in number than nonrefundable credits. After all available nonrefundable credits have been used to the extent possible to reduce the income tax calculated for the year, the refundable credits can be subtracted to reduce the remaining tax or to generate a tax refund. It is not necessary to carry refundable credits back or forward because they generate a tax benefit in the current year.

Note that the American Opportunity Tax Credit shown in **Exhibit 9.1** and **Exhibit 9.2** is refundable up to 40 percent unless the taxpayer claiming the credit is a child who:

1. is 18 or is under the age of 18 (or a full-time student under age 24) and has earned income less than one-half of his support
2. has at least one living parent
3. does not file a joint return

The Protecting Americans from Tax Hikes Act of 2015 (PATH 2015) clarified that erroneously claimed refundable credits may subject the taxpayer claiming the erroneous credit to accuracy related or fraud penalties. This provision of PATH 2015 expressly overruled the Tax Court's decision in *Rand*, 141 T.C. 327 (2012), which held that for purposes of determining the amount of an underpayment, the tax shown on the return may not be less than zero. While this provision of PATH 2015 will only affect taxpayers and tax preparers who are not complying with the requirements found in the tax code, it does increase the penalties for non-compliance and encourages a fairer administration of the tax laws.

Exhibit 9.2 | Refundable Tax Credits

Item	*IRC Section*	*IRS Publication*	*Reported on Form*
American Opportunity Tax Credit (formerly the Hope Scholarship Credit)	25A	970	8863/1040
Earned Income Credit	32	17/596	Sched. EIC
Credit for Tax on Undistributed Capital Gain From: A Mutual Fund A Real Estate Investment Trust (REIT)	852(b)(3)(D)(ii) 857(b)(3)(D)(ii)	17/564/550 17/550	2439 2439
Health Coverage Tax Credit	35	17/502	8885
Credit for Excise Taxes on Gasoline and Special Fuels	34	510	4136

Tax Credits vs. Tax Deductions

The benefit received by a taxpayer from a tax credit is not dependent on the taxpayer's marginal tax rate (tax bracket). A tax credit of $1,000 provides the same $1,000 tax reduction for a taxpayer in the 12 percent tax bracket or the 37 percent tax bracket. On the other hand, a reduction in tax liability generated by a tax deduction is entirely dependent on the marginal tax rate of the taxpayer. A tax deduction of $1,000 generates a tax reduction of $120 ($1,000 x 0.12) for a taxpayer in the 12 percent bracket and a tax reduction of $370 ($1,000 x 0.37) for a taxpayer in the 37 percent tax bracket.

Tax Policy Issues

The equal tax benefit (as measured in dollars) generated by tax credits for taxpayers with different marginal tax rates is one of the reasons for the increasing number of tax credits. Congress has created a variety of tax credits for social, economic, fairness (equity), environmental, and other purposes. For example, the earned income credit was enacted to encourage low-income taxpayers to seek gainful employment and to reward them for doing so (thereby, satisfying social, economic, and perhaps equity objectives). Residential energy credits were provided to encourage taxpayers to make energy-saving improvements to their homes (environmental and economic purposes).

Tax Credit Requirements

In order to claim a tax credit, a taxpayer must normally do the following:

- Meet eligibility requirements
- Determine the amount of the credit
- Apply any specified limitations to the credit
- Subtract the allowable credits from the tax in the proper sequence
- Carryback or carryforward any amounts disallowed for the current tax year, if permitted

Nonbusiness and Business Tax Credits

Tax credits can be conveniently divided into those that relate to business activities and those that do not. This chapter will present a discussion of a few of the many available tax credits in the following order:

- Nonrefundable credits of a personal nature
- Refundable credits
- The general business credit

The foreign tax credit is included in this section of the chapter even though this credit may relate to foreign source *business* income.

Quick Quiz 9.1

1. A tax credit is an amount that is added to a calculated tax.
   a. True
   b. False
2. Nonrefundable tax credits can reduce the tax on taxable income to zero, but they cannot generate a tax refund.
   a. True
   b. False
3. Nonrefundable tax credits must be used in a specific sequence.
   a. True
   b. False
4. The benefit of a tax credit depends on the taxpayer's marginal tax rate.
   a. True
   b. False

False, True, True, False.

Most of the credits available to businesses are built into the nonrefundable general business credit.

A few of the most common credits will be discussed in some detail, some less common credits will be described only briefly, and some are beyond the scope of this text.

NONREFUNDABLE CREDITS OF A PERSONAL NATURE

Foreign Tax Credit

A taxpayer who pays income and similar taxes to a foreign country (or a possession of the United States) on foreign source income, and also pays U.S. income taxes on the same income, is usually eligible to claim a **foreign tax credit** for some or all of the taxes paid to the foreign country. Alternatively, the taxpayer can claim an itemized deduction for the foreign income taxes paid (under TCJA, foreign property taxes are no longer deductible through 2025, but foreign income taxes remain deductible) as discussed in Chapter 7. The foreign tax credit is usually more beneficial to the taxpayer than a deduction for foreign taxes paid. The taxpayer should also consider future foreign income since the foreign tax credit can be carried back one year and carried forward ten years.

An individual is not allowed to claim a foreign tax credit for foreign taxes paid on income that is excluded from U.S. gross income. However, if foreign taxes are paid to a foreign government for earned income that exceeds the amount of the foreign earned income (and housing) exclusion, a foreign tax credit can be claimed for the excess. The foreign earned income exclusion is discussed in Chapter 5.

The amount of the foreign tax credit that can be offset against the U.S. federal income tax is typically 100 percent of the qualifying taxes paid to the foreign country on foreign source income, subject to limitations.

Key Concepts

1. Describe the requirements for claiming the foreign tax credit.
2. Explain the purpose and requirements of the credit for child and dependent care expenses.
3. Define employment-related dependent care expenses.
4. Describe the requirements for the credit for the elderly or disabled.

The foreign tax credit is intended to avoid double taxation of foreign source income, but it is not intended to reduce U.S. taxes on U.S. source income. Therefore, all of the foreign taxes paid on foreign source income can offset U.S. taxes if the foreign jurisdiction imposes taxes at the same rate as (or at a lower rate than) the United States. If the foreign country imposes taxes at a higher rate than the United States, however, not all of the foreign taxes will be allowed as a credit against the U.S. income tax. Without this limitation in place, it would be possible for the foreign tax credit to reduce the U.S. tax on U.S. source income. This limitation on the foreign tax credit is calculated using the following formula:

$$\frac{\textbf{Taxable Income from Sources Outside the U.S.}}{\textbf{Worldwide Taxable Income}} \times \begin{array}{c}\textbf{Pre-credit U.S. Tax}\\ \textbf{on Worldwide Income}\end{array} = \textbf{Maximum Credit}$$

Example 9.6

Walden earns taxable income of $100,000 in France. He has no other income for the year. His U.S. tax on that income is $24,000 (24%). France imposes an income tax of $35,000 (35%) on the same income. Walden will be allowed to claim a foreign tax credit of only $24,000 on his U.S. income tax return [($100,000/$100,000) x $24,000 = $24,000]. If he were allowed to claim a foreign tax credit of $35,000, the credit would reduce the U.S. income tax on any income earned in the United States for the year.

Example 9.7

Use the facts from **Example 9.6** and assume that France imposes an income tax of only $2,000 on the $100,000 of income that Walden earns in France. Walden will be allowed to claim a $2,000 foreign tax credit on his U.S. income tax return.

Example 9.8

Use the facts from **Example 9.6** (Walden earns foreign source income of $100,000 and pays $35,000 in income tax to France) and assume that Walden earned $25,000 of taxable income in the U.S. in addition to his income from France. Assume Walden's U.S. tax on $125,000 of income is $24,021.00 (24% marginal bracket). Walden will be allowed to claim a foreign tax credit of $19,216.80 [($100,000/$125,000) x $24,021.00 = $19,216.80].

Although the foreign tax credit is a nonrefundable credit, any unused credit for the current year can be carried back to the preceding year and carried forward for up to ten years.

The foreign tax credit is calculated on Form 1116 for individuals and Form 1118 for corporations. Individual taxpayers with investment income less than $300 ($600 on a joint return):

1. are not normally required to file Form 1116
2. are exempt from the foreign tax credit limitation (the limitation formula discussed above)

In such circumstances, foreign taxes withheld from dividends and other types of investment income earned outside the United States can be claimed as a foreign tax credit (without the limitation) directly on the Form 1040. A foreign tax credit is also available for businesses.

Credit for Child and Dependent Care Expenses

The **credit for child and dependent care expenses** is intended to provide some financial relief to individuals who incur employment-related expenses for the care of one or more qualifying individuals. The American Rescue Plan Act (ARPA) of 2021 substantially increases the benefits available to taxpayers who qualify for the child and dependent care expense credit in tax year 2021. Beginning in tax year 2022, the rules revert to the standards applicable before the American Rescue Plan Act of 2021 was enacted.

The amount of the credit is equal to employment-related expenses of up to the maximum limit outlined in **Exhibit 9.3**, multiplied by the applicable percentage explained below.

Exhibit 9.3 | Maximum Expenses Considered in Calculating the Child and Dependent Care Credit

	Expense Maximum for Tax Years Before and After 2021	*Expense Maximum for the 2021 Tax Year*
One Qualifying Child or Dependent	$3,000	$8,000
Two or More Qualifying Children or Dependents	$6,000	$16,000

Note that these are the maximum employment-related expenses to be considered, not the amount of the credit.

The dollar limits above are not inflation adjusted on an annual basis, and must be reduced by any excludable benefits received from an employer as dependent care assistance under IRC Section 129.

Qualifying Individual

A qualifying individual includes any of the following:

1. A dependent who is a qualifying child under the age of 13.[1]
2. A dependent of the taxpayer who:
   - is physically or mentally incapable of caring for himself, and
   - has the same principal place of abode as the taxpayer for more than half the year; or
3. The spouse of the taxpayer who:
   - is physically or mentally incapable of caring for himself, and
   - has the same principal place of abode as the taxpayer for more than half the year.

1. The requirements for a qualifying child are the same as those explained in Chapter 3.

Employment-Related Expenses

Employment-related expenses are expenses incurred for the care of qualifying individuals that enable the taxpayer to be employed.

Eligible Expenses

Eligible expenses include expenses for household services and expenses for the care of a qualifying individual.

Employment-Related

To qualify as employment-related expenses, the child and dependent care expenses must be incurred to enable the taxpayer to work or to actively look for work. The work can be as an employee or in the taxpayer's own proprietorship or partnership and can be either full-time or part-time.

Earned Income Limit

In order to claim the credit for child and dependent care expenses, the taxpayer (and spouse if married) must have earned income such as wages, salary, tips, net earnings from self-employment, and certain nontaxable fringe benefits. Although the credit is based on employment-related expenses up to the maximum dollar amounts listed in Exhibit 9.3, the eligible employment-related expenses cannot exceed the earned income of the taxpayer, or for married taxpayers, the earned income of the spouse with the lesser amount of earned income.

Example 9.9

Alan and Judith have earned income in 2021 of $30,000 and $2,000 respectively. Even though they pay $8,600 for child care expenses for their three-year-old daughter during the year, their eligible employment-related expenses amount for the year is limited to $2,000 (Judith's earned income). If Judith had earned $8,000 or more for the year, $8,000 of the child care expenses would qualify for the child and dependent care credit.

For each month that an unemployed spouse who lives with the taxpayer for more than half the year is:

1. a full-time student, or
2. is physically or mentally unable to care for himself, then the unemployed spouse is deemed to earn $250 monthly if the married couple pays for the care of one qualifying individual ($500 for two or more).

This treatment can only apply to one spouse in a given month. If both spouses are unemployed and are full-time students for a given month, only one of them can be treated as though he had earned income for the month. To be considered a student, an individual must be a full-time student during five months of the tax year.

Example 9.10

Charlie earned $32,000 during the year. His wife, Rose, was unemployed but she was a full-time student during five months of the year. They paid $200 per month for the care of their young son, Jake, who is their only child. Even though they paid $2,400 for child care during the year, their employment-related expenses for the child and dependent care credit will be limited to $1,250 ($250 x 5 months), the amount of income that Rose is deemed to have earned during the year.

Payments to Relatives

Payments for employment-related care that are made to relatives of the taxpayer may qualify for the dependent care credit even if the relatives live with the taxpayer. However, payments made to a person who can be claimed as a dependent or to a taxpayer's child who is under the age of 19 do not qualify.

Joint Return

Married taxpayers must normally file a joint return to claim the child and dependent care credit.

Amount of the Credit

The amount of the credit is the total of the qualifying employment-related expenses multiplied by the applicable rate in the exhibit below. The rate ranges from 20 percent to 50 percent for 2021 (20 percent to 35 percent for tax years beginning before or after 2021) of eligible expenses and declines as the taxpayer's adjusted gross income (AGI) increases. The AGI limits specified in the table below are not subject to inflation adjustment on an annual basis.

Exhibit 9.4 | Applicable Percentage for Child and Dependent Care Expenses Credit

For Tax Years Beginning Before or After 2021			For the 2021 Tax Year		
If AGI is Over	*But Not Over*	*Then the Percentage is*	*If AGI is Over*	*But Not Over*	*Then the Percentage is*
$0	$15,000	35%	$0	$125,000	50%
$15,000	$17,000	34%	$125,000	$127,000	49%
$17,000	$19,000	33%	$127,000	$129,000	48%
$19,000	$21,000	32%	$129,000	$131,000	47%
$21,000	$23,000	31%	$131,000	$133,000	46%
$23,000	$25,000	30%	$133,000	$135,000	45%
$25,000	$27,000	29%	$135,000	$137,000	44%
$27,000	$29,000	28%	$137,000	$139,000	43%
$29,000	$31,000	27%	$139,000	$141,000	42%
$31,000	$33,000	26%	$141,000	$143,000	41%
$33,000	$35,000	25%	$143,000	$145,000	40%
$35,000	$37,000	24%	$145,000	$147,000	39%
$37,000	$39,000	23%	$147,000	$149,000	38%
$39,000	$41,000	22%	$149,000	$151,000	37%
$41,000	$43,000	21%	$151,000	$153,000	36%
$43,000	No Limit	20%	$153,000	$155,000	35%
			$155,000	$157,000	34%
			$157,000	$159,000	33%
			$159,000	$161,000	32%
			$161,000	$163,000	31%
			$163,000	$165,000	30%
			$165,000	$167,000	29%
			$167,000	$169,000	28%
			$169,000	$171,000	27%
			$171,000	$173,000	26%
			$173,000	$175,000	25%
			$175,000	$177,000	24%
			$177,000	$179,000	23%
			$179,000	$181,000	22%
			$181,000	$183,000	21%
			$183,000	$400,000	20%
			$400,000	No limit	Reduce 20% by 1% for each $2,000 of AGI over $400,000

For the 2021 tax year, the ARPA of 2021 sets the maximum applicable percentage as 50 percent. This percentage is reduced by one percentage point for each $2,000 (or fraction thereof) by which the taxpayer's adjusted gross income exceeds $125,000; however once AGI reaches $183,000 and the applicable percentage has been reduced to 20 percent, there will be no further decrease until AGI reaches $400,000. For taxpayers with AGI of $400,000 or above in 2021, the applicable percentage of 20 percent is reduced by one percent for every $2,000 (or fraction thereof) by which AGI exceeds $400,000, until the credit is fully phased out.

The maximum credit for 2021 is $8,000 ($16,000 x 50%) for two or more children or dependents. The maximum credit for tax years beginning before or after 2021 is $2,100 ($6,000 x 35%) for two or more children or dependents.

Credit is Refundable in 2021 Only

For tax years beginning before or after 2021, any credit that cannot be used in the current year is lost. However, for the 2021 tax year, the child and dependent care tax credit is fully refundable if the taxpayer (or spouse if married filing jointly) has a principal place of abode in the United States for more than one half of the taxable year.

CASE STUDY 9.1

Earned Income Credit, Child Care Credit, and Child Tax Credit

Andre Keith Moore, Petitioners v. Commissioner of Internal Revenue, Respondent. T.C. Summary Opinion 2010-80 (June 21, 2010).

Respondent determined a $4,896 deficiency in Moore's 2007 federal income tax. After concessions, the issues for decision are: (1) Whether Moore is entitled to a dependency exemption deduction for S.S. (Ms. Saunders' son); (2) whether Moore is entitled to claim head of household filing status; (3) whether Moore is entitled to the child tax credit and additional child tax credit; (4) whether Moore is entitled to an earned income credit (EIC); and (5) whether Moore is entitled to a child care credit. Moore and his girlfriend, Lisa Saunders (Ms. Saunders), met in 1989 and began a relationship shortly thereafter. Ms. Saunders' son (S.S.) was born in 1994. Since 1998 Moore and Ms. Saunders have lived together with S.S. as a family. Although Moore holds Ms. Saunders out as his wife, Moore and Ms. Saunders have never been married. Moore is not listed as the father on S.S.'s birth certificate. Moore, Ms. Saunders, and S.S. lived together throughout 2007 in two rooms Moore rented.

Moore timely filed his 2007 income tax return and claimed total payments of $6,307, which was subsequently refunded to him. Respondent issued a notice of deficiency on November 28, 2008, determining a deficiency of $4,896. Respondent determined that Moore is ineligible for the claimed head of household filing status, the dependency exemption deductions, the EIC, the child tax credit, the additional child tax credit, and the child care credit.

In general, the Commissioner's determination set forth in a notice of deficiency is presumed correct, and the taxpayer bears the burden of showing that the determination is in error. A taxpayer bears the burden of proving entitlement to any deduction claimed.

CASE STUDY 9.1 CONTINUED

A taxpayer is required to maintain records sufficient to substantiate deductions claimed on his or her income tax return. Rather, an income tax return is merely a statement of the taxpayer's claim; it is not presumed to be correct.

S.S. is not a qualifying child because he is not related to Moore and is not an adopted or foster child. There are multiple reasons S.S. is not a qualifying relative. Since S.S. is the qualifying child of Ms. Saunders, S.S. cannot be a qualifying relative for purposes of Moore's claimed dependency exemption deduction.

Section 1(b) imposes a special tax rate on an individual taxpayer who files a federal income tax return as a head of household. Section 2(b) in pertinent part defines a head of household as an individual taxpayer who: (1) is unmarried as of the close of the taxable year and is not a surviving spouse; and (2) maintains as his home a household that constitutes for more than one-half of the taxable year the principal place of abode, as a member of such household, of a dependent for whom the taxpayer is entitled to a deduction under section 151. Since Moore does not have a dependent and has not provided evidence to show he maintained the household, he is not entitled to head of household filing status.

Section 24(a) provides a credit with respect to each qualifying child of the taxpayer. Section 24(c)(1) defines the term "qualifying child" as "a qualifying child of the taxpayer (as defined in Section 152(c)) who has not attained age 17."[1] The child tax credit may not exceed the taxpayer's regular tax liability. Where a taxpayer is eligible for the child tax credit, but the taxpayer's regular tax liability is less than the amount of the child tax credit potentially available under Section 24(a), Section 24(d) makes a portion of the credit, known as the additional child tax credit, refundable. Since S.S. is not petitioner's qualifying child, petitioner is not entitled to the child tax credit or the additional child tax credit.

An eligible individual is entitled to a credit against his federal income tax liability, calculated as a percentage of his earned income, subject to certain limitations. As previously discussed, S.S. is not Moore's qualifying child; thus, Moore is not entitled to the EIC with one qualifying child for 2007.[2]

Section 21(a) allows a taxpayer a credit for a certain percentage of employment-related expenses incurred to enable the taxpayer to be employed gainfully, including expenses for the care of a "qualifying individual." A qualifying individual must be the taxpayer's qualifying child or qualifying relative under the age of 13. Because Moore has no qualifying individuals, he is not entitled to the child care credit for 2007.

1. The credit is reduced by $50 for each $1,000 (or fraction thereof) by which an individual's modified adjusted gross income exceeds specified amounts not relevant herein. Sec. 24(b).
2. Moore's adjusted gross income for 2007 exceeded $12,590; accordingly he is also ineligible to claim an earned income credit under §32(c)(1)(A)(ii) as an individual without a qualifying child. See Rev. Proc. 2006-53, §3.07(1), 2006-2 C.B. 996, 1000.

Exhibit 9.5 | Summary of Eligibility Rules for the Credit for Child and Dependent Care Expenses (Excerpt from IRS Publication 503)

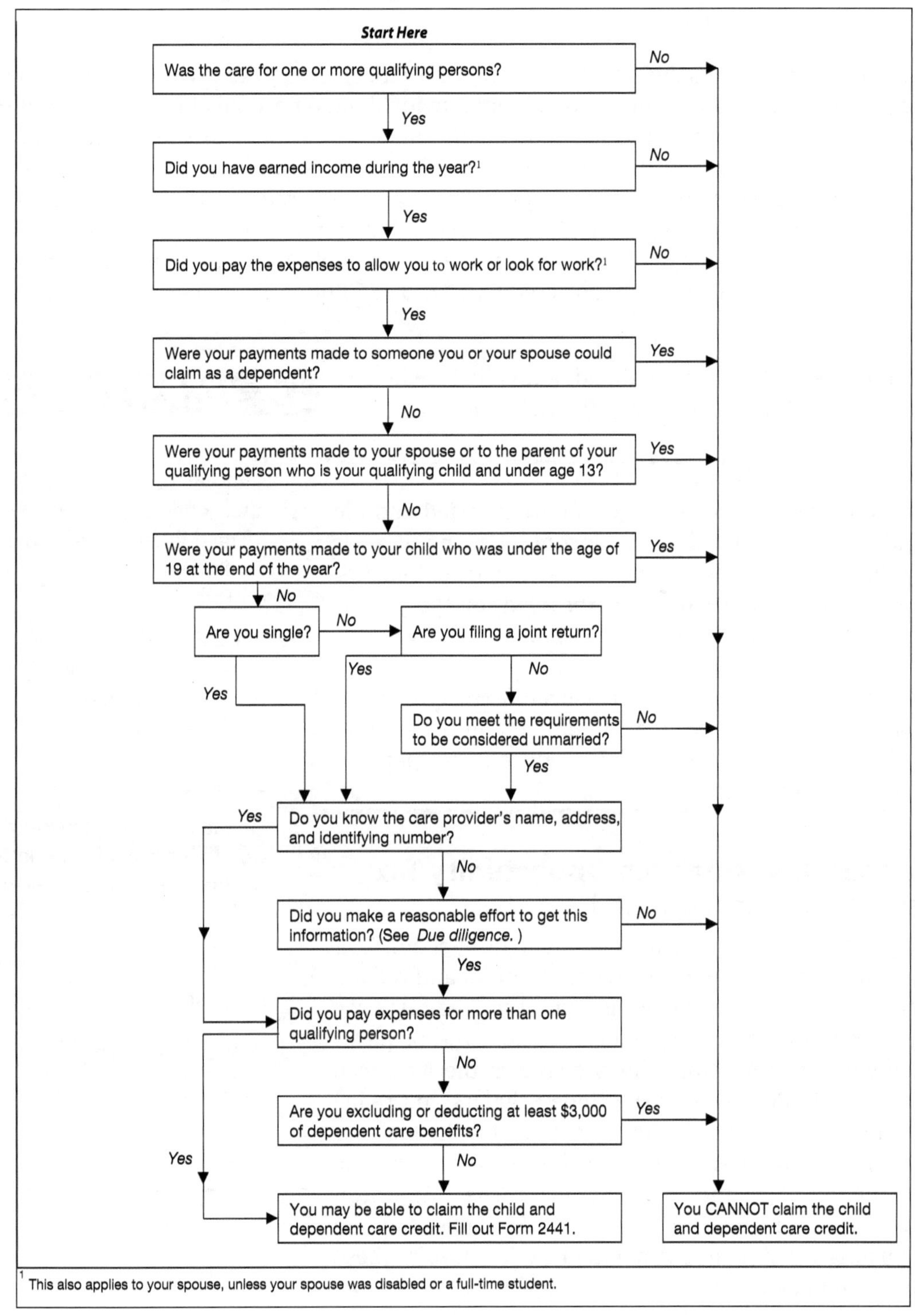

Credit for the Elderly or Disabled

The **credit for the elderly or disabled** is intended to provide financial assistance to elderly or disabled individuals with modest incomes.

The credit for the elderly or disabled is available to a U.S. citizen or resident who is a qualified individual and has income below specified limits. A qualified individual must normally be 65 or older at the end of the tax year. Certain permanently disabled individuals under the age of 65 are also eligible for the credit, provided that they receive taxable disability income and are younger than the mandatory retirement age of the employer at the beginning of the tax year. The maximum credit is 15% of a base amount. The initial base amount of $5,000 (single; or $7,500 married filing jointly) is reduced by both 1) one-half of AGI in excess of $7,500 (single; $10,000 MFJ), and 2) nontaxable Social Security benefits and certain other nontaxable income. The maximum credit is $750 ($5,000 x 15%) per year for an unmarried taxpayer.

The maximum credit for two qualified individuals who are married and file jointly is $1,125 ($7,500 x 15%) per year.

Example 9.11

Jesse (age 69) and Becky (age 67) are married and file jointly. Their adjusted gross income for the year is $9,500 and they receive no Social Security benefits. Their credit for the elderly or disabled for the year is $1,125 ($7,500 initial amount x 15%).

If they had received nontaxable Social Security benefits or if their AGI had exceeded $10,000, the initial amount of $7,500 would have been reduced or perhaps completely eliminated.

Quick Quiz 9.2

1. A taxpayer, who is eligible to claim a foreign tax credit may, in the alternative, claim an itemized deduction for the taxes paid.
   a. True
   b. False
2. The child and dependent care expenses credit is intended to provide financial relief to non-working individuals.
   a. True
   b. False
3. Payments for employment-related care that are made to relatives of the taxpayer may qualify for the child and dependent care expenses credit.
   a. True
   b. False
4. Only taxpayers age 65 or older qualify for the credit for the elderly or disabled.
   a. True
   b. False

True, False, True, False.

Education Credits (American Opportunity Tax and Lifetime Learning Credits)

Two education tax credits are available under IRC Section 25A to an individual taxpayer who pays qualified tuition and related expenses to an eligible educational institution for the taxpayer, the taxpayer's spouse, or a dependent for whom the taxpayer claims a dependency exemption. The two credits, the American Opportunity Tax Credit (formerly the Hope Scholarship Credit) and the Lifetime Learning Credit, are calculated for the tax year and then subjected to a limit based on the taxpayer's income (discussed under "Income Limitation"). The American Opportunity Tax Credit may be partially refundable, but the Lifetime Learning Credit is not. A detailed explanation of these credits is provided below.

Qualified Tuition and Related Expenses

Qualified tuition and related expenses consist of tuition and academic fees that are required for enrollment. Nonacademic fees such as student activity fees, athletic fees, insurance expenses, or other fees that are unrelated to a student's academic course of instruction are not eligible for the credit. Expenses for courses or education involving sports, games, or hobbies are not eligible for the credit unless the courses or education are part of the student's degree program. For the American Opportunity Tax Credit, "course materials" (including books, supplies, and equipment needed for a course of study) count as "qualified related expenses" whether or not the material is purchased from an educational institution as a condition of enrollment or attendance.

Qualified education expenses for a tax year must be paid during the year or for an academic period that begins during the first three months of the following tax year. When claiming the Lifetime Learning Credit, student activity fees and expenses for course-related books, supplies, and equipment costs must be paid directly to an educational institution as a condition of enrollment or attendance to be considered qualified education expenses.

For tax years beginning before December 31, 2015, Educational Institutions typically reported amounts billed for tuition and related expenses on Form 1098-T. In some instances, however, the taxpayer would not pay the amount billed during the year yet would attempt to claim tax credits for qualified educational expenses on their tax return. To avoid this abuse, The Protecting Americans from Tax Hikes Act of 2015 (PATH 2015) requires higher educational institutions issuing Form 1098-T to report only the amount of qualified tuition and related expenses actually paid by the student/taxpayer. An additional change to 1098-T reporting was also imposed for tax years beginning after December 31, 2015 to improve tracking and matching of 1098-T forms to amounts claimed by taxpayers to obtain educational credits. The educational institution issuing Form 1098-T must include their employer identification number on the form, and the taxpayer must include the employer identification number of the educational institution on their tax return in order to claim educational expense credits.

Exhibit 9.6 | Form 1098-T

FILER'S name, street address, city or town, state or province, country, ZIP or foreign postal code, and telephone number		1 Payments received for qualified tuition and related expenses $ 2	OMB No. 1545-1574 2021 Form 1098-T	**Tuition Statement**
FILER'S employer identification no.	STUDENT'S TIN	3		**Copy B** **For Student**
STUDENT'S name		4 Adjustments made for a prior year $	5 Scholarships or grants $	This is important tax information and is being furnished to the IRS. This form must be used to complete Form 8863 to claim education credits. Give it to the tax preparer or use it to prepare the tax return.
Street address (including apt. no.) City or town, state or province, country, and ZIP or foreign postal code		6 Adjustments to scholarships or grants for a prior year $	7 Checked if the amount in box 1 includes amounts for an academic period beginning January–March 2022 ☐	
Service Provider/Acct. No. (see instr.)	8 Checked if at least half-time student ☐	9 Checked if a graduate student ☐	10 Ins. contract reimb./refund $	

Form **1098-T** (keep for your records) www.irs.gov/Form1098T Department of the Treasury - Internal Revenue Service

No Double Benefit

A double benefit for the same expenses is not allowed. Qualified tuition and related expenses that are paid with scholarships, Pell grants, excludable employer-provided educational assistance, veterans' educational assistance, and similar sources of funding that are excluded from gross income are not eligible for the credit.[2] Therefore, total qualified tuition and related expenses must be reduced by such funding sources before the credits are calculated. However, qualified expenses do include tuition and related expenses paid with borrowed money or with money received as a gift or inheritance.

> **Key Concepts**
>
> 1. Explain the "no double benefit" rule.
> 2. Describe who can claim an education credit.
> 3. Explain the "eligible student" requirement of the American Opportunity Tax Credit.
> 4. Define the amount of credit available under the American Opportunity Tax Credit and the Lifetime Learning Credit.

Additional rules designed to prevent taxpayers from receiving a double benefit for educational costs prohibit a taxpayer from:

- deducting qualifying expenses as a business expense or otherwise and also claiming an education credit based on the same expenses;
- claiming an American Opportunity Tax Credit and a Lifetime Learning Credit based on the same qualified education expenses; or
- claiming an education credit based on the same expenses used to figure the tax-free portion of a distribution from a Coverdell Education Savings Account or qualified tuition program (Sec. 529 plan).

A taxpayer can claim both credits in the same year but not for the same student. If a student qualifies a taxpayer for both education credits, the taxpayer may claim either the American Opportunity Tax Credit or the Lifetime Learning Credit for that student for that year. For students who qualify, The American Opportunity Tax Credit is preferable to the Lifetime Learning credit, because it will generate a larger tax savings with a smaller cash outlay for qualified education expenses.

Eligible Educational Institution

An eligible educational institution is a college, university, vocational school, or other postsecondary educational institution that is eligible to participate in a student aid program administered by the federal Department of Education. Almost all accredited postsecondary institutions meet the eligibility requirements.

Income Limitation

Once the tentative amounts for the two credits are determined, they must be reduced ratably as the taxpayer's modified adjusted gross income (MAGI) for 2021 ranges between \$80,000 - \$90,000. The phaseout range for joint returns is \$160,000 - \$180,000 for 2021.[3] The credits are phased out over a \$10,000 range (\$20,000 for a joint return) and the lower limit is adjusted for inflation. For purposes of

2. Emergency financial aid grants received under the CARES Act of 2020 are not included in the gross income of the recipient and do not reduce the amount of qualified education expenses for purposes of the American Opportunity Tax Credit or Lifetime Learning Tax Credit (COVID-Related Tax Relief Act (COVIDTRA) of 2020, Sec. 277).
3. Prior to January 1, 2021, the Lifetime Learning credit phaseout thresholds were lower (scheduled to be \$59,000 - \$69,000 Single, \$119,000 - \$139,000 MFJ in 2021). In addition, an above-the-line deduction for qualified tuition and related expenses was available on a year-by-year basis (as extended by Congress). The Taxpayer Certainty and Disaster Tax Relief Act of 2020 permanently repealed the above-the-line deduction and permanently increased the phaseout of the Lifetime Learning Credit, bringing the LLC phaseout into alignment with that of the AOTC, for tax years beginning after December 31, 2020.

these education credits, MAGI is equal to adjusted gross income plus excluded income from foreign countries, specified U.S. possessions, and Puerto Rico.

Claiming the Credits

The education credits are normally claimed by a taxpayer who pays qualified education expenses for himself, his spouse, or his dependent for whom he claims an exemption. When the taxpayer pays qualified education expenses for a claimed dependent, any expenses paid by the dependent or even by a third party are considered to be paid by the taxpayer. If the taxpayer does not claim an exemption for a dependent (even if the taxpayer is entitled to do so), the dependent can claim the credit, but the taxpayer cannot. In this situation, any qualified education expenses paid by the taxpayer or another person are normally considered to be paid by the dependent. A person who is claimed as the dependent of another is not eligible to claim an education credit.

In order to claim the education credits, a married taxpayer must file a joint return.

Exhibit 9.7 | The American Opportunity Tax Credit and Lifetime Learning Credit Compared

Feature	*American Opportunity Tax Credit*	*Lifetime Learning Credit*
Base and Rate	$2,000 @ 100% plus $2,000 @ 25% (2021)	$10,000 @ 20%
Maximum Annual Credit	$2,500 per eligible student (2021)	$2,000 per tax return
General Availability	For the first four years of postsecondary education	For all years of postsecondary education and for courses to acquire or improve job skills
Years Available	Four years per student	Unlimited number of years
Degree Requirement	Student must pursue an undergraduate degree or other recognized education credential.	Student does not need to pursue a degree or education credential.
Half-time Requirement	Student must be enrolled at least half-time for one academic period during the year.	Student must take one or more courses.
Drug Conviction	No felony drug conviction on student's record.	Felony drug conviction rule does not apply.
Phaseout	$80,000 - $90,000 (Single) $160,000 - $180,000 (MFJ)	$80,000 - $90,000 (Single) $160,000 - $180,000 (MFJ)

American Opportunity Tax Credit

The **American Opportunity Tax Credit** is allowed for the qualified education expenses of an eligible student during the first four years of postsecondary education, and the credit can be claimed for only four tax years. The American Opportunity Tax Credit is not allowed for a student who has completed the first four years of postsecondary education before the beginning of the tax year.

Eligible Student

In order to qualify for the American Opportunity Tax Credit, an eligible student must be:

- enrolled at least half-time for one quarter, semester, or other academic period
- enrolled in a program leading to a degree, certificate, or other educational credential
- free of any federal or state felony conviction for possessing or distributing a controlled substance

Amount of the Credit

The amount of the American Opportunity Tax Credit is 100 percent of the first $2,000 of qualified tuition and related expenses plus 25 percent of the next $2,000 of qualified expenses for the 2021 tax year. Therefore, the maximum credit is $2,500 for 2021.

Example 9.12

Tanner, a married taxpayer filing jointly, paid $5,000 of qualified tuition and related expenses for each of his twin daughters (a total of $10,000), Ashley and Kate, during 2021. They finished their freshman year and started their sophomore year of college during 2021. Tanner claims both of his daughters as dependents. His modified adjusted gross income for the year is $70,000. His American Opportunity Tax Credit for 2021 is $5,000 (maximum credit of $2,500 x 2). Since the American Opportunity Tax Credit is available for each student, he can claim the maximum credit for each daughter. If he uses the expenses to claim the Lifetime Learning Credit instead, his maximum credit will be $2,000 (20% x $10,000).

Requirements Imposed on the AOTC by PATH 2015

For several years, the American Opportunity Tax Credit was scheduled to sunset and revert back to the rules that governed the HOPE Credit. PATH 2015 removed this uncertainty and made the American Opportunity Tax Credit permanent.

To help prevent erroneous claims of the American Opportunity Tax Credit, PATH 2015 imposed new requirements on both taxpayers and tax preparers, and created new consequences for intentional disregard of the tax laws when claiming the credit.

In order to claim the American Opportunity Tax Credit, the taxpayer for whom the credit is claimed must have a tax identification number (for individuals, a Social Security Number) that has been issued prior to the due date for filing the tax return for the taxable year the credit is claimed. The American Opportunity Tax Credit will not be available for any taxpayer whose tax ID number was issued after the due date for filing the tax return for the taxable year. Filing amended returns to obtain American Opportunity Tax Credits in prior tax years is no longer permitted (for tax periods beginning after December 31, 2015) if the taxpayer did not have a valid taxpayer identification number as of the due date of the tax return.

Over the past several years, the IRS has seen an increase in fraudulent claims of the American Opportunity Tax Credit. In an effort to help prevent this abuse, paid tax preparers who prepare tax returns where the American Opportunity Tax Credit is claimed must meet additional due diligence requirements that are similar to those imposed when claiming the Earned Income Credit. Tax preparers who fail to comply with these due diligence requirements will be subject to additional penalties and potential administrative action, which could include being barred from filing tax returns with the IRS as a paid preparer in the future.

In the event that the IRS determines that a taxpayer fraudulently claimed the American Opportunity Tax Credit, or claimed the credit with a reckless or intentional disregard of the tax rules, that taxpayer will be barred from claiming the American Opportunity Tax Credit for a period of two years. Recall that the American Opportunity Tax Credit is only available for the first four years of post-secondary education, so denying the credit for two years can result in depriving the taxpayer of at least half the benefit of the credit during that four year period. This provision is effective for tax years beginning after December 31, 2015.

Quick Quiz 9.3

1. A taxpayer may claim both the American Opportunity Tax Credit and the Lifetime Learning Credit based on the same qualified education expenses.
   a. True
   b. False
2. The education credits are normally claimed by the taxpayer who pays the qualified education expenses.
   a. True
   b. False
3. The felony drug conviction rule does not apply to the American Opportunity Tax Credit.
   a. True
   b. False
4. The maximum annual Lifetime Learning Credit is $2,000.
   a. True
   b. False

False, True, False, True.

Lifetime Learning Credit

The **Lifetime Learning Credit** is available to a taxpayer who pays qualified tuition and related expenses to an eligible institution for himself, his spouse, and his dependent for whom he claims a dependency exemption. The qualified expenses must relate to any course of instruction at an eligible educational institution to acquire or improve job skills of the individual.

No Eligible Student Requirement

With the Lifetime Learning Credit, there is no requirement for the student to:

1. seek a degree or certificate,
2. pay the expenses for the first four years of postsecondary education, or
3. be free of a felony conviction related to a controlled substance.

Qualified education expenses incurred to attend a regular class or a continuing education course at an eligible educational institution will qualify for this credit.

Amount of the Credit

The amount of the Lifetime Learning Credit is 20 percent of the first $10,000 of qualified tuition and related expenses for the year. Therefore, the maximum annual credit is $2,000. Both the rate and the $10,000 are fixed (no inflation adjustments). Unlike the American Opportunity Tax Credit, the Lifetime Learning Credit limits are based on the tax return rather than the number of eligible students. With the Lifetime Learning Credit, the qualified education expenses for all family members can be combined to calculate the credit.

Retirement Savings Contributions Credit (Saver's Credit)

The **retirement savings contributions credit** is intended to encourage lower-income taxpayers to save for retirement. The rate used in calculating the credit is reduced as modified adjusted gross income (MAGI) increases, until the rate reaches zero percent at MAGI of $66,000 on a joint return for 2021, $49,500 for a head of household for 2021, and $33,000 in all other cases for 2021. For purposes of this credit, MAGI is defined in IRS Publication 590 as adjusted gross income less any exclusion or deduction claimed for the year for foreign earned income, foreign housing costs, income for bona fide residents of American Samoa, or income from Puerto Rico.

The retirement savings contributions credit is available to an eligible individual who makes qualified retirement savings contributions of up to $2,000 for a tax year. An eligible individual is a person who is 18 or older at the end of the tax year if that person is not allowed to be claimed as a dependent of another person for the year and is not considered to be a full-time student.

The amount of the credit is determined by multiplying a taxpayer's qualified retirement savings contributions (after the reduction for certain distributions) by the applicable percentage from **Exhibit 9.8**.

Exhibit 9.8 | Applicable Percentage for Qualified Retirement Savings Contributions Credit (2021)

Applicable Percentage	*Joint Return Modified AGI*		*Head of a Household Modified AGI*		*All Other Cases Modified AGI*	
	Over	**Not over**	**Over**	**Not over**	**Over**	**Not over**
50%	$0	$39,500	$0	$29,625	$0	$19,750
20%	$39,500	$43,000	$29,625	$32,250	$19,750	$21,500
10%	$43,000	$66,000	$32,250	$49,500	$21,500	$33,000
0%	$66,000	--	$49,500	--	$33,000	--

The maximum credit is $1,000 per person each year, or $2,000 on a joint return. Any credit that cannot be used in the current year is lost.

Example 9.13

Stephanie contributed $4,000 to her Roth IRA for 2021. She had MAGI of $15,000 for 2021 and used the single filing status. She has never taken a distribution from a retirement plan. Her maximum credit for 2021 is $1,000 ($2,000 x 50%).

Assume the same facts as above, except that Stephanie contributes $5,000 to her Roth IRA for 2021. Also assume that her MAGI was $20,000 for 2021, then her maximum credit is $400 ($2,000 x 20%).

Child Tax Credit (IRC Section 24)

A **child tax credit** is available to an individual taxpayer for each qualifying child under the age of 17 (in tax years beginning before or after 2021; age 18 in 2021). In order to claim the credit, the taxpayer must provide the name and Social Security number of each child on the tax return. For tax years before and after 2021, the credit is nonrefundable; however, for the 2021 tax year, the credit is fully refundable for a taxpayer or spouse with a principal place of abode in the United States for more than one-half of the tax year, or for a taxpayer who is a bona fide resident of Puerto Rico for the tax year (ARPA 2021).

Key Concepts

1. Describe a qualifying child.
2. Explain the child tax credit limitation on income.
3. Describe the circumstances under which the child tax credit is a refundable credit.

A Qualifying Child

A qualifying child is defined in a manner similar to that for a dependency exemption, as discussed in Chapter 3. A qualifying child for the child tax credit is a person who:

- Is the son, daughter, stepchild, foster child, brother, sister, stepbrother, stepsister, half brother, half sister, or a descendant of any of them (for example, grandchild).
- Was under the age of 17 (in tax years beginning before or after 2021; under age 18 in 2021) at the end of the tax year.
- Did not provide over half of his own support for the tax year.
- Lived with the taxpayer for more than half the year (see exceptions below).
- Was a U.S. citizen, a U.S. national, or a resident of the United States.

Adopted Child

An adopted child is always treated as the taxpayer's own child. An adopted child includes a child who has been lawfully placed with the taxpayer for adoption.

Exceptions to Time Lived with the Taxpayer

A child who is born or dies during the year is considered to have lived with the taxpayer for the entire year if he lived with the taxpayer for the entire time he was alive during the year. A child is also considered to have lived with the taxpayer for any period during which the child is temporarily absent from the taxpayer's residence attending school, in military service, receiving medical care, being detained in a juvenile facility, or other similar purposes.

Quick Quiz 9.4

1. A 19-year-old person may be a qualifying child for the purposes of the child tax credit.
   a. True
   b. False
2. The child tax credit phaseout range begins at $400,000 for taxpayers who are married filing jointly.
   a. True
   b. False

False, True.

Amount of the Credit

A base credit of up to $2,000 per child is available for taxpayers who meet the qualification rules. The American Rescue Plan Act of 2021 temporarily expanded the amount of the child tax credit to $3,600 per child under the age of six, and $3,000 per child up the age of 17 for tax year 2021. The enhanced portion of the child tax credit (the extra $1,600 per child under age six and $1,000 per child under age 18 over the base child tax credit) is subject to separate phaseout rules.

Limitation Based on Income

The allowable base child tax credit (the base child tax credit is $2,000 per qualifying child) amount is reduced $50 for each $1,000 (or fraction of $1,000) that a taxpayer's modified adjusted gross income (MAGI) exceeds the following amounts:

Married filing jointly*	$400,000
All other filing statuses*	$200,000

** Not adjusted for inflation*

For the child tax credit, MAGI is equal to adjusted gross income increased by excluded income from foreign countries, specified U.S. possessions, and Puerto Rico.

In the 2021 tax year, the allowable enhanced portion of the child tax credit ($1,600 for children under age 6, and $1,000 for children under age 18) is subject to phaseout at lower MAGI levels, as follows:

Married filing jointly*	$150,000
Head of Household*	$112,500
Single*	$75,000

** Phaseout for the enhanced portion of the credit in 2021*

The total credit amount (as opposed to the credit amount per child) is reduced by $50 for every $1,000 (or fraction thereof) by which MAGI exceeds the threshold; therefore, the MAGI level at which the credit is fully phased out will vary depending on the number of children eligible for the credit. Taxpayers with MAGI over these thresholds, but under the phaseout thresholds for the base child tax credit may claim the base child tax credit (but a reduced or eliminated enhanced child tax credit) on their 2021 tax return.

Example 9.14

Heinrich and Gardenia Fischer have three children, ages 5, 7, and 15 in 2021. The Fischers' MAGI for 2021 is $170,000. The amount of child tax credit for each child, without consideration of any phaseout, is as follows:

Child	*Base Child Tax Credit*	*Enhanced Child Tax Credit (2021)*
Age 15	$2,000	$1,000
Age 7	$2,000	$1,000
Age 5	$2,000	$1,600
Total	**$6,000**	**$3,600**

Since the Fichers' MAGI is below $400,000, the base amount of the child tax credit (a total of $6,000) is unaffected by any phaseout. The enhanced portion of the credit, however, is phased out at a rate of $50 per $1,000 (or fraction thereof) by which MAGI exceeds $150,000. Therefore, the enhanced portion of the credit is reduced from $3,600 to $2,600 [($170,000 - $150,0000)/$1,000 = 20 x $50 = $1000 reduction]. Their total child tax credit for 2021 is $8,600 ($6,000 base credit + $2,600 enhanced credit for 2021). If the Fischers' MAGI remains the same in 2022, the child tax credit will be $6,000.

After any reduction of the credit because MAGI exceeds the limits, in tax years that begin before or after 2021, the remaining child tax credit is refundable up to $1,400 per eligible child. For tax year 2021, the entire child tax credit that a taxpayer is eligible to claim is refundable. In addition, one half of the credit will be paid in advance to taxpayers by the IRS as a monthly installment beginning in July 2021 and ending in December 2021. The other half of the credit will be claimed when the taxpayer files their 2021 tax return.

Additional Child Tax Credit Before 2018

For tax years before 2018, a taxpayer who was unable to use all of the otherwise allowable nonrefundable child tax credit because the tax has been reduced to zero by nonrefundable credits could qualify to use some or all of the unused child tax credit as a refundable credit called the additional child tax credit. The determination of the additional child tax credit was complicated, and was calculated using Form 8812. TCJA 2017 repealed the additional child tax credit, and as a substitute made part of the child tax credit refundable.

Refundable Child Tax Credit

Beginning with tax year 2018, up to $1,400 of the $2,000 Child Tax Credit is refundable. The refundable portion of the child tax credit is available for each eligible child. For tax year 2021, the entire child tax credit that a taxpayer is eligible to claim is refundable.

Example 9.15

Penelope is a divorced mother. She has three children under the age of 10 in 2022, has custody of the children, claims them as dependents, uses the head of household filing status, and does not itemize deductions. She earns a salary of $38,792 for 2022 and has federal income tax in the amount of $2,000 withheld from her salary. Her adjusted gross income for the year is $38,792. Her taxable income is $20,142, calculated as follows:

$38,792	Salary (for tax year 2022)
- $18,800	Standard Deduction (HH) (assume same as 2021)
- 0	Personal Exemption
- 0	Dependency Exemption (child 1)
- 0	Dependency Exemption (child 2)
- 0	Dependency Exemption (child 3)
$19,992	**Taxable Income**

Penelope's tax before credits and withholding is $2,115 (per tax rate schedule; assume same as 2021). She has no nonrefundable credits other than the child tax credit. She is eligible for a child tax credit of up to $6,000. She will use a child tax credit of $2,115 to reduce her tax liability to $0. The child tax credit is refundable up to $1,400 per eligible child. When the $3,885 (the remaining child tax credit) of the refundable child tax credit ($1,400 x 3 = limit of $4,200) is added to the $2,000 of federal income taxes withheld from her salary, Penelope will receive a tax refund of $5,885. The earned income credit is ignored for purposes of this example. ($2,000 + $6,000 - $2,115 = $5,885)

Exhibit 9.9 | Form 8812

SCHEDULE 8812
(Form 1040)

Department of the Treasury
Internal Revenue Service (99)

Additional Child Tax Credit

▶ Attach to Form 1040, 1040-SR, or 1040-NR.

▶ Go to *www.irs.gov/Schedule8812* for instructions and the latest information.

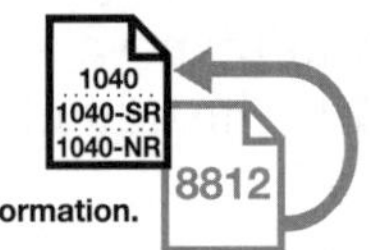

OMB No. 1545-0074

2020

Attachment Sequence No. **47**

Name(s) shown on return | **Your social security number**

Part I All Filers

Caution: If you file Form 2555, **stop here;** you cannot claim the additional child tax credit.

1	If you are required to use the worksheet in Pub. 972, enter the amount from line 10 of the Child Tax Credit and Credit for Other Dependents Worksheet in the publication. Otherwise, enter the amount from line 8 of your Child Tax Credit and Credit for Other Dependents Worksheet. (See the instructions for Forms 1040 and 1040-SR, line 19, or the instructions for Form 1040-NR, line 19.)	1	
2	Enter the amount from line 19 of your Form 1040, Form 1040-SR, or Form 1040-NR	2	
3	Subtract line 2 from line 1. If zero, **stop here;** you cannot claim this credit	3	
4	Number of qualifying children under 17 with the required social security number: ________ x $1,400. Enter the result. If zero, **stop here;** you cannot claim this credit. **TIP:** The number of children you use for this line is the same as the number of children you used for line 1 of the Child Tax Credit and Credit for Other Dependents Worksheet.	4	
5	Enter the **smaller** of line 3 or line 4	5	
6a	Earned income (see instructions) — 6a		
b	Nontaxable combat pay (see instructions) — 6b		
7	Is the amount on line 6a more than $2,500? ☐ **No.** Leave line 7 blank and enter -0- on line 8. ☐ **Yes.** Subtract $2,500 from the amount on line 6a. Enter the result — 7		
8	Multiply the amount on line 7 by 15% (0.15) and enter the result	8	
	Next. On line 4, is the amount $4,200 or more? ☐ **No.** If line 8 is zero, **stop here;** you cannot claim this credit. Otherwise, skip Part II and enter the **smaller** of line 5 or line 8 on line 15. ☐ **Yes.** If line 8 is equal to or more than line 5, skip Part II and enter the amount from line 5 on line 15. Otherwise, go to line 9.		

Part II Certain Filers Who Have Three or More Qualifying Children

9	Withheld social security, Medicare, and Additional Medicare taxes from Form(s) W-2, boxes 4 and 6. If married filing ointly, include your spouse's amounts with yours. If your employer withheld or you paid Additional Medicare Tax or tier 1 RRTA taxes, see instructions — 9		
10	Enter the total of the amounts from Schedule 1 (Form 1040), line 14, and Schedule 2 (Form 1040), line 5, plus any taxes that you identified using code "UT" and entered on Schedule 2 (Form 1040), line 8 — 10		
11	Add lines 9 and 10 — 11		
12	**1040 and 1040-SR filers:** Enter the total of the amounts from Form 1040 or 1040-SR, line 27, and Schedule 3 (Form 1040), line 10. **1040-NR filers:** Enter the amount from Schedule 3 (Form 1040), line 10. — 12		
13	Subtract line 12 from line 11. If zero or less, enter -0-	13	
14	Enter the **larger** of line 8 or line 13 **Next,** enter the **smaller** of line 5 or line 14 on line 15.	14	

Part III Additional Child Tax Credit

15	**This is your additional child tax credit**	15	

1040 / 1040-SR / 1040-NR ◀ *Enter this amount on Form , ne 8; Form -SR, ne 8; or Form -NR, ne 8.*

For Paperwork Reduction Act Notice, see your tax return instructions. Cat. No. 59761M **Schedule 8812 (Form 1040) 2020**

Child Tax Credit Anti-Abuse Provisions Imposed by PATH 2015

As a partially refundable credit, the Child Tax Credit has been a popular one with those who wish to abuse the tax rules, and the IRS has reported a significant increase in non-compliance with the IRC requirements. To help prevent erroneous claims of the Child Tax Credit, PATH 2015 imposed new requirements on both taxpayers and tax preparers, and created new consequences for intentional disregard of the tax laws when claiming the credit.

In order to claim the Child Tax Credit, the taxpayer for whom the credit is claimed must have a tax identification number (for individuals, a Social Security Number) that has been issued prior to the due date for filing the tax return for the taxable year the credit is claimed. The Child Tax Credit will not be available for any taxpayer whose tax ID number was issued after the due date for filing the tax return for the taxable year. Filing amended returns to obtain Child Tax Credits in prior tax years will no longer be permitted (for tax periods beginning after December 31, 2015) if the taxpayer for whom the credit is claimed did not have a valid taxpayer identification number as of the due date of the tax return.

Over the past several years, the IRS has seen an increase in fraudulent claims of the Additional Child Tax Credit. In an effort to help prevent this abuse, paid tax preparers who prepare tax returns where the Additional Child Tax Credit is claimed must meet additional due diligence requirements that are similar to those imposed when claiming the Earned Income Credit. Tax preparers who fail to comply with these due diligence requirements will be subject to additional penalties and potential administrative action, which could include being barred from filing tax returns with the IRS as a paid preparer in the future.

In the event that the IRS determines that a taxpayer fraudulently claimed the Child Tax Credit, or claimed the credit with a reckless or intentional disregard of the tax rules, that taxpayer will be barred from claiming the Child Tax Credit for a period of ten years. Recall that the Child Tax Credit is only available for a dependent under the age of 17, so denying the credit for ten years can result in depriving the taxpayer of more than half the benefit of the credit. This provision is effective for tax years beginning after December 31, 2015.

Other Dependent Credit (ODC)

TCJA 2017 created a new Other Dependent Credit (also called the Family Tax Credit) available for tax years beginning after December 31, 2017. Taxpayers with dependents other than qualified children (for purposes of claiming the Child Tax Credit) may claim a $500 non-refundable credit for each dependent. The Other Dependent Credit does not apply to the taxpayer, or the taxpayer's spouse.

Example 9.16

Derek and Morgan have two children, Emily and Derek, Jr. In 2021, Emily turned age 18, and Derek, Jr. turned 14. Emily just started attending Excel University, and is registered as a full time student. Derek and Morgan file their tax return as a married couple filing jointly, and have adjusted gross income of $150,000. In 2021, they will be able to claim a child tax credit for Derek Jr. of $3,000. In addition, they will be able to claim the Other Dependent Credit for Emily, since she is their dependent (as a full time student under the age of 24), of $500. Derek and Morgan may not, however, claim a $500 credit for themselves on their tax return. Their total child and other dependent credit, therefore, will be $3,500.

Residential Energy Property and Residential Energy Efficient Property Credits

The American Recovery and Reinvestment Act of 2009 provided energy saving incentives for taxpayers. The **Residential Energy Property Credit** increases the energy tax credit for energy efficient improvements made to a taxpayer's existing home. The credit rate is 30 percent of the cost of all qualifying improvements (i.e., adding insulation, energy efficient heating and air conditioning systems, and energy efficient exterior windows) with a maximum combined credit limit of $1,500.

The credit for nonbusiness energy property is not a permanent credit but has been extended through December 31, 2023 by various Acts of Congress throughout the years (subject to rate reductions in later years).

The **Residential Energy Efficient Property Credit** is a nonrefundable energy tax credit that helps an individual taxpayer pay for qualified residential alternative energy equipment. Previously imposed dollar caps on the residential alternative energy equipment have been removed leaving a credit equal to 10 or 30 percent of the cost of qualified property (see **Exhibit 9.10**).[4]

Key Concepts

1. Define qualified adoption expenses.
2. Explain the standards for considering a child to be a special needs child.
3. Describe the phaseout range for the qualified adoption expenses credit.

Exhibit 9.10 | Residential Energy Efficient Property Credit

Qualified Energy-Efficient Products at 10% Rate	*Qualified Energy-Efficient Products at 30% (26% in 2021) Rate*
Insulation	Solar electric property
Exterior Doors, Windows and Skylights	Solar water heating property
Water Heaters and Heat Pumps	Fuel cell property
Central Air Conditioners	Wind energy property
Furnaces	Geothermal heat pump property
Hot Water Boilers	Qualified biomass fuel property
Advanced Main Air Circulating Fans	
Metal or Asphalt Roof with Pigmented Coatings or Cooling Granules Designed to Reduce Heat Gain	

The limits in the table above apply to each residence. If a taxpayer has more than one residence, the limits for qualified solar electric property and qualified solar water heating property apply to each residence. Any limits for qualified fuel cell property limits apply only to the taxpayer's principal residence.

4. For property placed in service during 2021 and 2022, the 30% rate is reduced to 26%. For property placed in service during 2023, the 30% rate is reduced to 22%.

If more than one taxpayer occupies a residence, each taxpayer may have to report his qualifying expenditures for the year on his own return and the limits for the residence in the table above may have to be allocated to the eligible taxpayers. For obvious reasons, an allocation is not necessary for married taxpayers filing a joint return.

The amount of the annual credit is equal to the sum of the credits for each type of qualifying expenditure. Any amount of the credit that cannot be used in the current year because the nonrefundable credits have reduced the year's income tax to zero can be carried forward to the next year. For fuel cell property, the maximum credit is $500 per each half-kilowatt of capacity.

Example 9.17

In 2021, Tara paid $8,000 for qualified solar electric property for her vacation home and also paid $6,000 for qualified fuel cell property with one kilowatt of capacity for her principal residence. Her maximum residential energy efficient property credit for 2021 is $3,080 [($8,000 x 26% = $2,080) + (lesser of, $6,000 x 26% = $1,560 or $500 x 2 = $1,000)].

Qualified Adoption Expenses Credit

The **adoption expenses credit** is designed to encourage the adoption of children. More generous provisions apply if an adopted child is a U.S. citizen or resident with special needs. If a child is not a citizen or resident of the U.S. at the time the adoption process begins, no credit is allowed unless the adoption becomes final.

An adoption expenses credit is allowed for qualified adoption expenses paid by an individual to adopt an eligible child. Qualified adoption expenses include adoption fees, court costs, attorney fees, and travel expenses (including amounts spent for meals and lodging) while away from home. An eligible child is a child under 18 or a child who is physically or mentally incapable of caring for himself.

Although the adoption expenses credit is now a nonrefundable credit, it was refundable for 2010 and 2011.

Qualifying adoption expenses do not include any of the following expenses:

- expenses that violate state or federal law,
- expenses for carrying out any surrogate parenting arrangement,
- expenses for the adoption of a spouse's child,
- expenses for which the taxpayer received funds under any federal, state, or local program,
- expenses allowed as a credit or deduction under any other federal income tax rule, or
- expenses paid or reimbursed by the taxpayer's employer or any other person or organization.

Quick Quiz 9.5

1. Expenses for the adoption of a spouse's child are not qualifying adoption expenses.
   a. True
   b. False
2. The maximum credit (subject to income limitations) is allowed for the adoption of a child with special needs even if the adopting parent has no qualified adoption expenses.
   a. True
   b. False
3. For 2021, the qualified adoption expenses credit begins to phaseout for MAGI above $216,660.
   a. True
   b. False

True, True, True.

The maximum credit (subject to income limitations) is allowed for the adoption of a child with special needs even if the adopting parent has no qualified adoption expenses. For a child to be considered a child with special needs:

1. the child must be a citizen or resident of the United States (including U.S. possessions) at the time the adoption process begins,
2. the state must have determined that the child cannot or should not be returned to his parents, and
3. the state has determined that the child will not be adopted due to a physical, mental, or emotional handicap, age, or one of several other specified factors unless assistance is provided to the adopting parents.

For expenses paid or incurred in a tax year before the adoption becomes final, the credit is allowed for the following year. For expenses paid or incurred during or after the tax year the adoption becomes final, the credit is allowed for the year of the expense.

The amount of the adoption expenses credit is 100 percent of the qualified adoption expenses up to $14,440 for 2021 for the adoption of each child. The amount of the credit for the adoption of a child with special needs is $14,440 for 2021 regardless of the amount of the qualified adoption expenses. Portions of the credit may be claimed in different years.

Whether the adopted child is a child with special needs or not, the maximum amount of the credit is phased out if the taxpayer's modified adjusted gross income (MAGI), as defined in IRC Section 23, exceeds $216,660 for 2021. The maximum credit is ratably phased out as the taxpayer's MAGI ranges between $216,660 and $256,600 for 2021, the $40,000 phaseout range.

Example 9.18

During 2021, Meredith and Derek Campbell paid $16,000 of adoption expenses to adopt their new daughter, Zola. The adoption was final in October of 2021. Their modified adjusted gross income for 2021 was $220,000. Their maximum allowable adoption expenses credit is $13,234 for 2021 as calculated below.

1. Maximum credit (2021)		$14,440
2. Excess MAGI:		
MAGI	$220,000	
Lower MAGI limit	$216,660	
Excess	$3,340	
3. Reduction of maximum credit:		
$\frac{\$3,340}{\$40,000}$ x $14,440 =		$1,206
4. Maximum (the difference between 1 and 3)		$13,234

If the MAGI of the Campbells had been $120,000 for 2021 they would have been allowed to claim an adoption expenses credit of $14,440 for 2021. If their MAGI had been $120,000 and they had paid qualifying adoption expenses of only $9,000 during 2021, their adoption expenses credit would have been $9,000.

Any portion of the adoption expenses credit that cannot be used in the tax year can be carried forward for up to five years using a first-in, first-out (FIFO) method. The FIFO method allows the taxpayer to use the oldest credits first.

REFUNDABLE CREDITS

Once nonrefundable credits have been used to the extent possible to reduce the tax calculated on taxable income, refundable credits can be used in the current year to further reduce the year's tax liability and/or to generate a tax refund.

Credits for Taxes Paid

Quite appropriately, any federal income taxes paid in advance by a taxpayer will generate a refundable **credit for the taxpayer**. Advance payments of taxes include:

1. federal income taxes withheld by employers and others
2. estimated federal income taxes paid by the taxpayer
3. refunds from prior tax years that have been retained by the Internal Revenue Service at the request of the taxpayer
4. excess Social Security taxes (OASDI) withheld when a taxpayer has more than one employer

Key Concepts

1. Describe the available credits for taxes paid.
2. Explain the purpose of the earned income credit.
3. Define "eligible individual" for the purposes of the earned income credit.
4. Describe the other available refundable tax credits.

For 2021, Social Security or OASDI taxes of 6.2 percent must be withheld by the employer on the first $142,800 of salary or wages earned by an employee. This wage base is adjusted upward each year due to inflation. Each employer is required to withhold this tax and remit it to the federal government. If the combined compensation subject to Social Security taxes exceeds the wage base for the year, excess taxes may be withheld and should be repaid to the taxpayer.

Example 9.19

Callie earns a salary of $150,000 from Company A during 2021. For purposes of this example, assume that the Social Security wage base is $142,800. Company A withholds OASDI taxes in the amount of $8,854 (0.062 x $142,800). Callie also earns $10,000 of wages from Company B. Company B withholds OASDI taxes in the amount of $620 (0.062 x $10,000). Callie will be allowed to take a $620 refundable credit against income taxes for the excess Social Security taxes withheld from her compensation during the year.

If a taxpayer has only one employer and that employer withholds too much in Social Security taxes from his or her compensation for the year, the taxpayer is not allowed to take a refundable credit for the excess. The taxpayer must seek a reimbursement from his or her employer for the excess taxes withheld.

In addition to the federal income taxes withheld from compensation by employers, federal income taxes are often withheld and paid to the government on retirement plan distributions, traditional IRA distributions, and annuities.

Earned Income Credit

The **earned income credit** is intended to motivate lower-income taxpayers to earn income. The credit increases as the individual's earned income increases up to a maximum level of earned income. This generous refundable credit provides a tax refund to many people who have not paid in any federal income taxes through withholding or otherwise. In one sense, it is effectively a negative or reverse income tax since money is paid out to the taxpayer by the government rather than having the taxpayer pay taxes to the government. It is slightly more generous for taxpayers who are married filing jointly than for those who are not. It is much more generous for a taxpayer who has one qualifying child than for a taxpayer who has no qualifying child, and most generous for a taxpayer who has three or more qualifying children.

The earned income credit is available to an eligible individual who has earned income for the tax year provided his income does not exceed specified limits. As income increases beyond the maximum level of earned income, the credit remains level until a phaseout level of income is reached. The credit is then gradually decreased as higher levels of income are earned until the credit is reduced to zero. The relevant income levels, credit rates, and phaseout rates are dependent on filing status and the number of qualifying children of the taxpayer. These income levels and rates are presented in the following exhibits.

Exhibit 9.11 | Earned Income Tax Credit (EITC) Summary (2021)

EITC Situation	*No Children*	*With 1 Child*	*With 2 Children*	*With 3+ Children*
1. Earned Income Amount (minimum income earned required to claim credit)	\$7,100[1]	\$10,640	\$14,950	\$14,950
2. Earned Income Credit Percentage	7.65%[2]	34%	40%	45%
3. Maximum Amount of Credit	\$543[3]	\$3,618	\$5,980	\$6,728
4. Phaseout Threshold Amount Begins (for Single, SS, or Head of Household)	\$8,880[4]	\$19,520	\$19,520	\$19,520
5. Phaseout Amount When Credit Ends (for Single, SS, or Head of Household)	\$15,980[5]	\$42,158	\$47,915	\$51,464
6. Phaseout Threshold Amount Begins (for Married Filing Jointly)	\$14,820	\$25,470	\$25,470	\$25,470
7. Phaseout Amount When Credit Ends (for Married Filing Jointly)	\$21,920[6]	\$48,108	\$53,865	\$57,414

1. Increased to \$9,820 for tax year 2021 by ARPA 2021.
2. Increased to 15.3% for tax year 2021 by ARPA 2021.
3. Increased to \$1,502 for tax year 2021 by ARPA 2021.
4. Increased to \$11,610 for tax year 2021 by ARPA 2021.
5. Increased number (under ARPA 2021) not yet released by the IRS as of the time of printing. Estimated to be \$21,426 for tax year 2021.
6. Increased number (under ARPA 2021) not yet released by the IRS as of the time of printing. Estimated to be \$24,636 for tax year 2021.

The earned income credit of eligible individuals who are married filing jointly with three or more qualifying children is zero when earned income is zero. As earned income increases up to the maximum level of earned income (rows 5 and 7 in **Exhibit 9.11**), the credit is determined by multiplying earned income by the credit percentage (row 2). At the $14,950 minimum level of earned income for 2021, the maximum credit is $6,728 ($14,950 x 45%). That maximum credit is allowed until the phaseout amount of income is reached (rows 5 and 7).

The income level at which the credit phaseout begins is based upon the greater of earned income or adjusted gross income (AGI). The MFJ phaseout begins at $25,470 of income for three or more children (2021). The phaseout amount is subtracted from the $6,728 maximum credit (2021). The phaseout amount is equal to the income (the greater of earned income or AGI) of the taxpayer in excess of the phaseout amount multiplied by the phaseout percentage. For tax year 2021, ARPA 2021 allows the taxpayer to elect to use earned income from the 2019 tax year if it is higher than earned income in 2021 and will result in a higher credit amount. This election does not change the taxpayer's gross income or impact any other portion of the tax formula calculation for the 2021 tax year.[5]

The table, summary, and explanation above are intended to illustrate the concepts behind the determination of the earned income credit. In filing a tax return, the taxpayer may determine the amount of the earned income credit by filling in the applicable worksheets and referring to a table for the amount of the credit or may simply use a computer program to calculate the credit. IRS Publication 596 contains several examples with filled-in schedules and worksheets.

Eligible Individual

All eligible individuals must meet the following requirements:

- Taxpayer (or spouse if married) must have earned income.
- Earned income and adjusted gross income must each be less than the phaseout end amount (rows 5 or 7 of **Exhibit 9.11**).
- Taxpayer (and spouse if married) must have a valid Social Security number.
- Filing status generally cannot be married filing separately.[6]
- Taxpayer (and spouse if married) must be a U.S. citizen or resident alien all year.
- Cannot claim a foreign earned income exclusion for the year.
- Cannot be a qualifying child of another person.
- Investment income must be $10,000 or less for 2021.[7]

Additional requirements for a taxpayer with a qualifying child:

- The child must meet relationship, age, and residency tests.
- The qualifying child cannot be used by more than one person to claim the earned income credit.

Additional requirements for a taxpayer with no qualifying child:

- Taxpayer (or spouse if married) must be at least age 25 but under age 65. The American Rescue Plan Act (ARPA) of 2021 temporarily reduced the lower age limit from 25 to 19 and eliminated the upper age limit for taxpayers with no qualifying children, for the 2021 tax year.
- Taxpayer cannot be the dependent of another person.
- Taxpayer must have lived in the United States more than half of the year.

5. The Taxpayer Certainty and Disaster Tax Relief Act of 2020 similarly allows a taxpayer to elect to use 2019 earned income in determining their 2020 earned income tax credit, if the 2019 earned income was higher and will result in a larger tax credit.
6. Limited exceptions apply for taxpayers who do not file jointly with a spouse if the taxpayer does not live with the spouse and the taxpayer maintains a home for a qualifying child. IRC §32(d).
7. Permanently increased from $3,650 by ARPA 2021. The $10,000 will be indexed for inflation for tax years beginning after 2021.

Qualifying Child

A qualifying child of an eligible individual must meet relationship, age, and residency tests that are almost identical to those required to claim a dependency exemption for a qualifying child. These relationship, age, and residency tests are briefly summarized below. A qualifying child for the earned income credit is a person who:

- **Relationship:** Is the son, daughter, stepchild, foster child, brother, sister, stepbrother, stepsister, half brother, half sister, or a descendant of any of them
- **Age:** Was under the age of 19 as of the end of the calendar year, a student under the age of 24 as of the end of the calendar year, or permanently and totally disabled at any time during the year
- **Residency:** Lived with the taxpayer in the United States for more than half the year

> ### *Quick Quiz 9.6*
>
> 1. A taxpayer who has too much OASDI tax withheld may only take a refundable credit if he has more than one employer.
>   a. True
>   b. False
> 2. The earned income credit is not a refundable credit.
>   a. True
>   b. False
>
> True, False.

EITC Fraud

The Government Accountability Office has listed the Earned Income Tax Credit (EITC) Program as having the third highest dollar amount of improper payments of all federal programs. The Internal Revenue Service (IRS) has made little improvement in reducing EITC improper payments since 2003 when it was first required to report estimates of these payments to Congress. IRS continues to report an enormous error rate for EITC payments. In Fiscal Year 2019, the IRS estimated that 25.3 percent, or $17.4 billion, of these program payments were improper.

In an attempt to combat EITC fraud, PATH 2015 imposed a new requirement for claiming the EITC. In order to claim the EITC, the taxpayer for whom the credit is claimed must have a tax identification number (a Social Security number) that has been issued prior to the due date for filing the tax return for the taxable year the credit is claimed. The EITC will not be available for any taxpayer whose tax ID number was issued after the due date for filing the tax return for the taxable year. Filing amended returns to obtain earned income tax credits in prior tax years will no longer be permitted (for tax periods beginning after December 31, 2015) if the taxpayer for whom the credit is claimed did not have a valid taxpayer identification number as of the due date of the tax return.

GENERAL BUSINESS CREDIT

The **general business credit** is a combination of more than thirty different nonrefundable tax credits. These credits are intended to promote social, economic, environmental, and other objectives favored by Congress.

Like the nonbusiness credits that are nonrefundable, the components of the general business credit must be considered in sequence. Any portion of the general business credit that cannot be used in the current year can be carried back to the preceding year and then carried forward for up to twenty years if necessary.

> ### *Key Concepts*
>
> 1. Describe the carryforward and carryback rules for the general business credit.
> 2. List the components of the general business credit.

In a given tax year, the general business credit may consist of credit amounts carried forward to the current year, the business credit generated in the current year, and credit amounts carried back to the current year. These credits are used in a first-in, first-out (FIFO) sequence.

The credits are to be used in the following order:

- The business credit carryforwards to the current year
- The amount of the current year business credit
- The business credit carrybacks to the current year

This sequence is favorable to the taxpayer because it gives the taxpayer the best opportunity to use the general business credit carryforwards before they expire.

The general business credit may not be allowed to offset all of the income tax remaining after the application of the nonrefundable credits discussed earlier in this chapter. A limit must be calculated to determine how much of the general business credit can be used in the current year. The components of the general business credit are listed in **Exhibit 9.12**.

The general business credit is reported on Form 3800.

A brief discussion of a few of the components of the general business credit follows.

Exhibit 9.12 | General Business Credit

General Business Credit (Nonrefundable)
Unused Credit: Carryback 1 Year; Carryforward 20 Years
See IRS Publication 334, Tax Guide for Small Business

Item	Credit Sequence	IRC §	Reported on Form
General Business Credit		38	3800
Investment Credit	1	46	3468
Work Opportunity Credit	2	51(a)	5884
Biofuel Producer Credit	3	40	6478
Research Credit (Credit for Increasing Research Activities)	4	41(a)	6765
Low-income Housing Credit	5	42(a)	8586
Enhanced Oil Recovery Credit	6	43(a)	8830
Disabled Access Credit	7	44(a)	8826
Renewable Electricity, Refined Coal, & Indian Coal Production Credit	8	45	8835
Empowerment Zone Employment Credit	9	1396	8844
Indian Employment Credit	10	45A(a)	8845
Employer Social Security Credit	11	45B(a)	8846
Orphan Drug Credit	12	45C(a)	8820
New Markets Credit	13	45D(a)	8874
Small Employer Pension Plan Startup Costs Credit	14	45E(a)	8881
Employer-Provided Child Care Credit	15	45F(a)	8882
Qualified Railroad Track Maintenance Credit	16	45G(a)	8900
Biodiesel and Renewable Diesel Fuels Credit	17	40A(a)	8864
Low Sulfur Diesel Fuel Production Credit	18	45H(a)	8896
Credit for Oil and Gas Production from Marginal Wells	19	45I(a)	carry fwd only
Distilled Spirits Credit	20	5011(a)	8906
Nonconventional Source Fuel Production Credit	21	45K(a)	8907
Energy Efficient Home Credit	22	45L(a)	8908
Energy Efficient Appliance Credit	23	45M(a)	8909
Alternative Motor Vehicle Credit	24	30B(g)(1)	8910
Alternative Fuel Vehicle Refueling Property Credit	25	30C(d)(1)	8911
Mine Rescue Team Training Credit	26	45N(a)	8923
Credit for Employer Differential Wage Payments	27	45P	8932
Carbon Oxide Sequestration Credit	28	45Q	8933
Qualified Plug-In Electic Drive Motor Vehicle Credit	29	30D	8936
Credit for Small Employer Health Insurance Premiums	30	45R	8941
Employee Retention Credit (Qualified Disaster Areas)	31	38*	5884-A
Employer Credit for Paid Family and Medical Leave	32	45S	8994
Credit for Auto-Enrollment in Small Employer Retirement Plan	33	45T	8881

* Public Law 116-94, Div. Q, Sec. 203

Investment Credit

The **investment credit** consists of the sum of five different credits:

- the rehabilitation credit
- the energy credit
- the qualifying advanced coal project credit
- the qualifying gasification project credit
- the qualifying advanced energy project credit

Only the rehabilitation credit will be discussed here.

Rehabilitation Credit

This rehabilitation credit is intended to promote the improvement and continued use of older buildings. The credit is allowed for qualified rehabilitation expenditures made for any qualified rehabilitated building if the building is substantially rehabilitated.

Prior to TCJA 2017, there was a two-tier credit for rehabilitation expenditures – a 20 percent credit for certified historic structures and a 10 percent credit for qualified rehabilitated buildings that were placed in service prior to 1936. The TCJA 2017 eliminated the 10 percent credit and modified the 20 percent credit to be claimed ratably over a five-year period.

The new law also provides transitional rules for qualified rehabilitation expenditures (for a pre-1936 building) with respect to any building owned or leased by the taxpayer at all times on and after January 1, 2018, the 24-month period (over which rehabilitation expenses are incurred) selected by the taxpayer is to begin no later than the end of the 180-day period beginning on the date of the enactment of the TCJA 2017.

The total of the four components of the investment credit is calculated on Form 3468 and then carried to Form 3800, the general business credit form.

Work Opportunity Credit

The **work opportunity credit** is intended to promote the hiring of targeted groups of people who have special needs or high unemployment rates. The credit is allowed on up to $6,000 of qualified first-year wages paid to an employee in a targeted group. A targeted group employee must be certified by a state employment security agency to be a member of one of the following ten targeted groups:

1. a qualified IV-A recipient (recipients of assistance under Temporary Assistance for Needy Families (TANF))
2. veterans
3. ex-felons
4. designated community residents, age 18 to 40, who live in an empowerment zone, enterprise community, or renewal community
5. vocational rehabilitation referrals
6. summer youth employees, age 16 or 17, who live in an empowerment zone, enterprise community, or renewal community
7. supplemental nutrition assistance program benefits (food stamp) recipients, or
8. supplemental security income (SSI) recipients
9. long-term family assistance recipient
10. qualified long-term unemployment recipient

The amount of the credit is 40 percent of the qualified first-year wages up to $6,000 ($3,000 for a summer youth employee) paid to a targeted group employee. This 40 percent rate applies only if the employee works at least 400 hours during the year. For an employee who work at least 120 hours but less than 400 hours, the rate is 25 percent. The amount of first-year wages may be increased to $12,000, $14,000, or $24,000 for qualified veterans.

Wages expense for the tax year must be reduced by the amount of the work opportunity credit of the taxpayer.

The work opportunity credit was scheduled to expire after December 31, 2019, but was extended through December 31, 2020 by the Taxpayer Certainty and Disaster Tax Relief Act of 2019 and further extended through December 31, 2025 by the Consolidated Appropriations Act of 2021.

Credit for Increasing Research Activities

The **credit for increasing research activities** is intended to encourage businesses to conduct research and to increase their research expenditures. The credit is allowed for specified increases in qualified research expenditures.

The credit is really the sum of three components. First, the amount of the incremental research activities credit is 20 percent of a specified increase in qualified research expenditures over a base amount. Second, the amount of energy research portion is 20 percent of business expenses paid to an energy research consortium. Third, the amount of the basic research component is 20 percent of a specified increase in certain basic research payments over a base amount. The third component is available only to regular corporations (C corporations). It is not available to individuals.

Research expenses for the tax year must be reduced by the amount of the research credit determined for the tax year.

For tax years 2009-2014, the research tax credit was subject to a sunset provision. The PATH 2015 permanently extended the research and development credit. In addition, PATH 2015 permits research credits of eligible small businesses to offset both regular and alternative minimum tax liabilities.

Low-Income Housing Credit

The **low-income housing credit** is intended to promote the construction of housing for low-income residents. The credit is based on the qualified basis or cost of the building and the portion of the units that are rented to low-income tenants.

The amount of the credit is the qualified basis of the building multiplied by an applicable percentage rate that is updated by the IRS on a monthly basis. The resulting credit is allocated over a ten-year period if the building continues to meet qualification requirements.

Disabled Access Credit

The **disabled access credit** is intended to encourage small businesses to make their buildings accessible to persons with disabilities. The credit is available to eligible small businesses for eligible access expenditures of up to $10,250. Eligible access expenditures are expenditures made by small businesses to comply with requirements under the Americans with Disabilities Act of 1990.

The amount of the credit is 50 percent of the eligible access expenditures in excess of $250 and not in excess of $10,250. Therefore, the maximum credit is $5,000 [50% x ($10,250 - $250)].

Small Employer Pension Plan Startup Costs Credit

The **small employer pension plan startup costs credit** is intended to encourage small employers to set up retirement plans for employees. The credit is based on qualified startup costs paid or incurred by the employer for the first three years of the plan. Qualified startup costs include the costs of setting up and administering the plan and the cost of retirement-related education for employees with respect to the employer plan.

The amount of the credit is 50 percent of the qualified startup costs for the tax year, not to exceed the greater of:

1. $500, or
2. the lesser of:
   - $250 multiplied by the number of non-highly compensated employees of the eligible employer who are eligible to participate in the plan, or
   - $5,000.

The maximum credit is therefore $5,000 per year.[8] The credit is allowed for the first three years of the employer plan.

The taxpayer's deduction for startup costs must be reduced by the amount of the credit for the tax year.

Quick Quiz 9.7

1. The components of the general business credit can be used in whatever order is most advantageous to the taxpayer.
   a. True
   b. False
2. All components of the general business credit are reported on Form 3800.
   a. True
   b. False
3. The work opportunity credit is intended to promote the hiring of targeted groups of people who have special needs or high unemployment rates.
   a. True
   b. False
4. The disabled access credit may not exceed $5,000.
   a. True
   b. False

False, True, True, True.

Employer-Provided Child Care Credit

The **employer-provided child care credit** is intended to encourage employers to help provide and promote appropriate child care for their employees.

The amount of the credit is equal to the sum of 25 percent of the qualified child care facility expenditures and 10 percent of the qualified child care resource and referral expenditures of the taxpayer for the tax year. The maximum amount of the credit allowed is $150,000 per year.

The basis of a purchased child care facility must be reduced by the amount of any related credit. The deduction for other child care expenditures must be reduced by the amount of the related credit.

8. Increased from $500 by the SECURE Act of 2019 for tax years beginning after December 31, 2019.

Tax Credits from the 2010 Health Care Legislation

The 2010 Health Care Legislation requires taxpayers to purchase and maintain health insurance beginning January 1, 2014. In an effort to assist lower income taxpayers in meeting this obligation, a new **Premium Assistance Credit** (IRC Section 36B) became available beginning in 2014. The Premium Assistance credit is a refundable tax credit available for eligible taxpayers who enroll in a plan offered through a state-sponsored health benefit exchange. The amount of the premium assistance credit, as well as eligibility to claim the credit, depends on the taxpayer's income. To be eligible for the credit, a taxpayer must have income between 100 percent and 400 percent of the federal poverty level, and must not receive health insurance through an employer. When a taxpayer qualifies for the credit, the Treasury will pay the allowable premium assistance credit directly to the health plan in which the taxpayer is enrolled, and the taxpayer will pay the difference between the plan cost and the premium assistance credit directly to the health insurance company sponsoring the plan. Alternatively, eligible taxpayers could elect to pay the full premium amount, and receive payment for the premium assistance credit when they file their income tax return. Inflation adjustments to the credit amount are based on the rate of premium growth for the preceding year over the Consumer Price Index.

In an effort to encourage small businesses to provide health insurance coverage for their employees, the 2010 Health Care Legislation also created a "**Small Business Health Coverage Tax Credit**" by expanding the General Business Credit. A "small business" is a business with 25 or fewer employees and average annual wages of less than $55,600 in 2021. Under IRC Section 45R, the Small Business Health Coverage Tax Credit is up to 50 percent of the nonelective contributions the business makes on behalf of its employees for insurance premiums. For tax exempt organizations, a 35 percent credit against payroll taxes applies (tax exempt organizations are not generally required to pay income tax, so to provide an incentive for those organizations to offer health insurance coverage to their employees, the credit is used to offset payroll tax). Businesses with 10 or fewer employees and average wages of less than $27,800 qualify for 100 percent of the credit. Availability of the credit begins to phaseout once the number of employees exceeds 10, or average wages of the employees exceed $27,800 in 2021.

KEY TERMS

Adoption Expenses Credit – A nonrefundable credit allowed for qualified adoption expenses paid by an individual to adopt an eligible child.

American Opportunity Tax Credit (formerly Hope Scholarship Credit) – A credit (a portion of which is refundable) allowed for the qualified education expenses of an eligible student during the first four years of post-secondary education.

Child Tax Credit – A partially refundable tax credit of $2,000 (in tax years before and after 2021), which is available to an individual taxpayer for each qualifying child under the age of 17 (refundable up to $1,400 per eligible child).

Credit for Child and Dependent Care Expenses – A nonrefundable credit intended to provide some financial relief to individuals who incur employment-related expenses for the care of one or more qualifying individuals. The credit is refundable in 2021 (ARPA 2021).

Credit for Increasing Research Activities – A component of the general business credit intended to encourage businesses to conduct research and increase their research expenditures.

Credit for the Elderly or Disabled – A nonrefundable credit intended to provide financial assistance to elderly or disabled individuals with modest incomes.

Credits for Taxes Paid – Refundable credits generated by federal income taxes paid in advance.

Disabled Access Credit – A component of the general business credit intended to encourage small businesses to make their buildings accessible to persons with disabilities.

Earned Income Credit – A refundable credit intended to reward lower-income taxpayers for earning income.

Employer-Provided Child Care Credit – A component of the general business credit intended to encourage employers to help provide and promote appropriate child care for their employees.

Foreign Tax Credit – A nonrefundable tax credit available to qualifying taxpayers who pay income taxes to a foreign country on foreign source income and also pay U.S. income taxes on the same income.

General Business Credit – A combination of more than thirty different nonrefundable tax credits that must be considered in a specific sequence.

Investment Credit – Part of the general business credit consisting of the sum of five different credits, (1) the rehabilitation credit, (2) the energy credit, (3) the qualifying advanced coal project credit, (4) the qualifying gasification project credit, and (5) the qualifying advanced energy project credit.

Lifetime Learning Credit – A nonrefundable credit available to taxpayers who pay qualified tuition and related expenses to an eligible institution for themselves, their spouses, and their dependents for whom a dependency exemption is claimed.

Low-Income Housing Credit – A component of the general business credit intended to promote the construction of housing for low-income residents.

Nonrefundable Tax Credits – Tax credits that can reduce the tax on taxable income to zero, but cannot generate a tax refund.

Premium Assistance Credit - A credit created by the 2010 Health Care Legislation to provide assistance to low income taxpayers who purchase health insurance through a state-sponsored health benefit exchange.

Refundable Tax Credits – Tax credits that can be used not only to reduce or eliminate the current year's tax, but also to generate a tax refund.

Residential Energy Efficient Property Credit – A nonrefundable energy tax credit that helps an individual taxpayer pay for qualified residential alternative energy equipment.

Residential Energy Property Credit – A credit that increases the energy tax credit for energy efficient improvements made to a taxpayer's existing home.

Retirement Savings Contribution Credit – A nonrefundable credit intended to encourage lower-income taxpayers to save for retirement.

Small Business Health Coverage Tax Credit – A tax credit for organizations that employ 25 or fewer employees who have annual compensation of $55,600 or less. The credit is designed to encourage employers to provide health care benefits to employees.

Small Employer Pension Plan Startup Costs Credit – A component of the general business credit intended to encourage small employers to set up retirement plans for employees.

Tax Credit – An amount that reduces the calculated tax liability of the taxpayer.

Work Opportunity Credit – Part of the general business credit intended to promote the hiring of targeted groups of people who have special needs or high unemployment rates.

DISCUSSION QUESTIONS

SOLUTIONS to the discussion questions can be found exclusively within the chapter. Once you have completed an initial reading of the chapter, go back and highlight the answers to these questions.

1. Compare and contrast nonrefundable and refundable tax credits.
2. Why is a tax credit generally more beneficial than a tax deduction of the same amount?
3. What are the requirements for claiming a tax credit?
4. Can a taxpayer take both a deduction for foreign taxes paid and take the foreign tax credit?
5. Who is a qualifying individual for the purpose of the credit for child and dependent care expenses?
6. Who is a qualified individual for the purpose of the credit for the elderly or disabled?
7. Define qualified tuition and related expenses.
8. Who is an eligible student for the purpose of the American Opportunity Tax Credit (formerly Hope Scholarship Credit)?
9. What is the maximum amount of the Lifetime Learning Credit?
10. What is the purpose of the retirement savings contribution credit and to whom is it available?
11. Who is a qualifying child for the purpose of the child tax credit?
12. Describe the earned income credit.
13. What is the general business credit?
14. Can the general business credit offset all income?
15. What is the purpose of the work opportunity credit?

MULTIPLE CHOICE PROBLEMS

A sample of multiple choice problems is provided below. Additional multiple choice problems are available at money-education.com by accessing the Student Practice Portal.

1. Miranda is a single mom with 2 children, Alex and Bailey. Alex is 14 years old and Bailey is 3 years old. Miranda has AGI of $50,000. She paid the following expenses for child care in 2022:
   - $300 to Alex to care for Bailey so Miranda could go out to dinner with friends.
   - $1,000 for an after-school program for Alex.
   - $3,500 to Miranda's mother for the care of Bailey during the day.

   What is Miranda's available child and dependent care credit in 2022?
   a. $0.
   b. $200.
   c. $600.
   d. $700.

2. Owen, who is single, contributed $6,000 to his Roth IRA for 2021. He had MAGI of $17,000 for 2021 and used the single filing status. Owen has never taken a distribution from a retirement plan. What is his maximum retirement savings credit for 2021?
   a. $0.
   b. $200.
   c. $1,000.
   d. $2,000.

3. Jackson's second wife, Avery, died several years ago. Jackson and Avery had two children together, Lexi and Levi (twins, age 6) and they had adopted a child Preston (age 10). Jackson also had a child, April, age 18, with his first wife. Jackson's fiancé (who also lives with Jackson) gave birth to Jackson's biological child, Teddy, in November of the current year. All five children live with Jackson and he claims all of them as dependents. Jackson's AGI for 2022 is $60,000 and he files head of household. What is Jackson's available child tax credit in 2022?
   a. $2,000.
   b. $4,000.
   c. $8,000.
   d. $10,000.

4. Adele earns a salary of $150,000 from Hospitals, Inc. as a hospital administrator during 2021. Hospitals, Inc. withholds OASDI taxes in the amount of $8,853. She also earns $20,000 of wages from CPR Experts where she teaches CPR. CPR Experts withholds OASDI taxes in the amount of $1,240. What is Adele's available credit for excess Social Security taxes withheld, assuming Adele's tax due before application of the credit is $800?
   a. $0.
   b. $440.
   c. $800.
   d. $1,240.

5. Which of the following statements concerning business credits is correct?
    a. The investment credit consists of the sum of two different credits, (1) the rehabilitation credit, and (2) the qualifying gasification project credit.
    b. The amount of the rehabilitation credit is 20 percent of the qualified rehabilitation expenditures for certified historic structures.
    c. The work opportunity credit is a credit for employees of certain high risk jobs to provide them with an additional benefit because of the risks involved in their job (for example, police officers).
    d. The employer-provided child care credit allows a credit for employer provided payments to 3rd party caregivers.

Additional multiple choice problems are available at *money-education.com* by accessing the Student Practice Portal. Access requires registration of the title using the unique code at the front of the book.

QUICK QUIZ EXPLANATIONS

Quick Quiz 9.1

1. False. A tax credit is an amount that is subtracted from a calculated tax.
2. True.
3. True.
4. False. The benefit received by a taxpayer from a tax credit is not dependent on the taxpayer's marginal tax rate. The benefit received by a taxpayer from a tax deduction, on the other hand, is entirely dependent on the marginal tax rate of the taxpayer.

Quick Quiz 9.2

1. True.
2. False. Because the child and dependent care expenses credit is intended to provide relief for employment-related expenses for the care of one or more qualifying individuals, it is intended to benefit taxpayers who are either working or who are looking for work.
3. True.
4. False. For the purpose of the credit for the elderly or disabled, a qualified individual must be 65 or older at the end of the tax year or under age 65 and (1) retired on total and permanent disability, (2) the recipient of taxable disability benefits, and (3) younger than the mandatory retirement age of the employer at the beginning of the tax year.

Quick Quiz 9.3

1. False. Under the double benefit rule, a taxpayer may not claim both the American Opportunity Tax Credit and the Lifetime Learning Credit for the same expenses.
2. True.
3. False. The felony drug conviction rule applies to the American Opportunity Tax Credit, but not to the Lifetime Learning Credit.
4. True.

Quick Quiz 9.4

1. False. To be a qualifying child for the purposes of the child tax credit, the qualifying child must be under the age of 17 (in tax years beginning before or after 2021; under age 18 in 2021) at the end of the tax year.
2. True.

Quick Quiz 9.5

1. True.
2. True.
3. True.

Quick Quiz 9.6

1. True.
2. False. The earned income credit is a refundable credit intended to reward lower-income taxpayers for earning income.

QUICK QUIZ EXPLANATIONS

Quick Quiz 9.7

1. False. The components of the general business credit must be considered in a specific sequence.
2. True.
3. True.
4. True.

10

BASIS RULES, DEPRECIATION, & ASSET CATEGORIZATION

LEARNING OBJECTIVES

1. Describe how gain or loss is calculated.*
2. Define the purpose of basis.
3. Identify the uses of basis.*
4. Determine the cost basis of an asset.*
5. Identify items that increase basis and items that decrease basis.*
6. Calculate adjusted basis for a taxpayer.*
7. Calculate a taxpayer's gain or loss upon the sale of an investment.*
8. Explain the purpose of depreciation.
9. Identify when a taxpayer may take depreciation deductions.*
10. Calculate the basis of inherited property.*
11. Calculate the basis of gifted property.*
12. Calculate the basis of property transferred between spouses.*
13. Identify the effect of related party transactions on asset basis.*
14. Determine the taxable gain or loss on the sale of property that the taxpayer received as a gift.*
15. Identify the methods of depreciation.*
16. Describe how depreciation deductions are determined for a given asset.*
17. Describe the conventions used to determine depreciation deductions in the first year property is placed in service and in the year the property is sold.*
18. Calculate Section 179 expense, additional first year depreciation, and depreciation under MACRS.*
19. Define amortization.*
20. Define listed property and describe its tax treatment.*
21. Describe the planning benefits of making a Section 179 election.*
22. Identify the various categories of assets for income tax purposes.*
23. Describe a capital asset.*
24. Identify ordinary income assets.*
25. Define Section 1231 assets.*
26. Explain the tax consequences associated with the various asset classes.*

**Ties to CFP Certification Learning Objectives*

INTRODUCTION TO BASIS

In order to comprehend taxation of property transactions, it is first necessary to understand the purpose of basis in the tax system and the manner in which assets are categorized. Recall from Chapter 1 that basis represents previously taxed income that is invested in an asset, which is exempt from tax to prevent the taxpayer from being subject to a double tax on the same income. This chapter will review these rules, and will lay the groundwork for several chapters to come.

Calculating Gain or Loss

Before we can discuss basis rules and the categorization of assets for tax purposes, a general understanding of the calculation of taxable gain or loss on an asset is necessary. This concept will be developed more fully later in this textbook, but the basic rules are needed to understand the material included in this chapter.

The formula for calculating gain or loss on the sale of a capital asset is set forth in §1001 of the Internal Revenue Code. The amount of money plus the value of any property received in a sale or exchange of an asset is referred to as the **amount realized**. To calculate gain or loss, the taxpayer's adjusted basis is subtracted from the amount realized. The concept of basis is developed in this chapter. Future chapters will deal with the issue of the amount realized in more depth.

Example 10.1

Logan purchased 100 shares of XYZ stock for $10,000. Last week, he sold all 100 shares for $13,000. The amount realized in the transaction is what Logan received, $13,000. His adjusted basis is $10,000 (what he paid for the stock, in this case). Therefore, Logan's gain on the sale of the stock is $3,000, calculated as follows:

Amount Realized	$13,000
Less: Adjusted Basis	($10,000)
Equals: Gain	$3,000

Example 10.2

Logan purchased 100 Shares of ABC stock for $12,000. Last week, he sold all 100 shares for $5,000. The amount realized in the transaction is $5,000 (what Logan received). Logan's adjusted basis is $12,000 (what he paid for the stock, in this case). Therefore, Logan's loss on the sale of the stock is $7,000, calculated as follows:

Amount Realized	$5,000
Less: Adjusted Basis	($12,000)
Equals: Loss	($7,000)

Purpose of Basis

In the United States, an individual's income is subject to income tax only once. The portion of income retained after income tax is paid is referred to as capital. Capital is not subject to further income tax.

Perhaps the two most common ways to earn income are through employment and through ownership of investments. While the full amount received by a taxpayer as salary or wages is fully subject to income tax, only part of the amount received from the sale of an investment is subject to income tax. When an investment is sold, the investor is permitted to recoup his or her basis tax-free; only the amount received in excess of basis is subject to income tax. The purpose of basis is to keep track of after-tax dollars an individual invests so that upon the sale of an investment, income is not taxed twice.

Example 10.3

Ryan took a job last year earning $30,000 for the year. The full amount of his income is included for purposes of his income tax and will be reported on form W-2. After paying his expenses throughout the year, he has managed to save $2,000 by the end of the year. This $2,000 represents after-tax savings, or capital. At the beginning of this year, Ryan invests $1,000 of his capital in AMZN. Assume that two years later, Ryan sells his shares in the AMZN for $3,000. He has a return of basis of $1,000, representing the capital he invested, and a capital gain of $2,000, representing the increase in the investment, which is subject to tax.

Assume in the alternative that at the end of two years, Ryan sells his original investment in AMZN for $400. The $400 represents a return of his basis, or at least what is left of his basis (or capital). Because he has sold his investment for $400 after investing $1,000, he has a recognized loss of $600.

Basis represents capital (or after-tax income) that a taxpayer uses to purchase an investment. An easy way to remember this is to recall the a toll-booth analogy. Picture yourself driving along a highway with a car full of cash earned in your most recent business deal. As you drive along, you come upon a toll booth (representing the income tax system). All the cash that approaches the toll booth is income. Once you pay the toll (the tax on the income), all of the cash that comes out the other side of the toll booth is capital. You can choose to consume your capital or reinvest it in other income producing assets. If a taxpayer invested capital in income producing assets, and had to pay income tax on that same amount again when the asset was sold, the taxpayer would be paying tax on income twice - once when income was earned and again when the investment was sold. To avoid this trap, taxpayers keep track of the capital that was used to purchase the investment, or basis, so that the capital can be recovered without the imposition of a second income tax.

Quick Quiz 10.1

1. The taxpayer's adjusted basis is subtracted from the amount realized to calculate gain or loss.
   a. True
   b. False
2. The purpose of basis is to make sure that income is only taxed twice.
   a. True
   b. False
3. Basis may be used to determine a taxpayer's depreciation deductions.
   a. True
   b. False

True, False, True.

Uses of Basis

Basis is the income tax system's method of keeping track of capital in an investment, and is used in several different ways. First, as we have already seen, basis is used to determine gain or loss on an investment when it is sold. An investor would subtract his or her basis from the sales proceeds of the investment to determine the taxable gain or loss. Second, basis is used to determine depreciation deductions that an investor can take on an investment. Depreciation will be discussed in more depth later in this chapter. Third, basis is used to determine the amount an investor has "at risk," which limits loss deductions for income tax purposes under the at risk and passive activity loss rules. The at risk and passive activity rules will be discussed in more depth in Chapter 14.

DETERMINING BASIS

Cost Basis

Cost basis is the initial value of an asset acquired by an investor using capital to purchase the investment. As explained above, cost basis represents the amount of after-tax dollars that the investor has dedicated to purchasing an investment. For most investments, the initial basis in an investment is the cost basis.

Example 10.4

Nina believes that the antique car market will be strong for the next several years, and purchases a 1926 Rolls-Royce for $400,000 in cash. Nina's initial basis in the car is $400,000. Her basis establishes whether she will have a gain or loss once she sells the Rolls-Royce.

Cost basis includes not only the cash paid by the taxpayer to purchase the investment, but also the amount of recourse debt that the investor incurs to purchase the investment. **Recourse debt** is debt that the taxpayer is personally liable to repay, regardless of whether or not the investment produces a return for the investor. Creditors holding recourse debt may receive payment on the debt from the personal resources of the taxpayer if the investment does not provide a sufficient return to cover the outstanding liability. Whenever a taxpayer incurs recourse debt, that debt must be repaid with after-tax dollars. The taxpayer must earn money, pay tax on those earnings, and use the after-tax earnings to make debt payments.[1] As a result, recourse debt assumed by the taxpayer is added to the cash invested to determine the taxpayer's cost basis in an investment.

Key Concepts

1. Define the cost basis of an asset.
2. Identify items that increase basis.
3. Identify items that decrease basis.

Example 10.5

In our previous example, Nina purchased a Rolls-Royce for $400,000 in cash. Assume that instead of paying the full purchase price, she decides to obtain a recourse loan from Jarvis Savings Bank. Nina pays $80,000 in cash, and Jarvis Savings Bank gives her a promissory note for $320,000. Nina will have to pay back the $320,000 loan with after-tax dollars, so her initial basis in the car is still $400,000.

Nonrecourse debt is debt that is secured by the investment itself and/or other collateral, and is not an obligation of the investor (taxpayer). In the event that the loan is in default, the lender may seek to recover from the collateral securing the debt but cannot recover from the personal assets of the taxpayer. Because nonrecourse debt does not subject the taxpayer to risk, it is generally not treated as basis. Nonrecourse debt is far less risky to the investor (taxpayer) than recourse debt because with nonrecourse debt, the lender has to satisfy claims using the collateral rather than pursuing the personal assets of the taxpayer.

Example 10.6

Continuing with **Example 10.5**, assume that instead of a recourse note, Nina obtains a nonrecourse note from Jarvis Savings Bank. If the antique car market declines, and the value of the car drops dramatically causing Nina to default on the note, Jarvis Savings Bank's only recourse is to repossess the car, sell it, and use the sales proceeds to satisfy the note. The bank cannot seek repayment from Nina's personal assets. In this circumstance, since the bank, not Nina, is taking the risk of loss for the amount of the nonrecourse loan, Nina will not be able to take a loss in excess of what she actually paid

1. Recall that the payment of the principal debt payments is not deductible, but the interest on the debt is generally deductible for tax purposes.

for the car. Furthermore, Nina can only take the loss when she transfers the car to the bank in satisfaction of the debt.

Nina's basis in this scenario is $80,000, which is the cash she paid. Nina's basis will not include the amount of debt assumed with the purchase since she is not personally responsible for the debt, and her risk is limited to her investment (which, in this case, is $80,000).

The amount paid for an asset includes not only its purchase price, but also any amounts paid for sales tax, freight, installation and testing of the asset, and any other costs necessary to acquire the asset and get it into operations. All of the items below are included in the cost basis of the asset.

Items Included in Basis
Purchase Price
Sales Tax
Freight
Installation and Testing Costs
"All costs to get the asset into operations"

If the investor engages in certain types of transactions, such as a Section 1031 like-kind exchange, the investor's basis in the property may not equal the economic cost of the property acquired in the exchange. When a Section 1031 exchange is used, any gain that the taxpayer had in the property that was given up in the exchange would be deferred into the new property and would not be taxed until the property received in the exchange is subsequently sold. Section 1031 exchanges will be discussed in more detail in Chapter 13.

Adjustments to Basis

Once an asset is acquired and its initial cost basis is established, that basis may be adjusted over the holding period of the asset, resulting in an adjusted basis for income tax purposes.

Increases in Basis

The first and most frequently encountered adjustment to basis is an upward adjustment to cost basis for additions to the investment. If additional capital is added to the investment, the cost basis is increased to reflect this additional investment, so that upon sale, the investor receives all of his or her capital back without being subjected to additional tax. Examples of capital infusions that increase a taxpayer's basis in an investment include subsequent investments in the same vehicle, additions to the investment, or changes to the investment and capital contributions to partnerships and corporations.

Example 10.7

Five years ago, Tom and Gerri built their first house. At that time they had one child, with another child on the way; so they built their house with three bedrooms. Recently, Gerri found out that she will be having a third child. Tom, in anticipation of the new arrival, has finished plans for an addition to the house to add a new bedroom for their third child.

The costs that they incur in adding the new bedroom to the house will increase their basis in the house by the cost of the new addition.

Example 10.8

Donald was trained well by his Uncle Scrooge, and he has made prudent investments throughout his lifetime. Instead of taking dividend distributions from stocks and mutual funds that he owns, he reinvests those dividends by purchasing additional shares of the investments. In December of this year, a mutual fund that Donald owns made a long-term capital gain distribution of $450, which was automatically reinvested for him on the day of distribution into additional shares of the same fund. Early next year, the mutual fund company will send an IRS Form 1099 to Donald showing that he had a $450 capital gain distribution, and Donald will report that capital gain on his income tax return. Since the $450 distribution went through the "tax toll booth" (Donald paid tax on the distribution even though he did not receive it in cash), Donald's total basis in the mutual fund will increase by $450.

Another item that can cause an increase in basis is amortization of the discount on bonds purchased below face value. Due to fluctuations in interest rates, a bond may sell for more or less than its face value. If the bond sells for less than its face value, the investor's return will consist of two components: (1) the periodic interest payments on the bond; and (2) the difference between the face amount (maturity value) of the bond and the bond's purchase price, or discount. While individuals are cash-basis taxpayers and generally pay tax on income when it is received, the income tax rules include a special exception to that general rule which requires the discount on bonds to be amortized over the remaining life of the security.

The reasoning for the amortization of any discount is quite simple. The purchaser of a bond held to maturity expects to receive the full maturity value (usually $1,000 per bond) at the maturity date. The investor will periodically collect the coupon interest rate times the maturity value and then the full face value at maturity. The Internal Revenue Code requires taxpayers to recognize two types of interest income for discount bonds. The first type is for the annual or semiannual coupon payments when they are received. The second type of interest is for the amortization of the discount from par value. The difference between the par value and the discounted price of the bond will be received at maturity. However, taxpayers must recognize this difference each year the bond is held until it matures. This income is often referred to as phantom income because it represents income to the taxpayer without corresponding cash flow. Taxpayers calculate the phantom income by using the yield to maturity (YTM) for the bond. Since the amount amortized each year passes through the tax toll booth and is subject to income tax, the investor's basis in the bond is increased by the amount of the annual discount subject to tax. For income tax purposes, bonds (other than U.S. savings bonds) sold at a discount are called **"Original Issue Discount (OID)" bonds**, and the rules governing the tax treatment of these bonds are referred to as the OID rules.

Example 10.9

Mickey purchased a $1,000 face value bond this year for $939.43 with an annual coupon rate of 9% when the prevailing interest rate was 11.5%. The bond will mature in exactly 3 years. The coupon rate of the bond Mickey purchased was lower than the current market rate, causing the price discount of $60.57. This year, Mickey will report Original Issue Discount (OID) interest (the amortizable discount for the current year) of $18.03 on his tax return. The OID interest of $18.03 is determined by figuring the interest in total on the value of the bond based on its purchase price and then subtracting the actual coupon payments received.

- Year 1 interest based on the YTM: $939.43 x 11.5% = $108.03
- Less coupon payments received of $90.00 equals $18.03.
- The OID interest for Year 2 and Year 3 is $20.11 and $22.43 respectively, which totals to $60.57 for the three years.

Because Mickey paid tax on $18.03 of the bond discount, his basis in the bond will increase by $18.03, from $939.43 to $957.46 (rounded). The increase in basis will prevent Mickey from paying income tax on the $18.03 twice – once in the current year when he has phantom income due to the imposition of the OID rules, and once in the year the bond matures and he receives payment of the full $1,000. The interest in this example is calculated using the real (or effective) interest method rather than a straight-line amortization method.

The profit (or loss) of pass-through entities also results in an increase (or decrease) in the basis that each owner has in his or her ownership interest. **Pass-through entities** are not treated as separate taxable entities for income tax purposes, and the income that the entity earns is generally taxed to each of the owners in proportion to their ownership interest. The owner of the entity pays tax on the business earnings. Consequently, the earnings have passed through the tax toll booth, and the owner's basis in the business interest must be increased by a like amount. Pass-through entities include general partnerships, limited partnerships, limited liability companies (LLCs), limited liability partnerships (LLPs), S Corporations, and all unincorporated entities (other than trusts) that have two or more owners.

Example 10.10

Daisy acquired an interest in a newly formed company by purchasing a 20% interest in Lucky Heart, LLC (taxed as a partnership), which is an internet dating service. To acquire her interest, she paid $100,000. The owners agreed that no distributions would be made from the business during the first two years since the funds would be necessary to finance business expansion. In its first year of operation, Lucky Heart, LLC earned $50,000 and Daisy's share of the profits was $10,000 (20% of $50,000). This amount was reported to Daisy on Schedule K-1, and Daisy paid income tax on these earnings when she filed her personal income tax return. Daisy's basis in Lucky Heart, LLC, therefore, increased to $110,000 ($100,000 + $10,000) at the end of Year 1. In Year 2, Daisy's share of the profits was $25,000. Consequently, her basis at the end of Year 2 increased to $135,000 ($110,000 + $25,000) since she took no distributions in Year 1 or Year 2. Daisy has paid tax on the $35,000 of profits over the two-year period.

Decreases in Basis

If an individual's basis in an investment increases when capital is added to the investment, the opposite happens when capital is removed from an investment. When capital is removed from an investment, a basis reduction must occur because the taxpayer has received a refund of some of his or her capital. Capital can be taken out of an investment in several ways. Two of the most common methods of removing capital from an investment are: (1) distributions from business entities that have pass-through tax treatment (such as partnerships, LLCs, and S corporations), and (2) claiming depreciation deductions.

Example 10.11

Daisy owns a 20% interest in Lucky Heart, LLC, which is an internet dating service. Her original cost basis was $100,000 and while the company has been operating, it has never made a cash distribution to owners. Each year, as the company earned money, Daisy paid tax on her portion (20%) of the earnings even though she did not receive any distributions from the LLC. As a result, Daisy's basis in the LLC increased each year in an amount equal to her share of the company's earnings; and her adjusted basis in her LLC interest is currently $135,000. This year, the owners decided that they needed to enjoy some of their profits, so they made a distribution, and Daisy's share of the distribution was $25,000. The distribution from the partnership is not taxable, since the partners previously paid tax on the partnership income as it was being earned. Therefore, the$25,000 distribution to Daisy reflects a return of capital (after-tax income), and her basis in the LLC will be reduced by a like amount to $110,000 ($135,000 - $25,000). After the distribution, Daisy still has capital worth $135,000, but the character of the capital has changed. She has $110,000 of the capital in the LLC, and the remaining $25,000 of capital in cash, for a total of $135,000.

When an asset is used in a trade or business, or for the production of income, the owner of the asset is permitted to take depreciation deductions. **Depreciation** is a form of cost recovery designed to return capital to a business, presumably so that it can be reinvested in additional equipment for the business. The depreciation deduction causes a basis reduction in the asset for which depreciation is claimed. In the context of this discussion, the term "depreciation" encompasses not only the classic form of depreciation, but also amortization, depletion, and other "cost recovery" methods. Since the cost of these items is recovered through depreciation, the adjusted basis of the asset is decreased by the depreciation claimed each year. A more detailed discussion of depreciation occurs later in this chapter.

Just as bond discounts cause an upward adjustment in basis, bond premiums may cause a downward adjustment in basis. If an investor pays a premium upon the purchase of a bond (most likely due to a decline in interest rates compared to the coupon rate since the bond was issued), the investor may elect to amortize the bond premium over the lifetime of the bond. One difference between a

Quick Quiz 10.2

1. A taxpayer's cost basis does not include nonrecourse debt.
   a. True
   b. False
2. The earnings of a pass-through entity may increase the basis of the owner of that entity.
   a. True
   b. False
3. Depreciation deductions increase the basis of an asset.
   a. True
   b. False

True, True, False.

taxable bond premium and a discount is that the discount on a bond must be amortized (with a few rare exceptions, such as U.S. savings bonds), whereas the premium paid to acquire a bond is amortized only if the investor elects to do so (pursuant to IRC Section 1016). When a tax-exempt bond is purchased at a premium, Section 171(c) requires the premium to be amortized.

If the investor elects to amortize the premium paid on a taxable bond, the amount amortized is treated as an interest deduction, which is used to offset interest income taxed at ordinary income tax rates. Generally, making the election is favorable to the taxpayer, since the capital loss that will be generated by the bond upon maturity (equal to the difference between the purchase price and the maturity value of the bond) will offset capital gains, which may be taxed at a lower rate. If the election is made, and the taxpayer amortizes the bond premium, the amount amortized each year will reduce the taxpayer's basis in the bond.

Example 10.12

Kalani purchased a bond with a $1,000 face value for $1,040 (a premium of $40). The bond will mature in two years. If Kalani elects to do so, she may amortize the premium over the two-year period, and, in year one, take an interest expense deduction of $20. Assuming Kalani makes the election, at the end of year one her basis in the bond will be $1,020 (equal to the cost basis of $1,040 minus the amortization deducted for income tax purposes of $20). Since Kalani has recouped $20 of her capital through the deduction, she only has $1,020 left in basis to recoup in the future.

The $20 of amortized premium amount used in this example (half of the total) is used for simplicity. The actual calculation makes use of YTM in a similar manner as determining OID interest.

BASIS RULES FOR PERSONAL USE ASSETS

When an asset is purchased for personal use, its initial basis equals its cost. If the taxpayer adds capital into the asset (such as building an addition on a personal residence), the taxpayer's basis in the asset is increased by the same amount. This treatment allows the taxpayer to receive his or her capital back tax-free at a later point in time. Upward adjustments to cost basis are often observed for personal use assets.

Personal use assets, such as a personal residence, personal automobiles, furniture, and the like do not qualify for depreciation deductions because they are not employed for use in a trade or business or for the production of income. Taxpayers who hold personal use assets typically get their capital back only when they sell or dispose of the asset. Therefore, downward adjustments in basis are not typical with personal use assets.

There are exceptions, however. Perhaps the most common downward adjustment for basis in a personal use asset involves the use of part of a personal residence for business purposes. An individual who meets certain requirements can deduct costs associated with the use of his or her home for business purposes (the rules for the home office deduction are covered elsewhere in the text). Among the costs that may be deducted is depreciation. If the owner of a personal residence claims the home office deduction, a downward adjustment to basis in the home will be necessary to account for the partial return of capital.

Example 10.13

Rex is a consultant for pharmaceutical companies. He maintains an office in his home for his business. Earlier this year, Rex purchased his current principal residence for $350,000. Rex's expenses directly associated with his home office are $2,650 this year, of which $400 represents depreciation. Rex's adjusted basis in his home will be $349,600 (Cost basis of $350,000 less $400 of depreciation) since he recovered $400 of his capital through the depreciation deduction.

TCJA 2017 suspended from 2018 through 2025 the deduction for miscellaneous itemized deductions subject to the two percent hurdle. One of these deductions is the home office deduction for employees. However, a deduction for a home office used in a trade or business, such as the example above, could still be taken on Schedule C.

SPECIAL BASIS RULES

In addition to the general rules governing the basis of assets discussed above, some special rules apply when property is gifted or inherited, and when property is sold to a related party.

Basis of Inherited Property

The basis of property that passes through a decedent's estate is stepped to the fair market value of the asset on the date of the decedent's death, or, if elected by the executor of the decedent's estate, to the fair market value of the asset on the alternate valuation date. This **step-to fair market value** may result in an increase (step-up) or decrease (step-down) in the basis of the asset, depending on the asset's value at the decedent's date of death (or the alternate valuation date).[2] Section 1014 simply states that the basis in the hands of the recipient of inherited property is the value at which it was included in the gross estate.

Due to the temporary repeal of the estate tax in 2010, executors of estates of decedents who died in 2010 had the option to take a carry-over basis and not be subject to estate tax, or could opt out of this treatment subjecting the estate to a federal estate tax but qualifying for a step up in basis. Advisors and clients should be cognizant of the different treatment of assets inherited from individuals who died in 2010, and use the income tax basis that is appropriate depending on the executor's election.

Example 10.14

Barbie recently received an inheritance from her Uncle Ken. The inheritance consisted of a 40% ownership interest in Malibu's Funeral Home, a family business started by Barbie's father, Skip, and his Uncle Ken. Uncle Ken paid $10,000 for his 40% ownership interest in the business, and it was worth $250,000 at the time of his death. Barbie's basis in the 40% inherited business interest she receives through Uncle Ken's estate is $250,000. Barbie's step-to fair market value resulted in an increase in basis of $240,000 ($250,000 - $10,000). The capital appreciation of $240,000 avoids income taxation.

2. The alternate valuation date is six months after the date of death of the decedent. For assets that are sold by the estate within six months of the date of death, the value equals the sales price of the asset sold.

Example 10.15

Wally, a self-proclaimed expert on investments and finance, died last month. At the height of the last bull market, Wally made a significant investment in Fly-By-Nite WebCo. (FBN), an internet-based company. Wally's basis in his FBN interest was $250,000. Wally left his entire portfolio to his son, Wally Jr. The value of the FBN interest held by Wally's estate as of the date of his death was $10,000. Wally Jr.'s basis in the FBN interest he receives through his father's estate is $10,000. Wally Jr.'s step-to fair market value resulted in a decrease in basis of $240,000 ($250,000 - $10,000). The decline in value of the stock cannot be taken as a loss for income tax purposes.

The rationale for the Section 1014 "step-to fair market value" basis provision is two pronged. First, since the asset is included in the estate of a decedent, and is subject to estate tax (which historically was assessed at a rate higher than income tax rates), it is fair to match the basis to the estate tax value, since taxes are being paid on that amount. Second, the provision is one of convenience. It is difficult and, in many cases, impossible, to track basis when assets are passed through an estate. Very few individuals keep detailed records of the cost of the assets they acquire, and assets held for the longest holding periods are not often transferred with complete basis information. By setting the basis equal to the value in the estate, the need for detailed records spanning several generations simply to compute taxable gain or loss on the sale of an asset is diminished, and eases the administrative burden on both the taxpayer and the government.

Key Concepts

1. Calculate the basis of inherited property.
2. Describe how the basis of gifted property is determined.
3. Identify the basis of property transferred between spouses incident to divorce.
4. Identify the effect of related party transactions on asset basis.

The Highway and Transportation Funding Act of 2015 (HTFA 2015) imposed consistent basis reporting standards for property that receives a Section 1014 step-to basis. Under HTFA 2015, when an estate beneficiary sells an asset received through the estate of a decedent, the beneficiary's basis cannot exceed the final value that had been used for estate tax purposes. To effectuate the requirements of HFTA 2015, estate executors and administrators must furnish a statement to each beneficiary identifying the value of the property included in the decedent's estate so that the beneficiary can report his or her basis upon sale of the property in a manner consistent with the value of that property used by the estate in determining estate tax liability.

IRD (income in respect of a decedent) assets do not receive a step-to fair market value at the death of the transferor. IRD assets were not subject to ordinary income tax during the life of the transferor. To prevent these assets from escaping income taxation, they do not receive a step-to fair market value basis at death; rather the decedent's basis carries over to the beneficiary of the asset. Some examples of IRD assets are IRAs, annuities, installment notes, and back wages payable to the decedent.

Death Bed Gifts - Modification to Step-to Fair Market Value at Death

Another exception to the step-to fair market value basis provision occurs when a donor (transferor) makes a gift of appreciated property to a donee, who later dies and leaves the property to the original transferor or the spouse of the transferor, and whose death occurs within one year of the gift. When this type of death-bed gift is made, the step-to fair market value rule will not apply, and the transferee's basis will be the original basis of the transferor.

Example 10.16

Clever Colin owns $1 million worth of highly appreciated AAPL stock with a basis of $45. Colin would like to donate the stock to his favorite Uncle Robbie, have the stock receive an upward adjustment in its basis at the date of Robbie's death, and then receive it back as an inheritance from Uncle Robbie so that he avoids a large capital gain. However, this type of transaction will not receive an adjustment in basis if the decedent (Robbie) dies within one year of the gift.

Basis of Gifted Property

When an individual (donor) gives property to another person (donee), the donor's basis typically carries over to the donee. No gain or loss is recognized at the time of the gift, but when the donee sells the gifted property, recognition will occur and income tax will be paid on any gain. There are some situations, however, when the basis of property in the hands of the donee will differ from the donor's basis. This may occur when (1) the donor pays gift tax on the transfer; or (2) when the donor gifts property that has a fair market value less than the donor's adjusted basis as of the date of the gift.

The gift tax is a tax on the donor's right to transfer the property during his or her lifetime. When a transfer is made at the death of a decedent, an estate tax and "step-to fair market value" basis rule applies. If appreciated property is transferred during lifetime and a gift tax is paid on the transfer, an adjustment in the basis of the property should be made since the gift and estate tax are designed to serve similar functions. When a donor is required to pay gift tax, the portion of the gift tax paid that represents appreciation in the value of the property that occurred while in the hands of the donor may be added to the donor's original basis when determining the basis of the donee. The formula that is used to calculate this increase in basis is:

$$\frac{\textbf{Appreciation in the Property}}{\textbf{FMV of Property at Date of Gift}} \times \textbf{Gift Tax Paid} = \textbf{Increase in Basis for Donee}$$ [3]

Example 10.17

Fred gives ABC Stock to his daughter, Wilma. Fred's basis in the stock is $5,000 and the stock is worth $8,000 on the date he transfers it to Wilma. Fred made no other gifts to Wilma this year. Since the transfer qualifies for the gift tax annual exclusion (it is a present interest gift of no more than $15,000), Fred did not have to pay any gift tax on the transfer. Wilma's basis in the ABC stock is $5,000.

3. The "FMV of Property at Date of Gift" is the amount of the taxable gift, which includes a deduction for any gift exclusion taken for the particular gifted property.

Example 10.18

Betty, a successful attorney and security consultant, transfers $100,000 of XYZ stock to her son, Barney. Betty's basis in the stock is $60,000 and she believes that it has substantial appreciation potential. Betty has already used her lifetime exemption for gift tax purposes ($11,700,000 in 2021) and has already made gifts to Barney this year that qualify for and fully use the annual exclusion of $15,000 (2021). Assume Betty pays $40,000 in gift taxes to transfer the XYZ stock to Barney. Barney's income tax basis will equal $76,000, which is Betty's original basis of $60,000 plus $16,000 (40% of $40,000) from the payment of gift tax, calculated as follows:

$$\frac{\$40{,}000 \text{ Appreciation}}{\$100{,}000 \text{ FMV}} \times \begin{matrix}\$40{,}000 \\ \text{Gift Tax Paid}\end{matrix} = \$16{,}000 \text{ (increase in basis for donee)}$$

The second circumstance causing the basis of gifted property to differ from the donor's basis occurs when gifted property has a fair market value that is lower than the donor's basis. When this occurs, the **double basis rule**, which states that the asset owner will have one basis for loss purposes and another basis for gain purposes, applies. The double basis rule is sometimes referred to as the split basis rule, dual basis rule, or bifurcated basis rule. When gifted property has a fair market value that is less than the donor's basis, the donee's basis for gain purposes equals the donor's original basis, and the donee's basis for loss purposes equals the fair market value of the property on the date of the gift. If the property is later sold by the donee at a price between the donor's original basis and the value on the date of the gift, there is no gain or loss to the donee.

Exhibit 10.1 | Double Basis Rule

(OCCURS WHEN FAIR MARKET VALUE < DONOR'S BASIS AT DATE OF GIFT)

If the donee's sale price is...	less than FMV	between the original basis and FMV	greater than the original basis
Then the donee's basis used is ...	the loss basis, which is the FMV at the date of the gift	no gain or loss	the gain basis, which is the donor's original basis

Example 10.19

Sully purchased 100 shares of Hyde, Inc. five years ago for $5,000. He just gave those shares to his son, Randall, and the value of the 100 shares of stock on the date of the gift was $1,000. Sully's son will have a double basis in the stock, determined as follows:

If the donee's sale price is...	less than FMV	between the original basis and FMV	greater than the original basis
Then the donee's basis used is ...	$1,000 (Loss Basis)	no gain or loss	$5,000 (Gain Basis)

If Randall sells the stock for $5,500 he can use the gain basis of $5,000 (Sully's original basis), for purposes of calculating gain or loss. In this case, Randall will have to pay tax on a $500 gain ($5,500 amount realized less $5,000 adjusted gain basis).

If Randall sells the shares for $750, his loss is $250. In this case, since the stock was sold for less than the value on the date of the gift, the loss basis must be used for purposes of calculating loss. The $750 amount realized, less his loss basis of $1,000 yields a loss of $250.

If Randall sells the shares for $3,000 he will have no gain or loss to report, since the sales price was between the gain and loss basis.

As illustrated in these examples, the gift of property in a loss position followed by a subsequent sale at less than the donor's adjusted basis in the property results in a loss of capital, since nobody will be able to take a loss deduction for the difference between the amount realized and the gain basis of the gift. In the last part of this example, for instance, the $2,000 difference between the donor's cost basis of $5,000 and the sale price of $3,000 will never be recovered. A better tax strategy would be for the donor to sell the property and recognize a $4,000 taxable loss, and subsequently transfer the $1,000 in sale proceeds to the donee. The donee could then buy the stock on the market for $1,000. If this was done, all of the capital (after-tax dollars) would be recovered through the loss deduction plus the proceeds received at the sale. The holding period for assets acquired by gift is discussed more fully in Chapter 11.

Example 10.20

If Lola has stock with a basis of $100,000 and gives it to her son, Rico, when the fair market value is $80,000, Rico will have a double basis in the stock. If Rico sells the stock for $50,000 he will use the FMV on the date of the gift, $80,000, as his basis and his loss will be $30,000. If Rico sells the stock for $120,000, he will use Lola's carryover basis of $100,000 as his basis, and his gain will be $20,000. If Rico sells at a price between $80,000 and $100,000, his basis will be equal to the sale price and there will be no gain or loss.

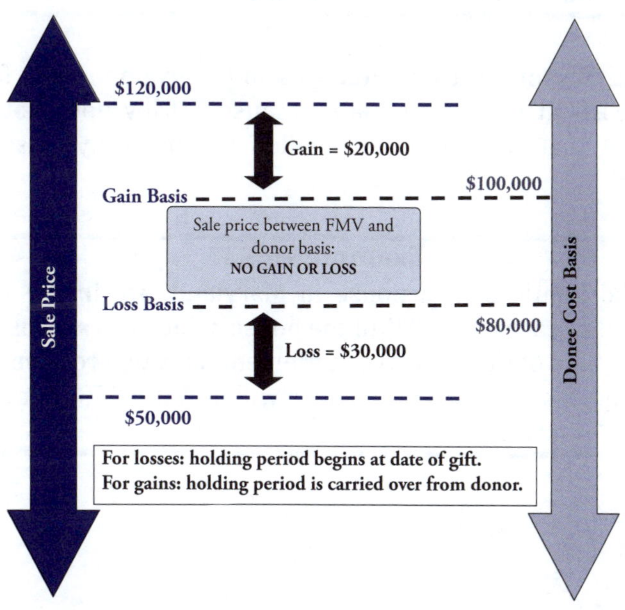

Basis of Property Transferred Between Spouses or Incident to Divorce

A special rule, found under Section 1041 of the IRC, governs the treatment of basis for all assets transferred between spouses or incident to a divorce. Section 1041 states that, regardless of whether property is sold or given to a spouse, the basis of the original owner spouse will carry over to the new owner spouse. This treatment is mandatory; it is not an election of the taxpayer.

Example 10.21

Archie and Veronica have been married for 10 years. In celebration of their 10th anniversary, Archie gives Veronica a diamond ring valued at $20,000. The ring belonged to Archie's grandmother, and he inherited it from her estate. At the time his grandmother died, the ring had a fair market value of $15,000. Archie's basis, which is $15,000, will carry over to Veronica. If Veronica sells the ring for $20,000 she will have to recognize a $5,000 gain. When a gift is made from one spouse to another, Section 1041 does not require different treatment from the normal rule covering the basis of gifted property – both rules require a carry-over basis.

Example 10.22

Raj and Shirley have been married for 10 years. Shirley decides to sell her beach house to Raj. Shirley purchased the beach house 15 years ago for $400,000. The current fair market value of the beach house is $1,500,000. Raj transfers $1,500,000 in cash to Shirley's account, and Shirley signs over the deed to the beach house to Raj. If Raj sells the beach house for $1,500,000, he will recognize a $1,100,000 gain on the property. Raj's basis in the beach house is $400,000 and this amount subtracted from the amount realized yields a gain of $1,100,000. Even though the property was sold, and Raj paid full and fair consideration for the property, he only receives a carry-over basis because he was married to Shirley on the date of the sale.

Example 10.22 illustrates that spouses are treated as a single economic unit for tax planning purposes. Raj receives a carry-over basis at the time of sale because Shirley does not pay any tax on the gain inherent in the property at that time. It is only when the property is sold to a non-spouse that recognition occurs.

Example 10.23

Vinny and Lisa, who jointly own a house in Maryland, are in the process of getting divorced. Vinny and Lisa each own 50% of the house, which has a basis of $100,000 and a FMV of $175,000. As part of their divorce settlement, Lisa will receive sole ownership of the house in Maryland. Lisa's basis in the house will be $100,000 (her $50,000 basis plus $50,000 of carryover basis from Vinny).

Related Party Transactions (Sales, Gifts, and Basis-IRC Section 267)

When property is sold to a related party (other than the seller's spouse), and the sale will result in a gain to the selling party, the normal basis rules apply. That is, the selling party will recognize gain and the purchasing party will acquire a basis in the property equal to the price he or she paid for the property. Related parties include a taxpayer's lineal ascendants (e.g., parents and grandparents), lineal descendants (e.g., children and grandchildren), and brothers and sisters (of whole or half blood). The definition of a related party also includes certain business entities and trusts, although this information is beyond the scope of this textbook. Collateral relatives (aunts, uncles, nephews, nieces, cousins, stepchildren, step-parents, or in-laws) are not considered to be related parties.

Example 10.24

Gonzo sells stock in Baseball Enterprises, Inc. to his son, Scooter. Gonzo purchased the stock 5 years ago for $1,500 and the current fair market value of the stock is $2,000. Since Gonzo believes that the stock will experience significant growth (and he does not want that growth to increase his taxable estate), he sells the stock to Scooter for its current fair market value. Gonzo will recognize a gain of $500 ($2,000 amount realized minus the $1,500 basis), and Scooter's basis in the stock will be $2,000, which equals the amount he paid to acquire it.

If property is sold to a related party (other than the seller's spouse) at a loss, however, the seller is not permitted to deduct the loss and the double basis rule applies. As a result, the purchaser will have one basis for purposes of calculating gain and another basis for purposes of calculating loss, and the seller will not be permitted to recognize the loss for tax purposes. The gain basis will equal the seller's original basis in the property, and the loss basis will equal the fair market value of the property at the time of the sale. The holding period used to determine whether gains or losses are short-term or long-term are based on the purchaser's holding period. The significance of holding period will be discussed in the next chapter.

Example 10.25

Gonzo sells stock in Baseball Enterprises, Inc. to his son, Scooter. Gonzo purchased the stock five years ago for $2,000 and the current fair market value of the stock is $1,500. On the date of sale, Gonzo will not be permitted to recognize a $500 loss on his tax return (the difference between his purchase price of $2,000 and the sale price of $1,500). Scooter's gain or loss on subsequent disposition of the stock will be dependent on the selling price of the stock, and there are three possible outcomes from a related party sale.

If Scooter sells the stock to Kermit (an unrelated party) for $2,500, he uses his gain basis for purposes of determining gain. Recall that Scooter's gain basis is the same as Gonzo's basis. As long as the property is ultimately sold for more than the original purchaser's basis, the result is the same as the normal carry-over basis rule. Upon the sale to Kermit, Scooter will realize and recognize a $500 gain ($2,500 amount realized less $2,000 gain basis).

If Scooter sells the stock to Kermit for $900, he uses his loss basis for purposes of determining loss. Scooter's loss basis equals the fair market value on the date of the original sale from Gonzo to Scooter, or in this case, $1,500. Upon the sale to Kermit,

Scooter will realize a $600 loss on the stock ($900 amount realized less $1,500 loss basis). This is a bad result for the family, because the $500 loss incurred during Gonzo's holding period is never deductible – Gonzo is not permitted to deduct the $500 when he sells the property to Scooter (a related party), and Scooter is not permitted to deduct that loss on the sale to Kermit because Scooter is required to use his loss basis to determine the amount of his loss.

If Scooter sells the stock for $1,750, or, in fact, for any amount between his gain and loss basis, there will be no gain or loss recognition on the sale. In this instance, the sale is said to occur within the "no gain/no loss corridor." This is still a bad result for the family, since the actual loss suffered by the family as a whole is still not deductible (calculated by subtracting the sale price in the "no gain/no loss corridor" from the basis of the original seller).

The purpose of applying the double basis rule to related party transactions is to prevent families from allocating losses to the family member with the best ability to use them. If, using the above example, Gonzo had $750,000 of carry-forward losses, triggering a loss on the sale of the stock will not give him an additional tax benefit, since he can only take a maximum of $3,000 of capital losses against ordinary income in any one year. If the double basis rule did not apply, he might be encouraged to sell the stock to his son and let his son take the loss, which would generate an immediate income tax benefit for his son, and, therefore, be better for the family unit as a whole.

Assuming that a taxpayer does not have a large carry-forward loss position for income tax purposes, a better course of action is to sell the property, recognize the loss, and give the proceeds to the related party. This course of action will allow loss recognition, and, therefore, recovery of capital for the losses generated during the first owner's holding period.

Recall that the double basis rule may also apply to gifts. One significant difference between the double basis rule for sales and gifts is that for sale transactions, the holding period for determining the nature of the gain or loss starts anew on the date of sale. If loss property is gifted to a related party, the holding period only starts anew if, on disposition of the property, the loss basis is used to determine the donee's loss.

Quick Quiz 10.3

1. A taxpayer's basis in inherited property is the same as the decedent's basis in the property.
   a. True
   b. False
2. Gift tax paid never affects the donee's basis in gifted property.
   a. True
   b. False
3. Property transferred between spouses has a carryover basis.
   a. True
   b. False
4. If property is sold to a related party at a loss, the double basis rule applies.
   a. True
   b. False

False, False, True, True.

Example 10.26

Moira purchased 100 Shares of International Security, Inc. for $2,000 five years ago. She gives the stock to her daughter, Alexis, when the fair market value of the stock is $1,750. Since this is a gift transaction, a carry-over basis generally applies; but in this case, Moira is gifting loss property to Alexis, so Alexis will have a different basis for purposes of gain and loss.

If Alexis sells the stock for $2,500 she will use her gain basis to calculate gain. Alexis's gain basis would equal Moira's basis in the stock, or $2,000. Therefore, upon sale, Alexis would recognize a $500 gain (the $2,500 amount realized less the $2,000 gain basis).

The character of the gain would be long-term gain regardless of Alexis's holding period. Since gifted property was sold at a gain, the donor's holding period tacks on to the donee's holding period. In this case, Moira held the stock for 5 years, so the character of the gain would be long-term capital gain. Note that this is no different than if Moira gifted the property to Alexis at a time when the stock was in a gain position – both the donor's basis and holding period carry over to the donee.

If Alexis sells the stock for $1,500 she will use her loss basis to calculate loss. Alexis's loss will be $250 ($1,500 amount realized less her loss basis of $1,750). The character of the loss, however, will be dependent on Alexis's holding period. If Alexis held the stock for at least a year and a day from the date of the gift, she will recognize a long-term capital loss. If, however, she sold the stock within a year from the date of the gift, the character of the loss will be short-term.

As the above example illustrates, the use of the double basis rule works the same way for both sales and gifts with one major exception: If gifted property is subsequently sold at a gain, the holding period of the donor tacks onto the holding period of the donee for purposes of determining the character of the gain, and in a sale it does not.

Basis of Jointly Held Property

If property is held jointly (such as joint tenants with rights of survivorship, tenants in common, or community property), each owner's basis usually follows the actual contribution rule that each owner's basis equals their original contribution toward purchasing the property. However, if the joint owners are married and the property is titled in joint tenancy with right of survivorship, tenancy by the entirety, or community property, the basis of each spouse equals one half of the total basis regardless of their actual contribution. If the interest in joint tenancy was acquired by gift, then the gift basis rules are followed.

DEPRECIATION

Depreciation is a method of capital recovery that allows a taxpayer to receive his or her capital back over the useful life of the asset. We have already seen that assets purchased for personal use are not entitled to depreciation deductions. Assets held for productive use in a trade or business, or held for the production of income, however, generate depreciation deductions for their owner. As we have seen in our discussion of basis, depreciation deductions cause a downward adjustment in basis, since the taxpayer receives his or her capital back over the lifetime of the asset through the depreciation deductions.

Key Concepts

1. Identify the purpose of depreciation.
2. Identify the methods of depreciation.
3. Identify the various asset classes.

Purpose

When a taxpayer employs an asset in productive use in a trade or business or for the production of income, he or she becomes a partner of the government. As that asset is used to generate income (and, hopefully, profit), some of the profits go to the taxpayer, and some go to the government through the income tax system.

Keeping machinery and equipment or assets used to produce income up to date and in working order is in the interest of both the taxpayer and the government. Both parties profit from the employment of the asset in a profit seeking venture. Since the asset is being used to generate income subject to tax, the government permits the taxpayer to recoup his capital earlier than the date the asset is sold or discarded. As depreciation deductions are taken, the taxpayer can use the recovered capital to reinvest in other assets that can be employed in a trade or business or for the production of income, thereby increasing the income potential of the activity. Depreciating the asset over its useful life is consistent with Generally Accepted Accounting Principles (GAAP), since it ties the expenses incurred in acquiring the asset to the income earned on the asset. In financial accounting, depreciation is a form of asset allocation since it allocates the cost of the asset to the accounting periods that report income from the use of that asset.

Methods of Depreciation

For financial accounting purposes, many methods of depreciation can be used. For federal income tax purposes, depreciation methods are set by law. Therefore, tax depreciation and financial accounting depreciation are often different. For tax depreciation, three distinct sets of depreciation rules have been used over the last four decades. Prior to 1981, a variety of depreciation methods were used depending upon the type of asset, whether the asset was new or used, and several other factors. The Economic Recovery Tax Act of 1981 created the accelerated cost recovery system (ACRS) which accelerated and simplified tax depreciation for assets placed in service after 1980. This method or set of rules applied from 1981 through 1986. The Tax Reform Act of 1986 modified ACRS for assets place in service after 1986. This modified depreciation system is called the **modified accelerated cost recovery system (MACRS)** and is still in use today. The discussion in this textbook focuses primarily on the MACRS rules.

Real Estate

For real estate, the depreciation period depends on the use of the property. Under current law, if the real estate is used for residential rental purposes, the property is depreciated according to the **straight-line depreciation** method over 27½ years. If the real estate is used for commercial purposes, other than residential rentals, depreciation occurs on a straight-line basis over 39 years. The value of land cannot be depreciated; only the value of improvements to land qualify for depreciation.

Example 10.27

David purchases an 8-unit rental apartment unit for $900,000. The value of the land is determined to be $60,000. Since the property is used for residential rental purposes, David will be able to depreciate the building (at a value of $840,000, which equals the purchase price of $900,000 less the land value of $60,000) over a 27½ year period. Therefore David's annual depreciation deduction will be $30,545.

Example 10.28

Twyla purchases an office building that she plans to rent out. The building costs $1.4 million, and $200,000 of the purchase price is attributed to the land. Since the property is used for commercial rental purposes, Twyla can depreciate the building (at a value of $1.2 million, which equals the purchase price of $1.4 million less the land value of $200,000) on a straight-line basis over a 39 year period. Therefore, Twyla's annual depreciation deduction will be $30,769.23.

Personal Property

Personal property, sometimes referred to as personalty, is any property other than real property. The depreciation of personal property is determined with reference to its recovery period, or class life, which is defined by statute. The following exhibit lists the various asset classes and examples of assets included in each class.

Exhibit 10.2 | MACRS Asset Classes

3-Year Class Life Assets	Automobiles used as taxis, hogs used for breeding, racehorses, qualified rent to own property, tractors and some manufacturing tools.
5-Year Class Life Assets	Most cars, trucks and airplanes, heavy construction equipment, assets used for the manufacturing of apparel and other finished products, timber cutting equipment, electronic office equipment (such as computers, calculators, adding machines, typewriters, and copiers), information systems, alternative energy equipment (solar and wind), cattle used for breeding and dairy purposes, and sheep and goats used for breeding.
7-Year Class Life Assets	Office furniture, fixtures, and equipment; agricultural machinery and equipment; cotton ginning assets; breeding and work horses under 12 years old; equipment used for mining, quarrying, and milling; assets used in the manufacturing of furniture and wood products, assets used in printing and publishing industries; assets used for the manufacture of jewelry and athletic goods; recreational assets.
10-Year Class Life Assets	Vessels, barges, tugs and water transportation equipment; single purpose agricultural or horticultural structures; property used in petroleum refining.
15-Year Class Life Assets	Improvements to land (such as sidewalks, roads, canals, waterways, docks, fences, shrubbery); pipelines; billboards.
20-Year Class Life Assets	Farm buildings; municipal sewers.

The TCJA 2017 made several changes to the class lives of assets, including:

- The class life for farming machinery and equipment changed from 7-year to 5-year.
- The definition of "qualified leasehold improvements, qualified restaurant and qualified retail improvements" were eliminated. "Qualified improvement property" will have a a 15-year recovery period and will use straight line depreciation.
- ADS recovery period for residential rental property was reduced from 40 years to 30 years.

While it is not necessary for a tax practitioner to commit the various class life categories to memory, it is important to understand that the law attempts to assign a class life to an asset that is roughly the same as its useful life. The use of class lives is for both the taxpayer's and the government's convenience. Without standard classifications, it would be necessary to value each asset used by a business at the end of each year, compare it to the value at the beginning of the year, and take a tax deduction for the actual decline in value of the asset. While this system would certainly make some appraisers happy, it is not a practical way to administer either a business or the tax system. Once an asset is classified into a particular class life, the depreciation deduction for that asset each year is fixed, which eases the administrative burden for both the business and the government. When an asset is sold, an accounting must be made for the difference between the depreciation taken on the asset for tax purposes, and the actual decline in value of the asset. The depreciation recapture rules are designed to take care of this issue when an asset is sold. These rules will be covered in Chapter 12.

The normal depreciation method for personalty used under MACRS is an accelerated depreciation system unlike the straight-line depreciation used for real property. Assets that have a 3, 5, 7, or 10 year class life are depreciated under a depreciation method known as the **double declining balance** (or "200 percent declining balance") **method**, with a switch to straight-line depreciation when the straight-line method produces a larger deduction than the double declining balance method. If used in farming, these 3, 5, 7, or 10 year class assets are usually depreciated using the 150 percent declining balance method. Property in the 15 and 20 year class lives are depreciated under the **150 percent declining balance method**, but also switch to straight-line depreciation when the straight-line method would produce a greater deduction for the current tax year. One notable exception from these rules is the depreciation of software, which is depreciated on a straight-line basis over three years.

Accelerated depreciation is generally more favorable for a taxpayer than straight-line depreciation because it results in a larger deduction, lower income, and therefore, lower taxes in the first few years compared with straight-line depreciation. If given the choice, a taxpayer would typically choose to use the accelerated method available under MACRS. Prior to 2018, if the taxpayer was subject to AMT (alternative minimum tax), much of the benefit of accelerated depreciation would be lost. The TCJA 2017 eliminated AMT for C corporations and minimized its impact for individuals after 2017.

Furthermore, a taxpayer may choose an alternative method of depreciation so that the depreciation system used for tax purposes matches the system used for financial reporting purposes. If a taxpayer so chooses, he or she can elect out of MACRS and can depreciate the assets used in his or her trade or business in one of the following ways:

1. The taxpayer can elect straight-line depreciation for property that is otherwise eligible for the declining-balance method of depreciation. If a taxpayer chooses to use straight-line depreciation, depreciation will not cause any potential problems with the alternative minimum tax (discussed in Chapter 15).
2. The taxpayer can elect the alternative depreciation system (ADS). Under ADS:
    - Property that would have been depreciated under the 200 percent double declining balance method under MACRS will be depreciated using the 150 percent declining balance method, over the MACRS class life (for property placed in service after December 31, 1998).
    - Property that would have been depreciated under the 150 percent declining balance method under MACRS will be depreciated on a straight-line basis.
    - Real estate will be depreciated over a 40 year period on a straight-line basis with the exception of residential rental property, for which the recovery period was reduced to 30 years by TCJA 2017.

Depreciation Conventions

When depreciable assets are placed in service, certain **conventions** govern the amount of the depreciation deduction available for the first year. For personalty (assets with a class life of 20 years or less), a "half-year" convention is used. The half-year convention assumes that the asset was placed in service half-way through the year, regardless of the date it was actually employed; and therefore a half-year of depreciation is allowed in the year in which the asset is placed in service. To prevent businesses from engaging in too much tax planning (by purchasing all of their assets in December and claiming a half-year of depreciation deductions for the year), a special rule applies for a year in which more than 40 percent of all depreciable personalty (based on cost) is placed in service in the last three months of the taxable year. When this occurs, a "mid-quarter" convention is used, which states that the first-year depreciation deduction for the property will be calculated as if each asset purchased during that year was placed in service in the middle of the quarter in which it was actually placed in service.

> **Quick Quiz 10.4**
>
> 1. The purpose of depreciation is to allow the taxpayer to recoup part of his investment earlier than the date that the asset is sold.
>   a. True
>   b. False
> 2. Two methods of depreciation are straight-line and double-declining balance.
>   a. True
>   b. False
>
> True, True.

In order to better understand the MACRS conventions and in order to accurately calculate depreciation deductions, tables from IRS Publication 946 will be used in many of the following examples.[4] Appendix A of Publication 946 contains tables of rates used to calculate MACRS depreciation. Appendix B provides the class lives of many depreciable assets. **Example 10.29 - Example 10.31** are half-year convention examples and **Example 10.32 - Example 10.33** are mid-quarter convention examples.

Half-Year Convention Examples

Example 10.29

On April 10, Roland, a calendar-year taxpayer, buys a computer, a five-year class asset, for $10,000. He immediately places the computer in service in his business. What is his depreciation deduction for the first year? The first page of Appendix A indicates that Roland should use Publication 946 Table A-1 to determine the depreciation using the half year convention. Using the percentage in the 5-year column and the row for Year 1, Roland multiplies the $10,000 cost of the computer by 20% to determine the depreciation of $2,000 for Year 1. The table uses the 200% declining balance method and the half-year convention and switches to straight-line when straight-line depreciation is greater than the declining balance method.

Example 10.30

Using the information above for Roland, what is his depreciation deduction for Year 2? He will multiply the original cost of the computer by the percentage for 5-year property and Year 2. His depreciation for Year 2 is therefore $3,200 ($10,000 x 32%). Using the same method, his depreciation for the following years will be: $1,920 for Year 3, $1,152 for Year 4, $1,152 for Year 5, and $576 for Year 6. Notice that the five-year asset is depreciated over 6 years. Under the half-year convention, only one-half year of

4. Available at www.irs.gov/pub/irs-pdf/p946.pdf.

depreciation is taken in the first and last years. Conveniently, it is unnecessary to calculate the 200% declining balance depreciation amounts since the calculations have been summarized in the table.

Example 10.31

Using the information from **Example 10.29** , assume that Roland sells the computer on August 21 of Year 3. How much depreciation will he be allowed for the computer for Year 3? Since the computer is being depreciated using the half-year convention, the depreciation that is allowable for all of Year 3 is simply divided by 2. His depreciation for Year 3 is therefore $960 ($1,920/2).

Mid-Quarter Convention Examples

Example 10.32

Assume that Roland bought the computer from the three examples above on November 20 for $10,000 and that the only other depreciable personalty he purchased during the year was a desk, a seven-year class asset, with a cost of $2,000 (purchased in June). What amount of MACRS depreciation can Roland deduct for the computer in Year 1? Since the mid-quarter convention must be used ($10,000/$12,000 = 83.3% is greater than 40%), Roland will use Publication 946 Table A-5 (Mid-Quarter Convention for 4th Quarter). Using the percentage from the 5-Year column and the row for year one, his depreciation for the computer will be $500 ($10,000 x 5%) for Year 1. Since the desk was purchased in the second quarter of the year, Roland will use Publication 946 Table A-3 (Mid-Quarter Convention for 2nd Quarter). Using the 7-year column and the row for Year 1, his depreciation for the desk will be $357 ($2,000 x 17.85%) for Year 1. For the computer, the depreciation will be $3,800 for Year 2, $2,280 for Year 3, $1,368 for Year 4, $1,094 for Year 5, and $958 for Year 6.

Example 10.33

If Roland sells the computer from the preceding example on March 12 of Year 3, what amount of depreciation will be allowable in Year 3 for the computer? Since Roland sells the computer in the first quarter of the year and the mid-quarter convention applies, Roland will be deemed to have sold the computer in the middle of the first quarter. Therefore, his depreciation for Year 3 for the computer will be $285 (0.5/4 x $2,280). The depreciation for all of Year 3 (see the preceding example) is multiplied by a fraction with 0.5 quarters as the numerator and 4 quarters as the denominator. The same result is obtained by multiplying by a fraction with 1.5 months as the numerator and 12 months as the denominator.

For real property (property subject to 27½ and 39 year class lives), a mid-month convention is used. For purposes of calculating the depreciation deduction for real property placed in service, it is considered to be placed in service in the middle of the month it is actually employed. Depreciation can only be taken if the asset is actively being used in the trade or business.

Example 10.34

Johnny and Stevie bought a warehouse building for use in their business. The building was purchased on October 22 for $1,200,000 ($200,000 was for the land) and was immediately placed in service. How much depreciation can they claim for the first year? Real estate is not eligible for Section 179 treatment (discussed later in this chapter). Since the building is not residential real estate, Publication 946 Table A-7a (39-year depreciation period) is used to calculate depreciation using straight-line depreciation and the mid-month convention. Only the $1,000,000 cost of the building can be depreciated. Using column 10 (10th month) and row 1 (Year 1) of Table A-7a, the allowable depreciation deduction is $5,350 ($1,000,000 x 0.535%). The depreciation for each of the following 38 years is $25,640 ($1,000,000 x 2.564%) and the depreciation for the 40th year is $20,330 ($1,000,000 x 2.033%). If the property had been an apartment building, it would have been depreciated as residential rental property and Table A-6 would have been used to depreciate the building over a period of 27.5 years.

Example 10.35

If Johnny and Stevie in the preceding example sell the property on March 23 of Year 10, how much depreciation will they be able to deduct for Year 10? The mid-month convention used for real estate allows the owner to deduct depreciation from the beginning of the year until the middle of the month the property is sold. Therefore, Johnny and Stevie will be able to deduct depreciation for 2.5 months of Year 10. Since the depreciation for the entire year would have been $25,640, their depreciation for Year 10 is $5,341.67 ($25,640 x 2.5/12). The numerator of the fraction is the number of months the asset is deemed to be owned during the year and the denominator of 12 represents the number of months in the year.

Bonus Depreciation (Additional First Year Depreciation)

Bonus depreciation is a method of accelerated depreciation that allows businesses to take an immediate first-year deduction on the purchase of qualifying business property, in addition to other depreciation. Since 2001, Section 168(k) has provided taxpayers the ability to immediately deduct a percentage of the acquisition cost of qualifying assets as "bonus depreciation."

Under the prior tax law, the bonus depreciation deduction was limited to 50 percent of eligible new (new only) property. TCJA extended and modified bonus depreciation to allow businesses to immediately deduct 100 percent of eligible property placed in-service after September 27, 2017 and before January 1, 2023. In addition, the 100 percent bonus depreciation is extended through December 31, 2023 for certain property with longer production periods. However, the 100 percent depreciation will not remain indefinitely but rather will be phased out over time.

Exhibit 10.3 | Bonus Depreciation After September 27, 2017

Placed in Service Year	*Bonus Depreciation Percentage*	
	Qualified Property in General / Specific Plants	*Longer Production Period Property and Certain Aircraft*
Sept. 28, 2017 - Dec. 31, 2022	100%	100%
2023	80%	100%
2024	60%	80%
2025	40%	60%
2026	20%	40%
2027	None	20%
2028 and thereafter	None	None

Source: Conference report accompanying TCJA 2017.

Before MACRS deductions are calculated, bonus depreciation can be taken on qualifying new or used depreciable personalty for the year it is placed in service. Because of TCJA 2017, bonus deprecation is now 100 percent, which represents the full cost of the asset. Once 100 percent bonus depreciation is taken, there is no additional cost recovery available. Taxpayers can elect out of bonus depreciation if they so choose and then use MACRS. Taxpayers can also make an election to apply a 50 percent bonus deprecation rate in lieu of the 100 percent rate.

Quick Quiz 10.5

1. Most cars are depreciated over a period of seven years.
   a. True
   b. False
2. 100% bonus depreciation can be taken for assets placed in service after September 27, 2017 and before 2023.
   a. True
   b. False

False, True.

To take bonus depreciation, the property must either:

- be tangible personal property with a regular depreciation life of 20 years or less
- be computer software
- be water utility property
- be qualified film or television production
- be qualified live theatrical production

Used property placed in service after September 27, 2017, may qualify for bonus depreciation as long as it is the taxpayer's first use of the property.

Bonus depreciation will NOT be available to:

- vehicle dealers and other businesses that have floor-plan financing
- electrical energy, water, or sewage disposal services
- gas or steam through a local distribution system
- transportation of gas or steam by pipeline

Finally, bonus depreciation is not permitted on any asset that is required to be depreciated using the ADS method.

Example 10.36

Jocelyn buys a new business machine (7-year class) for $20,000 and places it in service on July 22 of 2017 (prior to the availability of 100% bonus depreciation). She uses first year 50% bonus depreciation as well as accelerated MACRS depreciation. What is her total depreciation deduction for the machine for 2017? Additional first year depreciation is available for 50% of the cost of new or used tangible personalty (not for real estate). MACRS depreciation can be taken on any remaining cost of the machine, once she takes 50% bonus depreciation. Her additional first year depreciation is $10,000 ($20,000 x 50%). Her MACRS depreciation is $1,429 ($10,000 x 14.29% from Publication 946 Table A-1). Therefore, her total depreciation deduction for the machine is $11,429 for 2017. Notice that the MACRS depreciation is only available for the remaining cost of the machine after the additional first year depreciation is taken. Therefore, in Year 2, her MACRS deduction for the machine is $2,449 ($10,000 remaining cost after bonus depreciation x 24.49% from Table A-1). If Jocelyn had elected to do so, she could have deducted the entire cost of the machine as a Section 179 expense (discussed later in this chapter). In that case, none of the cost would be available to claim additional first-year depreciation or MACRS depreciation.

In addition, if the property was placed in service after September 27, 2017 and before December 31, 2023, she could have taken 100 percent bonus depreciation.

Example 10.37

Assume that Jocelyn chose to take additional 50% first-year depreciation as in the preceding example, but that she chose to take straight-line depreciation on the balance. How much depreciation will she be allowed to deduct in 2017? The additional first year depreciation is the same as in the preceding example. For the MACRS straight-line depreciation and the half-year convention, Jocelyn will use Publication 946 Table A-8. Therefore, her straight-line depreciation will be $714 ($10,000 x 7.14%) and her total depreciation deduction will be $10,714 for 2017. In 2018, her depreciation deduction will be $1,429 ($10,000 x 14.29%). If Jocelyn had purchased the machine in the 4th quarter of the year and no other assets were purchased during the year, the mid-quarter convention would apply and the straight-line depreciation would be calculated using Table A-12.

Amortization of Intangible Assets

Intangible assets, such as the goodwill of a business, patents and copyrights acquired with the acquisition of a business interest, covenants not to compete, and franchises, trademarks, and tradenames acquired in connection with the acquisition of a business may be amortized on a straight-line basis over a 15 year (180 month) period. The term "**amortization**" is typically used to signify that cost recovery deductions are being taken for intangible assets.

Key Concepts

1. Define amortization.
2. Define listed property and describe its tax treatment.
3. Describe the planning benefits of making a Section 179 election.

Depletion of Natural Resources

The cost of many natural resources, such as oil, coal, gas, and precious metals can be recovered through depletion deductions. A method called cost depletion is normally used for financial accounting. Two different methods, cost depletion and statutory or percentage depletion, are available for federal income tax purposes.

Special Depreciation Issues

The general rules for depreciation discussed above apply in most circumstances, but there are a few special situations that are important to know. The first issue deals with "listed" property, and the second is an election available for small businesses known as the **Section 179 election**.

Listed Property

Listed Property can more accurately be described as suspect property, at least from the perspective of the IRS. Listed property includes automobiles weighing less than 6,000 pounds, as well as property generally used for entertainment, recreation, or amusement such as photographic equipment and electronic devices.[5] Listed property is considered suspect because it is easily used for both business and personal purposes, and taxpayers will be tempted to take a deduction for their personal use of the asset. Since only the business use of the asset qualifies for depreciation deductions, those taking deductions for such property will merit special review.

If listed property is used more than 50 percent for business purposes, the normal MACRS rules will apply, and the deduction will equal the allowable depreciation for the asset multiplied by its percentage of business use. If listed property is not used more than 50 percent for business purposes, depreciation must be computed under the alternative depreciation system (ADS) of MACRS and a straight-line depreciation method must be used. Furthermore, if use of listed property that was being depreciated under MACRS falls to 50 percent or less for any year, excess depreciation is recaptured (included in income). Excess depreciation, for this purpose, equals the depreciation actually claimed in prior years, less the amount of depreciation that would have been allowed under ADS.

In addition to the limitations placed on listed property, further limitations apply to the deductibility of automobiles that weigh less than 6,000 pounds. The additional limitations apply to both the depreciation deductions allowable and to first-year expensing under Section 179 (discussed later). Also, TIPA 2014 provides a bonus depreciation of $8,000 to first-year depreciation for both automobiles and trucks. The maximum depreciation deduction (based on 100 percent business use) is shown in the following exhibit. If a passenger automobile is acquired prior to September 27, 2017 and placed in service in 2018 or 2019, then the bonus deprecation equals $6,400 or $4,800, respectively, instead of $8,000.

5. TCJA 2017 removes computer or peripheral equipment from the definition of listed property. Such property is therefore not subject to the heightened substantiation requirements that apply to listed property.

Exhibit 10.4 | 2020 Maximum Depreciation Limitations for Automobiles[6] (Listed Property)

Tax Year	*Passenger Auto Limitations*	*Truck & Van Limits*
1st Year	$10,100	$10,100
1st Year with Bonus Depreciation	$18,100*	$18,100*
2nd Year	$16,100	$16,100
3rd Year	$9,700	$9,700
Each Succeeding Year	$5,760	$5,760

However, use of bonus depreciation will result in lower amounts of depreciation in years three through six than the (Section 280F) schedule (see example).

Example 10.38

Ronnie places a $65,000 automobile (below 6,000 lb. GVW) in service in January 2020 (5-year property). Ronnie elects to use first year bonus depreciation and will depreciate the auto in accordance with the safe harbor method for listed autos provided in Rev. Proc. 2019-13.

Under the safe harbor calculation, Ronnie will take the first year with bonus depreciation amount (under Sec. 280F, as listed in **Exhibit 10.4**) in the year the property is placed in service. In each subsequent year, Ronnie will recover the lesser of the MACRs depreciation amount (the applicable percentage from the MACRs table x the adjusted depreciable basis) or the Section 280F limit. Since Ronnie has unrecovered basis at the end of the 5-year recovery period, he can extend the recovery period until all basis is recovered; however, each year he will continue to be limited by the lesser of the Section 280F maximum deduction amount or the remaining unrecovered basis.

		A	*B*	*C*	*D*	*E*	*F*	*G*
		Section 280F (Maximum Allowable Depreciation; with Bonus Depreciation)	*Depreciation calculated Using MACRs (Column F x adjusted depreciable basis of $46,900)*	*MACRS %*	*Actual Deduction (Lesser of Column A or B)*	*Original Unadjusted Basis*	*Adjusted Depreciable Basis after Bonus Depreciation*	*Remaining Basis (end of year)*
2020 (Bonus)	1	$18,100	N/A	20%	$18,100	$65,000	$46,900	$65,000 - $18,100 = $46,900
2021	2	$16,100	$15,008	32%	$15,008			$46,900 - $15,008 = $31,892
2022	3	$9,700	$9,005	19.20%	$9,005			$31,892 - $9,005 = $22,887
2023	4	$5,760	$5,403	11.52%	$5,403			$22,887 - $5,403 =$17,484
2024	5	$5,760	$5,403	11.52%	$5,403			$17,484 - $5,403 = $12,081
2025	6	$5,760	$2,701	5.76%	$2,701			$12,081 - $2,701 = $9,380
2026	7	$5,760			$5,760			$9,380 - $5,760 = $3,620
2027	8	$5,760			$3,620			$3,620 - $3,620 =$0

6. Rev Proc. 2020-37, issued July 8, 2020.

Of course, the normal rule that limits the deduction to the percentage of business use applies; so, for example, if the car was used 60 percent for business purposes, only 60 percent of the above limit would be permitted as a depreciation deduction. Furthermore, if a taxpayer has unrecovered basis in a vehicle after the five year period has expired, the amount allowed in the 4th year for depreciation is allowed as a deduction in remaining years, until the vehicle is fully depreciated.

Section 179 Expense

Section 179 provides business owners with an option to elect to expense property placed in service during the year instead of capitalizing the assets and depreciating them over their MACRS class life, provided that certain requirements are met. To qualify for expensing under Section 179, an asset must be used more than 50 percent of the time in a trade or business (if the asset is used less than 100 percent of the time in a trade or business, only the percentage of business use may be expensed under Section 179).

A business owner may elect to immediately expense up to $1,050,000 (2021) of depreciable personalty (not real estate) placed in service during the year, unless the phaseout limit has been met. The amount that can be immediately expensed is subject to a phaseout, and is reduced dollar for dollar for the cost of depreciable personalty placed in service during the year that exceeds $2,620,000 (2021). The Section 179 expense was made permanent at $2,620,000 and $1,050,000 as indexed.

> **Quick Quiz 10.6**
>
> 1. Amortization is cost recovery for intangible assets.
>   a. True
>   b. False
> 2. The Section 179 election allows business owners to expense property placed in service during the year instead of capitalizing it.
>   a. True
>   b. False
> 3. Section 179 treatment cannot result in a loss for the business.
>   a. True
>   b. False
>
> True, True, True.

While real estate is not eligible for expensing under Section 179, the TCJA expanded the definition of qualified property to include certain improvements made to nonresidential property that are made after the property was first placed in service. This applies only to property placed in service in tax years beginning after December 31, 2017. Improvements that qualify include any improvements to the building's interior, roofs, heating and air conditioning systems, and fire protection systems. Some improvements, such as enlargement of the building, do not qualify.

Example 10.39

Raymond owns and operates a printing company. As the end of the year approaches, he reviews the financial results for the company operations for the year, and decides to purchase some new printing equipment. Since he anticipates a large increase in demand for his products, he decides to purchase a printing press at a cost of $550,000, which is the only depreciable property he places in service for the year. Raymond is able to make a Section 179 election for the printing press. The Section 179 deduction is reduced, dollar for dollar, by the amount of depreciable property placed in service during the year exceeding $2,620,000 (2021). Raymond gets the full benefit of his Section 179 deduction because the printing press did not cost more than $1,050,000. Raymond can take a $550,000 Section 179 deduction (2021).

Example 10.40

Continuing with the previous example, assume that Raymond decides to purchase a more expensive printing press for $900,000. Also assume that earlier in the year he placed $1,800,000 of depreciable property in service but did not elect Section 179 expensing for any of that property. The Section 179 deduction is reduced, dollar for dollar, by the amount of depreciable property placed in service during the year exceeding $2,620,000 (2021). The total placed in service is $2,7000,000 ($1,800,000 + $900,000), which exceeds the threshold by $80,000 ($2,700,000 - $2,620,000). Therefore, the maximum Section 179 deduction will be reduced to $970,000 ($1,050,000 – $80,000) for Raymond. Alternatively, Raymond can elect to use 100% bonus depreciation.

In addition, electing Section 179 treatment cannot result in a loss for the business, so the maximum Section 179 deduction that can be taken in any year is further limited by the income of the business. To the extent that a business owner makes an otherwise allowable Section 179 expense election that is limited in the current year by the income of the business, the elected expenses over the business income may be carried forward to future tax years, and applied against future income of the business.

Example 10.41

Debra recently opened a new business, and it is off to a good start. She anticipates that her profit at the end of the year will be $15,000. Looking forward, she knows she will have to invest in additional machinery and equipment to meet the growing demand for her products, so she purchases $125,000 (2021) of equipment this year. Debra has heard that she can elect to expense up to $1,050,000 (2021) of equipment placed in service, and asks you for confirmation of this fact. However, since the profit of Debra's business is only $15,000 she can only take a $15,000 Section 179 deduction for the current year. If she makes an election to expense the full amount, however, the remaining $110,000 of her Section 179 deduction can be carried forward to future years when she has profits to offset the additional expense deduction. She could have used 100% bonus depreciation but might have created a net operating loss (NOL) if she did not have other income to offset the loss.

Keep in mind that as a result of TCJA 2017, losses at the entity level may be limited. This topic is further discussed in Chapter 8.

There is an additional limitation on the Section 179 expense election that applies to the purchase of automobiles. If a vehicle weighing over 6,000 pounds but less than 14,000 pounds is purchased, the maximum Section 179 expense that can be elected with respect to that vehicle is limited to $26,200 (2021). This limitation was enacted as part of the 2004 tax legislation to close a perceived loophole allowing businesses owners to purchase SUVs and expense them immediately under Section 179.

Example 10.42

Robert, owner of Lucy Heart, LLC, has always wanted a yellow Hummer (weighing over 6,000 pounds). He recently purchased one, to be used solely in his business, paying $80,000. Robert can elect to expense up to $26,200 of the cost immediately under Section 179 if he meets all of the other requirements for application of that section. Alternatively, Robert can choose to depreciate the asset or use 100% bonus depreciation. Note that vehicles over 6,000 pounds are not listed property (as described above); therefore the Section 280F limitations do not apply.

It is clear that a taxpayer may have several options for recovering the cost of a depreciable asset. If a taxpayer is eligible for all three of the following cost recovery options and chooses to use all of them, they must be used in the following order:

- Section 179 expense of up to $1,050,000 (2021); election made on a property-by-property basis.
- Bonus depreciation (100% or 50%), if available. No maximum or phaseout, not limited by income, and applies automatically unless the taxpayer elects out for the entire class of property (e.g., all 7-year property).
- MACRS depreciation on the remaining cost basis after the Section 179 depreciation.

Exhibit 10.5 | Form 4562 (Page 1)

Form **4562**

Department of the Treasury Internal Revenue Service (99)

Depreciation and Amortization
(Including Information on Listed Property)

▶ Attach to your tax return.

▶ Go to *www.irs.gov/Form4562* for instructions and the latest information.

OMB No. 1545-0172

2020

Attachment Sequence No. 179

Name(s) shown on return	Business or activity to which this form relates	Identifying number

Part I Election To Expense Certain Property Under Section 179
Note: If you have any listed property, complete Part V before you complete Part I.

1	Maximum amount (see instructions)	1	
2	Total cost of section 179 property placed in service (see instructions)	2	
3	Threshold cost of section 179 property before reduction in limitation (see instructions)	3	
4	Reduction in limitation. Subtract line 3 from line 2. If zero or less, enter -0-	4	
5	Dollar limitation for tax year. Subtract line 4 from line 1. If zero or less, enter -0-. If married filing separately, see instructions	5	

6	(a) Description of property	(b) Cost (business use only)	(c) Elected cost
7	Listed property. Enter the amount from line 29	7	

8	Total elected cost of section 179 property. Add amounts in column (c), lines 6 and 7	8	
9	Tentative deduction. Enter the **smaller** of line 5 or line 8	9	
10	Carryover of disallowed deduction from line 13 of your 2019 Form 4562	10	
11	Business income limitation. Enter the smaller of business income (not less than zero) or line 5. See instructions	11	
12	Section 179 expense deduction. Add lines 9 and 10, but don't enter more than line 11	12	
13	Carryover of disallowed deduction to 2021. Add lines 9 and 10, less line 12 ▶	13	

Note: Don't use Part II or Part III below for listed property. Instead, use Part V.

Part II Special Depreciation Allowance and Other Depreciation (Don't include listed property. See instructions.)

14	Special depreciation allowance for qualified property (other than listed property) placed in service during the tax year. See instructions	14	
15	Property subject to section 168(f)(1) election	15	
16	Other depreciation (including ACRS)	16	

Part III MACRS Depreciation (Don't include listed property. See instructions.)

Section A

17	MACRS deductions for assets placed in service in tax years beginning before 2020	17	
18	If you are electing to group any assets placed in service during the tax year into one or more general asset accounts, check here ▶ ☐		

Section B—Assets Placed in Service During 2020 Tax Year Using the General Depreciation System

(a) Classification of property	(b) Month and year placed in service	(c) Basis for depreciation (business/investment use only—see instructions)	(d) Recovery period	(e) Convention	(f) Method	(g) Depreciation deduction
19a 3-year property						
b 5-year property						
c 7-year property						
d 10-year property						
e 15-year property						
f 20-year property						
g 25-year property			25 yrs.		S/L	
h Residential rental			27.5 yrs.	MM	S/L	
property			27.5 yrs.	MM	S/L	
i Nonresidential real			39 yrs.	MM	S/L	
property				MM	S/L	

Section C—Assets Placed in Service During 2020 Tax Year Using the Alternative Depreciation System

(a) Classification of property	(b) Month and year placed in service	(c) Basis for depreciation	(d) Recovery period	(e) Convention	(f) Method	(g) Depreciation deduction
20a Class life					S/L	
b 12-year			12 yrs.		S/L	
c 30-year			30 yrs.	MM	S/L	
d 40-year			40 yrs.	MM	S/L	

Part IV Summary (See instructions.)

21	Listed property. Enter amount from line 28	21	
22	**Total.** Add amounts from line 12, lines 14 through 17, lines 19 and 20 in column (g), and line 21. Enter here and on the appropriate lines of your return. Partnerships and S corporations—see instructions	22	
23	For assets shown above and placed in service during the current year, enter the portion of the basis attributable to section 263A costs	23	

For Paperwork Reduction Act Notice, see separate instructions. Cat. No. 12906N Form **4562** (2020)

FORM 4562 (PAGE 2)

Form 4562 (2020) Page 2

Part V **Listed Property** (Include automobiles, certain other vehicles, certain aircraft, and property used for entertainment, recreation, or amusement.)

Note: For any vehicle for which you are using the standard mileage rate or deducting lease expense, complete **only** 24a, 24b, columns (a) through (c) of Section A, all of Section B, and Section C if applicable.

Section A—Depreciation and Other Information (Caution: See the instructions for limits for passenger automobiles.)

24a Do you have evidence to support the business/investment use claimed? ☐ **Yes** ☐ **No** | **24b** If "Yes," is the evidence written? ☐ **Yes** ☐ **No**

(a) Type of property (list vehicles first)	(b) Date placed in service	(c) Business/ investment use percentage	(d) Cost or other basis	(e) Basis for depreciation (business/investment use only)	(f) Recovery period	(g) Method/ Convention	(h) Depreciation deduction	(i) Elected section 179 cost
25 Special depreciation allowance for qualified listed property placed in service during the tax year and used more than 50% in a qualified business use. See instructions .						**25**		
26 Property used more than 50% in a qualified business use:								
		%						
		%						
		%						
27 Property used 50% or less in a qualified business use:								
		%				S/L –		
		%				S/L –		
		%				S/L –		
28 Add amounts in column (h), lines 25 through 27. Enter here and on line 21, page 1 .						**28**		
29 Add amounts in column (i), line 26. Enter here and on line 7, page 1							**29**	

Section B—Information on Use of Vehicles

Complete this section for vehicles used by a sole proprietor, partner, or other "more than 5% owner," or related person. If you provided vehicles to your employees, first answer the questions in Section C to see if you meet an exception to completing this section for those vehicles.

	(a) Vehicle 1		(b) Vehicle 2		(c) Vehicle 3		(d) Vehicle 4		(e) Vehicle 5		(f) Vehicle 6	
30 Total business/investment miles driven during the year (**don't** include commuting miles) .												
31 Total commuting miles driven during the year												
32 Total other personal (noncommuting) miles driven												
33 Total miles driven during the year. Add lines 30 through 32												
	Yes	**No**	**Yes**	**No**	**Yes**	**No**	**Yes**	**No**	**Yes**	**No**	**Yes**	**No**
34 Was the vehicle available for personal use during off-duty hours?												
35 Was the vehicle used primarily by a more than 5% owner or related person? . .												
36 Is another vehicle available for personal use?												

Section C—Questions for Employers Who Provide Vehicles for Use by Their Employees

Answer these questions to determine if you meet an exception to completing Section B for vehicles used by employees who **aren't** more than 5% owners or related persons. See instructions.

	Yes	**No**
37 Do you maintain a written policy statement that prohibits all personal use of vehicles, including commuting, by your employees?		
38 Do you maintain a written policy statement that prohibits personal use of vehicles, except commuting, by your employees? See the instructions for vehicles used by corporate officers, directors, or 1% or more owners . .		
39 Do you treat all use of vehicles by employees as personal use?		
40 Do you provide more than five vehicles to your employees, obtain information from your employees about the use of the vehicles, and retain the information received?		
41 Do you meet the requirements concerning qualified automobile demonstration use? See instructions.		
Note: If your answer to 37, 38, 39, 40, or 41 is "Yes," don't complete Section B for the covered vehicles.		

Part VI **Amortization**

(a) Description of costs	(b) Date amortization begins	(c) Amortizable amount	(d) Code section	(e) Amortization period or percentage	(f) Amortization for this year
42 Amortization of costs that begins during your 2020 tax year (see instructions):					
43 Amortization of costs that began before your 2020 tax year				**43**	
44 Total. Add amounts in column (f). See the instructions for where to report				**44**	

Form **4562** (2020)

CASE STUDY 10.1

Expenses for the Business Use of a Car

Kevin E. and Sondra Ward, Petitioners v. Commissioner of Internal Revenue, Respondent, T.C. Summary Opinion 2011-67 (June 8, 2011).

Sondra Ward, a real estate agent for Century 21, purchased a 2006 BMW X5 on December 21, 2005 for $49,431.50 and immediately placed the car in service for Mrs. Ward's real estate business. In 2005, Sondra, and, on occasion, her husband, Kevin, drove the car 1,405.7 miles. On her Schedule C, Sondra claimed a depreciation expense of $2,349 for the BMW. The IRS chose to examine the return, and reduced the depreciation deduction claimed on the BMW to $528 (based on the calculated business use of the vehicle). Sondra and Kevin asserted that they were entitled to a $25,000 Section 179 expense deduction and a $1,099 depreciation deduction for the BMW in lieu of the deduction claimed on their return.

During the examination of their return, a mileage log was provided with 3 entries for 2005 totaling 47 miles for personal use of the BMW. The log had no entries with a business use purpose and no miles were allocated to business use. A log was later reconstructed using Sondra's mobile phone daily calendar. Based on the information provided during the examination of the return, the revenue agent determined that the business use percentage of the BMW for 2005 was 42.7%.

The tax court noted that an automobile is "listed property," and to claim a Section 179 deduction for listed property, strict substantiation requirements must be met (the taxpayer must substantiate the amount, time, place, and business purpose of the expenditures and provide adequate records or sufficient evidence to corroborate his own statement). While Sondra claims that she is entitled to a Sec. 179 deduction for the BMW because it was predominately used for business purposes, she failed to comply with the strict substantiation requirements, and the available evidence provided to the IRS and at trial indicated that the percentage of business use was only 42.7%. Since the car was not used at least 50% for business purposes, the court concluded that a section 179 deduction was not available.

Furthermore, given the evidence on business use of the car, the court concluded that the IRS was correct in reducing the depreciation expense for the BMW. Only that portion of the car that was actually used for business purposes would qualify for depreciation deductions. The portion of the car used for personal purposes is not considered when determining the allowable depreciation expense deduction.

CATEGORIZING ASSETS FOR INCOME TAX PURPOSES

Key Concepts

1. Identify the various categories of assets for income tax purposes.
2. Describe a capital asset.
3. Identify ordinary income assets.
4. Define Section 1231 assets.

Thus far we have reviewed the purpose of basis and the uses of depreciation in the income tax system; but to determine what the income tax consequences of a particular transaction are, we must categorize the asset that is being transferred. In the U.S. income tax system, there are only three types of assets: capital assets, ordinary income assets, and Section 1231 assets. Categorizing the asset is essential because the tax consequence resulting from the transfer of each of the three types of assets differ. In this chapter, we introduce the concept of categorizing the assets for income tax purposes and give a brief overview of the tax characteristics that apply to that asset.

Capital Assets

Most assets are **capital assets**. This category is the catch-all category. Capital assets are all assets that are not ordinary income assets or Section 1231 assets. Specifically, capital assets are defined in Section 1221 as everything in the world other than:

1. Accounts and Notes Receivable from a trade or business
2. Copyrights, literary, musical, and artistic creations and similar assets in the hands of the creator[7]
3. Inventory or stock in trade held for sale to customers in the ordinary course of business
4. Depreciable property or real property used in a trade or business
5. Publications of the United States Government
6. Supplies used in the ordinary conduct of a trade or business
7. Derivative instruments for commodities held by a dealer (subject to various restrictions)
8. Hedging transactions entered into in the normal course of business.

The TCJA 2017 excludes a patent, invention, model or design (whether or not patented), and a secret formula or process which is held either by the taxpayer who created the property or a taxpayer with a substituted or transferred basis from the taxpayer who created the property (or for whom the property was created) from the definition of a "capital asset." Thus, gains or losses from the sale or exchange of any of these assets will not receive capital gain treatment.

From an introductory tax and financial planning standpoint, the first four items in the list are the most important. The last four on the list, other than supplies used in business, apply to specialized situations that are beyond the scope of this textbook. An easy way to remember the definition of a capital asset is "everything in the world is a capital asset except ACID." ACID is constructed using the first letter of the items 1 - 4 on the list above.

7. IRC Section1221(b)(3) allows an election by musicians for musical compositions or copyrights. The taxpayer could elect for tax treatment of the composition or copyright as a capital gain or loss instead of inventory subject to ordinary income.

Example 10.43

Amy recently purchased a painting by Worthington, an aspiring artist, to hang in her dining room. Amy is not an art dealer, but rather a collector. The painting is a capital asset in Amy's hands, since it was not created by Amy, it is not being held as inventory for sale to her customers, and is not depreciable property used in a trade or a business.

If a capital asset is transferred or sold, the gain or loss recognized for tax purposes will depend on three items:

1. the holding period of the asset
2. the type of asset
3. the use of the asset

If a taxpayer disposes of a capital asset at a gain, and has held that asset for more than a year, he or she may qualify for a special capital gains tax rate, which is currently lower than the tax rate that applies to ordinary income. Capital gains tax rates currently range from zero percent to 20 percent (not including any surtaxes imposed by the Affordable Care Act of 2010). The specifics of capital transactions are covered in Chapter 11. While gains on personal capital assets are fully taxable, losses on personal capital assets are not fully deductible. When the asset generating a capital gain is a collectible, such as artwork, the special long-term capital gains rate does not apply. Under current law, the capital gains tax rate on the sale of collectibles held for more than one year is a maximum of 28 percent.

The benefit to having a capital asset with a long-term holding period (more than one year) disposed of at a gain is that a lower tax rate applies. While the lower tax rate also applies to losses (which is not such a good thing, since the taxpayer receives less of a tax benefit in this case), the deductibility of losses is limited. Capital losses in any year are fully deductible against capital gains in the same year. If a capital loss exceeds capital gains for the year, however, the maximum loss that may be deducted against other forms of income is a net capital loss of $3,000. Losses in excess of this amount may be carried forward indefinitely.

The bottom line for capital assets is that gains are good, (they typically result in paying tax at a lower rate) but losses are bad (losses are either limited, or result in a decreased tax benefit for the taxpayer when compared to other types of assets).

If capital assets include all assets other than those on the list above, the assets on the list are ordinary income assets or Section 1231 assets. These are listed in **Exhibit 10.6**.

CASE STUDY 10.2

Section 179

Stephen L. and Darlene G. Morgan, Petitioners v. Commissioner of Internal Revenue, Respondent, T.C. Summary Opinion 2011-92 (July 14, 2011).

Stephen worked in the Construction Business for most of his career. In 2006, Stephen sold his interest in JBS Enterprises, LLC for $1,206,806, which included a 2006 Dodge Ram Truck with a price of $33,836 and a travel trailer at a price of $16,836. After selling his business interest, Stephen began to purchase and renovate distressed properties. He purchased two properties in 2006, and sold them in 2007. He kept detailed expense logs, and used the 2006 Dodge Truck exclusively in his renovation activities. Given economic circumstances at the time, Stephen did not feel that purchasing additional properties was prudent.

On his 2006 income tax return, Stephen claimed a $33,836 Section 179 deduction on Schedule C for the Dodge Ram Truck. Since the properties were not sold until 2007, the Schedule C did not include any income for 2006. The IRS issued a notice of deficiency disallowing all of Stephen's Schedule C deductions, claiming that Steven's renovation activities did not qualify as a trade or business, and, even if they did, his Section 179 deduction would not be allowed since there was no income from the business activity.

The tax court determined that Stephen's activities did constitute a trade or business, stating that his "work" and behavior in connection with the search for, purchase, renovation, and sale of the two properties Cedar Hill and Nashville clearly established that he treated his activities as a trade or business. The court used several of the guidelines found in Treas. Reg. §1.183-2(b), which are frequently used in determining whether an activity is a business or a hobby, in coming to this conclusion.

Since Stephen conducted a trade or business, he is entitled to claim Section 179 deductions for property used in that trade or business. In 2006, two limitations applied to the use of the Section179 deduction: (1) an overall $100,000 cap; and (2) the deduction cannot exceed the "aggregate amount of taxable income of the taxpayer for such taxable year which is derived from the active conduct by the taxpayer of any trade or business." While Stephen's renovation business did not have income for 2006, he did have income allocated from JBS Enterprises, LLC. Since the second limitation of Section 179 applies to the "aggregate" of "any trade or business" during the taxable year, the Court concluded that Stephen had sufficient taxable income from the active conduct of a trade or business to claim the Section 179 expense deduction of $33,836. [Note that under current law, the Section 179 deduction for an automobile would be limited to $26,200. That limitation was not in place for the tax year covered in this case.]

Ordinary Income Assets

Ordinary Income Assets are, simply, assets that will generate tax at ordinary income rates when transferred. We know from our prior discussion that most assets are capital assets. The only assets that are not considered capital assets are listed in the following exhibit.

Exhibit 10.6 | Assets Not Considered Capital Assets

- Accounts and Notes Receivable from a trade or business
- Copyrights, literary, and artistic creations and similar assets in the hands of the creator
- Patents, inventions, models or designs (whether or not patented), as well as any secret formula or process that is held either by the taxpayer who created the property
- Inventory or stock in trade held for sale to customers in the ordinary course of business
- Depreciable property or real property used in a trade or business

The first four items in this list are the ordinary income assets. The last item (depreciable property or real property used in a trade or business) is a Section 1231 asset.

First, consider inventory. Inventory is purchased by a business or business person for sale to customers. When the inventory is sold, there is (hopefully) a gain for the business that will be subject to tax at the end of the tax year. All earnings from business operations are taxed at ordinary income tax rates. Therefore, inventory must be an ordinary income asset because it generates ordinary income when sold.

Copyrights, literary compositions, and artistic creations in the hands of the author are really a form of inventory. A writer who composes a novel does so for sale to customers. That sale is in the ordinary course of business, and therefore results in ordinary income tax on the gain. The same is true for an artist who paints a painting. By creating a work available for sale to a customer, the author of the work is creating his or her inventory.

Similar to artistic creations, patents and inventions are creations of a taxpayer that will generate ordinary income if sold after 2017 (TCJA 2017). In prior years, patents and inventions received favorable capital gain treatment.

Example 10.44

Robin is tired of transcribing Mike's bad handwriting as she has been doing it for 20 years. She invents a pen that clarifies the handwriting as the user writes on paper. If she sells this invention for $6 million, it will be ordinary income after 2017.

Accounts and notes receivable are items of inventory that have been sold in return for a customer's promise to pay for that item at some point in the future. They represent delayed payment for the sale of inventory, and the gain on the sale will be subject to ordinary income tax rates. Think of the tax planning that could occur if accounts and notes receivable were treated as capital assets – businesspeople would have great incentive to sell on account, meet the requisite holding period, and pay tax on the gain at capital, rather than ordinary tax rates. Because Congress does not want business people to be able to transform their ordinary income taxed at a higher rate to capital gains taxed at a lower rate, accounts and notes receivable are treated as ordinary income assets.

Example 10.45

Marie is a renowned artist in New England, and her work is sought after by the rich and famous. Marie has recently painted her newest masterpiece. The painting in Marie's hands is inventory, and is therefore an ordinary income asset.

Example 10.46

Frank is an art dealer, and has galleries in New Orleans, New York, and San Diego. Frank recently purchased a painting by Wentworth, and placed it in his New Orleans studio for sale. Because the painting is being held for sale to customers in the ordinary course of business, it is inventory, and, therefore, is an ordinary income asset.

Since we began our discussion of asset categorization, nearly all of the examples have dealt with one type of property – a painting. As the above examples illustrate, asset categorization does not depend on the asset, but rather, the use to which that asset is put. In **Example 10.43**, when Amy purchased a painting for use in her home, the painting was a capital asset. When Marie creates a painting for sale to her patrons (**Example 10.45**), or when Frank purchases a painting for sale to customers of his art gallery (**Example 10.46**), the paintings are ordinary income assets, and the tax consequences are different.

The consequence of classifying an asset as an ordinary income asset depends on whether the asset is transferred at a gain or at a loss. If the asset is transferred for a gain, ordinary income tax rates will apply. Ordinary income tax rates are the highest tax rates in our tax system, implying that ordinary income assets carry a higher tax burden when sold for a gain. If, however, an ordinary asset is sold for a loss, there is no decrease in the tax rate (as would occur, for example, if the asset was a capital asset and was held for a long-term holding period), so the loss will generate a higher tax benefit for the taxpayer. Furthermore, ordinary losses, unlike capital losses are not subject to deduction limitations.

The bottom line for ordinary income assets is this: gains are bad (from a tax perspective, not an economic perspective because they are taxed at the highest marginal income tax rate of the taxpayer), but losses are good (no income tax rate reductions or loss limitations apply).

If a taxpayer had a crystal ball and could tell which assets would generate gains and which would generate losses, the taxpayer would hold all of the assets that would generate gains as capital assets (to get the tax-rate break that long-term capital assets offer), and hold all of the assets that would generate a loss as ordinary income assets (since the losses would generate a bigger tax benefit and would not be limited, as is the case with capital losses). Unfortunately, this is a difficult planning feat to achieve.

Section 1231 Assets

The final type of asset in our income tax system is known as a **Section 1231 asset**, obviously named after the IRC section that defines it. Since capital assets consist of everything other than ordinary income assets and Section 1231 assets, and ordinary income assets include three of the four items in our list;

there is only one item left to constitute a Section 1231 asset: depreciable property or real property used for productive use in a trade or business or for the production of income.

Technically, Section 1231 assets include:

1. Depreciable property or real property used for productive use in a trade or business or for the production of income
2. Timber, coal, and iron to which Section 631 applies
3. Livestock held for draft, breeding, dairy or sporting purposes
4. Unharvested crops on land used in business
5. Purchased intangible assets eligible for amortization (such as goodwill)

Items 2-5 apply to very specific situations, and are therefore beyond the scope of this textbook. From a planning perspective, the most important Section 1231 asset is the first item: depreciable property or real property used for productive use in a trade or business or for the production of income.

You may recall from our discussion above that in order to be depreciable, the property must be used in a trade or business or for the production of income. Personal use property (such as a personal residence) is not eligible for depreciation deductions.

Example 10.47

Homer Headshrinker, a prominent psychiatrist, purchases new furniture for his office. Since the furniture is being used in Homer's trade or business, the furniture is categorized as a Section 1231 asset.

In addition to meeting the definition of a Section 1231 asset, to qualify for the tax advantages Section 1231 confers, the asset must have been held for a long-term holding period. The only exception to the long-term holding period requirement deals with un-harvested crops (a special exception that is beyond the scope of this textbook).

When engaging in tax planning, it is important to recognize that if you are dealing with depreciable property or land used in a trade or business, that property will be treated as a Section 1231 asset. If the property is not real or depreciable property used in a trade or business, it is not a Section 1231 asset.

Once an asset has been categorized as a Section 1231 asset, it is afforded special tax treatment. Gains on Section 1231 assets are treated as capital gains, and losses on Section 1231 assets are treated as ordinary losses. Section 1231 gives the taxpayer the best of capital and ordinary income asset treatment. Since gains are treated as capital gains, and, by definition, Section 1231 requires a long-term holding period, the long-term capital gains rates will apply, reducing the tax burden on the asset when compared to an ordinary income asset. If a Section 1231 asset is sold at a loss, ordinary loss treatment applies, granting the taxpayer a greater tax benefit (due to the higher tax rate that applies to ordinary income assets) and removing the limitation on losses that are associated with capital assets.

Quick Quiz 10.7

1. Generally, a copyright in the hands of the creator is a capital asset.
   a. True
   b. False
2. Inventory is an ordinary income asset.
   a. True
   b. False
3. Section 1231 assets are afforded special tax treatment.
   a. True
   b. False

False, True, True.

While Section 1231 grants the best of both worlds treatment (gains are capital; losses are ordinary), there are some limitations. Whenever an asset is categorized as a Section 1231 asset, there is the potential for depreciation recapture. Depreciation recapture will be discussed in Chapter 12.

Exhibit 10.7 | Asset Categories

	Capital Assets	*Ordinary Assets*	*1231 Assets*
Sold for Gain	Capital Gain Treatment	Ordinary Income Treatment	Capital Gain Treatment (part or all gain may require recapture)
Sold for Loss	Capital Loss Treatment (current loss may be limited)	Ordinary Loss Treatment	Ordinary Loss Treatment

SUMMARY

This chapter reviewed the purpose of basis rules, depreciation, and asset categorization in our income tax system. Basis is simply a way of keeping track of capital that has been invested in an asset; so that upon disposition of the asset, the capital can be returned income tax-free to the owner. Recall that capital represents after-tax income, and should not be subject to income tax again. Depreciation allows those who use assets in a trade or business or for production of income to receive their capital back earlier than the date the asset is sold; so that capital can be reinvested in the business, and as a result, the business will continue to make money upon which taxes will be due. Depreciation is not allowed on personal use assets. Finally, the chapter reviewed the categorization of assets for federal income tax purposes. All assets are either capital assets, ordinary income assets, or Section 1231 assets. To qualify as a Section 1231 asset, the asset must either be real property or depreciable personal property used in a trade or business. Section 1231 assets have the best of both worlds tax treatment, but may be subject to depreciation recapture rules.

KEY TERMS

Amortization - Cost recovery deductions for intangible assets.

Amount Realized - The amount of money plus the value of property received in the sale or exchange of an asset.

Basis - Represents the total capital from after-tax income used by a taxpayer to purchase an investment.

Bonus Depreciation - A form of accelerated depreciation, similar to what is available under Section 179. However, there are no income limitations or limitations on the value of assets placed in service. While these rules have changed since introduced in 2010, TCJA 2017 allows for 100% bonus depreciation for assets placed in service after September 27, 2017 and before 2023. The 100% bonus deprecation is phased out after 2022, and taxpayers are permitted to elect 50% bonus deprecation in lieu of 100% bonus depreciation.

Capital Assets - All assets that are not specified as ordinary income assets or Section 1231 assets.

Conventions - Rules that govern the amount of depreciation that may be deducted during the first year that an asset is put into service.

Cost Basis - The initial value of an asset acquired by an investor using capital to purchase the investment.

Depreciation - A return of capital to a business that results in a reduction in the basis of the asset for the amount of depreciation that is claimed.

Double Basis Rule - A rule that applies to gifts and related party transactions where the transferee has a basis of the fair market value for losses and the transferor's basis for gains. The rule applies when the asset that is transferred has a fair market value less than the transferor's basis at the time of the transfer. This rule does not apply to arm's-length unrelated party transactions. This rule may also be referred to as the split basis rule, dual basis rule, or bifurcated basis rule.

Double Declining Balance Method - An accelerated depreciation method used for MACRS assets with a 3, 5, 7, or 10 year class life in which the annual depreciation percentage is twice the annual depreciation percentage under the straight-line depreciation method.

Listed Property - Suspect property that is easily used for both business and personal purposes.

Modified Accelerated Cost Recovery System (MACRS) - An accelerated depreciation system under which assets are divided into specific classes according to their useful lives.

Nonrecourse Debt - Debt that is secured only by the asset pledged as security and not by any personal guarantee of the debtor.

150 Percent Declining Balance Method - An accelerated depreciation method used for MACRS assets with a 15 or 20 year class life in which the annual depreciation percentage is 150 percent of the annual depreciation percentage under the straight-line depreciation method.

Ordinary Income Assets - Accounts receivable, copyrights, and inventory, all of which generate gains that will be taxed at ordinary income tax rates.

Original Issue Discount (OID) Bonds - A bond that is issued for a price that is less than its face amount or principal amount on which interest is usually paid only at maturity.

Pass-Through Entities - Legal business forms that are not treated as separate taxable entities for income tax purposes. The income of a pass-through entity is taxed to each of the owners in proportion to their ownership interest.

Recourse Debt - Debt that the taxpayer is personally liable to repay regardless of whether the investment produces a return for the investor.

Section 1231 Assets - Depreciable property or real property used for productive use in a trade or business or for the production of income.

Section 179 Election - Provides to business owners, provided that certain requirements are met, the option of taking all of the depreciation deductions in the year the asset was placed into service, rather than over the MACRS class life.

Step-to Fair Market Value - The basis of inherited property, which is equal to the fair market value of the asset on the date of the decedent's death, or, if elected by the executor of the decedent's estate, the alternate valuation date.

Straight-Line Depreciation - A depreciation method under which the purchase price of the asset, less its expected salvage value, is divided by the expected useful life of the asset to determine the annual depreciation deduction.

DISCUSSION QUESTIONS

SOLUTIONS to the discussion questions can be found exclusively within the chapter. Once you have completed an initial reading of the chapter, go back and highlight the answers to these questions.

1. How is gain or loss calculated?
2. What is basis and what is its purpose?
3. Describe three uses of basis.
4. What is cost basis?
5. What is the difference between recourse debt and nonrecourse debt?
6. Name several items that increase basis.
7. Name several items that decrease basis.
8. What is depreciation?
9. How is the basis of inherited property determined?
10. What is the rationale for the step-to fair market value of the basis for inherited property?
11. What is the general rule for determining the basis of gifted property?
12. How is the basis of gifted property affected when the donor pays gift tax on the transfer?
13. How is the basis of gifted property determined when the donor gifts property that has a fair market value less than the donor's adjusted basis on the date of the gift?
14. How is the basis of property transferred between spouses determined?
15. Who is considered a related party?
16. What are the tax consequences of selling property to a related party at a loss?
17. How is real property depreciated?
18. What are the two methods of depreciation used with MACRS?
19. What is the 100% and 50% depreciation bonus?
20. How is the cost of an intangible asset recovered?
21. What is "listed property?"
22. What is the Section 179 deduction?

MULTIPLE CHOICE PROBLEMS

A sample of multiple choice problems is provided below. Additional multiple choice problems are available at money-education.com by accessing the Student Practice Portal.

1. Five years ago, Carlton purchased 1,000 shares of Ickingham Industries, Inc. for $10 per share. He signed an agreement with the company which allowed the company to use his dividend payments to purchase additional shares for him. Over the last 5 years, Carlton received a total of $1,200 in dividend payments, which purchased an additional 100 shares of stock. If Carlton sells all of his shares for $24,000, what is his taxable gain?
   a. $0.
   b. $12,800.
   c. $14,000.
   d. $24,000.

2. Which of the following items is not included in the cost basis of an investment?
   a. Cash used to purchase the investment.
   b. Recourse debt incurred in purchasing the investment.
   c. Nonrecourse debt incurred in purchasing the investment.
   d. The fair market value of property transferred to acquire the investment.

3. Uncle Phil died in 2021, he left his estate to his ungrateful cousin, Will. Uncle Phil's cost basis in his property was $2 million but, due to turbulent political and economic times, it was only worth $1 million at his death. Uncle Phil had reinvested approximately $250,000 of dividends during his holding period, and his estate paid $500,000 in transfer taxes at his death. What is Uncle Phil's basis in the property?
   a. $1,000,000.
   b. $2,000,000.
   c. $2,250,000.
   d. $2,750,000.

4. Two months after Hillary purchased Jazz Acres for $25,000, she died. The fair market value of Jazz Acres as of the date of Hillary's death was $32,000. She left Jazz Acres to her daughter, Vivian. Since Vivian was the only beneficiary of the estate and there were no estate taxes due, the title to the property was transferred to Vivian within one month of Hillary's death. Two weeks after receiving title to the property, Vivian sold Jazz Acres for $35,000. What is the amount of taxable gain that Vivian will realize on the sale?
   a. $3,000.
   b. $7,000.
   c. $10,000.
   d. $35,000.

5. All of the following statements concerning depreciation are correct EXCEPT:
    a. Depreciation is a method of cost recovery that allows a taxpayer to receive his capital back over the useful life of an asset.
    b. Assets purchased for personal use are eligible for depreciation deductions.
    c. Depreciation deductions cause a downward adjustment in the taxpayer's basis.
    d. Depreciation on real estate is taken on a straight-line basis.

Additional multiple choice problems are available at *money-education.com* by accessing the Student Practice Portal. Access requires registration of the title using the unique code at the front of the book.

QUICK QUIZ EXPLANATIONS

Quick Quiz 10.1

1. True.
2. False. The purpose of basis is to keep track of after-tax dollars an individual invests so that upon the sale of the investment, income is not taxed twice.
3. True.

Quick Quiz 10.2

1. True.
2. True.
3. False. Since the cost of an asset is recovered through depreciation, the adjusted basis of the asset must be decreased by the depreciation claimed each year.

Quick Quiz 10.3

1. False. The basis of property that passes through a decedent's estate is stepped to the fair market value of the asset on the date of the decedent's death, or, if elected by the executor of the decedent's estate, to the fair market value of the asset on the alternate valuation date.
2. False. When a donor pays gift tax, the portion of the gift tax paid that represents appreciation in the value of the property may be added to the donor's original basis to determine the basis in the hands of the donee. Therefore, gift tax paid increases the donee's basis in gifted property.
3. True.
4. True.

Quick Quiz 10.4

1. True.
2. True.

Quick Quiz 10.5

1. False. Most cars are 5-Year Class Life Assets.
2. True.

Quick Quiz 10.6

1. True.
2. True.
3. True.

Quick Quiz 10.7

1. False. Generally, a copyright in the hands of its creator is an ordinary income asset, not a capital asset.
2. True.
3. True.

11

THE TAXATION OF CAPITAL ASSETS

LEARNING OBJECTIVES

1. Identify assets classified as capital assets for income tax purposes.*
2. Explain the realization and recognition requirements associated with the taxation of capital assets.*
3. Calculate gain or loss on the sale of a capital asset.*
4. Identify items included in the amount realized on the sale of a capital asset.*
5. Identify the types of losses that are disallowed for income tax purposes.*
6. Determine the deductibility of losses for a given taxpayer.*
7. Calculate the tax impact of a wash sale for a given taxpayer.*
8. Explain the relationship between capital asset holding periods and tax rates.*
9. Determine the holding period of property that a taxpayer receives through a decedent's estate.*
10. Determine the holding period used for determining gain or loss when a taxpayer sells an asset received as a gift.*
11. Determine the holding period used for determining gain or loss when a taxpayer sells an asset that was purchased from a related party.*
12. Explain the holding period rule for nonbusiness bad debts.
13. Calculate the capital gains tax due when a taxpayer sells a piece of real estate that was used to produce rental income.*
14. Calculate the net capital gain/loss for a taxpayer given information on the taxpayer's asset sales.*
15. Describe the netting procedures for short and long-term capital gains and losses.*
16. Describe the annual limits on capital loss deductions for individual taxpayers.*
17. Calculate the allowable loss associated with a taxpayer's sale of small business stock.*

**Ties to CFP Certification Learning Objectives*

INTRODUCTION

As discussed in the previous chapter, the tax characteristics of a particular asset depend upon the categorization of the asset. There are three categories of assets in our income tax system: capital assets, ordinary income assets, and Section 1231 assets. This chapter covers the income tax rules associated with capital assets.

The **"capital asset"** classification is the catch-all (default) category in our income tax system; all assets that are not specified as ordinary income assets or Section 1231 assets are capital assets. IRC Section 1221 defines capital assets as all assets *other than*:

- accounts and notes receivable;
- a copyright, a literary, musical, or artistic composition, a letter or memorandum, or similar property, held by a taxpayer whose personal efforts created such property;
- gains or losses from the sale or exchange of a patent, invention, model, or design held by the taxpayer who created the property;
- inventory; and
- real property or depreciable personal property used in a trade or business.

A special election is available to taxpayers to treat musical compositions and copyrights in musical works as capital assets instead of ordinary income assets.[1]

While IRC Section1221 does specify that a few additional categories of assets are not capital assets, these categories deal with specialized transactions, and as such do not have general applicability from a planning perspective. Remember the asset categorization memory aid that was introduced in the prior chapter: *All assets are capital assets except ACID*:

- **A**ccounts Receivable
- **C**opyrights
- **I**nventory
- Real or **D**epreciable Personal Property used in a trade or business

Once an asset has been categorized, the tax attributes of that asset are defined. As discussed in Chapter 10, gains on capital assets are subject to favorable capital gain tax rates if the asset has a long-term holding period, but losses on capital assets are limited. The details of the tax rules governing capital assets are covered in this chapter.

REALIZATION AND RECOGNITION

Unlike ordinary income, which is subject to income tax when earned, gains on capital assets are subject to tax only when there has been both a **realization event** and a **recognition event**. Realization implies that the asset has been sold or exchanged, and recognition occurs when a realized gain is required to be included on a taxpayer's income tax return. Generally, all realized gains are recognized (that is, all realized gains are subject to current taxation) unless a provision can be found in the IRC that either exempts the gain from taxation or defers the gain to a future tax period. The various types of transactions that constitute tax-deferred and tax-free transfers will be discussed in Chapter 13.

Key Concepts

1. Describe a realization event and a recognition event.
2. Define the sale or exchange requirement.
3. Explain how to calculate gains and losses.
4. Define the amount realized.
5. Identify the disallowed losses.

Sale or Exchange Requirements

For a gain to be subject to income tax, there must first be a sale or exchange of the asset. Sometimes, as in the case of a sale, the **sale or exchange requirement** is both obvious and easily met. In other cases, it may be less obvious whether the sale or exchange requirement has been met.

First, consider the sale of an asset. When the owner of an asset sells that asset in exchange for another asset (which could include cash or any other property), a realization event occurs.

1. IRC Sec. 1221(b)(3).

Example 11.1

After conducting a thorough investment portfolio analysis, Eric decides that MNL, Inc. stock no longer fits into his asset allocation, and sells the shares of MNL that he owns. The sale constitutes a realization event. Eric will calculate any gain or loss and, absent a special IRC provision deferring or exempting any gain, will be required to recognize any gain on his individual income tax return.

In the case of the sale of an asset, it does not matter what type of asset is sold. It could be stocks, bonds, real estate, personal assets, business use assets, intangible assets, or antique furniture. Realization of gain or loss will occur on the sale, and recognition will occur in the same tax year unless a special provision of the IRC exempts or defers it from taxation in the current year.

In some cases, it may be less obvious that the sale or exchange requirement has been met. Consider the following examples.

Example 11.2

After finishing college, Ariel moved from New England to Louisiana. Over the past several years, Ariel has lost her home three times to forces of nature that have created havoc in the gulf region of the United States. When Hurricane Katrina passed through, destroying her home for the third time, Ariel decided to pack up what little she had left and move back to New England. When she receives her insurance check for the damage to her home in Louisiana, she deposits it into her savings account and does not rebuild or replace her home. In this instance, a realization event has occurred, and Ariel will be required to calculate gain or loss on her Louisiana home and may have to recognize that gain on her income tax return.

Natural disasters that destroy property cause a realization event for income tax purposes since the gain or loss in a particular property can be calculated at or around that time. It may be possible to defer recognition of the gain by following the rules of IRC Section 1033, which are discussed in Chapter 13. If those deferral rules are not followed, however, the gain or loss is recognized as well as realized, sometimes to the surprise of taxpayers who experience these types of losses.

Another event that could cause realization of a loss is the bankruptcy of a public company. When a company and its stock become worthless, a constructive sale of the stock held in the worthless company is deemed to have occurred on December 31 of the year in which the stock became worthless, forcing loss recognition in that year.

Example 11.3

On December 28 of last year, Jasmine purchased 1,000 shares in Jafar Industries, Inc. This investment was not one of Jasmine's best investments; the company declared bankruptcy on January 5 of the current year, and the security became immediately worthless. For federal income tax purposes, when a security becomes worthless, a constructive sale occurs on December 31 of that year. Therefore, Jasmine will have a recognition event due to the bankruptcy of Jafar Industries, Inc. as of December 31 of the current year.

There are special rules governing worthless securities, which were covered in Chapter 8. As the discussion illustrates, an event over which the taxpayer has no control, such as the bankruptcy of a company or the occurrence of a natural disaster, is considered a sale or exchange of an asset and may trigger a recognition event for federal income tax purposes.

Calculation of Gain or Loss

When a sale or exchange occurs, gain or loss must be determined. As explained in Chapter 10, IRC Section 1001 provides the formula used to calculate gain or loss on the sale or exchange of an asset. The gain or loss equals the amount realized by the taxpayer on the sale or exchange of the asset, less the taxpayer's adjusted basis in the asset. Mathematically, the formula is:

Amount Realized
Less: Adjusted Basis
Equals: Gain or (Loss)

The Amount Realized

The **amount realized** on a sale includes the cash received plus the fair market value of any other property received in exchange for the asset sold. While a sale generally involves cash, in some cases the party purchasing the asset may give cash plus other property or perhaps only property in the sale or exchange.

Example 11.4

Alvin owns an interest in Seville Farms, LLC. He inherited his interest from his grandfather and does not believe that it is the most efficient asset to include in his investment portfolio given his goals and objectives. On the date of his grandfather's death, the interest was worth $90,000. One year later, Alvin agrees to sell his interest in Seville Farms, LLC to his cousin in return for $20,000 cash plus a piece of raw land worth $90,000. Alvin would like to hold the land as an investment, since he believes that the value will increase substantially over the next 5 years. The amount that Alvin realized in this transaction is $110,000 (equal to the $20,000 in cash received, plus the fair market value of the land received, $90,000). To calculate his gain or loss, Alvin would have to subtract his adjusted basis ($90,000) from the amount realized in the transaction.

In the above example, an asset was transferred for cash plus other property, therefore the amount realized equals the cash plus the fair market value of the property received. Sometimes, instead of transferring property in exchange for assets, the parties to a transaction transfer debt. This can occur when, for example, the property being transferred has an assumable mortgage or has a liability attached to the property that will not be released until paid. In these circumstances, the transfer of debt is treated as the transfer of "other property" in the exchange and is included in the amount realized from the transaction. The party who is giving up, or "shedding," the debt will be deemed to have an additional amount realized; therefore, the party assuming the debt will be deemed to be paying that amount in the exchange.

Example 11.5

Continuing with **Example 11.4**, instead of receiving Seville Farms, LLC from his grandfather's estate, assume that Alvin purchased the interest years ago for $90,000. He paid $20,000 in cash, and obtained an assumable loan for the balance of the $70,000. Currently, the balance of the note is $50,000. Alvin is no longer interested in the business. His cousin, who also owns an interest in the company, agrees to purchase Alvin's interest for $60,000 in cash, and he will assume the $50,000 note. The amount realized in this transaction by Alvin is $110,000 (equal to the cash received, $60,000, plus the value of the "liability shed" by Alvin, $50,000, for a total of $110,000).

Sample Calculation of Gain or Loss

Basis represents capital invested in an asset, which is returned tax-free to the investor when he or she sells the asset. Basis must be subtracted from the amount realized to determine the amount of the gain or loss on the transaction. Issues associated with the determination of basis were discussed at length in Chapter 10.

Continuing with the example above, Alvin's basis in Seville Farms, LLC is $90,000 regardless of whether he received it from his grandfather's estate (**Example 11.4**), or he purchased the interest for $90,000 ($20,000 in cash plus the $70,000 note) (**Example 11.5**).

If Alvin received the interest from his grandfather's estate, his basis in the interest was stepped to the fair market value of the property on the date of the decedent's death.

If Alvin purchased the interest for $90,000 by paying $20,000 in cash and financing the rest of the acquisition, his basis is also $90,000. Since Alvin must pay back the note with after-tax dollars (he must earn money, pay taxes on those earnings, and use what is left to make payments on the note), the amount borrowed is included in his basis.

Therefore, since Alvin's basis is $90,000 in either case, he is entitled to recoup his capital of $90,000 tax-free when he sells the asset.

As discussed in the previous section, the amount realized from either transaction is $110,000. Alvin's gain in each case is $20,000, calculated as follows:

Amount Realized	$110,000
Less: Adjusted Basis	- 90,000
Equals: Gain or (Loss)	**$20,000**

Assuming that Alvin cannot find a provision in the IRC that allows him to defer or avoid the gain, he will have to recognize the gain in the current tax year.

What is Alvin's basis in his replacement asset?

In the first scenario (**Example 11.4**), when Alvin transferred the property in return for cash plus raw land worth $90,000, his basis in the cash is the face value of the cash, $20,000. His basis in the land is the fair market value of the land, or $90,000. When property is received in an exchange, and the entire gain realized on the exchange is recognized, the basis of the replacement property will be its fair market value on the date of the exchange. Therefore, Alvin recognizes $20,000 in gain and has a basis of $90,000 in the land received. In some cases, taxpayers can defer the gain realized on the sale of a capital asset if the like-kind exchange requirements are met. These rules are discussed in Chapter 13.

Quick Quiz 11.1

1. Capital gains are subject to tax upon either a realization event or a recognition event.
   a. True
   b. False
2. When a taxpayer sells an asset in exchange for cash, a realization event occurs.
   a. True
   b. False

False, True.

Recognition Rules

Recall, the default rule for income taxation is that all gains realized are recognized, unless a special provision of the IRC exempts or defers the gain from taxation. If a gain is realized upon transfer, the use of the asset (for personal or business purposes) will not prevent the gain from being recognized.

Example 11.6

Belle purchased a Ferrari 10 years ago for $80,000. She used the car for personal purposes and sold it earlier this year. Because the model she purchased was a limited edition, she was able to sell the car for $90,000 even though she used it for over 10 years. Belle's gain is calculated as follows:

Amount Realized	$90,000
Less: Adjusted Basis	- 80,000
Equals: Gain or (Loss)	**$10,000**

The realized gain of $10,000 must be recognized on his income tax return this year.

The same is not true for losses on personal use assets, however. In most cases, the general rule of recognition applies to losses as well as gains, but there are circumstances where losses that are realized are disallowed on either a permanent or temporary basis. The rules covering the disallowance of losses stem from congressional desire to prevent taxpayers from being able to manipulate their taxable income by incurring losses and to prevent taxpayers from allocating losses to family members who may be in a better position to take advantage of them.

Disallowed Losses

Losses that are realized, but not permitted to be recognized (**disallowed losses**) include:

- losses on the sale of personal use assets;
- losses on the subsequent sale of property gifted to anyone or sold to a related party when its fair market value is less than the original owner's adjusted basis; and
- wash sales.

The first type of loss disallowed for income tax purposes is a loss generated on property used for personal purposes. In order for a loss to be deductible for income tax purposes, the asset generating the loss must have been used in a trade or business or for the production of income. If the taxpayer is attempting to use the property to generate gains that will be subject to income tax, it seems appropriate that losses should be allowed to be deducted.

CASE STUDY 11.1

Capital Loss Carryover

Perry Dean Knowles, Petitioner v. Commissioner of Internal Revenue, Respondent, T.C. Memo 2011-23 (January 27, 2011).

Perry realized capital gains in 2005, and reported them on a timely filed tax return. The IRS issued a notice of deficiency for 2005. Perry filed an amended 2005 tax return, claiming to have carryforward losses from prior tax years before 2001, which were partially used to offset the gains he realized in 2005. The IRS did not accept the amended return, claiming that Perry was not entitled to use those losses to offset current gains.

The record in front of the court included tax returns for 2001, 2002, 2003, 2004, and 2005. Tax returns before 2001 were not available. In 2001, Perry reported no capital gain or loss. He reported long-term capital gains of $26,984, $15,265, and $171 for tax years 2002, 2003, and 2004, respectively. Perry claimed that he sustained net capital losses of about $9,000 and $6,000 in at least two years before 2001, but was unaware of the capital loss carryover rule and thus did not carry these amounts forward. When he became aware of the rule in 2007, he filed an amended 2005 tax return, but the IRS did not accept the return.

The tax court, citing IRC Section 6001 and the regulations thereunder, stated that taxpayers are required to keep sufficient records to establish the amount of deductions claimed on any federal tax return. Unfortunately, Perry did not provided credible evidence that he is entitled to a capital loss carryover. Even if he could substantiate the losses, the losses would not impact his 2005 income tax return. Capital losses are allowed to be deducted fully against capital gains, and can offset up to $3,000 of other income. Citing both IRC and prior cases, the court indicated that a taxpayer's capital loss carryover is reduced to the extent a deduction is allowed regardless of whether the taxpayer benefits from the deduction or chooses not to claim the deduction. Assuming that Perry had $15,000 of losses from years prior to 2001, he would have been allowed a $3,000 loss deduction in 2001 (a year in which he realized no capital gains), and the excess beyond $3,000 would then carryover to 2002 where he would exhaust the entire carryover since he reported $26,984 of long-term capital gains. Since tax years 2001 and 2002 were beyond the three-year statute of limitations, Perry could not file amended returns for those tax years.

As Perry found out the hard way, it is important to claim loss carryforwards when they are available. Failure to do so may result in a loss of the ability to claim the loss.

When an asset is used for personal purposes, however, any loss incurred during the period of personal use is considered a personal loss, and is not permitted as a tax deduction. In fact, a loss incurred while an asset is used for personal purposes will *never* be deductible and results in a permanent loss of capital for the taxpayer. This is one of the fundamental rules of income taxation – only losses incurred when the taxpayer is trying to make a profit may be deducted. Note that casualty losses attributable to a presidentially declared disaster, which were covered in more detail in Chapter 7, are an exception to this rule.

Example 11.7

Aurora purchased a personal residence six months ago for $325,000. Since Aurora purchased the home, the housing market slumped and prices began to fall. Wooster Enterprises, LLC informed Aurora that her presence will be required on a permanent basis in an office on the other side of the country beginning in three months. Aurora puts her house up for sale, but cannot sell it for what she paid. As her impending moving date approaches, she panics and agrees to sell the home for $310,000. Aurora's economic loss is calculated as follows:

Amount Realized	$310,000
Less: Adjusted Basis	- 325,000
Equals: Gain or (Loss)	**($15,000)**

Aurora will not be permitted to recognize the $15,000 loss for income tax purposes, since the asset was a personal-use asset and personal-use asset losses are not tax deductible.

Recall that most assets used in a trade or business or for the production of income are depreciable, which allows the owner to recoup his or her investment in the property before disposition so that the capital can be reinvested in the business to make more money (the only exception to this rule for trade or business or production of income assets is land). When property is put into use in a trade or business or for production of income, the amount that can be depreciated is the lesser of the taxpayer's cost basis or the fair market value of the property at the time it was converted to business use. If a personal-use asset has declined in value since it was purchased, the fair market value of the asset at the time of the asset's conversion (from personal to business use) will be used as the asset's adjusted basis for determining both depreciation deductions and any subsequent loss on the sale of the asset.

Example 11.8

Continuing with **Example 11.7**, assume that Aurora does not want to sell her home for a loss, which she cannot recognize for tax purposes because the asset is personal; so she begins to rent out the house after she moves across the country. Assuming that none of the purchase price was allocable to land, which is not depreciable, Aurora's depreciable basis in the property will be $310,000 or the fair market value of the property at the time it was converted to business use. The $15,000 loss was still incurred and will not be considered when calculating Aurora's depreciation deductions since that loss was personal, and was not related to a trade or business or to the production of income.

A second circumstance when realized losses are not currently recognized involves the gift of property to anyone, or the sale of property to a related party (other than a spouse), when the property has a fair market value that is less than the adjusted basis of the original owner. Related party transactions were discussed in Chapter 10. For property transferred by gift, the double basis rule results in the disallowance of part or all of a realized loss when the new owner disposes of the asset at a value less than the original owner's adjusted basis. The unrealized loss at the time of gift will *never* be deductible, resulting in a permanent loss of capital. In the event of a transfer by sale to a related party where the fair market value of the property is less than the adjusted basis of the transferor, the loss realized by the transferor is disallowed. However, if the transferee later sells or disposes of the property at a value above the purchase price paid by the transferee, the transferee will use the gain basis (under the double basis rule), which will allow the transferee to benefit from the previously disallowed loss.

Quick Quiz 11.2

1. The amount realized on a sale includes cash and the fair market value of any other property received.
   a. True
   b. False
2. Losses associated with wash sales are permanently disallowed.
   a. True
   b. False

True, False.

Example 11.9

Simon would like to dispose of one stock in his investment portfolio, Hawke, Inc., but he currently has a loss position in the company (he purchased the stock for $50 per share, and it is currently worth $40 a share). Simon's son, Theodore, has realized several gains on his portfolio this year; so Simon gives the stock to Theodore thinking that Theodore can sell the stock and offset some of his gains with the loss on the stock. Upon receiving the stock, Theodore quickly sells it at a price of $42 per share. Theodore's loss basis was $40 (the fair market value of the stock on the date of the gift) and his gain basis is $50 (adjusted basis of the transferor), which means that his economic gain is $2 (calculated by subtracting his loss basis of $40 from the amount realized of $42). His taxable gain is zero because the sale occurs between the gain and loss basis. The $10 loss that occurred during Simon's holding period (calculated by subtracting Simon's basis of $50 from the fair market value on the date of the gift, or $40) will never be recognized but Theodore benefited by not having to recognize his $2 economic gain.

A third situation where a realized loss is not recognized is a **wash sale**. A wash sale occurs when a taxpayer sells a stock or security, and purchases (or enters into an agreement to purchase) substantially identical stock or security within a 30 day period before or after the sale. Including the day of sale, there is actually a 61 day window during which a wash sale can occur. If a wash sale transaction results in gain realization, the gain must be recognized. If, however, the wash sale results in realization of a loss, the loss is not recognized and is temporarily disallowed. The unrecognized loss will be added to the basis of the replacement securities, so that recognition will occur on the subsequent sale of the replacement securities. Unlike the situation described above with respect to personal assets and related party sales and gifts, the realized loss is permitted to be recognized, but is deferred until the replacement securities are eventually sold.

Example 11.10

On December 28, 2021, Tiana reviews her investment portfolio and finds out that she has had a very profitable year. To offset some of her gains, Tiana sells 100 shares of Orion Industries, Inc. for $10,000. She purchased those shares for $15,000 two years earlier. On January 24, 2022, Tiana learns that Orion Industries, Inc. is expected to patent a new synthetic that will be in great demand if available, and that the announcement of the new product may be made soon. If the patent is in fact issued, the value of Orion Industries, Inc. stock will increase substantially. Second-guessing the wisdom of selling the company shares, she purchases 100 shares of Orion Industries, Inc. for $8,000 on that same day. Since Tiana purchased and sold substantially identical securities within 30 days, a wash sale has occurred. Her realized loss on the December 28 transaction is calculated as follows:

Amount Realized	$10,000
Less: Adjusted Basis	- 15,000
Equals: Gain or (Loss)	**($5,000)**

Due to the wash sale classification, however, Tiana is not permitted to recognize the loss in the year it was incurred. Instead, the realized but unrecognized loss of $5,000 is added to the basis of the replacement securities. Tiana purchased the replacement securities for $8,000 so adding the unrecognized loss increases her basis to $13,000. By increasing basis in the amount of the unrecognized loss, Tiana will receive both the $8,000 cost and the $5,000 unrecognized loss as a tax-free return of her investment when she ultimately sells the stock.

In **Example 11.10**, Tiana's original basis in the stock was $15,000. After she engaged in the wash sale, her new basis is $13,000. What happened to the $2,000 difference? The $2,000 is in her pocket. If the stock goes up later, Tiana made a wise investment choice, she sold the stock when it was worth $10,000 and repurchased it when it was worth $8,000. By doing so, Tiana avoided incurring $2,000 of additional losses. If the $2,000 avoided loss is added to the basis of the replacement securities, Tiana still has the same amount of capital that she originally had, but it is now spread between two assets – Orion Industries, Inc. stock, and cash.

CAPITAL ASSET HOLDING PERIODS AND TAX RATES

One of the benefits of categorizing an asset as a capital asset is that if a gain is realized, it is potentially subject to a lower income tax rate than the taxpayer's ordinary marginal income tax rate. The taxpayer's holding period for the asset determines whether or not the lower tax rate applies. In this section, we will review the holding period rules, followed by a discussion of the tax rates that apply to sales of capital assets.

Holding Periods

The **holding period** for an asset can be either short-term or long-term. If a taxpayer holds an asset for a year or less, the taxpayer has a short-term holding period for that asset. If the holding period is more than one year, it is a long-term holding period.

Exhibit 11.1 | Holding Period Summary

Capital Gain/Loss	Holding Period
Long-Term Capital Gain/Loss	> 1 Year
Short-Term Capital Gain/Loss	≤ 1 Year

Example 11.11

Merlin purchased 100 shares of Lucky Bubbles, Inc. stock on March 17 for $5,000. Fearing that the stock market would experience a downturn due to recent political events, Merlin sold the stock for $5,150 on September 30 of the same year. Since Merlin held the stock for less than a year, his $150 gain on the stock ($5,150 amount realized less $5,000 adjusted basis) is a short-term capital gain.

Example 11.12

Dory purchased 100 shares of CrushCo, Inc. stock on March 17 for $8,000. She sold the stock for $8,500 on March 17 of the following year. Dory's gain of $500 ($8,500 amount realized less $8,000 adjusted basis) is a short-term capital gain, since she did not hold the stock for *more than* one year.

As the prior example illustrates, holding an asset for exactly one year does not characterize the gain or loss as long term. To achieve long-term capital treatment, the asset must be held for *more than* one year. As a practical matter, this means that a **long-term holding period** begins when the asset is held for a year and one day. If the asset is sold in the current year on the same day it was purchased in the prior year, the result is a **short-term holding period**.

Example 11.13

Gill purchased 100 shares of Reef Novelties, Inc. stock on March 17 for $10,000. On March 18 of the following year, he sold the stock for $12,000. Gill's $2,000 gain on the stock ($12,000 amount realized less $10,000 adjusted basis) is a long-term capital gain, since Gill held the stock for *more than* one year.

Property Acquired by Inheritance

There are a few special rules concerning holding periods that are worth noting. First, whenever property is received from a decedent's estate, it is deemed to have a long-term holding period, regardless of when the asset was acquired by the decedent. An easy way to remember this rule is to recall that "death is long term."

Example 11.14

Wilbur died two months ago and left his entire estate to his only daughter, Charlotte. A week before Wilbur died, he purchased a new building for $300,000 that he planned to lease to his business. Wilbur held the title to the building personally, and it was included in his estate when he died. The appraiser valued the building at $310,000 on the date of Wilbur's death. The deed to the building was just transferred to Charlotte by the executor of the estate, and Charlotte decides that another building would be more appropriate for use by the business. Charlotte sells the building for $325,000 one week after she received title. Charlotte's gain on the building is calculated as follows:

Amount Realized	$325,000	
Less: Adjusted Basis	- 310,000	(value at date of death)
Equals: Gain or (Loss)	**$15,000**	

The character of the gain is long-term capital gain, despite the fact that the building was purchased by Wilbur only three months before Charlotte sold it. The reason, of course, is that all property acquired by inheritance has a deemed long-term holding period.

Gifted Property

The second special rule concerning holding periods applies to gifted property. When gifted property has a fair market value in excess of the donor's basis in the property on the date of the gift, the donee's holding period will tack onto the donor's holding period. In other words, the donee's holding period begins on the date the donor acquired the property.

Example 11.15

Anna purchases 100 shares of Texco stock on January 1, 2021 for $1,000, or $10 per share. On June 1, 2021, the price of the Texco stock has risen to $12 per share and Anna decides to gift all 100 shares to her sister, Elsa. If Elsa sells the Texco stock on August 1, 2021, any gain from the sale of the stock will be a short-term capital gain.

Example 11.16

Continuing with **Example 11.15**, if instead of selling the stock on August 1, 2021, Elsa decided to sell the stock on February 1, 2022, any gain from the sale of the stock will be a long-term capital gain. Even though Elsa had personally owned the stock for less than one year, her holding period began on January 1, 2021 (the date that Anna, the donor, acquired the stock).

If the gifted property has a fair market value on the date of the gift that is less than the donor's basis in the property, the donee's holding period will not necessarily tack onto the donor's holding period. As discussed in prior chapters, the double basis rule would apply. If the donee subsequently disposes of the property at a gain, then the donee's holding period tacks onto the donor's holding period, resulting in the same outcome illustrated in **Example 11.15** and **Example 11.16**. However, if the donee subsequently disposes of the property at a loss, the donee's holding period begins on the date of the gift.

Example 11.17

Dax purchased 50 shares of Clark Co. five years ago for $2,000. He just gave those shares to his daughter, Kristen, and the value of the 50 shares of stock on the date of the gift was $500. Kristen will have a double basis in the stock, determined as follows:

If the donee's sale price is...	less than FMV	between the original basis and FMV	greater than the original basis
Then the donee's basis used is ...	$500 (Loss Basis)	no gain or loss	$2,000 (Gain Basis)

If Kristen sells the stock one month later for $3,000 she can use the gain basis of $2,000 (Dax's original basis), for purposes of calculating gain or loss. In this case, Kristen will have a long-term capital gain of $1,000 because her holding period tacks to Dax's holding period.

If Kristen sells the shares one month later for $300, her loss is $200. In this case, since the stock was sold for less than the value on the date of the gift, the loss basis must be used for purposes of calculating loss. In addition, Kristen's loss will be treated as a short-term capital loss because her holding period for loss purposes began on the date of the gift (one month ago).

If Kristen sells the shares for $1,000 she will have no gain or loss to report, since the sales price was within the no gain/no loss corridor. Consequently, Kristen's holding period is not relevant when determining the tax consequence of the sale.

Property Acquired in a Related Party Transaction

The third special holding period rule applies to property acquired in a related party transaction. When property is sold to a related party (other than the seller's spouse), the holding period used to determine whether any subsequent gains or losses are short-term or long-term is based solely on the purchaser's holding period. In other words, when property is sold to a related party, the holding period of the seller does not tack onto the holding period of the purchaser. This rule applies without regard to whether the property is subsequently sold by the purchaser at a gain or a loss.

Example 11.18

Jessie sells stock in Baseball Enterprises, Inc. to her son, Andy, for $2,000. Jessie purchased the stock three years ago for $3,000 and the current fair market value of the stock is $2,000. If Andy sells the stock six months later for $3,500, he uses his gain basis for purposes of determining gain. Upon sale, Andy will realize and recognize a $500 gain ($3,500 amount realized less $3,000 gain basis) that will be classified as a short-term capital gain because Andy has only held the stock for six months.

If Andy sells the stock six months after the date of his purchase from Jessie for $1,200, he uses his loss basis for purposes of determining loss. Andy's loss basis equals the fair market value on the date of sale, or in this case, $2,000. Upon sale, Andy will realize a $800 loss on the stock ($1,200 amount realized less $2,000 loss basis). In addition, the loss will be characterized as a short-term capital loss because Andy only held the stock for six months.

If Andy sells the stock 14 months after the date of his purchase from Jessie for $3,700, he will have a long-term capital gain of $700. Andy's gain is long-term because he held the property for more than one year. Note that in all of these scenarios, the fact that Jessie previously held the property for three years does not impact Andy's holding period. From a planning point of view, Jessie should not have sold the property to a related party when the fair market value was less than her basis because she would be denied the benefit of the tax loss. Jessie would have been better off selling the stock in an arm's-length transaction to a non-related party and taking the tax loss.

Nonbusiness Bad Debts

A fourth special rule dealing with holding periods applies to nonbusiness bad debts. A nonbusiness bad debt is any debt created by a person who is not in the business of loaning money or who has not established the debt in the conduct of his or her trade or business. All nonbusiness bad debts are treated as short-term capital losses, regardless of how long the debt was outstanding. Nonbusiness bad debts are only deductible when they become completely worthless – a deduction for partial worthlessness is not allowed.

Example 11.19

Uncle Dale loaned money to his nephew, Chip, two years ago. The loan and promissory note were well documented. Chip was having trouble meeting the payroll for his household staff, and when his butler threatened to leave his employment, Chip turned to his Uncle Dale for help. Unfortunately, over the last few years, the situation has not improved for Chip. Uncle Dale is beginning to realize that Chip will not repay the loan. Uncle Dale determines that the loan is worthless when Chip files bankruptcy. Uncle Dale writes off the loan to Chip as a capital loss. Capital treatment is required since Uncle Dale is not in the business of making loans (if he was, the loan would be treated as an ordinary asset), and the loan is not depreciable (precluding Section 1231 treatment). Despite the fact that the loan has been outstanding for two years, it is treated as a short-term capital loss.

Exhibit 11.2 | Summary of Holding Period Rules

Property acquired by:	Will have the following holding period / treatment:
Inheritance	Long-term holding period.
Gift	Holding period will tack to donor's holding period if the gain basis is used. If the loss basis is used, the donee's holding period begins on the date of the gift.
Related Party Transaction	The holding period starts on sale date.
Nonbusiness Bad Debts	Treated as short-term capital losses.

Capital Gains Tax Rates

The capital gains tax rate that applies to a particular transaction is a function of the holding period of the asset.

Short-term gains and losses are subject to tax at the taxpayer's ordinary marginal income tax rate. There is no tax rate benefit afforded to assets held for a short-term holding period.

Exhibit 11.3 | Summary of Capital Gain Rates (2021)

Long-Term Capital Gains Rates	*Single Taxpayers*	*Married Filing Jointly*	*Head of Household*	*Married Filing Separately*
0%	Up to $40,400	Up to $80,800	Up to $54,100	Up to $40,400
15%	$40,401 - $445,850	$80,801 - $501,600	$54,101 - $473,750	$40,401 - $250,800
20%	Over $445,850	Over $501,600	Over $473,750	Over $250,800
Special Rates			**Capital Gain Rate**	
Unrecaptured 1250 Straight-Line Depreciation			25%	
Sale of Collectibles			28%	

Income thresholds in this table are based on taxable income

The rates illustrated in **Exhibit 11.3** do not include any applicable surtaxes imposed by the Affordable Care Act of 2010 (discussed below).

If the asset sold was held for a long-term holding period, the gain or loss is subject to long-term capital gains tax rates, which are lower than the taxpayer's ordinary marginal income tax rate. Generally speaking, if the transaction results in a gain, this is a good result since the taxpayer will pay less tax on the gain. If the transaction results in a loss, however, the taxpayer will receive less of a tax benefit. As discussed in our review of asset categorization, capital gains are good, but capital losses are bad for the taxpayer.

The maximum long-term capital gains tax rate is 20 percent. The lower capital gains rates (0 percent and 15 percent) are available to taxpayers in lower income tax brackets. If that were not the case, those in the 10 percent marginal ordinary income tax bracket would have to pay a higher tax rate on their capital gains than on their ordinary income. To ensure that all taxpayers receive a tax break for long-term capital gains, Congress eliminated the long-term capital gains tax rate for lower income taxpayers.

Net Investment Income Tax (NIIT)

The Affordable Care Act of 2010 imposes a 3.8 percent Medicare surtax on net investment income for taxpayers with modified adjusted gross income in excess of the following amounts:

Filing Status	*Threshold Amount*
Married filing jointly	$250,000
Married filing separately	$125,000
Single	$200,000
Head of household (with qualifying person)	$200,000
Qualifying widow(er) with dependent child	$250,000

Net investment income is a broadly defined term that includes gross income from interest, dividends, annuities, royalties, and rents other than such income derived from the ordinary course of a trade or business, **plus** other trade or business income, for which the entity is a passive activity (or if the entity is trading financial instruments or commodities), **plus** net gain attributable to the disposition of property other than property held in a trade or business. It should be noted that net investment income does not include any distribution from a 401(k), 403(b), 457(b) plan or an IRA or Roth IRA. However, such distributions may cause a taxpayer to exceed the threshold amounts.

The NIIT applies to the lesser of the net investment income or the amount by which modified adjusted gross income (MAGI) exceeds the threshold.

Exhibit 11.4 | 3.8% Medicare Tax

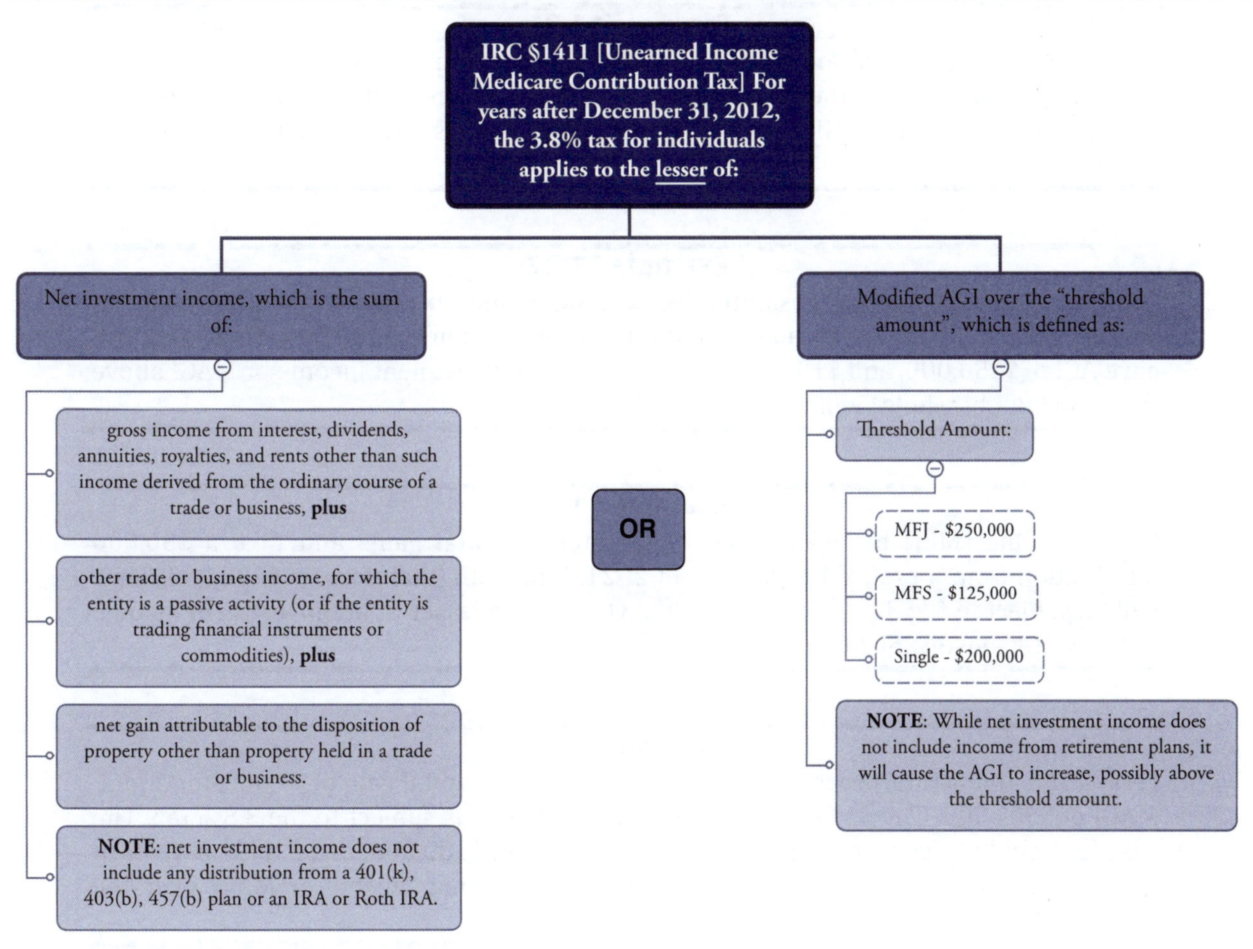

Example 11.20

Bruce, a single filer, has $180,000 of wages. Bruce also received $90,000 taxed as a short-term capital gain on the sale of property, which is considered net investment income. Bruce's modified adjusted gross income is $270,000.

Bruce's modified adjusted gross income (MAGI) exceeds the threshold of $200,000 for single taxpayers by $70,000. His net investment income is $90,000.

The net investment income tax (NIIT) is based on the lesser of $70,000 (the amount that Bruce's modified adjusted gross income exceeds the $200,000 threshold) or $90,000 (Bruce's net investment income). Bruce owes NIIT of $2,660 ($70,000 x 3.8%).

Example 11.21

In 2021, Roger and Anita (MFJ) have $250,000 of long-term capital gains income, which is their only income for the year. In this case, they are not subject to the 3.8% net investment income tax (NIIT) because their MAGI does not exceed the $250,000 threshold.

Example 11.22

Continuing with the previous example, assume Roger and Anita convert a traditional IRA to a Roth IRA in 2021. The taxable amount of the conversion is $100,000. Thus, they will have AGI of $350,000, and $100,000 (the lesser of net investment income or MAGI above the $250,000 threshold) will be subject to the 3.8% NIIT.

Example 11.23

Carl and Ellie (MFJ) have $250,000 of long-term capital gains and take a $50,000 distribution from a pretax 401(k) plan in 2021. Their AGI, therefore, is $300,000. They will be subject to the 3.8% tax on $50,000, which is the lesser of net investment income or the MAGI above $250,000.

Example 11.24

Fergus and Elinor (MFJ) each earn $250,000 and have a capital gain of $1,000, for a total MAGI of $501,000. The $1,000 of net investment income is subject to the 3.8% tax. The answer would not change if they each made $125,000, $500,000, or $1 million. In each case, there would be $1,000 (the lesser of net investment income or MAGI over the $250,000 threshold) subject to the 3.8% tax.

Individuals, estates, and trusts use Form 8960 to compute net investment income tax. Individuals will then report the tax on Form 1040 and estates and trusts report the tax on Form 1041.

Exhibit 11.5 | Form 8960

Form **8960**
Department of the Treasury
Internal Revenue Service (99)

Net Investment Income Tax—Individuals, Estates, and Trusts

► Attach to your tax return.
► Go to *www.irs.gov/Form8960* for instructions and the latest information.

OMB No. 1545-2227
2020
Attachment Sequence No. **72**

Name(s) shown on your tax return | **Your social security number or EIN**

Part I Investment Income ☐ Section 6013(g) election (see instructions)
☐ Section 6013(h) election (see instructions)
☐ Regulations section 1.1411-10(g) election (see instructions)

1	Taxable interest (see instructions)			1	
2	Ordinary dividends (see instructions)			2	
3	Annuities (see instructions)			3	
4a	Rental real estate, royalties, partnerships, S corporations, trusts, etc. (see instructions)	4a			
b	Adjustment for net income or loss derived in the ordinary course of a non-section 1411 trade or business (see instructions)	4b			
c	Combine lines 4a and 4b			4c	
5a	Net gain or loss from disposition of property (see instructions)	5a			
b	Net gain or loss from disposition of property that is not subject to net investment income tax (see instructions)	5b			
c	Adjustment from disposition of partnership interest or S corporation stock (see instructions)	5c			
d	Combine lines 5a through 5c			5d	
6	Adjustments to investment income for certain CFCs and PFICs (see instructions)			6	
7	Other modifications to investment income (see instructions)			7	
8	Total investment income. Combine lines 1, 2, 3, 4c, 5d, 6, and 7			8	

Part II Investment Expenses Allocable to Investment Income and Modifications

9a	Investment interest expenses (see instructions)	9a			
b	State, local, and foreign income tax (see instructions)	9b			
c	Miscellaneous investment expenses (see instructions)	9c			
d	Add lines 9a, 9b, and 9c			9d	
10	Additional modifications (see instructions)			10	
11	Total deductions and modifications. Add lines 9d and 10			11	

Part III Tax Computation

12	Net investment income. Subtract Part II, line 11, from Part I, line 8. Individuals, complete lines 13–17. Estates and trusts, complete lines 18a–21. If zero or less, enter -0-			12	
	Individuals:				
13	Modified adjusted gross income (see instructions)	13			
14	Threshold based on filing status (see instructions)	14			
15	Subtract line 14 from line 13. If zero or less, enter -0-	15			
16	Enter the smaller of line 12 or line 15			16	
17	Net investment income tax for individuals. Multiply line 16 by 3.8% (0.038). **Enter here and include on your tax return** (see instructions)			17	
	Estates and Trusts:				
18a	Net investment income (line 12 above)	18a			
b	Deductions for distributions of net investment income and deductions under section 642(c) (see instructions)	18b			
c	Undistributed net investment income. Subtract line 18b from 18a (see instructions). If zero or less, enter -0-	18c			
19a	Adjusted gross income (see instructions)	19a			
b	Highest tax bracket for estates and trusts for the year (see instructions)	19b			
c	Subtract line 19b from line 19a. If zero or less, enter -0-	19c			
20	Enter the smaller of line 18c or line 19c			20	
21	Net investment income tax for estates and trusts. Multiply line 20 by 3.8% (0.038). **Enter here and include on your tax return** (see instructions)			21	

For Paperwork Reduction Act Notice, see your tax return instructions. Cat. No. 59474M Form **8960** (2020)

There are exceptions to the maximum 20 percent tax rate that applies to long-term capital gains. These exceptions are designed to minimize tax planning opportunities for taxpayers. The two exceptions are: (1) a 25 percent capital gains tax rate for unrecaptured Section 1250 depreciation, and (2) a 28 percent capital gains tax rate on the sale of collectibles, as described below. The 3.8 percent Medicare surtax is added to the capital gains tax rate for unrecaptured Sec. 1250 depreciation and collectibles if a taxpayer has adjusted gross income over the levels specified above.

CASE STUDY 11.2

Classification of Real Estate Activities

Mark S. and Cheryl R. Gardner, Petitioners v. Commissioner of Internal Revenue, Respondent (June 20, 2011)

Mark and Cheryl are married, and Mark is self-employed. His Schedule C indicated that his business was "Carpentry/Site contracting." Over a 26 year period, Mark purchased and sold 16 parcels of real property. Some of these properties were purchased as raw land, and Mark would build a single-family home on the land, and then sell the property. Other properties were purchased to build multifamily housing, or were improved properties with multifamily housing that Mark would update. Mark did not immediately sell the multifamily housing properties, but rather kept them for rental income.

In March, 2004, Mark purchased property from his brother, which had been approved for subdivision into five lots. Mark built a road on the property, and conveyed to his brother one of the lots on which he constructed a house. In November, 2004, Mark sold three of the remaining lots for $750,000 and reported the gain (of $373,841) from the sale of those three lots on Schedule D. The IRS recharacterized the sale as the sale of property held for sale to customers in the ordinary course of Mark's business, requiring the gain to be reported on Schedule C. By moving the gain from Schedule D to Schedule C, the IRS sought to collect additional self-employment taxes (there would have been no difference in the income tax rate that applied to the transaction, since they constituted short-term capital gains taxable at ordinary income tax rates). Mark argued that the three lots sold were duplex lots, and that his original intention was to develop the properties and rent them out (hold them for investment), but due to the costs of the road, he had no choice but to sell them.

Quoting ***Mathews v. Commissioner, 315 F.2d 101 (6th Cir. 1963)***, the tax court found that "It is true... that a taxpayer may hold lands primarily for sale to customers in the ordinary course of his trade or business and, at the same time, hold other lands for investment." The Matthews court indicated that the factors to be considered include: (1) the purpose for which the property was acquired; (2) the purpose for which it was held; (3) improvements made to the property; (4) the frequency and continuity of sales; (5) the extent and substantiality of the transactions; (6) the nature and extent of the taxpayer's business; (7) the extent of advertising to promote sales; and (8) listing of the property for sale directly or through brokers. After finding that Mark was a credible witness, the Tax Court accepted his testimony and found that he purchased the property for investment purposes. Mark's history of holding multifamily units for investment was also noted by the court. Consequently, the court classified the property as a capital asset, resulting in short-term capital gains tax treatment and no self-employment income.

Unrecaptured Section 1250 Depreciation

The rules concerning depreciation recapture will be covered in detail in Chapter 12 which covers property transactions for business assets. A brief discussion of this issue is provided here to describe the purpose of the special 25 percent tax rate.

One of the tax benefits of purchasing real estate for use in a business or for the production of income (rental real estate) is the ability to take depreciation deductions for the cost basis of the property (less the portion of cost basis allocated to land) over the useful life of the asset. Because real estate used for these purposes is depreciable, it is not considered to be a capital asset, but rather a Section 1231 asset. Under Section 1231, gains are treated as capital gains, and losses are treated as ordinary losses – the "best of both worlds" treatment is obtained. Under current law, all depreciation taken on real estate is taken on a straight-line basis. When a depreciation deduction is taken, it offsets what would otherwise be ordinary income taxed at ordinary rates. That is, business income is reduced by depreciation deductions if a business owns real estate, or the profit on a rental activity is reduced when depreciation deductions are taken on "production of income" property. In both cases, the income of these activities would be subject to ordinary income tax rates. Despite the fact that depreciation is allowed on real estate used for these purposes, the value of real estate tends to increase, not decrease. By taking depreciation deductions, a real estate investor could reduce his or her ordinary income but would not really suffer an economic loss provided that the value of real property increases over time. When the value of the property is increasing, not decreasing, depreciation deductions allow a real estate investor to transform income that would otherwise be treated as ordinary income into capital gains. Congress believed that this result is unfair, especially in light of the ordinary loss treatment that is accorded to real estate investments if the property does not increase in value due to the imposition of Section 1231, and consequently they imposed a special capital gains tax rate on straight-line depreciation taken on real estate. That special tax rate is 25 percent.

The terminology in this area is sometimes confusing, but can be explained in the following manner. Straight-line depreciation is *not* recaptured under IRC Section1250. The special 25 percent capital gains rate only applies to the straight-line depreciation taken on a real estate investment. Therefore, the 25 percent capital gains tax rate applies to "**unrecaptured Section 1250 depreciation**."

Example 11.25

Doc supplements his income by making strategic real estate investments. He purchases properties, improves them, and rents them out to generate additional cash flow for himself and his family. Assume Doc's other income places him in the 35% marginal income tax bracket. He purchased one of his properties for $200,000 and spent approximately $50,000 on improvements. Over the years, he has taken $40,000 of straight-line depreciation deductions on the property. Doc has accepted an offer to sell the property to a national franchise for $450,000, a price he believes exceeds the fair market value of the property.

Doc's adjusted basis in the property is $210,000 (equal to his cost basis of $200,000 plus the improvements of $50,000 less the depreciation deductions of $40,000). His gain on the sale may be calculated as follows:

Amount Realized	$450,000
Less: Adjusted Basis	- $210,000
Equals: Gain or (Loss)	**$240,000**

Doc's gain will be split into two pieces for tax purposes. First, the straight-line depreciation that Doc claimed for tax purposes will be taxed at 25%. In this case, Doc took straight-line depreciation deductions of $40,000 so the first $40,000 of the gain will be taxed at 25%. The remaining portion of the gain, $200,000 will be taxed at Doc's long-term capital gains rate. Note that since Doc is in the 35% marginal tax bracket, his adjusted gross income is above the applicable threshold; thus, the Affordable Care Act Medicare surtax (net investment income tax) of 3.8 percent will apply, raising his tax rate on Unrecaptured Sec. 1250 gains to 28.8% (25% + 3.8%) and his regular capital gains tax rate on the remaining gain to 18.8% (15% + 3.8%) (assuming he is a 15% capital gains rate taxpayer).

Analysis of Gain:		Tax Rate*
From straight-line depreciation	$40,000	25%
From sale price in excess of purchase price plus additions	$200,000	15%
Total	**$240,000**	

** Does not include the Affordable Care Act's Medicare surtax.*

A few issues illustrated by the previous example are worth noting. First, when real estate is sold, the straight-line depreciation is taxed at 25 percent *before* the remaining portion of the gain qualifies for the special long-term capital gains tax rate. If the gain is less than the straight-line depreciation taken, all of the gain will be taxed at 25 percent (assuming, for the sake of simplicity that there is no recapture under IRC Section 1250).

Second, note that the actual increase in the value of the property qualifies for the long-term capital gains tax rate. In the above example, the actual increase in the value of Doc's property is the difference between what he sold the property for, and what he paid for the property without taking into consideration the depreciation deductions. This can be calculated as follows:

Sale Price	$450,000
Less: Cost of Building Plus Improvements	- $250,000
Equals: Gain or (Loss)	**$200,000**

Of Doc's $240,000 gain, the only portion that is taxed at a higher rate is the portion of the gain that resulted from taking depreciation deductions. By crafting the "Unrecaptured Section 1250 Depreciation" rule in this way, Congress is preserving an investor's right to receive a special tax rate on actual increases in value, but captures part of the tax benefit received from the depreciation deductions upon sale of the property.

While the "Unrecaptured Section 1250 Depreciation" rule appears to subject a taxpayer to additional tax, if the taxpayer is in a marginal tax bracket that exceeds 25 percent, the taxpayer still wins. Recall that depreciation deductions are claimed against ordinary income. In the example, Doc was assumed to be in the 35 percent marginal income tax bracket. When he claimed depreciation deductions on his property, Doc offset income that would have been taxed at 35 percent. When Doc sells the property, he only has to pay a 25 percent tax on the portion of the gain which results from those depreciation deductions. Therefore, Doc has achieved a tax arbitrage of 10 percent (less 3.8% if the Medicare Surtax applies). Each year when he takes depreciation deductions, Doc gets a tax benefit of 35 percent, and he pays only part of that tax benefit back (due to the lower tax rate of 25 percent on the unrecaptured Section 1250 depreciation) when he ultimately sells the property. Doc has saved 10 percent in taxes (assuming that his income for the year is not high enough for the Affordable Care Act surtax to apply) and has the benefit of time value on the other 25 percent that he has to pay back when he sells the property.

As is the case with regular long-term capital gains, if a taxpayer is in a marginal ordinary income tax bracket of less than 25 percent, instead of imposing a 25 percent rate on the unrecaptured Section 1250 depreciation, the taxpayer's regular ordinary tax rate applies to that portion of the gain.

Example 11.26

Violet is proud of her only nephew, Charlie. Charlie is currently attending WW University; and to provide him with a source of funds to cover his social and living expenses, Violet transfers an apartment house that she owns that is located next to WW University. She paid $400,000 for the apartment house, and over her period of ownership she took $10,000 in straight-line depreciation deductions. Charlie has no other source of income, and even with the profits earned from his new rental activity, Charlie is in the 12% tax bracket. During his time at WW University, Charlie claimed another $10,000 in depreciation deductions. Since Charlie will be completing his schooling within the next six months, Aunt Violet encourages him to sell the property, and Charlie does so on January 1. Aside from the gain on the property, Charlie will have no other income in the year of sale. The selling price was $405,000 and Charlie plans to use those funds to establish himself both socially and in his new career. Charlie's gain on the apartment house is calculated as follows:

Amount Realized	$405,000
Less: Adjusted Basis	- $380,000
Equals: Gain or (Loss)	**$25,000**

Charlie's adjusted basis equals the original purchase price of $400,000 less the depreciation that Aunt Violet claimed ($10,000) and the depreciation that he claimed ($10,000).

In this case, $20,000 of the gain will be taxed at 12%, and $5,000 of the gain will be taxed at 0%. Because Charlie is in the 12% ordinary income tax bracket, and the special rate that applies to unrecaptured Section 1250 depreciation cannot exceed the ordinary tax rate, the straight-line depreciation claimed is taxed at 12%. Charlie qualifies for the special 0% capital gains tax rate on the remaining portion of the gain since his taxable income is below the maximum threshold for the 0% capital gains rate.

The concept of depreciation recapture will be discussed again in Chapter 12. Remember that the form of depreciation recapture covered in this chapter – "unrecaptured Section 1250 depreciation" – only applies to straight-line depreciation taken on real estate. If depreciation on real estate was taken on an accelerated basis (which was only available for property placed in service between 1981-1986), the accelerated portion of the depreciation will be recaptured under Section 1250, and a different tax result occurs for that portion of the depreciation.

Capital Gains Tax Rates on Collectibles

A second exception to the tax rate on long-term capital gains applies when collectibles are sold at a gain. The capital gains tax rate that applies to the sale of collectibles is 28 percent. As with unrecaptured Section 1250 depreciation, however, if a taxpayer is in a marginal ordinary income tax bracket of less than 28 percent, instead of imposing a 28 percent rate on the entire collectible gain, the taxpayer's regular ordinary tax rate applies to that portion of the gain.

Single taxpayers with adjusted gross income in excess of $200,000 and married taxpayers filing jointly with adjusted gross income in excess of $250,000 must add the Affordable Care Act surtax of 3.8 percent to the tax rate on collectibles, raising the maximum capital gains tax rate on the sale of collectibles held for more than one year to 31.8 percent.

Collectibles include items such as coins, stamps, Hummels, antique furniture, oriental rugs, and similar assets. Usually, these assets are held for personal use and are rarely held by the taxpayer for use in a trade or business or for the production of income. If a collectible is held for personal use and is sold at a loss, the taxpayer may not recognize the loss for income tax purposes because the loss was personal in nature. If the asset is sold at a gain, however, the realized gain must be recognized.

Before 1997, the special capital gains tax rate that applied to any long-term capital gain was 28 percent. In the Taxpayer Relief Act of 1997, Congress lowered the long-term capital gains tax rates for most assets to 20 percent (which was later lowered to 15 percent), but did not extend the lower rate to collectibles. In excluding collectibles from the new, lower rate, Congress recognized that these assets are typically used for personal use purposes and did not want to give gains on personal assets the same tax treatment as gains on assets purchased for use in a trade or business or for the production of income. Consequently, the pre-TRA '97 capital gains rates continue to apply to collectibles. Whenever a collectible is sold for a gain, the capital gains rate is 28 percent.

Quick Quiz 11.3

1. An asset held for exactly one year has a long-term holding period.
   a. True
   b. False
2. All taxpayers are subject to capital gain tax rates of 15%.
   a. True
   b. False
3. Unrecaptured Section 1250 depreciation applies to all depreciable property.
   a. True
   b. False
4. Capital gains are taxed at the same rate under the AMT system as they are under the regular income tax system.
   a. True
   b. False

False, False, False, True.

In some circumstances, collectibles are used in a trade or business, or for production of income. Examples might include the oriental rug in the CEO's office or a portfolio of investment grade rare coins held by an investment manager with the objective of making a profit. Gains on the disposition of these assets, even though the assets are used in a trade or business or for the production of income, are still subject to the 28 percent collectibles capital gains tax rate.

CASE STUDY 11.3

Are State Tax Credits a Capital Asset?

William M. McNeil and Catherine A. McNeil, Petitioners v. Commissioner of Internal Revenue, Respondent (May 23, 2011).

In 2003 and 2005, William and Catherine donated conservation easements over property they owned to the State of Colorado. Colorado law provided a tax credit for donation of conservation easements, and specifically stated that unused tax credits could be carried forward for up to 20 successive tax years, or transferred by sale. When they filed their tax return, William and Catherine reported a $173,991 long-term capital gain from the sale of the 2003 Colorado state tax credit. Their 2005 tax returns (which included partnership returns, since a partnership owned by the couple had title to the land subject to the conservation easement) reported $113,429 as a long-term capital gain from the sale of the 2005 state tax credit. The IRS sent a notice of deficiency to the taxpayers, recharacterizing the gains as ordinary income rather than long-term capital gain, and, by implication, indicating that the tax credits were not capital assets. How should tax credits be classified?

The tax court, citing prior cases, held that Colorado state credits are, in fact, capital assets, but held that the holding period for classifying the gain as long-term or short-term commences when the taxpayers receive the credits, not when they acquired the real property that was subject to the conservation easement. The court specifically referred to IRC Section 1221, which defines a capital asset as everything in the world other than specifically excluded categories, and noted that tax credits were not in the list of exclusions. The tax court noted that the benefits arising from the tax credits came into being when the credits were granted, not when the underlying land later subject to the conservation easement was purchased, and therefore started the holding period on the date of the grant. As a consequence, William and Catherine were required to treat the gains as short-term capital gain subject to ordinary income tax rates, not as long-term capital gain subject to preferential rates.

Capital Gains and the AMT

The alternative minimum tax (AMT) system was created in 1986 to prevent wealthy taxpayers from eliminating their current income tax through use of tax planning strategies. The AMT will be covered in depth in Chapter 15, but a brief introduction and discussion of the AMT and capital gains tax rates is warranted here. Under the AMT tax system, income is taxed at a flat 26 percent or 28 percent rate depending upon the income of the taxpayer. Since capital gains are currently subject to tax at a rate lower than the AMT tax rate, it would be possible, absent a special exception, for a taxpayer with large capital gains to be subject to the AMT tax rate. Generally, whenever a taxpayer has too much income taxed at a rate lower than the taxpayer's AMT tax rate, imposition of the AMT may be possible.

Due to tax policy reasons for subjecting capital gains to a lower tax rate, Congress has applied the special capital gains tax rates to both regular and AMT tax. Therefore, most capital gains will be taxed at either the 15 or 20 percent rate (or zero percent for those in the lowest marginal tax brackets), as outlined previously in **Exhibit 11.3**.

DETERMINING NET CAPITAL GAINS AND LOSSES

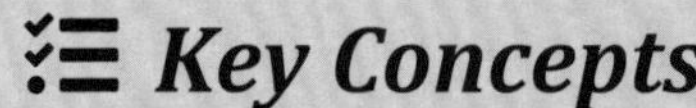

Key Concepts

1. Describe the netting procedures for short and long-term capital gains and losses.

Capital gains and losses must be systematically combined to determine their net income tax consequences.

As a threshold matter, all capital gains and losses are categorized as short-term or long-term. Recall that a long-term gain or loss results from holding an asset for more than one year. Short-term losses are offset against short-term gains, and long-term losses are offset against long-term gains.

Example 11.27

Sylvester has been adjusting his investment portfolio to meet his target asset allocation and has realized several capital gains and losses this year. He categorized the capital gains and losses into short-term and long-term and netted each type of gain/loss together. The results are as follows:

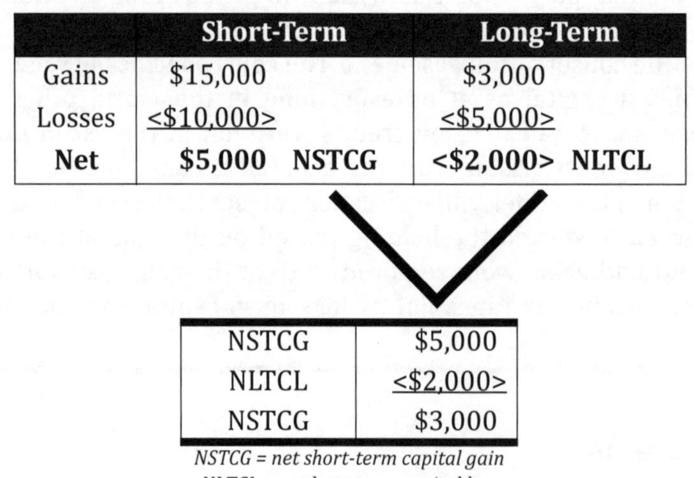

	Short-Term	Long-Term
Gains	$15,000	$3,000
Losses	<$10,000>	<$5,000>
Net	**$5,000 NSTCG**	**<$2,000> NLTCL**

NSTCG	$5,000
NLTCL	<$2,000>
NSTCG	$3,000

NSTCG = net short-term capital gain
NLTCL = net long-term capital loss

The first step in the netting process is to calculate the net short-term and net long-term gain or loss. In the previous example, Sylvester has a net short-term capital gain of $5,000 ($15,000 in gains less $10,000 in losses) and a net long-term capital loss of $2,000 ($3,000 in gains less $5,000 in losses).

Once net short-term and net long-term gains or losses are calculated, a comparison of the short-term and long-term results must be made. If both the net short-term and net long-term results are gains, or both are losses, no further action is necessary. As discussed above, short-term gains and losses are subject to ordinary tax rates, and long-term gains and losses are subject to a special capital gains tax rate. If short-term and long-term gains or losses were added together to find a total gain/loss, the tax result would be distorted.

If, however, the net results are of different signs (gain for one and loss for other), the net short-term gain/loss is combined with the net long-term gain or loss. This can only occur in two circumstances: (1) when there is a net short-term capital gain and a net long-term capital loss; or (2) when there is a net short-term capital loss and a net long-term capital gain. The character (short-term or long-term) of the resulting gain or loss is determined by the larger net number, not taking into account whether it was a gain or loss.

Example 11.28

Continuing with **Example 11.27**, Sylvester had a net short-term capital gain of $5,000 and a net long-term capital loss of $2,000. Since the net results are of different signs (one is a gain and one is a loss), they are netted against each other. Sylvester's result is a $3,000 net short-term capital gain (NSTCG).

To illustrate the characterization process, assume instead that Sylvester had a $5,000 short-term capital loss and a $2,000 long-term capital gain. The net result would be a $3,000 short-term capital loss ($5,000 is bigger than $2,000 and the $5,000 amount applied to short-term losses).

In summary, when netting capital gains and losses, if net short-term and net long-term results are either both gains or both losses, no further action is required. If the net results are of different signs, however (one is a gain and the other is a loss), the net short-term and net long-term results are netted together.

LIMITATIONS ON RECOGNITION OF CAPITAL LOSSES

The netting process does not end the inquiry for taxation of capital assets. There are further limitations that must be applied to determine how much of a gain or loss is taxable (is recognized) in a given tax year.

If a series of transactions results in a net capital gain, the net capital gain is recognized in the current tax year regardless of its size. In this instance, the taxpayer has received income, and the amount and character of the income could be precisely calculated, so recognition is required.

Key Concepts

1. Describe the annual limits on loss deductions for individual taxpayers.
2. Identify the loss rules associated with small business stock.

If a series of transactions results in a net capital loss, however, the amount of that loss that may be recognized in the current tax year is limited. Under current law, up to $3,000 of net capital losses (either short or long-term) may be recognized against other forms of income in any one tax year.

This limitation is a liberalization of the general rule of taxation that says that losses in one income category can only be offset against gains in that income category. If the general rule applied, no loss deduction would be allowed in the current tax year if a taxpayer had a net loss on capital transactions. The $3,000 net capital loss limitation rule is a special exception to the general rule and allows taxpayers to take up to $3,000 of losses currently against other income. If losses exceed $3,000 and the taxpayer has both short-term and long-term losses, then the short-term losses are used up first. The balance of any losses, short or long-term, carry over indefinitely and may be used in a subsequent year.

Recall that in our tax system there are three types of income: (1) ordinary (active) income; (2) portfolio income; and (3) passive income. Capital gains and losses fall into the portfolio "bucket." The general rule limits loss deductions to the income within that bucket, but the special rule allows a portion of that loss to be deducted against other income. This concept is illustrated graphically in **Exhibit 11.6**.

Exhibit 11.6 | Types of Income

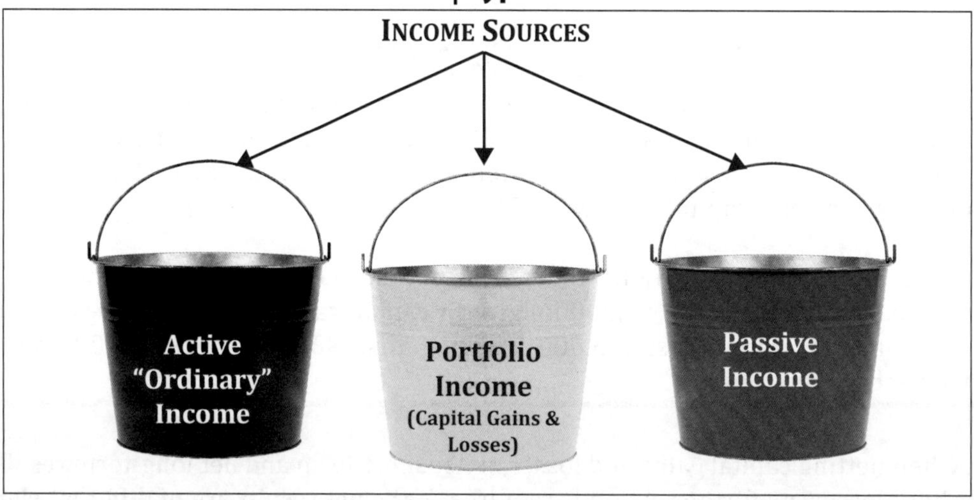

If a capital loss is realized in a given tax year, but is not recognized due to the imposition of the loss limitation rule, the remaining loss is carried forward indefinitely and may be used to offset future capital gains, or, alternatively, generate a $3,000 loss deduction against other income each subsequent year until the loss is eventually used up.

Example 11.29

Merida, upon being hired as executive vice president of The Amazing Company, Inc., purchases $2 million of The Amazing Company stock without researching the viability of the business. The Amazing Company, despite its name, goes bankrupt, and Merida loses her entire investment. Merida has no other capital gains or losses in the current year. She will be able to write-off $3,000 of the $2 million loss this year and will carry forward the remaining $1,997,000 loss to future years. In the unlikely event that Merida has gains in future years, she can offset those gains dollar for dollar with the carryforward loss. Alternatively, she could continue to deduct $3,000 per year until she dies, or until the remaining loss is completely written off.

In addition to the special rule that allows up to $3,000 of capital losses to be offset against other income, another rule re-categorizes capital losses on **small business stock (1244 stock)** into ordinary losses if certain requirements are met. Under IRC Section 1244, a single taxpayer can deduct up to $50,000 ($100,000 for married individuals filing jointly) of the loss on small business stock as an ordinary loss in any given year if the following requirements are met:

1. The stock represents ownership in a domestic corporation.
2. The corporation was a small business corporation (less than $1 million in total capital contributions plus paid-in capital) at the time the stock was issued.
3. The company was incorporated after November 6, 1978.

4. The loss was sustained by the original owner of the stock (the person to whom the stock was issued by the corporation), who is not a corporation, trust, or estate.
5. The stock was issued to the original owner in exchange for money or property. Stock issued in return for services or other stock does not qualify.
6. For the five years prior to the loss, the corporation must have earned more than 50 percent of it's gross receipts from sources other than royalties, rents, dividends, interest, annuities, and capital gains.

Example 11.30

Jasper, a single individual, was an original investor in Monarch, Inc. When the company was formed, it had $500,000 in initial capitalization. While the company did well for a few years, its performance has slipped, and earlier this year it declared bankruptcy. Jasper's ownership interest in the company was 20%. All of the other requirements for Section 1244 treatment have been met.

Since Jasper owned 20% of the company, his initial capital contribution was $100,000 (20% of $500,000). This year, the company became worthless, so a constructive sale will occur on December 31. Jasper's loss is $100,000. Out of the $100,000 loss, Jasper can treat $50,000 as an ordinary loss, leaving the other $50,000 to be treated as a capital loss. There is no loss limitation on ordinary losses, so the entire $50,000 ordinary loss is deductible in the current year. In addition, assuming he has no other capital gains or losses in the current year or carryforward losses from prior years, Jasper will be able to deduct $3,000 of the capital loss against his other income. The remaining $47,000 capital loss will be carried forward to future tax years.

Small Business Stock (Section 1202)

The PATH Act of 2015 retroactively renewed and permanently extended the 100 percent capital gains exclusion relating to qualified **small business stock (1202 stock)** to non-corporate taxpayers. For stock (C Corporations only) acquired after September 27, 2010 and held at least five years, the gain exclusion is 100 percent. The maximum gain exclusion is the greater of $10,000,000 (reduced by the amount of gain eligibility for exclusion in prior years for stock issued by the corporation) or 10 times the taxpayer's adjusted basis.

Type of Stock	C Corporation, $50,000,000 or less
Acquired	After 9/27/2010
Holding Period	5 years minimum
Exclusion of Gain	100%
Acquired by	Money, property, or sweat equity
Gain	Excluded if qualified
AMT	Gain is not an AMT preference
Applies to	Stock acquired by the taxpayer at its original issue
Amount Excluded	Greater of 10 times the taxpayer's basis in the stock or $10 million

In addition, for qualified small business stock acquired before February 18, 2009, the exclusion is 50 percent and for qualified small business stock acquired between February 18, 2009 and September 27, 2010, the exclusion is 75 percent. However, a portion of these (50 and 75 percent) exclusions will continue to be treated as a preference item for AMT.

SUMMARY

This chapter has introduced the tax principles associated with capital assets. In particular, the calculation of gain or loss, holding period requirements, tax rates, and special rules were reviewed. The overriding principal of taxation in the capital asset arena is that all realized gains will be recognized, but may be taxed at different rates depending on the character of the gain. The rules introduced in this chapter will apply to most capital transactions, but there are some additional rules that may alter the results illustrated here. These additional rules deal with deferral of gain, or in some instances, nonrecognition of gain, and will be discussed in detail in Chapter 12.

Quick Quiz 11.4

1. A taxpayer with a $20,000 long-term capital gain and a $5,000 short-term capital loss has a net $15,000 short-term capital gain.
   a. True
   b. False
2. $3,000 of net capital losses may be recognized against other income each year.
   a. True
   b. False
3. A single taxpayer can deduct up to $50,000 of the loss from a small business stock as an ordinary loss if certain requirements are met.
   a. True
   b. False

False, True, True.

KEY TERMS

Amount Realized - The amount of money plus the value of property received in the sale or exchange of an asset.

Capital Asset - All assets that are not specified as ordinary income assets or Section 1231 assets.

Disallowed Losses - Losses that are realized, but are not permitted to be recognized, including losses on the sale of personal use assets (except for casualty losses), losses on the subsequent sale of property gifted or sold to a related party when its FMV is less than the original owner's adjusted basis, and losses associated with a wash sale.

Holding Period - The period over which a taxpayer owns an asset.

Long-Term Holding Period - Occurs when an asset is owned by a taxpayer for more than one year.

Realization Event - Generally occurs when an asset has been sold or exchanged. Gains on capital assets are subject to tax only when there has been both a realization event and a recognition event.

Recognition Event - Occurs when a realized gain is included on a taxpayer's income tax return. All realized gains are generally recognized unless a provision in the IRC provides otherwise.

Sale or Exchange Requirement - One of the requirements for a gain to be subject to income tax.

Short-Term Holding Period - Occurs when an asset is owned by a taxpayer for one year or less.

Small Business Stock (1202 Stock) - Stock that is eligible for a 100% capital gains exclusion.

Small Business Stock (1244 Stock) - Stock in a company initially capitalized with $1 million or less that permits special ordinary loss recognition.

Unrecaptured Section 1250 Depreciation - The portion of gain that is attributable to non-recaptured depreciation (up to the amount of straight-line depreciation deductions taken) for depreciable real estate that is taxed at 25 percent upon the sale or exchange of the property (plus the net investment income tax of 3.8% if applicable).

Wash Sale - Occurs when a taxpayer sells a stock or security at a loss and purchases substantially identical stock or securities within a 30 day period before or after the sale.

DISCUSSION QUESTIONS

SOLUTIONS to the discussion questions can be found exclusively within the chapter. Once you have completed an initial reading of the chapter, go back and highlight the answers to these questions.

1. What is a capital asset?
2. When are gains on capital assets subject to tax?
3. Give several examples of events that satisfy the sale or exchange requirement of a realization event.
4. How is the gain or loss on the sale of a capital asset calculated?
5. What is the amount realized?
6. How is the amount realized affected when the parties transfer debt in addition to cash or other property?
7. What is the default recognition rule?
8. Define a disallowed loss and give several examples of a disallowed loss.
9. Why are losses on the sale of personal use assets disallowed?
10. How is a realized loss affected when the property is sold or gifted to a related party?
11. What is a wash sale and what are its tax consequences?
12. What is the difference between a short-term and long-term holding period?
13. How is the holding period determined for property received from a decedent's estate?
14. How is the holding period determined for nonbusiness bad debts?
15. What is the difference between the tax rate for short-term capital gains and long-term capital gains?
16. What are the two exceptions to the 20% maximum capital gains tax rate?
17. What items generally qualify as collectibles and what is the tax treatment of these items?
18. How do capital gains affect the AMT?
19. How are net capital gains determined?
20. What is the limitation on the recognition of capital losses?

MULTIPLE CHOICE PROBLEMS

A sample of multiple choice problems is provided below. Additional multiple choice problems are available at money-education.com by accessing the Student Practice Portal.

1. Which of the following statements concerning the taxation of assets is correct?
    a. Ordinary income may qualify for a special 0% rate.
    b. Capital gains are always taxed at the taxpayer's marginal tax rate.
    c. Gains on Section 1231 assets are taxed at ordinary rates, and losses are taxed at capital rates.
    d. Gains on Section 1231 assets are taxed at long-term capital gains tax rates, and losses are taxed at ordinary income tax rates.

2. Which of the following statements correctly identifies when income is subject to tax?
    a. Capital gains must be realized before they can be recognized on a tax return.
    b. Realization occurs when the gain on an asset is reflected on the taxpayer's return.
    c. As a general rule, realized gains are not recognized unless a provision in the IRC requires recognition.
    d. Recognition occurs when an asset has been sold or exchanged.

3. All of the following are included in the amount realized upon disposition of an asset EXCEPT:
    a. The cash received.
    b. The fair market value of property received in the exchange.
    c. A transfer of obligation to pay debt from the seller to the buyer.
    d. The taxpayer's adjusted basis.

4. Anastasia purchased a home in Connecticut three years ago for $300,000. She had been working in Connecticut for the past 10 years. Yesterday, her employer decided to transfer her to the San Diego, California branch, effective next month. Unfortunately, the real estate market has weakened over the past few years, and Anastasia is only able to sell her home for $270,000. Which of the following statements correctly identifies her tax consequences of the sale:
    a. Anastasia is not permitted to deduct the loss on her income tax return.
    b. Anastasia's loss will be reflected as a long-term capital loss on her tax return.
    c. Anastasia's loss will be reflected as a short-term capital loss on her tax return.
    d. Anastasia will recognize an ordinary loss of $30,000.

5. Gus purchased a home for $300,000 three years ago, and was recently transferred by his employer to an office located across the country. He made $20,000 of improvements to the residence, but if he sold the home today, he would only be able to receive $260,000 for the house due to a weak real estate market. Instead of selling the home and realizing a loss, Gus rents the home to a tenant. What is Gus's basis for depreciation purposes?
    a. $260,000.
    b. $270,000.
    c. $300,000.
    d. $320,000.

QUICK QUIZ EXPLANATIONS

Quick Quiz 11.1

1. False. Capital gains are subject to tax when there has been both a realization event and a recognition event.
2. True.

Quick Quiz 11.2

1. True.
2. False. If a wash sale results in realization of a loss, the loss is not currently recognized and is temporarily disallowed. The unrecognized loss will be added to the basis of the replacement securities, so that on sale of the replacement securities, recognition will occur. Therefore, losses associated with a wash sale are not permanently disallowed.

Quick Quiz 11.3

1. False. To achieve long-term treatment, the asset must be held for *more than* one year. As a practical matter, this means that a long-term holding period begins if the asset is held for a year and one day. If the asset is sold in the current year on the same day it was purchased in the prior year, the result is a short-term holding period.
2. False. The maximum long-term capital gains tax rate is 20% and the lowest is 0%. In addition, there are special 25% and 28% capital gains rates. These rates do not include any applicable net investment income tax (Medicare surtax) imposed by the Affordable Care Act of 2010.
3. False. Unrecaptured Section 1250 depreciation applies to depreciable real estate used in a trade or business or for the production of income.
4. True.

Quick Quiz 11.4

1. False. The taxpayer has a net $15,000 long-term capital gain. The character (short-term or long-term) of a net gain or loss is determined by the larger net number, not taking into account whether it was a gain or loss.
2. True.
3. True.

12
BUSINESS ASSETS

LEARNING OBJECTIVES

1. Identify ordinary income assets.*
2. Explain the tax treatment of income generated by ordinary income assets.*
3. Explain the tax treatment of gains and losses generated by the sale or exchange of ordinary income assets.*
4. Explain the tax advantages and disadvantages associated with Section 1231 assets.*
5. Explain the tax advantages and disadvantages associated with the sale of Section 1231 assets by corporations.*
6. Explain the depreciation recapture rules for personal property.*
7. Determine the tax consequences of the sale of Section 1231 personal property.*
8. Explain the depreciation recapture rules for real property.*
9. Determine the tax consequences resulting from the sale of Section 1231 real property.*
10. Determine the impact of the depreciation recapture rules when property is acquired by gift.*
11. Determine the impact of the depreciation recapture rules when property is acquired through a like-kind exchange, or through an involuntary conversion.*
12. Determine the impact of the depreciation recapture rules when property is acquired from a decedent.*
13. Discuss the impact of the depreciation recapture rules on installment sales.*
14. Calculate the tax impact of the 5-year lookback rule for a given client.*

**Ties to CFP Certification Learning Objectives*

INTRODUCTION

In prior chapters, we examined the general rules governing the taxation of property transactions and how the sale of capital assets is treated within the income tax system. In that discussion, we learned that there are three types of assets in our tax system – ordinary income assets, capital assets, and Section 1231 assets. The prior chapter dealt with capital assets, which is the catch-all (default) asset category. For income tax purposes, everything in the world is a capital asset except for those items specified in Section 1221. For tax planning purposes, remember that everything in the world is a capital asset except "ACID" (accounts receivable, creative works held by the creator, inventory, and depreciable property or real property used in a trade or business). This chapter deals with the taxation of the other two asset categories: ordinary income assets and Section 1231 assets.

Key Concepts

1. Identify ordinary income assets.
2. Define what kind of income is generated by the sale or exchange of an ordinary income asset.

ORDINARY INCOME ASSETS

Ordinary income assets generate gains that are taxed at ordinary income tax rates. If an individual engages in business by selling goods or services, for example, the income generated from that business activity is taxed at ordinary income tax rates.

Out of the items not defined as capital assets under IRC Section 1221 (ACID), the first three items (accounts receivable, creative works held by the creator, and inventory) are ordinary income assets. These items simply represent potential future or earned ordinary income and the IRC will not allow taxpayers to change the characterization of that income simply by changing the nature of the asset.

You may recall that accounts and notes receivable, the first type of ordinary income asset, represent ordinary income receipts that are deferred into the future. The sale of a good or service in the ordinary course of business generates ordinary income. Transforming that transaction from cash to an account or note receivable does not change the ordinary income nature of the transaction.

Inventory is held for resale to customers in the normal course of business and therefore generates ordinary income upon sale. Consequently, any inventory held by a business is considered an ordinary income asset. Copyrights, musical compositions, and artistic creations in the hands of the author are ordinary income assets because they are a form of inventory.[1] An artist creates a masterpiece with the intent of selling it and is therefore creating inventory for his business, which is the creation and sale of pieces of art. Recall from our discussion in earlier chapters, however, that copyrights, musical compositions, and artistic creations in the hands of someone other than the creator may not be considered ordinary income assets. Rather, they may be considered capital assets or Section 1231 assets.

Quick Quiz 12.1

1. Notes receivable are ordinary income assets.
   a. True
   b. False
2. The deductibility of ordinary losses is limited to $3,000 per year.
   a. True
   b. False

True, False.

Real estate may be classified as a capital asset or as inventory if the real estate is held primarily for sale to customers in a real estate business. Specifically, subdivided land may be treated as inventory or as a capital asset.

When a taxpayer generates ordinary income, it is taxed at ordinary income tax rates, which, under current law, are the highest tax rates in our income tax system. If a loss is incurred in the conduct of business, the loss may be deducted as an ordinary loss and will be available to reduce ordinary income, up to the limits imposed on business losses for noncorporate taxpayers in tax years 2018 - 2025 ($262,000 single, $524,000 MFJ, in 2021 as discussed in Chapter 8). Excess business losses not deductible in the year incurred due to the business loss limitation are carried forward as net operating losses in subsequent years. The CARES Act of 2020, however, allows business losses for noncorporate taxpayers to be deducted without limitation in tax years 2018, 2019, and 2020.

Under current law, net operating losses (NOLs) can be carried forward indefinitely and used to offset future income. When carrying an NOL forward, the amount that can be used to offset income in that year is limited to 80 percent of taxable income. NOLs incurred in farming business and by insurance companies may also be carried back to prior years to generate tax refunds. The CARES Act of 2020 also permitted businesses to carry back up to five years NOLs arising in tax years 2018, 2019, or 2020.

1. Treas. Reg. §1.1221(b)(3) allows an election by musicians for musical compositions or copyrights. The taxpayer could elect for tax treatment of the composition or copyright as a capital gain or loss upon the sale of the property instead of inventory subject to ordinary income (effective 5/17/06).

While the generation of a loss is not the objective of a well-run business, if a loss does occur, a taxpayer would prefer to have that loss treated as an ordinary loss so that he or she can make current use of that loss to offset other ordinary income.

SECTION 1231 ASSETS

As discussed in our review of asset categorization, accounts receivable, copyrights and creative compositions in the hands of the creator, and inventory are classified as ordinary income assets. The only type asset that can be classified by the IRC as a **Section 1231 asset** is depreciable real or personal property used in a trade or business or for the production of income. The owner of depreciable real and personal property used in a trade or business or for the production of income must have a long-term holding period for the asset to be classified as a Section 1231 asset.

There are two types of property that receive 1231 treatment - personal property (also called personalty) and real property. Depreciable tangible personal property used in a trade or business or held for the production of income purposes is sometimes referred to as Section 1245 property. Section 1250 property is depreciable real property used in a trade or business or held for the production of income. As used in Sections 1245 and 1250, real property (realty) is defined as land and anything permanently attached to the land, while personal property (personalty) is defined as any property not meeting the definition of real property.

From our discussion of basis rules, we know that any asset used in a trade or business or for the production of income that is expected to decline in value qualifies for depreciation deductions. Personal use assets cannot be depreciated. Only trade or business assets and production of income assets subject to depreciation are Section 1231 assets.

Benefits of Section 1231

The significance of Section 1231 is that once an asset is categorized as a Section 1231 asset, gains generated from the sale of the asset are treated as capital gains, and losses generated from the sale or other disposition of the asset are treated as ordinary losses. Therefore, gains will qualify for favorable long-term capital gains tax rates, and losses will not be subject to the limitations that typically apply to capital assets.

Key Concepts

1. Identify Section 1231 assets.
2. Explain the advantages of Section 1231.
3. Describe the disadvantages of Section 1231.

Gains on Section 1231 assets qualify for the long-term capital gains tax rate since the owner of the asset held the asset for more than one year (recall that a long-term holding period is required for an asset to be categorized as a Section 1231 asset). Section 1231 losses, however, are treated as ordinary losses and will therefore not be subject to the net $3,000 loss limitation that applies to capital losses.

By achieving a lower tax rate on gains, and avoiding limitations on loss deductions, Section 1231 gives the taxpayer what is often referred to as the best of both worlds tax treatment. Given a choice, taxpayers would characterize all of their losses as ordinary losses because the only limitation that applies to the loss deduction is the $262,000 (single, $524,000 MJF in 2021) limitation on business losses for noncorporate taxpayers, as discussed in Chapter 8, and the higher ordinary tax rate generates a greater tax benefit from the loss. In addition, given a choice, taxpayers would characterize all of their gains as capital gains to take advantage of the lower long-term capital gains tax rates. Section 1231 gives the appearance of tax nirvana, but further discussion (below) will explain why Congress has given taxpayers what appears to be, at first glance, too good to be true.

The tax treatment of Section 1231 assets also differs depending on whether an individual (acting as a sole proprietor, partner, S corporation shareholder, or member of an LLC) or a C corporation generates the Section 1231 gain or loss.

If an individual generates a Section 1231 gain, the favorable, lower capital gains rate (currently 20 percent is the maximum) will apply. If the taxpayer is in a low ordinary income tax bracket, the zero percent capital gains tax rate will apply. Conversely, if a loss is generated, the taxpayer can write off that loss as an ordinary loss, subject to the $262,000 (single, $524,000 MJF in 2021)limitation on business losses for noncorporate taxpayers (discussed in Chapter 8), against other forms of income for the current, and possibly, future tax years. Had the loss been categorized as a capital loss and not a Section 1231 loss, the net $3,000 loss limitation rule would have applied, and the loss may not be fully utilized by the taxpayer in the current tax year.

C corporations do not qualify for the lower, favorable tax rate on capital gains. Therefore, the generation of a Section 1231 gain will not result in a tax benefit for the corporation. If a corporation generates a Section 1231 loss, however, the loss will be considered an ordinary loss and may be deducted in full against other income. For corporations, capital losses may not be deducted against other forms of income – capital losses can only be used to offset capital gains. Categorizing an asset as a Section 1231 asset, therefore, allows the corporation to recognize losses without having to generate capital gains to offset them.

Entities that are taxed as pass-through vehicles, such as partnerships, limited liability companies, limited liability partnerships, and S corporations "pass-through" their tax results to their owners, so the individual, not the corporate rules, apply. Owners of these entities qualify for the capital gains tax rate on their Section 1231 gains and can deduct the losses from ordinary income.

The Catch - Depreciation Recapture

Section 1231 looks almost too good to be true, and it would be if the analysis ended at asset categorization. Once the taxpayer has categorized an asset as a Section 1231 asset, however, an additional consideration must be addressed – **depreciation recapture**. Depreciation recapture is the inclusion of a portion, or all, of the previously taken depreciation deductions in the current year's income as ordinary income if a gain is associated with the sale or exchange of property. For example, if tangible personal property is purchased for $20,000, depreciated by $12,000 (resulting in an adjusted basis of $8,000), and is later sold for $10,000, then $2,000 of the $12,000 of depreciation taken on the asset will be recaptured as ordinary income.

In order to be classified as a Section 1231 asset, the asset must be "depreciable property or real property used in a trade or business." When an asset that was subject to depreciation is sold, depreciation recapture may apply. In order to understand depreciation recapture, it is first necessary to review the purposes and uses of depreciation.

The purpose of depreciation is to allow individuals and businesses who use property in productive use or in a trade or business to recoup their capital investment in the asset over the useful life of that asset.

This is accomplished by reducing ordinary income with depreciation deductions, representing a return of capital, so that capital can be reinvested to generate more income.

In an ideal world, the depreciation expense deduction claimed by the taxpayer each year would be the actual decline in value of the asset, representing the portion of the asset that was used up in that tax year. Doing this, however, would be impractical – it would require every asset to be appraised each year, followed by a comparison of the end-of-year value to the beginning-of-year value simply to ascertain the current year depreciation deduction.

Recognizing that it would be impractical to require taxpayers to value each asset they own annually to justify their depreciation deductions, Congress developed a statutory scheme for depreciation. In this statutory scheme, each asset acquired is classified into a specific class life based on the rules set forth in the IRC. The class lives of various types of assets were discussed in Chapter 10. Once the class life is determined, a statutorily defined deduction is taken for depreciation of the asset, regardless of the actual decline in value of the asset from year to year. Since the depreciation deduction is not based on the actual decline in the value of the asset, it could be thought of as an estimate based on averages calculated by the IRS. This real world approach that generates an estimated depreciation value is convenient and relatively easy to apply, but generates tax results that would not be obtained in an ideal world, where depreciation deductions are based on the actual decline in the value of each asset each year.

Many assets purchased for use in a trade or business are completely used up in that trade or business and are then disposed of at the end of their useful life. Often, upon disposal, the taxpayer receives nothing in return for the asset. When this happens, the taxpayer has recouped his or her capital investment in that asset over the useful life of that asset, and there is nothing to be concerned about for income tax purposes.

Quick Quiz 12.2

1. Depreciable personal property used in a trade or business is Section 1231 property.
   a. True
   b. False
2. Gains from the sale of Section 1231 property are always taxed as ordinary income.
   a. True
   b. False
3. Losses on Section 1231 property are treated as ordinary losses.
   a. True
   b. False
4. Depreciation recapture applies upon the sale or exchange of a capital asset.
   a. True
   b. False

True, False, True, False.

Example 12.1

Piper, a highly sought after financial planner in her community, opened a new office several years ago. She purchased computers for use by her staff, and the computers were classified as 5-year class life property. Over the next six years, Piper and her staff used the computers, at which time they were replaced with new computers. The old computers were disposed of at no value. Piper was able to recover her capital investment in the computers over the 5-year class life through the depreciation expense deductions, which reduced ordinary income. She received nothing upon disposition of the computers.

Consequently, the disposal of the computers does not trigger any income tax consequences.

When an asset is sold, a realization event occurs for income tax purposes and the gain or loss must be calculated. When the asset sold is a Section 1231 asset, the taxpayer may breathe a sigh of relief, since he or she knows that the optimal tax treatment will be afforded. Before that can happen, however, depreciation recapture must be taken into consideration. Section 1231 treatment only applies to the economic (i.e., ideal world) results of the transaction. Before Section 1231 applies, we must first make sure that the depreciation deduction taken in the real world (by using the estimated value based on the class life of the asset) equals the depreciation deduction that would have been taken in the ideal world (where the deduction equals the actual decline in value each year).

From a planning standpoint, whenever a Section 1231 asset is sold, the taxpayer must first consider the possibility of depreciation recapture before the "best of both worlds" tax treatment can apply. The only time that depreciation recapture is an issue is when the asset has been categorized as a Section 1231 asset. If the asset is a capital asset or an ordinary income asset, depreciation recapture does not apply.

RECAPTURING DEPRECIATION ON PERSONAL PROPERTY (SECTION 1245)

The sole purpose of depreciation recapture is to ensure that, when an asset is sold, the taxpayer receives his or her capital back tax free – no more, and no less. The rules for depreciation recapture differ depending upon the type of property sold.

If personal property used in a trade or business is sold, Section 1245 sets forth the rules for depreciation recapture.

Personal property, as used in Section 1245, means anything that is not real property. The depreciation recapture provisions of the IRC (Sections 1245 and 1250) use the legal definition of property. **Real property** is land and anything permanently attached to the land (such as buildings, trees, and swimming pools). **Personal property** is everything else in the world (i.e., anything other than land or things permanently attached to the land). Used in this context, personal property does not imply that the property is used for personal, as opposed to business, purposes. As described in Chapter 3, both real and personal property can be used in one of three ways for income tax purposes:

1. personal use (a personal residence and furnishings),
2. production of income use (the residential rental building and furnishings that a taxpayer owns), or
3. trade or business use (the office building and furniture used in a taxpayer's trade or business).

One special exception to this rule classifies silos and greenhouses, which are typically classified as real property, as Section 1245 property.

Key Concepts

1. Explain depreciation recapture for personal property.
2. Identify the four possible results of Section 1245.

When personal property is used in a trade or business or for the production of income, it is depreciable and therefore becomes a Section 1231 asset. When that property is sold, Section 1245 governs the depreciation recapture rules. Simply put, Section 1245 states that when personal Section 1231 property is sold, depreciation is recaptured as ordinary income to the extent of the gain or the amount of depreciation taken, whichever is less. This means that before capital gains treatment can result under Section 1231, all of the depreciation which was previously deducted from ordinary income must be recaptured or subjected to ordinary income tax. Since depreciation was taken as a deduction against ordinary income, when depreciation is recaptured, it will be treated as an addition to ordinary income.

There are only four potential outcomes that result from the application of Section 1245. While the numbers in each example or problem will change, identifying which of the four scenarios applies will assist in quickly ascertaining the tax consequences. The best way to describe the application and purpose of Section 1245 is by example.

Exhibit 12.1 | Results of Section 1245

If Sale Price:	AR = AB*	AR < AB*	AR > AB* and Gain < Depreciation	AR > AB* and Gain > Depreciation
Tax Consequences	No gain or loss, no depreciation recapture, **no tax consequences.**	Resulting loss is always treated as an **ordinary loss.**	Section 1245 treats the gain as **ordinary gain.**	**Gain up to amount of depreciation** taken is treated as **ordinary gain** under Section 1245. **Gain in excess of depreciation** taken is treated as **capital gain** under Section 1231.
Resulting from Economics	Accounting estimate of depreciation equals economic reality.	Not enough depreciation was taken.	Too much depreciation was taken.	Too much depreciation was taken and the asset appreciated.
Illustrated By	**Example 12.3**	**Example 12.4**	**Example 12.5**	**Example 12.6**

**AR = Amount Realized; AB = Adjusted Basis*

When faced with a property transaction question, the first step is to ascertain what type of asset is being dealt with.

Example 12.2

Kasey, a high school student, decided to apply some of the principles of entrepreneurship that have been taught to him by his uncle and opened the KB Lawnmowing Service, LLC. Kasey purchased several pieces of equipment and hired his high school friends to help him provide lawn mowing services. One of the items Kasey purchased when he opened the business two years ago was a riding mower. He paid $1,500 for the mower and has since taken $400 in depreciation deductions. Due to the popularity of the company's service, Kasey now needs a heavy-duty mower and has decided to sell his existing riding mower to purchase the heavy-duty equipment. Kasey would like to know what the tax consequences of such an action would be and has asked you, his financial advisor, for advice.

In this case, Kasey purchased a lawnmower for use in his trade or business and has been taking depreciation deductions on that asset. Consequently, the asset is a Section 1231 asset. The asset Kasey proposes to sell is a lawnmower, which is a personal asset (it is not land or anything permanently attached to the land), so the depreciation recapture rule that applies will be found in Section 1245.

The next step is to calculate the gain or loss on the sale of the asset.

Example 12.3

Continuing with **Example 12.2**, what is the tax result if Kasey sells the riding lawnmower for $1,100?

In this example, the amount realized from the sale is $1,100. To calculate gain or loss, we must subtract Kasey's adjusted basis in the asset from the amount realized in the transaction. Kasey's adjusted basis is his cost basis of $1,500 reduced by his depreciation deductions (or return of capital) of $400. Kasey's adjusted basis, therefore, is $1,100.
Using the formula for calculating gain or loss found in IRC Section 1001, we find the following:

Amount Realized	$1,100
Less: Adjusted Basis	$1,100
Equals: Gain or (Loss)	$0

Since there is no gain or loss, there is no depreciation recapture, and no tax consequence.

Out of the four possible outcomes for the sale of personal Section 1231 property, **Example 12.3** illustrates the simplest result – the example where there are no tax consequences. This result will rarely occur in real life, but it does illustrate an important point. This example shows what happens when the "ideal world" and the "real world" meet. Despite the fact that the depreciation deductions taken by Kasey were formula amounts based on averages set forth in the Internal Revenue Code, the actual depreciation in the asset equaled the amount of depreciation claimed for income tax purposes. Kasey purchased the asset for $1,500. He received his entire investment back through depreciation deductions ($400) and proceeds from the sale of the asset ($1,100). Since there is no gain or loss, there is no tax consequence. **Example 12.3** illustrates the rare occurrence where the conventions used in the IRC to calculate depreciation deductions match the actual decline in the value of an asset perfectly.

Since the convergence of the "ideal" and "real" world is rare, it is in the other three situations (as illustrated by **Example 12.4** - **Example 12.6**) that the impact of the depreciation recapture rule for personal property is demonstrated. Note that the preliminary steps of categorizing the asset and identifying the potential type of depreciation recapture is presumed in each of the following three examples.

Example 12.4

Continuing with **Example 12.2**, what is the tax result if Kasey sells the riding lawnmower for $1,000? Using the formula for calculating gain or loss found in IRC Section 1001, we find the following:

Amount Realized	$1,000
Less: Adjusted Basis	$1,100
Equals: Gain or (Loss)	($100)

Kasey's adjusted basis is the same as in **Example 12.3**, and equals his cost basis reduced by the actual depreciation deductions he claimed on the asset. In this instance, Kasey has realized a $100 loss on the sale. Consequently, there is no depreciation recapture, since Section 1245 requires recapture of the depreciation to the extent of the *gain*. Strictly applying the language of Section 1245, no recapture occurs, but the lawnmower was a Section 1231 asset. Section 1231 states that losses on the sale of Section 1231 assets are treated as ordinary losses, so Kasey's $100 loss will be treated as an ordinary loss. The loss will not be reported as a capital transaction and will be used to offset other ordinary income.

The application of the IRC in this instance simply allows Kasey to recoup all of his capital investment tax free. Capital is income that was already subject to tax, so it should be returned to the owner without assessing an additional tax. Depreciation is supposed to permit a taxpayer who uses an asset in productive use in a trade or business or for the production of income to receive his or her capital back, tax free, as the value of the asset is used up in the activity. In this circumstance, the actual decline in value of the asset while it was being used in Kasey's trade or business was:

Cost Basis	$1,500
Less: Amount Realized	$1,000
Decline in Value	$500

Although the actual decline in value was $500, Kasey was only allowed to deduct $400 of depreciation on the asset due to the asset-life rules set forth in the IRC. If he would have been allowed a deduction based on the actual decline in the value of the asset, his depreciation deduction would have equaled $500, but the deduction contrived by application of the IRC was only $400. If Kasey had taken the full decline in value as a depreciation deduction, it would have offset ordinary income from his business operations. Therefore, Kasey should be permitted to take an ordinary loss deduction of $100 for the additional amount of depreciation he experienced but could not take due to the application of the depreciation rules found in the IRC. This is why Section 1231 treats losses on the sale of Section 1231 assets as ordinary losses. If a Section 1231 asset is sold at a loss, the taxpayer did not take enough depreciation over the holding period of the asset, and, upon sale, the additional depreciation (represented by the loss on the sale) may be taken as an ordinary deduction so that the results experienced in the ideal and real worlds are equivalent. After the application of Section 1231, Kasey has received all of his capital back tax free: $400 through depreciation deductions, $1,000 upon sale of the asset, and $100 of Section 1231 loss, which is really a catch-up depreciation deduction. **Example 12.4** is summarized below.

	Ideal World	Real World	Notes for Real World
Cost Basis	$1,500	$1,500	
Amount Realized	$1,000	$1,000	
Actual Decline	$500	$500	
Depreciation Deduction	$500	$400	Specified by IRC
Amount Realized from Sale	$1,000	$1,000	
Adjusted Basis	$1,000*	$1,100	$1,500 cost basis less $400 depreciation
Gain/Loss	$0	($100)	Ordinary Loss
Totals After 1231 Treatment			
Depreciation	$500	$500	$400 per tax code plus $100 per Section 1231

* The adjusted basis of the asset in the "Ideal World" example is calculated as follows:
Cost Basis $1,500 – Depreciation Deduction $500 = $1,000.

Example 12.4 illustrates the following rule: If a Section 1231 asset is sold at a loss, the resulting loss will ALWAYS be treated as an ordinary loss. Section 1231 allows this treatment so that the taxpayer can deduct the actual depreciation in the value of the asset from his or her ordinary business income.

Example 12.5

Continuing with **Example 12.2**, what is the tax result if Kasey sells the riding lawnmower for $1,200? Using the formula for calculating gain or loss found in IRC Section 1001, we find the following:

Amount Realized	$1,200
Less: Adjusted Basis	$1,100
Gain/(Loss)	$100

In **Example 12.5**, Kasey has a gain on the sale of the lawnmower, which is personal property and a Section 1231 asset. Section 1231 states that all gains on the sale of Section 1231 assets are capital gains, but before we can apply that rule we have to consider depreciation recapture under Section 1245. Section 1245 states that depreciation is recaptured as ordinary income to the extent of the gain. In this example, the depreciation Kasey took on the lawnmower was $400. His gain on the sale was $100. Since the gain of $100 is less than the depreciation taken, the gain is treated as an ordinary gain. Kasey would not be able to get capital gains treatment on any of the gain until all of the depreciation was recaptured.

In **Example 12.3**, we saw the rare occurrence of the real world and ideal world merging. In **Example 12.4**, the sale of a personal Section 1231 asset resulted in a loss because not enough depreciation was taken on the asset during the holding period. **Example 12.5** illustrates what happens when too much depreciation is taken on the asset for tax purposes.

In **Example 12.5**, the real decline in the value of the asset can be calculated as follows:

Cost Basis	$1,500
Less: Amount Realized	$1,200
Decline in Value	$300

Nevertheless, Kasey claimed $400 in depreciation deductions as specified in the IRC. Recall that the purpose of the depreciation recapture rules is to ensure that the appropriate amount of depreciation is taken at the time that the asset is sold. If too much depreciation was allowed under the IRC, the "excess depreciation" must be added back to ordinary income so that the depreciation deduction in the real world equals the depreciation deduction in the ideal world upon sale of the asset. **Example 12.5** is summarized below.

	Ideal World	*Real World*	*Notes for Real World*
Cost Basis	$1,500	$1,500	
Amount Realized	$1,200	$1,200	
Actual Decline	$300	$300	
Depreciation Deduction	$300	$400	Specified by IRC
Amount Realized from Sale	$1,200	$1,200	
Adjusted Basis	$1,200*	$1,100	$1,500 cost basis less $400 depreciation
Gain/Loss	$0	$100	Ordinary Income
Totals After 1231 Treatment			
Depreciation	$300	$300	$400 per IRC less $100 "recaptured" per Section 1231

** The adjusted basis of the asset in the "Ideal World" example is calculated as follows: Cost Basis $1,500 – Depreciation Deduction $300 = $1,200.*

As **Example 12.5** illustrates, when a personal Section 1231 asset is sold at a gain, the gain (to the extent of the prior depreciation deduction taken) is treated as ordinary income to offset the excess depreciation taken over the holding period. The excess depreciation is $100 ($400 depreciation taken - $300 actual decline in value of the asset). The only way to ensure that the actual amount of depreciation taken on the asset equals the actual decline in value of the asset is to reverse out $100 of the depreciation deduction by adding it to ordinary income. Once this is done, a $300 depreciation deduction results, and Kasey recoups the remaining portion of his capital, $1,200, from the amount realized in the sale.

Example 12.5 illustrates the application of the following rule: Whenever a personal Section 1231 asset is sold at a gain, compare the gain to the depreciation taken over the life of the asset. If the gain is equal to or less than the depreciation taken, Section 1245 treats the gain as ordinary income (and it is sometimes referred to as a Section 1245 gain).

Example 12.6

Continuing with **Example 12.2**, what is the income tax result if Kasey sells the riding lawnmower for $1,700? Using the formula for calculating gain or loss found in IRC Section 1001, we find the following:

Amount Realized	$1,700
Less: Adjusted Basis	$1,100
Gain/(Loss)	$600

In **Example 12.6**, Kasey has a gain on the sale of the lawnmower, which is personal property and a Section 1231 asset. Section 1231 states that all gains on the sale of Section 1231 assets are capital gains, but before we can claim that for tax purposes we have to consider depreciation recapture under Section 1245. Section 1245 states that depreciation is recaptured as ordinary income to the extent of the gain. In this example, the depreciation Kasey took on the lawnmower was $400. His gain on the sale was $600. Since the gain of $600 is greater than the depreciation taken, the gain is split into two pieces. Under Section 1245, the gain to the extent of depreciation taken is ordinary income. Kasey took $400 of depreciation on the lawnmower, so the first $400 of the gain is treated as ordinary income. The remaining portion of the gain, $200, qualifies for capital gains tax treatment because the lawnmower is a Section 1231 asset. In this case, since Kasey recaptured all of the depreciation deductions that he had taken, the remaining gain is taxed as a capital gain under Section 1231.

Quick Quiz 12.3

1. If a Section 1231 asset is sold at a loss, the resulting loss is always a capital loss.
   a. True
   b. False
2. When a personal Section 1231 asset is sold at a gain, the gain is always ordinary income.
   a. True
   b. False

False, False.

In practice, it is rare to come across a situation like that illustrated in **Example 12.6**. Most assets purchased for productive use in a trade or business or for production of income are wasting assets – they tend to wear out as they are used to generate income. The very fact that they wear out is what justifies the depreciation deduction, which allows the taxpayer to recoup his capital as the asset is being used up to generate income. In some instances, this gain situation may occur, however. Using the facts of the current case, assume that the manufacturer of the lawnmower Kasey purchased made such good mowers that they eventually drove themselves out of business because nobody ever needed to purchase a replacement mower. Eventually, the company could not sell enough to justify continued operations, so it closed. Nevertheless, the reputation of the company's product persists, and people in the market for mowers will now pay a premium for one produced by that company since they anticipate that it will be the last mower they will have to purchase in their lifetime. Due to this fact, Kasey was able to sell the mower for more than he paid for it, despite the fact that he had claimed depreciation deductions. A more common example of this phenomenon occurs with investment real estate. Depreciation deductions are allowed on the structures purchased, even though, over time, those structures may tend to appreciate in value. The depreciation recapture rules for real property differ from those that apply to personal property and are covered in more depth later in this chapter.

In **Example 12.6**, observe that there is no decline in the value of the asset, so in the ideal world, no depreciation deductions should have been taken. The IRC, however, allowed Kasey to take depreciation deductions on the mower totaling $400. Since Kasey took those depreciation deductions against ordinary income, when he sells the mower for more than the amount he paid for it he will have to recapture the depreciation deductions by treating the first $400 of the gain as ordinary income. The remaining portion of the gain is capital gain, since the mower is a Section 1231 asset. **Example 12.6** is summarized below.

	Ideal World	*Real World*	*Notes for Real World*
Cost Basis	$1,500	$1,500	
Amount Realized	$1,700	$1,700	
Actual Decline	$0	$0	
Depreciation Deduction	$0	$400	Specified by IRC
Amount Realized from Sale	$1,700	$1,700	
Adjusted Basis	$1,500*	$1,100	$1,500 cost basis less $400 depreciation
Gain/Loss	$200	$600	$400 depreciation recapture plus $200 capital gain
Totals After 1231 Treatment			
Depreciation	$0	$0	$400 per IRC less $400 "recaptured" per Section 1231/1245

** The adjusted basis of the asset in the "Ideal World" example is calculated as follows: Cost Basis $1,500 – Depreciation Deduction $0 = $1,500.*

Another way of viewing the application of Section 1245 in this case is to compare the original cost basis (purchase price) of the asset to the sale price of the asset. If the sale price exceeds the purchase price, the difference between the sale price and purchase price will be treated as capital gain, and all of the depreciation will be recaptured as ordinary income under IRC Section 1245.

In fact, the only time that part of the gain on a Section 1231 asset will achieve capital gains treatment under Section 1245 is when the sales price of an asset exceeds the cost basis.

Example 12.6 illustrates the following rule: Whenever a personal Section 1231 asset is sold at a gain, compare the gain to the depreciation taken on the asset. If the gain exceeds the depreciation taken, Section 1245 treats the depreciation taken as ordinary income (and it is sometimes referred to as a Section 1245 gain), and Section 1231 treats the remaining gain as capital gain.

The prior example set illustrates why asset categorization is important and should always be the first step you consider when looking at the taxation of property transactions. If an asset is characterized as a personal Section 1231 asset (personal asset used in a trade or business or for the production of income), there are four possible tax results, three of which are likely to occur in the real world that differ from the results that would apply if the asset was categorized as a capital asset or ordinary income asset. While the numbers can change, every transaction resulting from the sale of Section 1231 personal property must fall into one of these four categories. See **Exhibit 12.2**.

Exhibit 12.2 | Summary of Examples 12.3 - 12.6

	Example 12.3	*Example 12.4*	*Example 12.5*	*Example 12.6*
Amount Realized	$1,100	$1,000	$1,200	$1,700
Adjusted Basis	$1,100	$1,100	$1,100	$1,100
Gain/(Loss)	$0	($100)	$100	$600
Tax Impact	None	Ordinary loss	Ordinary gain (Gain is less than depreciation taken.)	Part ordinary gain ($400), part capital gain ($200) (Gain is more than depreciation taken.)
Economic Reality	Depreciation estimate was perfect.	Taxpayer took too little depreciation.	Taxpayer took too much depreciation.	Taxpayer took too much depreciation and asset appreciated.

RECAPTURING DEPRECIATION TAKEN ON REAL ESTATE (SECTION 1250)

If real property used as a Section 1231 asset is sold, the recapture rules are a bit different. IRC Section 1250 governs recapture of depreciation on real property that is a Section 1231 asset. Under Section 1250, depreciation taken on real estate that exceeds straight-line depreciation is recaptured at ordinary income tax rates.

Key Concepts

1. Identify the property affected by Section 1250.
2. Define "unrecaptured Section 1250 depreciation."

Under current law, all depreciation on real estate is taken on a straight-line basis. If the real estate is used for residential purposes, the recovery period is 27½ years, and if the real estate is used as commercial property, the recovery period is 39 years. Real estate that was purchased and placed in service for production of income or for business use before 1981 or after 1986 must be depreciated on a straight-line basis. Unlike accelerated depreciation, **straight-line depreciation** allows the owner to take a constant, monthly allowance for depreciation during the recovery period. Since Section 1250 requires only the depreciation taken in excess of straight-line depreciation to be recaptured at ordinary income tax rates, real property placed in service before 1981 or after 1986 will not be affected by Section 1250.

Between 1981 and 1986, real estate placed in service for business or production of income use qualified for accelerated depreciation over a 15 - 19 year period. **Accelerated depreciation** allowed the owner of the property to front-load the depreciation deductions so that more of the depreciation deduction was taken in the early years, and less was taken in later years. When real property that was depreciated on an accelerated basis is sold, Section 1250 requires the excess depreciation, calculated by subtracting straight-line depreciation from accelerated depreciation, to be recaptured at ordinary income tax rates.

Section 1250 is quickly becoming a non-issue for income tax planning purposes. First, only real property that could have been depreciated on an accelerated basis will be affected by the provisions of Section 1250. As noted above, since 1986, real estate has not qualified for accelerated depreciation. Second, as time goes by, the total depreciation taken on an accelerated basis approaches the total depreciation taken on a straight-line basis, so that at the end of the recovery period, the total cumulative depreciation deductions taken by the taxpayer under either system are the same. The recovery period for almost all pieces of real property for which accelerated depreciation could have been claimed expired in 2016; therefore, the imposition of Section 1250 no longer results in additional tax revenue. It is a rare occurrence where an advisor will have to deal with Section 1250 for planning purposes, but it can still be an issue for compliance purposes. Section 1250 recapture applies to real property that has been owned for more than one year. If real property is held for one year or less, all depreciation taken (whether straight-line or accelerated) is subject to recapture rules.

Prior to the American Taxpayer Relief Act (ATRA 2012), capital gains were taxed at 15 or zero percent, except in two situations. The first exception, covered in Chapter 11, was a 28 percent capital gains tax rate on collectibles. The second exception was a 25 percent capital gains tax rate on **unrecaptured Section 1250 depreciation**. ATRA added a 20 percent capital gains rate for individuals in the 39.6 percent tax bracket. In addition, high income taxpayers are also subject to the 3.8 percent net investment income tax (discussed in Chapter 11). TCJA 2017 lowered maximum income tax rates to 37 percent for ordinary income but the 3.8 percent net investment income tax remains. In addition, the capital gains rates no longer perfectly align with the ordinary income tax rates.

Based on our discussion above, it is clear that depreciation in excess of straight-line depreciation is recaptured at ordinary income rates due to the imposition of Section 1250. Consequently, the depreciation that is not recaptured under Section 1250, otherwise known as the "unrecaptured Section 1250 depreciation," is straight-line depreciation. The recapture of straight-line depreciation taken after 1997 on real estate used as a Section 1231 asset is taxed at a maximum 25 percent rate (plus net investment income tax, if applicable) upon the sale or exchange of the asset.

To the extent that the gain on the sale of real Section 1231 property exceeds the total depreciation taken (both the "excess" portion from accelerated depreciation and the straight-line portion), any remaining gain is taxed at capital gains tax rates, as set forth in IRC Section 1231. An alternative way of looking at this is that capital gain tax treatment is limited to the excess of the sale price over the original purchase price.

From a planning standpoint, whenever a real Section 1231 asset is sold, the gain will be treated as shown in **Exhibit 12.3**.

Exhibit 12.3 | Treatment of Gain Under Section 1231 for Real Property

1. The smaller of the gain or the difference between depreciation taken and straight-line depreciation will be taxed as ordinary income. (This is recapture of "excess" depreciation under Section 1250).
2. If the gain exceeds the amount in (1), the smaller of the remaining gain or the straight-line depreciation taken on the property will be taxed at 25% (this is the "unrecaptured Section 1250 depreciation").
3. Any gain in excess of (1) and (2) is taxed at long-term capital gains tax rates (0%, 15%, or 20%) plus the net investment income tax of 3.8%, if applicable.

Example 12.7

Lorna owns a residential apartment building, and has grown weary of the constant management issues that confront her concerning the property. She purchased the property for $750,000, and took depreciation deductions of $400,000. Assume that straight-line depreciation on the property would have been $375,000. What are the tax consequences if Lorna sells the property for $2,000,000?

As a threshold matter, we are dealing with a residential apartment building, which Lorna used for the production of income. Therefore, the asset is real property used for production of income, is depreciable, and is therefore classified as a Section 1231 asset. Since the property is real estate, the depreciation recapture rules that apply will be found under Section 1250.

Before we can apply the depreciation recapture rules, however, we must first calculate the gain or loss generated on the sale. Using the formula for calculating gain or loss found in IRC Section 1001, we find the following:

Amount Realized	$2,000,000
Less: Adjusted Basis	$350,000
Gain/(Loss)	$1,650,000

Adjusted basis, in this example, equals the cost basis of $750,000 less the depreciation deductions actually taken of $400,000.

The next step is to determine if any of the gain will be taxed at ordinary rates under Section 1250. In this case, Lorna took $400,000 of depreciation deductions, and straight-line depreciation would have been $375,000. Therefore, Lorna took $25,000 in excess depreciation deductions. This amount is recaptured as ordinary income under Section 1250.

$25,000 of the $1,650,000 gain has been characterized as ordinary income, leaving $1,625,000. The next step is to subject the unrecaptured Section 1250 depreciation to a tax rate of 28.8% (since Lorna's adjusted gross income will exceed the threshold for the imposition of the 3.8% net investment income tax).

Lorna took total depreciation deductions of $400,000 and $25,000 of that amount was recaptured under Section 1250. Consequently, the $375,000 of straight-line depreciation was not recaptured under Section 1250, and will be taxed at 25% plus the 3.8% net investment income tax (NIIT).

The remaining portion of the gain, $1,250,000 will be taxed at long-term capital gains tax rates (plus the 3.8% NIIT) due to the imposition of Section 1231. These steps can be summarized as follows:

Sale Price Adjusted Basis Gain	$2,000,000 ($350,000) **$1,650,000**	Total Gain = $1,650,000	
Amount of Gain	(1st) $25,000	(2nd) $375,000	(3rd) $1,250,000
Treatment of Gain	Ordinary Income	28.8% Tax Rate	Capital Gain
Explanation of Calculation and Treatment	Excess Depreciation (Total Depreciation less Straight-Line Depreciation)	Straight-Line Depreciation taxed at 28.8%	Excess Gain under Section 1231 as Capital Gain

Purchase Price	**$750,000**	
Less Depreciation	($400,000)	(Straight-line depreciation would be $375,000)
Adjusted Basis	**$350,000**	
Sales Price	$2,000,000	
Less Adjusted Basis	($350,000)	
Gain	$1,650,000	
Less Ordinary Income	($25,000)	(Recapture accelerated vs. straight-line depreciation)
Less 25% Tax Rate	($375,000)	(For straight-line depreciation)
Section 1231 Gain	**$1,250,000**	(Note: 1231 Gain is sales price > Purchase price)

Example 12.8

Bennett sold a residential apartment building that he owned for $800,000. He originally purchased it for $800,000. Bennett had taken a total of $400,000 in depreciation deductions over the period he held the real estate. The straight-line depreciation would have been $375,000. What is the tax result of Bennett's total gain of $400,000?

Bennett's excess depreciation is $25,000 (total depreciation of $400,000 less straight-line depreciation of $375,000), which is subject to recapture under Section 1250 at ordinary income tax rates. The remainder of the gain ($375,000) is taxed at the unrecaptured Sec. 1250 gains rate, plus the net investment income tax, because it represents the straight-line depreciation. There is no capital gain (1231).

Example 12.9

Assume the same facts as **Example 12.8**, except that Bennett sells the property for $850,000. What are the tax consequences?

As noted above, the first $25,000 will be recaptured under Section 1250 at ordinary income tax rates. The $375,000 of Bennett's $450,000 gain will be taxed at the unrecaptured Sec. 1250 gains rate, plus the net investment income tax, since this amount represents unrecaptured Section 1250 depreciation. The remaining $50,000 is Section 1231 capital gain.

In **Example 12.8**, none of the gain qualifies for the favorable long-term capital gains tax rates. Those rates can only apply once all of the depreciation is recaptured under Section 1250 or taxed as an "unrecaptured Section 1250 gain."

An alternative way of approaching the taxation of real Section 1231 assets is to recognize that the difference between the amount realized and the original purchase price equals the capital gain. Recall that this rule also applies for personal Section 1231 assets.

In **Example 12.7**, Lorna paid $750,000 for the property and she sold it for $2,000,000. The difference of $1,250,000 is taxed as a capital gain under Section 1231.

Quick Quiz 12.4

1. Real property placed in service after 1986 is generally not subject to depreciation recapture.
   a. True
   b. False
2. Unrecaptured Section 1250 depreciation is equal to the lesser of the gain or the straight-line depreciation.
   a. True
   b. False

True, True.

The next step is to split the depreciation taken on the property into two pieces: the straight-line depreciation that is taxed at 25 percent and the depreciation in excess of straight-line that is taxed at ordinary income tax rates.

In **Example 12.7**, straight-line depreciation would have been $375,000. This amount will be taxed at the unrecaptured Section 1250 depreciation tax rate. Excess depreciation was $25,000 ($400,000 of depreciation taken, less straight-line depreciation of $375,000), which will be taxed at ordinary rates as recapture under Section 1250.

CASE STUDY 12.1

1250 Recapture

Philip and Margery Skalka, Petitioners v. Commissioner of Internal Revenue, Respondent. T.C. Summary Opinion 2003-107 (July 29, 2003).

The IRS determined a deficiency of $4,860 in the Skalkas' federal income tax for the taxable year 1997. The cover page of the notice of deficiency shows a deficiency of $14,341 for the year at issue. The $9,481 discrepancy relates to tax previously assessed because of computational errors on the Skalkas' 1997 federal tax return. At trial, the parties orally stipulated that $32,029 of gain from the sale of business real estate, which was not included in income on the Skalkas' tax return, is includible in income as a capital gain. The testimony of Philip Skalka corroborated this further stipulation. However, the parties dispute at which capital gains tax rate the $32,029 capital gain is to be taxed.

The issue for decision for the 1997 taxable year is the capital gains tax rate applicable to the Skalkas' capital gains. Using Schedule D, Capital Gains and Losses, the Skalkas determined their 1997 federal income tax using the maximum capital gains rates. In the tax computation, the Skalkas reported $27,159 of unrecaptured Section 1250 gain, to which they applied a 25-percent capital gains tax rate. The Skalkas did not include the $32,029 of reported Section 1250 gain in the Schedule D tax computation. The Skalkas argue that the $32,029 of gain not previously included in income should be taxed at only 20 percent. The IRS asserts that the $32,029 is unrecaptured Section 1250 gain subject to a Section 1(h) tax rate of 25 percent. The Skalkas assert that long-term capital gains are taxed at a maximum 20-percent rate; therefore, the entire gain from the sale of their investment property should be taxed at only 20 percent. While the Taxpayer Relief Act of 1997 did reduce the maximum capital gains rate on net capital gains from 28 percent to 20 percent, the Skalkas' assertion fails to take into consideration all of the relevant changes made by the 1997 Act. The 1997 Act made several changes to the capital gains tax. For the 1997 tax year, the capital gains tax rates vary depending on the type, nature, and amount of the gain. In addition, the length of time the asset was held before its disposition and the date of the disposition affect the capital gains tax rates for 1997. Accordingly, the Skalkas claim that their entire gain from the sale of the property is taxed at a maximum rate of 20 percent is without merit. The Skalkas' claim is made without a clear understanding of Section 1(h) and its interaction with Section 1250. For the 1997 tax year, the maximum capital gains rate is generally 20 percent on the gain from the disposition of a capital asset held more than 18 months and sold after July 28, 1997. However, the 20-percent rate does not apply to unrecaptured Section 1250 gain, which is subject to a 25-percent tax rate.

On July 6, 1977, petitioners purchased a two-story residential property (investment property) at 7708 Bay Parkway, Brooklyn, New York. For approximately 20 years, petitioners rented the two-family investment property to various tenants. In addition, the testimony of Philip Skalka (petitioner) maintained his dental office on the second floor. Petitioner testified that he depreciated the investment property over a 20-year period.

CASE STUDY 12.1 CONTINUED

On October 27, 1997, petitioners sold the investment property for a gross sale price of $297,500. Petitioners reported the property sale on Form 4797, Sale of Business Property. On Form 4797, petitioners reported a cost or other basis in the property of $85,611.69 and depreciation allowed or allowable of $59,187.69. Accordingly, petitioners reported an adjusted basis of $26,242, for a total gain from the sale of $271,076. Petitioners further reported on Form 4797 that $32,029 of the total gain was from section 1250 property. Petitioners subtracted the $32,029 of reported section 1250 gain from the total gain amount to arrive at a capital gain of $239,047. Petitioners included the $239,047 of capital gain as income on their 1997 tax return. However, petitioners did not include the $32,029 of section 1250 gain in income.

The property is Section 1231 property. If, as here, the Section 1231 gains exceed the Section 1231 losses for the year, the gains and losses shall be treated as long-term capital gains and long-term capital losses, respectively. Accordingly, the gain the Skalkas recognized on the sale of the investment property is long-term capital gain. Pursuant to Section 1250(c), Section 1250 property is any real property subject to the allowance for depreciation that is not Section 1245 property. Therefore, the Skalkas' investment property is also Section 1250 property. Gain realized on the disposition of Section 1250 property is recaptured as ordinary income, rather than capital gains, to the extent that the depreciation amount allowed or allowable exceeds the amount of depreciation that would have resulted under the straight-line method. The 1997 Act amended Section 1(h) to include Section 1(h)(1)(B), which taxes unrecaptured Section 1250 gain at a capital gains tax rate of 25 percent. Pursuant to the pertinent part of Section 1(h)(6)(A), the term "unrecaptured Section 1250 gain" means the amount of long-term capital gain which would be treated as ordinary income if Section 1250(b)(1) included all depreciation.

Under the 1998 Act, the definition of unrecaptured Section 1250 gain was amended to include long-term capital gain that is not otherwise treated as ordinary income. The amendment to the definition took effect as if included in the 1997 Act. Therefore, for the 1997 tax year, if long-term capital gain is subject to Section 1250, the Section 1250 gain is recaptured at ordinary income tax rates, and the remaining depreciation claimed is unrecaptured Section 1250 gain taxed at the 25-percent rate.

Here, the parties have stipulated that none of the long-term capital gain attributable to depreciation claimed on the investment property is Section 1250 gain recaptured at ordinary income tax rates. Therefore, the remaining $32,029 of depreciation claimed is subject to the Section 1250 gain rules and the unrecaptured Section 1250 gain rules. However, since the parties have stipulated that none of the $59,188 of depreciation is to be recaptured as ordinary income under Section 1250, the entire $59,188 is considered unrecaptured Section 1250 gain. Accordingly, the $32,029 of gain at issue is unrecaptured Section 1250 gain subject to the capital gains tax rate of 25 percent.

THE IMPACT OF TAXATION OF BUSINESS ASSETS ON PLANNING

The depreciation recapture rules for business assets affect the tax rate that applies to gains on the sale of business assets. In addition, depreciation recapture must be considered when engaging in various types of tax planning. When assets subject to recapture are transferred, potential depreciation may be transferred as well.

Depreciation recapture may be an issue with any of the following types of transfers, which will be discussed briefly below:

1. Gifts
2. Nontaxable exchanges
3. Transfers at death
4. Charitable contributions
5. Installment sales

> ***Key Concepts***
>
> 1. Identify the types of transfers affected by depreciation recapture.
> 2. Explain the 5-year lookback rule.

Gifts

When property is gifted, the value of the gift is the fair market value of the property on the date of the gift, but the basis in the hands of the donee is typically the donor's basis, adjusted for any gift tax paid. Gifts are said to have a "carryover" basis, since the donor's basis is transferred to the donee. The same is true for depreciation recapture. If the donor held the asset for productive use in a trade or business or for the production of income, and depreciation was allowed on the asset, any recapture potential will carryover to the donee. If the gifted asset was personal property, the donee's gain, to the extent of the depreciation taken, will be taxed at ordinary income tax rates. If the gifted asset was real property, the excess depreciation to the extent of the gain will be taxed at ordinary income tax rates, the straight-line depreciation will be taxed at the unrecaptured Section 1250 gains rate and any remaining gain will be taxed at capital gains tax rates. Understanding that depreciation recapture will carryover may impact the donor's choice of the appropriate property to give to the donee.

Example 12.10

Nicky purchased a desk for use in his business. The desk cost $500, and Nicky has taken $250 of depreciation deductions on the desk. Nicky's daughter, Suzanne, is in college and needs a desk to work on her course assignments. Nicky transfers the desk to Suzanne when the fair market value of the desk is $260. No gift tax was paid on the transfer. After Suzanne finishes college, she sells the desk to her roommate for $300. What is Suzanne's gain, and how is it taxed?

Since Nicky gifted the desk to Suzanne, and the desk had a fair market value in excess of Nicky's basis ($250 = $500 cost basis - $250 in depreciation), Suzanne has a carryover basis in the desk of $250. Suzanne also has a carryover of the potential depreciation recapture (requiring the first $250 of gain to be taxed at ordinary income tax rates).

When Suzanne sells the desk, the gain can be calculated as follows:

Amount Realized	$300
Less: Adjusted Basis	$250
Gain/(Loss)	$50

In Suzanne's hands, the desk is a capital asset, which is normally subject to capital gains tax treatment. Simply looking at this fact might lead one to conclude that the gain will be taxed as a capital gain. Despite the fact that the asset is a capital asset in Suzanne's hands, she received the asset as a gift from Nicky, who held the asset, at least for a time, as depreciable personal property used in a trade or business. The potential recapture, therefore, carried over with the gift. Since Suzanne's gain is less than the potential recapture amount, the entire gain is taxed at ordinary income tax rates.

Given these facts, this result could be good or bad. If Suzanne does not have substantial income (she was a college student and was not working full-time), she may be in a low ordinary income tax bracket, perhaps 10 percent. If Nicky sold the desk for $300, he would have had to pay 24 percent on the gain (his marginal ordinary income tax rate), but Suzanne would only have to pay 10 percent on that same gain. From a family income tax planning perspective, gifting the desk was a wise strategy, since it reduced the income taxes that the family, as a group, has to pay. If Suzanne was in the 37 percent ordinary income tax bracket (and the sale would generate tax at a higher rate), Nicky may want to consider selling the desk and paying the tax himself (at the lower rate), and giving either the proceeds of the sale, or another asset, to Suzanne.

Nontaxable Exchanges

When property is exchanged for another property in a nontaxable exchange (such as a Section 1031 like-kind exchange, or a Section 1033 involuntary conversion), potential recapture on the asset carries over to the replacement property.

Example 12.11

Maritza owns an office building that was destroyed by a hurricane. She purchased the office building for $450,000, had taken straight-line depreciation deductions of $150,000, and the fair market value of the property at the time it was destroyed was $800,000. Maritza received a check from her property insurance carrier for $800,000 and immediately purchased a replacement office building for $850,000. Maritza's basis in the original building was $300,000 (equal to $450,000 cost basis less $150,000 in depreciation deductions), and she had potential unrecaptured Section 1250 depreciation in the original building of $150,000 (all depreciation had been straight-line). Since Maritza meets the requirements for nonrecognition of gain for an involuntary conversion, her adjusted basis in the old building, plus the potential recapture, will carryover to the new building. In this example, Maritza also put another $50,000 into the property, which will add to her basis (she paid $850,000 for the new property, but only received $800,000 from the insurance company – the other $50,000 had to come out of her after-tax income, so this amount increases her basis). Therefore, Maritza's basis in the new property is $350,000; she has $150,000 of potential unrecaptured Section 1250 depreciation from the old office building that will be taxed at the unrecaptured Sec. 1250 tax rate when she disposes of the replacement property in a taxable exchange.

Exchanging properties in like-kind exchanges under IRC Section 1031 or in involuntary conversions under IRC Section 1033 does not extinguish the potential depreciation recapture that applies to the original property. As depicted in the prior example, it postpones the potential recapture until a taxable exchange occurs.

Transfers at Death

One way for a taxpayer to eliminate potential depreciation recapture is to transfer property subject to recapture at the taxpayer's death, through their estate. Property transferred through the estate of a decedent receives a step-to fair market value in basis under IRC Section 1014, and, by receiving the step-to fair market value, depreciation recapture is extinguished. This fact can, in some planning situations, be valuable to consider. In the estate planning process, to the extent that a client will have assets included in his gross estate, holding those assets at death will eliminate the depreciation recapture. Other assets, not subject to recapture, could be used as gifts since all the gain will be taxed as capital gain. Structuring the transfer of the estate in this way may minimize the overall tax (income, estate, and gift tax combined) that is paid by a family on the transfer of their assets.

Charitable Contributions

Potential depreciation recapture may also affect the size of the charitable deduction a taxpayer may take for gifts of property to qualified charitable organizations. When a gift of tangible personal property or real estate is made to a charitable organization that will use that property in their charitable function, the deduction for income tax purposes is generally the fair market value of the property on the date of the gift. When property subject to depreciation recapture is given to a charitable organization, and the deduction would otherwise be based on the fair market value of the property, the fair market value (and the resulting income tax deduction) is reduced by the potential depreciation recapture on the asset. By making this adjustment, the government is indirectly recouping the depreciation taken by limiting the donor's income tax deduction.

Example 12.12

Prior to his retirement, Pablo owned and operated his own business (a sole proprietorship) for 30 years. He purchased a van for the business several years ago for $30,000. During the time that he used the van in his business, he took depreciation deductions of $10,000. When he closed the business, he kept title to the van personally. An animal rescue charity has been looking for a new van to be used to transport rescued animals, and thinks that Pablo's van would be ideal. Pablo has no use for the van, and has always supported animal rescue charities, so he decides to give the van to the charity. The value of the van at the time of the transfer is $17,000. Normally, Pablo would receive a $17,000 charitable deduction for a transfer of tangible personalty to a charity that will use it in its tax-exempt purpose, but this van has potential depreciation recapture, so the charitable deduction is reduced by the amount of the recapture. Pablo can take a charitable deduction of $7,000 ($17,000 FMV - $10,000 depreciation taken) for the gift he made to the animal rescue charity.

Installment Sales

Another planning device that can be affected by potential depreciation recapture on property is the installment sale (including, for our discussion here, regular installment sales, self-canceling installment notes (SCINs), and private annuities). Note that on October 18, 2006, the Treasury and the IRS proposed regulations pertaining to the taxation of private annuities under Section 72. These regulations, which have not been finalized, state that the seller's entire gain or loss must be recognized when an annuity is acquired in exchange for a substantially appreciated asset, rather than ratably over the seller's life expectancy. If these regulations are finalized without changes, they will have a significant detrimental effect on the utility of private annuities.

When an asset is transferred, gain is usually realized and recognized. Recognition of gain on the sale of an asset in return for an installment note can typically be deferred under the installment reporting provisions of the IRC. For example, if an asset is sold today, but equal principal payments plus interest will be made over a ten year period, the seller can elect to report 10 percent ($1/10^{th}$) of the gain he realized this year in each of the next ten years instead of paying tax on all of the gain in the year that realization occurs. Installment reporting of the gain is helpful from a planning standpoint, since it allows the taxpayer to smooth his or her income, report less of a gain in each year during the installment period (possibly staying in a lower tax bracket) and defer tax.

Example 12.13

On January 1 of this year, Tasha sold a piece of real estate to Yvonne for $150,000 under an installment note in which Yvonne would pay her 10% down, plus installment payments at the end of each year for the next nine years, at 8% interest. Tasha's basis in the property is $82,500 (for the sake of simplicity, assume no depreciation was taken). To determine the tax consequences for Tasha in the year of sale, the following steps will apply:

Step 1: Determine the gross profit. Tasha sold the property for $150,000 and her cost basis is $82,500, resulting in a gross profit of $67,500.

Step 2: Determine the gross profit percentage. The gross profit is $67,500 and the sale price is $150,000. $67,500/$150,000 = 45%.

Step 3: Determine the amount of the down payment that is subject to tax. The down payment is 10% x $150,000 = $15,000. Of this amount, 45% (the gross profit percentage) is subject to tax. 45% x $15,000 = $6,750 taxed as a capital gain. The remaining $8,250 is tax-free return of basis.

Step 4: Determine the amount of the annual payment. Using a financial calculator: PV = $135,000 (the sale price of $150,000 less the down payment of $15,000), I = 8, N = 9, solve for PMT (on END mode) = $21,610.76.

Step 5: Determine the tax treatment of the payment to be received on December 31 of the current year. The interest is $10,800 (8% on the outstanding balance of $135,000 during the year), taxed as ordinary income. The principal amount of the payment is $10,810.76 (payment of $21,610.76 less interest of $10,800). The profit portion of the principal payment is 45% x $10,810.76 = $4,864.84 to be included in income as capital gain. The remaining $5,945.92 is a tax-free return of basis.

The total tax consequence for Tasha in the year of sale is capital gain of $11,614.84 ($6,750 from the down payment + $4,864.84 from the end of year payment), plus ordinary income of $10,800 from the interest received as part of the end-of-year payment. She also received a tax-free return of basis equal to $14,195.92 ($8,250 from the down payment + $5,945.92 from the December payment).

The gross profit percentage will continue to apply to the principal portion of each subsequent payment, allowing each payment over the nine-year period to be taxed partially as capital gain and partially as tax-free return of basis, plus ordinary income on the interest portion of the payment.

The installment reporting provisions, however, do not apply to potential ordinary income depreciation recapture on Section 1231 property sold in return for an installment note. The ordinary income depreciation recapture, to the extent of the gain, must be recognized in the year the gain is realized. The unrecaptured Section 1250 depreciation may be deferred under the installment reporting provisions, but all of the gain in each installment reporting year will be taxed at the 25 percent unrecaptured Section 1250 rate until all of the straight-line depreciation has been recaptured. Once the portion of the gain representing unrecaptured Section 1250 depreciation has been fully reported, any remaining gain will be taxed at the applicable long-term capital gains tax rate, plus net investment income tax, if applicable.

Example 12.14

After 20 years of managing his rental apartment building, Sam decides it is time to retire from the landlord business – he no longer enjoys the hassles of management. He purchased the apartment building for $1,500,000 and $100,000 of the purchase price was allocated to land. Total depreciation taken on the building was $1,000,000 and straight-line depreciation would have been $800,000. The apartment complex is now worth $8,100,000. Sam has agreed to sell the apartment complex to a young business associate, Stella, for its current fair market value to be paid in an installment note over 20 years. The note carries an interest rate that matches the IRS published rate necessary to avoid gift-loan status. While Sam will be able to defer some of his gain over the 20 year period, the potential ordinary income depreciation recapture cannot be deferred. In this case, the potential ordinary income recapture is $200,000 ($1,000,000 in total depreciation less straight-line depreciation of $800,000). Despite the presence of the installment sale, Sam will be required to pay ordinary income tax on $200,000 in the year of sale. As Sam receives payments over the first several years, the gain portion of each payment will be treated as the unrecaptured Section 1250 gain ($800,000) and will be taxed at the unrecaptured Sec. 1250 gains tax (plus the net investment income tax) until the tax on the unrecaptured Section 1250 gain has been paid in full. Any remaining gain will be taxed at the long-term capital gain rate (plus net investment income tax).

Observe that this could create a cash flow problem for Sam. If Stella only pays 1/20th of the purchase price plus interest to Sam this year as the installment agreement requires, but Sam has to pay up to 37 percent on $200,000 in the year of sale, plus tax on the interest and the tax imposed on part of the unrecaptured Section 1250 gain received in this year's installment payment. Sam may not have sufficient cash flow from the sale necessary to meet all of his tax obligations. This could be an important consideration when recommending the structure of an installment sale to a client. For example, if a cash flow problem would occur, Stella could make a down payment equal to (at a minimum) the tax that will be due as a result of the recapture. This would ensure that Sam does not have to utilize his other assets to pay the income tax on the sale.

As these examples illustrate, depreciation recapture is important in ways other than simply determining which tax rate applies. In many cases, the presence of potential depreciation recapture may change the planning options that may be optimal for the client. Understanding why this happens and the situations to be aware of allow advisors to give better, more competent advice to their clients.

Quick Quiz 12.5

1. Depreciation recapture carries over to the donee for gifted property.
   a. True
   b. False
2. Sales of tangible personalty but not involuntary conversions are affected by the carryover of depreciation recapture.
   a. True
   b. False
3. Depreciation recapture is extinguished upon death.
   a. True
   b. False
4. Under the 5-year lookback rule, net Section 1231 losses in the current tax year will be subject to ordinary loss rules to the extent of the 1231 gains of the last five years.
   a. True
   b. False

True, False, True, False.

The 5-Year Lookback Rule

The astute planner, having learned how the depreciation recapture rules work, might have spotted a potential planning opportunity. Similar to the netting process for capital gains, all Section 1231 gains for the year are added together, and all Section 1231 losses for the year are added together, and losses are offset against gains to determine the net Section 1231 gain or loss. Since gains are treated as capital gains (subject, at least for individuals, to a lower tax rate) and losses are treated as ordinary losses, it would be beneficial, from a tax planning standpoint, to generate Section 1231 losses in one year, and Section 1231 gains in another year. By separating gains and losses, all of the gains would be taxed at the lower capital gains tax rate in one year, and all of the losses will generate a tax benefit at a higher ordinary tax rate in another year instead of offsetting each other.

Unfortunately, Congress thought of this planning option as well. To help combat this form of planning, there is a **5-year lookback rule** that applies for Section 1231. The lookback rule states that a net Section 1231 gain in the current tax year (which should be taxed at capital gains tax rates) will be taxed at ordinary income tax rates to the extent of any unrecaptured Section 1231 losses claimed during the last five years. The lookback rule forces the netting process to occur over a five-year period. Note that for the lookback rule to apply:

1. there must be a net Section 1231 gain in the current year, and
2. there must have been Section 1231 losses in the last five years.

If there is a net Section 1231 loss in the current year, or if there are no unrecaptured Section 1231 losses in the last five tax years, the lookback rule does not apply.

Example 12.15

Blanca has a Section 1231 gain for the current year (2021) of $15,000. In prior years, Blanca had the following net Section 1231 transactions:

	Year	*Net Section 1231 Transaction*
5-Year Lookback Period	2020	$4,000 Section 1231 Loss
	2019	$2,000 Section 1231 Loss
	2018	No Section 1231 Transactions
	2017	No Section 1231 Transactions
	2016	No Section 1231 Transactions
	2015	$8,000 Section 1231 Gain
	2014	$2,000 Section 1231 Gain

Blanca would have to recognize $6,000 of her 2021 gain as ordinary income since in 2020 and 2019 she had Section 1231 losses. The remaining $9,000 of Blanca's Section 1231 gain ($15,000 - $6,000) would be treated as a Section 1231 capital gain.

KEY TERMS

5-Year Lookback Rule - A net Section 1231 gain in the current tax year (which should be taxed at capital gain tax rates) will be taxed at ordinary income tax rates to the extent of any unrecaptured Section 1231 losses claimed during the last five years.

Accelerated Depreciation - Allows the owner of an asset to front-load the depreciation deductions so that more of the depreciation deduction is taken in the early years, and less is taken in later years.

Depreciation Recapture - Special tax consequences that occur when a Section 1231 asset is sold for an amount greater than its adjusted basis.

Inventory - Assets that are held for resale to customers in the normal course of business.

Ordinary Income Assets - Accounts receivable, creative works in the hands of the creator, and inventory, all of which generate gains that will be taxed at ordinary income tax rates.

Personal Property - Any property that is not real property.

Real Property - Land and anything permanently attached to it (such as buildings, trees, and swimming pools).

Section 1231 Asset - Depreciable property or real property used for productive use in a trade or business or for the production of income.

Straight-Line Depreciation - A depreciation method under which the purchase price of the asset, less its expected salvage value, is divided by the expected useful life of the asset to determine the annual depreciation deduction.

Unrecaptured Section 1250 Depreciation - The portion of gain that is attributable to non-recaptured depreciation (up to the amount of straight-line depreciation deductions taken) for depreciable real estate that is taxed at a maximum 25 percent upon the sale or exchange of the property (plus the net investment income tax of 3.8% if applicable).

DISCUSSION QUESTIONS

SOLUTIONS to the discussion questions can be found exclusively within the chapter. Once you have completed an initial reading of the chapter, go back and highlight the answers to these questions.

1. What is an ordinary income asset?
2. Describe the taxation of ordinary income assets for noncorporate taxpayers.
3. What is a Section 1231 asset?
4. What is the advantage of being classified as a Section 1231 asset?
5. How are corporations affected by Section 1231 assets?
6. What is the purpose of depreciation recapture?
7. What is the difference between real and personal property?
8. What are the four possible results when personal property used in a trade or business or for the production of income is sold?
9. How is depreciation recaptured under Section 1250?
10. What is the difference between straight-line depreciation and accelerated depreciation?
11. Why is Section 1250 not as important to tax planning as it used to be?
12. What is unrecaptured Section 1250 depreciation, and how is it taxed?
13. How is gain from the sale of a Section 1231 real property asset treated?
14. How is depreciation recapture affected when a Section 1231 asset is gifted?
15. How is depreciation recapture affected by a nontaxable exchange of a Section 1231 asset?
16. What happens to potential depreciation recapture when the owner of a Section 1231 asset dies?
17. How can a charitable contribution be affected by potential depreciation recapture?
18. What are the tax consequences when a Section 1231 asset is sold in an installment sale?
19. How can potential depreciation recapture create a cash-flow problem for the seller of an asset in an installment sale?
20. Describe the impact of the 5-year lookback rule.

MULTIPLE CHOICE PROBLEMS

A sample of multiple choice problems is provided below. Additional multiple choice problems are available at money-education.com by accessing the Student Practice Portal.

1. Janae, a 12 year old middle school student, just agreed to take over a paper route to deliver Newsday to her extended neighborhood on a daily basis. To deliver the papers, she purchases a new bike with a specially equipped basket to transport the papers each morning. How is the bike classified for income tax purposes?
   a. The bike is an ordinary income asset.
   b. The bike is a capital asset.
   c. The bike is a Section 1231 asset.
   d. The bike is a personal asset.

2. Custom Framing, Inc., a C corporation, sold a wood cutting machine used in their business for $2,700. They originally purchased the machine for $2,000 and had taken $1,400 in depreciation deductions. When the company that made the machine went out of business, the machine became a collectors item, and the company sold the machine for more than they paid for it to purchase other equipment. Which of the following statements concerning the tax impact of the sale transaction is correct?
   a. The company will recognize $2,100 of ordinary income.
   b. The company will recognize $1,400 of ordinary income.
   c. The company will recognize a capital gain of $700 that will be taxed at the favorable long-term capital gains tax rate.
   d. The company will recognize a short-term capital gain of $700.

3. Ten years ago, Joel purchased an industrial sewing machine used in his business, Danbury Dolls, LLC, for $10,000. He had taken depreciation deductions of $9,000 over this period, and sold the machine for $12,000 after he purchased a new state-of-the-art industrial sewing machine. How much ordinary income will Joel recognize on the sale of the machine?
   a. $0.
   b. $1,000.
   c. $9,000.
   d. $11,000.

4. Leanne purchased an apartment building for $2 million several years ago. She has claimed depreciation deductions totaling $950,000 during the holding period, and straight-line depreciation would have been $900,000. What is Leanne's long-term capital gain (taxed at the highest capital gains tax rate) that will be recognized for income tax purposes if she sells the building for $2.5 million?
   a. $0.
   b. $50,000.
   c. $500,000.
   d. $1,450,000.

5. After 35 years in business for herself, Freida retired and closed the doors of her office. She gave her desk to her nephew, Desi, who recently completed his degree in a similar field and is opening up his practice. Freida originally paid $12,000 for the desk, and it was fully depreciated by the time she gave it to Desi. Desi used the desk for two years, and then sold it (for $6,000) when he decided to redecorate his office. How will Desi treat the proceeds from the sale of the gift for income tax purposes?
    a. Since Desi received the desk as a gift, there is no need to pay taxes on the proceeds from the sale.
    b. Since the desk was given to Desi when it was fully depreciated, it is "loss property," and the $6,000 proceeds will not be taxable because it fell between Desi's gain basis and loss basis in the transaction.
    c. Desi will recognize $6,000 of ordinary income on the sale.
    d. Desi will recognize $6,000 of long-term capital gain on the sale.

Additional multiple choice problems are available at *money-education.com* by accessing the Student Practice Portal. Access requires registration of the title using the unique code at the front of the book.

QUICK QUIZ EXPLANATIONS

Quick Quiz 12.1

1. True.
2. False. Unlike a capital loss, an ordinary loss may be taken against ordinary income and is not subject to limitations.

Quick Quiz 12.2

1. True.
2. False. Gains on Section 1231 assets will qualify for the long-term capital gains tax rate because the owner of the asset held the asset for more than one year (recall that a long-term holding period is required for an asset to be categorized as a Section 1231 asset).
3. True.
4. False. Depreciation recapture applies upon the sale or exchange of a Section 1231 asset.

Quick Quiz 12.3

1. False. If a Section 1231 asset is sold at a loss, the resulting loss is treated as an ordinary loss.
2. False. When personal property is used in a trade or business or for the production of income, it is depreciable and therefore becomes a Section 1231 asset. When that property is sold, Section 1245 governs the depreciation recapture rules. Simply put, Section 1245 states that when personal Section 1231 property is sold, depreciation is recaptured as ordinary income to the extent of the gain. Gain in excess of depreciation is then taxed at capital gain rates.

Quick Quiz 12.4

1. True.
2. True.

Quick Quiz 12.5

1. True.
2. False. Sales of tangible personal property and involuntary conversions are subject to depreciation recapture that applies to the original property.
3. True.
4. False. The lookback rule states that a net Section 1231 gain in the current tax year (which should be taxed at capital gains tax rates) will be taxed at ordinary income tax rates to the extent of any Section 1231 losses claimed during the last five years.

13
NONTAXABLE EXCHANGES

LEARNING OBJECTIVES

1. Identify assets for which like-kind exchange treatment is available.*
2. Describe the requirements for like-kind exchange treatment.*
3. Calculate the tax consequences of like-kind exchange treatment.*
4. Describe the tax consequences of an involuntary conversion.*
5. Compare the requirements for like-kind exchanges under Section 1031 to involuntary conversions under Section 1033.
6. Identify the tests for characterizing replacement property for an involuntary conversion.
7. Identify the appropriate replacement period for various types of involuntary conversions.*
8. Identify the insurance policies that can be exchanged under Section 1035, and what they can be exchanged for without triggering recognition of gain.*
9. Describe the tax impact of re-possession of property subject to an installment note.
10. Discuss the tax treatment of transfers between spouses pursuant to a divorce.*
11. Explain the requirements for an exclusion of gain under Section 121.*
12. Describe the circumstances for which a reduced Section 121 exclusion is permissible.*
13. Calculate the Section 121 exclusion for a given taxpayer.*
14. Describe the impact of the Section 121 exclusion on depreciation recapture from a rental property that was later converted to a principal residence of the taxpayer.*
15. Describe the tax consequences of death benefits and loans from life insurance policies.*
16. Identify situations where the transfer for value rule applies, and state the five exceptions to the transfer for value rule.*
17. Identify the tax consequences of distributions from Roth IRAs and Roth accounts in 401(k) plans, 403(b) plans, and governmental 457(b) plans.*

**Ties to CFP Certification Learning Objectives*

INTRODUCTION

The 16th Amendment to the U.S. Constitution gives Congress the power to tax all income "from whatever source derived." Generally speaking, any accretion to wealth is income. A mere increase in the value of an asset, however, does not subject the wealth accretion to current taxation. As illustrated in prior chapters, a realization event (which fixes the taxpayer's gain or loss) must occur before the income must be recognized on the taxpayer's income tax return.

While Congress has the power to tax all income when realized, in some cases it has chosen to defer the collection of tax on that income. In other cases, Congress has decided not to tax the income at all. This chapter reviews those circumstances where a realized gain or loss is deferred, as well as the rare circumstances where realized gains are exempt from income tax. Even though gains from these realization events could be subject to current tax, Congress has chosen to defer or forgo that revenue for public policy reasons. Usually, the decision to defer or exempt taxation is an indication that Congress feels that either the activities that generate the gains should be encouraged, or it would be unfair to subject that income to tax at the current time.

LIKE-KIND EXCHANGES (SECTION 1031)

Key Concepts

1. Identify assets for which like-kind exchange treatment is available.
2. Describe the requirements for like-kind exchange treatment.
3. Identify the tax consequences of a like-kind exchange.

Perhaps the best known tax deferral transaction technique is the **like-kind exchange**, permitted under Section 1031 of the IRC. Prior to 2018, deferral of gain was permitted under Section 1031 for exchanges of trade or business equipment as well as for exchanges of real estate. For years after 2017, this deferral technique is now limited to real estate transactions (TCJA 2017). The Section 1031 exchange is embedded in one of the most popular board games of all time – Monopoly. In Monopoly, players trade little green houses for big red hotels. In real estate markets, investors often trade real estate properties to increase or decrease their position in real estate, and, if they follow the rules of Section 1031, they can often defer part or all of their gain to a future tax period.

A like-kind exchange resulting in tax deferral provides a benefit to investors by allowing the taxpayer to keep all of the proceeds of the sale and thus reinvest the full proceeds in a new property. By not paying the tax currently, the taxpayer is indirectly borrowing at a zero percent interest rate from the U.S. government, and hopefully generating greater returns on the investment.

Assets Subject to Like-Kind Exchange Treatment

As a threshold matter, like-kind exchange treatment after 2017 is only available for real property assets held for productive use in a trade or business, or for the production of income. This rule is consistent with a general theme in income taxation – only those items held to produce income that the U.S. government can tax will qualify for special tax benefits. Assets held for personal use do not qualify for like-kind exchange treatment. The sale of assets held by a taxpayer for personal use resulting in a realized gain must generally be recognized in the year of sale (unless special exceptions apply, such as the IRC Section 121 exclusion of gain on the sale of a principal residence). As discussed in prior chapters, losses from the sale of personal use assets are not deductible by the taxpayer.

Exhibit 13.1 | Assets that Qualify for Like-Kind Exchange Treatment

- Assets held for trade or business
- Assets held for production of income

Note: Personal use assets (e.g., personal residences) do NOT qualify for like-kind exchange treatment. However, personal residences are afforded special tax treatment under IRC Section 121.

Example 13.1

Winston owns 1,000 shares of Coca-Cola common stock. He believes that Pepsi has better current marketing programs, and anticipates that Pepsi will capture part of Coke's market share. Winston sells his 1,000 shares of Coca-Cola stock and reinvests the proceeds in Pepsi. While he has purchased and sold shares of stock in a similar industry, the transaction will not qualify for like-kind exchange treatment because the property is not real property. Winston will be required to recognize any gain that he realized on the sale of the stock.

CASE STUDY 13.1

Like-Kind Exchanges

Ralph E. Crandall, Jr., and Dene D. Dulin, Petitioners v. Commissioner of Internal Revenue, Respondent. T.C. Summary Opinion 2011-14 (February 15, 2011).

Ralph and Dene owned an undeveloped parcel of property with a basis of $8,500 in Lake Havasu City, Arizona, which was held for investment. On March 4, 2005, Ralph and Dene sold the property for $76,000. $10,000 was paid to Ralph and Dene, and the remaining $66,000 was placed in an escrow account with Capital Title Agency, Inc. Capital Title released $4,256.75 to Ralph and Dene, retaining $61,743.25 in escrow. The Capital Title escrow agreements did not reference a like-kind exchange under IRC Section 1031, nor did they expressly limit Ralph and Dene's right to receive, pledge, borrow, or otherwise obtain the benefits of the funds. The funds in the escrow account, plus additional deposits, were used to purchase an investment property in California. While Ralph and Dene treated the sale and purchase as a like-kind exchange under IRC Section 1031, the IRS asserted that the sale of the Arizona property was a taxable exchange, and assessed a tax deficiency.

The Tax Court stated that they had no doubt that Ralph and Dene intended to engage in a deferred like-kind exchange. Citing prior cases, however, the court noted that "it is well established that a taxpayer's intention to take advantage of tax laws does not determine the tax consequences of his transactions." Treas. Regs. §1.1031(k)-1(f)(2) states that "The taxpayer is in constructive receipt of money or property at the time the money or property is credited to the taxpayer's account, set apart for the taxpayer, or otherwise made available so that the taxpayer may draw upon it at any time." If a taxpayer has constructive receipt over sale proceeds, a deferred like-kind exchange is not permitted, and gain must be recognized on sale. To avoid constructive receipt, a taxpayer can use a qualified escrow account, as specified in the Treasury Regulations. A qualified escrow account is an escrow account where: (1) the escrow holder is not the taxpayer or a disqualified person; and (2) the escrow agreement expressly limits the taxpayer's right to receive, pledge, borrow, or otherwise obtain the benefits of the cash or cash equivalent held in the escrow account. While the Court found that the Arizona and California properties were like-kind properties, the escrow agreement did not contain the limitations necessary to avoid constructive receipt. Consequently, the court concluded that like-kind exchange treatment was not available, and the gain on the sale of the Arizona property must be recognized.

Taxpayers who wish to engage in like-kind exchanges must strictly follow the rules set forth in the IRC and Treasury Regulations to avoid constructive receipt of sale proceeds in a deferred like-kind exchange.

Requirements for Like-Kind Exchange Treatment

Like-kind exchange treatment, when available, is mandatory; the taxpayer may not choose whether to subject the transaction to current taxation or defer the gain or loss into the future. If a taxpayer would like to increase his basis for depreciation purposes, or anticipates higher capital gains tax rates in the future, recognition in the current year may be a better choice than deferral under Section 1031. Taxpayers who wish to subject their gains to current taxation should make sure that they avoid one or more of the requirements necessary to qualify for like-kind exchange treatment under Section 1031.

Example 13.2

Rose has a large carryforward loss that she realized from a recent stock market correction. She also owns a single family rental property, and has decided to purchase an apartment complex. If Rose engages in a tax-deferred exchange under Section 1031, her basis and, therefore, her depreciation deductions, will carryover to the new property. Of course, any additional funds she invests to purchase the larger rental property unit results in an increase in her basis. As an alternative, if Rose intentionally structures the transaction so that it does not qualify for tax-deferral treatment, she can offset the gain on the sale of her rental property with her carryforward loss. When she purchases the new property, the entire cost (less the portion that represents land) will be depreciable, increasing the current depreciation deductions Rose can take on the property.

Example 13.3

Curtis is considering the sale of a residential rental property that he owns, and may decide to invest the proceeds in another piece of real property. Under current law, capital gains tax rates are relatively low, and Curtis is unsure whether they will stay at that level in the future. Instead of deferring his gain into another property and potentially subjecting the gains to tax at a future higher capital gains tax rate, Curtis would like to pay the tax on any gain he realizes on the current property now. In order to do this, Curtis would have to ensure that at least one of the requirements necessary to trigger deferral under Section 1031 is not met.

Like-Kind Property

To qualify as a like-kind exchange, the asset received in the exchange must first be of the same nature and character as the asset given up in the exchange. Section 1031 does not require that the properties have similar uses. Since 2018, only real property held for investment or production of income can be exchanged tax-deferred under Section 1031.

When real property is exchanged, the type of property given or received will not matter, provided it is used for trade or business purposes, or for the production of income. Raw land held for investment, for example, could be exchanged for an apartment building, or an apartment building could be exchanged for an industrial warehouse. As long as the property is being used to generate taxable income, it will qualify for like-kind exchange treatment. One limitation on the tax-deferred exchange of real estate involves the transfer of U.S. real estate for foreign real estate. U.S. real estate and foreign real estate are not **like-kind assets** for income tax purposes, so a gain or loss realized on the transaction must be recognized in the year of transfer. However, foreign real estate is considered a like-kind asset when exchanged for other foreign real estate.

Example 13.4

Darrel inherited a piece of raw land from his great-grandfather, and decided to convert that property to income-producing property. Darrel later traded his raw land for an apartment building of equal value. Since he engaged in an exchange of like-kind property (realty for realty), any gain he realized on the raw land as of the date of the sale will be deferred into the apartment building under Section 1031.

Example 13.5

Blanche owns a hotel in Salem, Massachusetts. She has always wanted to own real estate abroad, and an opportunity arose for her to purchase the Killarney Hotel in Ireland. Both properties are worth the same amount of money, so Blanche trades her hotel in Salem for the Killarney Hotel. Despite the fact that both properties were used in a trade or business or for the production of income, U.S. and foreign real estate are not like-kind assets, and therefore Blanche must recognize any gain she realizes on the Salem hotel in the year of the transfer.

While it is possible to engage in a tax-deferred Section 1031 exchange by the simultaneous swapping of two properties, doing so would be almost impossible. It is unlikely that a taxpayer will be able to find an available property that he or she wants, while at the same time holding the property that the other party wants to obtain. Often, Section 1031 exchanges are completed in two transactions, separated by time, which is referred to as a non-simultaneous exchange. The requirements that must be met in order to defer the gain on the property transferred in a non-simultaneous exchange are summarized in **Exhibit 13.2**.

Exhibit 13.2 | Requirements for Deferral of Gain Under Section 1031

- The proceeds from the sale of the original property must be held by a qualified intermediary escrow agent (the proceeds may not be received by the property owner wishing to engage in the 1031 exchange).
- A replacement property must be identified within 45 days of the sale of the original property.
- The closing of the replacement property must take place by the earlier of (1) 180 days from the sale of the original property, or (2) the due date (including extensions) of the tax return for the year the original property was sold.

To obtain tax-deferred exchange treatment, these requirements must be strictly observed. Any deviation from the requirements will result in immediate recognition of any realized gain.

Related-Party Transactions

One additional situation that may result in a change to the normal rules associated with like-kind exchanges is a related-party transaction. If a like-kind exchange of property occurs between related parties, and either related party disposes of the property received in the exchange within two years, any deferred gain is recognized in the year of disposition. The deferred gain will not be accelerated upon disposition of property received in a like-kind exchange between related parties if the disposition is due to the death of a related party, or due to an involuntary conversion (discussed later in this chapter). A **related party** (defined under Section 267(b)), includes brothers and sisters (of the whole and half blood or adopted), ancestors, and descendants. A spouse is considered a related party as well, but all transactions between spouses result in a carryover basis (under Section 1041), so the provisions of Section 1031 do not apply to spousal transactions. In a business context, a related party also includes a controlled corporation (a corporation in which the taxpayer owns more than 50 percent of the equity interest), or, for example, two corporations who are members of the same controlled group.

Example 13.6

Dallas, owner of a large apartment building, engaged in a like-kind exchange with his son, Cade, who owned a smaller rental property. Part of the gain on Dallas's large apartment building was deferred in a like-kind exchange under Section 1031 into the new, smaller property. The next year, Cade announced that he sold the apartment building he received in a like-kind exchange. Since Cade was a related party, and he disposed of the property received in the like-kind exchange within two years of the transfer, Dallas will be required to recognize any remaining gain he realized on the transfer of the large apartment building in the same year.

Example 13.7

Sophia owns 55% of the equity interest in Cimbel Corporation. Sophia and Cimbel agree to enter into a like-kind exchange of a high-rise condominium owned by Cimbel for a warehouse owned by Sophia. Sophia subsequently sells the high-rise condominium 18 months later. Cimbel will be required to recognize the deferred gain on the transfer of the high-rise condominium since Sophia is a related party (a taxpayer who owns more than 50 percent of the equity interest in the corporation) and the property received in the like-kind exchange was sold within two years of the original exchange transaction.

Tax Consequences of Like-Kind Exchanges

When considering the tax consequences of a Section 1031 exchange, it is helpful to think of an investment as a single investment solution. To visualize this, picture a beaker containing a chemical solution in a laboratory. The first layer of solution in the beaker is the cost of the investment, which becomes the taxpayer's adjusted basis and is reduced over time by any depreciation deductions.

Example 13.8

Ten years ago, Keegan purchased a residential rental property for $200,000. He has taken $70,000 in depreciation deductions over his holding period, resulting in an adjusted basis of $130,000. Graphically, Keegan's investment solution would look like this:

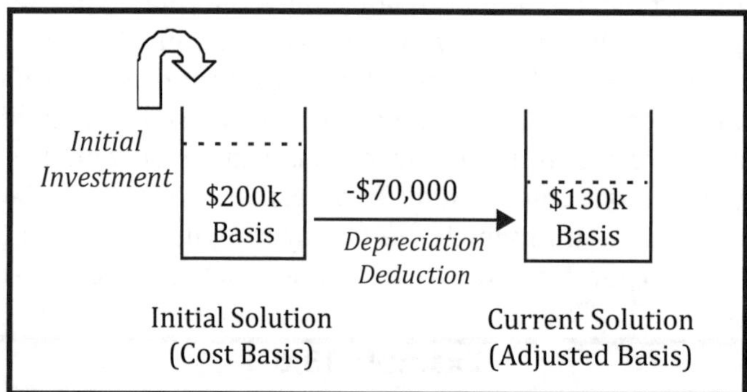

Over time, the value of some investments tends to increase, adding a second layer to the investment solution that represents unrealized gain on the investment.

Example 13.9

Assume that the building Keegan purchased now has a fair market value (FMV) of $450,000. Keegan's investment solution would appear as follows:

FMV	$450,000
Less Adjusted Basis	$130,000
Potential Gain	**$320,000**

This text refers to deferred or unrealized gain or loss as potential gain or loss.

In allowing realized gains on assets transferred in a like-kind exchange to be exempt from current taxation, Congress is recognizing that while the asset held by the taxpayer is changing, the taxpayer's investment solution is the same. Alternatively stated, swapping assets, as long as those assets comprise the same investment solution, does not trigger gain recognition.

The tax consequences of engaging in a Section 1031 exchange will depend on the property received in the exchange. If the only asset the taxpayer receives in a like-kind exchange is like-kind property, there will be no immediate tax consequence. The taxpayer's basis in the original property, and his or her holding period, will carryover to the new property. If an additional investment is made to acquire the new property, the additional investment amount will increase the acquiring taxpayer's basis.

Example 13.10

Continuing with our example, assume that Keegan decides to swap his rental property for a larger rental property. The property he is interested in acquiring is worth $600,000. Keegan gives his current property, worth $450,000, plus $150,000 in cash, for the new property. Provided that Keegan meets the requirements for a tax-deferred like-kind exchange, his new investment solution will be as follows:

Before Exchange		*Keegan Adds Cash to Basis	After Exchange	
FMV	$450,000		FMV	$600,000
Basis	$130,000	→	New Basis*	$280,000
Potential Gain	**$320,000**	$150,000	**Potential Gain**	**$320,000**

Note that Keegan is trading up – he is adding to his investment solution. Since he qualified for like-kind exchange treatment, all of his potential gain in the old property is carried over to the new property (it stays in the investment solution), but Keegan's basis in the investment has been increased by $150,000. The basis increase results from his transfer of $150,000 of additional capital into the investment solution. Keegan's holding period will not be determined by referring to the length of time he held the asset, but rather to the length of time he held the investment solution.

Whenever a taxpayer engages in an exchange and receives only like-kind property, the tax treatment under Section 1031 defers all gain realized on the transfer. This type of exchange will occur when the taxpayer engages in an equivalent value exchange, or trades up. The only change that occurs when the taxpayer trades up is his or her basis in the investment solution increases.

Boot

If a taxpayer receives non-like-kind property in exchange for the asset, he is not keeping all the assets in the same investment solution. Non-like-kind property received in an exchange, which may come in the form of cash, property, or debt, is referred to as **boot**. The recognition rule that applies when boot is received is that any realized gain is taxable to the extent of boot received. The taxpayer has "booted" part of the investment into another investment solution, so that portion of the gain will be subject to tax. This rule applies when the taxpayer is trading down, or decreasing his investment in a particular investment solution.

Example 13.11

Instead of trading his $450,000 property for a $600,000 rental property, Keegan decides to engage in an exchange where he will receive a property worth $350,000 plus $100,000 in cash. Based on these facts, Keegan is trading down, which means that the gain, to the extent of boot received, is subject to income tax. The transaction could be illustrated as follows:

Before Exchange (Old Property)		After Exchange (New Property)	
FMV	$450,000	FMV	$350,000
Basis	$130,000	Carryover Basis	$130,000
Potential Gain	**$320,000**	**Potential Gain**	**$220,000**

Boot Received $100,000 (Cash)

Recognized Gain $100,000

Since Keegan traded down, he has booted $100,000 out of the investment solution. When this happens, the top layer of the investment solution, the deferred gain in the property, is reduced by a like amount, and is contemporaneously recognized for income tax purposes. Keegan's basis in the like-kind property received remains $130,000 (the basis is carried over, since the amount booted out of the solution did not dip into the basis layer), and his basis in the "boot" (cash, in this case) is $100,000 since that amount was subject to income tax recognition.

Recall that the recognized gain may be subject to income tax at different rates. If the asset exchanged is real estate, the gain realized may be treated partly as a Section 1250 gain (for recapture of excess depreciation on real estate), partly as unrecaptured Section 1250 depreciation (taxed at a 25% rate, plus the 3.8 percent Affordable Care Act surtax, if applicable), and partly as capital gain. Refer to the rules on taxation of business assets for review of these concepts.

Note that in the above example, Keegan has still deferred part of his gain under Section 1031. The gain remaining in the investment solution was realized on the transfer, but will not be recognized. Whenever boot is received, deferred gain (top layer) is recognized to the extent of boot received. If the boot received exceeds the deferred gain, the taxpayer will reduce his basis in the replacement property by a like amount. This portion of the boot (the excess) will not be subject to income tax.

Quick Quiz 13.1

1. Assets held for personal use qualify for like-kind exchange treatment.
   a. True
   b. False
2. IRC Section 1031 requires that exchanged properties have the same use.
   a. True
   b. False
3. If the only asset a taxpayer receives in a like-kind exchange is like-kind property, there will not be any immediate tax consequences.
   a. True
   b. False

False, False, True.

Example 13.12

Instead of trading his $450,000 property for a $600,000 rental property, Keegan decides to engage in an exchange where he will receive a property worth $100,000 plus $350,000 in cash. Based on these facts, Keegan is trading down, which means that the gain, to the extent of boot received, is subject to income tax.

The transaction could be illustrated as follows:

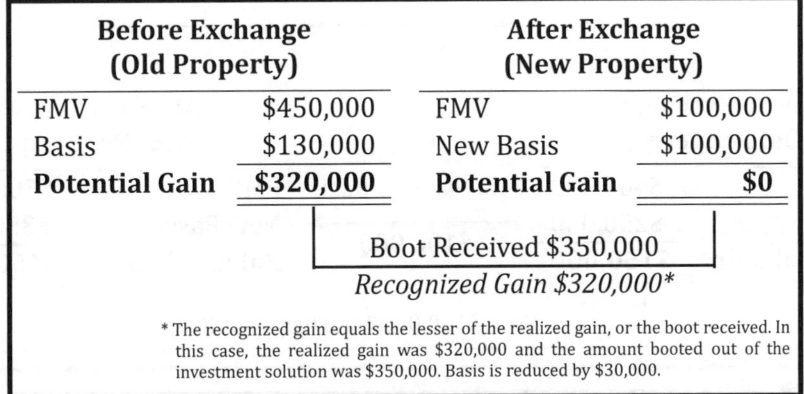

Before Exchange (Old Property)		After Exchange (New Property)	
FMV	$450,000	FMV	$100,000
Basis	$130,000	New Basis	$100,000
Potential Gain	**$320,000**	**Potential Gain**	**$0**

Boot Received $350,000

*Recognized Gain $320,000**

* The recognized gain equals the lesser of the realized gain, or the boot received. In this case, the realized gain was $320,000 and the amount booted out of the investment solution was $350,000. Basis is reduced by $30,000.

As this example illustrates, once the top layer of the investment solution - the deferred gain - has been recognized for income tax purposes, the remaining boot received is treated as a return of basis and is not taxable, and the potential gain in the new asset is zero.

Assumption of Debt

One last important issue to review concerning the taxation of like-kind exchanges is the consequences of liability relief, or liability assumption, as part of the exchange transaction. In some real estate transactions, the mortgage on the real estate is transferred with the property. When a mortgage is transferred with the property, the party transferring the mortgage is treated as having received boot equal to the amount of debt relief, and the party undertaking the mortgage obligation is treated as giving boot. The IRC treats the transaction this way since liability relief is the equivalent of receiving cash (boot) in the exchange, followed by use of the cash to pay off the outstanding liability.

Example 13.13

Reilly and Ryan engage in a like-kind exchange. Reilly transfers real estate with a fair market value of $400,000 and an adjusted basis of $250,000 to Ryan. Ryan transfers real estate worth $500,000 and an adjusted basis of $200,000, plus a $100,000 mortgage on the property, to Reilly. Including the mortgage, the exchange is an equivalent economic value transfer. The following illustrates the tax consequences for Reilly and Ryan:

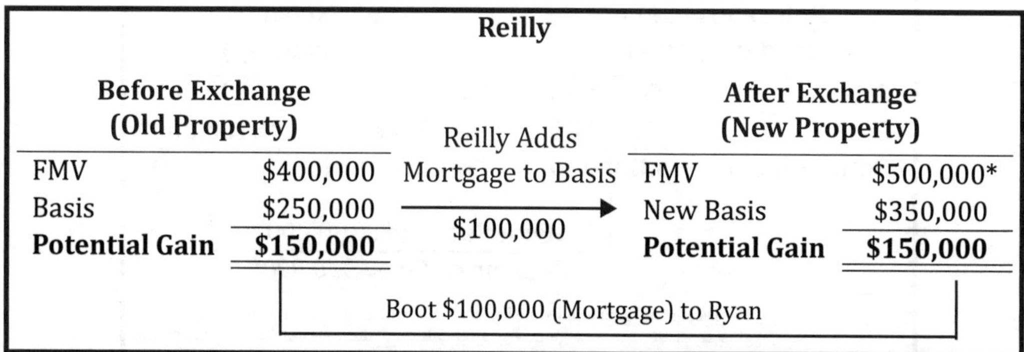

Ryan

Before Exchange (Old Property)		**After Exchange (New Property)**	
FMV	$500,000*	FMV	$400,000
Basis	$200,000	Carryover Basis	$200,000
Potential Gain	$300,000	**Potential Gain**	**$200,000**

*Subject to Mortgage

Boot Received $100,000 (Mortgage) from Reilly

Recognized Gain equal to debt relief of $100,000

Since Reilly was trading up, there is no recognized gain. Reilly's basis equals his basis in his original investment, plus the $100,000 in debt that he assumed in the Section 1031 exchange. Reilly will have to pay the $100,000 debt back with after-tax dollars, so the full amount of the loan will increase his basis in the investment solution. After the transaction, Reilly has a building with a fair market value of $500,000 and an adjusted basis of $350,000.

Ryan traded down in this transaction – he gave up a property with a fair market value of $500,000 and received a like-kind property with a fair market value of $400,000. Ryan will be able to defer part of his gain under Section 1031, but the portion of the transaction that represents liability relief will be recognized. Instead of simply transferring the liability, Ryan could have received $100,000 in cash in the transaction, and paid off the outstanding debt. If Ryan had received the $100,000 in cash, it would have been treated as boot and would be taxable to the extent of the gain. The tax result should not be different when liabilities are relieved.

Losses on Section 1031 Exchanges

So far, we have reviewed the rules covering the recognition/nonrecognition of gain when a transaction qualifies for like-kind exchange treatment. The rule is a little different for losses under a like-kind exchange. In this case, receiving boot does not result in recognition of a realized loss, but rather a reduction of basis.

Example 13.14

Ten years ago, Dorothy purchased a residential rental property for $200,000. She has taken $70,000 in depreciation deductions over her holding period, resulting in an adjusted basis of $130,000. The fair market value of the property is $120,000. Dorothy engages in a Section 1031 exchange for a new property worth $100,000, and receives cash in the amount of $20,000.

The transaction could be illustrated as follows:

Before Exchange (Old Property)		After Exchange (New Property)	
FMV	$120,000	FMV	$100,000
Basis	$130,000	New Basis*	$110,000
Potential Loss	**($10,000)**	**Potential Loss**	**($10,000)**

*Basis Reduced by Boot

Cash Boot Received $20,000

No Gain or Loss Recognized

Since losses on Section 1031 exchanges are not recognized, the $20,000 in boot must be taken out of the basis layer of the investment solution. After the transaction, Dorothy has a property with a fair market value of $100,000 and an adjusted basis of $110,000 resulting in a deferred loss of $10,000. (An alternative way to calculate the basis on a Section 1031 exchange resulting in a realized loss is to take the fair market value of the replacement property, and add the disallowed loss. In this case, the fair market value of the replacement property is $100,000 and the disallowed loss is $10,000, resulting in a basis of $110,000.) No loss can be recognized on the exchange. The loss will be recognized when the replacement property is eventually sold which is one advantage to a Section 1031 deferral of losses.

The following exhibit summarizes the income tax consequences of a Section 1031 exchange.

Exhibit 13.3 | Tax Consequences of a Section 1031 Exchange

1. Determine whether the taxpayer is trading up or down. Taxpayers who receive only like-kind property in the exchange will not have any current income tax consequences. The basis that they have in their investment solution is increased by any additional capital investment made in the investment solution.
2. The party trading down (receiving less like-kind property than given up) is required to recognize gain to the extent of any boot received. If the boot received exceeds the gain, the amount of the boot in excess of gain is treated as a return of capital.
3. Debt relief is treated as boot, requiring gain recognition for the party no longer responsible for the debt. The party assuming the debt will increase their basis in the replacement property by an amount equal to the debt assumed.
4. Losses realized in a like-kind exchange are not recognized until the replacement property is sold. The taxpayer's basis in the replacement property equals the fair market value of the property received in the exchange plus any disallowed loss.

EXCHANGE OF STOCK FOR PROPERTY (SECTION 1032)

When a corporation receives money or property in return for its stock (including common, preferred, and treasury stock), no gain or loss is recognized. Sale of stock to investors is treated as an infusion of capital, and is not subject to income tax under Section 1032.

INVOLUNTARY CONVERSIONS (SECTION 1033)

In some cases, a taxpayer may not voluntarily choose to transfer property and cause a realization event to occur for income tax purposes. Instead, either a natural disaster or a government action converts their property to cash proceeds (through insurance proceeds for the destruction of property due to a natural disaster or eminent domain payments received when the government takes the taxpayer's property). When a realization event is outside of the control of the taxpayer, the event is referred to as an **involuntary conversion**. Examples of involuntary conversions include natural disasters (e.g., hurricanes, tornadoes, or fires), theft, condemnation, seizure, or sale of property under threat of condemnation. In all of these instances, the taxpayer does not have control over the timing of the realization event. Consequently, Congress has determined it would be unfair to subject the taxpayer to income tax on the gain realized if the taxpayer reinvests those proceeds in a like-kind investment. Granting taxpayers time to reinvest the proceeds of such events is consistent with the general philosophy embedded in the law of like-kind exchanges. Voluntary acts, such as destruction of the property by the taxpayer, however, will not qualify for involuntary conversion treatment.

Key Concepts

1. Define involuntary conversion.
2. Identify the tests for characterizing replacement property.
3. Define the reinvestment period.

To avoid recognition of the gain on an involuntary conversion, the taxpayer must invest the proceeds in a replacement property that has a similar use to the property that was involuntarily converted. Note that the similar use requirement under Section 1033 differs from the property class requirement that is normally associated with Section 1031 like-kind exchanges. Two different rules for characterizing the replacement property apply, depending on how the original property was held by the taxpayer.

If the owner of the property also used the property, the **functional use test** applies. The functional use test requires the replacement property to serve the same functional use as the original property in order for any gain realized to be deferred.

Example 13.15

Neville owned a warehouse in New Orleans that he used to store his company's product for distribution to customers. A hurricane destroyed the warehouse and Neville used the insurance proceeds to purchase a new warehouse to store his company's product for distribution to customers. Since the replacement property had the same functional use (warehouse facility for his company) as the original property, Neville will be able to defer recognition of gain. Had Neville invested the insurance proceeds in manufacturing facilities, in rental properties, or in any property which could be "used" in a different capacity, he would be required to recognize gain at the time of conversion.

If the owner of the property did not use the property directly, but rather held the property for investment, the **taxpayer use test** applies. The taxpayer use test requires replacement property to be used by the taxpayer in an activity which is treated the same for income tax purposes (i.e., real property held for investment) as the property that was lost, in order for any gain realized to be deferred.

Example 13.16

Nola owned a warehouse in New Orleans that she leased to several local businesses. After sustaining damage in several hurricanes in the past, it was completely destroyed by Hurricane Katrina. Nola decided that she did not want to reinvest in New Orleans, but instead took her insurance proceeds and purchased an apartment building in Michigan. Both of the properties were rental properties. Since Nola was an owner-investor in the old warehouse and also in the new apartment building, she will be able to defer recognition of the gain if she purchases the apartment building within the statutory period.

Under IRC Section 1033, the taxpayer must reinvest the proceeds from the involuntary conversion within a statutorily specified period in order to defer the realized gain. The **reinvestment period** varies depending upon the type of conversion the taxpayer experienced. The default reinvestment period begins on the date of conversion and ends on the last day of the tax year that is two years after the realization event. This gives the taxpayer two years from the end of the year in which the realization event (not the date of conversion) occurred to replace the property with similar use property. When considering the impact of the nonrecognition rules, the date of the conversion does not matter. Instead, the last day of the year in which the realization event occurs starts the two-year time period.

Example 13.17

Gordie owned a summer home in Florida, which was destroyed by a hurricane on August 1, 2021. Gordie paid $150,000 for the home, and it was insured for its full fair market value of $275,000, and he received the payment from the insurance company on October 1, 2021. Receipt of the check from the insurance company is the realization event; therefore, to avoid recognition of gain on the Florida home, Gordie must replace the property with other similar use property by December 31, 2023. If Gordie had received the check from the insurance company on January 5, 2022, he must replace the property with other similar use property by December 31, 2024. As we will more fully discuss later in this chapter, Gordie will not qualify for the Section 121 exclusion of gain on the property, since he did not use the property as his principal residence.

A special rule applies to involuntary conversions due to governmental action, or condemnation. When a property is condemned by the local, state, or national government through the eminent domain process, the taxpayer has one additional year to find replacement property in order to avoid recognition of gain. Therefore, instead of two years from the end of the year in which the realization event occurred, the taxpayer has three years from that time to purchase the replacement property.

Example 13.18

Teddy owned a summer home in Florida. The State of Florida condemns the property, paying Teddy the current fair market value of the property on January 5, 2021. Teddy has until December 31, 2024 to reinvest the proceeds in a replacement property in order to avoid recognition of gain on the conversion.

Another special rule applies to natural disasters that destroy principal residences. If the natural disaster becomes a Presidentially designated disaster, then the replacement period is four years instead of two.

Quick Quiz 13.2

1. The sale of property as a result of the owner's bankruptcy is an example of an involuntary conversion.
   a. True
   b. False
2. Replacement property must only satisfy the functional use test.
   a. True
   b. False
3. Taxpayers who lose property by eminent domain have three years from the date of the conversion to replace the property.
   a. True
   b. False

False, False, False.

When the involuntary conversion results in a replacement of the converted property with new property, nonrecognition treatment is mandatory. This type of transaction is sometimes referred to as a direct conversion. If cash is received, non-recognition treatment is available at the election of the taxpayer and this type of conversion is sometimes referred to as an indirect conversion. To avoid nonrecognition treatment in an indirect conversion, however, the taxpayer must refrain from purchasing a like-kind replacement property within the statutory period. Avoiding nonrecognition may be appropriate when a taxpayer has large carryforward losses, or expects capital gains tax rates to increase in the future.

Example 13.19

Teddy owned a summer house in Florida. The State of Florida condemns the property, giving Teddy a piece of beach-front property in a resort location that has a value of $600,000 within the statutory period. While Teddy's original property was only worth $375,000, none of the gain on the conversion will be recognized, because there was a direct conversion of the property.

Example 13.20

Vern, a vice president at The Phoenix Company, fancied himself as an investment guru, and made large investments in trendy stocks right before the last market decline. As a result, Vern realized over $1,000,000 in capital losses. Vern is 67 years old, and has decided he has had enough with the stock market, so he will not make any future equity investments. Vern will be permitted to use $3,000 of his loss each year against his other taxable income. Recently, the State of California condemned Vern's vacation home to put in a new 12-lane highway, and paid Vern $750,000 for his property. His basis in the property was $200,000. Instead of electing nonrecognition treatment, Vern could wait to replace the property for three years from the end of the year the realization occurred, and use his carryforward loss to offset his $550,000 of capital gain. When Vern purchases a new vacation property in the future, his basis will be equal to his investment in the house.

Example 13.21

Jules owned a vacation home in Avalon, NJ that was destroyed by a storm surge on August 1, 2021. Jules believes that Congress will increase capital gains rates in the near future due to pressing budget concerns. Instead of buying a replacement property, Jules waits until the statutory period expires, and triggers recognition of gain.

The bottom line with involuntary conversions is that since the taxpayer has no control over the timing of gain realization, extra time should be afforded to allow the taxpayer to replace the property and defer the gain.

INSURANCE POLICIES (SECTION 1035)

As client needs and objectives change, it may be appropriate to change the insurance coverages that the client maintains to better serve the client's goals. Some insurance products have cash-value features, which permits amounts invested to grow on a tax-deferred or tax-free basis. Absent a special rule allowing deferral of gain, the surrender or sale of an insurance product would result in realization of gain or loss on the contract. IRC Section 1035 provides an opportunity to exchange insurance products for like-kind products while deferring recognition of gain.

Key Concepts

1. Identify the three insurance products subject to Section 1035.
2. Describe which products can be exchanged without triggering recognition of gain.

There are three types of insurance products that can be exchanged in a way that will avoid gain recognition. These products include life insurance contracts, modified endowment contracts, and annuities.

Life insurance contracts are contracts where the insurance company promises to pay a specified amount upon the death of the insured. In return for this promise, the insured pays a premium, often on an annual basis over a period of years or for his or her lifetime. One of the attractive features of a cash value life insurance policy is that lifetime and death benefits on the policy are income tax free if the policy remains in force until the death of the insured. At certain times it may be suitable to replace a client's life insurance policies as costs may change within the policy or the client's needs may change. IRC Section 1035 permits a taxpayer to defer any gain recognition and retain the tax benefits of the old policy within the new policy.

Modified Endowment Contracts (MECs) are also life insurance contracts, but these life insurance contracts have taxable lifetime benefits because they were paid up too quickly. To prevent individuals from using life insurance contracts as a vehicle to temporarily defer tax on investment growth, Congress came up with a set of rules that defines a MEC as a life insurance policy that does not pass the 7-pay test or the corridor rule. These tests and rules are complex, and are beyond the scope of this text. As a consequence of the MEC rules, when the owner of a modified endowment contract takes a policy loan, the policy loan will trigger recognition of income to the extent that there is gain on the policy. Policy loans from a life insurance policy that has not been classified as a MEC will not trigger recognition of income as long as the policy remains in force. Death benefits on MECs, like non-MECs, are income tax free if received by reason of the death of the insured, provided that there has not been a transfer-for-value (discussed later in this chapter).

Annuity contracts allow individuals to invest a lump sum or stream of payments with an insurance company, and defer recognition of income on the investment growth inside the contract until the owner begins to take distributions from the annuity. All distributions of growth from an annuity contract are taxed at ordinary income tax rates. Annuity contracts are Income in Respect of a Decedent (IRD) assets, and therefore do not qualify for a step-up in basis on the death of the owner. This means that any gains distributed from an annuity contract are subject to income tax. Out of the three types of insurance contracts covered under IRC Section 1035, annuity contracts are the least favorable, since all of the gains will be subject to income tax at ordinary rates.

Quick Quiz 13.3

1. Of the three types of insurance contracts, life insurance contracts offer the best tax benefits to owners.
   a. True
   b. False
2. A MEC may be exchanged for either a MEC or an annuity, but it may not be exchanged for a life insurance policy.
   a. True
   b. False

True, True.

From an income tax standpoint, of the three types of insurance contracts covered under IRC Section 1035, modified endowment contracts are not quite as good as life insurance policies (since lifetime benefits may trigger income tax), but are better than annuity contracts (since the death benefit, if received by reason of the death of the insured, is income tax free). **Exhibit 13.4** illustrates the three contracts on a ladder, with the most tax advantageous contract at the top, and the least tax advantageous contract at the bottom.

Exhibit 13.4 | Insurance Products Ladder

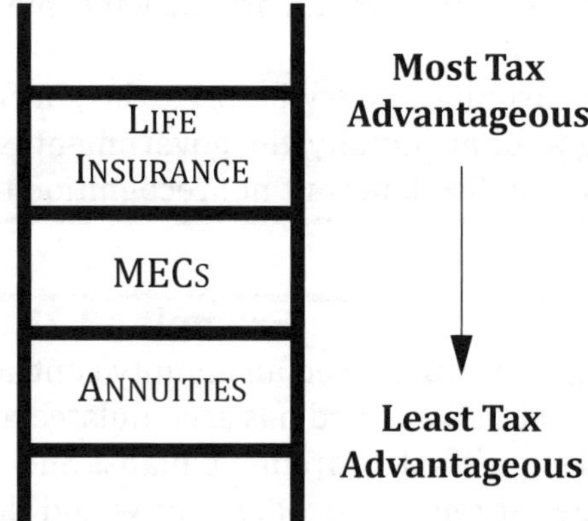

Under IRC Section 1035, the exchange of insurance contracts will achieve nonrecognition treatment if the contract is replaced with another contract of the same type, or with another type of contract that is lower on the ladder than the contract given up. A simple way to remember this rule is that the exchange is allowed if the result is neutral or better for the government, but not if it is better for the taxpayer. The following table shows how insurance contracts can be exchanged without causing recognition of gain:

Exhibit 13.5 | Exchanging Insurance Products

This type of contract:	*May be exchanged without tax recognition for:*
Life Insurance	Life Insurance Modified Endowment Contract Annuity
Modified Endowment Contract	Modified Endowment Contract Annuity
Annuity	Annuity

As **Exhibit 13.5** illustrates, when a client exchanges something that would be tax free for something that will create ordinary income, there is no immediate recognition of gain. However, there will be a recognition of gain if the contract given up in the exchange created ordinary income and the new contract has tax-free benefits.

Example 13.22

Demi owns a life insurance policy that she purchased when her children were young to provide security for her family in the event of her early death (in particular, the policy was intended to pay off the mortgage, pay for children's college, and provide retirement income to her spouse). She does not need the policy for estate planning purposes, and she has paid off her mortgage, finished paying for her children's college education, and has fully funded her retirement. Demi would like to supplement her retirement income to allow her to travel a bit more frequently, and she exchanges the life insurance policy for an annuity. The exchange of the policy will not cause recognition of gain, since Demi is exchanging a tax-free contract for an ordinary income contract.

If she kept the life insurance policy in force, the government would not tax the benefits, but by exchanging it for an annuity, the government is now able to subject the growth to income tax. Section 1035 will permit nonrecognition treatment in this case.

Example 13.23

Early in her career, Demi purchased an annuity contract to partially fund her retirement. Demi has been very successful, and has accumulated a substantial amount of wealth both inside and outside qualified retirement plans. She does not really need the annuity contract to provide retirement income, and would like to convert the annuity contract into a life insurance policy. She paid $30,000 for the annuity, and it is currently worth $100,000. If Demi surrenders the annuity to purchase the life insurance policy, she will have to recognize the $70,000 realized gain. Demi cannot avoid gain recognition when going up the insurance ladder – it is only possible to avoid gain recognition when going down the insurance ladder.

CORPORATE RECAPITALIZATIONS (SECTION 1036)

Corporate recapitalizations are often used to achieve estate planning and business succession planning goals for small and family-owned businesses. Typically, the recapitalization involves a restructuring of equity interests from voting common stock to nonvoting common stock in the same corporation. IRC Section 1036 states that a shareholder does not recognize gain or loss upon recapitalization of a corporation when common stock is exchanged for other common stock in the same corporation, or when preferred stock is exchanged for other preferred stock in the same corporation.

Example 13.24

Denny owns 100% of Emerald Isle, Inc., and would like to gift shares to his children to facilitate his estate plan. Denny is concerned, however, about the influence that his children's spouses may have on the business. Prior to gifting shares of stock to his children, Denny recapitalizes the corporation, and receives one voting share and 9 non-voting shares of common stock for every 10 shares of common stock he currently holds in the company. He gives the non-voting shares to his children, and keeps the voting shares. Denny will not be required to recognize gain on the recapitalization, since he exchanged common stock for other common stock in the same corporation.

In most cases, recapitalizations that involve an exchange of common stock for a combination of common and preferred stock usually result in recognition of gain for income tax purposes.

REACQUISITIONS OF REAL PROPERTY (SECTION 1038)

A common way of deferring gain on the sale of appreciated property is to structure an installment sale. Under the installment reporting provisions, a taxpayer can elect to pay the tax on the realized gain over the life of the installment obligation. Installment sales are often used in family situations, and in some estate planning situations to:

1. allow the purchaser of the asset (usually a younger generation family member) to pay for the asset at least partly with the income generated by the asset, and
2. permit the senior generation to defer a large part of the gain and recognize it ratably over the life of the installment note to smooth their taxable income over the years.

One feature of an installment sale that is particularly attractive for older-generation family members is the ability to take a security interest in the property sold subject to the installment note. Particularly in situations where the seller is relying on the payments to fund or supplement their retirement income, a security interest is necessary. If the purchaser stops making the agreed-upon payments, the seller may repossess the property so that the property can be resold, or the income on the property can be used as a substitute for the installment note income.

Under IRC Section 1038, repossession of property subject to an installment note will not cause recognition of the remaining, deferred gain on the property. When the repossessed property is sold, any remaining gain will be taxed at that time.

Example 13.25

Andie, a recently retired small business owner, decided to sell her office building to her daughter, Trina. Andie needs to supplement her retirement income, so she sells the office building to Trina on an installment sale basis. Andie's gain on the building was $1,000,000, which, per the amortization schedule, will be recognized in $100,000 increments over the 10-year installment note. Three years after the office building was sold, Trina declares bankruptcy and defaults on the note. Andie repossesses the building in satisfaction of the note. At the time she repossessed the building, she had recognized $300,000 of the $1,000,000 gain under the installment reporting provisions, leaving $700,000 of gain that still needs to be recognized. Since Andie repossessed the building, IRC Section 1038 will allow her to defer the remaining $700,000 gain until she sells the building.

CASE STUDY 13.2

Transfers During Marriage and Incident to Divorce

John L. and Myrna L. Parsley, Petitioners, v. Commissioner of Internal Revenue, Respondent, T.C. Summary Opinion 2011-35 (March 24, 2011).

John, a real estate broker, married Myrna, a real estate agent, in 2000. This was Myrna's second marriage. Her ex-husband, Joseph, purchased a property for $320,000 in June, 1990 while married to Myrna, that was titled in his name alone. In 1992, Myrna found out about this, and confronted Joseph, at which time he deeded her an undivided interest in the property as a tenant in common. In 1998, Joseph and Myrna divorced, and as part of the divorce settlement, Joseph was ordered to deed his remaining ownership interest in the property to Myrna, making her the sole owner of the property. Joseph quitclaimed his remaining interest in the property to Myrna in September, 2000.

In 2006, Myrna sold the property for $700,000. She told her tax preparer that she did not know what the basis in the property was, but had estimated the fair market value of the property for purposes of taking depreciation deductions of approximately $500,000. Myrna used this amount for calculating gain, resulting in a reported capital gain of $256,272. The IRS recomputed the capital gain on sale, and determined it to be $488,071. The record in the case did not include details on the depreciation deductions claimed, which explains the difference in the gain calculated by both the taxpayer and the IRS and the purchase/basis numbers reported.

The court found that Myrna's basis in the property was $320,000 - not the $500,000 that she used for taking depreciation deductions. Citing §1041, the court noted that the transfer of property in 1992 during her marriage to Joseph, and the transfer in 2000 that was ordered pursuant to their divorce resulted in a carryover basis. Section 1041 provides that for the carryover basis provisions to apply, the transfer must occur within one year after the date of the cessation of the marriage or must be "related to the cessation of the marriage." (§1041(c)). After finding that the transfer was related to the cessation of their marriage, the court determined that a carryover basis applied, and sustained the IRS' determination of capital gain. The court also permitted the IRS to assess an accuracy related penalty for failure to properly report the gain in large part because "the petitioner's experience, knowledge, and education strongly suggest that she either knew or should have known that the basis on which petitioners computed their gain from the sale of the property in 2006 was inflated."

TRANSACTIONS BETWEEN SPOUSES INCIDENT TO DIVORCE (SECTION 1041)

Under IRC Section 1041, all transactions between spouses or incident to a divorce result in a carryover basis and a carryover of holding periods.

Example 13.26

Prior to getting married, Phoebe owned a beach house worth $1,000,000. Her basis in the beach house was $400,000. To restructure their estates, Phoebe sells the beach house to her husband, Joey, for $1,000,000. Three years later, Joey sells the home for $1,200,000, and his taxable gain is $800,000. Despite the fact that Joey paid $1,000,000 for the property, Phoebe's basis was carried over to him when he purchased the home, since Phoebe and Joey were married at the time.

Example 13.27

Ross and Rachel are getting divorced. As part of the divorce settlement, Rachel receives a vacation home worth $800,000 that the couple paid $300,000 for many years earlier. Rachel's basis in the home is $300,000. If she sells the property, she will recognize gain to the extent any sale proceeds from the home exceed this amount.

SALE OF PERSONAL RESIDENCE (SECTION 121)

Perhaps the most widely used type of nontaxable exchange occurs when an individual sells his or her principal residence. IRC Section 121 excludes up to $500,000 of the gain from the sale of a principal residence from income tax if certain requirements are met.

The amount of the available exclusion will depend on the filing status of the individual who claims the exemption. For married couples filing jointly, up to $500,000 of any gain is excluded from income tax. All other individuals may exclude up to $250,000 of any gain from income tax. A gain on the sale of a principal residence in excess of these amounts is subject to income tax, typically as long-term capital gains.

Key Concepts

1. Explain the requirements for an exclusion of gain under Section 121.
2. Describe the circumstances under which a reduced exclusion is available.
3. Compute the reduced exclusion.

Qualifications

To qualify for the exclusion of gain under IRC Section 121, two requirements must be met. First, the taxpayer must have owned and used the home as his principal residence for two out of the last five years (the ownership and use test). Ownership implies that the taxpayer holds title to the home outright, or the home is owned by a grantor trust.[1] If the home is owned by a partnership, family limited partnership, or irrevocable trust, the taxpayer is not deemed to own the home for purposes of claiming the Section 121 exclusion.[2] Second, to claim the exemption, the taxpayer must not have excluded gain on the sale of

1. Ltr. Rul. 199912026.
2. Ltr. Rul. 200029046 and Ltr. Rul. 200104005.

a principal residence within the last two years. An individual will qualify for this exclusion as often as the individual can meet these two requirements.

Example 13.28

At the time of his retirement, Chandler owned a principal residence and a vacation home. Needing some rest and relaxation, Chandler moves into his vacation home, and, after two and a half-years, decides that he really enjoys living there and will sell his principal residence. Chandler knows that he must meet the two out of five year rule in order to exclude the gain on the sale of his principal residence, so he immediately puts his old home on the market, and sells it by the close of the year. He is able to exclude all of the gain on the sale of the home under Section 121. In January of the following year, Chandler and his wife decide that they are growing weary of keeping up the large vacation home that has now become their principal residence, so Chandler puts that home up for sale as well, hoping to be able to move into a smaller residence. The second home sells after Chandler and his wife have been in the home for three years. Even though they meet the two out of five year requirement, Chandler and his wife will not be able to exclude the gain on the sale of his current residence from income tax under IRC Section 121 because they had excluded the gain from the sale of a principal residence in the prior tax year.

Example 13.29

Monica, who is single, recently retired and decided to move from New York, where she has been living for the past 15 years, to Connecticut. She immediately sells her home in New York, and realizes a $250,000 gain. Despite the fact that Monica has a realized and recognized gain of $250,000, IRC Section 121 exempts the gain from being taxed because Monica has used the home as her principal residence for two out of the last five years. In addition, if Monica were married, up to a $500,000 gain would be considered nontaxable. Absent a special provision in the IRC exempting the gain from tax (such as Section 121), the gain on the sale of any personal asset must be recognized in the year of sale.

Married couples who wish to claim up to the $500,000 exclusion must meet conditions in addition to the two requirements set forth above. For the $500,000 exclusion to apply for a married couple, they must file a joint tax return for the year (filing status must be married filing jointly), and both spouses must have used the residence for two out of the previous five years as a principal residence (referred to as the use test). Only one of the spouses must have owned the residence for two out of the previous five years (the ownership test). Furthermore, if either spouse claimed the Section 121 exclusion within the previous two years, the gain cannot be excluded from income taxation.

If, however, a couple is getting divorced and are filing separate returns, and a principal residence is sold, each spouse can exclude up to $250,000 of gain from the sale if the ownership and use tests are otherwise met.

Example 13.30

Arturo and Katarina recently married. About four years prior to their marriage, Arturo purchased a townhouse which the couple used as their residence after they were married. Knowing that they would purchase a new residence when they started their family, Arturo never added Katarina's name to the title of the property. Three years after they were married, they decided to start their family and look for a new home. When the townhouse is sold, Arturo and Katarina may exclude up to $500,000 of the gain from the sale since Arturo met the ownership test (he owned the principal residence for two years) and both Arturo and Katarina met the use test (they both used the residence as a principal residence for two out of the last five years).

Proration of the Exclusion

If a principal residence is sold before the two-year ownership and use test is met, or if the exclusion was used during the last two years, it may be possible to qualify for a reduced exclusion. A reduced exclusion will be available when the sale of the principal residence is caused by: (1) a change of employment, (2) a change of health, or (3) an unforeseen circumstance. When one of these exceptions apply, the amount of the exclusion is determined by dividing the number of months the taxpayer used the home as a principal residence, or the number of months since the exclusion was used last, by 24 (the number of months in a two year period), and multiplying that result by the otherwise applicable exclusion. The formula for calculating the partial exclusion may be expressed as:

$$\frac{\text{\# of months of use (or last exclusion)}}{24} \times \text{Applicable Exclusion (\$250,000 or \$500,000)}$$

Change of Employment

The most frequently applied exception to the two-year rule is a change in employment. If the taxpayer, the taxpayer's spouse, a co-owner of the home, or a person whose principal residence is the same as the taxpayer's changes employment, and the two-year rule has not been met, a prorated exclusion is available.

Example 13.31

After their marriage, Katarina moved into Arturo's home. Arturo had purchased the home five years prior to the marriage, and before that did not own a residence. Six months after their marriage, Katarina is offered a career opportunity that will require her to relocate across the country. Arturo sells the home and seeks employment in the city where Katarina will be working. Despite the fact that only Arturo has met the two-year use test, a partial exclusion will be available for Katarina, since the move was conditioned on a change of employment. The total exclusion would be calculated as follows:

Arturo has met the ownership and use test, so he is permitted to exclude up to $250,000 of the gain.

Katarina's exclusion will be:

$$\frac{\text{6 months of use}}{24} \text{ x Applicable Exclusion (\$250,000) = \$62,500}$$

Therefore, the total amount that can be excluded by them from the gain is $312,500 ($250,000 + $62,500).

If, upon sale, the gain realized was $312,500 or less, none of the gain would be taxable. Gain in excess of $312,500 would be subject to tax at long-term capital gains rates (since Arturo owned the home for more than one year).

To prevent abuse of the change in employment exception to the two-year use rule, the law provides a safe harbor that is based on the distance of the new job from the taxpayer's current home. If the distance of the new job to the old home is 50 miles greater than the distance from the old job to the old home, the reduced exclusion will be available. Note that the safe harbor test used here matches the distance test that applied to moving expenses when they were deductible.

Change of Health

For the partial exclusion to apply due to a change in health, the residence must be sold to facilitate the taxpayer's, the taxpayer's dependent, or specified family member's treatment for the diagnosis, cure, or mitigation of an illness. The sale of the home to improve the taxpayer's general health does not qualify, unless a physician recommends a change in residence due to health concerns.

Unforeseen Circumstances

The unforeseen circumstance exception is the most difficult to apply, but the Treasury regulations do provide some guidance and safe-harbors. If any of the following situations apply, a partial exemption will be available:

1. The taxpayer, spouse, co-owner of the home or a person who also uses the home as a primary residence dies, loses their job, divorces, or separates from their spouse.
2. The government condemns the home through use of eminent domain.
3. The home is affected by a natural disaster or act of war or terrorism resulting in a casualty to the home.

Exhibit 13.6 lists some of the events that the IRS has accepted as unforeseen circumstances.

Exhibit 13.6 | Unforeseen Circumstances

- *PLR 200702032:* Taxpayer was bothered by excessive noise from a nearby airport.
- *PLR 200652041:* Taxpayer/co-owner became pregnant, but was no longer in a relationship with the father/other co-owner of the house.
- *PLR 200613009:* Taxpayer needed a larger house in order to provide a separate bedroom for an adopted child.
- *PLR 200601022:* Taxpayer's new spouse's child lost ride to school when sibling graduated and taxpayer and spouse then had a baby, making house too small.
- *PLR 200601023:* Taxpayer needed to move out of an age-restricted community so that taxpayer's daughter (who had lost her job) and grandchild could move in with the taxpayer.
- *PLR 200403049:* A member of the taxpayer's family was on house arrest/probation, to which the neighbors were hostile.
- *PLR 200630004:* Taxpayer was accosted at gunpoint outside his residence and forced to withdraw money from ATMs.
- *PLR 200601009:* Taxpayers and son were assaulted in separate events in new neighborhood.
- *PLR 200615011:* Taxpayer's address was discovered by the associates of a drug dealer that taxpayer had arrested.
- *PLR 200504012:* Taxpayer was assigned to a K-9 unit, but his homeowner's association prohibited kennels.

Other Provisions Related to Section 121

The ability to take the Section 121 exclusion may be affected if the property was acquired in a like-kind exchange. If the home currently being used as the taxpayer's principal residence is sold within five years of acquiring the property through a like-kind exchange, the Section 121 exclusion is not available. While it is not possible to exchange personal residences and defer recognition of the gain under IRC Section 1031, conversion of a residence from rental use to personal use may invoke application of this rule.

Example 13.32

Four years ago, Dean engaged in a Section 1031 exchange of an apartment building for a rental house. One year after the Section 1031 exchange occurred, the tenant moved out and Dean had a difficult time finding a new tenant. Since he liked the property, he decided to move in and make it his principal residence. Dean has used the home as a principal residence for three years. Despite the fact that Dean meets both the ownership and use tests, if he sells the home he will not be able to exclude the gain under the Section 121 exclusion. To be able to exclude the gain, Dean would have to sell the home five years or more after he acquired it in the Section 1031 exchange.

One final issue should be addressed concerning the application of Section 121. In cases where rental property is converted to use as a principal residence, the Section 121 exclusion will permit some or all of the capital gain on the sale to be excluded from income taxation, but will not shield depreciation recapture from taxation. You may recall from the property transactions chapters that accelerated depreciation taken on real estate is recaptured at ordinary tax rates, and that straight-line depreciation (referred to as "unrecaptured Section 1250 gain") is taxed at a 25 percent long-term capital gain tax rate (plus the 3.8% Affordable Care Act surtax, if applicable). The tax on any depreciation recapture must be paid before the Section 121 exclusion comes into effect.

Quick Quiz 13.4

1. Married couples may exclude up to $500,000 of gain under Section 121.
   a. True
   b. False
2. All taxpayers are entitled to a reduced exclusion if they have not lived in their principal residence for two years.
   a. True
   b. False
3. If a taxpayer's principal residence was acquired within the last five years by a like-kind exchange, nonrecognition of gain under Section 121 is not available.
   a. True
   b. False

True, False, True.

Gain Allocated to Nonqualified Use

Gain from the sale or exchange of a principal residence allocated to periods of nonqualified use is not excluded from gross income. The amount of gain allocated to periods of nonqualified use is the amount of gain multiplied by a fraction the numerator of which is the aggregate periods of nonqualified use during the period the taxpayer owned the property and the denominator of which is the period the taxpayer owned the property.

A period of nonqualified use means any period (not including any period before January 1, 2009) during which the property is not used by the taxpayer or the taxpayer's spouse or former spouse as a principal residence. Examples of nonqualified use include vacation property or rental property. The period of nonqualified use does not include any portion of the 5-year testing period that occurs after the last date that the property is used as a principal residence by the taxpayer or spouse. If any gain is attributable to depreciation, the exclusion does not apply to that amount of gain.

Example 13.33

Goldie bought a vacation home on the beach for $300,000 ten years ago. Three years ago, Goldie retired and made the beach house her principal residence. She recently sold the house for $450,000, realizing a gain of $150,000. The gain attributed to nonqualified use is 70% (7 years out of the 10 years of ownership), or $105,000, and does not qualify for the Section 121 exclusion. The remaining gain ($45,000; which is less than the $250,000 maximum exclusion) may be excluded from income under Section 121.

Example 13.34

Assume that Kurt buys a property for $400,000, and uses it as rental property for two years claiming $20,000 of depreciation deductions. Kurt then converts the property to his principal residence. Four years after the purchase, he moves out, and sells the property for $700,000 one year later (after five years). In this case, $20,000 of the gain attributable to the depreciation deductions is included in income. Of the remaining $300,000 gain, 40% of the gain (2 years divided by 5 years), or $120,000, is allocated to nonqualified use and is not eligible for the exclusion. Since the remaining gain of

$180,000 is less than the maximum gain of $250,000 that may be excluded, gain of $180,000 is excluded from gross income. The net gain equals $140,000 ($120,000 plus $20,000).

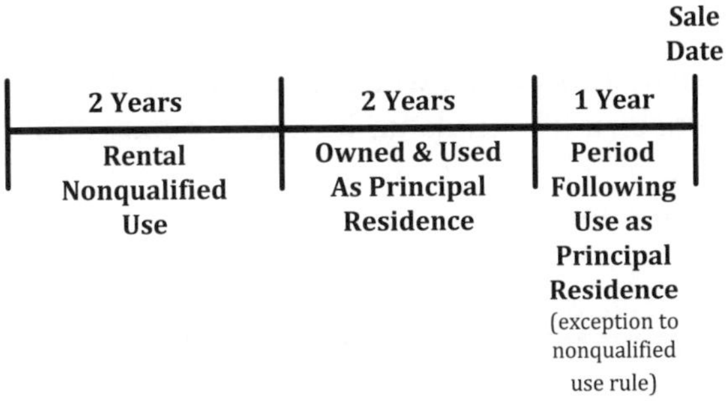

2 Years	2 Years	1 Year (Sale Date)
Rental Nonqualified Use	Owned & Used As Principal Residence	Period Following Use as Principal Residence (exception to nonqualified use rule)

Example 13.35

Assume that Russell buys a principal residence for $400,000, moves out ten years later. Assume Russell sells the property for $600,000 two years later. The entire $200,000 gain is excluded from gross income because the two-year period after the last qualified use does not constitute nonqualified use. The nonqualified use rules became effective for sales and exchanges after December 31, 2008.

DEATH BENEFITS AND LOANS FROM LIFE INSURANCE

Death Benefits

Under IRC Section 101, the death benefit on a life insurance policy received by reason of the death of the insured is exempt from income tax provided that the policy has not been transferred for valuable consideration. This exception to the tax-free receipt of a life insurance death benefit is referred to as the **transfer-for-value rule**. If there is a transfer for value, the death benefit of a life insurance policy is subject to income tax. Transfers for value occur when the policy is sold, or is otherwise transferred in return for some other form of economic benefit.

Key Concepts

1. Describe the tax consequences of death benefits and loans from life insurance policies.
2. Identify the five exceptions to the transfer-for-value rule.
3. Identify the tax consequences of distributions from Roth IRAs/Roth 401(k)s.

The code does provide five exceptions to the transfer-for-value rule. The five exceptions are:

1. A transfer to the insured
2. A transfer to a corporation in which the insured is a shareholder
3. A transfer to a partnership in which the insured is a partner
4. A transfer to a partner of the insured
5. A transfer to a transferee who takes the transferor's basis

If a life insurance policy has been transferred for valuable consideration, but one of these exceptions apply, the death benefit will be received by the beneficiary income tax free. The following examples give common scenarios where a transfer of a life insurance policy for valuable consideration does not cause the death benefit of the life insurance policy to be subject to income tax.

Example 13.36

Hudson is Chief Security Officer of BioTech, Inc. Because of his unique training and skills, BioTech considers Hudson to be a key person for the corporation, and purchased a life insurance policy on Hudson's life to compensate the corporation in the event he dies prior to retirement. Hudson retired last week, and BioTech no longer has need for the life insurance policy on Hudson's life. Hudson, however, needs additional life insurance to support his estate plan. BioTech sells the life insurance policy to Hudson for the value of the policy (the interpolated terminal reserve plus unearned premium). Despite the fact that a transfer for value has occurred, the sale of the policy was to the insured (Hudson), so the beneficiary will receive the death benefit income tax free.

Example 13.37

Kate is a one-third owner of KRK, Inc. As part of the company's business succession plan, KRK has entered into an entity-type buy-sell agreement, which requires the estates of deceased owners to sell their shares back to the corporation. To fund this buy-sell agreement, KRK plans on purchasing enough life insurance so that, upon the death of each owner, it will have sufficient funds to purchase the stock. Kate happens to have an existing life insurance policy in force that she no longer needs for her other planning objectives. The death benefit on the policy is approximately the amount the company would need to purchase to fund Kate's part of the buy-sell agreement. Kate sells her life insurance policy to the corporation so that it can be used to fund the buy-sell agreement. Despite the fact that there has been a transfer of the policy for valuable consideration, the death benefit will be received by the corporation income tax free, since the transfer was from a shareholder of the corporation to the corporation.

Example 13.38

Refer to the facts from the previous example, but assume that KRK is not a corporation, but rather a partnership. The same result would occur. While there has been a transfer for value, the transfer was made to a partnership in which the insured was a partner. The partnership would receive any death benefits income tax free.

Example 13.39

Kate is a 50% owner of KRK, LLC. As part of the company's business succession plan, Kate and her partner have entered into a cross-purchase type buy-sell agreement, which requires the estates of deceased owners to sell their shares back to the surviving LLC member. To fund this buy-sell agreement, Kate and her partner plan on purchasing enough life insurance on the life of the other owner so that, upon the death of each owner, sufficient funds will be available to purchase the deceased owner's interest. Kate happens to have an existing life insurance policy in force that she no longer needs for her other planning objectives. The death benefit on the policy matches the amount of insurance that her partner would have to purchase to fund the cross-purchase buy-sell agreement. Kate sells her life insurance policy to her partner so that it can be used to fund the buy-sell agreement. Despite the fact that there has been a transfer of the policy for valuable consideration, the death benefit will be received by the partner income tax free, since the transfer was to a partner of the insured.

Policy Loans

While a life insurance policy is in force, the owner of the policy may borrow from the policy's cash value without triggering any income tax consequences. Borrowing from a policy, therefore, is a tax-free event, which gives the owner access to capital without any tax cost. If the policy is later surrendered, however, the amount borrowed from the cash value of a life insurance policy will be considered part of the distribution upon surrender, and will be subject to income tax. If the policy is kept in force until the death of the insured, there are no income tax consequences for policy loans.

DISTRIBUTIONS FROM ROTH IRAs AND ROTH ACCOUNTs

Roth IRAs and Roth accounts in 401(k) plans, 403(b) plans and governmental 457(b) plans provide individuals with the opportunity to accumulate money for retirement on a tax-free basis. Unlike traditional retirement savings plans that give the taxpayer the ability to defer taxation on income until distributions are received from the retirement account, Roth savings vehicles must be funded with after-tax dollars. All of the investment growth, however, is tax free if the account has been in existence for five years, and the distributions are made after the time the owner reaches age 59½. Roth IRAs and Roth accounts give taxpayers a rare opportunity to completely avoid income tax on investment gains and income.

Quick Quiz 13.5

1. A transfer to the insured is one of the exceptions to the transfer-for-value rule.
   a. True
   b. False
2. All distributions from a Roth IRA or a Roth account after five years are tax free.
   a. True
   b. False

True, False.

CONCLUSION

Tax-deferred exchanges give taxpayers the opportunity to determine the time when income is recognized, and tax-free exchanges exempt the taxpayer from income tax liability on certain types of income. These provisions give incentives for investment, and should be carefully considered by individuals when engaging in property transactions. Congress can, and sometimes does, change the rules governing these provisions. Tax-deferred and tax-free exchanges are matters of legislative grace; without express provisions in the IRC to exempt or defer taxation, these transactions would trigger taxable income for taxpayers engaging in them.

KEY TERMS

Annuity Contract - A contract under which an individual invests a lump sum or stream of payments with an insurance company and the income on the investment growth is deferred until the owner begins to take distributions from the annuity.

Boot - Non-like-kind property received in an IRC Section 1031 exchange, usually cash, property or a reduction in debt.

Corporate Recapitalization - Restructuring the equity interests of a corporation, often in an effort to achieve estate planning or business succession goals.

Functional Use Test - Requires the replacement property to serve the same functional use as the original property.

Involuntary Conversion - A realization event that occurs outside of the control of the taxpayer.

Life Insurance Contract - A contract under which the insurance company promises to pay a specified amount upon the death of the insured.

Like-Kind Assets - Property of the same nature and character that may be exchanged in a like-kind exchange. After 2017, only real property is permitted for Section 1031 like-kind exchange treatment.

Like-Kind Exchange - A tax deferral technique in which real estate assets held for productive use in a trade or business are exchanged.

Modified Endowment Contracts (MECs) - Life insurance contracts that do not pass the 7-pay test or the corridor rule.

Reinvestment Period - Period during which the taxpayer must acquire replacement property.

Related Party - Anyone defined under IRC Section 267(b) including brothers and sisters (of whole or half blood or adopted).

Taxpayer Use Test - Requires that the replacement property be used by the taxpayer within activities which are treated the same for tax purposes.

Transfer-for-Value Rule - An exception to the general rule that life insurance death benefits are received tax free.

DISCUSSION QUESTIONS

SOLUTIONS to the discussion questions can be found exclusively within the chapter. Once you have completed an initial reading of the chapter, go back and highlight the answers to these questions.

1. What is a like-kind exchange?
2. What types of assets are eligible for like-kind exchange treatment?
3. How can taxpayers avoid like-kind exchange treatment when it is available?
4. What types of assets are considered like-kind under IRC Section 1031?
5. What are the requirements for the deferral of gain when a like-kind exchange is not accomplished by a simultaneous exchange of like-kind property?
6. How is a like-kind exchange affected by being a related party transaction?
7. What are the tax consequences of a Section 1031 exchange?
8. What happens if a taxpayer receives non-like-kind property in exchange for an asset?
9. What happens when a mortgage is part of a like-kind exchange?
10. Describe the tax consequences of exchanging property for stock.
11. What is an involuntary conversion?
12. What reinvestment period applies to involuntary conversions?
13. Name and describe the three types of insurance products that can be exchanged in a way that will avoid gain recognition.
14. How can the above types of insurance products be exchanged without realizing gain?
15. What is a corporate recapitalization and what are its tax consequences?
16. What are the tax consequences of transfers between spouses incident to divorce?
17. What are the requirements for the exclusion of gain on the sale of a principal residence?
18. Under what circumstances is a reduced exclusion available under Section 121 and how is that reduced exclusion calculated?
19. What is the transfer-for-value rule and what are the exceptions to this rule?
20. What are the tax consequences of distributions from Roth IRAs and Roth accounts?

MULTIPLE CHOICE PROBLEMS

A sample of multiple choice problems is provided below. Additional multiple choice problems are available at money-education.com by accessing the Student Practice Portal.

1. Which of the following could qualify as a residence, for principal residence exclusion from gain?
   1. A condominium.
   2. An RV.
   3. A boat.
   4. Vacant land adjacent to personal residence regularly used by the taxpayer.
      a. 4 only.
      b. 1 and 4.
      c. 1, 2, and 3.
      d. 1, 2, 3, and 4.

2. Meg wants to sell her rental beach home and purchase rental property in the mountains. Her friend, Ryan, tells her he can do a nonsimultaneous tax-free exchange as long as the fair market value of mountain property is equal to or greater than the fair market value of the beach property. How long after selling his beach property does Meg have to identify and purchase the mountain property?
   a. The mountain property must be identified within 45 days of the closing of the beach property and must be closed within 180 days of the closing of the beach property.
   b. The mountain property must be identified within 30 days of the closing of the beach property and must be closed within 120 days of the closing of the beach property.
   c. The mountain property must be identified within 60 days of the closing of the beach property and must be closed within 180 days of the closing of the beach property.
   d. The mountain property must be identified within 90 days of the closing of the beach property and must be closed within 180 days of the closing of the beach property.

3. In which of the following circumstances would a taxpayer be able to get a partial exemption for the sale of a personal residence when the taxpayer did not meet the two year ownership and use test?
   a. The taxpayer decides to move from Florida to Arizona to possibly look for a new job.
   b. The taxpayer changes jobs to a town that is 10 miles away from the former house and 10 miles away from the former job.
   c. The taxpayer sold the house in Milwaukee because the gray days were affecting her sunny disposition and general health.
   d. The taxpayer suffered anxiety attacks after a home invasion where the taxpayer was held at gunpoint for three days.

4. Steven, a single taxpayer, has been transferred by his company to Portland. He sold his house for $650,000 and he had an adjusted basis of $330,000. Steven owned and lived in the home for 18 months. What is his capital gain from the sale of the personal residence?
   a. $0.
   b. $132,500 LTCG.
   c. $187,500 LTCG.
   d. $320,000 LTCG.

5. Assume Liv and Tyler bought a ski condo 10 years ago for $100,000. They treated it as a vacation home for eight years but used it as their personal residence for the last two years. They recently sold the condo for $450,000. How much gain can they exclude from the sale of their personal residence?
   a. $70,000.
   b. $210,000.
   c. $250,000.
   d. $350,000.

Additional multiple choice problems are available at *money-education.com* by accessing the Student Practice Portal. Access requires registration of the title using the unique code at the front of the book.

QUICK QUIZ EXPLANATIONS

Quick Quiz 13.1

1. False. Like-kind exchange treatment is only available for real property assets held for productive use in a trade or business, or for the production of income. Assets held for personal use do not qualify.
2. False. To qualify as a like-kind exchange, the asset received in the exchange must be of the same nature and character as the asset given up in the exchange. Section 1031 does not require that the properties have similar uses.
3. True.

Quick Quiz 13.2

1. False. An involuntary conversion is a realization event that occurs outside of the control of the taxpayer. Examples of involuntary conversions include theft, condemnation, seizure, or sale of property under threat of condemnation. Bankruptcy is not an example of an involuntary conversion.
2. False. To avoid recognition of the gain on an involuntary conversion, the taxpayer must invest the proceeds in a replacement property that has a similar use to the property that was converted. Either the taxpayer use test or the functional use test must be satisfied.
3. False. Taxpayers who lose property by eminent domain have three years from the end of the year in which the realization event occurred to purchase the replacement property.

Quick Quiz 13.3

1. True.
2. True.

Quick Quiz 13.4

1. True.
2. False. Taxpayers who have not lived in their principal residence for two years may be entitled to a reduced exclusion if the sale of the principal residence is caused by (1) a change of employment, (2) a change of health, or (3) an unforeseen circumstance.
3. True.

Quick Quiz 13.5

1. True.
2. False. For distributions to be tax free from a Roth IRA or Roth account, taxpayers must meet the five year rule AND the distribution must be after the attainment of age 59½ (or on account of a few other exceptions).

14
PASSIVE ACTIVITY RULES

LEARNING OBJECTIVES

1. Identify the three categories of income and losses.*
2. Describe Congress' reason for establishing the passive activity loss rules.
3. Identify the taxpayers to whom the passive activity loss rules apply.*
4. Distinguish between material participation and active participation in an activity.*
5. Explain how passive activities can be grouped for income tax reporting purposes.
6. Identify the three primary limitations imposed on the deductibility of passive losses.*
7. Describe the basis limitation.
8. Explain the at-risk rules and how debt affects the amount that is considered at risk.*
9. Describe the passive activity loss rules.*
10. Given the facts facing a taxpayer, calculate the portion of a taxpayer's passive loss suspended under the at-risk limitation, and the portion of the passive loss suspended under the passive activity loss rule.*
11. Identify six exceptions to the passive categorization of tangible property that is used for rental purposes.*
12. Identify the two circumstances where real estate activities can be classified as active businesses.*
13. Describe the requirements for the individual investor exception to the passive activity loss rules.*
14. Calculate the amount of passive losses that can be deducted against active and portfolio income for a given taxpayer under the individual investor exception to the passive activity loss rules.*
15. Determine under what circumstances the 3.8 percent Medicare tax applies to net investment income.*

**Ties to CFP Certification Learning Objectives*

INTRODUCTION

The passive activity rules are a classic example of anti-abuse provisions adopted by Congress to address the planning excesses of taxpayers. They were adopted as part of the 1986 Tax Reform Act to limit the ability of high income taxpayers to manipulate their taxable income by generating losses to offset other income. While the rules appear to be complex, an appreciation of the objective of the passive activity rules makes the analysis of transactions falling under these rules much easier to understand. The impact of the passive activity rules is to restrict or limit the current deductibility of losses resulting from passive activities. The rules do not eliminate passive losses, but rather suspend them until later, making loss deductibility a timing issue.

Key Concepts

1. Identify the three categories of income and losses.
2. Describe Congress' reasons for establishing the passive activity loss rules.

Background to the Passive Activity Loss Rules

Prior to 1986, all income received by a taxpayer was classified as either earned income or portfolio income. **Earned income** included wages, salaries, and income from the conduct of business activities.

Portfolio income included income generated through the investment of capital, such as dividends, interest, and capital gains.

When the passive activity rules were adopted by Congress in 1986, a new category of income was created – passive income. **Passive income** includes income generated from investments in real estate, rental activities, and income generated by businesses entities when the owner does not materially participate (defined later in this chapter) in the conduct of that business. After 1986, all income or losses received by a taxpayer must fall into one of three categories: active, portfolio, or passive.

Real estate and business investments have the potential to generate large gains over the long run, but may also generate large losses in the short run. Before 1986, wealthy taxpayers would often invest in real estate and start-up business entities that were managed by others to generate losses that could be used to offset their active income that otherwise would be taxed at high marginal tax rates. By making these investments, therefore, a taxpayer could manage his or her taxable income, and could also manage his or her marginal income tax rate.

In the 1980s, the sale of real estate limited partnerships and interests in start-up businesses was promoted as a way to minimize or eliminate federal income tax liability. In fact, it was possible to purchase real estate limited partnership interests that would generate a tax write-off greater than the investment made by the taxpayer. This ability to create tax write-offs that could eliminate taxable income became a major concern of Congress.

Example 14.1

In 1983, Ari anticipated his adjusted gross income to be $150,000. Ari has a high net worth, and decides that his income tax rates are too high. At the end of the tax year, he purchases a 10% interest in a real estate limited partnership interest for $100,000. The real estate limited partnership uses its initial $1 million in capital, plus a nonrecourse bank loan of $20 million to purchase an apartment building. At the time of the purchase (the early 1980s), the apartment building could be depreciated on an accelerated basis, and the first year depreciation on the apartment building is $1,500,000. The partnership has no other income for the year (since it was not created until the end of the tax year), and has no other expenses. Since Ari owns a 10% limited partnership interest, 10% of the depreciation is allocated to him, which he is able to deduct for income tax purposes. Since Ari's allocation of the depreciation expense ($150,000) equals his adjusted gross income for the year, he has completely offset his income with the loss generated on the real estate rental activity, and is not required to pay any income tax in the current year.

While these tax planning options were certainly favorable for high income taxpayers who wanted to minimize current income taxes, most taxpayers (middle-class and low-income individuals) could not afford to purchase these types of investments, and were left paying their income tax bill. Furthermore, the Treasury, the IRS, and Congress did not like the idea that income taxes for the wealthy were essentially becoming voluntary, so they took action to limit this type of tax planning. Congress solved this problem by imposing new limitations on deductions in three ways. First, they changed the basis rules; second, at-risk rules were imposed; and third, limitations were placed on passive activity losses and the deductibility of investment interest expense. Remember that the intent of Congress was not to eliminate deductibility but rather to manage the timing of each deduction.

Net Investment Income Tax

The **net investment income tax** (NIIT) is imposed by Section 1411 of the Internal Revenue Code (IRC). NIIT is a Medicare surtax that applies at a rate of 3.8 percent to certain net investment income of individuals, estates and trusts that have income above the statutory threshold amounts. Individual taxpayers will owe the tax if they have net investment income and also have modified adjusted gross income over the following thresholds, which are not indexed for inflation:

Filing Status	*Threshold Amount*
Married filing jointly	$250,000
Married filing separately	$125,000
Single	$200,000
Head of household (with qualifying person)	$200,000
Qualifying widow(er) with dependent child	$250,000

In general, investment income includes, but is not limited to: interest, dividends, capital gains, rental and royalty income, nonqualified annuities, income from businesses involved in trading of financial instruments or commodities, and businesses that are passive activities to the taxpayer (within the meaning of IRC Section 469). Net investment income is investment income less certain expenses properly allocable to the income.

Taxpayers with income above the NII thresholds must include income from their passive activities in the calculation of the NII tax. Passive activities include rental real estate activities and most limited partnership activities.

Example 14.2

Jackson is married to Shelby, and they file a joint tax return each year. This year, their adjusted gross income is $300,000, which is comprised of Jackson's salary from work of $280,000 and $20,000 in income from an apartment house that Jackson and Shelby own. The rental of the apartment house is a passive activity, and the income derived from the rental will be subject to the net investment income tax, since Jackson and Shelby's adjusted gross income exceeds the threshold amount.

As a result of these rules, passive income is not only subject to ordinary income tax rates, it may also be subject to an additional 3.8 percent tax. These rules increase the importance of qualifying as a material participant, which is discussed later in the chapter.

APPLICATION OF THE RULES

The passive activity loss rules apply to individuals, estates and trusts, certain personal service corporations, and closely held regular corporations.

The passive activity loss rules do not apply to publicly held corporations. The purchase of an interest in a publicly held corporation will generate investment income or loss, not passive income or loss. Dividends and capital gains derived from a publicly held corporation fall into the portfolio income bucket.

Three Types of Income

As you have learned in prior chapters, subsequent to the imposition of the passive activity rules in 1986, there are three types of income (or loss) that can be generated in our income tax system (active, portfolio, or passive). All income (or loss) earned by a taxpayer must fall into one of the three categories.

Exhibit 14.1 | Types of Income

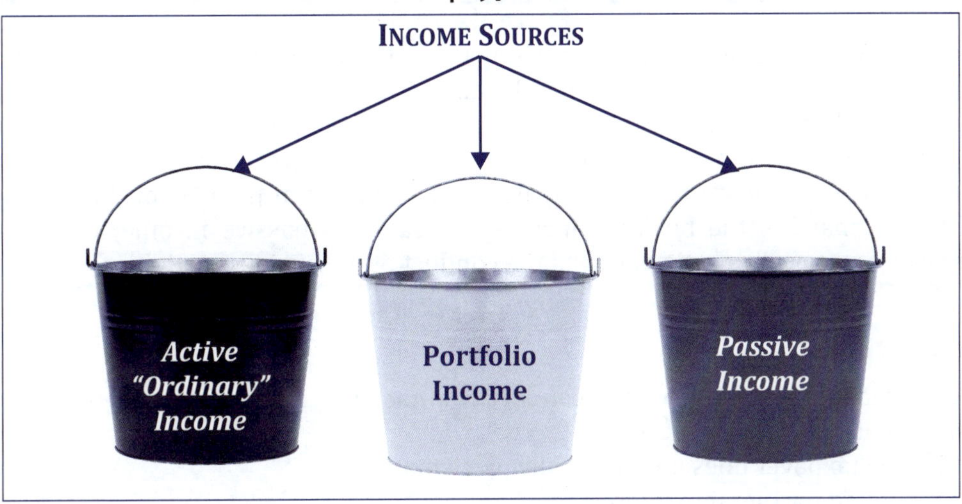

Active Income

Active income is income earned through the active conduct of a trade or business and earned from the provision of labor. Salaries, wages, and income from self employment, S corporations and partnerships in which the taxpayer materially participates is considered active income. Generally, active income is taxed at ordinary income tax rates.

Portfolio Income

Portfolio income is income derived from the investment of capital. Interest, dividends, and capital gains are forms of portfolio income. Some forms of portfolio income, such as interest, annuity payments, royalties, short-term capital gains and nonqualified dividends, are subject to ordinary income tax rates. Other types of portfolio income, such as qualified dividends and long-term capital gains are taxed at favorable income tax rates.

> ### *Key Concepts*
>
> 1. Identify the taxpayers to whom the passive activity loss rules apply.
> 2. Describe the different types of income.
> 3. Define material participation.
> 4. Explain how passive activities are grouped for the purpose of imposing limits.

Passive Income

Passive income generally includes income generated from all rental and real estate activities (unless specific exceptions are met) and income generated from trade or business activities when the taxpayer receiving the income does not materially participate in the conduct of that trade or business. Distributive shares of income from S corporations and partnerships (including general partnerships, limited partnerships, limited liability companies, and limited liability partnerships) may be classified as passive income or active income depending on material participation standards.

The creation of the passive activity rules may result in different treatment of business income from the same business for different taxpayers. If a taxpayer regularly participates in the conduct of the business generating the income/loss, that income/loss will be allocated to the active income bucket. If the taxpayer does not regularly participate in the conduct of the business activities, the income/loss for that taxpayer is allocated to the passive bucket.

Example 14.3

Kenny and Roger are brothers, and each owns a 10% interest in JarvCo, LLC, a closely held family business. Kenny is the general manager of JarvCo's local office. Roger decided to become a physician, and does not participate in the operation of the family business. The distributive share of the business income that Kenny receives is treated as active income since Kenny materially participates in the conduct of JarvCo's business. Roger's distributive share of the business income is treated as passive income/loss because Roger is not materially participating in the conduct of the business activities.

Passive Activities

Passive income or loss is derived from the conduct of a **passive activity**. Section 469 defines a passive activity as any activity:

- in which the taxpayer does not materially participate,
- that is a limited partnership interest, or
- that is a rental activity, even if the taxpayer materially participates in the activity.

Material Participation

Material participation requires involvement in the conduct of the trade or business on a regular, continuous, and substantial basis. Mere management approval of decisions made by others does not constitute material participation. Treasury Regulation 1.469-5T sets forth seven tests to determine whether or not a person materially participates in the conduct of a trade or business. All of these tests are designed to give taxpayers a safe harbor rule for classifying income. If one of the tests is met, material participation is presumed and the income is generally considered to be active income (there are a few exceptions, covered below). The seven tests for material participation are:

1. The taxpayer dedicates more than 500 hours of effort to the activity each year.
2. The taxpayer dedicates more than 100 hours to the activity, but no less than anyone else.
3. The taxpayer dedicates more than 100 hours to each of several activities, and more than 500 hours in total for those activities not including any activity for which he is a material participant.
4. The taxpayer is the only person substantially participating in the operation of the activity.
5. The taxpayer has materially participated in the activity for five out of the last 10 years.
6. If the activity is a personal service activity, the taxpayer has materially participated in that personal service activity for at least three years. A personal service activity includes any trade or business where capital is not a material income producing factor, and professional services (law, accountancy, medicine, engineering, performing arts, and the like).
7. The facts and circumstances surrounding the case indicate that the taxpayer has been regularly, continuously, and substantially involved in the activity.

Exhibit 14.2 | Summary of Material Participation

1. >500 hours devoted to activity.
2. >100 hours devoted to activity and the most of any participant.
3. >100 hours devoted to several activities that add to more than 500 hours.

Recall that the passive activity rules, and, thus, the tests for material participation only apply to the owners of closely held businesses. Publicly traded corporations are exempt from the application of the passive activity rules. Most closely held businesses are structured as proprietorships, partnerships (general partnerships, limited partnerships, LLCs, and LLPs) or S corporations.

Quick Quiz 14.1

1. The passive activity loss rules do not apply to publicly held corporations.
   a. True
   b. False
2. A taxpayer who dedicates 400 hours to an activity is presumed to materially participate in that activity.
   a. True
   b. False
3. If grouped, passive activity limits apply on a group, rather than a per-unit, basis.
   a. True
   b. False

True, False, True.

Special rules apply when determining whether a limited partner is materially participating in a trade or business. If the owner of the interest is a limited partner, he or she will be considered to materially participate in the operation of the business only if he or she meets the 500 hour test (number 1, above), the five of 10 years test (number 5, above), or the three year test for personal service companies (number 6 above). The other tests are not available for limited partners.

Material participation of a limited partner may be problematic if the limited partner is attempting to maintain limited liability status. To the extent that a limited partner participates in management decisions for the partnership, limited liability protection is lost. If the limited partner does not have management control, limited liability is maintained. Limited partners participating in the operation of the business need to be mindful of this distinction to maintain the asset protection features of their ownership interest. The Treasury Regulations may be particularly problematic in this regard since the regulations indicate that work that is not normally performed by owners or whose principal purpose is to avoid the passive activity rules will not be considered when applying the tests for material participation. In addition, work done as an investor that does not involve direct day-to-day management of the operation (e.g., reviewing financial statements) will not be considered when applying the tests for material participation.

Proprietors, general partners, S corporation owners, and LLC members may meet any of the seven tests for material participation to qualify the income generated by the business entity as active income in their hands.

For married taxpayers, the participation of both spouses may be combined when calculating the number of hours necessary to meet the material participation tests. Unlike most other provisions in the IRC, the hours of involvement by each spouse may be added together to determine material participation even if the couple files separately for income tax purposes.

Example 14.4

Buddy and Holly are married and file jointly. Holly works 300 hours in Activity A and Buddy works 250 hours in Activity A. They are material participants in Activity A with 550 hours between them.

Grouping of Passive Activities

To make the tax rules surrounding the use of passive activities a bit more user-friendly, it is possible to group several passive activities into an "appropriate economic unit." Once grouped into an appropriate economic unit, the limitations imposed on passive activities (discussed below) will apply on a group basis, as opposed to per-unit basis. This can be useful, from a compliance and simplicity view, if the taxpayer has one activity generating passive gains that can be grouped with another activity that generates passive losses so the losses can offset the gains directly, thus decreasing the likelihood of an IRS challenge.

The factors that should be considered in grouping activities into appropriate economic units includes:

- the similarities and differences in the types of business,
- the extent of common control of the business entities,
- the extent of common ownership of the business entities,
- geographic location, and
- the interdependencies between the various activities.

Once chosen, the activities grouped into the appropriate economic unit cannot be changed without IRS approval. Typically, the IRS will not give approval for a change unless the original grouping was clearly inappropriate, or there has been a material change in facts and circumstances since the activities were grouped together.

Example 14.5

Miguel participates in 3 activities (A, B, and C). He dedicates 120 hours to Activity A, 150 hours to Activity B, and 270 hours to Activity C. He can group the three together to be a material participant in all (120 + 150 + 270 = 540).

There are two forms of groupings that are not appropriate:

1. groupings of rental and non-rental activities unless one activity is substantially related to the other, and
2. groupings of rental activities that involve real and personal property, unless the personal property rental activity is provided in tandem with the real estate rental activity.

The IRS has the authority to reallocate groupings if it determines that the groupings are not appropriate economic units.

LIMITATIONS IMPOSED ON PASSIVE LOSSES

Passive losses are subject to three primary limitations: the basis limitation, the at-risk limitation, and the passive activity loss rules. When a taxpayer generates a loss that is considered passive, each of these limitations must be applied in sequence.

Key Concepts

1. Identify the three primary limitations on passive income.
2. Describe the basis limitation.
3. Explain the at-risk rules and how debt affects the amount that is considered at risk.
4. Describe the passive activity loss rules.

The Basis Limitation

The first limitation that is imposed on the deductibility of passive losses is the basis limitation. The **basis limitation** states that the maximum allowable loss that the taxpayer can deduct is equal to his or her basis in the investment. This limitation generally applies to all investments including those generating passive activity losses.

Basis is used to keep track of the after-tax dollars invested in an investment vehicle. In our tax system, a loss cannot be claimed in excess of basis (a notable exception to this rule is percentage depletion).

There are three ways that the basis of an investment can be increased. First, basis in an investment can be increased by adding more capital to the investment (stated differently, a taxpayer may make a further investment in the entity). Second, when a pass-through business entity earns money, each owner's basis in that business entity is increased by the owner's proportionate share of the undistributed business income because the owners recognize the income on their personal tax return. Finally, an owner's basis in a proprietorship or partnership may be increased by having the proprietorship or partnership incur debt. Since the proprietorship or partnership is not a separate legal entity, any increase in partnership debt is really an increase in the debt of each owner in proportion to his or her ownership interest in the entity. Since debt is paid back with after-tax dollars (while a deduction is allowed for interest payments, no deduction is allowed for the principal portion of debt payments) and each owner or partner is responsible for the debt, an increase in the debt of a proprietorship or partnership results in a pro-rata increase in the basis of each partner.

At-Risk Rules

Once the basis rule has been applied to the loss from the activity, a second test must be met in order to claim a loss deduction – the "at-risk" rule. The **at-risk rule** states that a taxpayer may not deduct, in the current tax year, more than the amount that he/she is "at risk" for in the investment. Unlike the basis limitation, which simply states that the maximum deduction is the taxpayer's basis in the investment, the at-risk limitation only allows a deduction equal to the taxpayer's economic investment in the activity. Generally, basis and at-risk amounts are the same.

There are two basic forms of debt: recourse debt and nonrecourse debt. **Recourse debt** is secured by the property purchased with the loan proceeds (usually, the lender will take a secured interest in this property) and by the personal guarantee of the debtor. If the debtor defaults on a recourse loan, the lender can take possession of the asset purchased and, if that is not enough to satisfy the outstanding note balance, may seek to attach the personal assets of the borrower. In contrast, **nonrecourse debt** only allows the lender to take possession of the property that was the object of the loan.

A taxpayer is considered at risk for qualified nonrecourse financing secured by real property used in an activity of holding real property. Qualified nonrecourse financing is financing for which no one is personally liable for repayment and that is:

- borrowed by the taxpayer in connection with the activity of holding real property,
- secured by real property used in the activity,
- non-convertible from a debt obligation to an ownership interest, and
- loaned or guaranteed by any federal, state, or local government, or borrowed by the taxpayer from a qualified person.

Before 1986, a basis increase was permitted for debt assumption without regard to the type of debt that was assumed by the partnership. As illustrated in the first example in this chapter, it was common for real estate limited partnerships to solicit capital financing for use as a down payment, and then obtain a loan to purchase a large rental real estate property. Obtaining the loan resulted in a basis increase for each partner equal to the partner's proportionate share of the loan balance, since, presumably, the loan would have to be paid back with after-tax dollars. This transaction gives the investor a basis increase without any capital outlay. Typically, however, these loans were issued on a nonrecourse basis. If the investment was not successful, the investors could walk away, leaving the bank to deal with the property and any resulting loss despite the fact that the investors took depreciation deductions on the entire value of the property, including the loan balance that resulted in an increase in basis. When investors walked away from the property, they often had accumulated income tax deductions in excess of the actual capital invested in the venture.

Quick Quiz 14.2

1. A taxpayer may deduct losses on an investment up to 150% of his basis in that investment.
   a. True
   b. False
2. Nonrecourse debt does not increase a taxpayer's maximum allowable loss for a given investment.
   a. True
   b. False

False, True.

Example 14.6

In 1983, Hayden, a high net worth individual, invested in a real estate limited partnership. She purchased a 10% interest for $100,000. The real estate limited partnership uses its initial $1 million in capital plus a nonrecourse bank loan of $20 million to purchase an apartment building. At the time of the purchase (the early 1980s), the apartment building could be depreciated on an accelerated basis, and the losses claimed in the first several years of operation were $5,500,000. Since Hayden owns a 10% limited partnership interest, 10% of the losses were allocated to her, which she deducted for income tax purposes. In 1986, the real estate market turned sour, and the investors decide to walk away from their investment. For Hayden's $100,000 investment, she was able to generate $550,000 in tax deductions, and she was not personally liable to pay back any of the outstanding balance on the note assumed by the partnership.

To prevent wealthy taxpayers from purchasing investments to generate tax deductions, two limitations apply. First, as outlined above, the basis rule sets the maximum loss that a taxpayer can claim on a given activity within one tax year. Second, that maximum loss determined by the basis rule must be reduced by nonrecourse financing to arrive at the amount at risk under the at-risk rules. The impact of the at-risk rule is to prevent nonrecourse debt from increasing the taxpayer's maximum allowable loss for a given investment.

Example 14.7

In 2021, Brent, a high net worth individual, invested in Real Estate, LP, a real estate limited partnership. He purchased a 10% interest for $100,000. Real Estate, LP uses its initial $1 million in capital, plus a nonrecourse bank loan of $20 million to purchase an apartment building. While the nonrecourse loan will increase Brent's basis in the investment, it will be ignored under the at-risk limitation since Brent is not personally liable to pay back the loan. During the first year of operations the partnership incurred a $1,100,000 loss. Brent's share of this loss is $110,000. The maximum amount of loss Brent can deduct in the current tax year is limited to his basis of $100,000.

Brent's Passive Income Bucket

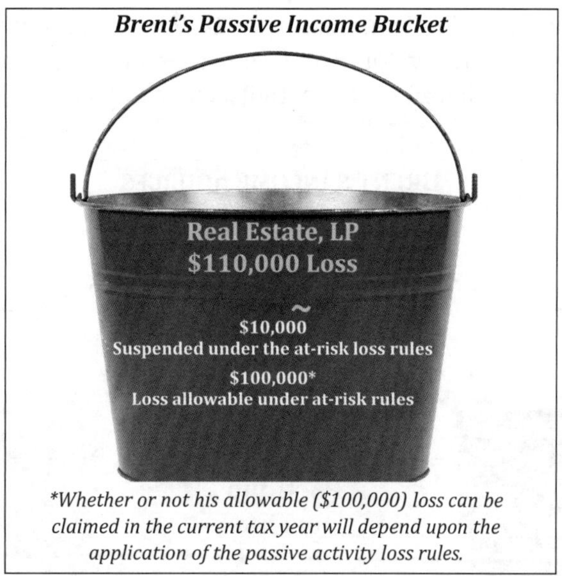

**Whether or not his allowable ($100,000) loss can be claimed in the current tax year will depend upon the application of the passive activity loss rules.*

To deduct the additional $10,000 loss, Brent would have to increase his basis by making an additional capital investment. Alternatively, the partnership could either generate a gain that would be allocated to partners or incur a recourse debt, either of which would result in a basis increase for the partners.

Any losses that are disallowed are carried forward until the at-risk amount is increased, at which time they may be deductible for income tax purposes provided that they are also deductible under the passive activity loss rules.

At-risk limitations are computed separately for each passive activity owned by a taxpayer.

Recall that the only time the at-risk limitation will differ from the basis limitation is when an investment is encumbered by a nonrecourse debt that has not been classified as a "qualified nonrecourse debt." Consequently, in most instances, the basis limitation is the same as the at-risk limitation.

Passive Activity Loss Rules

After application of the basis limitation rules and the at-risk rules, one additional test must be met before a taxpayer may deduct a passive loss for federal income tax purposes. The **passive activity loss rule** states that losses falling into the passive activity bucket from a passive activity can only be offset against gains that are in the passive activity bucket, unless special exceptions apply.

If a taxpayer's passive losses are smaller than his or her passive gains, the losses are offset by the gains, and only the net gain is included in gross income on the income tax return.

On the other hand, if the taxpayer's passive losses are larger than his or her passive gains, the excess losses are suspended under the passive activity rules, and may not be used as a deduction against active or portfolio income in the current tax year. Instead, the losses will remain in the passive activity bucket, and can be deducted in future tax years when the taxpayer's passive activities generate gains (income) or when the activity that generated the loss is disposed of or sold.

Example 14.8

Continuing with the information from **Example 14.7**, assume that the real estate limited partnership is a passive activity for Brent (he does not materially participate in the operation of the business), therefore, the activity will be placed in Brent's passive income bucket.

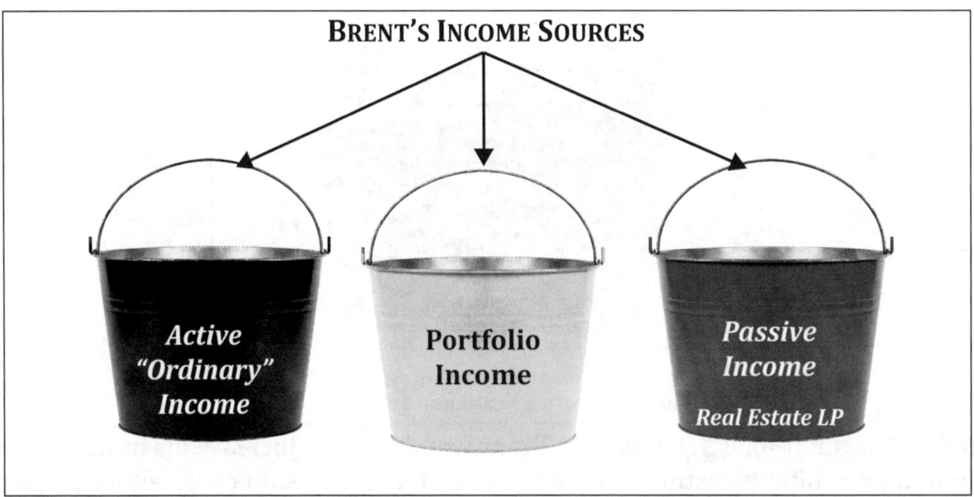

Within the passive bucket, two tests will limit Brent's ability to deduct losses. The first test that applies is the basis test. The basis test will limit Brent's deduction this year to his adjusted basis in the property. The at-risk limitation, however, states that losses cannot be taken for that portion of basis that represents nonrecourse debt. Therefore, given the facts of this case, Brent's maximum allowable loss is $100,000 despite the fact that $110,000 of losses had been allocated to him on the partnership tax return. The $10,000 that Brent cannot deduct is referred to as the suspended at-risk loss. The suspended at-risk loss will be carried forward to future years and to the extent that Brent's amount at risk in that investment increases, the suspended at-risk loss may be deducted. The $10,000 loss suspended by the at-risk limitation is trapped within the investment and cannot be released until additional at-risk amounts are generated. The remaining $100,000 of loss that can be deducted under the at-risk rules moves into the passive activity bucket, and will be subject to the passive activity rules. Brent's income tax deduction will be determined when the third test - the passive activity loss rule - is applied to the gains and losses in the passive bucket.

Passive Activity Income	$0
Passive Activity Loss	$100,000
Loss Suspended Under Passive Activity Rule	**$100,000**
Loss Suspended Under the At-Risk Limitation	$10,000

Example 14.9

Continuing our **Example 14.8**, Brent has a $100,000 potentially deductible passive loss from his real estate limited partnership. Since he did not have any passive gains this year, he is not permitted to deduct any of that loss and it will be suspended and remain in the passive bucket until he either generates passive income or sells (or otherwise disposes of) the real estate limited partnership.

Now assume that Brent is a 10 percent owner in HLQ, LLC in addition to his passive activity in the Real Estate, LP. Also assume Brent does not materially participate in HLQ, LLC. Brent's at-risk amount and loss/income for the current year is as follows:

Real Estate, LP: At risk = $100,000; Loss of $110,000

HLQ, LLC: At risk = $250,000; Income of $70,000

Brent's actual loss deduction available for the current year is $70,000. As previously indicated, of the $110,000 loss from Real Estate LP, $100,000 is potentially deductible and $10,000 is suspended under the at-risk rules. The $70,000 of passive income is available (from HLQ, LLC) in the current year to offset the current $100,000 at-risk rule loss. This allows use of the passive loss on Real Estate, LP to offset the income from HLQ, LLC, with the remaining $70,000 and $30,000 suspended under the passive activity loss rule.

Passive Activity Income	$70,000
Passive Activity Loss	$100,000
Loss Suspended Under Passive Activity Rule	**$30,000**
Loss Suspended Under the At-Risk Limitation	$10,000

The passive loss rules reflect the general rule discussed earlier that losses in one income category may be used to offset against gains in the same income category, but may not be used to offset other forms of income unless a special exception applies.

The planning impact of the passive activity rule is that high income taxpayers can no longer manage their income tax liability by generating losses from passive activities to offset other forms of income.

Excess passive losses may be carried forward indefinitely and may be used to offset future passive gains. Alternatively, the passive losses on an activity may be accelerated by disposing of the activity that generated the losses. Sale of the passive investment will allow passive losses generated on that investment to be used first against any gain on the sale of the passive activity. To the extent that the losses are not offset by any gain, they may be used to offset other passive income generated in the current year. If there is still a remaining loss, the remaining loss may be used to offset other active or portfolio income. Note that this ordering rule requires the taxpayer to allocate the passive losses first to income that may qualify for favorable capital gains tax rates. Only to the extent that the lower-taxed gain is eliminated can the losses be used to offset active income.

Separate Treatment of Publicly Traded Partnership Losses

A special exception to the bucket approach discussed above, where all passive activities fall into the same passive activity bucket, is for income and losses from **publicly traded partnerships** (PTPs; partnerships that trade on an active securities market) in which the owner does not materially participate. Each PTP is separated from all other passive investments and from all other PTPs, as if each PTP were the only passive activity for the investor.[1] A loss from one PTP cannot be used to offset income from another PTP or any other passive investment. Likewise, a loss from another passive investment, including another PTP, cannot offset the income from any PTP. All losses from a particular PTP will be suspended until they can be used to offset income generated from that same PTP or until the PTP is disposed of. Upon disposal of the PTP any suspended losses can then be utilized to offset other types of income.

Quick Quiz 14.3

1. At-risk limitations are computed separately for each passive activity owned by a taxpayer.
   a. True
   b. False
2. Excess passive activity losses are deductible against other income.
   a. True
   b. False

True, False.

Example 14.10

Alexandra, whose AGI is $250,00, owns an interest in several businesses in which she does not materially participate and all of which are passive activities. The businesses and Alexandra's share of their corresponding gains or losses are as follows:

1. Publicly traded partnership A - income $50,000
2. Publicly traded partnership B - loss $60,000
3. Limited partnership X - income $7,000
4. Limited partnership Y - loss $25,000
5. Rental Z - income $3,000

Assume that Alexandra has sufficient basis in each investment such that she is not restricted by the at-risk rules.

Alexandra has three separate passive activity categories: one for PTP A, one for PTP B, and one for non-PTP passive investments (limited partnerships X and Y, and rental Z).

	PTP A	*PTP B*	*Non-PTP Passive Investments (LPs X and Y, and rental Z)*
Income	$50,000	$0	$10,000 ($7,000 + $3,000)
Loss	$0	$60,000	$25,000
Net Result	$50,000 income	$60,000 suspended loss	$15,000 suspended loss

1. IRC §469(k)

Note that Alexandra cannot offset the income from PTP A with losses from either of the other categories. The suspended losses for PTP B will continue to carry forward until PTP B produces income which can be offset by the suspended loss, or until Alexandra disposes of PTP B and the remaining suspended losses can be used against other income. The suspended loss from limited partnership Y can be used to offset passive income from any other non-PTP passive investment in future years, or until Alexandra disposes of limited partnership Y and the remaining suspended losses can be used against other income.

CASE STUDY 14.1

When can rental expenses be claimed when there is no rental income?

Hattie M. Bonds, Petitioner v. Commissioner of Internal Revenue, Respondent, T.C. Summary Opinion 2011-122 (October 17, 2011).

In 1988, Hattie moved to Minnesota from Kansas City, Missouri. In the early or mid 1980s, Hattie purchased a single family home in Kansas City and lived in it until she relocated to Minnesota. Hattie kept the Kansas City house and has not made personal use of it since moving to Minnesota. Instead, she rented the house to various tenants through 2004 or 2005. Since then, the house was not rented due to Hattie's claim that a number of factors, including the economy, made rental impractical. Hattie never listed the property for sale. In 2006 and 2007, Hattie reported various rental expenses (including advertising, mortgage interest, taxes, depreciation and utilities) on a Schedule E even though she received no rental income for those years. The IRS disallowed the claimed rental expenses for 2006 and 2007, asserting that: (1) the Kansas City house was not held for the production of income; (2) the losses resulted from a passive activity; and (3) the losses lacked substantiation.

The Tax Court concluded that Hattie was entitled to claim expenses for the property, even though she did not receive any rental income for the years at issue. Citing Treas. Reg. §1.212-1(b), the court noted that "ordinary and necessary expenses paid or incurred in the management, conservation, or maintenance of a building devoted to rental purposes are deductible notwithstanding that there is actually no income therefrom in the taxable year." The court found that the record established that Hattie converted the house from personal use to production of income use when she relocated to Minnesota around 1988, and is entitled to claim substantiated expenses. The court reviewed the expenses claimed by Hattie, permitting some to be deducted while others were set aside because there was no substantiation for those expenses. The court also noted that Hattie may qualify for the $25,000 individual investor exception to the passive activity loss rules, since she owned more than 10 percent of the home and actively participated in the management of the home during those tax years.

As this case illustrates, failure to receive rental income does not eliminate loss deductions from rental properties, provided, of course, that those expenses can be substantiated.

PASSIVE ACTIVITY LOSS RULES UPON TRANSFER

Passive activity losses can be used to offset passive activity gains, and can be used to offset other income when the asset that generates the passive losses is sold. There are several ways of transferring an asset other than by sale of the asset and a competent financial advisor should be able to counsel his or her client on the application of the passive activity loss rules to those transactions.

If, when a taxpayer dies, there are remaining suspended passive activity losses that have not been used by the taxpayer, IRC Section 469(g) states that those suspended losses will be deductible on the decedent's final income tax return. The suspended losses will be deductible to the extent they exceed any step to fair market value in basis received by the passive assets under IRC Section 1014 as they pass through the estate of the decedent. If a decedent has suspended losses and the asset basis gets stepped to fair market value at death, the suspended loss is reduced by the change in basis and the remaining suspended loss is deductible. If the asset gets stepped to fair value and the decedent's basis in the asset was greater than the fair market value of the asset, the full suspended loss is deductible, but the decrease in basis is not deductible.

Exhibit 14.3 | Suspended Losses when Taxpayer Dies

- If asset value is stepped up, reduce the suspended losses by the amount stepped up.
- If asset value is stepped down, deduct the full suspended loss.

Example 14.11

Manny dies when he has Asset A with a basis of $600,000 and suspended losses of $520,000. The fair value of Asset A at Manny's death is $1,000,000. The suspended loss deduction on Manny's final return is $120,000.

FMV $1,000,000	$520,000	Suspended loss
↑	$400,000	Reduction for step-up
BASIS $600,000	$120,000	Suspended loss deduction

Example 14.12

Eddie died last week. Throughout his life, he relied on the advice of his friend, Murphy, and purchased a series of passive investments that persistently generated losses and had little prospect of increasing in value. Eddie's total basis in the passive investments was $150,000. As of the date of his death, Eddie had $150,000 in suspended passive losses, and the fair market value of his passive investments was $20,000. Since Section 1014 will result in a new basis of $20,000 (a step down) in the hands of the estate beneficiary who receives the investments, Eddie is permitted to deduct the entire $150,000 suspended loss on his final income tax return.

When a passive activity that has generated a suspended passive activity loss is gifted to another person, the donor is not permitted to take the loss against other income. Instead, the donee's basis in the gift is increased by the suspended passive activity loss.

Sometimes, a passive asset will be sold subject to an installment note. While immediate sale of the passive activity will allow the taxpayer to trigger the suspended passive activity loss for the current tax year, an installment sale results in a deferral of the recognition of the passive activity loss over the term of the note. The portion of suspended loss deductible is the same percentage as the total gain recognized in each year the installment note is in existence.

Finally, the taxpayer may dispose of the passive activity in a nontaxable exchange. Perhaps the most frequently observed nontaxable exchange of passive activity assets is a Section 1031 exchange of real estate. Provided the requirements for a like-kind exchange are met, the suspended losses are carried over into the replacement property, and the income generated from the replacement property can be used to offset those suspended passive losses. Of course, if the requirements for a like-kind exchange are not met, the transfer of the property will result in a taxable gain/loss and the suspended passive losses may be used to offset other income.

EXCEPTIONS TO THE PASSIVE ACTIVITY RULES

In the passive activity loss arena, as in other areas of tax planning, the best opportunities for clients are often presented in exceptions to the general rule.

Key Concepts

1. Identify the six exceptions to the passive categorization of tangible property that is used for rental purposes.
2. Identify the two circumstances where real estate activities can be classified as active businesses.

Rental Activities

In defining a passive activity, the IRC includes any activity that is a rental activity even if a taxpayer materially participates in the activity. If this was the final word on categorizing assets into the passive category, there would be few, if any, planning options for those purchasing rental property.

The Treasury Regulations provide six exceptions to the passive categorization of tangible (real or personal) property that is used for rental purposes. If a taxpayer does **not** meet one of the exceptions, the activity is classified as a passive activity. If one of the exceptions applies, the taxpayer must still meet the material participation test to convert the asset from a passive asset to an asset used in an active trade or business.

The first exception states that if the average period of customer use is seven days or less, the activity could be considered an active trade or business. This exception is necessary to allow certain industries to treat their short-term rental activities as an active trade or business.

Example 14.13

Randy is the general manager and owner of The Beachcomer Hotel, a national hotel chain. Most of his customers rent rooms in his hotels for a five-day period. Because the average period of customer use is less than seven days, the activity can be considered an active trade or business, assuming that Randy materially participates in the operation of the hotel. If Randy does not materially participate in the operation of the hotel chain, any year in which the company generated a loss, that loss cannot be used to offset other forms of income since the activity will be classified as passive activity.

Under the second exception to the rental activity rule, if the average period of customer use is 30 days or less and the taxpayer provides significant personal services in concert with the rental activity, the activity may be classified as an active trade or business provided that the taxpayer materially participates in the operation of the company.

Example 14.14

Continuing with **Example 14.13**, even if the average period of customer use of The Beachcomer Hotel was 14 days, since Randy provides significant personal services (such as maid service, room service, and management of recreational facilities) as well as rents the room, he can still treat operation of the hotel as an active trade or business provided that he materially participates in the operation of the company.

The third exception further expands the first two exceptions and states that the period of customer use is not of consequence if extraordinary personal services are provided by the company. When this exception applies, the customer's use of the property is incidental to the special services provided.

Example 14.15

Maura is a part owner in a private hospital located in Long Island, NY (organized as an LLC). This year, the hospital realized a small loss and Maura is curious if she can use her pro-rata share to offset other income on her taxes this year. At a recent investment seminar, Maura found out that rental activities were classified as passive activities and she is concerned that she will not be able to recognize the loss against other income this year. While the hospital does rent beds to patients, the rental of the beds to patients is merely incidental to the personal services being provided to the patients. Therefore, provided Maura materially participates in the operation of the activity, she can classify it as an active trade or business and use the loss to offset other income.

The fourth exception, which is very similar to the third exception covered above, states that the activity will be considered an active trade or business if the rental of property is incidental to a non-rental activity of the taxpayer.

The fifth exception classifies a rental activity that the taxpayer customarily makes available during business hours for nonexclusive use by customers as the active conduct of a trade or business, provided that the owner materially participates in the activity.

The sixth and final regulatory exception states that if the taxpayer provides the property for use in a non-rental activity by a partnership, S corporation, or joint venture in which the taxpayer is an owner, and the taxpayer materially participates in the operation of the entity, none of the partnerships distributive share of partnership income is income from a rental activity.

Exhibit 14.4 | Summary of Rental Property Exceptions to Passive Categorization

1. Customer use ≤ 7 days
2. Customer use ≤ 30 days and significant personal services provided
3. Extraordinary personal services are provided
4. Rental activities incidental to non-rental activity
5. Rental activity available during business hours for nonexclusive use of customers
6. Rental property used in an activity conducted by partnership, etc. where the taxpayer is the owner and an active participant

Real Estate Exceptions

There are two circumstances where real estate activities can be classified as active businesses. The first situation involves real estate professionals and the second involves the individual investor exception.

Real Estate Professionals Exception

Prior to 1993, all real estate activities were classified as passive activities regardless of whether or not the owner of the activity materially participated in the operation of the activity. Seven years after creating the passive activity rules, Congress realized that this categorization was unfair to those who spent most of their time in real estate activities and created the **real estate professionals exception**.

A real estate professional may treat a real estate activity as an active trade or business provided that the taxpayer meets the following requirements:

1. More than one-half of the taxpayer's personal services performed during the year are in real property trades or businesses in which the taxpayer materially participates, taking into consideration all of the trade and business activities engaged in by the taxpayer.
2. The taxpayer performed at least 750 hours of service in real-estate-related activities.

Closely held C corporations are also eligible if more than 50 percent of the gross receipts of the corporation are derived from real property trades or businesses in which the corporation materially participates. While this exception is available for C corporations, a special rule applies for those C corporations who wish to take advantage of it. Any excess passive activity losses generated by a C corporation that qualifies for the exception may be used to offset active, but not portfolio, income of the company. Due to the imposition of this special exception, closely held C corporations have a partial exemption from the passive activity loss rules.

CASE STUDY 14.2

Rental Activities as a Trade or Business

Victor and Francisca Ani, Petitioners v. Commissioner of Internal Revenue, Respondent. T.C. Summary Opinion 2011-119 (October 11, 2011).

In 2005 and 2006, Victor worked as a barber and Francisca worked as a nurse. Victor and Francisca also owned five rental properties which Victor managed. He negotiated leases, dealt with tenants, collected rent, coordinated repairs, and paid bills associated with the properties. They reported income and expenses on Schedule E, and deducted losses of $64,856 (for 2005) and $125,510 (for 2006) claiming that Victor was a real estate professional. Victor claimed that he spent 1,377 hours on barber activities and 956 hours on real estate activities in 2005. Likewise, Victor claimed he spent 1,380 hours on barber activities and 886 hours on real estate activities in 2006. The IRS disallowed the real estate losses under the passive activity rules of IRC Section 469.

After reviewing the basic tax rules that apply to passive activities, the court stated that the relevant issue in this case is the determination of whether or not Victor can be classified as a real estate professional. IRC Section 469(c)(7)(B) indicates that a taxpayer must meet the following requirements to be considered a real estate professional: (1) more than one-half of the personal services performed in trades or businesses by the taxpayer during the year are performed in real property trades or businesses in which the taxpayer materially participates; and (2) the taxpayer performs more than 750 hours of services during the taxable year in real property trades or businesses in which the taxpayer materially participates. Based on these requirements, the court found that Victor did not meet the definition of a real estate professional because the number of hours spent on his activities were ballpark guesstimates; furthermore, the documents submitted in court showed that Victor spent more time working as a barber than he did managing rental properties.

While Victor did not meet the definition of real estate professional, he did actively participate in the management of the properties. As such, the court determined that Victor and Francisca were entitled to deduct part of their losses (up to $25,000 against other income, as specified in IRC Section 469(i)), but that deduction may be subject to a partial or complete phaseout if their adjusted gross income exceeds $100,000.

Individual Investor Exception

Even after the imposition of the passive activity loss rules, Congress recognized that many middle-income families used real estate investing as a way to increase their net worth. The passive activity loss rules were intended to put an end to the games that high-income taxpayers were playing to wipe out exposure to tax. Congress never really intended to discourage investment in real estate for the moderate income groups. To provide an inducement for middle-income groups to invest in real estate, Congress created the **individual investor exception** to the passive loss rules.

The individual investor exception allows individual taxpayers who actively participate in rental real estate activities to deduct up to $25,000 of losses from that activity against non-passive income for the year. Like the rule that allows taxpayers to deduct $3,000 of capital losses against other forms of income each year, this rule is a special exception to the general rule that requires losses in one income bucket to be offset only against gains in the same income bucket. The exceptions to the general rule may be illustrated as follows:

There are some limitations to the $25,000 loss deduction, however. In order to qualify, the taxpayer must:

1. actively participate in the activity,
2. own at least 10% of the value of the real estate, and
3. have AGI equal to or less than $100,000 (the loss deduction is ratably phased out for AGI between $100,0000 and $150,000. Taxpayers with income over $150,000 are not eligible for any loss deduction under the individual investor exception to the passive activity rules).For most of this chapter, we have been referring to the material participation rules. Material participation in an activity generally allows the activity to be classified as an active trade or business as opposed to a passive activity. As previously discussed, material participation requires substantial, continuous involvement in the operation of the activity.

To qualify for the individual investor exception to the passive activity loss rules, however, the taxpayer does not have to materially participate in the activity. Active participation is required. **Active participation** means that the taxpayer participates in making management decisions concerning the property, but is not substantially and continuously involved in the operation of the activity (recall that substantial and continuous involvement is the standard that applies for material participation). A taxpayer who hires a property manager to manage the property will meet the active participation standard if he or she retains the right to have the final say on all management decisions.

As you can see by the ownership requirement, the taxpayer does not have to own the entire property, but must have a minimum of a 10 percent ownership interest in the property to take advantage of the exception. This allows taxpayers to invest with others, yet still qualify for the special individual investor exception.

When enacting the passive activity rules, Congress did not want to take away the ability of moderate income taxpayers to deduct losses by enacting the passive activity rules. Wealthy individuals were the primary target. How does Congress define a moderate income taxpayer? The answer is a taxpayer who has AGI less than $100,000. The $25,000 maximum allowable deduction is reduced by 50 cents for each dollar of adjusted gross income exceeding $100,000. Once the taxpayer reaches an AGI of $150,000, there is no remaining loss deduction available, and any losses generated by the activity will be either trapped in the activity under the at-risk limitation or trapped in the passive income bucket under the passive loss rules (unless, of course, there is other passive income that can be used to offset the passive losses).

A few items concerning the phaseout of the $25,000 loss deduction are worthy of note. First, the $100,000 - $150,000 phaseout range applies to adjusted gross income, regardless of filing status. Both single individuals, and dual-income married couples are subject to the same phaseout range. Consequently, Congress has imposed a significant marriage penalty. Second, the phaseout range and deduction amount ($25,000) is not inflation adjusted, so the same phaseout range and deduction amount has remained in place since 1986. Due to the lack of inflation adjustments to the phaseout range and deduction amount, and as incomes have increased over time, fewer and fewer taxpayers are able to make use of this exception to the passive activity loss rules.

Quick Quiz 14.4

1. If a taxpayer meets one of the six exceptions for rental activities, he does not have to meet the material participation test.
   a. True
   b. False
2. An individual taxpayer who actively participates in rental real estate activities and meets certain other qualifications may deduct up to $25,000 of losses against non-passive income.
   a. True
   b. False
3. Active participation is a higher standard than material participation.
   a. True
   b. False

False, True, False.

Example 14.16

Giorgio, a single taxpayer, has AGI of $90,000 and has losses from a rental real estate property of $20,000. Giorgio can deduct the full $20,000 against his $90,000 AGI.

Example 14.17

Ralph and Lauren, a married couple, have AGI of $138,000 and have a loss of $30,000 from a rental real estate property. Since they are beyond the $100,000 in AGI they can only deduct 50¢ for every dollar of loss that they are below the $150,000.

$150,000 - $138,000 = $12,000 / 2 = $6,000 deduction

Therefore, Ralph and Lauren can deduct $6,000 against ordinary income. The remainder of the loss is suspended under the passive activity rules.

CASE STUDY 14.3

Material Participation Standards

Tom and Nancy Miller, Petitioners v. Commissioner of Internal Revenue, Respondent, T.C. Memo 2011-219 (September 8, 2011).

Tom worked professionally as a ship pilot and in his spare time provided construction services, including kitchen remodeling, replacing home siding, building decks, building fences, and replacing windows. Tom and Nancy owned six rental real estate properties during 2005, and seven during 2006. They conceded that they did not materially participate in one rental real estate activity, and therefore the losses from that property are passive losses. They contended, however, that the losses from their remaining rental properties are not passive activity losses. The IRS issued a notice of deficiency, disallowing Schedule E rental real estate losses.

The Millers maintained contemporaneous time logs showing hours spent in their various production of income activities. If the Millers can show that they are qualified real estate professionals and materially participated in the operation of their properties, the losses are deductible notwithstanding the passive activity loss rules.

On the basis of the record and the testimony provided at trial, the court found that Tom had spent more than 750 hours performing significant construction work as a contractor and on his rental real estate activities; furthermore, the court found that he spent more time on his construction work and rental properties than he spent piloting vessels during the tax years at issue.

Since Tom spent more time on real estate activities than non-real-estate activities, and spent more than 750 hours during the year on rental real estate activities, the Court concluded that he is a qualified real estate professional.

In order to be able to deduct the losses on the real estate activities, however, the Court also needs to consider whether Tom materially participated in the rental activities. Material participation requires regular, continuous, and substantial involvement in the business operations (IRC Section 469(h)(1)). There are seven tests for material participation provided for in the Treasury Regulations, two of which are relevant in this case: (1) if the taxpayer's participation during the taxable year constitutes substantially all of the participation in the activity for the year, the material participation standard is met; and (2) a taxpayer is treated as having materially participated if the taxpayer participates in the activity for more than 100 hours during the taxable year and the taxpayer's participation in the activity for the taxable year is not less than the participation of any other individual.

CASE STUDY 14.3 CONTINUED

Since Tom and Nancy did not make an election to treat all of their rental properties as a group, the court applied these standards to each property individually. The court concluded that there was material participation in two of the properties (permitting them to claim the losses for tax purposes). For the remaining four properties, Tom and Nancy failed to carry the burden of proving that they met the material participation standards, and, consequently, the losses on those properties are subject to the passive activity rules.

As this case illustrates, individuals who have multiple rental properties and who wish to avoid imposition of the passive activity loss rules should determine whether it makes sense to group the multiple rental properties together as an appropriate economic group, and keep records to substantiate the material participation requirements. Strategically making appropriate elections and maintaining contemporaneous time records to justify material participation go a long way when arguing with the IRS over the imposition of the passive activity loss rules.

PASSIVE CREDITS

Some passive activities are deemed by Congress to be desirable from a public policy perspective despite the characterization of the activity as a passive activity. To encourage individuals to engage in these types of passive activities, Congress has made **passive credits** available. Passive credits may be used to offset any tax attributed to taxable income. The passive credits are, however, non-refundable credits, so in order to get a benefit from the credit, the taxpayer must have taxable income in the year the passive credit is generated.

The passive credits currently available include the low-income housing credit, the rehabilitation credit, and the research credit. Other passive credits may be used to offset income tax only on passive activity income and are also subject to the at-risk rules.

CONCLUSION

The passive activity loss rules are anti-abuse provisions designed to prevent high-income individuals from manipulating their exposure to tax. Once an activity has been designated a passive activity, any losses generated from that activity can only be offset against gains from other activities in the passive income bucket. To determine how much of the loss can potentially be used to offset other passive income, a three-part test is employed. First, the overall loss limitation is the taxpayer's basis in the property. Second, the maximum allowable loss will be limited to the amount that the taxpayer has at risk. Finally, the passive activity loss rule applies and states that, in most cases, passive losses may only be offset against passive gains.

The exceptions to the passive activity loss rules provide planning opportunities for individuals. Accordingly, it is important for advisors to understand the passive activity loss rules. In particular, the individual investor exception allowing deduction of up to $25,000 in real estate rental losses against other forms of income may be a valuable planning tool for clients.

KEY TERMS

Active Participation - Requires participation in making management decisions concerning the property, but is not substantially and continuously involved in the operation of the activity (the standard that applies for material participation).

At-Risk Rule - Provides that a taxpayer may not deduct, in the current tax year, more than the amount that he or she has at risk.

Basis Limitation - Provides that the maximum allowable loss that the taxpayer can deduct is equal to his or her basis in the investment.

Earned Income - Income received by a taxpayer in the form of wages, salaries, and income from the conduct of business activities.

Individual Investor Exception - Allows individual taxpayers who actively participate in rental real estate activities to deduct up to $25,000 of losses from that activity against non-passive income for the year.

Material Participation - Requires involvement in the conduct of the trade or business on a regular, continuous, and substantial basis.

Net Investment Income Tax (NIIT) - Applies at a rate of 3.8 percent to certain net investment income of individuals, estates and trusts that have income above the statutory threshold amounts.

Nonrecourse Debt - Debt that is secured only by the asset pledged as security and not by any personal guarantee of the debtor.

Passive Activity - Any activity in which a taxpayer does not materially participate, that is a limited partnership interest, or that is a rental activity (even if the taxpayer materially participates in the activity).

Passive Activity Loss Rule - Provides that passive losses may only be used to offset gains from passive activities and may not be used to offset other types of income.

Passive Credits - Non-refundable tax credits designed to encourage individuals to engage in certain types of passive activities. Passive credits may be used to offset any tax attributed to taxable income.

Passive Income - Income received by a taxpayer including income generated from investments in real estate and income generated by business entities in which the owner does not materially participate.

Portfolio Income - Income received by a taxpayer through the investment of capital, such as dividends, interest, and capital gains.

Publicly Traded Partnership (PTP) - A partnership that trades on an active securities market.

Real Estate Professional Exception - Provides that if a taxpayer meets certain requirements, he is considered a real estate professional and may treat a real estate activity as an active trade or business.

Recourse Debt - Debt that the taxpayer is personally liable to repay regardless of whether the investment produces a return for the investor.

DISCUSSION QUESTIONS

SOLUTIONS to the discussion questions can be found exclusively within the chapter. Once you have completed an initial reading of the chapter, go back and highlight the answers to these questions.

1. Describe the new category of income created by Congress in 1986.
2. Explain to whom the passive activity loss rules do and do not apply.
3. Name and describe the three types of income.
4. How is a passive activity defined by Section 469 of the Internal Revenue Code?
5. Describe the seven tests for material participation.
6. Why are the material participation standards problematic for limited partners?
7. What factors are considered when grouping passive activities?
8. What are the ways in which it is inappropriate to group passive activities?
9. What are the three types of limits that are generally imposed on passive losses?
10. What is the basis limitation?
11. What is the at-risk rule and how is it different from the basis limitation?
12. What is the difference between recourse and nonrecourse debt?
13. What is the passive activity loss rule?
14. Describe the passive loss limitations for publicly traded partnerships.
15. What happens when a taxpayer dies with suspended passive activity losses and the asset gets stepped up to fair market value?
16. What happens when a passive activity that has generated a suspended passive activity loss is gifted to another person?
17. What are the six exceptions to the passive categorization of tangible (real or personal) property that is used for rental purposes?
18. What is the real estate professionals exception?
19. What is the individual investor exception?
20. What is the difference between active participation and material participation?
21. What is the purpose of a passive credit?

MULTIPLE CHOICE PROBLEMS

A sample of multiple choice problems is provided below. Additional multiple choice problems are available at money-education.com by accessing the Student Practice Portal.

1. Tito and Chuck are good friends. They decide to open a sports equipment store together because of their love of the outdoors. They each own 50 percent in SportsCrazy, LLC, which is taxed as a partnership. Chuck manages the business. Tito has a thriving tax practice and therefore does not participate in the operation of the business. Which of the following is true?
    a. Only the income distributed to Chuck is considered passive income.
    b. Only the income distributed to Tito is considered passive income.
    c. The income distributed to both Chuck and Tito is considered passive income.
    d. The income distributed to both Chuck and Tito is considered active income.

2. Brad, Tom, Katie, and Angelina are partners in MovieMakers, LLC. They all participate in the business to some extent and there are no other employees. Given the following activities, which of these individuals are clearly material participants?
    - Brad has a job outside of the business but does provide about 125 hours a year to help market the business.
    - Tom devotes all of his time to the business and generally devotes 60 hours per week to the business.
    - Katie has materially participated in the business for the last seven years, however she only dedicated about 50 hours this year because she had a baby in January.
    - Angelina devotes very little time to the business and only helps on an as-needed basis. She rarely helps more than two or three hours per month.

    a. Tom only.
    b. Tom and Katie.
    c. Tom and Brad.
    d. Tom, Katie, Brad and Angelina.

3. Keke owns a 10 percent interest in CreativeWorks, LLP. She originally invested $500,000 and has personally taken losses from the partnership of $200,000. The partnership took out a nonrecourse loan of $800,000. What is Keke's at-risk amount?
    a. $300,000.
    b. $500,000.
    c. $1,100,000.
    d. $1,300,000.

4. Elton is a 20 percent owner in CheerSquad, LLC, a local gym for middle school and high school cheerleaders. The gym provides private coaches to help young cheerleaders learn stunts and improve their overall cheer performance. Elton does not materially participate. Elton contributed $200,000 initially. During the prior years he has been allocated $200,000 in income and $300,000 in losses. After a freak accident during the current year in which one of the cheerleaders was critically injured doing a stunt, the business lost many customers. The business allocated a $150,000 loss to Elton for the current year. What is Elton's suspended loss due to at-risk rules?
   a. $0.
   b. $50,000.
   c. $100,000.
   d. $150,000.

5. Norma Jean is a 10 percent owner in HKAccounting, LLC, a review company for the CPA exam. She is also a 20 percent owner in MyPuppy, LLC, a rescue organization for dogs. Norma Jean does not materially participate in either company. Her at-risk amount and loss/income for the current year is as follows:
   - HKAccounting – At risk = $800,000; Income of $150,000
   - MyPuppy – At risk = $200,000; Loss of $350,000

   Norma Jean also has wage income of $75,000. How much of the loss can she write off in the current year?
   a. $150,000.
   b. $200,000.
   c. $225,000.
   d. $350,000.

Additional multiple choice problems are available at *money-education.com* by accessing the Student Practice Portal. Access requires registration of the title using the unique code at the front of the book.

QUICK QUIZ EXPLANATIONS

Quick Quiz 14.1

1. True.
2. False. In terms of hours, a taxpayer must dedicate more than 500 hours of effort to an activity each year in order to be considered a material participant. In the alternative, the taxpayer may dedicate more than 100 hours to the activity, but no less than anyone else, to be considered a material participant. The question, however, does not mention that anyone else is involved in the activity, so the 500 hour rule would apply.
3. True.

Quick Quiz 14.2

1. False. The basis limitation states that the maximum allowable loss that the taxpayer can deduct is generally equal to his or her basis in the investment.
2. True.

Quick Quiz 14.3

1. True.
2. False. The passive activity loss rule states that losses falling into the passive bucket from a passive activity can only be offset against gains that are in the passive bucket. Excess passive losses may be carried forward indefinitely, and may be used to offset future passive gains, but may not be used to offset other income.

Quick Quiz 14.4

1. False. The Treasury Regulations provide six exceptions to the passive categorization of tangible (real or personal) property that is used for rental purposes. If none of the exceptions are met, the property is classified as a passive activity. If one or more of the exceptions applies, the taxpayer must still meet the material participation test to convert the asset from a passive asset to an asset used in an active trade or business.
2. True.
3. False. Active participation means that the taxpayer participates in making management decisions concerning the property, but is not substantially and continuously involved in the operation of the activity (the standard that applies for material participation). Therefore, active participation is a lower standard than material participation.

15

THE ALTERNATIVE MINIMUM TAX

LEARNING OBJECTIVES

1. Describe the purpose of the alternative minimum tax (AMT).
2. Identify the taxpayers most likely to be affected by the AMT.*
3. Explain how the AMT is calculated.
4. Identify the phaseout thresholds for AMT exemptions.
5. Discuss the difference between exclusion items and deferral items.*
6. Describe the general effect of adjustments and preferences on alternative minimum taxable income (AMTI).*
7. Identify how itemized deductions are affected by the AMT.*
8. Explain how the exercise of incentive stock options (ISOs) affects AMT.*
9. Calculate a taxpayer's AMT preference created by the exercise of ISOs.
10. Identify business-related items that are deferral or exclusion items for AMT purposes.*
11. Describe the AMT impact on private activity municipal bond interest that is received by a taxpayer.*

**Ties to CFP Certification Learning Objectives*

INTRODUCTION

The **alternative minimum tax (AMT)**, like the passive activity rules, was enacted in 1986 to curb perceived abuses by high-income taxpayers attempting to minimize their current income tax liability. The AMT is the ultimate tax oxymoron. It is neither alternative (it *must* be used to calculate tax liability), nor is it minimum (the imposition of the AMT means that the taxpayer will have to pay *more* tax than that calculated using the regular tax system). Understanding why, and how, the AMT is imposed is important for tax planners who are advising clients who may be caught in its snares.

Key Concepts

1. Describe the purpose of the alternative minimum tax.
2. Identify the taxpayers most likely to be affected by the AMT.
3. Explain how the AMT is calculated.
4. Identify the phaseout thresholds for AMT exemptions.

As an anti-abuse technique, the AMT is designed primarily to change the timing of tax payments, although in some cases, imposition of the AMT results in a permanent increase in tax. Long ago taxpayers learned that it is generally preferable or beneficial to pay less tax now, and defer tax liability into the future. Several planning techniques were developed to do just that, resulting in a loss of current tax revenue for Congress. Congress would rather have taxpayers pay more now, and less later, since this fills federal coffers and minimizes the need to borrow to fund government expenditures. Furthermore, Congress believed it unfair to allow wealthy taxpayers to participate in many of these activities that reduce or eliminate their current tax liability in ways that were not available to lower and middle-income taxpayers. The AMT is designed to offset the timing impact of tax deductions, so that those impacted by it will have to pay more tax now, and correspondingly less in the future. Generally, those impacted by the AMT are taxpayers who take advantage of "items of tax preference."

For many years, Congress made ad hoc changes to the exemption used in calculating the AMT. The American Taxpayer Relief Act of 2012 (ATRA) imposed indexing for AMT exemptions and tax brackets in an attempt to prevent the AMT from inadvertently affecting middle-income taxpayers. It also allows for nonrefundable credits against the AMT.

Prior to 2018, AMT was primarily an issue for those with income in excess of $200,000 and affected taxpayers who itemized and who had more children. However, AMT is one of the least favorite parts of the Internal Revenue Code (IRC) and one that many politicians on both sides of the isle had promised to eliminate for the American people.

Many people were hoping that the TCJA 2017 would finally eliminate AMT for everyone. Unfortunately, while the House bill included a provision eliminating AMT for individuals and for corporations, the conference agreement did not abolish AMT for individuals. The new law did eliminate AMT for corporations and it made changes that will result in fewer individuals and families being subject to AMT.

The TCJA 2017 increased the AMT exemption by approximately 30 percent and increased the phaseout amounts significantly for years from 2018 through 2025. In addition, the law suspended dependency exemptions. As a result of these changes, most individual taxpayers will not be impacted by AMT. These positive changes expire in 2026 unless Congress extends these modifications or eliminates AMT altogether.

HOW THE AMT WORKS

The AMT is an alternative tax calculation. The AMT applies to everyone, but it does not create additional tax for everyone and therefore does not increase an unaffected taxpayer's tax liability. When a taxpayer prepares his income tax return, the taxpayer must complete two tax calculations, the regular tax and the AMT. The first calculation will use the regular tax system, and is calculated on Form 1040. Prior chapters in this textbook have reviewed, in detail, the calculation of tax under the regular income tax system. The second calculation that must be completed each year is the alternative minimum tax, which is calculated separately on Form 6251. A taxpayer is liable for the greater of the regular tax liability or the tentative minimum tax calculated for AMT on Form 6251.

To calculate the AMT, the taxpayer starts with his taxable income from the Form 1040. The AMT system requires certain changes be made to taxable income. These changes are referred to as adjustments or preferences. **Adjustments** can either increase or decrease **alternative minimum taxable income (AMTI)**, while **preferences** always result in an addition to AMTI. Once all adjustments and preferences have been accounted for, AMTI is calculated. An exemption (discussed below) is subtracted from AMTI to arrive at the AMT tax base, to which the AMT rate is applied. For individuals, the AMT rate is 26 percent on the first $199,900 of income ($99,950 for those married filing separately), and 28 percent on the excess. The result at this point is referred to as the tentative minimum tax, which is further reduced by any foreign tax credit that the taxpayer may claim, and the taxpayer's regular tax liability from Form 1040. The detailed AMT formula described above is illustrated in **Exhibit 15.1**.

Exhibit 15.1 | Alternative Minimum Tax Formula

Taxable Income
Add: Adjustments that increase AMTI
Less: Adjustments that decrease AMTI
Add: Preferences
Alternative Minimum Taxable Income (AMTI)
Less: AMT Exemption
AMT Tax Base
Application of Appropriate AMT Rate
Tentative Minimum Tax
Less: Foreign Tax Credit
Less: Regular Tax Liability (Form 1040)
Alternative Minimum Tax (AMT)

The applicable exemption used within the AMT calculation depends on the taxpayer's filing status and the taxpayer's AMTI. The following exhibit contains the AMT exemption amounts for 2021.

Exhibit 15.2 | AMT Exemption Amounts

Filing Status	*2021*
Single and Head of Household	$73,600
Married Filing Jointly and Surviving Spouse	$114,600
Married Filing Separately	$57,300
Estates and Trusts	$25,700

These exemptions are subject to phaseout. When the taxpayer's AMTI begins to exceed certain amounts, the phaseout rule states that the exemption amount is reduced by 25 percent of the amount by which AMTI exceeds the beginning of the phaseout range. This reduction continues until the end of the phaseout range at which point the taxpayer's AMT exemption is reduced to zero and the taxpayer is not entitled to any AMT exemption. The phaseout levels are sufficient to ensure that very few individual taxpayers will lose their AMT exemption.

Exhibit 15.3 | AMT Exemption Phaseout Thresholds

Filing Status	*2021*
Single and Head of Household	$523,600 - $818,000
Married Filing Jointly and Surviving Spouse	$1,047,200 - $1,505,600
Married Filing Separately	$523,600 - $752,800
Estates and Trusts	$85,650 - $188,450

The structure of the phaseout affects high-income taxpayers, who may have their AMT exemption limited, or eliminated, in the calculation of their alternative minimum tax.

Example 15.1

Carmela is a single taxpayer with an AMTI of $560,300 in 2021. Because her AMTI is above the phaseout threshold for single taxpayers of $523,600, Carmela's AMT exemption for 2021 must be reduced. The phaseout rule states that the exemption amount is reduced by 25% of the amount by which the taxpayer's AMTI exceeds the threshold. Therefore, Carmela's AMT exemption amount must be reduced by 25% of $36,700 ($560,300 - $523,600) or $9,175. Consequently, her AMT exemption for 2021 is $64,425 ($73,600 - $9,175).

Example 15.2

Tony is a married filing jointly taxpayer with an AMTI of $1,345,600 in 2021. Because Tony's AMTI is above the phaseout threshold for married filing jointly taxpayers of $1,047,200, his AMT exemption must be reduced by $74,600[($1,345,600 - $1,047,200) x 25%]. The maximum AMT exemption amount is $114,600 for a married filing jointly taxpayer. Therefore, Tony's AMT exemption for 2021 is $40,000 ($114,600 - $74,600).

Now assume the same facts except that Tony has an AMTI of $1,550,000 for 2021. Tony's AMT exemption must be reduced by $125,700 [($1,550,000 - $1,047,200) x 25%]. Because the 2021 maximum AMT exemption amount is $114,600, Tony is not entitled to any exemption this year.

In some cases, triggering the AMT causes a permanent increase in tax. In other cases, the AMT merely changes the timing of the tax payment. Adjustments and preferences are classified as either exclusion items or deferral items. **Exclusion items** result in a permanent increase in tax. **Deferral items** result in a tax credit equal to the additional tax that must be paid in the current year, and this credit can be used to offset tax liability in a future year when the taxpayer is no longer subject to the AMT. There is an unlimited carryforward for the AMT credit generated from deferral items, but the credit may not be carried back and applied against regular tax liability in past years. From a planning standpoint, therefore, deferral items are better to have than exclusion items.

Quick Quiz 15.1

1. The AMT was designed to curb abuses by high-income taxpayers.
   a. True
   b. False
2. The AMT is most likely to affect low-income taxpayers.
   a. True
   b. False
3. The Foreign Tax Credit increases the tentative minimum tax.
   a. True
   b. False
4. In some cases, the AMT merely changes the timing of a tax payment.
   a. True
   b. False
5. The TCJA 2017 eliminated AMT for individuals.
   a. True
   b. False

True, False, False, True, False.

Additionally, capital gains are taxed at the same rate for AMT purposes as they are for regular tax purposes. As a result, even though capital gains have a lower tax rate (0-20%) than the AMT rates, capital gains do not have an impact on whether a taxpayer will become an AMT taxpayer.

ADJUSTMENTS AND PREFERENCES

As illustrated in the AMT formula, the key planning issues surrounding the AMT involve the adjustments and preferences that are either added or subtracted in arriving at alternative minimum taxable income (AMTI). For simplicity, we will review these adjustments and preferences in four categories: (1) exemptions and standard deduction changes; (2) itemized deduction changes; (3) investment-related changes; and (4) business-related changes.

Personal and Dependency Exemptions and the Standard Deduction

While personal and dependency exemptions were allowed for regular tax purposes before 2018 (and will be allowed again beginning in 2026 after the sunset of TCJA 2017), personal and dependency exemptions are preference items in the calculation of AMT.

The standard deduction, including the additional standard deduction for the aged or blind, is also a preference item in the calculation of the AMT. However, the additional standard deduction for qualified disaster-related personal casualty losses (when available) is not a preference item and, therefore, does not increase AMTI.[1]

Itemized Deduction Changes

From an individual tax planning standpoint, itemized deduction changes are perhaps the most important changes for clients. Many taxpayers itemize deductions, and it is important to understand how these deductions are treated differently under the regular tax system as compared to the AMT system.

Exhibit 15.4 | Summary of Itemized Deductions

	Deductible for Regular Tax	*Deductible for AMT*	*Differences in Deductions*
Home Mortgage Interest	Qualified mortgage interest only	Qualified mortgage interest only	None
Medical	Excess above 7.5% AGI	Excess above 7.5% AGI	None
Taxes	Property/sales/use/ and ad valorem taxes are deductible	Taxes are not deductible, except tax on qualified motor vehicles	Lose all tax deductions under AMT (Add all back except tax on qualified motor vehicles)
Miscellaneous	Regular rules (TCJA 2017 eliminated miscellaneous deductions subject to 2%)	Same as regular rules	None
Charitable	Regular rules	Same as regular rules	None
Casualty	Regular rules	Same as regular rules	None

1. The additional standard deduction for qualified disaster-related personal casualty losses is not a permanent part of the tax code. It is only available through Congressional action, usually on a year-by-year basis for specified Presidentially-declared major disasters.

Due to TCJA changes to regular tax rules for the deductibility of mortgage interest for tax years 2018 - 2025, there is no AMT adjustment to qualified mortgage interest during those years.

There is not a difference in the deductibility of medical itemized expenses between regular tax and AMT. The limit is 7.5 percent of AGI for 2021 and beyond due to the passage of the Consolidated Appropriations Act of 2021.

Any state or local income taxes, property taxes, or sales taxes claimed as a deduction for regular tax purposes must be added back to income to determine AMTI. No deduction is allowed for state and local taxes once the taxpayer becomes an AMT taxpayer. There is only one exception to this rule, and that is tax on qualified motor vehicles.

Key Concepts

1. Describe the general effect of adjustments and preferences on AMTI.
2. Identify how itemized deductions are affected by AMT.
3. Explain how the exercise of ISOs affects AMT.
4. Identify business-related items that are deferral or exclusion items for AMT.

After 2017, miscellaneous itemized deductions subject to two percent are no longer deductible and therefore have no effect on AMT. Those miscellaneous itemized deductions that are not subject to two percent, such as gambling losses and unrecovered basis in annuities at the time of death, are treated the same for regular tax and for AMT.

Exhibit 15.5 summarizes the itemized deductions that must be added back to income to calculate AMTI.

Exhibit 15.5 | Deductions Lost Using AMT

- 100% of state and local income taxes
- 100% of property taxes
- 100% of sales taxes

Deductions for charitable contributions and casualty losses claimed as itemized deductions for regular tax are not impacted in any way by the AMT rules, and they do not have to be added back into income when calculating AMTI.

If an individual does not itemize deductions, the standard deduction is added back to taxable income when calculating AMTI. Only the allowable itemized deductions noted above may be used as deductions for AMT purposes.

Once the changes for itemized deductions necessary to calculate AMTI have been made, the next important inquiry is whether they are an exclusion or deferral item. Unfortunately, all of the itemized deduction changes are classified as exclusion items. Any additional tax generated by adding these items to calculate AMTI will not result in the creation of a credit that can be used against regular tax liability in the future, but will rather result in a permanent increase in tax liability for the taxpayer.

CASE STUDY 15.1

AMT

James A. and Nancy B. Wiese, Petitioners v. Commissioner of Internal Revenue, Respondent. T.C. Summary Opinion 2005-91 (July 19, 2005).

James and Nancy Wiese timely filed a joint Form 1040 for 2002 using the cash method of accounting. They itemized deductions for the following expenses: (1) medical and dental expenses (in excess of 7.5 percent of adjusted gross income) in the amount of $2,914;[1] (2) State and local income taxes in the amount of $32,099; and (3) real estate taxes in the amount of $20,445.[2] They reported taxable income in the amount of $9,631 and reported tax of $963. They neither completed nor attached to their 2002 return Form 6251, Alternative Minimum Tax-Individuals, nor did they report any liability for the AMT on their return.[3] The IRS determined that the Wieses are liable for the AMT computed in the following manner:

Form 1040, line 39[1]	$18,631
plus: adjustments and preferences	
(1) medical / dental expenses[2]	$2,021
(2) State / local income taxes	$32,099
(3) real estate taxes	$20,445
Alternative Minimum Taxable Income	$73,196
less: Exemption Amount	$49,000
Taxable Excess	$24,196
Applicable AMT Rate	26%
Tentative Minimum Tax	$6,291
less: regular tax[3]	$963
AMT	$5,328

1. Line 39 of the 2002 Form 1040 represents adjusted gross income less itemized deductions as reported by petitioners on their return. Line 39 precedes the line on which personal exemptions are claimed; thus, the AMT computation effectively serves to disallow all personal exemptions.
2. Medical expenses in excess of 7.5 percent, but less than

The Wieses contend that the AMT should not apply to them under the circumstances of their case, and they ask for a waiver from such tax on equitable grounds. In this regard, the Wieses point out that they had no items of tax preference in 2002. They also point out that they are neither wealthy nor the high-income taxpayers for whom the AMT was intended, having faced a financially-disastrous business failure in the mid-1990s from which they are still struggling to recover.

1. The 7.5% was changed to 10% in 2013.
2. Prior to 2018 there was no dollar limit on the deduction of state and local taxes in the regular tax calculation.
3. Typically, AMT would have been reported on line 43 of Form 1040.

CASE STUDY 15.1 CONTINUED

The AMT is the difference between the "tentative minimum tax" and the regular tax. The adjustments provided in section 56(b) are threefold. First, §56(b)(1)(A)(ii) provides that in computing alternative minimum taxable income, no deduction shall be allowed for any state and local income taxes or real estate taxes.

Second, §56(b)(1)(B) provides that medical and dental expenses shall be deductible in computing alternative minimum taxable income only to the extent that such expenses exceed 10 percent of the taxpayer's adjusted gross income.

Third, §56(b)(1)(E) provides that no personal exemptions shall be allowed in computing alternative minimum taxable income.

After taking into account the foregoing three adjustments, the Wiese's alternative minimum taxable income for 2002 equals $73,196; i.e., taxable income of $9,631 plus adjustments of $63,565. Alternative minimum taxable income exceeds the applicable exemption amount of $49,000 by $24,196. The Wiese's "tentative minimum tax" is therefore 26% of the taxable excess; i.e., 26% of $24,196, or $6,291. Because the tentative minimum tax exceeds the regular tax of $963, the Wieses are liable for the AMT in the amount of such excess, i.e., $6,291 less $963, or $5,328.

The AMT serves to impose a tax whenever the sum of specified percentages of the excess of alternative minimum taxable income over the applicable exemption amount exceeds the regular tax for the taxable year. If Congress had intended to tax only items of tax preference, it would have defined "alternative minimum taxable income" differently, for example, solely by reference to items of tax preference. They are liable for the AMT as determined by respondent in the notice of deficiency.[1]

1. Petitioners should regard as their good fortune the fact that the IRS did not determine AMT for 2001 if, as suggested by petitioners, they claimed significant state and local income taxes and real estate taxes on their return for that year. In this regard, suffice it to say that the Commissioner's acceptance of a taxpayer's return for a prior year does not estop or otherwise preclude the Commissioner from raising the issue in a return for a subsequent year. See Ekren v. Commissioner, T.C. Memo. 1986-509 (and cases cited at n.6).

Investment-Related Changes

Certain investment activities may also have an impact on AMT. The two most important considerations from a planning standpoint are (1) interest on private activity municipal bonds, and (2) the exercise of incentive stock options (ISOs).

Interest on Private Activity Municipal Bonds

Private Activity Municipal Bonds are securities issued by or on behalf of local governments that bear interest which is tax-exempt for regular tax purposes and are used to provide debt financing for private projects (as opposed to public/governmental projects). Projects that may be financed by private activity municipal bonds include airports, residential rental projects, sports stadiums, and qualified hazardous waste facilities, just to name a few. Interest earned on private activity municipal bonds is excluded from tax for regular income tax purposes, but is potentially taxable under the AMT. This interest must be added back to regular taxable income to arrive at AMTI. Recall that if a client would like to purchase a municipal bond that will be fully exempt from income tax (both regular and AMT), he or she could purchase a public purpose municipal bond.

For tax years beginning in 2008, tax-exempt interest received on certain types of municipal bonds are not considered items of tax preference and are therefore not subject to the AMT if the bonds were issued after 2008. Municipal bonds that qualify for this exemption from AMT include:

- an exempt facility bond for which 95% or more of the net proceeds are to be used to provide qualified residential rental projects,
- a qualified mortgage bond,
- a qualified veterans mortgage bond, or
- any refunding bond of the bond being refunded (or in the case of a series of refunded bonds, the original bond) is one of the bonds listed above issued after July 30, 2008.

Furthermore, tax-exempt interest on specified private activity bonds issued in 2009 and 2010 are exempt from the AMT. You may recall that, as a general rule, taxpayers can only deduct expenses for income tax purposes if the amount claimed had already been brought into income. Applying this general rule to municipal bonds, we learned that investment interest expense associated with acquiring a portfolio of municipal bonds is not deductible for regular tax purposes since the income generated by the bonds is exempt from tax. (Alternatively stated, since the taxpayer purchasing municipal bonds was not sharing his or her gains with the government, the government does not allow a tax deduction for the interest incurred to acquire the investment.) When municipal bond interest becomes taxable under the AMT system, however, any investment interest paid to acquire the bonds will be deductible when arriving at AMTI. This adjustment for investment interest expense used to acquire the municipal bond portfolio is in concert with the general rule that allows deductions for expenses incurred in purchasing investments where the gains from the investment will be shared with the government in the form of tax revenue.

The add-back of the interest on private activity municipal bonds (unless issued after June 30, 2008 and excluded from this treatment), and the deduction permitted for investment interest incurred to acquire those bonds, are considered to be AMT exclusion items. As a result, any increase in tax caused by the adjustments for private activity bonds will be a permanent increase in tax for the taxpayer, and no credit will be available to offset future regular tax liability.

Quick Quiz 15.2

1. If a taxpayer's medical expenses equal 5% of their AGI, this will not affect the calculation of AMTI.
   a. True
   b. False
2. Charitable contributions must be added back to calculate AMTI.
   a. True
   b. False
3. All itemized deduction changes are deferral items.
   a. True
   b. False

True, False, False.

Exercise of Incentive Stock Options

Another investment related activity that could have an impact on a taxpayer's AMT liability is the exercise of incentive stock options.

There are two types of stock options:

- Nonqualified Stock Options
- Incentive Stock Options

A **Nonqualified Stock Option (NQSO)** is a right to purchase shares of company stock at a given strike price (generally set at the market price of the stock on the day the option is granted). The exercise of a

NQSO results in ordinary income for the taxpayer equal to the difference between the value of the stock on the day of exercise and the strike price of the option. When a NQSO is granted to an employee, the employer must withhold taxes on exercise, including employment (Social Security) taxes. Since a NQSO results in ordinary income tax treatment, it is not a preference item for AMT purposes and does not have to be added back to taxable income to arrive at AMTI (it is already included in taxable income).

An **Incentive Stock Option (ISO)** has different tax characteristics. To qualify as an ISO, the issuing company must comply with a host of special rules. The advantage of an ISO, as compared to a nonqualified stock option, is that if the taxpayer meets the holding period requirement, the gain on the option will be taxed as capital gain instead of ordinary income. To qualify for capital gain tax treatment, the stock must be held a minimum of two years from the date of the grant of the ISO, and one year from the date of the exercise of the option. If either part of this two-pronged holding period test is not met, the taxpayer will have to report the gain as ordinary income. At the exercise of an ISO, therefore, there is no immediate regular income tax consequence since it is not possible to determine, at that time, whether the gain will be taxed as ordinary income or as a capital gain. If the taxpayer exercises the option and sells the stock within one year (referred to as a disqualifying disposition), the gain will be taxed at ordinary rates because the holding period was not met, and the ISO will be treated similarly to an NQSO.

While the exercise of an ISO does not impact the taxpayer's regular tax liability, it may result in the imposition of the AMT. The difference between the value of the stock on the date of exercise and the strike price of the option must be added to taxable income to arrive at AMTI. When a taxpayer exercises a large number of options in one tax year, and does not sell the stock (thereby triggering a disqualifying disposition and imposing ordinary income tax on the gain), there is a danger of becoming an AMT taxpayer.

Example 15.3

Paulie, a single individual, who is an executive at Cobb's Consulting, Inc., was granted 1,000 ISOs on Cobb's stock two years ago when the price per share was $15. The last few years have resulted in tremendous growth for Cobb's and the stock is now trading at $95 per share. Paulie exercised the ISOs, but did not sell the stock. He plans on holding the shares for at least a year so he can pay the lower capital gains tax rate on the growth. Even though exercise of the options did not result in a taxable event for regular tax purposes this year, Paulie will have to add $80,000 to his taxable income when computing AMTI. If there are no other transactions this year that could reduce AMTI, it is likely that Paulie will become an AMT taxpayer for the year, since the tax preference item – the gain on the exercise of the ISO – is greater than his exemption for AMT purposes.

Example 15.4

Assume the same facts as **Example 15.3**, except that Paulie exercises the options and immediately sells the shares. In this case, since there was a disqualifying disposition of the stock (Paulie did not meet the two year from date of grant/one year from date of exercise holding period), the gain will be taxed as ordinary income to Paulie this year. Since the gain is included in regular income, there is no adjustment to be made when calculating AMTI. In a circumstance such as this, it is unlikely that Paulie will become an AMT taxpayer in the current year.

From a planning standpoint, it may be wise to counsel clients with ISOs to exercise the ISOs in small amounts over time so that the AMT gain is not combined into one tax year.

Unlike the itemized deduction adjustments and the preferences for private activity bonds, the adjustments to taxable income from ISOs are considered deferral items (not exclusion items), and any AMT generated by including the ISOs in AMTI will become a credit that can be used to offset future, regular tax liability.

Exhibit 15.6 | Summary of AMT Investment Related Changes

	Regular Tax	*AMT*	*Differences*
Private Activities Municipal Bonds	Not taxable	Taxable	AMT preference item
NQSOs	At exercise W-2 income	At exercise W-2 income	None
ISOs	At exercise No regular tax	At exercise AMT income to extent fair market value > strike price	AMT at exercise

Other Investment-Related Changes

In addition to the AMT rules concerning private activity municipal bond interest and incentive stock options, adjustments must be made for certain transactions when the taxpayer moves to AMT status. In particular, gains or losses on the sale or disposition of property must be recalculated if the taxpayer's AMT basis in the asset is different than his or her regular basis. Likewise, loss limitations imposed by the amount at-risk limitation and the passive activity rules must be recalculated taking into account any adjustments required for AMT purposes. While calculation of these adjustments is beyond the scope of this text, you should be aware that these adjustments are often necessary due primarily to changes in allowable depreciation deductions, which will be discussed briefly below. When calculating AMTI, certain adjustments must be made to the depreciation deductions taken for regular tax purposes, and these adjustments must also be taken into account when considering gain/loss and passive limitations when calculating the alternative minimum tax.

Quick Quiz 15.3

1. Interest earned on private activity bonds is added back to taxable income to calculate AMTI.
   a. True
   b. False
2. Exercising a large number of ISOs and not selling the stock in the same tax year may result in the imposition of AMT.
   a. True
   b. False

True, True.

Business-Related Changes

One of the advantages of using an asset in the active conduct of a trade or business is the ability to claim depreciation deductions, which allows the taxpayer to recoup his investment over the useful life of the asset. Asset class lives and depreciation scales are provided for both real and personal property. When a taxpayer becomes an AMT taxpayer, however, the depreciation time period lengthens, requiring the taxpayer to add back some of the depreciation claimed for regular income tax purposes.

In addition to regular depreciation, the IRC allows quicker expensing of asset costs, and, in some cases, immediate expensing of asset costs for certain specified expenditures. Usually, Congress allows businesses to immediately expense costs in an effort to provide an incentive for investment in that area. Expenditures that qualify for these special rules include circulation costs (for publishers), intangible drilling costs (for oil and gas investors), mining costs (for natural resource extractors) and research and experimental costs (for scientific enterprises). If a taxpayer moves from regular status to AMT status, adjustments must be made to the expenses claimed on these activities so that, usually, the taxpayer will have to add part of the expense claimed back to taxable income in arriving at AMTI.

All of the depreciation and accelerated expense adjustments mentioned above are considered to be deferral items for AMT purposes. If any AMT is generated due to the inclusion of these items in AMTI, the taxpayer will receive a credit of a like amount that can be used against future regular tax liability. These adjustments change the timing of the payment of tax (they require the taxpayer to pay more now, less later), but do not result in a permanent increase in tax burden.

Two additional business related changes are exclusion items, resulting in a permanent change in tax burden if their inclusion causes the taxpayer to be subject to the AMT. The business related exclusion items are: (1) depletion, and (2) qualified small business stock (under Section 1202).

Depletion is a form of depreciation that applies to natural resources. As minerals are extracted from the earth, the owner of the mineral rights may claim a depletion deduction to recoup some of his capital used to acquire the mineral rights. When a taxpayer moves into AMT status, the deduction for depletion must be recalculated taking into consideration allowable AMT income and deductions from the activity. Once the taxpayer is subject to the AMT, the depletion deduction is further limited to the taxpayer's alternative minimum tax basis in the activity. Compared to the allowable depletion rules in the regular tax system, this rule severely limits the taxpayer's ability to claim deductions. As noted above, the depletion changes are exclusion items. Once the adjustment is made and the AMT applies, the taxpayer's tax burden has been permanently increased.

Quick Quiz 15.4

1. Depreciation is an exclusion item for AMT purposes.
   a. True
   b. False
2. Depletion is a deferral item for AMT purposes.
   a. True
   b. False

False, False.

In an effort to encourage individuals to capitalize small corporations, IRC Section 1202 allows investors of qualified small business stock to exclude up to 100 percent of the capital gain from income. If a taxpayer claiming a Section 1202 exclusion on stock acquired prior to September 28, 2010 becomes an AMT taxpayer, however, seven percent of the excluded gain must be added back to taxable income in arriving at AMTI. Section 1202 stock acquired after September 27, 2010 that qualifies for the 100 percent exclusion under regular tax is not subject to the AMT tax. If the gain on Section 1202 stock acquired before September 28, 2010 is large, the gain alone could cause a taxpayer to move into AMT status. Too much gain can trigger the AMT, exactly what Congress designed the AMT to do. The preference for Section 1202 stock is an exclusion item, resulting in a permanent increase in tax liability for the taxpayer.

Miscellaneous Adjustments

In addition to the major categories of changes described above, when a person becomes an AMT taxpayer, several other adjustments must be made to the tax return as well (to calculate AMTI). While these adjustments are beyond the scope of this text, you should be aware that adjustments will be made to Section 179 depreciation deductions, expenses associated with business use of the taxpayer's home, deductions for IRAs, Keogh, SEP, and SIMPLE plans, the self-employed health insurance deduction, and distributions from IRAs.

CORPORATIONS AND THE AMT

Prior to 2018, corporations with average gross receipts over $7.5 million were also subject to the AMT. The AMT tax rate that applied at the corporate level was 20 percent. Many of the adjustment and preference items discussed above with respect to individual taxpayers also applied to corporations, and there were additional corporate AMT rules that needed to be complied with.

The TCJA 2017 repealed the corporate AMT for years after 2017.

CONCLUSION

The AMT, like the passive activity rules, is designed to prevent abusive practices resulting in low current tax liability for wealthy individuals. While its application is complex, the idea is simple. Understanding the types of activities and events that may cause the imposition of the AMT gives advisors an edge in counseling clients who may find themselves subject to this alternative tax system.

KEY TERMS

Adjustments - AMT changes made to taxable income that either increase or decrease AMTI.

Alternative Minimum Tax (AMT) - An anti-abuse technique designed to change the timing of tax payments.

Alternative Minimum Taxable Income (AMTI) - Taxable income plus or minus certain adjustments and preferences.

Deferral Items - Adjustments and preferences that result in a tax credit that can be used in future years equal to the additional tax that must be paid in the current year.

Depletion - A form of depreciation that applies to natural resources.

Exclusion Items - Adjustments and preferences that result in a permanent increase in tax.

Incentive Stock Option (ISO) - A stock option that meets certain requirements and is granted by a corporation to an employee to purchase the stock of that corporation.

Nonqualified Stock Option (NQSO) - A right to purchase shares of company stock at a given strike price (generally set at the market price of the stock on the day the option is granted).

Preferences - AMT changes made to taxable income that increase AMTI.

Private Activity Municipal Bonds - Securities issued by or on behalf of local governments that bear tax-exempt interest for regular income tax and are used to provide debt financing for private projects. Private activity municipal bond income is an AMT preference item.

DISCUSSION QUESTIONS

SOLUTIONS to the discussion questions can be found exclusively within the chapter. Once you have completed an initial reading of the chapter, go back and highlight the answers to these questions.

1. Describe the purpose of the alternative minimum tax.
2. Describe, in general, how the AMT is calculated.
3. How do adjustments and preferences affect AMTI?
4. How is the AMT exemption phased out?
5. What is the difference between an exclusion item and a deferral item?
6. What itemized deduction items are lost by the application of the AMT?
7. How is qualified mortgage interest affected by the AMT?
8. What regular tax itemized deductions are not affected by AMT?
9. How are private activity municipal bonds affected by AMT?
10. How does the exercise of an ISO impact AMT?
11. Name three business-related items that can be affected by AMT.
12. Are corporations subject to AMT?

MULTIPLE CHOICE PROBLEMS

A sample of multiple choice problems is provided below. Additional multiple choice problems are available at money-education.com by accessing the Student Practice Portal.

1. HHH Company grants Willow one incentive stock option (ISO) on January 10, 2020. The exercise price is $10. The market price on the exercise date (June 12, 2021) is $33. What is the AMT consequence when Willow exercises the ISO?
    a. $0 AMT gain.
    b. $10 AMT gain.
    c. $23 AMT gain.
    d. $33 AMT gain.

2. Your client, A.J., who has a taxable income of $200,000, is concerned about being subject to the alternative minimum tax (AMT). The following income and deductions were included in computing taxable income. Select the one item that may be added to (or subtracted from) regular taxable income in calculating the AMT.
    a. A long-term capital gain of $90,000.
    b. A cash contribution to A.J.'s church of $18,000.
    c. Dividend income of $80,000.
    d. A state income tax deduction of $8,000.

3. In 2021, Adriana (a single taxpayer) has an AMTI of $175,000. What is Adriana's AMT exemption this year?
    a. $0.
    b. $45,875.
    c. $73,600.
    d. $103,300.

4. In 2021, Livia (a surviving spouse) has an AMTI of $1,289,100. What is Livia's AMT exemption this year?
    a. $0.
    b. $54,125.
    c. $114,600.
    d. $1,047,200.

5. Vito, age 50, has deductible medical expenses of $12,000 under the regular tax system and an AGI of $100,000. What are the tax consequences for computing Vito's AMTI?
    a. Vito's AMTI is not affected by his medical expenses.
    b. $300 of Vito's medical expenses must be added back to compute his AMTI.
    c. $2,500 of Vito's medical expenses must be added back to compute his AMTI.
    d. All of Vito's medical expenses must be deducted to compute his AMTI.

Additional multiple choice problems are available at *money-education.com* by accessing the Student Practice Portal. Access requires registration of the title using the unique code at the front of the book.

QUICK QUIZ EXPLANATIONS

Quick Quiz 15.1

1. True.
2. False. The AMT is more likely to affect wealthy taxpayers who take advantage of "items of tax preference."
3. False. The tentative minimum tax is reduced by any Foreign Tax Credit that the taxpayer may claim.
4. True.
5. False. The TCJA increased the exemption and phaseout amount for the years 2018 through 2025.

Quick Quiz 15.2

1. True.
2. False. Charitable contributions, like casualty losses, are itemized deductions for regular tax and are not impacted in any way by the AMT rules. In addition, they do not have to be added back into income (or, an alternative way of thinking of this is reversed out) when calculating AMTI.
3. False. All of the itemized deduction changes are classified as exclusion items, not deferral items.

Quick Quiz 15.3

1. True.
2. True.

Quick Quiz 15.4

1. False. Depreciation is considered to be a deferral item, not an exclusion item for AMT purposes.
2. False. Depletion, unlike depreciation, is an exclusion item for AMT purposes.

16

BUSINESS ENTITY SELECTION AND TAXATION

LEARNING OBJECTIVES

1. Distinguish the complexity, costs, and ease to form various types of business entities.*
2. Articulate the liability protection that various business entity forms offer to investors.*
3. Determine the reporting requirements for various business entity forms.
4. Understand the taxation of various business entity forms.*
5. Explain the similarities and differences between:*
   - sole proprietorships
   - general partnerships
   - limited partnerships
   - limited liability partnerships
   - family limited partnerships
   - limited liability companies
   - C corporations
   - S corporations
6. Understand how payroll taxes (Social Security) are treated in each type of business entity form.*
7. Understand the calculation of the qualified business income (QBI) deduction.*

**Ties to CFP Certification Learning Objectives*

INTRODUCTION

One of the most important decisions new business owners make is the selection of the entity type to be used for conducting the business activities of the enterprise.

The most common legal forms of business (entity types) used in the United States are the sole proprietorship, general and limited partnerships, including limited liability partnerships (LLPs) and family limited partnerships (FLPs), the limited liability company (LLC), the regular C corporation, and the S corporation.

The selection process includes consideration of the following factors:

1. Ease and cost of formation
2. Complexity of management and governance
3. How transferability and dissolution are achieved
4. Liability protection for owners' personal assets
5. Reporting requirements and taxation

Ease and Cost of Formation

Proprietorships and general partnerships are less complex, inexpensive, and easy to form, while the other entity types are more complex and more expensive to form. Entities are almost always formed under state law. Therefore, the state itself dictates the requirements for formation and the formalities that must be followed to maintain the entity's legal status.

Complexity of Management and Governance

Proprietorships are the least complex in terms of management and governance. The administrative requirements and formalities dictated by state law are the least burdensome for sole proprietorships. Proprietorships and general partnerships do not typically require an initial filing registration with the state and have fewer state-imposed annual filing requirements. Furthermore, proprietorships and general partnerships have fewer state-imposed operational requirements that must be met to assure continuation of the entity's legal status and the benefits that the legal status brings.

Key Concepts

1. Name the most common legal entities.
2. Identify the factors to be considered during the entity selection process.
3. Define "piercing the veil."

Transferability and Dissolution

Transferability of an ownership interest is easiest with a proprietorship and becomes increasingly more difficult as we move along a spectrum of business entities to the C corporation. Partnerships, limited partnerships, LLPs, FLPs, LLCs, S corporations, and smaller C corporations generally have limited or restricted transferability rights. Unlike other business forms, proprietorships can be dissolved at the election of the owner and do not require formal steps for dissolution.

Liability Protection for Owners' Personal Assets

Some business forms offer liability protection for investors. If liability protection is available, the investors in such business ventures or entities will not have their personal assets exposed to business (entity) debts or obligations. This protection, which may be the most important factor in entity choice, is not available to proprietorships or general partnerships, nor to general partners of a limited partnership and only to a limited extent for limited liability partnerships (LLP). We refer to this protection as limited liability protection.

There are situations in which an entity that has limited liability protection for its owners under state law can lose that protection. The state requires that for such protection to continue, the entity must alert the public to its status in a clear and identifiable manner so as to put business creditors on notice that the entity has such protection. Entities do this through markings on business correspondence such as invoices, letterhead, business cards, and through markings on vehicles (with the name and LLC or Inc. designated), which signals the limited liability status to the public. The entities receiving such protection usually are required to maintain a reasonable amount of liability insurance to protect the public (e.g., vehicle liability insurance) and are required to be vigilant in meeting any annual formalities to maintain the state-granted entity status.

General Liability Issues

Relying on the entity as the primary source of liability protection is dependent on the entity maintaining a clear and consistent identity as a corporation, limited partnership, or limited liability company. Failure to maintain that identity in contracts and correspondence could result in a court "**piercing the veil**" of liability protection, which could result in personal liability for the owner(s). Piercing the veil means disregarding the legal status of the entity that gives the owners limited liability. A secondary source of protection is liability insurance, which should be sufficient in amount and sufficiently comprehensive in risk coverage, to cover the claims of creditors.

To avoid piercing the veil, the entity should keep its books and records separate from the personal books and records of the owners, segregate activities of business from personal affairs, follow corporate formalities such as meeting requirements and filings, and address all content in contracts and correspondence from the view point of the business entity (rather than the owners').

Reporting Requirements and Taxation

States individually require annual filings and other types of reporting. All entities that have employees have payroll reporting at both the state and federal level. All entities that have retail sales have sales tax returns to prepare in states that impose sales taxes.

There are few, if any, other state reporting requirements for proprietorships and general partnerships. However, for all other types of entities there will be annual reporting requirements that are state-imposed to maintain the entity's legal status and thus its protections.

For federal income tax purposes, the income and expenses of a proprietorship or a single-member LLC are reported on the Schedule C of the individual owner's Form 1040. For all other types of entities, an entity-level tax return is filed. A partnership files Form 1065, an S corporation files Form 1120-S, and a C corporation files Form 1120. All of the returns other than the C corporation return are informational returns because there is no tax at the entity level. The income and losses of such entities "flow through" to the individual owners. Each owner's share of the entity's income or loss is reported to the owner on a Schedule K-1.

The C corporation is a separate entity for taxation and its income is taxed at the entity level. However, it does have the advantage of being able to accumulate profits at the corporate level without the owners having to pay income taxes on those profits until they are distributed as dividends to the owners by the corporation.

Quick Quiz 16.1

1. Not all entities are separate legal entities for the purposes of taxation.
   a. True
   b. False
2. "Piercing the veil" may occur if business owners fail to keep their personal records with their business records.
   a. True
   b. False

True, False.

Choosing the appropriate entity type requires an understanding of each type of the entity, its advantages and disadvantages, competing considerations including each of the factors above, and business loss considerations.

In general, the most important factors in entity selection are ease of formation, liability protection, and the manner of taxation. However, serious thought should be given to all of the factors to make the right choice for the nature of the business and the objectives of the owners.

It is also important to periodically review the choice of legal form (entity) to determine whether changes in circumstances may suggest a change in entity type.

SOLE PROPRIETORSHIPS

Sole proprietorships are business ventures owned and operated by a single individual. A sole proprietorship arises when an individual engages in a business for profit. A sole proprietorship can operate under the name of the owner or it can conduct business under a trade or fictitious name such as "The Corner Pocket." No filings are required with the secretary of state and no annual filing fees are required. There is no transfer of assets to the entity because the entity is considered a legal extension of the proprietor.

Formation

Formation is easy and inexpensive, although the proprietorship may be required to obtain a local business license. In addition, if the proprietorship will be collecting sales taxes, it must register with the state or local taxing authority. Operation is easy in that all decisions are made by the proprietor. Any trade names or assets are owned by the individual proprietor.

Key Concepts

1. Describe the formation and operation of a sole proprietorship.
2. Describe the liability issues associated with a sole proprietorship.
3. Explain how a sole proprietorship can raise capital.
4. Explain the tax attributes of a sole proprietorship.

Interest, Disposal of Interest, and Dissolution

A proprietor has a 100 percent interest in the proprietorship assets and income. It is relatively easy to sell assets of a proprietorship, but it does require finding a buyer. Dissolution is achieved by simply discontinuing business operations and paying creditors or by the death of the proprietor.

Capital

Capital for a proprietorship is limited to the resources of the proprietor including the proprietor's ability to borrow.

Liability

One of the major disadvantages of a sole proprietorship is the potential legal liability. The sole proprietor is personally legally liable for the debts and torts of the business. There is no separate legal entity under which limited liability protection for personal assets may be claimed.

Management/Operations

The proprietor has the day-to-day management and decision-making responsibilities, including the hiring and firing of employees. There is no guarantee of continuity beyond the proprietor's lifetime.

Income Taxation and Payroll (Social Security) Taxes

The cost of tax compliance is low because the proprietor simply adds a Schedule C to his Form 1040 (see **Exhibit 16.1**) and generally does not even obtain a separate federal taxpayer tax identification number (unless the proprietor hires employees, in which case an Employer Identification Number (EIN) must be obtained). Rather, the proprietor conducts business under his own Social Security number. There is no ability to allocate income to other taxpayers since there is only one owner. A sole proprietor does not have to pay unemployment taxes on himself, but he must pay unemployment taxes for his employees.

However, the proprietor does pay self-employment tax (up to 15.3 percent) on his own earnings (see **Exhibit 16.2**) and one-half of Social Security taxes for his employees.

Taking Deductions

The proprietor can deduct all ordinary and necessary business expenses from gross income. The business deductions are in Part II of Schedule C, lines 8-27 (2020). The net profit or loss from **line 31 of Schedule C** is then carried over to **line 3 of Schedule 1** of Form 1040 (identified by the arrow in **Exhibit 16.1** and the first arrow in **Exhibit 16.3**). The proprietor may also make deductible contributions to a qualified or other retirement plan, but these contributions are reported on his Form 1040 as a deduction for AGI on **line 15 of Schedule 1** of Form 1040 (identified by the second arrow in **Exhibit 16.3**).

Employer Deduction for Retirement Plans

The proprietor can usually deduct, subject to certain limitations, contributions made to a qualified plan for employees, including those made for the proprietor. The contributions (and the attributable earnings and gains) are generally not taxed to the proprietor or employee until distributed by the plan. The deduction limit for contributions to a qualified plan depends on the type of plan.

The deduction for contributions to a defined contribution plan cannot exceed 25 percent of the compensation paid or accrued during the year to eligible employees participating in the plan. The proprietor must reduce this limit in figuring the deduction for contributions made to his own account. Recall that the maximum compensation that can be taken into account when calculating plan funding for each employee is the covered compensation limit, $290,000 for 2021.

The deduction for contributions to a defined benefit plan is based on actuarial assumptions and computations. Consequently, an actuary must calculate the appropriate amount of mandatory funding.

In the case of an employer who maintains both a defined benefit plan and a defined contribution plan, the funding limit set forth is combined. The maximum deductible amount is the greater of:

- 25 percent of the aggregate covered compensation of employees, or
- The required minimum funding standard of the defined benefit plan.

This limit does not apply if the contributions to the defined contribution plan consist entirely of employee elective deferrals (elective contributions to the plan by employees). In other words, employee elective deferrals do not count against the plan limit.

Exhibit 16.1 | Form 1040 Schedule C

SCHEDULE C (Form 1040)
Department of the Treasury Internal Revenue Service (99)

Profit or Loss From Business
(Sole Proprietorship)

▶ Go to *www.irs.gov/ScheduleC* for instructions and the latest information.
▶ Attach to Form 1040, 1040-SR, 1040-NR, or 1041; partnerships generally must file Form 1065.

OMB No. 1545-0074
2020
Attachment Sequence No. 09

Name of proprietor | Social security number (SSN)

A Principal business or profession, including product or service (see instructions) | **B Enter code from instructions** ▶

C Business name. If no separate business name, leave blank. | **D Employer ID number (EIN)** (see instr.)

E Business address (including suite or room no.) ▶
City, town or post office, state, and ZIP code

F Accounting method: (1) ☐ Cash (2) ☐ Accrual (3) ☐ Other (specify) ▶

G Did you "materially participate" in the operation of this business during 2020? If "No," see instructions for limit on losses ☐ Yes ☐ No

H If you started or acquired this business during 2020, check here ▶ ☐

I Did you make any payments in 2020 that would require you to file Form(s) 1099? See instructions ☐ Yes ☐ No

J If "Yes," did you or will you file required Form(s) 1099? ☐ Yes ☐ No

Part I Income

1	Gross receipts or sales. See instructions for line 1 and check the box if this income was reported to you on Form W-2 and the "Statutory employee" box on that form was checked ▶ ☐	1	
2	Returns and allowances	2	
3	Subtract line 2 from line 1	3	
4	Cost of goods sold (from line 42)	4	
5	**Gross profit.** Subtract line 4 from line 3	5	
6	Other income, including federal and state gasoline or fuel tax credit or refund (see instructions)	6	
7	**Gross income.** Add lines 5 and 6 ▶	7	

Part II **Expenses.** Enter expenses for business use of your home **only** on line 30.

8	Advertising	8		18	Office expense (see instructions)	18	
9	Car and truck expenses (see instructions)	9		19	Pension and profit-sharing plans	19	
				20	Rent or lease (see instructions):		
10	Commissions and fees	10		a	Vehicles, machinery, and equipment	20a	
11	Contract labor (see instructions)	11		b	Other business property	20b	
12	Depletion	12		21	Repairs and maintenance	21	
13	Depreciation and section 179 expense deduction (not included in Part III) (see instructions)	13		22	Supplies (not included in Part III)	22	
				23	Taxes and licenses	23	
				24	Travel and meals:		
14	Employee benefit programs (other than on line 19)	14		a	Travel	24a	
15	Insurance (other than health)	15		b	Deductible meals (see instructions)	24b	
16	Interest (see instructions):			25	Utilities	25	
a	Mortgage (paid to banks, etc.)	16a		26	Wages (less employment credits)	26	
b	Other	16b		27a	Other expenses (from line 48)	27a	
17	Legal and professional services	17		b	**Reserved for future use**	27b	

28	**Total expenses** before expenses for business use of home. Add lines 8 through 27a ▶	28	
29	Tentative profit or (loss). Subtract line 28 from line 7	29	
30	Expenses for business use of your home. Do not report these expenses elsewhere. Attach Form 8829 unless using the simplified method. See instructions. **Simplified method filers only:** Enter the total square footage of (a) your home: ______ and (b) the part of your home used for business: ______. Use the Simplified Method Worksheet in the instructions to figure the amount to enter on line 30	30	
31	**Net profit or (loss).** Subtract line 30 from line 29. • If a profit, enter on both **Schedule 1 (Form 1040), line 3,** and on **Schedule SE, line 2.** (If you checked the box on line 1, see instructions). Estates and trusts, enter on **Form 1041, line 3.** • If a loss, you **must** go to line 32.	31	
32	If you have a loss, check the box that describes your investment in this activity. See instructions. • If you checked 32a, enter the loss on both **Schedule 1 (Form 1040), line 3,** and on **Schedule SE, line 2.** (If you checked the box on line 1, see the line 31 instructions). Estates and trusts, enter on **Form 1041, line 3.** • If you checked 32b, you **must** attach **Form 6198.** Your loss may be limited.	32a ☐ All investment is at risk. 32b ☐ Some investment is not at risk.	

For Paperwork Reduction Act Notice, see the separate instructions. Cat. No. 11334P **Schedule C (Form 1040) 2020**

See www.irs.gov/Forms-&-Pubs for the complete forms.

Exhibit 16.2 | Form 1040 Schedule SE

SCHEDULE SE (Form 1040)

Department of the Treasury Internal Revenue Service (99)

Self-Employment Tax

▶ Go to *www.irs.gov/ScheduleSE* for instructions and the latest information.
▶ Attach to Form 1040, 1040-SR, or 1040-NR.

OMB No. 1545-0074

2020

Attachment Sequence No. **17**

Name of person with self-employment income (as shown on Form 1040, 1040-SR, or 1040-NR)	Social security number of person with **self-employment** income ▶

Part I Self-Employment Tax

Note: If your only income subject to self-employment tax is **church employee income,** see instructions for how to report your income and the definition of church employee income.

A If you are a minister, member of a religious order, or Christian Science practitioner **and** you filed Form 4361, but you had $400 or more of **other** net earnings from self-employment, check here and continue with Part I . . . . ▶ ☐

Skip lines 1a and 1b if you use the farm optional method in Part II. See instructions.

Line	Description	Sub-line	Sub-amount	Line	Amount
1a	Net farm profit or (loss) from Schedule F, line 34, and farm partnerships, Schedule K-1 (Form 1065), box 14, code A			1a	
b	If you received social security retirement or disability benefits, enter the amount of Conservation Reserve Program payments included on Schedule F, line 4b, or listed on Schedule K-1 (Form 1065), box 20, code AH			1b	( )
	Skip line 2 if you use the nonfarm optional method in Part II. See instructions.				
2	Net profit or (loss) from Schedule C, line 31; and Schedule K-1 (Form 1065), box 14, code A (other than farming). See instructions for other income to report or if you are a minister or member of a religious order			2	
3	Combine lines 1a, 1b, and 2			3	
4a	If line 3 is more than zero, multiply line 3 by 92.35% (0.9235). Otherwise, enter amount from line 3			4a	
	Note: If line 4a is less than $400 due to Conservation Reserve Program payments on line 1b, see instructions.				
b	If you elect one or both of the optional methods, enter the total of lines 15 and 17 here			4b	
c	Combine lines 4a and 4b. If less than $400, **stop;** you don't owe self-employment tax. **Exception:** If less than $400 and you had **church employee income,** enter -0- and continue ▶			4c	
5a	Enter your **church employee income** from Form W-2. See instructions for definition of church employee income	5a			
b	Multiply line 5a by 92.35% (0.9235). If less than $100, enter -0-			5b	
6	Add lines 4c and 5b			6	
7	Maximum amount of combined wages and self-employment earnings subject to social security tax or the 6.2% portion of the 7.65% railroad retirement (tier 1) tax for 2020			7	137,700
8a	Total social security wages and tips (total of boxes 3 and 7 on Form(s) W-2) and railroad retirement (tier 1) compensation. If $137,700 or more, skip lines 8b through 10, and go to line 11	8a			
b	Unreported tips subject to social security tax from Form 4137, line 10	8b			
c	Wages subject to social security tax from Form 8919, line 10	8c			
d	Add lines 8a, 8b, and 8c			8d	
9	Subtract line 8d from line 7. If zero or less, enter -0- here and on line 10 and go to line 11 ▶			9	
10	Multiply the **smaller** of line 6 or line 9 by 12.4% (0.124)			10	
11	Multiply line 6 by 2.9% (0.029)			11	
12	**Self-employment tax.** Add lines 10 and 11. Enter here and on **Schedule 2 (Form 1040), line 4**			12	
13	**Deduction for one-half of self-employment tax.** Multiply line 12 by 50% (0.50). Enter here and on **Schedule 1 (Form 1040), line 14**	13			

Part II Optional Methods To Figure Net Earnings (see instructions)

Farm Optional Method. You may use this method **only** if **(a)** your gross farm income[1] wasn't more than $8,460, **or (b)** your net farm profits[2] were less than $6,107.

Line	Description	Line	Amount
14	Maximum income for optional methods	14	5,640
15	Enter the **smaller** of: two-thirds (2/3) of gross farm income[1] (not less than zero) **or** $5,640. Also, include this amount on line 4b above	15	

Nonfarm Optional Method. You may use this method **only** if **(a)** your net nonfarm profits[3] were less than $6,107 and also less than 72.189% of your gross nonfarm income,[4] **and (b)** you had net earnings from self-employment of at least $400 in 2 of the prior 3 years. **Caution:** You may use this method no more than five times.

Line	Description	Line	Amount
16	Subtract line 15 from line 14	16	
17	Enter the **smaller** of: two-thirds (2/3) of gross nonfarm income[4] (not less than zero) **or** the amount on line 16. Also, include this amount on line 4b above	17	

[1] From Sch. F, line 9; and Sch. K-1 (Form 1065), box 14, code B.

[2] From Sch. F, line 34; and Sch. K-1 (Form 1065), box 14, code A—minus the amount you would have entered on line 1b had you not used the optional method.

[3] From Sch. C, line 31; and Sch. K-1 (Form 1065), box 14, code A.

[4] From Sch. C, line 7; and Sch. K-1 (Form 1065), box 14, code C.

Exhibit 16.3 | Schedule 1 Form 1040

SCHEDULE 1 (Form 1040) Department of the Treasury Internal Revenue Service	**Additional Income and Adjustments to Income** ▶ Attach to Form 1040, 1040-SR, or 1040-NR. ▶ Go to *www.irs.gov/Form1040* for instructions and the latest information.	OMB No. 1545-0074 **2020** Attachment Sequence No. **01**
Name(s) shown on Form 1040, 1040-SR, or 1040-NR		**Your social security number**

Part I Additional Income

1	Taxable refunds, credits, or offsets of state and local income taxes	**1**	
2a	Alimony received	**2a**	
b	Date of original divorce or separation agreement (see instructions) ▶		
3	Business income or (loss). Attach Schedule C	**3**	
4	Other gains or (losses). Attach Form 4797	**4**	
5	Rental real estate, royalties, partnerships, S corporations, trusts, etc. Attach Schedule E	**5**	
6	Farm income or (loss). Attach Schedule F	**6**	
7	Unemployment compensation	**7**	
8	Other income. List type and amount ▶	**8**	
9	Combine lines 1 through 8. Enter here and on Form 1040, 1040-SR, or 1040-NR, line 8	**9**	

Part II Adjustments to Income

10	Educator expenses	**10**	
11	Certain business expenses of reservists, performing artists, and fee-basis government officials. Attach Form 2106	**11**	
12	Health savings account deduction. Attach Form 8889	**12**	
13	Moving expenses for members of the Armed Forces. Attach Form 3903	**13**	
14	Deductible part of self-employment tax. Attach Schedule SE	**14**	
15	Self-employed SEP, SIMPLE, and qualified plans	**15**	
16	Self-employed health insurance deduction	**16**	
17	Penalty on early withdrawal of savings	**17**	
18a	Alimony paid	**18a**	
b	Recipient's SSN ▶		
c	Date of original divorce or separation agreement (see instructions) ▶		
19	IRA deduction	**19**	
20	Student loan interest deduction	**20**	
21	Tuition and fees deduction. Attach Form 8917	**21**	
22	Add lines 10 through 21. These are your **adjustments to income.** Enter here and on Form 1040, 1040-SR, or 1040-NR, line 10a	**22**	

For Paperwork Reduction Act Notice, see your tax return instructions. Cat. No. 71479F **Schedule 1 (Form 1040) 2020**

Deduction Limit for Self-Employed Individuals (Keogh Plans)

Sole proprietors who file a Schedule C, partners of a partnership, and members of an LLC are generally treated as self-employed individuals for tax purposes. In contrast, owners of C corporations or S corporations are typically treated as employees of those entities. While self-employed individuals may adopt almost any qualified plan, they cannot normally choose a stock bonus plan or an employee stock ownership plan (ESOP) because there is no stock involved with sole proprietorships, partnerships, or LLCs. A qualified retirement plan selected by a self-employed individual is referred to as a **Keogh plan**. A Keogh plan is simply a qualified plan for a self-employed person usually structured as a profit sharing plan, a money purchase pension plan (MPPP), or a combination of both. (Note that self-employed individuals may also be able to establish a 401(k) plan.) An important characteristic of a Keogh plan is the reduced contribution that can be made on behalf of the self-employed individual. The employees of a firm that maintains a Keogh plan will generally be treated in the same manner as if the plan were not a Keogh plan. Employees will generally receive a benefit based on their W-2 income. The reason for the distinction is that self-employed individuals do not receive a W-2 form and will instead file a Schedule C or receive a K-1 which details the owner's earnings.

There is a special computation needed to calculate the maximum contribution and tax deduction for a Keogh plan on behalf of a self-employed individual. Since self-employed individuals do not have W-2s, the IRC uses the term "earned income" to denote the amount of compensation that is earned by the self-employed individual.

Earned income is defined as net earnings from self-employment less one-half of self-employment tax less the deduction for contributions to the qualified plan on behalf of the self-employed person. Through this process, the IRC attempts to treat self-employed individuals as if they were corporations instead of self-employed individuals. An employer and an employee each pays one-half of the employee's Social Security taxes; however, in the case of self-employed individuals, they are required to pay both halves. If the company was a corporation, then it would deduct one half of the self-employment taxes paid on behalf of the individual in arriving at net income. Therefore, earned income for self-employed individuals is the self-employment income reduced by one-half of self-employment tax. Similarly, a corporation would deduct the contribution made to a qualified retirement plan in arriving at net income. Therefore, calculating earned income for a self-employed individual also requires a reduction for the amount of the contribution to the Keogh plan.

> **Quick Quiz 16.2**
>
> 1. Sole proprietorships are never required to register with the state in which they do business.
>   a. True
>   b. False
> 2. One of the major disadvantages of a sole proprietorship is the potential legal liability.
>   a. True
>   b. False
> 3. The ordinary and necessary expenses of a sole proprietorship are reported on Schedule C of the owner's Form 1040.
>   a. True
>   b. False
>
> False, True, True.

The two primary parts of the Social Security system are OASDI (Old Age Survivor Disability Insurance) and Medicare. Both employers and employees contribute to the system through FICA tax payments that generally consists of 6.2 percent for OASDI and 1.45 percent for Medicare. The OASDI portion of 6.2 percent applies to income up to the Social Security wage base ($142,800 for 2021) while the Medicare portion applies to all income with no limit.

The deduction for the self-employed person's own plan contribution and his net earnings are interrelated. For this reason, the self-employed person must determine the deduction for his own contributions by using simultaneous equations, or a circular calculation, or by using the simpler method described below that adjusts the plan contribution rate for the self-employed person.

To calculate the self-employed individual's 2021 contribution to the Keogh plan, utilize the following formulas:

1. Calculate the self-employed individual's contribution rate:

$$\text{Self-Employed Contribution Rate} = \left(\frac{\text{Contribution Rate to Other Participants}}{1 + \text{Contribution Rate to Other Participants}}\right)$$

2. Calculate Self-Employment Tax:

Net Self-Employment Income
Times: 92.35%
Equals Net Earnings subject to Self-Employment Tax
Times: 15.3% up to $142,800 Plus: 2.9% over $142,800
Equals: Self-Employment Tax

3. Calculate the self-employed individual's contribution:

Net Self-Employment Income
Less: ½ of Self-Employment Taxes
Equals: Adjusted Net Self-Employment Income (Earned Income)
Times: Self-Employed Contribution Rate
Equals: Self-Employed Individual's Qualified Plan Contribution

Example 16.1

Lana has Schedule C net income of $200,000 and wants to know the maximum amount she can contribute to a Keogh profit sharing plan. In this instance Lana can contribute $37,694 to the plan. The contribution is calculated as follows:

1. Calculate the self-employed individual's contribution rate:

$$\text{Self-Employed Contribution Rate} = \left(\frac{25\%}{1 + 25\%}\right)$$

$$\text{Self-Employed Contribution Rate} = 20\%$$

2. Calculate Self-Employment Tax:

2021	
$200,000	Net Self-Employment Income
x 0.9235	Times: 92.35%
$184,700	**Net Earnings subject to Self-Employment Tax**
x 15.3%/2.9%	Times: 15.3% up to $142,800 + 2.9% over $142,800
$23,064	**Equals: Self-Employment Tax ($21,849 + $1,215) for 2021**

3. Calculate the self-employed individual's contribution:

2021	
$200,000	Net Self-Employment Income
$11,532	Less: ½ of Self-Employment Taxes (50% x $23,064)
$188,468	**Equals: Adjusted Net Self-Employment Income**
x 0.20	Times: Self-Employed Contribution Rate
$37,694	**Equals: Self-Employed Individual's Qualified Plan Contribution**

Check figure:

2021

$$\frac{\$37,694}{\$188,468 - \$37,694} = 25\%$$

When solving the Keogh contribution calculation, it is important to understand that while 25 percent of compensation is the limit for deductible employee contributions, the self-employed individual maximum contribution is 25 percent of the self-employed individual's earned income. The 25 percent of earned income effectively translates to 20 percent of net self-employed income less one-half of self-employment tax.

Example 16.2

In **Example 16.1**, Lana's earned income is calculated as follows:

2021	
$200,000	Schedule C net income
- $11,532	Less: ½ self-employment taxes
- $37,694	Less: Keogh contribution
$150,774	Earned income
x 0.25	Times: 25% to determine Keogh contribution
$37,694	**Total Keogh contribution**

Notice that the maximum Keogh contribution for 2021 is exactly 25% of the earned income for each respective year.

Example 16.3

Cargile Co., a sole proprietorship, employs B, C, D, and E as well as the sole proprietor, A, who files a Schedule C 1040 for his business.

	Compensation	*Contributions*
A*	$150,000	See note below
B	$100,000	$15,000
C	$80,000	$12,000
D	$50,000	$7,500
E	$20,000	$3,000

*A's compensation is Schedule C net income

Cargile maintains a Keogh profit sharing plan with a 15% contribution to each employee (not the owner). In spite of the fact that each employee receives exactly 15%, A is limited to receiving 13.04% (0.15/1.15) of $150,000 less one-half of the self-employment taxes due on his earnings.

$150,000	Schedule C net income
$10,597	Less: ½ self-employment taxes
$139,403	Self-employment income
x 0.1304	Contribution rate (0.15/1.15)
$18,183	**Contribution on behalf of A ***

** Rounding was not utilized when applying the contribution rate. (Actual rate = 0.130434783)*

The special calculation is required because Schedule C net income must be reduced by both the self-employed person's qualified plan contribution and one-half of his self-employment tax before the reduced contribution rate is applied. For all of the other employees, their contribution is calculated based upon 15% of their compensation.

Exhibit 16.4 | A Summary of Advantages and Disadvantages of Sole Proprietorships

Advantages
• Easy to form • Simple to operate • Easy to sell business assets • Few administrative burdens • Income is generally passed through to the owner on Schedule C of Form 1040
Disadvantages
• Generally have limited sources of capital • Unlimited liability • No guarantee of continuity beyond the lifetime of the proprietor • Business income is subject to self-employment tax

GENERAL PARTNERSHIPS

Partnerships are joint business ventures among two or more persons or entities to conduct a business as co-owners under their names or under a trade or fictitious name. A partnership is automatically created when two or more individuals conduct business for a profit. There are different types of partnerships and we will examine each type, including general partnerships and limited partnerships. Typically, **general partnerships** are not required to be registered with the secretary of state in the state of formation, but limited partnerships are required to register.

Formation

Although partnerships are easy to form, state law will govern the relative rights and obligations of the partners (including equal sharing of profits and losses regardless of contributions of property or effort), unless there is a contrary agreement among the partners. Ownership of a general partnership may be in the form of partnership units, shares, or percentages.

Key Concepts

1. Discuss the formation and operation of a general partnership.
2. Explain why disposing of a general partnership interest may be difficult.
3. Describe the sources of liability for a general partnership.
4. Explain the tax attributes of a general partnership.

Interest, Disposal of Interest, and Dissolution

A partner's interest in a partnership is frequently referred to as his partnership percentage interest. The partners usually have voting power in proportion to their ownership interest. Thus, majority voting rules generally apply.

It is typically difficult to dispose of a partnership interest because any buyer will not only have to evaluate the business, but also the other partners. In addition, partnership agreements often require the approval of non-selling partners before a partner's share can be sold to an outside party.

Partnership dissolution is either voluntary or judicial (ordered by a court). Partners usually vote for voluntary dissolution and, if affirmed, pay creditors and then distribute remaining assets to partners in accordance with either the partnership agreement or in proportion to their individual partnership interests. Judicial dissolution may be necessary when the partners cannot agree on how to conduct the business or whether to dissolve the entity. This situation is most likely to arise when partnership votes are required to be unanimous.

Capital

The amount of capital contributed usually determines the ownership interest of a partner in a partnership. However, sometimes partners allocate ownership interest differently from capital contributed. Such a situation could occur when one partner brings ideas and talent and the other brings money. Whenever partners are deviating from ownership based on capital contributed, there should be a written partnership agreement that clarifies partnership interests and each partner's distributive share of partnership profits and losses. If a partnership wants to divide profits and/or losses in a proportion that does not equal partnership interest, it will be considered a special allocation. There must be a sound business purpose for a special allocation and partners are well advised to seek the counsel of an attorney or CPA.

Liability

The co-owner partners share the risks and rewards of the business. Each partner is jointly and severally liable for partnership obligations. Like a sole proprietorship, a partner's personal assets can be seized to satisfy partnership obligations.

A principal disadvantage of the general partnership arrangement is that all general partners in a partnership are subject to joint and several liability for the debts and obligations of the partnership. These liabilities can arise from:

1. negligence and acts of employees
2. negligence of other partners
3. commercial liabilities (e.g., loans) to the partnership
4. commercial obligations to other trade creditors

Management/Operations

Partnerships are typically managed equally by all partners. It is possible to name a "**managing partner**" to have responsibilities for some specific task or day-to-day operations. Partnerships can even appoint presidents and vice presidents as officers. If so, these should be spelled out in the written partnership agreement. Partnerships are not required to have annual meetings of partners, but rather have a relatively relaxed set of rules regarding formalities.

Employees of general partnerships are eligible to receive a wide variety of tax-free fringe benefits provided by the employer such as health care. This is not so for partners since partners are not considered to be employees for most employee fringe benefit purposes. However, partners can participate in company-sponsored retirement plans, but they have the same limitations as proprietors in terms of calculations (see discussion under proprietorships).

Quick Quiz 16.3

1. General partnerships are governed by federal law.
   a. True
   b. False
2. The owners of a general partnership have limited liability from the debts and obligations of the partnership.
   a. True
   b. False
3. General partnerships are pass-through entities for tax purposes.
   a. True
   b. False

False, False, True.

Income Taxation and Payroll (Social Security) Taxation

Partnerships are not subject to entity level taxation. Partnerships file a Form 1065 (**Exhibit 16.6**), including Schedule K (**Exhibit 16.7**), which is the summary of all distributive items to individual partners. Income and losses are then "passed through" to the individual partners in proportion to their partnership interests on Form 1065 Schedule K-1 (**Exhibit 16.8**) regardless of whether the income is distributed to partners in the form of cash. Each partner then reports their share of partnership income or loss on Form 1040 Schedule E, which ultimately flows to line 5 of Schedule 1 of Form 1040 (see Exhibit 16.3). Partnership taxation may be complex because of the tax rules related to basis, as discussed below. All partnership business net income is subject to self-employment tax up to 15.3 percent. Partnerships are legal entities and thus are required to obtain a Federal Employer Identification Number (FEIN). The year-end for tax purposes is usually the calendar year-end.

Partnerships can deduct all "ordinary and necessary" business expenses from their income. Partners can deduct partnership losses against other ordinary income to the extent of their investment (or their at-risk amount, as discussed in Chapter 14). However, passive partners (those not actively involved in the enterprise) may not be able to deduct losses due to passive activity rules even if they are at-risk. Partners' Basis in a Partnership

When a partnership is formed by partners contributing assets to the partnership in return for an interest in it, the transfer is generally tax-free to the partners. This is true even if the assets which the partners contribute have market values greater than the contributing partners' basis. The partners then have basis in the partnership shares equal to their basis in the property contributed. Thus, any gain realized on the contribution of appreciated property to the partnership is reflected in the lower basis of the partners' interests and will be deferred until the partnership interest is sold.

If the partners contribute assets which are subject to liabilities to the partnership, the transfer is still tax-deferred. A partner's basis in his or her partnership interest is equal to the basis the partner had in the property contributed, less the share of the liability assumed by new partners.

Example 16.4

Tate contributes a building with a $120,000 value and a basis of $80,000, subject to a mortgage of $40,000, to an equal partnership with Misty. Tate will not recognize gain on the transaction, and his basis in the partnership interest is the $80,000 basis from the building less the $20,000 (half) of the mortgage assumed by Misty.

If a partner contributes services to a partnership in return for a partnership interest, the market value of the services is taxable to the partner as compensation income. However, the partner's basis in the partnership interest is increased by this ordinary income.

Increases and Decreases of Basis

A partner's basis is increased by all items of income allocated to the partner and by any subsequent contributions. Basis is reduced by items of loss allocated to a partner, by any distributions of money or property to a partner, and by charitable contributions allocated to a partner. A partner's basis is increased by the partner's share of the partnership's liabilities. Changes in the liabilities of the partnership will affect the partner's basis.[1]

A partner cannot have basis reduced below zero. Any distributions that exceed a partner's basis will be treated as capital gain to the partner. Any losses that exceed a partner's basis will not be deductible until the business entity creates income in future years or capital contributions are made which increase the partner's basis sufficiently to absorb the losses.

1. A partner's at-risk basis increases for the partner's share of recourse debt and for the partner's share of qualified nonrecourse debt. Qualified nonrecourse debt is debt that is used by the taxpayer in the activity of holding real property, is secured by the real property, and is borrowed from a person or entity who is actively and regularly engaged in the business of lending money. See IRC Sec. 465(b).

Example 16.5

Joe and his brother decide to form a partnership to open a deli. Joe will contribute property with a basis of $50,000 and fair market value of $75,000 in exchange for his interest in the partnership. Joe's brother will contribute $112,500 of cash in exchange for his interest in the partnership. Joe owns 40% of the partnership and all income and expenses are allocated to each partner based on the partner's percentage of ownership. Joe's original basis in his partnership interest is $50,000.

In the first year of operation, the partnership income is $30,000. Joe receives a Schedule K-1 showing his $12,000 share of the partnership income ($30,000 x 40% = $12,000). The partnership made a $10,000 distribution to Joe in the same year. Joe's basis is increased by the partnership income allocated to him, but is decreased by the distribution made to him. His basis at the end of the first year is $52,000 ($50,000 + $12,000 - $10,000 = $52,000).

During the following year, the partnership takes out a loan for $22,500. At the end of the year, the partnership shows a loss of $8,000 and Joe receives a Schedule K-1 indicating his share of the loss is $3,200. Joe's basis in the partnership interest is increased by $9,000 ($22,500 x 40%) due to the loan, but is decreased by the $3,200 loss. His basis at the end of the second year is $57,800 ($52,000 + $9,000 - $3,200 = $57,800).

Exhibit 16.5 | A Summary of Advantages and Disadvantages of Partnerships

Advantages
• More sources of initial capital than proprietorships. • Usually have more management resources available than proprietorships. • Have fewer administrative burdens than corporations. • Income and losses are generally passed through to the partners for tax purposes.
Disadvantages
• Transfer of interests is more difficult than for proprietorships. • Unlimited liability - each partner is liable for partnership debts and obligations. • Partnership income tax and basis adjustment rules can be complex. • Business net income is subject to self-employment tax. • Partners are entitled to few tax-free fringe benefits that are generally available to employees.

Exhibit 16.6 | Form 1065

Form **1065** | **U.S. Return of Partnership Income** | OMB No. 1545-0123

Department of the Treasury
Internal Revenue Service

For calendar year 2020, or tax year beginning ________, 2020, ending ________, 20____.

▶ Go to *www.irs.gov/Form1065* for instructions and the latest information.

2020

A Principal business activity	Type or Print	Name of partnership	D Employer identification number
B Principal product or service		Number, street, and room or suite no. If a P.O. box, see instructions.	E Date business started
C Business code number		City or town, state or province, country, and ZIP or foreign postal code	F Total assets (see instructions) $

G Check applicable boxes: (1) ☐ Initial return (2) ☐ Final return (3) ☐ Name change (4) ☐ Address change (5) ☐ Amended return

H Check accounting method: (1) ☐ Cash (2) ☐ Accrual (3) ☐ Other (specify) ▶

I Number of Schedules K-1. Attach one for each person who was a partner at any time during the tax year ▶

J Check if Schedules C and M-3 are attached . . . ▶ ☐

K Check if partnership: (1) ☐ Aggregated activities for section 465 at-risk purposes (2) ☐ Grouped activities for section 469 passive activity purposes

Caution: Include **only** trade or business income and expenses on lines 1a through 22 below. See instructions for more information.

Income	1a	Gross receipts or sales	1a			
	b	Returns and allowances	1b			
	c	Balance. Subtract line 1b from line 1a			1c	
	2	Cost of goods sold (attach Form 1125-A)			2	
	3	Gross profit. Subtract line 2 from line 1c			3	
	4	Ordinary income (loss) from other partnerships, estates, and trusts (attach statement)			4	
	5	Net farm profit (loss) (attach Schedule F (Form 1040))			5	
	6	Net gain (loss) from Form 4797, Part II, line 17 (attach Form 4797)			6	
	7	Other income (loss) (attach statement)			7	
	8	**Total income (loss).** Combine lines 3 through 7			8	
Deductions (see instructions for limitations)	9	Salaries and wages (other than to partners) (less employment credits)			9	
	10	Guaranteed payments to partners			10	
	11	Repairs and maintenance			11	
	12	Bad debts			12	
	13	Rent			13	
	14	Taxes and licenses			14	
	15	Interest (see instructions)			15	
	16a	Depreciation (if required, attach Form 4562)	16a			
	b	Less depreciation reported on Form 1125-A and elsewhere on return	16b		16c	
	17	Depletion **(Do not deduct oil and gas depletion.)**			17	
	18	Retirement plans, etc.			18	
	19	Employee benefit programs			19	
	20	Other deductions (attach statement)			20	
	21	**Total deductions.** Add the amounts shown in the far right column for lines 9 through 20			21	
	22	**Ordinary business income (loss).** Subtract line 21 from line 8			22	
Tax and Payment	23	Interest due under the look-back method—completed long-term contracts (attach Form 8697)			23	
	24	Interest due under the look-back method—income forecast method (attach Form 8866)			24	
	25	BBA AAR imputed underpayment (see instructions)			25	
	26	Other taxes (see instructions)			26	
	27	**Total balance due.** Add lines 23 through 26			27	
	28	Payment (see instructions)			28	
	29	**Amount owed.** If line 28 is smaller than line 27, enter amount owed			29	
	30	**Overpayment.** If line 28 is larger than line 27, enter overpayment			30	

Sign Here

Under penalties of perjury, I declare that I have examined this return, including accompanying schedules and statements, and to the best of my knowledge and belief, it is true, correct, and complete. Declaration of preparer (other than partner or limited liability company member) is based on all information of which preparer has any knowledge.

▶ Signature of partner or limited liability company member ▶ Date

May the IRS discuss this return with the preparer shown below? See instructions. ☐ **Yes** ☐ **No**

Paid Preparer Use Only	Print/Type preparer's name	Preparer's signature	Date	Check ☐ if self-employed	PTIN
	Firm's name ▶			Firm's EIN ▶	
	Firm's address ▶			Phone no.	

For Paperwork Reduction Act Notice, see separate instructions. Cat. No. 11390Z Form **1065** (2020)

Exhibit 16.7 | Form 1065 Schedule K

Form 1065 (2020) Page 4

Section	Line	Schedule K — Partners' Distributive Share Items		Total amount
Income (Loss)	1	Ordinary business income (loss) (page 1, line 22)		1
	2	Net rental real estate income (loss) (attach Form 8825)		2
	3a	Other gross rental income (loss)	3a	
	b	Expenses from other rental activities (attach statement)	3b	
	c	Other net rental income (loss). Subtract line 3b from line 3a		3c
	4	Guaranteed payments: a Services 4a b Capital	4b	
		c Total. Add lines 4a and 4b		4c
	5	Interest income		5
	6	Dividends and dividend equivalents: a Ordinary dividends		6a
		b Qualified dividends 6b c Dividend equivalents	6c	
	7	Royalties		7
	8	Net short-term capital gain (loss) (attach Schedule D (Form 1065))		8
	9a	Net long-term capital gain (loss) (attach Schedule D (Form 1065))		9a
	b	Collectibles (28%) gain (loss)	9b	
	c	Unrecaptured section 1250 gain (attach statement)	9c	
	10	Net section 1231 gain (loss) (attach Form 4797)		10
	11	Other income (loss) (see instructions) Type ▶		11
Deductions	12	Section 179 deduction (attach Form 4562)		12
	13a	Contributions		13a
	b	Investment interest expense		13b
	c	Section 59(e)(2) expenditures: (1) Type ▶ (2) Amount ▶		13c(2)
	d	Other deductions (see instructions) Type ▶		13d
Self-Employment	14a	Net earnings (loss) from self-employment		14a
	b	Gross farming or fishing income		14b
	c	Gross nonfarm income		14c
Credits	15a	Low-income housing credit (section 42(j)(5))		15a
	b	Low-income housing credit (other)		15b
	c	Qualified rehabilitation expenditures (rental real estate) (attach Form 3468, if applicable)		15c
	d	Other rental real estate credits (see instructions) Type ▶		15d
	e	Other rental credits (see instructions) Type ▶		15e
	f	Other credits (see instructions) Type ▶		15f
Foreign Transactions	16a	Name of country or U.S. possession ▶		
	b	Gross income from all sources		16b
	c	Gross income sourced at partner level		16c
		Foreign gross income sourced at partnership level		
	d	Reserved for future use ▶ e Foreign branch category ▶		16e
	f	Passive category ▶ g General category ▶ h Other (attach statement) ▶		16h
		Deductions allocated and apportioned at partner level		
	i	Interest expense ▶ j Other ▶		16j
		Deductions allocated and apportioned at partnership level to foreign source income		
	k	Reserved for future use ▶ l Foreign branch category ▶		16l
	m	Passive category ▶ n General category ▶ o Other (attach statement) ▶		16o
	p	Total foreign taxes (check one): ▶ Paid ☐ Accrued ☐		16p
	q	Reduction in taxes available for credit (attach statement)		16q
	r	Other foreign tax information (attach statement)		
Alternative Minimum Tax (AMT) Items	17a	Post-1986 depreciation adjustment		17a
	b	Adjusted gain or loss		17b
	c	Depletion (other than oil and gas)		17c
	d	Oil, gas, and geothermal properties—gross income		17d
	e	Oil, gas, and geothermal properties—deductions		17e
	f	Other AMT items (attach statement)		17f
Other Information	18a	Tax-exempt interest income		18a
	b	Other tax-exempt income		18b
	c	Nondeductible expenses		18c
	19a	Distributions of cash and marketable securities		19a
	b	Distributions of other property		19b
	20a	Investment income		20a
	b	Investment expenses		20b
	c	Other items and amounts (attach statement)		

Form 1065 (2020)

Exhibit 16.8 | Form 1065 Schedule K-1

651119

☐ Final K-1 ☐ Amended K-1

OMB No. 1545-0123

Schedule K-1 (Form 1065) **2020**

Department of the Treasury
Internal Revenue Service

For calendar year 2020, or tax year

beginning / / 2020 ending / /

Partner's Share of Income, Deductions, Credits, etc. ▶ See separate instructions.

Part I Information About the Partnership

A Partnership's employer identification number

B Partnership's name, address, city, state, and ZIP code

C IRS Center where partnership filed return ▶

D ☐ Check if this is a publicly traded partnership (PTP)

Part II Information About the Partner

E Partner's SSN or TIN (Do not use TIN of a disregarded entity. See instructions.)

F Name, address, city, state, and ZIP code for partner entered in E. See instructions.

G ☐ General partner or LLC member-manager ☐ Limited partner or other LLC member

H1 ☐ Domestic partner ☐ Foreign partner

H2 ☐ If the partner is a disregarded entity (DE), enter the partner's:

TIN ______ Name ______

I1 What type of entity is this partner? ______

I2 If this partner is a retirement plan (IRA/SEP/Keogh/etc.), check here ☐

J Partner's share of profit, loss, and capital (see instructions):

	Beginning	Ending
Profit	%	%
Loss	%	%
Capital	%	%

Check if decrease is due to sale or exchange of partnership interest . . ☐

K Partner's share of liabilities:

	Beginning	Ending
Nonrecourse . .	$	$
Qualified nonrecourse financing . . .	$	$
Recourse . . .	$	$

☐ Check this box if Item K includes liability amounts from lower tier partnerships.

L **Partner's Capital Account Analysis**

Beginning capital account . . . $ ______
Capital contributed during the year . . $ ______
Current year net income (loss) . . . $ ______
Other increase (decrease) (attach explanation) $ ______
Withdrawals & distributions . . . $ ( )
Ending capital account . . . . $ ______

M Did the partner contribute property with a built-in gain or loss?
☐ **Yes** ☐ **No** If "Yes," attach statement. See instructions.

N **Partner's Share of Net Unrecognized Section 704(c) Gain or (Loss)**
Beginning . . . . $ ______
Ending . . . . $ ______

Part III Partner's Share of Current Year Income, Deductions, Credits, and Other Items

1	Ordinary business income (loss)	15	Credits
2	Net rental real estate income (loss)		
3	Other net rental income (loss)	16	Foreign transactions
4a	Guaranteed payments for services		
4b	Guaranteed payments for capital		
4c	Total guaranteed payments		
5	Interest income		
6a	Ordinary dividends		
6b	Qualified dividends		
6c	Dividend equivalents	17	Alternative minimum tax (AMT) items
7	Royalties		
8	Net short-term capital gain (loss)		
9a	Net long-term capital gain (loss)	18	Tax-exempt income and nondeductible expenses
9b	Collectibles (28%) gain (loss)		
9c	Unrecaptured section 1250 gain		
10	Net section 1231 gain (loss)		
11	Other income (loss)	19	Distributions
		20	Other information
12	Section 179 deduction		
13	Other deductions		
14	Self-employment earnings (loss)		

21 ☐ More than one activity for at-risk purposes*

22 ☐ More than one activity for passive activity purposes*

*See attached statement for additional information.

For IRS Use Only

For Paperwork Reduction Act Notice, see Instructions for Form 1065. www.irs.gov/Form1065 Cat. No. 11394R **Schedule K-1 (Form 1065) 2020**

LIMITED PARTNERSHIPS (LP)

Limited partnerships are associations of two or more persons as co-owners to carry on a business for profit except that one or more of the partners have limited participation in the management of the venture and thus limited risk exposure. If the limited partners participate in the management of the enterprise, they become general partners for liability purposes. In the normal limited partnership, there is at least one general partner. Because limited partners are passive investors in the enterprise, their liability is normally limited to the amount of their investment. A limited partner's personal assets cannot normally be seized to satisfy partnership obligations.

Key Concepts

1. Describe the ways in which a limited partnership is different from a general partnership.
2. Explain the advantages and disadvantages of a limited partnership.

Formation

Limited partnerships are generally required to file a partnership agreement or any other required documentation with the domiciliary state to establish the limited partnership. Those states that require initial filings also require annual filings to maintain the entity status. The written partnership agreement specifies which partners are limited partners and which partners are general partners.

Interest, Disposal of Interest, and Dissolution

The dissolution and transfer of an interest in a limited partnership is essentially the same as for a general partnership. Although the limited liability feature might attract more buyers, the inability for limited partners to have a say in the day-to-day operations of the company is likely to make the transfer of a limited partnership share very difficult.

Quick Quiz 16.4

1. Limited partnerships are generally required to register with the state.
   a. True
   b. False
2. Limited partnerships offer limited liability for all partners.
   a. True
   b. False

True, False.

Capital

It is easier to raise capital in a limited partnership than in a general partnership because of the availability of the liability shield for the non-managing limited partners. However, the limited liability may negatively affect the partnership's ability to obtain outside financing. Third party lenders may desire personal guarantees from the partners (which would partially defeat the benefits associated with the limited liability feature).

Liability

Liability for limited partners is limited as long as they refrain from participating in the management of the enterprise. The general partners, who are responsible for the day-to-day operations in a limited partnership, have unlimited liability for enterprise debts and obligations.

Management/Operations

A limited partnership is somewhat of a hybrid entity. The general partners run the business and are exposed to personal liability. The limited partners must avoid making management decisions to protect their limited liability status.

Income Taxation and Payroll (Social Security) Taxes

Limited partners are not usually subject to self-employment tax since they are passive investors who do not participate in management. The general partners in a limited partnership have self-employment income. As with the general partnership, the entity files a Form 1065 and issues Schedule K-1s to both its general and limited partners.

Exhibit 16.9 | A Summary of Advantages and Disadvantages of Limited Partnerships

Advantages
• Favorable pass-through partnership taxation status. • Flexibility in structuring ownership interests. • Limited partners are not personally liable for the debts and obligations of the limited partnership as long as they do not engage in management.
Disadvantages
• Must file with the state to register. • In most states, general partners are liable for debts and other obligations of the limited partnership. • Losses for limited partners are generally passive losses (subject to special tax rules limiting deductibility (see Chapter 14)).

LIMITED LIABILITY PARTNERSHIPS (LLP)

A **limited liability partnership (LLP)** is a hybrid entity that provides partial liability protection to its members and may be taxed as either a corporation or partnership. LLPs are similar to LLCs, but may not offer complete liability protection. The limited liability partnership is generally one comprised of licensed professionals such as accountants, attorneys, and doctors who practice together. The partners may enjoy liability protection from the acts of their other partners, but each partner remains personally liable for his own acts with respect to malpractice.

Key Concepts

1. Explain who can form a limited liability partnership.
2. Explain the ways in which an LLP differs from a general partnership.

Formation

Limited liability partnerships are generally required to file with the domiciliary state to establish the limited liability partnership. Those states that require initial filings also require annual filings to maintain the entity status.

Interest, Disposal of Interest, and Dissolution

The dissolution and transfer of an interest in a limited partnership is essentially the same as for a general partnership. If the LLP is comprised of licensed professionals, however, transfer of an interest will usually be more difficult because such interest may only be transferred to another similarly licensed professional.

Capital

The amount of capital contributed usually determines the ownership interest in a partnership. However, sometimes partners allocate ownership interest differently from capital contributed. Such a situation could occur when one partner brings ideas and talent and the other brings money. Whenever partners are deviating from ownership based on capital contributed, there should be a written partnership agreement that clarifies partnership interests and each partner's distributive share of the profits and losses. If a partnership divides profits and/or losses in a proportion that does not reflect partnership interests, the arrangement is considered to be a special allocation. There must be a sound business purpose for special allocations and partners are well advised to seek the counsel of an attorney or CPA.

Liability

A principal disadvantage of the general partnership arrangement is that all general partners in a partnership are subject to joint and several liability for the debts and obligations of the partnership. These liabilities can arise from:

1. liability for the negligence and acts of employees
2. negligence of other partners
3. commercial liabilities (e.g., loans) to the partnership
4. commercial obligations to other trade creditors

However, general partners of an LLP can insulate themselves from liabilities arising from the acts of other partners. General partners of an LLP will not be personally liable for the debts and obligations arising from errors, omissions, negligence, incompetence, or acts committed by another partner or representative of the partnership who is not under the supervision or direction of the first partner. It is important to note that general partners remain personally liable for commercial and trade obligations. If the partners wish to insulate themselves from these obligations, they should consider an LLC and once formed, they should not personally guarantee commercial obligations.

Quick Quiz 16.5

1. Limited liability partnerships are generally owned by licensed professionals.
   a. True
   b. False
2. The transferability of an interest in an LLP is the same as for any other type of partnership.
   a. True
   b. False

True, False.

Management/Operations

The management of an LLP is generally the same as for any general partnership. Note that unlike a limited partnership, the LLP confers limited liability status on all partners, not just limited partners.

Income Taxation and Payroll (Social Security) Taxes

For federal income tax purposes, the entity may elect to file as a corporation or as a partnership. This choice is known as "**checking the box**." Choosing to be taxed as a C corporation allows owners to take advantage of tax-free fringe benefits which may be provided by C corporations. Operating as a partnership has the disadvantages of subjecting income to employment taxes and limited fringe benefits for owners. If the entity files as a partnership it will file Form 1065. If it files as a corporation, it will file either the Form 1120-S (if it elects S corporation status) or Form 1120 (if it files as a C corporation).

Exhibit 16.10 | A Summary of Advantages and Disadvantages of Limited Liability Partnerships

Advantages
• Favorable pass-through partnership taxation status available. • Flexibility in structuring ownership interests. • Partners can insulate themselves from the acts of other partners.
Disadvantages
• Required to file with the state to register. • Unlimited liability for own acts of malpractice.

FAMILY LIMITED PARTNERSHIPS (FLP)

A **family limited partnership** (FLP) is a special type of limited partnership created under state law with the primary purpose of transferring assets to younger generations using annual exclusions and valuation discounts for minority interests and lack of marketability.

Formation

Usually, one or more family members transfer highly appreciated property that is expected to continue to appreciate to a limited partnership in return for both a small (one percent, for example) general and a large (99 percent, for example) limited partnership interest. In a limited partnership, the general partner has unlimited liability and the sole management rights of the partnership, while the limited partners are passive interest holders with limited liability and no management rights.

Key Concepts

1. Describe how the tax attributes of an FLP can be useful.
2. Explain the advantages of using an FLP to protect family assets.

Exhibit 16.11 | Family Limited Partnership

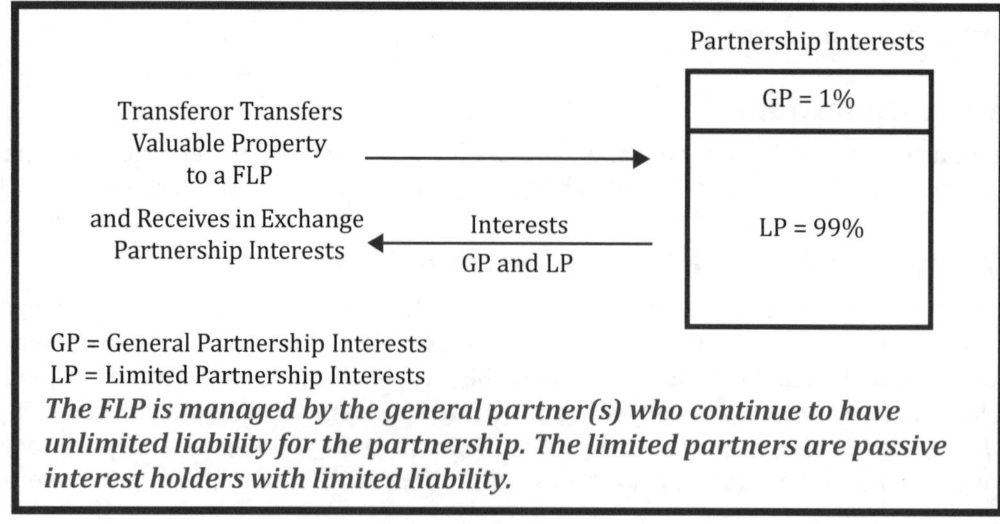

Interest, Disposal of Interest, and Dissolution

Upon creation of the partnership (FLP), there are neither income nor gift tax consequences because the entity created (the limited partnership and all of its interests, both general and limited) is owned by the same person, or persons, who owned it before the transfer.

Once the FLP is created, the owner of the general and limited partnership interests values the limited partnership interests. Since there are usually transferability restrictions on the limited partnership interests (lack of marketability), and since the limited partners have little control of the management of the partnership (lack of control), limited partnership interests are usually valued at a substantial discount from their fair market values. It is not uncommon for the discount of such interests to range between 20 and 40 percent for the purpose of calculating gift taxes payable by the transferor. The original transferor (grantor) then begins an annual gifting program utilizing the discounts, the gift tax annual exclusions, and gift-splitting (where applicable) to transfer limited partnership interests to younger generation family members at reduced transfer costs.

Example 16.6

Ferris, age 52, is married to Sloan, and they have three children and nine grandchildren. The three children are happily married and Ferris and Sloan think of their children's spouses as their own children. Ferris transfers a 100% interest in a business with a fair market value of $3,200,000 to a family limited partnership. Ferris, in return, receives a general partnership interest of one percent and 158.40 units of limited partnership interests representing 99 percent, at $20,000 (($3,200,000 x 99%) / 158.40) per unit. He then transfers two limited partnership units to each child, the spouse of each child, and each grandchild using a 25 percent discount, the annual exclusion ($15,000 in 2021), and the gift-splitting election.

FMV Per Unit	$20,000
x 2 Units Per Family Member = Value Per Donee	$40,000
x 15 Donees = Total Value Transferred	$600,000
Gift Value Per Unit (with 25% Discount to FMV)	$15,000
x 2 Units Per Family Member = Total Gift Value Per Donee	$30,000
x 15 Donees = Total Value for Gift Tax Purposes	$450,000

In this scenario, Ferris does not pay any gift tax due to the annual gift tax exclusion. It will take six years with this level of gifting for Ferris to transfer his entire limited partnership interest to his children, their spouses, and his grandchildren without paying any gift taxes.

Capital

One of the unique features of the FLP, and perhaps its most important non-tax benefit, is that the original owner/transferor can maintain control of the property transferred to the limited partnership by only retaining a small general partnership interest. If the FLP is funded with a business interest, the general partner could remain president of the business, direct the company's strategic plan, receive reasonable compensation and fringe benefits, hire and fire employees, receive executive perks, and generally control the limited partners' interests. As with all limited partnerships, the limited partners have no control over any of these enumerated management decisions.

> ### Quick Quiz 16.6
>
> 1. Only a limited partner can manage a family limited partnership.
>   a. True
>   b. False
>
> 2. At formation of a family limited partnership, the founder is subject to gift tax on the transfer of the property interest to the family limited partnership.
>   a. True
>   b. False
>
> False, False.

The FLP is often undertaken as a series of transfers, including an initial nontaxable contribution of property to the partnership followed by annual exclusion gifts of limited partnership interests. While a general partner has control over partnership affairs, an individual who transfers his property to an FLP needs to be financially secure without the transferred property, both from a net worth and cash flow perspective. The transferor of the property to the FLP that can sustain himself without accessing the FLP's assets will provide a strong defense to a potential IRS challenge regarding inclusion in the gross estate due to a retained interest in or economic benefit from the property.

Liability

The use of the FLP structure can also help protect family assets. By placing the assets in the FLP and only making gifts of limited partnership interests to heirs, judgments or liens entered against a donee (limited partner) will not jeopardize the assets of the partnership. A donee's creditor would not be able to force the donee to liquidate his interest, since the donee does not have the right to force the liquidation of a limited partnership interest.

Transferring limited partnership interests to children and children's spouses can also help protect assets from divorce claims. If the child and his spouse divorce, even if the divorced spouse received a limited partnership interest, he or she could not force distributions from the partnership, participate in management, require his or her interest to be redeemed, or force a liquidation of the partnership.

Taxation

The creation of family limited partnerships and the use of discounts to transfer value at a lower gift tax cost has been regularly contested by the IRS. However, in several cases, the courts have ruled in favor of the taxpayer and upheld discounts on the valuation of limited partnership interests in the range of 10 percent to 40 percent, as long as the FLP was operated like a separate business. The IRS has won, and the valuation discounts have not been allowed, in cases where the family withdrew money from the business at leisure, shared checking accounts with the business, had the FLP pay medical or other ordinary living expenses for the family, and when other non-business transactions were prevalent within the FLP.

The estate planning benefits of the FLP are lost and expenses are increased (as the result of legal fees) when the IRS successfully contests the use of the FLP arrangement. To mitigate against this risk and to ensure the use of the favorable discounts, the FLP should possess economic substance by having its own checking accounts, tax identification number, payroll (including payment of reasonable compensation to the general partner if he is managing the business), and should not allow family members to withdraw funds at will, nor should the FLP pay for personal expenses of its owners.

A FLP is taxed as a partnership and the entity files a Form 1065 and issues Schedule K-1s to both general and limited partners. The general partner may be a corporation or an individual. The treatment of payroll taxes will be determined by whether the general partner is an individual or a corporation. The limited partners are passive and not subject to employment tax.

Exhibit 16.12 | Advantages and Disadvantages of Family Limited Partnerships

Advantages
• Control retained by senior family member. • Valuation discounts are available for minority interests. • Annual exclusion gifts are generally used to transfer interests to family members. • Some creditor protection. • Restrictions can be placed on transferability of limited partnership interests of junior family members. • FLP is commonly used as an estate planning strategy.
Disadvantages
• Attorney setup fees and costs. • Periodic valuation costs. • Operational requirements. • Potential IRS challenges regarding valuations and discounts.

LIMITED LIABILITY COMPANIES (LLC)

Limited Liability Companies are separate legal entities formed by one or more individuals by meeting state statutory requirements necessary for the formation of an LLC.

Formation

LLCs are formed in much the same way as corporations. They are chartered entities registered with the secretary of state in the state of organization. The charter document is called **Articles of Organization** and the state requires the entity to have a resident agent. In addition, the state will require annual filings.

Key Concepts

1. Discuss the formation and operation of an LLC.
2. Discuss the liability protection offered by an LLC.
3. Explain the tax attributes of an LLC.

Interest, Disposal of Interest, and Dissolution

Usually, owners' contributions determine the ownership percentage of an LLC. However, sometimes the organization will want to divide the ownership interests in an amount differently than the initial contributions. They can do this in a variety of ways, including revaluing assets or issuing units for some obligation.

Disposal or transferability of interests may be difficult and may be restricted to transferring only to named parties. Such restrictions are clarified in the operating agreement.

Capital

Capital is easier to raise in an LLC than in a proprietorship. Ease of raising capital in an LLC is similar to the ease of raising capital in a partnership.

Capital Structure

There is no limitation on the number of members or the types of members in an LLC. Members may include foreign (nonresident aliens) individuals, estates, trusts, corporations, etc. LLCs may allocate items of income and gains in any manner agreed to by the members in the operating agreement and can also create different classes of ownership interests which have different rights.

Liability

The most important feature of an LLC is that the LLC's individual owners are protected from personal liability for the LLC's debts and obligations unless they personally guarantee such obligations.

The liability protection is not absolute. Piercing the veil and alter ego concepts give courts the power to disregard the LLC liability protection in extraordinary cases of owner/manager abuse or failure to maintain a clear and continuing identity.

Management/Operations

An LLC usually is managed by virtue of an **operating agreement**. The operating agreement is similar to corporate bylaws and may be amended from time to time. The agreement specifies how and who will manage the LLC, how interests may be transferred, etc. Operating agreements are not filed with the state. Operating agreements sometimes specify simple majority rules for some decisions, super majority rules for other decisions (e.g., 2/3 or 3/4 to take on debt in excess of certain amounts) and unanimous votes for special situations (e.g., changing the operating agreement). Caution should be used with unanimous agreement provisions because they essentially give a minority owner (member) a veto power over all other members.

Note that an LLC is not legally required to have an operating agreement. If an LLC does not have an operating agreement, it will (by default) be governed by the state laws regarding LLCs. Although this might be sufficient for some LLCs, it is generally best to have a written operating agreement signed by all members that specifies the rules and regulations pertinent to the LLC.

Income Taxation and Payroll (Social Security) Taxes

An LLC which has a single member/owner is typically a disregarded entity for federal income tax purposes. In this case, the owner files a Schedule C of Form 1040 for the LLC, the same as for a proprietorship. Such an LLC owner has the same issues as proprietors with respect to self-employment tax, unemployment compensation, and fringe benefits. Alternatively, a single member LLC may elect for federal income tax purposes to be taxed as an S corporation (Form 1120-S with Schedule K-1), or a C corporation (Form 1120 with W-2 income to the owner).

An LLC with two or more members can elect to be taxed for federal income tax purposes as a partnership (Form 1065 with Schedule K-1s), an S corporation (Form 1120-S with Schedule K-1s), or a C corporation (Form 1120 with W-2 income to the owners).

Taxation of Income

The LLC is not taxed at the entity level if it is taxed as a partnership. As a pass-through entity, an LLC's income is taxed to members at their personal rates. LLC losses are deductible on personal income tax returns to the extent of basis and may be limited by the passive activity rules. A unique characteristic of LLCs is that no gain or loss is recognized upon the distribution of appreciated property from an LLC to an LLC member. Gain will only be recognized to the extent that cash received exceeds the members adjusted basis.

Fringe Benefits

LLCs are usually taxed as partnerships. Therefore, members are not generally allowed to exclude from gross income the value of fringe benefits paid on their behalf by the LLC.

Quick Quiz 16.7

1. There is no limitation on the number of members of a LLC.
   a. True
   b. False
2. A written operating agreement is an important element of the management of a LLC.
   a. True
   b. False

True, True.

Employment Tax on Income

LLCs are usually taxed as partnerships. Income earned by the LLC members is normally subject to self-employment tax on the tax returns of individual members. There are exceptions: (1) for LLC income derived from rental real estate, and (2) for LLC members who are not the managing member and are the equivalent of limited partners.

Once elected, the tax status (partnership, S corporation, or C corporation) will dictate the handling of self-employment tax and fringe benefits.

Exhibit 16.13 | A Summary of Advantages and Disadvantages of LLCs

Advantages
• Members have limited liability. • Number of members is unlimited but a single member LLC is typically a disregarded entity for tax purposes (File Form 1040 Schedule C). • Members may be individuals, corporations, trusts, other LLCs, and other entities. • Income is passed through to the members, usually on Schedule K-1. • Double taxation affecting most C corporations is avoided if partnership tax status is elected. • Members can participate in managing the LLC. • Distributions to members do not have to be directly proportional to the members' ownership interests as they do for S corporations. • Can have multiple classes of ownership. • Entity may elect to be taxed as a partnership, an S corporation, or a C corporation.
Disadvantages
• May have limited life (often by termination on the death or bankruptcy of a member). • Transfer of interests is difficult and sometimes limited by operating agreement. • Some industries or professions may not be permitted to use LLC status. • Laws vary from state to state regarding LLCs. • Laws are relatively new for LLCs; therefore, precedent from prior court cases are limited. • For tax purposes, the complex partnership rules generally apply. • Members not meeting exceptions are subject to self-employment tax on all earned income if partnership status is elected.

CASE STUDY 16.1

Disregarded Entity

Tony L. Robucci, Petitioners, v. Commissioner of Internal Revenue, Respondent, T.C. Memo 2011-19 (January 24, 2011).

Tony Robucci, a psychiatrist, sought advice from Mr. Carson, a CPA, specializing in tax planning for small businesses, as to how he might minimize the tax liability arising from his practice. Mr. Carson restructured Mr. Robucci's practice from a sole proprietorship to a limited liability company (LLC) with two members: Tony Robucci owning 95% and a "manager" corporation (PC) owning 5%. Carson also organized a second corporation (W) to perform services associated with Robucci's practice. Robucci's 95% interest in LLC was divided between a 10% general partner interest and an 85% limited partner interest attributable to intangibles associated with the practice. Robucci paid self-employment tax only on distributions associated with his 10% general partner interest, whereas, as a sole proprietor, he was required to pay self-employment tax on the entire net income from his psychiatric practice.

The IRS alleges that PC and W are without substance and must be disregarded for federal tax purposes. As a result, LLC becomes a single-member LLC, which, because it did not elect association status, also must be disregarded for federal tax purposes, and therefore, Robucci's practice must be treated as a sole proprietorship.

The court held that because the organization of PC and W accomplished no significant business purpose and because PC and W were, in substance, hollow corporate shells formed primarily for tax avoidance, they are disregarded for federal tax purposes and Robucci is taxable as a sole proprietor for 2002 - 2004.

C CORPORATIONS

Corporations are chartered legal entities formed by one or more individuals by meeting state statutory requirements necessary for the formation of a corporation. There are two types of corporations: the C corporation and the S corporation. For tax purposes, S corporations are simply C corporations with a special tax election and will be discussed in the next section.

Formation

Corporations can only be created by filing a charter document with the state of incorporation (called **articles of incorporation**). The articles of incorporation generally require a corporation to disclose its name, number of shares, and the purpose of the corporation. The corporation's purpose may be broad (e.g., to engage in any lawful activity) or specific (e.g., to sell textbooks). In addition, the corporation will be required to name a registered agent located in the state of incorporation.

Interest, Disposal of Interest, and Dissolution

Ownership interests in a corporation are held by a shareholder and are evidenced by shares of stock certificates. Shares may be easy to transfer if there is a market, but certain small corporations restrict the transfer of shares through a shareholder agreement. The shares of stock issued by the corporation may be all one class or several classes. Different classes of stock generally have different values and/or voting rights.

Capital

Corporations can raise capital more easily than a proprietorship or partnership. The limited liability protection afforded corporations appeals to outside non-employee owner/investors.

Key Concepts

1. Describe the formation and operation of a corporation.
2. Discuss the tax attributes of a corporation.
3. Discuss the ability of a corporation to raise capital.

Liability

Liability in corporations is limited to the invested capital. Individual shareholders of the corporation have limited liability, presuming the corporation behaves in such a way as to clearly and consistently maintain its identity and complies with state-mandated requirements.

Management/Operations

Corporations are managed by one or more officers appointed by the board of directors. The board of directors is the governing body of a corporation. The board of directors appoints various officers to run the corporation (usually includes president, chief financial officer, secretary, treasurer). The board of directors acts, or should act, in a very formal way and is required under the corporate charter to meet and follow certain formalities. Observing corporate formalities, and maintaining good standing with the secretary of state in the state of incorporation, is an ongoing requirement.

Income Taxation and Payroll (Social Security) Taxes

A corporation is taxed as a C corporation unless S corporation status is elected. C corporations must file Form 1120 (**Exhibit 16.16**) and pay taxes on their own income on a calendar or fiscal year basis. The owner/employees of both C corporations and S corporations are treated as employees for payroll tax purposes. Therefore, the entity withholds 7.65 percent of the employee's pay for Social Security and Medicare taxes and matches such withholding for Social Security and Medicare taxes. The owner/employee's compensation is not considered to be self-employment income.

Distributions of cash and other assets to a shareholder/employee in his capacity as a shareholder rather than as an employee are considered to be dividends. A C corporation is not allowed to take a tax deduction for dividends distributed to shareholders, but shareholders must include the dividends in gross income. Therefore, the income of a C corporation can be taxed two times, once at the corporation level and a second time at the shareholder level when dividends are distributed. In a closely-held corporation, careful tax planning can minimize or even eliminate this double taxation.

Quick Quiz 16.8

1. A corporation's purpose must be narrowly defined in the articles of incorporation.
   a. True
   b. False
2. In-kind distributions of appreciated assets by a C corporation are treated as a deemed sale by the corporation.
   a. True
   b. False

False, True.

When non-cash distributions of appreciated property are made to shareholder/employees, gain must be recognized at the corporate level as though the property had been sold and the cash proceeds distributed. For a C corporation, this gain must be recognized at the corporation level. For an S corporation, the gain is passed through to shareholders and taxed on their individual income tax returns based on their ownership interests in the S corporation. Unlike this corporation treatment, appreciated assets can be distributed by an LLC or by any entity taxed as a partnership without any gain recognition at the time of the distribution.

Exhibit 16.14 | Tax Formula for C Corporation

Total Income (From Whatever Source Derived)	$XX,XXX
Less: Exclusions From Gross Income	(X,XXX)
Gross Income	$XX,XXX
Less: Deductions	(X,XXX)
Taxable Income	$XX,XXX

Prior to TCJA 2017, C corporations paid graduated federal income-tax rates of 15% to 39%. For tax years beginning after Dec. 31, 2017, TCJA 2017 established a flat 21% corporate rate. In addition, the TCJA placed limitations on certain deductions, such as interest expense, and eliminated the ability to carry back NOLs.[2]

Exhibit 16.15 | Advantages and Disadvantages of C Corporations

Advantages
• Relative ease of raising capital. • Limited liability of shareholders. • Unlimited life of entity. • Ease of transfer of ownership interests. • Generally more management resources. • Shareholder/employees may receive the full array of employer-provided tax-free fringe benefits.
Disadvantages
• Potential for double taxation due to entity level taxation. • Administrative burdens (e.g., filings). • More difficult to form and dissolution can cause taxable gains. • Borrowing may be difficult without stockholder personal guarantees, which negates part of the advantage of limited liability. • Requires a registered agent. • Requires a federal tax ID number.

2. The CARES Act of 2020 allows net operating losses arising in tax years 2018, 2019, or 2020 to be carried back up to five years.

Exhibit 16.16 | Form 1120

Form **1120**
Department of the Treasury
Internal Revenue Service

U.S. Corporation Income Tax Return

For calendar year 2020 or tax year beginning ________, 2020, ending ________, 20 ____

▶ Go to *www.irs.gov/Form1120* for instructions and the latest information.

OMB No. 1545-0123

2020

A Check if:	TYPE OR PRINT		
1a Consolidated return (attach Form 851) ☐		Name	B Employer identification number
b Life/nonlife consolidated return ☐		Number, street, and room or suite no. If a P.O. box, see instructions.	C Date incorporated
2 Personal holding co. (attach Sch. PH) ☐		City or town, state or province, country, and ZIP or foreign postal code	D Total assets (see instructions) $
3 Personal service corp. (see instructions) ☐			
4 Schedule M-3 attached ☐	E Check if: (1) ☐ Initial return	(2) ☐ Final return (3) ☐ Name change	(4) ☐ Address change

Income	1a	Gross receipts or sales	1a			
	b	Returns and allowances	1b			
	c	Balance. Subtract line 1b from line 1a			1c	
	2	Cost of goods sold (attach Form 1125-A)			2	
	3	Gross profit. Subtract line 2 from line 1c			3	
	4	Dividends and inclusions (Schedule C, line 23)			4	
	5	Interest			5	
	6	Gross rents			6	
	7	Gross royalties			7	
	8	Capital gain net income (attach Schedule D (Form 1120))			8	
	9	Net gain or (loss) from Form 4797, Part II, line 17 (attach Form 4797)			9	
	10	Other income (see instructions—attach statement)			10	
	11	**Total income.** Add lines 3 through 10 ▶			11	
Deductions (See instructions for limitations on deductions.)	12	Compensation of officers (see instructions—attach Form 1125-E) ▶			12	
	13	Salaries and wages (less employment credits)			13	
	14	Repairs and maintenance			14	
	15	Bad debts			15	
	16	Rents			16	
	17	Taxes and licenses			17	
	18	Interest (see instructions)			18	
	19	Charitable contributions			19	
	20	Depreciation from Form 4562 not claimed on Form 1125-A or elsewhere on return (attach Form 4562)			20	
	21	Depletion			21	
	22	Advertising			22	
	23	Pension, profit-sharing, etc., plans			23	
	24	Employee benefit programs			24	
	25	Reserved for future use			25	
	26	Other deductions (attach statement)			26	
	27	**Total deductions.** Add lines 12 through 26 ▶			27	
	28	Taxable income before net operating loss deduction and special deductions. Subtract line 27 from line 11			28	
	29a	Net operating loss deduction (see instructions)	29a			
	b	Special deductions (Schedule C, line 24)	29b			
	c	Add lines 29a and 29b			29c	
Tax, Refundable Credits, and Payments	30	**Taxable income.** Subtract line 29c from line 28. See instructions			30	
	31	Total tax (Schedule J, Part I, line 11)			31	
	32	2020 net 965 tax liability paid (Schedule J, Part II, line 12)			32	
	33	Total payments, credits, and section 965 net tax liability (Schedule J, Part III, line 23)			33	
	34	Estimated tax penalty. See instructions. Check if Form 2220 is attached ▶ ☐			34	
	35	**Amount owed.** If line 33 is smaller than the total of lines 31, 32, and 34, enter amount owed			35	
	36	**Overpayment.** If line 33 is larger than the total of lines 31, 32, and 34, enter amount overpaid			36	
	37	Enter amount from line 36 you want: **Credited to 2021 estimated tax** ▶		**Refunded** ▶	37	

Sign Here

Under penalties of perjury, I declare that I have examined this return, including accompanying schedules and statements, and to the best of my knowledge and belief, it is true, correct, and complete. Declaration of preparer (other than taxpayer) is based on all information of which preparer has any knowledge.

▶ Signature of officer | Date | ▶ Title

May the IRS discuss this return with the preparer shown below? See instructions. ☐ Yes ☐ No

Paid Preparer Use Only	Print/Type preparer's name	Preparer's signature	Date	Check ☐ if self-employed	PTIN
	Firm's name ▶			Firm's EIN ▶	
	Firm's address ▶			Phone no.	

For Paperwork Reduction Act Notice, see separate instructions. Cat. No. 11450Q Form **1120** (2020)

S CORPORATIONS

An **S corporation** is normally created under state law by first forming a C corporation and then filing an "S" election with the IRS. The incorporation is normally the same as for a C corporation. There are, however, significant ways in which an S corporation differs from a C corporation.

Interest, Disposal of Interest, and Dissolution

Like a C corporation, the ownership interests in an S corporation are held by shareholders and are evidenced by shares of stock. Transferability of shares may be restricted by a shareholders' agreement.

Capital

It is easier to raise capital in an S corporation than in a proprietorship or partnership because of the limited liability protection but the limited number of allowable shareholders may have a negative affect on the ability to raise capital. The IRC does, however, allow close family members to be treated as a single shareholder.

Key Concepts

1. Explain how an S corporation differs from a C corporation.
2. Discuss the advantages and disadvantages of an S corporation.

Liability

An S corporation offers the same limited liability protection as a C corporation or an LLC.

Management/Operations

Corporations are managed by one or more officers appointed by the board of directors. The board of directors is the governing body of a corporation. The board of directors appoints various officers to run the corporation. The board of directors acts, or should act, in a very formal way and is required under the corporate charter to meet and follow certain formalities. Observing corporate formalities and maintaining good standing with the secretary of state in the state of incorporation is an ongoing requirement.

The number of shareholders of an S corporation is limited to 100 and the S corporation can only have one class of stock. LLCs, partnerships, and other corporations are prohibited from becoming S corporation shareholders. Additionally, nonresident aliens and most trusts may not be S corporation shareholders.

Income Taxation and Payroll (Social Security) Taxes

The income of an S corporation is passed through to shareholders and is not taxed at the corporation level. Therefore, an S corporation provides many of the benefits of a corporation without any double taxation of income earned by the corporation.

The owner/employees of S corporations are employees for payroll tax purposes. Therefore, the entity withholds 7.65 percent of the employees' pay for Social Security and Medicare taxes and matches such withholding for Social Security and Medicare taxes. The owner/employee compensation is not considered self-employment income. Additional distributions to shareholders beyond reasonable compensation are treated as dividends not subject to payroll tax.

Since the income of an S corporation is taxed to the shareholders for the year in which it is earned, dividend distributions to shareholders are normally not subject to income tax at the time they are distributed. Stated differently, S corporation dividends normally represent the distribution of income that has previously been taxed to the shareholder.

As indicated in the C corporation discussion, in-kind distributions of appreciated assets will be treated as a deemed sale; thus, such distributions will generate a capital gain in the case of an S corporation to all shareholders in proportion to their ownership even if the asset was only distributed to one shareholder.

Generally, S corporations file Form 1120-S (**Exhibit 16.18**) on a calendar year basis and provide each shareholder with a Form 1120-S Schedule K-1 (**Exhibit 16.19**). Each shareholder then reports their share of S corporation income or loss on Form 1040 Schedule E, which ultimately flows to line 5 of Schedule 1 of Form 1040 (see **Exhibit 16.3**).

Quick Quiz 16.9

1. The number of S corporation shareholders is limited to 100.
   a. True
   b. False
2. All payments from an S corporation to an S corporation shareholder will be treated as income subject to payroll taxes.
   a. True
   b. False

True, False.

S Corporation Owners' Basis

The S corporation owner's initial basis is generally the amount of cash paid for the shares or value of property contributed to the corporation. In a manner similar to partnership basis adjustments, the stock basis of an S corporation owner will be adjusted each year based on the flow-through of income or loss, as well as distributions. Income and additional capital contributions increase basis while losses, deduction items, charitable contributions, and distributions decrease basis. Unlike partnership basis, an S corporation shareholder's basis will increase for amounts the shareholder loans to the corporation, but not for a guarantee of a loan made to the corporation by a third party. Additional rules regarding adjustments to S corporation stock basis can be rather complex, and are beyond the scope of this textbook.

Exhibit 16.17 | Advantages and Disadvantages of S Corporations

Advantages
• Income is passed through to the shareholders for federal income tax purposes. • Income is taxed at the individual level which may be a lower tax rate than the applicable corporate rate. • Shareholders have limited liability. • Distributions from S corporations are exempt from the payroll tax system, assuming the corporation provides adequate compensation to those shareholders who are employees of the corporation.
Disadvantages
• Limited to 100 shareholders. • Only one class of stock is permitted. • Cannot have corporate, partnership, certain trust, or nonresident alien shareholders. • Shareholder employees owning more than two percent of the company must pay taxes on a range of employee fringe benefits that would be tax-free to a shareholder/employee of a C corporation. • The tax rate of the individual shareholder may be higher than the corporate tax rate (even considering the new 20% deduction for flow-through entities). • Borrowing may be difficult without stockholder personal guarantees, which negates part of the advantage of limited liability.

Exhibit 16.18 | Form 1120-S

Form **1120-S**

Department of the Treasury
Internal Revenue Service

U.S. Income Tax Return for an S Corporation

▶ Do not file this form unless the corporation has filed or is attaching Form 2553 to elect to be an S corporation.
▶ Go to *www.irs.gov/Form1120S* for instructions and the latest information.

OMB No. 1545-0123

2020

For calendar year 2020 or tax year beginning , 2020, ending , 20

	TYPE OR PRINT	
A S election effective date	Name	D Employer identification number
B Business activity code number (see instructions)	Number, street, and room or suite no. If a P.O. box, see instructions.	E Date incorporated
C Check if Sch. M-3 attached ☐	City or town, state or province, country, and ZIP or foreign postal code	F Total assets (see instructions) $

G Is the corporation electing to be an S corporation beginning with this tax year? ☐ Yes ☐ No If "Yes," attach Form 2553 if not already filed

H Check if: **(1)** ☐ Final return **(2)** ☐ Name change **(3)** ☐ Address change **(4)** ☐ Amended return **(5)** ☐ S election termination or revocation

I Enter the number of shareholders who were shareholders during any part of the tax year . . . . ▶

J Check if corporation: **(1)** ☐ Aggregated activities for section 465 at-risk purposes **(2)** ☐ Grouped activities for section 469 passive activity purposes

Caution: Include **only** trade or business income and expenses on lines 1a through 21. See the instructions for more information.

Income	1a	Gross receipts or sales	1a			
	b	Returns and allowances	1b			
	c	Balance. Subtract line 1b from line 1a			1c	
	2	Cost of goods sold (attach Form 1125-A)			2	
	3	Gross profit. Subtract line 2 from line 1c			3	
	4	Net gain (loss) from Form 4797, line 17 (attach Form 4797)			4	
	5	Other income (loss) (see instructions—attach statement)			5	
	6	**Total income (loss).** Add lines 3 through 5 ▶			6	
Deductions (see instructions for limitations)	7	Compensation of officers (see instructions—attach Form 1125-E)			7	
	8	Salaries and wages (less employment credits)			8	
	9	Repairs and maintenance			9	
	10	Bad debts			10	
	11	Rents			11	
	12	Taxes and licenses			12	
	13	Interest (see instructions)			13	
	14	Depreciation not claimed on Form 1125-A or elsewhere on return (attach Form 4562)			14	
	15	Depletion **(Do not deduct oil and gas depletion.)**			15	
	16	Advertising			16	
	17	Pension, profit-sharing, etc., plans			17	
	18	Employee benefit programs			18	
	19	Other deductions (attach statement)			19	
	20	**Total deductions.** Add lines 7 through 19 ▶			20	
	21	**Ordinary business income (loss).** Subtract line 20 from line 6			21	
Tax and Payments	22a	Excess net passive income or LIFO recapture tax (see instructions)	22a			
	b	Tax from Schedule D (Form 1120-S)	22b			
	c	Add lines 22a and 22b (see instructions for additional taxes)			22c	
	23a	2020 estimated tax payments and 2019 overpayment credited to 2020	23a			
	b	Tax deposited with Form 7004	23b			
	c	Credit for federal tax paid on fuels (attach Form 4136)	23c			
	d	Reserved for future use	23d			
	e	Add lines 23a through 23d			23e	
	24	Estimated tax penalty (see instructions). Check if Form 2220 is attached ▶ ☐			24	
	25	**Amount owed.** If line 23e is smaller than the total of lines 22c and 24, enter amount owed			25	
	26	**Overpayment.** If line 23e is larger than the total of lines 22c and 24, enter amount overpaid			26	
	27	Enter amount from line 26: **Credited to 2021 estimated tax ▶** **Refunded ▶**			27	

Sign Here

Under penalties of perjury, I declare that I have examined this return, including accompanying schedules and statements, and to the best of my knowledge and belief, it is true, correct, and complete. Declaration of preparer (other than taxpayer) is based on all information of which preparer has any knowledge.

▶ Signature of officer | Date | ▶ Title

May the IRS discuss this return with the preparer shown below? See instructions. ☐ Yes ☐ No

Paid Preparer Use Only	Print/Type preparer's name	Preparer's signature	Date	Check ☐ if self-employed	PTIN
	Firm's name ▶			Firm's EIN ▶	
	Firm's address ▶			Phone no.	

For Paperwork Reduction Act Notice, see separate instructions. Cat. No. 11510H Form **1120-S** (2020)

Exhibit 16.19 | Form 1120-S Schedule K-1

671120

☐ Final K-1 ☐ Amended K-1 OMB No. 1545-0123

Schedule K-1 (Form 1120-S) **2020**
Department of the Treasury
Internal Revenue Service

For calendar year 2020, or tax year

beginning / / 2020 ending / /

Shareholder's Share of Income, Deductions, Credits, etc. ► See separate instructions.

Part I Information About the Corporation

A Corporation's employer identification number

B Corporation's name, address, city, state, and ZIP code

C IRS Center where corporation filed return

Part II Information About the Shareholder

D Shareholder's identifying number

E Shareholder's name, address, city, state, and ZIP code

F Current year allocation percentage . . . ______ %

G Shareholder's number of shares
Beginning of tax year . . . . . . ______
End of tax year . . . . ______

H Loans from shareholder
Beginning of tax year . . . . . . $ ______
End of tax year . . . . $ ______

For IRS Use Only

Part III Shareholder's Share of Current Year Income, Deductions, Credits, and Other Items

1	Ordinary business income (loss)	13	Credits
2	Net rental real estate income (loss)		
3	Other net rental income (loss)		
4	Interest income		
5a	Ordinary dividends		
5b	Qualified dividends	14	Foreign transactions
6	Royalties		
7	Net short-term capital gain (loss)		
8a	Net long-term capital gain (loss)		
8b	Collectibles (28%) gain (loss)		
8c	Unrecaptured section 1250 gain		
9	Net section 1231 gain (loss)		
10	Other income (loss)	15	Alternative minimum tax (AMT) items
11	Section 179 deduction	16	Items affecting shareholder basis
12	Other deductions		
		17	Other information

18 ☐ More than one activity for at-risk purposes*
19 ☐ More than one activity for passive activity purposes*

* See attached statement for additional information.

For Paperwork Reduction Act Notice, see the Instructions for Form 1120-S. www.irs.gov/Form1120S Cat. No. 11520D Schedule K-1 (Form 1120-S) 2020

Comparison of S Corporations and LLCs

Many business owners know that they want limited liability and a flow-through tax entity, but cannot distinguish between an S corporation and a LLC. Below is a side-by-side comparison of these two very important entity types.

Exhibit 16.20 | Comparison of S Corporations and LLCs

	S Corporation	*LLC*
Double taxation	No	No
Pass through tax losses	Yes	Yes
Availability of preferred return for certain investors (1 class of stock in S)	No	Yes
Partnerships, corporations, and trusts can be entity owners	No	Yes
Foreign investors	No	Yes
Distribute in-kind appreciated assets to owners without gain recognition	No	Yes
Ability to transfer interest to trust for estate planning	No	Yes
Low filing fees	Yes (Generally)	No
Self-employment tax on all income for owner/ employees	No	Yes (Generally)
Limited number of owners	Yes (100)	No
Owner's basis for deductibility of losses includes pro-rata share of loans to entity by third parties	No	Yes
The law is well settled pertaining to the entity	Yes	No
Filing date with extensions	September 15th	September 15th

Exhibit 16.21 | Entity Comparison

	Proprietorship	General Partnership	Limited Partnership	LLP	FLP	LLC	S Corp.	C Corp.
Cost to create (money & time)	Low	Medium	Medium-High	High	High	High	High	High
Personal liability of investors for enterprise debt	Yes	Yes	Yes (if GP) No (if LP)	Yes	Yes	No	No	No
Annual state filing requirement	No	Generally Not	Yes	Yes	Yes	Yes	Yes	Yes
Maximum owners	One	Unlimited	Unlimited	Unlimited	Unlimited	Unlimited	100	Unlimited
Owners are known as	Owner	Partner	Partner or Limited Partner	Partner or Limited Partner	Partner or Limited Partner	Member	Shareholder	Shareholder
Tax filing alternatives	Schedule C 1040	Form 1065 K-1 flows to Schedule E of Form 1040	Form 1065 K-1 flows to Schedule E of Form 1040	May file as corporation or partnership	Form 1065 K-1 flows to Schedule E of Form 1040	If one member, entity is disregarded and owner files Schedule C of Form 1040. If two or more members, choice of Form 1065 (Partnership), Form 1120-S (S Corporation), or Form 1120 (C Corporation)	Form 1120-S K-1 flows to Schedule E of Form 1040	Form 1120
Federal Tax ID required	No	Yes	Yes	Yes	Yes	No, if one member Yes, if two or more members	Yes	Yes
Taxation concept	Individual	Flow Through	Flow Through	Flow Through	Flow Through	Flow Through	Flow Through	Entity
Owners income	Self Employment	Self Employment	Self employment but limited partners/ members are not subject to Soc. Sec. tax unless they perform personal services for the entity	Self employment but limited partners/ members are not subject to Soc. Sec. tax unless they perform personal services for the entity	Self employment but limited partners/ members are not subject to Soc. Sec. tax unless they perform personal services for the entity	Depends on filing choice, but limited partners/members are not subject to Soc. Sec. tax unless they perform personal services for the entity	W-2 and ordinary income Excess profits distributed are not subject to Soc. Sec. tax	W-2 and dividend income

CASE STUDY 16.2

Disregarded Entity and S Corporations

John E. and Frances L. Rogers, Petitioners, v. Commissioner of Internal Revenue, Respondent, T.C. Memo 2011-277 (November 23, 2011).

Rogers is a tax attorney with over 40 years of experience. He received a law degree from Harvard University in 1967 and a master's degree in business administration from the University of Chicago. He worked in the tax department of Arthur Andersen for over 24 years before serving for seven years as the tax director and assistant treasurer at FMC Corp. In 2003 Rogers was a partner with the law firm Altheimer & Gray until its bankruptcy on June 30, 2003. Rogers promoted to clients "tax advantaged" transactions that dealt with the acquisition of, and sales of indirect interests in, Brazilian consumer receivables.

Rogers set up three business entities to manage numerous holding and trading companies used in the Brazilian receivable transactions. The first, PPI, was incorporated under the laws of Illinois on April 1, 1989, and elected on January 1, 1992, to be treated as an S corporation under §1361(a)(1). Rogers was its sole shareholder. The second, Jetstream Business Limited (Jetstream), a British Virgin Islands limited company, was formed by Rogers with PPI as its sole shareholder. Rogers was Jetstream's only director. In 2003, Jetstream was treated as a disregarded entity for federal tax purposes. The third, Warwick Trading, LLC (Warwick), an Illinois limited liability company (LLC), was formed in 2001. In 2003 Jetstream was the managing member of Warwick. Consequently, in 2003 Rogers had sole control over PPI, Jetstream, and Warwick.

In 2003, Warwick entered into transactions directly and through affiliated entities for, in effect, purchasing Brazilian consumer receivables and selling interests in them to numerous investors through trading and holding companies. The investors paid an aggregate of $2,381,000, all apparently for acquiring such interests. Of the $2,381,000, Warwick received and transferred $1,190,500 to Multicred Investamentos Limitada (Multicred), a Brazilian collection company. The other $1,190,500 was deposited directly in PPI's bank account on behalf of Jetstream. Neither Warwick, Jetstream, nor PPI had any obligation to transfer the $1,190,500 deposited directly in PPI's bank account to anyone, hold the funds in escrow, or segregate the funds from any other use.

PPI distributed $732,000 to Rogers in 2003. Rogers deposited this amount in his joint bank account with his wife. PPI deducted $513,501 of this amount as legal and professional fees paid to Rogers. In turn, Rogers included the $513,501 he received from PPI as income on his Schedule C, Profit or Loss From Business. Rogers did not report the remaining $218,499 distribution as income in 2003.

Rogers had no obligation to transfer the $218,499 to anyone, hold the funds in escrow, or segregate the funds from any other use.

CASE STUDY 16.2 CONTINUED

PPI's gross income for 2003 is its reported gross receipts or sales of $1,958,877, plus $450,000 from L&R, less the $1,190,500 that was transferred to Multicred, for a total of $1,218,377. Inconsistent with PPI's 2003 Form 1120-S, as prepared by Rogers, Rogers argued that the $1,190,500 PPI received from investors was not income to PPI. Rather, that the $1,190,500 was: (1) held in trust on behalf of Warwick or Jetstream; or (2) income to Warwick. The court concluded that neither of these contentions had merit.

Jetstream was also a disregarded entity in 2003 for federal tax purposes. Because both Warwick and Jetstream were disregarded entities for federal tax purposes, the $1,190,500 received from the investors is attributable only to PPI. On its face, the $218,499 transfer from PPI to Rogers is a distribution from an S corporation to a shareholder. Generally, §1368(b) provides that distributions from an S corporation with no accumulated earnings and profits (E&P) of a predecessor C corporation are not included in the gross income of the shareholder to the extent that they do not exceed the adjusted basis of the shareholder's stock.

Rogers argued that he held the $218,499 distribution from PPI in trust pursuant to a duty of loyalty to Warwick under the Illinois Limited Liability Company Act (Illinois LLC Act). Rogers' reliance on the Illinois LLC Act is illogical and misguided. PPI, and not Warwick, distributed the $218,499 in question to Rogers. PPI is an S corporation and is not subject to the Illinois LLC Act.

The $218,499 distribution from PPI to Rogers was nothing more than a distribution from an S corporation to a shareholder. PPI was incorporated on April 1, 1989, but did not elect to be treated as an S corporation until January 1, 1992. As a result, it is possible that PPI has accumulated E&P from its predecessor C corporation. Pursuant to the S corporation rules discussed above, if PPI has accumulated E&P then the $218,499 distribution is a dividend to Rogers to the extent it exceeds PPI's accumulated adjustments account (AAA) but does not exceed its accumulated E&P. If PPI does not have accumulated E&P, then the $218,499 distribution must be treated as a gain from the sale or exchange of property to the extent it exceeds Rogers' basis in his PPI stock.

TCJA 2017

As discussed in prior chapters, the TCJA 2017 made significant changes to the taxation of individuals, including the lowering of tax rates from a top rate of 39.6 percent to 37 percent, the significant increase in the standard deduction for all filing statuses, and elimination of both the personal and dependency exemptions. The TCJA also made significant changes to the taxation of C corporations and flow-through entities, such as partnerships, sole proprietorships, and S corporations.

The TCJA 2017 modified the corporate tax rates and modified certain deductions. The law eliminated the graduated corporate rate structure that had a top rate of 39 percent and replaced it with a flat 21 percent rate for years after 2017. The law also imposed a 30 percent limit on the amount of interest expense that can be deducted and eliminated NOL carrybacks incurred after 2017.[3] The law did, however, increase and extend bonus depreciation to 100 percent for both new and used equipment.

The Qualified Business Income (QBI or Section 199A) Deduction

One of the characteristics of flow-through entities is that the income of the entity is passed through to the individual owner, while retaining its character, and is taxed at individual rates. This tax treatment is beneficial in that it avoids the double taxation inherent in C corporations. However, the highest individual rates have historically exceeded the highest corporate rates. The reduction of the corporate tax rate to 21 percent reduces the benefit of avoiding the C corporation double taxation. In response, the TCJA created a 20 percent deduction for qualified business income that has the effect of lowering the tax burden of taxpayers who own an interest in a flow-through entity.

For tax years before 2018 and after 2025, net taxable income was passed through to owners and taxed at the owner level at standard rates. For tax years beginning after December 31, 2017 and before January 1, 2026, certain individuals, estates, and trusts are allowed a 20 percent deduction of qualified business income (QBI) from domestic (U.S.) pass-through business entities.[4] As discussed in Chapter 7, the QBI deduction is not allowed in calculating the owner's adjusted gross income (AGI), but reduces taxable income, similar to an itemized deduction. Therefore, it does not reduce AGI for purposes of other deductions or credits that are dependent on AGI. The deduction is available to taxpayers who itemize as well as those who do not itemize. While this new provision is fairly complex, it is discussed briefly below.

Calculating the QBI Deduction

In Chapter 7, the QBI deduction was introduced in terms of a taxpayer who owns a single qualified pass-through entity. If the taxpayer owns more than one qualified business, the deductible QBI amount is first calculated for each business, then these amounts are netted to determine the "combined QBI" amount.The deduction is then limited to the lesser of:

1. the combined QBI, or
2. 20 percent of adjusted taxable income (excluding net capital gains).

As the vocabulary is somewhat confusing, the following definitions will help in understanding the calculation of the QBI deduction:

3. The CARES Act of 2020 increased the deduction limit for interest expense from 30 percent to 50 percent for tax years beginning in 2019 and 2020 and allows NOLs arising in 2018, 2019, and 2020 to be carried back up to five years.
4. Subject to restrictions that can apply at higher income levels.

"**Qualified Business Income**" is defined as the net amount of income, gain, deductions, and losses with respect to a trade or business (being an employee does not qualify). Specified investment-related items are not included within the definition of QBI, such as capital gains or losses, dividends, interest income (unless the interest is properly allocable to the business). Also, QBI does not include reasonable compensation received from an S corporation or a guaranteed payment from a partnership. Consistent with the Keogh calculation discussed previously in this chapter, in determining the qualified business income, the owner's share of net income from the business is reduced by the proportionate share of above-the-line deductions (such as the deduction for ½ of the self-employment tax, the deduction for self-employed health insurance premiums, and the deduction for self-employed retirement plan contributions) attributable to that business.

"Deductible QBI" is determined for each business separately, and is generally 20 percent of qualified business income.

"Combined QBI" is the net amount of "deductible QBI" for all qualifying businesses owned by the taxpayer. In other words, combined QBI has already factored in the 20 percent of QBI for each business as the deductible amount.

"Adjusted taxable income" is the taxable income after allowable deductions not related to the business (AGI calculated without the deduction for ½ of the self-employment tax, self-employed health insurance, or self-employed retirement plan contribution; minus either the standard or itemized deductions); minus net capital gains. Taxable income includes all income of the taxpayer and spouse, but is calculated without regard to the Section 199A deduction.

"Net Capital Gains" equal the taxpayer's net long-term capital gains + qualified dividends for the taxable year, less the net short-term capital loss for the year.

Example 16.7

Jerry's share of "qualified business income" from each of his two partnership interests is:

Partnership A: $30,000
Partnership B: $40,000

His "deductible QBI" from each is:

Partnership A: $30,000 x 20% = $6,000
Partnership B: $40,000 x 20% = $8,000

Jerry's "combined QBI" is:

$6,000 + $8,000 = $14,000

Jerry is single and his adjusted taxable income from all sources (after taking above-the-line deductions and either the standard or itemized deduction, but before taking the 20% deduction for QBI) is $130,000, of which $10,000 is "net capital gain."

Jerry's Section 199A deduction is the lesser of:

1. the combined QBI, which is $14,000, or
2. 20% of adjusted taxable income (excluding net capital gains), which is: 20% x $120,000 = $24,000.

Jerry's deduction is $14,000.

If the net amount of QBI from all qualified trades or businesses during the taxable year is a loss, it is carried forward as a loss from a separate qualified trade or business in the next taxable year.

Example 16.8

Dorothy has qualified business income of $20,000 from qualified business A and a qualified business loss of $50,000 from qualified business B in Year 1. Dorothy is not permitted a deduction for Year 1 and has a carryover qualified business loss of $30,000 to Year 2. In Year 2, Dorothy has qualified business income of $20,000 from qualified business A and qualified business income of $50,000 from qualified business B. To determine the deduction for Year 2, Dorothy reduces the 20 percent deductible amount determined for the qualified business income of $70,000 from qualified businesses A and B by 20 percent of the $30,000 carryover qualified business loss. Therefore, Dorothy's combined QBI for Year 2 equals $8,000 ($14,000 less $6,000).

Any losses from a trade or business that are suspended (such as by the passive activity rules) and not available in computing taxable income for the year are not included in QBI for that year.

The QBI deduction has two major limitations: the W-2 wage limitation and the service business limitation. These limitations do not apply until an individual owner's taxable income exceeds $164,900 or $329,800 for a married filing jointly in 2021. Above those income levels, the limitation is phased in over a $50,000 phase-in range for individuals or a $100,000 range for married filing jointly. As long as an individual's taxable income is under the applicable threshold, neither limitation applies and the full 20 percent QBI deduction may be used.

W-2 Wage Limitation

For pass-through entities, other than sole proprietorships, the QBI deduction generally cannot exceed the greater of:

1. 50 percent of the W-2 wages (including owner-employees) with respect to the qualified trade or business (W-2 wage limitation); or
2. the sum of 25 percent of W-2 wages (including owner-employees) plus 2.5 percent of the unadjusted basis, immediately after acquisition (UBIA), of all "qualified property."

Note that W-2 wages of S corporation owner-employees are not counted in the definition of QBI, but are included when calculating the W-2 wage limitation.

Qualified property is defined as tangible, depreciable property (including real estate) owned by a qualified trade or business at the close of the tax year, which is used by the business at any point during the tax year for the production of qualified business income. Qualified property that is contributed to a partnership or S corporation in a nonrecognition transaction will retain the UBIA of the transferor (increased by any money paid by the partnership or S corporation, or decreased by any money received by the transferor).

The limitations above are based on each owner's allocable share of W-2 wages and UBIA.

Example 16.9

A taxpayer (who is subject to the limit) operates her widget-making business as a sole proprietorship. The business buys a widget-making machine for $100,000 and places it in service in the year 2021. The business has no employees in 2021. The limitation in 2021 is the greater of (a) 50 percent of W-2 wages, or $0, or (b) the sum of 25 percent of W-2 wages ($0) plus 2.5 percent of the unadjusted basis of the machine immediately after its acquisition: $100,000 x 0.025 = $2,500. The amount of the limitation on the taxpayer's deduction is $2,500.

Example 16.10

Rod and Marcee are married and file a joint return on which they report adjusted taxable income of $300,000 (determined without regard to the QBI deduction). Rod is a partner in a qualified trade or business that is not a specified service business ("qualified business A"). Marcee has a sole proprietorship qualified trade or business that is a specified service business ("qualified business B").

Rod's allocable share of qualified business income from qualified business A is $120,000, such that 20 percent of the qualified business income with respect to the business is $24,000. Rod's allocable share of wages paid by qualified business A is $100,000, such that 50 percent of the W-2 wages with respect to the business is $50,000. As Rod and Marcee's taxable income is not above the threshold amount for a joint return, the application of the wage limit for qualified business A is not relevant. Rod's deductible amount for qualified business A is $24,000.

Marcee's qualified business income and W-2 wages from qualified business B, which is a specified service business, are $150,000 and $120,000, respectively. Rod and Marcee's taxable income is not above the threshold amount for a joint return. Marcee calculates the deductible amount for qualified business B by taking 20 percent of $150,000 ($30,000). Her deductible amount for qualified business B is $30,000.

Rod and Marcee's combined qualified business income deduction amount of $54,000 is comprised of the deductible amount for qualified business A of $24,000 and the deductible amount for qualified business B of $30,000.

Since the phaseout is based on the taxable income of each owner separately, it is possible that one owner may be entitled to the deduction, while another is not.

Specified Service Trade or Business (SSTB) Limitation

The service business limitation is designed to deter high-income taxpayers from attempting to convert wages for personal services into income eligible for the deduction. As described in Chapter 7, the QBI deduction is not available for income from specified service businesses, such as most professional practices (financial, law, medical, athletics, brokerage services, consulting), when taxable income exceeds the phaseout amount.

Real Estate Safe Harbor

Revenue Procedure 2019-38 provides a safe harbor test for a rental real estate enterprise to qualify for the Section 199A deduction. Rental real estate enterprises that do not qualify under the safe harbor provision may still qualify for the deduction if it otherwise meets the definition of trade or business in Section 199A.

For purposes of the safe harbor, a rental real estate enterprise is an interest in real property held for the production of rents. A rental real estate enterprise may consist of an interest in multiple properties, although residential and commercial real estate may not be part of the same enterprise. The individual or relevant pass-through entity relying on the safe harbor must hold the interest directly or through a disregarded entity. If the taxpayer used the property as a vacation home, however, the safe harbor will not be available.

The following requirements must be met to qualify for the safe harbor:

1. Separate books and records must be maintained for each rental real estate enterprise.
2. a. For rental real estate enterprises that have been in existence less than four years: 250 or more hours of rental services (defined below) are performed per year with respect to the rental real estate enterprise.
   b. For rental real estate enterprises that have been in existence at least four years: in any three of the last five consecutive years, 250 or more hours of rental services are performed per year with respect to the rental real estate enterprise.
3. Contemporaneous records must be kept, including time logs regarding dates and hours for all services performed and who performed the services.
4. A statement must be attached to the taxpayer's timely filed tax return in each taxable year in which the taxpayer relies on the safe harbor. The statement must include a description of all properties held in the rental real estate enterprise, a description of properties acquired and disposed of during the year, and a representation that the requirements of Revenue Procedure 2019-38 have been satisfied.

For purposes of the above requirements, rental services include:

1. advertising to rent the real estate,
2. negotiating and executing leases,
3. verifying information in prospective tenant applications,
4. collection of rent,
5. daily operation, maintenance, and repair of the property, including purchase of materials and supplies,
6. management of the real estate, and
7. supervision of employees.

Rental services do not have to be performed directly by the owners. Rental services also include the above services that are performed by employees, agents, or independent contractors of the owner.

Tax Analysis: C Corporation versus Pass-Through Entity with QBI Deduction

The net result of the QBI deduction is to reduce the tax rate on qualified business income by 20 percent. For example, for a taxpayer in the highest marginal bracket (37 percent in 2021), the tax on the deductible amount of qualified business income is effectively reduced to 29.60 percent (37% x (1 – 0.20) = 29.60%).

Even though corporate earnings are subject to double taxation, there is still some potential for income tax reduction as a result of incorporating a business. Taxpayers in the higher marginal income tax brackets may want to incorporate a profitable business as a C corporation to take advantage of the lower tax rate of 21 percent on corporate taxable income.

By creating a separate tax entity, the owners can take advantage of the lower tax rate, as well as the special tax breaks available to corporations. The tax savings can be retained and reinvested in the company for growth. If the company is sold later, the gains will be taxed at the same favorable capital gains rates that apply to dividends, or may qualify for exclusion under Section 1202 (as discussed in Chapter 11).

When flow-through entities retain earnings, those earnings are still taxed to the owners even when no distribution is made. When a C corporation retains earnings, however, those earnings are taxed only to the entity, relieving the owners of paying tax on that retained income. For this reason, a profitable business that retains earnings for growth is a good candidate for incorporation as a C corporation.

If earnings are expected to be distributed, the comparison becomes complicated by the Section 199A qualified business income deduction. The earnings of sole proprietorships, partnerships, and S corporations are taxed directly to the participating individual or individuals at their marginal tax rate, which may be as high as 37 percent (a net rate of 29.6 percent on the business income if the pass-through income is fully eligible for the Section 199A qualified business income deduction). C corporation income is taxed at a flat 21 percent, although the double taxation when distributed must also be considered if it is likely that distributions will be made. If dividends are distributed to an owner in the highest marginal tax bracket, the combined corporate tax, dividend rate, and 3.8 percent Medicare tax will be 39.80 percent [0.21 + ((1-0.21)(0.238))]. An analysis of an individual's situation will be required in order to determine the most favorable tax treatment, as well as to evaluate other features of the various entities. If losses are expected, the flow-through entities will generally be more advantageous because the business losses can offset an owner's income from other sources (subject to limitations on excess business losses).

PROTECTING OWNERS FROM EACH OTHER

As the old saying goes "there is risk in the future." The choice of entity provides certain advantages and disadvantages to the partner, member, or shareholder. However, there are certain recurring situations where a little forethought could have prevented a bad result. Some of these situations are unexpected events like death or disability of an owner, divorce, bankruptcy, retirement, or a voluntary or involuntary disassociation with the entity.

Each owner faces the above risks. In entities where there are multiple owners, a written shareholder agreement, partnership agreement, or operating agreement addressing the listed issues and any others that are of concern should be considered.

Protecting Minority Shareholders/Members

A minority shareholder or member who is also an employee should have two protections from termination by having an employment agreement (rather than being an employee at will) and should also have a shareholder agreement with a buyout provision in the event of termination.

Elements of Shareholder/Partnership Agreements

For each risk there should be a method provided for valuing the entity and the departing owner's interest. For example:

- For the first five years, the departing owner gets nothing.
- After five years, the departing owner is entitled to his proportional share. The company shall be valued at 1.5 times the average revenues for the three previous years.
- If the departing owner is terminated for cause, the company shall be valued at 50 percent of the average revenues for the last three years.

It is not enough to identify the risk and the valuation; a funding method must also be provided. While cross purchase or entity life insurance may work for untimely death, life insurance does not work for voluntary termination. A payout over time that will not burden the remaining owners and entity may be a solution. Whatever the solution, it needs to be clearly articulated in the shareholder agreement, the operating agreement, or partnership agreement.

Issues Regarding Additional Capital Required

In the situation where multiple owners have made a certain initial investment into a business enterprise, there is always the chance that additional capital will be needed. What happens if one of the investors refuses to pay his proportional share of such new capital? Can the partners or shareholders compel the unwilling owner to pay? At the outset of an entity the initial owners should prepare an analysis of the risks of needing additional capital (e.g., debt service is certain). If additional capital is likely or even possibly needed, the joint owners should prepare for it. One way to do so is to have all owners put up a negotiable letter of credit for a reasonable period of time to assure cash calls will be met. Additionally, a provision should be put in the partnership agreement, shareholder agreement, or operating agreement to the effect that any owner who defaults on a cash call obligation automatically forfeits his original investment and such default makes the letter of credit immediately due and payable.

KEY TERMS

Articles of Incorporation - The charter document for a corporation that must be filed with the secretary of state in the state of organization.

Articles of Organization - The charter document of an LLC that must be filed with the secretary of state in the state of organization.

Checking the Box - When an eligible entity chooses to be taxed as either a corporation or a partnership.

Corporations - Chartered legal entities formed by one or more individuals by meeting state statutory requirements necessary for the formation of a corporation.

Family Limited Partnership - A special type of limited partnership created under state law with the primary purpose of transferring assets to younger generations using annual exclusions and valuation discounts for minority interests and lack of marketability.

General Partnership - A joint business venture among two or more persons/entities to conduct business as co-owners in which all owners have unlimited liability with regard to the debts and obligations of the partnership.

Keogh Plan - A qualified plan for a self-employed person. An important distinction of Keogh plans is the reduced contribution that can be made on behalf of the self-employed individual.

Limited Liability Company - Separate legal entity formed by one or more individuals by meeting state statutory requirements necessary for the formation of an LLC that may be taxed as a sole proprietorship, partnership, or corporation.

Limited Liability Partnership - A hybrid entity generally comprised of licensed professionals that provides partial liability protection to its members and may be taxed as either a corporation or partnership.

Limited Partnerships - Associations of two or more persons as co-owners to carry on a business for profit except that one or more of the partners have limited participation in the management of the venture and thus limited risk exposure.

Managing Partner - A partner named to have responsibilities for specific tasks or for day-to-day operations.

Operating Agreement - A written agreement similar to corporate bylaws that specify the rules and regulations for the operation of an LLC.

Piercing the Veil - Occurs when a court disregards the status of the entity that gives the owners limited liability because the owners failed to maintain a clear and consistent identity for the entity.

Qualified Business Income (QBI) - The net amount of income, gain, deductions, and losses with respect to a pass-through trade or business, which is used in determining the below-the-line deduction of 20% of QBI.

S Corporation - A corporation formed under state law that elects to be taxed under Subchapter S of the Internal Revenue Code.

Sole Proprietorship - A business venture owned and operated by a single individual.

Specified Service Trade or Business (SSTB) - A trade or business involving performance of services in the fields of health, law, accounting, actuarial services, consulting, performing arts, athletics, financial services, investing, investment management, trading or dealing in securities, and any trade or business where the principal asset of the business is the reputation or skill of one or more of its owners. SSTBs are permitted only limited use of the QBI deduction.

DISCUSSION QUESTIONS

SOLUTIONS to the discussion questions can be found exclusively within the chapter. Once you have completed an initial reading of the chapter, go back and highlight the answers to these questions.

1. What are the different types of legal entities from which a business owner can conduct business?
2. How is a general partnership taxed?
3. What are the differences between a general and a limited partnership?
4. How do different types of business entities differ from each other with regard to the personal liability of owners for business obligations?
5. How is a C corporation taxed?
6. What type of business entity should be chosen if the owners expect losses in the first few years and the owners want limited personal liability?
7. How is a limited liability company taxed if it has one or more owners?
8. Compare an S corporation to a limited liability company.
9. How can an entity avoid having a court "pierce the veil?"
10. Why is it often difficult to dispose of an interest in a partnership?
11. What is the principal disadvantage of the general partnership arrangement?
12. How does the limited partnership arrangement affect an entity's ability to raise capital?
13. Define "checking the box."
14. How is a family limited partnership usually formed?
15. What are the risks associated with the taxation of an FLP?
16. What is an operating agreement and why is it important to have this document?
17. What are some of the advantages of a corporation?
18. What are some of the disadvantages of an S corporation?
19. Describe the purpose and general calculation of the qualified business income (QBI) deduction.

MULTIPLE CHOICE PROBLEMS

A sample of multiple choice problems is provided below. Additional multiple choice problems are available at money-education.com by accessing the Student Practice Portal.

1. Doralee, an architect, performed services for Judy and Violet and, in lieu of her normal fee, accepted a 10 percent interest in a partnership with a fair market value of $10,000. How much income from this arrangement should Doralee report on her income tax return?
    a. Doralee does not have any currently taxable income.
    b. Doralee has realized $10,000 in capital gains.
    c. Doralee must recognize $10,000 in compensation income.
    d. Doralee has realized $10,000 in compensation income, but does not have to recognize it until she sells her interest in the partnership.

2. An S corporation has the following information for the taxable year:

Net Income (before the items below)	$90,000
Warner's Salary	($38,000)
Other Income	$29,000
Other Expenses	($14,000)
Net Income	$67,000

    Warner is a 20 percent owner of the S corporation and he performs services for the business as an employee. What is Warner's self-employment income?
    a. $0.
    b. $52,000.
    c. $67,000.
    d. $90,000.

3. On August 1, 2021, Elle bought a five percent interest (5 shares) in XYZ, an S corporation that files as a calendar-year taxpayer. In 2021, the S corporation income was $160,000. How much will be reported to Elle on her 2021 1120-S Schedule K-1?
    a. $0.
    b. $3,333.
    c. $3,353.
    d. $8,000.

4. At the beginning of the current year, Emmett's basis in his partnership interest was $100,000. At the end of the year, Emmett received a K-1 from the partnership that showed the following information:

Cash Withdrawn	$31,000
Partnership Taxable Income	$60,000
Charitable Contribution	$1,000

What is Emmett's basis in his partnership interest at year-end?

a. $128,000.
b. $129,000.
c. $159,000.
d. $160,000.

5. Which entity does <u>not</u> have all of the following characteristics?
1. Limited liability.
2. Ability to distribute in-kind appreciated assets to owners without gain recognition.
3. Can have foreign investors.

a. LLC.
b. S corporation.
c. Limited partnership.
d. LLP.

Additional multiple choice problems are available at *money-education.com* by accessing the Student Practice Portal. Access requires registration of the title using the unique code at the front of the book.

QUICK QUIZ EXPLANATIONS

Quick Quiz 16.1

1. True.
2. False. To avoid piercing the veil, the entity should keep books and records separate from the personal books and records of the owners, segregate activities of business from personal affairs, follow corporate formalities such as meeting requirements and filings, and address all content in contracts and correspondence from the viewpoint of the business entity (rather than the viewpoint of the owners).

Quick Quiz 16.2

1. False. A proprietorship may be required to obtain a local business license or register with the state or local taxing authority if it will be collecting sales tax.
2. True.
3. True.

Quick Quiz 16.3

1. False. General partnerships are governed by the laws of the state in which they are formed.
2. False. A principal disadvantage of the general partnership arrangement is that all general partners in a partnership are jointly and severally liable for the debts and obligations of the partnership.
3. True.

Quick Quiz 16.4

1. True.
2. False. Limited partnerships offer limited liability for the limited partners. The general partners run the business and are exposed for personal liability.

Quick Quiz 16.5

1. True.
2. False. If the LLP is comprised of only licensed professionals, transfer of an interest will usually be more difficult because such interest may only be transferred to another similarly licensed professional.

Quick Quiz 16.6

1. False. Only a general partner can manage a family limited partnership.
2. False. Upon creation of the partnership (FLP), there are neither income nor gift tax consequences because the entity created (the limited partnership and all of its interests, both general and limited) is owned by the same person, or persons, who owned it before the transfer.

Quick Quiz 16.7

1. True.
2. True.

QUICK QUIZ EXPLANATIONS

Quick Quiz 16.8

1. False. The corporation's purpose may be broad (e.g., to engage in any lawful activity) or specific (e.g., to sell textbooks).
2. True.

Quick Quiz 16.9

1. True.
2. False. Additional distributions to shareholders beyond reasonable compensation are treated as dividends not subject to payroll tax. In-kind distributions of appreciated assets will be treated as a deemed sale; thus, such distributions will generate a capital gain in the case of an S corporation to all shareholders in proportion to their ownership even if the asset was only distributed to one shareholder.

APPENDIX

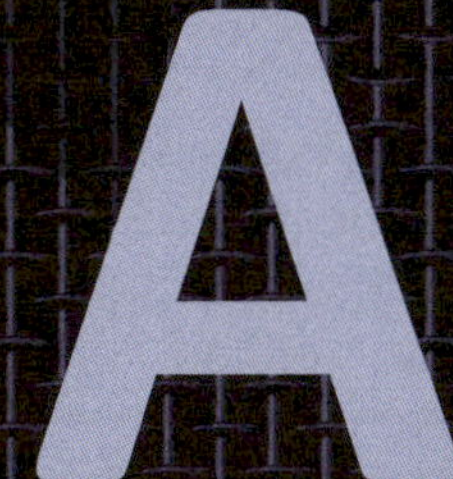

TAX RATE SCHEDULES

2021 Unmarried Individuals

If taxable income is over--	But not over--	The tax is:
$0	$9,950	10% of taxable income
$9,950	$40,525	$995 plus 12% of the amount over $9,950
$40,525	$86,375	$4,664 plus 22% of the amount over $40,525
$86,375	$164,925	$14,751 plus 24% of the amount over $86,375
$164,925	$209,425	$33,603 plus 32% of the amount over $164,925
$209,425	$523,600	$47,843 plus 35% of the amount over $209,425
$523,600	no limit	$157,804.25 plus 37% of the amount over $523,600

2021 Married Filing Jointly or Surviving Spouse

If taxable income is over--	But not over--	The tax is:
$0	$19,900	10% of taxable income
$19,900	$81,050	$1,990 plus 12% of the amount over $19,900
$81,050	$172,750	$9,328 plus 22% of the amount over $81,050
$172,750	$329,850	$29,502 plus 24% of the amount over $172,750
$329,850	$418,850	$67,206 plus 32% of the amount over $329,850
$418,850	$628,300	$95,686 plus 35% of the amount over $418,850
$628,300	no limit	$168,993.50 plus 37% of the amount over $628,300

2021 Head of Household

If taxable income is over--	But not over--	The tax is:
$0	$14,200	10% of taxable income
$14,200	$54,200	$1,420 plus 12% of the amount over $14,200
$54,200	$86,350	$6,220 plus 22% of the amount over $54,200
$86,350	$164,900	$13,293 plus 24% of the amount over $86,350
$164,900	$209,400	$32,145 plus 32% of the amount over $164,900
$209,400	$523,600	$46,385 plus 35% of the amount over $209,400
$523,600	no limit	$156,355 plus 37% of the amount over $523,600

2021 Married Filing Separately

If taxable income is over--	But not over--	The tax is:
$0	$9,950	10% of taxable income
$9,950	$40,525	$995 plus 12% of the amount over $9,950
$40,525	$86,375	$4,664 plus 22% of the amount over $40,525
$86,375	$164,925	$14,751 plus 24% of the amount over $86,375
$164,925	$209,425	$33,603 plus 32% of the amount over $164,925
$209,425	$314,150	$47,843 plus 35% of the amount over $209,425
$314,150	no limit	$84,496.75 plus 37% of the amount over $314,150

2021 Estates and Trusts

If taxable income is over--	But not over--	The tax is:
$0	$2,650	10% of taxable income
$2,650	$9,550	$265 plus 24% of the amount over $2,650
$9,550	$13,050	$1,921 plus 35% of the amount over $9,550
$13,050	no limit	$3,146 plus 37% of the amount over $13,050

2021 Basic Standard Deduction Amounts

Filing Status	Basic	Additional
Single	$12,550	$1,700
Married Filing Jointly/Surviving Spouse	$25,100	$1,350
Head of Household	$18,800	$1,700
Married Filing Separately	$12,550	$1,350

APPENDIX B

GLOSSARY

A

Above-the-Line Deductions – Deduction for adjusted gross income, also known as adjustments to income.

Accelerated Depreciation – Allows the owner of an asset to front-load the depreciation deductions so that more of the depreciation deduction is taken in the early years, and less is taken in later years.

Accountable Expense Reimbursement Plan – A plan under which an employer reimburses employees for certain actually incurred expenses and requires the employee to substantiate the expenditures by producing receipts.

Accountable Plan - A reimbursement plan that reimburses employees only for actual expenses incurred, and requires the employees to provide proof of, or "account for" their expenditures.

Accrual Method – An accounting method under which income is reported when it is earned rather than when it is received in cash, and expenses are reported when they are incurred rather than when they are paid.

Accuracy-Related Penalty – A penalty of 20 percent of the underpayment amount imposed on taxpayers who file incorrect tax returns in certain situations.

Acquisition Indebtedness – Indebtedness that is secured by the home and is used to acquire, construct, or improve the taxpayer's primary residence and one additional residence.

Active Participation – Requires participation in making management decisions concerning the property, but is not substantially and continuously involved in the operation of the activity (the standard that applies for material participation).

Activities of Daily Living – Eating, bathing, dressing, toileting, transferring, and continence.

Adjusted Gross Income – Gross income less above-the-line deductions.

Adjustments – AMT changes made to adjusted gross income that either increase or decrease AMTI.

Adoption Assistance Program – An employer plan that assists employees with the cost of adoption and may not discriminate in favor of highly compensated or key employees.

Adoption Expenses Credit – A nonrefundable credit allowed for qualified adoption expenses paid by an individual to adopt an eligible child.

Alimony – A separate maintenance payment that is intended to replace income lost by one spouse as the result of a divorce and may be included in the gross income of the payee. Alimony will be included in income of the payee for divorce decrees signed prior to 2019.

Alimony Recapture – Rules designed to prevent taxpayers from transforming property settlements into deductible alimony payments.

Alternative Minimum Tax (AMT) – An anti-abuse technique designed to change the timing of tax payments.

Alternative Minimum Taxable Income (AMTI) – Adjusted gross income plus or minus certain adjustments and preferences.

American Opportunity Tax Credit (formerly Hope Scholarship Credit) – A credit (a portion of which is refundable) allowed for the qualified education expenses of an eligible student during the first four years of post-secondary education.

Amortization – Cost recovery deductions for intangible assets.

Amount Realized – The amount of money plus the value of property received in the sale or exchange of an asset.

Annuitized – When regular periodic payments on an annuity contract begin for life or for a specified period of time in excess of one year.

Annuity Contract – A contract under which an individual invests a lump sum or stream of payments with an insurance company and the income on the investment growth is deferred until the owner begins to take distributions from the annuity.

Archer Medical Savings Accounts (MSAs) – Tax-favored savings accounts for medical expenses that were established by HIPAA in 1996, but cannot be established after 2005.

Articles of Incorporation – The charter document for a corporation that must be filed with the secretary of state in the state of organization.

Articles of Organization – The charter document of an LLC that must be filed with the secretary of state in the state of organization.

At-Risk Rule – Provides that a taxpayer may not deduct, in the current tax year, more than the amount that he or she has at risk.

B

Bartering – An exchange of property and/or services for other property and/or services.

Basis – Represents the total capital from after-tax income used by a taxpayer to purchase an investment.

Basis Limitation – Provides that the maximum allowable loss that the taxpayer can deduct is equal to his or her basis in the investment.

Below-the-Line Deductions – Deductions from adjusted gross income. Also known as itemized deductions. Personal and dependency exemption amounts are also deducted below-the-line. However, they have been suspended by the TCJA 2017 until 2026. In addition, the new 20% deduction for flow-through entities introduced in the TCJA 2017 is also a deduction that is below the line.

Bona Fide Resident Test – Requirement for the Foreign Earned Income exclusion that requires the taxpayer to generally intend to work and reside in the foreign country for an indefinite period of time.

Bonus Depreciation - A form of accelerated depreciation, similar to what is available under Section 179. However, there are no income limitations or limitations on the value of assets placed in service. While these rules have changed since introduced in 2010, TCJA 2017 allows for 100% bonus depreciation for assets placed in service after September 27, 2017 and before 2023. The 100% bonus deprecation is phased out after 2022, and taxpayers are permitted to elect 50% bonus deprecation in lieu of 100% bonus depreciation.

Boot – Non-like-kind property received in a Section 1031 exchange, usually cash, property or a reduction in debt.

C

Cafeteria Plan – A written plan under which an employee may choose to receive either cash or taxable benefits as compensation or qualified fringe benefits that are excludable from wages.

Capital Asset – All assets that are not specified as ordinary income assets or Section 1231 assets.

Cash Receipts and Disbursements Method – An accounting method under which income items are reported for the tax year in which they are received in cash and expenses are deducted in the year in which they are paid with cash.

Casualty Loss Deduction – Deduction allowed for losses or damages to a taxpayer's property resulting from a sudden or unexpected event, such as fire, storm, shipwreck, or theft.

Checking the Box – When an eligible entity chooses to be taxed as either a corporation or a partnership.

Child Tax Credit – A nonrefundable tax credit of $2,000 (in tax years before and after 2021), which is available to an individual taxpayer for each qualifying child under the age of 17 (refundable up to $1,400 per eligible child).

Community Property – A regime in which married individuals own an equal, undivided interest in all of the property accumulated, using either spouse's earnings, during the marriage.

Compensation – Salary, wages, and fringe benefits received in exchange for providing services to an employer.

Compensatory Damages – Monetary award intended to compensate for damage to property, for recovery of expenses incurred, for income lost, or for personal injury.

Conventions – Rules that govern the amount of depreciation that may be deducted during the first year that an asset is put into service.

Corporate Recapitalization – Restructuring the equity interests of a corporation, often in an effort to achieve estate planning or business succession goals.

Corporations – Chartered legal entities formed by one or more individuals by meeting state statutory requirements necessary for the formation of a corporation.

Cost Basis – The initial value of an asset acquired by an investor using capital to purchase the investment.

Coverdell Education Savings Account – Plan similar to a college savings plan that allows taxpayers to contribute up to $2,000 per beneficiary per year to an account.

Credit for Child and Dependent Care Expenses – A nonrefundable credit intended to provide some financial relief to individuals who incur employment-related expenses for the care of one or more qualifying individuals. The credit is refundable in 2021 (ARPA 2021).

Credit for Increasing Research Activities – A component of the general business credit intended to encourage businesses to conduct research and increase their research expenditures.

Credit for the Elderly or Disabled – A nonrefundable credit intended to provide financial assistance to elderly or disabled individuals with modest incomes.

Credits for Taxes Paid – Refundable credits generated by federal income taxes paid in advance.

D

De Minimis Fringe Benefit – Fringe benefits that are so small or insignificant that accounting for them would be unreasonable or administratively impracticable.

Deductions – Items that are subtracted from gross income, either below or above the line, in order to arrive at taxable income.

Deferral Items – Adjustments and preferences that result in a tax credit that can be used in future years equal to the additional tax that must be paid in the current year.

Dependency Exemption – A deduction from adjusted gross income allowed for each person who is a qualifying child or relative of the taxpayer for tax years before 2018 and after 2025.

Depletion – A form of depreciation that applies to natural resources.

Depreciation – A return of capital to a business that results in a reduction in the basis of the asset for the amount of depreciation that is claimed.

Depreciation Recapture – Special tax consequences that occur when a Section 1231 asset is sold for an amount greater than its adjusted basis.

Determination Letter – A letter issued by a district director of the IRS advising a taxpayer on how to report a transaction for tax purposes.

Disability Insurance – Provides benefits in the form of periodic payments to a person who is unable to work due to sickness or accidental injury.

Disabled Access Credit – A component of the general business credit intended to encourage small businesses to make their buildings accessible to persons with disabilities.

Disallowed Losses – Losses that are realized, but are not permitted to be recognized, including losses on the sale of personal use assets (except for casualty losses), losses on the subsequent sale of property gifted or sold to a related party when its FMV is less than the original owner's adjusted basis, and losses associated with a wash sale.

Discriminant Inventory Function System – A computer program used by the IRS to identify tax returns for audit.

Distance Test – In order to qualify for a moving expense deduction for tax years before 2018 and after 2025, the distance between the taxpayer's old home and new job location must be at least 50 miles greater than the distance between the old home and the old job location.

Dividend Income – A distribution of corporate earnings to shareholders, usually in cash.

Doctrine of Constructive Receipt – A cash method taxpayer must report income when it is credited to the taxpayer's account or when it is made available without restriction.

Double Basis Rule – A rule that applies to gifts and related party transactions where the transferee has a basis of the fair market value for losses and the transferor's basis for gains. The rule applies when the asset that is transferred has a fair market value less than the transferor's basis at the time of the transfer. This rule does not apply to arm's-length unrelated party transactions. This rule may also be referred to as the split basis rule, dual basis rule, or bifurcated basis rule.

Double Declining Balance Method – An accelerated depreciation method used for MACRS assets with a 3, 5, 7, or 10 year class life in which the annual depreciation percentage is twice the annual depreciation percentage under the straight-line depreciation method.

E

Earned Income – Income received by a taxpayer in the form of wages, salaries, and income from the conduct of business activities.

Earned Income Credit – A refundable credit intended to reward lower-income taxpayers for earning income.

Educational Assistance Program – A separate written plan that establishes a program through which an employer provides educational assistance to employees.

Employee Business Expenses – Expenses that include professional and union dues of employees, travel, supplies and services, professional books and journals, job related educational expenses, work clothes and uniforms, and job hunting expenses in the same line of work, which may be deductible as a miscellaneous itemized deduction subject to the 2 percent floor if they are not reimbursed by the employer (for tax years before 2018 and after 2025).

Employer-Provided Child Care Credit – A component of the general business credit intended to encourage employers to help provide and promote appropriate child care for their employees.

Endowment Contract – A type of insurance contract that pays a specified death benefit to a beneficiary upon the death of the insured owner, but also pays a specified benefit (in lieu of the death benefit) to the owner of the policy if the insured person lives to a specified age or date.

Estimated Tax Payments – Quarterly payments that are paid to the IRS and may be claimed as a credit against tax.

Exclusion Items – Adjustments and preferences that result in a permanent increase in tax.

Exclusions – Income items that are specifically exempted from income tax.

F

Failure to File Penalty – A penalty of 5 percent of the unpaid tax balance for each month or part thereof that a tax return is late.

Failure to Pay Penalty – A penalty of 0.5 percent per month or part thereof that a taxpayer fails to pay tax that is owed.

Family Limited Partnership – A special type of limited partnership created under state law with the primary purpose of transferring assets to younger generations using annual exclusions and valuation discounts for minority interests and lack of marketability.

Federal Insurance Contributions Act (FICA) – A law that dictates the amount to be withheld from an employee's pay for OASDI benefits.

Final Regulations – Regulations issued by the Treasury that have been adopted formally after compliance with the requirements of the Administrative Procedures Act.

5-Year Lookback Rule – A net Section 1231 gain in the current tax year (which should be taxed at capital gain tax rates) will be taxed at ordinary income tax rates to the extent of any unrecaptured Section 1231 losses claimed during the last five years.

Flexible Spending Account (FSA) – A type of cafeteria plan that is funded through employee salary reductions. The FSA limit is $2,750 (2021).

Foreign Earned Income – Income earned by a qualifying citizen or resident of the United States in exchange for personal services rendered in a foreign country. The foreign earned income limit is $108,700 (2021).

Foreign Tax Credit – A nonrefundable tax credit available to qualifying taxpayers who pay income taxes to a foreign country on foreign source income and also pay U.S. income taxes on the same income.

Fraud – Implies that the taxpayer intentionally disregarded tax rules or misstated information included on the return.

Fringe Benefits – Non-cash benefits provided to an employee by an employer in addition to wages and salary.

Functional Use Test – Requires the replacement property to serve the same functional use as the original property.

G

General Business Credit – A combination of more than thirty different nonrefundable tax credits that must be considered in a specific sequence.

General Partnership – A joint business venture among two or more persons/entities to conduct business as co-owners in which all owners have unlimited liability with regard to the debts and obligations of the partnership.

Gross Income – All income from whatever source derived unless it is specifically excluded by some provision of the Internal Revenue Code.

H

Head of Household Filing Status – A filing status that provides a basic standard deduction and tax bracket sizes that are less favorable to the taxpayer than those for the surviving spouse status, but more favorable than those for the single filing status.

Health Reimbursement Arrangements (HRAs) – Employer-funded plans that reimburse employees for medical expenses and allow employees to carry any unused balance forward to be used in future years.

Health Savings Account (HSA) – Accounts that allow individuals who have high deductible health insurance plans to save on a tax-free basis to fund their medical expenses.

Highly Compensated Employees – Those employees who are either a greater than five percent owner or have compensation in excess of $130,000 (2021).

Hobby Activity – Any activity that a taxpayer engages in without a profit motive. No deductions are permitted for hobbies after 2017.

Holding Period – The period for which a taxpayer owns an asset.

Home Equity Indebtedness – Additional debt secured by the home that exceeds the amount of acquisition indebtedness.

Hybrid Method – An accounting method that includes any other method of reporting that is permitted by the Code and regulations as long as it is deemed to clearly reflect income.

I

Imputed Interest – A payment deemed to be made by the borrower to the lender when the interest rate on a loan is less than the applicable federal rate.

Incentive Stock Option (ISO) – A tax-favored stock option that meets certain requirements and is granted by a corporation to an employee to purchase the stock of that corporation.

Income – Broadly defined as the gross amount of money, property, services, or other accretion to wealth received, but it does not include borrowed money or a return of invested dollars.

Individual Investor Exception – Allows individual taxpayers who actively participate in rental real estate activities to deduct up to $25,000 of losses from that activity against non-passive income for the year.

Interest Income – Gross income generated by a variety of debt instruments, including bank accounts, money market instruments, and bonds.

Interpretive Regulations – Official interpretations of the Internal Revenue Code by the Treasury.

Inventory – Assets that are held for resale to customers in the normal course of business.

Investment Credit – Part of the general business credit consisting of the sum of five different credits, (1) the rehabilitation credit, (2) the energy credit, (3) the qualifying advanced coal project credit, (4) the qualifying gasification project credit, and (5) the qualifying advanced energy project credit.

Involuntary Conversion – A realization event that occurs outside of the control of the taxpayer.

K

Keogh Plan – A qualified plan for a self-employed person. An important distinction of Keogh plans is the reduced contribution that can be made on behalf of the self-employed individual.

Key Employee – An employee who is (1) a greater than five percent owner, (2) a greater than one percent owner with compensation in excess of $150,000, or (3) an officer with compensation in excess of $185,000 (2021).

Kiddie Tax – A tax on the net unearned income of a child at the parent's marginal tax rate.

L

Legislative Regulations – Regulations in which the Treasury determines the details of the law.

Life Insurance Contract – A contract under which the insurance company promises to pay a specified amount upon the death of the insured.

Lifetime Learning Credit – A nonrefundable credit available to taxpayers who pay qualified tuition and related expenses to an eligible institution for themselves, their spouses, and their dependents for whom a dependency exemption is claimed.

Like-Kind Assets – Property of the same nature and character that may be exchanged in a like-kind exchange. After 2017, only real property is permitted for Section 1031 like-kind exchange treatment.

Like-Kind Exchange – A tax deferral technique in which assets held for productive use in a trade or business are exchanged, only real property is permitted for 1031 like-kind exchange treatment.

Limited Liability Company – Separate legal entity formed by one or more individuals by meeting state statutory requirements necessary for the formation of an LLC that may be taxed as a sole proprietorship, partnership, or corporation.

Limited Liability Partnership – A hybrid entity generally comprised of licensed professionals that provides partial liability protection to its members and may be taxed as either a corporation or partnership.

Limited Partnerships – Associations of two or more persons as co-owners to carry on a business for profit except that one or more of the partners have limited participation in the management of the venture and thus limited risk exposure.

Listed Property – Suspect property that is easily used for both business and personal purposes.

Long-Term Care Insurance – Provides benefits when the insured is unable to perform some of the activities of daily living.

Long-Term Holding Period – Occurs when an asset is owned by a taxpayer for more than one year.

Low-Income Housing Credit – A component of the general business credit intended to promote the construction of housing for low-income residents.

M

Managing Partner – A partner named to have responsibilities for specific tasks or for day-to-day operations.

Married Filing Jointly Filing Status – A filing status that allows married couples to combine their gross incomes and deductions.

Married Filing Separately Filing Status – A filing status used when married couples do not choose to file a joint return.

Material Participation – Requires involvement in the conduct of the trade or business on a regular, continuous, and substantial basis.

Medical Savings Account (MSA) – Accounts authorized by HIPAA 1996 which allowed contributions to the account to grow tax-free if funds distributed from the account were used to pay for medical expenses.

Mixed-Use Rental Activity – Rental activity in which the real estate is rented for 15 days or more per year and the owner's personal use of the property is more than the greater of 14 days per year or 10 percent of the rental days.

Modified Accelerated Cost Recovery System (MACRS) – An accelerated depreciation system under which assets are divided into specific classes according to their useful lives.

Modified Endowment Contracts (MECs) – Life insurance contracts that do not pass the 7-pay test or the corridor rule.

Municipal Bonds – Debt instruments issued by states and their political subdivisions, the interest income from which is generally excluded from federal gross income.

N

Necessary Expense – An expense that a prudent business person would incur in the conduct of business.

Net Investment Income Tax (NIIT) – Applies at a rate of 3.8 percent to certain net investment income of individuals, estates and trusts that have income above the statutory threshold amounts.

Net Operating Losses – Occur when trade or business activities generate higher expenses than income in a given year. Occurs when trade or business activities generate higher expenses than income in a given year. After 2020, NOLs can generally only be carried forward and can only offset up to 80 percent of income for any one year.

Net Unearned Income (NUI) – The amount of unearned income of a child that is subject to tax at the parent's marginal tax rate. NUI is equal to the unearned income of the child, less $1,100 (the basic standard deduction of a dependent) and the greater of $1,100 or the amount of the deductions allowed in producing the unearned income (2021 threshold).

No-Additional-Cost Services – A fringe benefit provided by employers that may be excluded from the employee's gross income if the service is (1) offered for sale to customers, (2) in the line of business in which the employee works, and (3) does not cause the employer to incur any substantial costs (including foregone revenue) in providing the service to the employee.

Non-Accountable Reimbursement Plans – Plans in which the employer gives the employee a specified sum of money out of which the employee will cover all of the business related expenses.

Nonqualified Stock Option (NQSO) – A right to purchase shares of company stock at a given strike price (generally set at the market price of the stock on the day the option is granted).

Nonrecourse Debt – Debt that is secured only by the asset pledged as security and not by any personal guarantee of the debtor.

Nonrefundable Tax Credits – Tax credits that can reduce the tax on taxable income to zero, but cannot generate a tax refund.

Nontaxable Rental Activity – Rental activity in which the real estate is rented for less than 15 days per year.

O

150 Percent Declining Balance Method – An accelerated depreciation method used for MACRS assets with a 15 or 20 year class life in which the annual depreciation percentage is 150 percent of the annual depreciation percentage under the straight-line depreciation method.

Operating Agreement – A written agreement similar to corporate bylaws that specify the rules and regulations for the operation of an LLC.

Ordinary Expense – An expense that is typically incurred in the normal, usual, or customary conduct of businesses in the same line of operations.

Ordinary Income Assets – Accounts receivable, copyrights, and inventory, all of which generate gains that will be taxed at ordinary income tax rates.

Original Issue Discount – The difference between the redemption price at maturity and the purchase price for debt instruments issued at a discount.

Original Issue Discount (OID) Bond – A bond that is issued for a price that is less than its face amount or principal amount on which interest is usually paid only at maturity.

P

Passive Activity – Any activity in which a taxpayer does not materially participate, that is a limited partnership interest, or that is a rental activity (even if the taxpayer materially participates in the activity).

Passive Activity Loss Rule – Provides that passive losses may only be used to offset gains from passive activities and may not be used to offset other types of income.

Passive Credits – Non-refundable tax credits designed to encourage individuals to engage in certain types of passive activities. Passive credits may be used to offset any tax attributed to taxable income.

Passive Income – Income received by a taxpayer including income generated from investments in real estate and income generated by business entities in which the owner does not materially participate.

Pass-Through Entities – Legal business forms that are not treated as separate taxable entities for income tax purposes. The income of a pass-through entity is taxed to each of the owners in proportion to their ownership interest.

Personal Exemption – A deduction from adjusted gross income for the taxpayer and the taxpayers spouse for tax years before 2018 and after 2025.

Personal Property – Any property that is not real property.

Phantom Income – Income imputed to taxpayer without a corresponding receipt of cash.

Physical Presence Test – Requirement for the Foreign Earned Income exclusion that requires the taxpayer to be present in a foreign country or countries for at least 330 full days during any period of 12 consecutive months.

Piercing the Veil – Occurs when a court disregards the status of the entity that gives the owners limited liability because the owners failed to maintain a clear and consistent identity for the entity.

Portfolio Income – Income received by a taxpayer through the investment of capital, such as dividends, interest, and capital gains.

Preferences – AMT changes made to adjusted gross income that increase AMTI.

Premium Assistance Credit – A credit created by the 2010 Health Care Legislation to provide assistance to low income taxpayers who purchase health insurance through a state-sponsored health benefit exchange.

Primarily Rental Use Activity – Rental activity in which the real estate is rented for 15 days or more per year and the owner's personal use of the property is less than the greater of 14 days per year or 10 percent of the rental days.

Private Activity Municipal Bonds – Securities issued by or on behalf of local governments that bear tax-exempt interest for regular income tax and are used to provide debt financing for private projects. Private activity municipal bond income is an AMT preference item.

Private Charities – Corporations or trusts structured to further the charitable intentions of a donor or the donor's family.

Private Letter Ruling – Rulings issued by the IRS that are binding on the IRS only with respect to the transaction and the taxpayer that are the subject of the ruling.

Procedural Regulations – Housekeeping instructions indicating how the Treasury and IRS will conduct their affairs.

Profit Motive – An actual and honest, even though unreasonable or unrealistic, profit objective in engaging in an activity.

Proposed Regulations – Regulations that have been drafted by the Treasury, but have not yet been adopted.

Public Charities – Charitable organizations that receive support from a wide cross-section of the population, such as the Red Cross or the YMCA.

Publicly Traded Partnership (PTP) - A partnership that trades on an active securities market.

Punitive Damages – Payments intended to punish the offending party.

Q

Qualified Business Income (QBI) – The net amount of income, gain, deductions, and losses with respect to a pass-through trade or business, which is used in determining the below-the-line deduction of 20% of QBI.

Qualified Charitable Organization – An organization that is operated exclusively for religious, charitable, scientific, literary, or educational purposes, or for the prevention of cruelty to animals or children.

Qualified Dividends – Dividends subject to favorable tax rates.

Qualified Education Expenses – Educational expenses that receive favorable tax treatment. Such expenses may vary depending on the type of program or tax benefit.

Qualified Employee Discounts – Employer-provided discounts on qualified property and services that can be excluded from an employee's gross income.

Qualified Moving Expense Reimbursement – Direct or indirect payments by an employer to pay the cost of moving an employee's family and belongings (TCJA 2017 limited this provision to members of the Armed Forces after 2017).

Qualified Residence Interest Deduction – Tax deduction that permits taxpayers to deduct the interest on up to $750,000 of home indebtedness.

Qualified Retirement Planning Services – Any retirement planning advice or information provided to an employee and his spouse by an employer maintaining a qualified employer-sponsored retirement plan.

Qualified Transportation Fringe Benefits – Benefits in the form of (1) transportation between an employee's residence and the place of employment in a commuter highway vehicle, (2) any transit pass, or (3) qualified parking. After 2017, employers are no longer permitted to take a deduction for qualified transportation fringe benefits, unless the benefit is provided for the safety of the employee.

Qualified Tuition Programs – Also known as 529 Plans, they permit taxpayers to save for elementary, secondary, and post-secondary education expenses of family members on a tax-favored basis through either a prepaid tuition program or a college savings plan.

Qualifying Child – A person who meets the relationship test, abode test, age test, support test, joint return test, and citizenship test, and may be claimed as a dependent of the taxpayer.

Qualifying Relative – A person who meets the relationship test, gross income test, support test, joint return test, and citizenship test; is not a qualifying child of the taxpayer; and may be claimed as a dependent by the taxpayer.

R

Real Estate Professional Exception – Provides that if a taxpayer meets certain requirements, he is considered a real estate professional and may treat a real estate activity as an active trade or business.

Real Property – Land and anything permanently attached to it (such as buildings, trees, and swimming pools).

Realization Event – Generally occurs when an asset has been sold or exchanged. Gains on capital assets are subject to tax only when there has been both a realization event and a recognition event.

Reasonable Expense – An expense that is incurred in a trade or business that is considered by the IRS to be reasonable based on the facts and circumstances surrounding the expense.

Recognition Event – Occurs when a realized gain is included on a taxpayer's income tax return. All realized gains are generally recognized unless a provision in the IRC provides otherwise.

Recourse Debt – Debt that the taxpayer is personally liable to repay regardless of whether the investment produces a return for the investor.

Refundable Tax Credits – Tax credits that can be used not only to reduce or eliminate the current year's tax, but also to generate a tax refund.

Reinvestment Period – Period during which the taxpayer must acquire replacement property.

Related Party – Anyone defined under Section 267(b) including brothers and sisters (of whole or half blood or adopted).

Reserve Method – A method of deducting bad debts used by some businesses in which bad debt deductions are taken based on a percentage of accounts receivable representing the historical percentage of accounts that go bad.

Residential Energy Efficient Property Credit – A nonrefundable energy tax credit that helps an individual taxpayer pay for qualified residential alternative energy equipment.

Residential Energy Property Credit – A credit that increases the energy tax credit for energy efficient improvements made to a taxpayers existing home.

Retirement Savings Contribution Credit – A nonrefundable credit intended to encourage lower-income taxpayers to save for retirement.

Revenue Procedures – Statements issued by the IRS which detail internal practices and procedures within the IRS and make important announcements to taxpayers.

Revenue Rulings – Rulings issued by the IRS based on a set of facts common to many taxpayers and binding on the IRS.

S

S Corporation – A corporation formed under state law that elects to be taxed under Subchapter S of the Internal Revenue Code.

Sale or Exchange Requirement – One of the requirements for a gain to be subject to income tax.

Section 1231 Asset – Depreciable property or real property used for productive use in a trade or business or for the production of income.

Section 179 Election – Provides to business owners, provided that certain requirements are met, the option of taking all of the depreciation deductions in the year the asset was placed into service, rather than over the MACRS class life.

Short-Term Holding Period – Occurs when an asset is owned by a taxpayer for one year or less.

Single Filing Status – A filing status used by an unmarried taxpayer who does not qualify as a surviving spouse or head of household.

16th Amendment – Amendment to the U.S. Constitution adopted on February 25, 1913 that gave Congress the power to lay and collect taxes on income.

Small Business Health Coverage Tax Credit – A tax credit for organizations that employ 25 or fewer employees who have annual compensation of $55,600 or less. The credit is designed to encourage employers to provide health care benefits to employees.

Small Business Stock (1202 Stock) - Stock that is eligible for a 100% capital gains exclusion.

Small Business Stock (1244 Stock) - Stock in a company initially capitalized with $1 million or less that permits special ordinary loss recognition.

Small Employer Pension Plan Startup Costs Credit – A component of the general business credit intended to encourage small employers to set up retirement plans for employees.

Sole Proprietorship – A business venture owned and operated by a single individual.

Specific Charge-Off Method – Allows businesses to deduct bad debts as an ordinary loss in the year in which the debt becomes partially or wholly worthless.

Specified Service Trade or Business (SSTB) – A trade or business involving performance of services in the fields of health, law, accounting, actuarial services, consulting, performing arts, athletics, financial services, investing, investment management, trading or dealing in securities, and any trade or business where the principal asset of the business is the reputation or skill of one or more of its owners. SSTBs are permitted only limited use of the QBI deduction.

Standard Deduction – A standard amount that is specified by Congress and includes inflation adjustments. Taxpayers may deduct the greater of the standard deduction or allowable itemized deductions.

Statute of Limitations – Specified time within which the IRS may examine an income tax return.

Step-to Fair Market Value – The basis of inherited property, which is equal to the fair market value of the asset on the date of the decedent's death, or, if elected by the executor of the decedent's estate, the alternate valuation date.

Straight-Line Depreciation – A depreciation method under which the purchase price of the asset, less its expected salvage value, is divided by the expected useful life of the asset to determine the annual depreciation deduction.

Substantial Omission – An omission from a tax return of more than 25 percent of the gross income reported.

Surviving Spouse Filing Status – A filing status for a surviving spouse with a qualifying child that affords the same basic standard deduction and tax rates as the married filing jointly status.

T

Tax Court – A special purpose court that sits in Washington, D.C. and only hears tax cases. The judges within the court travel throughout the U.S. to hear the cases.

Tax Credit – An amount that reduces the calculated tax liability of the taxpayer.

Tax Relief, Unemployment Insurance Authorization, and Job Creation Act of 2010 (TRA 2010) – Tax act signed December 2010 that extended various income and estate tax provisions of EGTRRA, increased the tax credit equivalency amount for gift, estate, and generation skipping purposes, set the maximum transfer tax rate at 40%, and introduced portability.

Tax Year – Normally a period of 12 months.

Taxable Income – Determined by subtracting allowable deductions from gross income.

Taxpayer Use Test – Requires that the replacement property be used by the taxpayer within activities which is treated the same for tax purposes.

Temporary Regulations – Regulations that have the same authority as final regulations and are issued when guidance must be provided quickly to taxpayers.

Transfer for Value Rule – An exception to the general rule that life insurance death benefits are received tax-free.

Treasury Regulations – An administrative source of tax law that are official interpretations of the Internal Revenue Code and give taxpayers insight as to how the Code will be enforced by the IRS.

U

U.S. Court of Federal Claims – Court that may preside over tax controversies and only hears cases in Washington, D.C.

U.S. District Court – Trial court of the federal judicial system which has general jurisdiction and is the only option for tax controversies in which the taxpayer would like a jury trial.

Unrecaptured Section 1250 Depreciation – The portion of gain that is attributable to non-recaptured depreciation (up to the amount of straight-line depreciation deductions taken) for depreciable real estate that is taxed at 25 percent upon the sale or exchange of the property (plus the net investment income tax of 3.8% if applicable).

W

Wash Sale – Occurs when a taxpayer sells a stock or security at a loss, and purchases substantially identical stock or securities within a 30 day period before or after the sale.

Work Opportunity Credit – Part of the general business credit intended to promote the hiring of targeted groups of people who have special needs or high unemployment rates.

Working Condition Fringe Benefit – Any property or service provided to an employee to help the employee perform his job better.

Z

Zero Coupon Bond – A bond that is sold at a deep discount, pays not coupons (or periodic interest payments), and matures at its face value.

APPENDIX

INDEX

A

B

C

D

E

F

G

H

I

J

K

L

Q

R

S

T

U

V

W

Z